Table of Contents

5. Tables R.1. Concessions Received (continued)

6. Tables R.2. Concessions Receieved: Exporting Group by Product Category   *147*

7. Tables R.3. Concessions Received: Product Category by Exporting Economy or Group   *155*

1

Introduction

This publication provides summaries of the tariff liberalization agreed at the Uruguay Round negotiations of the General Agreement on Tariffs and Trade (GATT). The tables provide measures of reductions, bindings, and levels of most-favored-nation (MFN) customs tariff rates. They do not provide estimates of how exports and imports will change as a result of these liberalizations, nor do they gauge margins of tariff preferences or how the Uruguay Round concessions will affect those margins.

The first group of tables presents tariff reductions and bindings from the perspective of the economy or group that gave the concession. For example, Australia agreed to bind its tariff rates on 97.2 percent of its imports and to reduce its rates on 43.3 percent of its imports.

The second group of tables looks at the tariff concessions that each economy or group received from its trading partners. Concessions received are the reverse image of concessions given: Australia's concessions received are the concessions given by Australia's trading partners on products they import from Australia. For example, Australia's trading partners agreed to bind their tariff rates on 92.1 percent of Australia's exports and to reduce their rates on 20.5 percent of its exports.

Data Description and Data Sources

These tables could not have been prepared without the cooperation and the support of the GATT Secretariat, particularly its Statistics and Information Systems Divisions. The GATT Secretariat, as authorized by GATT's member countries, provided access to the Integrated Data Base (IDB), which contains the basic records of the outcome of the Uruguay Round tariff negotiations.

The economies or groups included in the IDB are those GATT/WTO (World Trade Organization) members that submitted requisite information to the Secretariat. According to GATT, the IDB covers all industrial and transition economies that participated in the Uruguay Round, plus twenty-six of ninety-four developing economy participants.[1] The IDB data cover 100 percent of non-petroleum imports of North America, Western Europe, and GATT members in Central and Eastern Europe; 90 percent of Asia's non-petroleum imports; 80 percent of Latin America's non-petroleum imports; and 30 percent of Africa's non-petroleum imports. The level of coverage is low for Africa because few African countries participate in the IDB.

The import data, customs duties, and final concessions contained in the IDB were assembled by the GATT Secretariat from information that is publicly available in each GATT/WTO member country. The GATT Secretariat converted these data into a uniform format and performed several simplifications and adjustments described below.

The Integrated Database

All of our data for tariff rates on industrial goods and part of our information on agricultural goods came from the IDB. Table 1 summarizes the contents of the

Table 1. Years of the Available Trade and Tariff Information in the Integrated Database (IDB)

Economy or Group	Trade	MFN 01	MFN 02	MFN 03 [a]	MFN 09B	MFN 09F	Customs nomenclature	Group [b]	Ad valorem equivalents in industrial goods (percent) [c]
Argentina	1986	1986	1986	1993 T	1986	1999	CCCN10	LMIE	100.0
Australia	1988	1988	1988	-	1986	1999	HS-6+2	HIE	100.0
Austria	1988	1988	1988	-	1988	1999	HS-6+7	HIE	97.3
Brazil	1989	1989	1989	1993 T	1986	1999	HS-6+4	LMIE	98.8
Canada	1988	1988	1988	-	1988	1999	HS-6+2	HIE	100.0
Chile	1986	1986	1986	1991 T	1986	1999	CCCN-8	LMIE	100.0
Colombia	1991	1991	1992	-	1991	1999	HS-4+6	LMIE	100.0
Czech Republic	1990	1993	1992	-	1993	1999	HS-6	LMIE	100.0
El Salvador	1989	1991	1991	-	1991	1999	CCCN-8	LMIE	97.1
European Union	1988	1988	1988	1988	1988	1999	HS-6+2	HIE	100.0
Finland	1988	1988	1988	-	1988	1999	HS-6+2	HIE	99.9
Hong Kong	1992	1992	1992	-	1986	1999	HS-6+2	HIE	100.0
Hungary	1991	1993	1992	-	1993	1999	HS_6+3	LMIE	100.0
Iceland	1988	1988	1988	-	1986	1999	HS_6+2	HIE	99.9
India	1988	1994	1990	1992 T	1986	1999	HS-6	LMIE	90.5
Indonesia	1989	1989	1989	-	1989	1999	HS_6+3	LMIE	100.0
Jamaica	1991	-	1991	-	1991	1999	HS-4+3	LMIE	100.0
Japan	1988	1988	1988	1989	1988	1999	HS-6+3	HIE	100.0
Korea, Republic of	1988	1988	1988	1988	1986	1999	HS-6+4	LMIE	99.9
Macau	1991	-	1991	-	1991	1999	HS-6+2	LMIE	98.0
Malaysia	1988	1988	1988	-	1986	1999	HS-6+3	LMIE	98.9
Mexico	1988	1988	1988	1991 T	1986	1999	HS-4+4	LMIE	100.0
New Zealand	1991	1991	1992	-	1986	1999	HS-6+2	HIE	99.4
Norway	1988	1988	1988	-	1988	1999	HS-6+2	HIE	99.5
Peru	1986	1983	1986	1993 T	1986	1999	CCCN-8	LMIE	100.0
Philippines	1991	1991	1991	-	1986	1999	HS-6+2	LMIE	100.0
Poland	1989	-	1989	-	1986	1999	HS-6	LMIE	100.0
Romania	1991	1992	1992	-	1992	1999	HS-6+1	LMIE	89.0
Senegal	1989	1986	1986	-	1986	1999	CCCN-6	LMIE	100.0
Singapore	1989	1989	1989	-	1989	1999	HS-6+3	HIE	99.1
Sri Lanka	1991	1991	1990	-	1991	1999	HS-6+2	LMIE	100.0
Sweden	1988	1988	1988	-	1988	1999	HS-6+2	HIE	99.9
Switzerland	1988	1988	1988	-	1988	1999	HS-6+2	HIE	99.9
Thailand	1988	1988	1988	-	1988	1999	HS-6+4	LMIE	94.9
Tunisia	1989	-	1990	1990	1990	1999	HS-6+1	LMIE	100.0
Turkey	1989	1989	1989	-	1989	1999	HS-6+2	LMIE	100.0
United States	1989	1989	1989	-	1989	1999	HS-6+2	HIE	100.0
Uruguay	1987	1987	1988	1992 T	1986	1999	CCCN-8	LMIE	100.0
Venezuela	1990	1990	1991	1992 T	1990	1999	HS-4+6	LMIE	99.2
Zimbabwe	1987	1987	1982	-	1986	1999	CCCN-8	LMIE	94.2

- = Not available.

a. For entries that are marked with "T", the tariff data are based on four digit averages from UNCTAD's Trade Analysis and Simulation System (TRAINS 2.0 A 1994).

b. LMIE = low- and middle-income economy; HIE = high-income economy.

c. This column lists the coverage of imports in industrial goods with ad valorem equivalent tariff rates. In the following tabulations all industrial tariff averages and reductions are based on these available ad valorem equivalents.

IDB. The various files provide for each reporter economy or group the following trade and MFN tariff information:

I. *Trade*: Value of imports, by tariff line by economy or group of origin, for the year stated in table 1

II. *MFN01*: MFN GATT bound duty before the Uruguay Round, for the year stated in table 1

III. *MFN02*: MFN statutory rate, for the year stated in table 1

IV. *MFN03*: MFN applied rate, for the year stated in table 1

V. *MFN09B*: Uruguay Round MFN base rate, for the year stated in table 1

VI. *MFN09F*: Uruguay Round MFN final offer rate, for the year stated in table 1.

The economies or groups that participated in the IDB calculated ad valorem equivalents for most specific, compound, and mixed duties on manufactures, based on import value and quantity data for the years indicated in table 1. A few duties took complex forms such as "2.95 cents per meter, not to exceed 11.3 percent." For these, we used the appropriate ad valorem part — in the example 11.3 percent. We used these IDB ad valorem equivalents to calculate tariff changes and tariff averages for all product categories except for agricultural commodities of the product category "Agriculture excluding Fish: Estimate 1" described below. For categories with relatively few available ad valorem equivalents, namely "Agriculture excluding Fish: Estimate 2"[2] and "Petroleum Oils",[3] one should use caution when interpreting the statistics. For some countries the tariff averages and reductions might be based on few tariff lines with relatively small trade weights. Table 1 lists in the last column the coverage of imports in manufactures (All product categories except Agriculture and Petroleum oils) with ad valorem equivalent tariff rates. The coverage of all forty IDB markets with ad valorem equivalent tariffs in industrial products is 99.7 percent.

"Before" and "After"

To measure tariff changes agreed at the Round, we converted the categories of data available in the IDB into categories that could reasonably be interpreted as measures of rates "before" and "after" the Round. In doing so we followed conventions employed by the GATT Secretariat in preparing reports on the outcome of the Round.[4]

There is no "official" measure of the tariff reductions exchanged at the Round. Strictly speaking, each country agreed to bind its tariff rates at the levels notified — the levels reported in series MFN09F, the final offer rates. These bound levels are "official" — each country's commitment is to maintain its rates at or below the agreed levels.

A number of countries, particularly in Latin America,[5] introduced substantial unilateral reductions of their tariff rates before or during the years of the Uruguay Round. These unilateral changes were reflected in the MFN applied rate (MFN03). In those cases we updated the MFN applied rate with four-digit simple averages from the TRAINS database. Our objective in defining "before" and "after" as we did was to include in our measured tariff change all reductions that were agreed at the Uruguay Round, but to exclude the unilateral reductions that were not conditioned on reciprocal reductions by trading partners and that were, by accident of timing, introduced between the beginning and the end of the Round. By the same token we did not account for any regional integration such as Austria, Finland, and Sweden joining the European Union in January 1995.

We have thus measured "before" and "after" applied rates, hence the change of applied rates attributable to commitments undertaken at the Uruguay Round. Because many countries', particularly developing countries', post-Uruguay Round applied rates are below their bound rates; and because developing countries' commitments at the Round were in large part to bind rates that were not bound before, we concluded that changes of applied rates would be more interesting than changes of bound rates.

The basic source for tariff rates "before" the Uruguay Round concessions was the MFN applied rate (MFN03). If a country did not report MFN03, but reported the MFN statutory rate (MFN02) or the

Uruguay Round base rate (MFN09b) we interpreted the lower of these two as the "before" rate.[6]

Developing a series for "after" entailed a similar complication. Many developing countries agreed at the Round to tariff bindings that are above the tariff rates they actually apply; thus it would be inappropriate to interpret their post-Uruguay Round bound rates (MFN09F) as the "after-UR" applied rates. Instead, we adopted the following convention: our "after" rate presumes that when a Uruguay Round bound rate is below the pre-Uruguay Round applied rate, the country's "after" Uruguay Round rate will be that bound rate (Figure 1a).

If, however, the "before" applied rate is below the post-Uruguay Round bound rate (MFN09F), we assume the "before" applied rate to be the "after" applied rate (Figure 1b). In short, we measure the "after" rate as the minimum of the "before" rate (as defined above) and the Uruguay Round MFN final offer rate (MFN09F).

The Uruguay Round agreement allows for year-by-year staged introduction of tariff reductions. Generally, the MFN final offer rates will be effective no later than January 1, 1999, but some countries have, for some commodities, negotiated later deadlines. The MFN09F rates are the final rates—after all stages are completed.

Free Trade Agreements

The objective of this exercise is to describe MFN tariff rates and changes of those MFN rates. Measures of coverage will therefore be tabulated over the values of trade that are charged those rates, and, likewise, averages will be weighted by the values of imports that are assessed those MFN rates. To do this, we must leave out those trade flows that benefit from preferential arrangements.

While the IDB notes participation in free trade agreements, it does not provide the product coverage of these agreements. Indeed, Braga and Yeats, in their analysis of trade flows under preferential arrangements, found line-by-line information on the products that receive preferential treatment under free trade arrangements difficult to obtain, and they resorted to an approximation of the coverage of such arrangements.[7] We have followed their lead, assuming —with one group of exceptions — that the free trade agreements in existence cover all merchandise imports. The exceptions are the arrangements between the European Union and other countries. These arrangements, we presume, cover all manufactured goods categories but no categories of agricultural products.

Based on this assumption, we made the following adjustments: (1) tariff averages and average tariff

Figure 1a. Applied Tariff "Before" Is Greater than Applied Tariff "After" (Cut in Applied Tariff Rate)

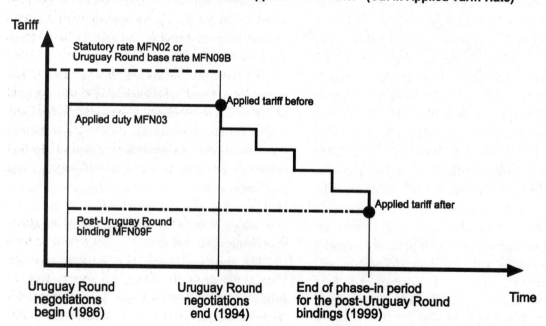

Figure 1b. Tariff "Before" Equals Tariff "After" (No Cut in Applied Tariff Rate)

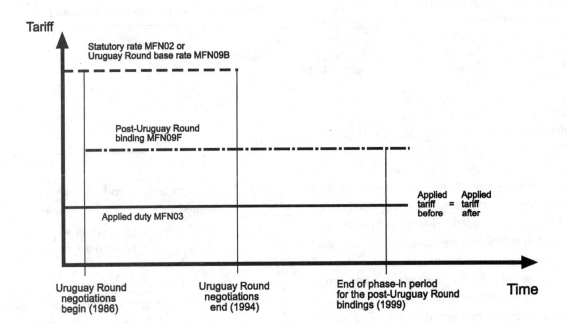

reductions are weighted by MFN, that is, "non-free trade agreement" imports; (2) coverage of tariff reductions includes only MFN imports; and (3) coverage of tariff bindings include both MFN and free trade agreement imports in the category of bindings above applied rates. To provide an indication of the significance of imports under free trade agreements, we report the value of imports both excluding and including the trade with free trade agreement partners. The free trade agreements covered by this methodology are listed in table 2.

Since the EU-EFTA free trade agreement excludes agriculture, we constrained the above analysis in the respective markets to the non agricultural product categories. Trade in agricultural products among EU and EFTA countries is treated purely on MFN basis. Therefore, in agriculture we weighted coverage, tariff, average and reduction by all imports including those from EU-EFTA free trade agreement partners.

Agriculture

One of the major accomplishments of the Uruguay Round was the agreement to convert all non-tariff restrictions (for example, quantitative restrictions, variable levies) on imports of agricultural products to tariff equivalents. Though percentages varied

among countries, for the OECD countries as a whole, the tariffication requirement covered about 30 percent of agricultural imports.

Because imports of agricultural products were subject, before the Uruguay Round, to many non-tariff restrictions, to compare "before" tariff rates with "after" tariff rates would provide a misleading account of the outcome of the Round: The "after" rates would include the equivalents of non-tariff restrictions, the "before" rates would not. We have therefore provided two alternative estimates of "before" and "after" levels of tariffs on agricultural products, along with two alternative measures of Uruguay Round reductions. The first of these, labeled "Estimate 1," includes the tariff equivalents of non-tariff restrictions both "before" and "after." The second, labeled "Estimate 2," covers only tariff rates; that is, it excludes the tariff equivalents of non-tariff restrictions, both "before" and "after".

Estimate 1

The Uruguay Round agreement provided guidelines converting their non-tariff restrictions to tariff equivalents. For industrialized countries, conversion was to be based on the observed difference between domestic prices and world prices, and was to provide the same level of protection as prevailed in 1986-1988.

Table 2. Free Trade Agreements Included in Calculations

EEA	MERCOSUR	NAFTA	US-Israel	Australia-New Zealand
Austria	Argentina	Canada	Israel	Australia
European Union	Brazil	Mexico	United States	New Zealand
Finland	Paraguay	United States		
Iceland	Uruguay			
Norway				
Sweden				
Switzerland				

Countries could express the level of protection as an ad valorem rate, a specific rate, or a mixed rate (a rate with both specific and ad valorem components). Tariffication by developing countries was not required to follow these guidelines, but was subject to the give and take of the negotiating process. A high rate notified by one country might incite criticism from other countries or trigger retaliation in the form of high rates on products of interest to the offender.[8]

In practice, countries took liberties with the guidelines. We therefore have not used the ad valorem equivalents of the notified rates as the "before" rates and have instead used Merlinda Ingco's estimates of the actual tariff equivalents of agricultural protection — both tariff and non-tariff — before the Uruguay Round. In computing these equivalents, she followed the guidelines of the Uruguay Round Agreement.[9]

Ingco took data on world and domestic prices from several sources, including the Organization for Economic Cooperation and Development (OECD), US Department of Agriculture (USDA), the Food and Agriculture Organization (FAO), and the World Bank. These sources were complemented by information on internal and reference prices in 1986-88 that were reported in the supplementary tables to the Uruguay Round schedules submitted by the GATT member countries. The tariff equivalent of border protection includes only the effects of market price support measures (price support, tariffs, quotas, and other non-tariff barriers) and excludes direct and indirect income transfers and assistance provided in forms other than border protection. The tariff equivalents based on data about market price support measures from the OECD and USDA databases are calculated as follows:

"After" rates from Ingco's work are based on the schedules of tariffied rates that countries submitted. To convert specific rates to ad valorem equivalents, she used World Bank price projections for the year 2000.

When the post-Uruguay Round tariffs in country submissions were for aggregates of tariff lines[10] and when Ingco's calculated "before" tariff equivalents were at an aggregated level, we used the same tariff equivalent rate for each tariff line contained in an aggregate category. In this way we kept the averaging process for agricultural products parallel with that for manufactured products.

We were able to calculate "before" and "after" tariff rates for more than 95 percent of agricultural tariff lines. In calculating coverage ratios and averages we treated the agricultural tariff lines for which we had no tariff estimate as if there were no trade in these products; that is, we left them out of both the numerator and the denominator of the average or the coverage ratio.

Estimate 2

The second estimate of protection rates on agricultural products does not include tariff equivalents of non-tariff restrictions. These estimates are those provided in the IDB, as converted to ad valorem equivalents (where the tariff rates were specific or mixed rates) by the GATT secretariat. Again, some values are missing; the source provides data for about 85 percent of agricultural imports.[11] As with Estimate 2, in calculating coverage ratios and averages we treated the agricultural tariff lines for which we had no tariff estimate as if there were no trade in these products.

Content of the Tables

All tabulations were made in the legal nomenclature of the economy or group, then aggregated into the product categories used in the tables. Table 3 provides definitions of the product aggregates; table 5, definitions of the groups; and table 1, the year of the import data we used. All of the tariff average and tariff coverage series presented for an economy or group were calculated using import data for the specified year; for example, the "before" and "after" tariff averages were calculated from "before" and "after" tariff rates, but used import weights from the same year.

As to measures of tariff levels and concessions given and received, we have provided six groups of tables:

Concessions given:

Group G.1. Importer economy or group by product category

Group G.2. Importer group by product category

Group G.3. Product category by importer economy or group

Concessions received:

Group R.1. Exporter economy or group by product category

Group R.2. Exporter group by product category

Group R.3. Product category by exporter economy or group

Information on concessions given is provided only for the forty economies whose data are included in the IDB. This means that tables for concessions given, by importing economy or group (group G.1) can be provided for these forty economies only. Thus the tables for concessions given, by importing group (group G.2) include only the forty IDB economies. The group G.2 tables are aggregates not on all of the economies in a particular region, but only over the IDB economies in that region. For example, the table in group G.2 for "South Asia" aggregates data from India and Sri Lanka only because these are the only South Asian economies that reported to the IDB. Each table in group G.2 identifies, in a footnote, the economies included in the aggregates.

Similarly, the reader should be aware that the information we provide for concessions received is for concessions received from the forty IDB economies, not from the entire list of economies that participated in the Uruguay Round.

Concessions Given: The Tables in Groups G.1, G.2 and G.3

These tables provide, for each IDB economy, a profile of the economy's applied tariff levels, along with tariff bindings and tariff reductions agreed at the Uruguay Round. Each coverage ratio or average can be expressed as a ratio of sums of the following type:

$$Column\ Entry = \frac{\sum\limits_{\substack{exporting\ tariff \\ countries\ lines}} \sum Variable_{numerator}}{\sum\limits_{\substack{exporting\ tariff \\ countries\ lines}} \sum Variable_{denominator}}$$

Group G.1. Concessions Given, Importing Economy or Group by Product Category

Table 4 lists the specifics of each element of the tables of Group G.1— the variables from which the sums are constructed along with the range of exporting countries and tariff lines over which the variables are summed.

More precisely, table 4 describes the elements in a row of the "Concessions given" tables of Group G.1. The rows of table 4 correspond with the columns of the Group G.1 tables. For example, the percentage of Australia's imports of "Metals" that were GATT-bound, pre-Uruguay Round is made up of the following numerator and denominator:

- Numerator: the value of Australia's imports summed over (a) all exporters, and (b) over all tariff lines that (i) fall into the product category "Metals" and (ii) were GATT-bound, pre-Uruguay Round.

- Denominator: the value of Australia's

Table 3. Definition of Industrial Product Categories

Category description	Harmonized system nomenclature	CCCN nomenclature
Agriculture, excluding Fish: Estimate 1	0105, 0201-04, 0206-07, 210, 0401-08, 0701-09, 0714, 0801-04, 0808, 0901-2, 0901-02 1001-08, 1201-07, 1404,1505, 1507-15, 1602, 1701, 1801-03, 1805,2101,2304-06,2401, 2403 5201-03,5303-04	0105, 0201,0401-05, 0701, 0706 0801, 0805-06, 0901-02 1001-08, 1201, 1223,1505, 1507, 1509-10, 1602, 1701,1801-03, 1805, 2102 2101, 2304-06, 2401, 5201-03 5502, 5703, 5704
Agriculture, excluding Fish: Estimate 2	Ch. 01-24 (exept Ch. 03 0509, 1504, 1603-05, 2301.20	Ch. 01-24 (except Ch. 3, 0513 1603-05)
Petroleum oils	2709-10	2709-10
Fish and fish products	Ch. 03, 0509, 1504, 1603-05, 2301.20	Ch. 03, 0513, 1504, 1603-05, 2301
Wood, pulp, paper, and furniture	Ch. 44, 45, 47, 4801-14, 4816-23, Ch. 49, 9401-04 (except 9404.90)	Ch. 44, 45, 47, 4801-11, 4813-21, Ch. 49 and 94
Textiles and clothing	3005.90, 3921.12-3004, 13, 3921.90, 4202.12, .22, .32 and .92, Ch. 50-63 (except 5001-03, 5101-03, 5201-02, 5301-02), 6405.20, 6406.10 and .99 6501-05, 6601, 7019.10-20, 8708.21, 8804, 9113.90, 9404.90, 9502.91 and 9612.10	Ch. 50-63 (except 5001-03, 5301-03, 5501, 5503, 5401 and 5701), 6404, 6501- 05, 6601, 7020, 8804 and 9808
Leather, rubber, footwear, and travel goods	Ch. 40, 41 (except 4101-03), 4201-05 (except 4202.12, .22, .32, .92), Ch. 43 (except 4301) and 64 (except 6406.10, .99) and 9605	Ch. 40, 41 (except 4101), 4201-05, Ch. 43 (except 4301) and 64 (except 6404)
Metals	2601-17, 2620, Ch. 72, 7301-20, 7323- 26, Ch. 74-76, 78- 82, 8301-03 and 8306-11	2601, 2603, 7301- 35, 7338-40, Ch. 74-82, 8301-03 and 8306-15

(Continued on the next page)

Table 3. Continued

Category description	Harmonized system nomenclature	CCCN nomenclature
Chemicals and photographic supplies	2705, Ch. 28-30 (except 2905.43-44 and 3005.90), 32 and 33 (except 3301), 3401-02, 3404-05,3407, 3506-07, 3601-04 and Ch. 37-39 (except 3809.10, 3823.60, 3921.12-13, 3921.90)	2705, Ch. 28-30 (except 2904, 3004), 32 and 33 (except 3301), 3401-02, 3404-05, 3407, 3506-07, 3601-05, 3607 and Ch. 37-39 (except 3812 and 3919)
Transport equipment	8601-07, 8609, 8701-08 (except 8708.21), 8711-14, 8716, 8801-03 and 8902-08	8601-09, 8701-06, 8709-12, 8714, 8801-03 and Ch. 89
Non-electric machinery	7321-22, Ch. 84, 8608 and 8709	7336-37, Ch. 84, 8610 and 8707
Electric machinery	8501-18 and 8525-48	Ch. 85
Mineral products and precious stones and metals	Ch. 25, 2701-04, 2706-08, 2711-15, Ch. 31, 3403, 6801-06, 6808-15, Ch. 69-71 (except 7019.10-20) and 9113 (except 9113.90)	Ch. 25, 2701-04, 2706-08, 2711-16, Ch. 31, 3403, 3804, 6801-07, 6809-16 and Ch. 69-72 (except 7020)
Manufactured articles not elsewhere specified	2716, 3406, 3605-06, 4206, 4601-02, 4815, 6506-07, 6602-03, 6701-04, 6807, 8304-05, 8519-24, 8710, 8715, 8805, Ch. 90, 9101-12, 9114, Ch. 92-93, 9405-06 and Ch. 95-97 (except 9502.91 and 9612.10)	2717, 3406, 3606, 3608, 4206, 4601-03, 4812, 6506-07, 6602-03, Ch. 67, 6808, 8304-05, 8708, 8713, 8805, Ch. 90, 9101-11, Ch. 92-93 and Ch. 95-99 (except 9808).

imports summed over (a) all exporters and (b) over all tariff lines that fall in the product category "Metals."

Coverage of Bindings. The tables in Group G.1 report, in the first two columns, tabulations of the percentage of imports that are bound under GATT, pre- and post-Uruguay Round. The third through fifth columns separate the post-Uruguay Round binding into those "above," "at" and "below" the recorded applied rates; that is,

- Above: includes all tariff lines in which the Uruguay Round bound rate is above the "before" Uruguay Round applied rate,

Table 4. Content of the Tables in Group G.1: Concessions Given, Importing Economy or Group by Product Category

Column of table	Variable	Sum over	
		Exporters	Tariff lines
Percentage of imports GATT-bound [a]			
1. Total, pre-Uruguay Round			
Numerator	M	All	All in the product category that were bound, pre-Uruguay Round
Denominator	M	All	All in the product category
2. Total, post-Uruguay Round			
Numerator	M	All	All in the product category that are bound, post-Uruguay Round
Denominator	M	All	All in the product category
3. Above applied rate			
Numerator	M	Not FTA partners	All tariff lines in the product category for which $MFN09F > Tb$
		FTA partners [b]	All tariff lines in the product category for which $MFN09F > 0$
Denominator	M	All	All in the product category
4. At applied rate			
Numerator	M	Not FTA partners	All tariff lines in the product category for which $MFN09F = Tb$
		FTA partners [c]	All tariff lines in the product category for which $MFN09F = 0$
Denominator	M	All	All in the product category
5. Below applied rate			
Numerator	M	Not FTA partners [b]	All tariff lines in the product category for which $MFN09F < Tb$
Denominator	M	All	All in the product category
Levels and changes of MFN rates; imports from the world excluding FTA [a]			
6. Post-Uruguay Round applied rate			
Numerator	$Ta \times M$	Not FTA partners	All in the product category
		FTA partners [c]	All tariff lines in the product category for which $Ta = 0$ [d]
Denominator	M	Same as for the numerator	
7. Tariff reduction			
Numerator	$dT \times M$	Not FTA partners	All in the product category for which $dT > 0$
Denominator	M	Same as for the numerator	
8. Post-Uruguay Round bound rate			
Numerator	$MFN09F \times M$	All	All in the product category that are bound, post-Uruguay Round
Denominator	M	Same as for the numerator	

(Continued on the next page)

Table 4. Continued

		Sum over	
Column of table	*Variable*	*Exporters*	*Tariff lines*

Changes and levels of MFN rates; imports from LMIE's, excluding FTA [a]

9. Post-Uruguay Round applied rate

Numerator	$Ta \times M$	LMIEs that are not FTA partners	All in the product category
		LMIEs that are FTA partners	All tariff lines in the product category on which $Ta = 0$
Denominator	M	Same as for the numerator	

10. Tariff reduction

Numerator	$dT \times M$	LMIEs that are not FTA partners	All in the product category for which $dT > 0$
Denominator	M	Same as for the numerator	

Value of imports in millions of U.S. dollars for the specified year [e]

11. From LMIEs (excluding FTA)	M	LMIEs that are not FTA partners	All in the product category
12. From World (excluding FTA)	M	All that are not FTA partners [c]	All in the product category
13. From World (including FTA partner)	M	All	All in the product category

na=Not applicable.
FTA=Free trade area.
LMIEs=Low- and middle-income economies.

a. A few agricultural tariff lines for which tariff rates could not be determined were left out of both the numerator and the denominator in Estimate 1 and Estimate 2.

b. For trade with (free trade area) partners, the applied rate, before and after, is zero. The binding is therefore above the applied rate for all product categories for which the bound rate, MFN09F, is greater than zero. As the EEA free trade area does not cover agricultural goods, agricultural imports by one EEA partner from another were treated as non-FTA imports.

c. Agricultural imports by one EEA partner from another were treated as non-FTA imports.

d. Tariff averages are of MFN rates, and are weighted by imports that are assessed these MFN rates. Imports from a FTA partner are duty free: that is, they are assessed the MFN rate only when the MFN rate is zero.

e. Includes the agricultural tariff lines for which tariff rates could not be determined.

Each of the following variables is specified per tariff line, per economy of origin:
M = value of imports
Tb = The before-Uruguay Round applied MFN tariff rate [MFN03, or if MFN03 is not available, the minimum of (MFN02, MFN09B)]
Ta = The after-Uruguay Round applied MFN tariff rate [Minimum of (Tb, MFN09F)]
dT = Tariff reduction as determined by $(Tb - Ta)/[1 - 1/2(Tb + Ta)] \times 100$.

- At: includes all tariff lines in which the Uruguay Round bound rate is at the "before" Uruguay Round applied rate

- Below: includes all tariff lines in which the Uruguay Round bound rate is below the "before" Uruguay Round applied rate. This column reports the percentage of imports with tariff cuts.[12]

For trade with free trade agreement partners, the applied rate, before and after, is zero. A binding is therefore above the applied rate for all product categories for which the bound rate, MFN09F, is greater than zero. Likewise, a binding is at the applied rate when the bound rate is zero. As the EEA free trade area does not cover agricultural goods, agricultural imports by one EEA partner from another were treated as non-free trade agreement imports.

Tariff Levels and Tariff Reductions. Columns six to nine provide weighted average tariff levels and reductions on imports from all non free trade agreement partners. The series in column six are the "after" applied rates, as we have defined them above. Tariff rates are specified and tariff reductions calculated by tariff line. Averages are weighted by the value of imports that are assessed these rates.[13] Because we are measuring the level of and changes of MFN rates, the weights are based on the flows of imports that bear these MFN rates. Details of what is covered are provided in table 4.

The user should note that we have defined the tariff reduction as the change divided by unity plus the ad valorem tariff rate: in symbols, $dT/(1+T)$.[14] For many purposes this is a better measure of the impact of the tariff cut than the percentage change of the ad valorem rate, dT/T. For a small country, one whose imports do not affect world prices, $dT/(1+T)$ measures the percentage by which the domestic price of the imported product will decline as a result of the tariff cut.[15] It would be inappropriate, for example, to treat the halving of a 2 percent tariff as equivalent to the halving of a 50 percent tariff. The latter change would allow a 20 percent reduction of domestic price, the former less than a 1 percent reduction — as the $dT/(1+T)$ measures.

The average tariff reductions cover only those tariff lines on which there were tariff reductions (tariff lines with zero changes are not included in the averages). Australia, for example has agreed to reductions of 8.0 percent on 43.3 percent of its imports of all merchandise — and implicitly, to cuts of zero percent on 56.7 percent of its imports.

Because the bound rate is averaged over only those tariff lines for which rates are bound and the "after" applied rates over all tariff lines, the tables sometimes indicate that the average "after" applied rate will be above the average post-Uruguay Round bound rate. For example, the G.1 table for Poland reports for petroleum products a zero average post-Uruguay Round bound rate, but an average post-Uruguay Round applied rate of 2.9 percent This does not imply any GATT violation — it does not suggest that for any tariff line, the applied rate will be above the bound rate. The explanation is that Poland has bound its duties on some petroleum products, and these bound rates are zero. But duties on other petroleum products, which account for 24.3 percent of Poland's imports of petroleum products, are not bound, and carry positive applied rates.

Columns nine and ten repeat the projected applied rates and tariff reductions, but this time they are weighted by the value of imports from non FTA low and middle income countries. These columns measure tariff levels and tariff reductions on the basket of goods that the subject country imports from developing countries. Finally, to provide a sense of proportion across the import categories, column eleven, twelve and thirteen provide information on import values.

Group G.2. Concessions Given, Importing Group by Product Category

The tables in Group G.2 are, in concept, similar to those of Group G.1, except that they are summed over groups of importing countries.

For each variable (i.e., for each column in the G.2 tables) the numerator and denominator, as specified in table 6, are summed across the designated group of importing countries: the group that makes up that particular World Bank analytical group. The makeup of these groups is listed in table 5.

Table 5. Regionally Aggregated Import Markets (Concessions Given)

High-Income Economies	*East Asia*	*Latin America*	*Rest of Europe*
Australia	Indonesia	Argentina	Turkey
Austria	Korea, Republic of	Brazil	
Canada	Macao	Chile	
European Union	Malaysia	Colombia	
Finland	Philippines	El Salvador	
Hong Kong	Thailand	Jamaica	
Iceland		Mexico	
Japan		Peru	
New Zealand		Uruguay	
Norway		Venezuela	
Singapore			
Sweden			
Switzerland			
United States			
Eastern Europe	*North Africa*	*South Asia*	*Sub-Saharan Africa*
Czech and Slovak CU	Tunisia	India	Senegal
Hungary		Sri Lanka	Zimbabwe
Poland			
Romania			

Group G.3. Concessions Given, Product Category by Importing Economy or Group

The product tables in Group G.3 report generally the same information as the country tables in Group G.1, but there are two important differences:

- The first three columns provide simple average; that is, unweighted, tariff levels and reductions,

- We report in columns 5 and 8, weighted average tariff reduction for the entire product category. While the average tariff reduction figures in the tables of Group G.1 cover only tariff lines on which there was a reduction (i.e., assign a zero weight to tariff lines on which there was no reduction), the averages in columns 4-8 in the tables of Group G.3 include the zero cuts (i.e., weigh zero cuts by the percentage of imports in tariff lines whose rates were not reduced).[16]

Table 6 provides details of the content of the tables in Group G.3.

Concessions Received: The Tables in Group R.1, R.2, and R.3

The "concessions received" by, say, Indonesia are the tariff reductions and bindings of the countries that import from Indonesia: that is, the concessions reported in the "concessions given" tables of all countries except Indonesia, weighted by the distribution of Indonesia's exports across these countries. Likewise for the average post-Uruguay Round tariff faced by Indonesia's exports.

Concessions received from high-income economies (HIEs) are analyzed separately from concessions received from low-and middle-income economies (LMIEs). Of course, the coverage of "from" is limited to the countries in the IDB, for which we have information on concessions given. This includes all major high-income countries, but a smaller proportion of the low-and middle-income economies.

While the tabulations provided here take into account the existence of free trade agreements, they do not take into account various schemes of preferences for developing countries such as the Generalized System of Preferences. To the extent that exports from developing countries are charged such preferential duties rather than MFN rates, these tables overstate

Table 6. Content of the Tables in Group G.3: Concessions Given, Product Category by Importing Economy or Group

Column of table	Variable	Sum over	
		Exporters	Tariff lines

Simple average MFN tariff rates [a]

1. Post-Uruguay Round applied rate

Numerator	Ta	na	All in the product category
Denominator	Number of tariff lines in the product category	na	na

2. Tariff reduction

Numerator	dT	na	All in the product category
Denominator	Number of tariff lines in the product category	na	na

3. Post-Uruguay Round bound rate

Numerator	MFN09F	na	All in the product category that are bound, post-Uruguay Round
Denominator	Number of tariff lines in the product category for which the post-UR rate is bound	na	na

Levels and changes of MFN rates, weighted by imports from the world, excluding FTA partners [a]

4. Post-Uruguay Round applied rate

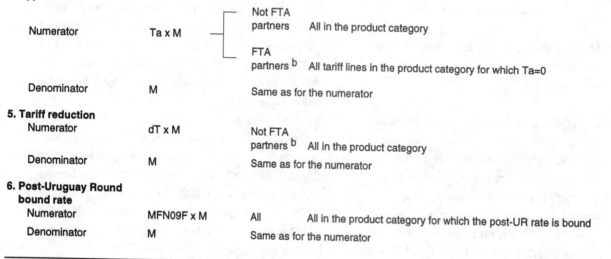

Numerator	Ta x M	Not FTA partners	All in the product category
		FTA partners [b]	All tariff lines in the product category for which Ta=0
Denominator	M	Same as for the numerator	

5. Tariff reduction

Numerator	dT x M	Not FTA partners [b]	All in the product category
Denominator	M	Same as for the numerator	

6. Post-Uruguay Round bound rate

Numerator	MFN09F x M	All	All in the product category for which the post-UR rate is bound
Denominator	M	Same as for the numerator	

(Continued on the next page)

Table 6. Continued

Column of table	Variable	Sum over	
		Exporters	*Tariff lines*

Levels and changes of MFN rates, weighted by imports from LMIEs, excluding FTA partners [a]

7. Post-Uruguay Round applied rate

Numerator	$T_a \times M$	LMIEs that are not FTA partners	All in the product category
		LMIEs that are FTA partners	All in the product category on which $T_a=0$
Denominator	M	Same as for the numerator	

8. Tariff reduction

Numerator	$dT \times M$	LMIEs that are not FTA partners	All in the product category for which $dT > 0$
Denominator	M	Same as for the numerator	

Value of 1988 imports in millions of U.S. dollars [c]

9. From LMIEs (excluding FTA)

	M	LMIEs that are not FTA partners	All in the product category

10. From World (excluding FTA)

	M	All that are not FTA partners [b]	All in the product category

11. From World (including FTA)

	M	All	All in the product category

---

n.a.=not applicable.

a. A few agricultural tariff lines for which tariff rates could not be determined were left out of both the numerator and denominator in Estimate 1 and in Estimate 2.

b. Agricultural imports by one EEA partner from another were treated as non-FTA imports.

c. Includes the agricultural tariff lines for which tariff rates could not be determined.

Each of the following variables is specified per tariff line, per economy of origin
M = Value of imports
T_b = The before-Uruguay Round applied MFN tariff rate [MFN03, or if MFN03 is not available, the minimum of (MFN02, MFN09B)]
T_a = The after-Uruguay Round applied MFN tariff rate [Minimum of (T_b, MFN09F)]
dT = Tariff reduction determined by (T_b - T_a)/ [1 - 1/2(T_b + T_a)] x 100.

Table 7. Content of the Tables in Group R.1: Concessions Received, Exporting Economy or Group by Product

Column of table	Variable [a]	Sum over	
		Importers [b]	Tariff lines
Levels and changes of MFN rates, weighted by subject country's exports to the world excluding FTA partners			
1. Percentage of exports affected by cuts			
Numerator	X	All non-FTA partner IDB countries [c]	All in the product category for which MFN09F < Tb [d]
Denominator	X	All IDB countries	All in the product category
2. Post-Uruguay Round applied rate			
Numerator	T_a x X	All non-FTA partner IDB countries [c]	All in the product category
		All FTA partner IDB countries	All in the product category for which $T_a=0$ [d]
Denominator	X	Same as for the numerator	
3. Tariff reduction			
Numerator	dT x X	All non-FTA partner IDB countries [c]	All in the product category for which dT > 0 [d]
Denominator	X	Same as for the numerator	
4. Post-Uruguay Round bound rate			
Numerator	MFN09F x X	All IDB countries for which the tariff rate is bound, post-Uruguay Round	All in the product category
Denominator	X	Same as for the numerator	
5. Percentage of exports affected			
Numerator	X	All non-FTA partner IDB LMIEs	All in the product category for which MFN09F < Tb [d]
Denominator	X	All IDB LMIEs	All in the product category
6. Post-Uruguay Round applied rate			
Numerator	T_a x X	All non-FTA partner IDB LMIEs	All in the product category
Denominator	X	Same as for the numerator	

(Continued on the next page)

Table 7. Continued

Column of table	Variable [a]	Sum over	
		Importers [b]	Tariff lines
7. Tariff reduction			
Numerator	dT x X	All non-FTA partner IDB LMIEs	All in the product category for which dT > 0 [d]
Denominator	X	Same as for the numerator	
8. Post-Uruguay Round bound rate			
Numerator	MFN09F x X	All IDB LMIEs	All tariff lines in the product category for which the tariffs are bound, Post-Uruguay Round
Denominator	X	Same as for the numerator	
Value of subject country's exports in millions of U.S. dollars			
9. To LMIEs (excluding FTA)	M	All non-FTA-partner LMIEs	All in the product category
10. To World (excluding FTA)	M	All non-FTA partner IDB economies [c]	All in the product category
11. To World (including FTA)	M	All IDB economies	All in the product category

FTA= Free Trade Agreement; LMIEs=Low- and middle-income economies.

a. The tariff rates and import values are those of the importing economies (the economies referred to in the third column).

b. The sum, of course, does not cover the subject exporter.

c. Agricultural exports by one EEA partner to another were treated as non-FTA exports.

d. Refers to the tariff of the importing economy, not of the economy whose concessions received are being tabulated.

Each of the following variables is specified per tariff line, per importing economy:
Tb = The before-Uruguay Round applied MFN tariff rate [MFN03, or if MFN03 is not available, the minimum of (MFN02, MFN09B)]
Ta = The after-Uruguay Round applied MFN tariff rate [Minimum of (Tb, MFN09F)]
dT = Tariff reduction determined by (Tb - Ta)/[1 - 1/2(Tb + Ta)] x 100
X = Value of exports (measured by the value of imports as reported by the importing country).

Table 8. Regionally Aggregated Export Markets (Concessions Received)

Developing Europe and Central Asia	*High-Income Economies*	*Latin America*	*Sub-Saharan Africa*
	Andorra	Antigua and Barbuda	Angola
Albania	Australia	Argentina	Benin
Armenia	Austria	Aruba	Botswana
Azerbaijan	Bahamas, The	Barbados	Burkina Faso
Belarus	Belgium	Belize	Burundi
Bosnia and Herzegovina	Bermuda	Bolivia	Cameroon
Bulgaria	Brunei	Brazil	Cape Verde
Croatia	Canada	Chile	Central African Republic
Czech and Slovak CU	Denmark	Colombia	Chad
Estonia	Faeroe Islands	Costa Rica	Comoros
Georgia	France	Cuba	Congo
Gibraltar	French Polynesia	Dominica	Côte d'Ivoire
Greece	Finland	Dominican Republic	Djibouti
Hungary	Germany	Ecuador	Equatorial Guinea
Kazakstan	Greenland	El Salvador	Eritrea
Kyrgyz Republic	Hong Kong	French Guyana	Ethiopia
Latvia	Iceland	Grenada	Gabon
Lithuania	Ireland	Guadeloupe	Gambia, The
Macedonia, FYR	Israel	Guatemala	Ghana
Malta	Italy	Guyana	Guinea
Moldova	Japan	Haiti	Guinea-Bissau
Poland	Kuwait	Honduras	Kenya
Portugal	Liechtenstein	Jamaica	Lesotho
Romania	Luxembourg	Martinique	Liberia
Russian Federation	Netherlands	Mexico	Madagascar
Slovenia	New Zealand	Netherlands Antilles	Malawi
Tajikistan	Norway	Nicaragua	Mali
Turkey	Quatar	Panama	Mauritania
Turkmenistan	San Marino	Paraguay	Mauritius
Ukraine	Singapore	Peru	Mayotte
Uzbekistan	Spain	Puerto Rico	Mozambique
Yugoslavia, Fed. Rep. of	Sweden	Saint Kitts and Nevis	Namibia
	Switzerland	Saint Lucia	Niger
	Taiwan (China)	St. Vincent and the Grenadines	Nigeria
	United Arab Emirates	Suriname	Reunion
East Asia and Pacific	United Kingdom	Trinidad and Tobago	Rwanda
American Samoa	United States	Uruguay	São Tomé and Principe
Cambodia	US Virgin Islands	Venezuela	Senegal
China			Seychelles
Fiji			Sierra Leone
Guam			Somalia
Indonesia			South Africa
Kiribati	*Middle East*		Sudan
Korea, Dem. Peoples' Rep.			Swaziland
Korea, Rep. of	Algeria		Tanzania
Lao PDR	Bahrain		Togo
Macao	Egypt, Arab Rep.		Uganda
Malaysia	Iran, Islamic Rep.		Zaire
Marshall Islands	Iraq		Zambia
Micronesia, Fed St. of	Jordan		Zimbabwe
Mongolia	Lebanon		
Myanmar	Libya		
New Caledonia	Morocco		
Northern Mariana Isl.	North Africa		*South Asia*
Papua New Guinea	Oman		
Philippines	Saudi Arabia		Afghanistan
Samoa	Syrian Arab Rep.		Bangladesh
Solomon Islands	Tunisia		Bhutan
Thailand	Yemen, Rep. of		India
Tonga			Maldives
Vanuatu			Nepal
Vietnam			Pakistan
			Sri Lanka

Table 9. Content of Columns 1, 2, 5 and 9 of the Tables in Group R.3: Concessions Received, Product Category by Exporting Economy or Group

		Sum over	
Column of table	Variable [a]	Importers [b]	Tariff lines

Percentage of exports GATT-bound

1. Pre-Uruguay Round

Numerator	X	All IDB economies	All in the product category that were bound, pre-UR
Denominator	X	All IDB economies	All in the product category

2. Post-Uruguay Round

Numerator	X	all IDB economies	All in the product category that are bound, post-UR
Denominator	X	all IDB economies	All in the product category

Average levels and changes of MFN rates, weighted by value of exports to the world excluding FTA partners [c]

5. Tariff reduction

Numerator	dT x X	All non-FTA partner IDB economies [d]	All in the product category
Denominator	X	Same as for the numerator	

Average levels and changes of MFN rates, weighted by value of exports to LMIEs excluding FTA partners [c]

9. Tariff reduction

Numerator	dT x X	All non-FTA-partner IDB LMIEs	All in the product category
Denominator	X	Same as for the numerator	

a. The tariff rates and import values are those of the importing economies (the economies referred to in the third column).

b. The sum, of course, does not cover the subject exporter.

c. A few agricultural tariff lines for which tariff rates could not be determined were left out of both the numerator and the denominator in Estimate 1 and Estimate 2.

d. Agricultural imports by one EEA partner from another were treated as non-FTA imports.

Each of the following is specified per tariff line, per exporting economy:

X = Value of exports (measured by the value of imports as reported by the importing economy)

T_b = The before-Uruguay Round applied MFN tariff rate [MFN03, or if MFN03 is not available, the minimum of (MFN02, MFN09B)]

T_a = The after-Uruguay Round applied MFN tariff rate [Minimum of (T_b, MFN09F)]

dT = Tariff reduction determined by $(T_b - T_a)/[1 - 1/2(T_b + T_a)] \times 100$.

the average level of tariffs that are in fact charged on developing countries' exports. Likewise, our calculation of the tariff reduction on a developing country's exports — because it is a calculation of the reduction of the importer's MFN rates — will overstate the reduction of the duties that are in fact paid.

Groups R.1 and R.2. Concessions Received: Exporting Economy or Group, by Product Category

Details of the contents of the tables in Group R.1 and R.2 are provided in table 7. Again, each coverage ratio or average rate is a ratio of sums of the following form:

$$
Column\ Entry = \frac{\displaystyle\sum_{\substack{exporting\ tariff \\ countries\ lines}} \sum Variable_{numerator}}{\displaystyle\sum_{\substack{exporting\ tariff \\ countries\ lines}} \sum Variable_{denominator}}
$$

Table 7 identifies the variables in the numerator and in the denominator of each ratio, along with the range of tariff rates and importing countries for each sum.

The information in the "concessions received" tables has, as its base, the information that underlies the "concessions given" tables. For example, "percent of exports affected" in column 1 is a tabulation of the subject country's exports on which its trading partners have reduced their tariffs. The average tariff reduction in the third column is the average of foreign cuts, weighted by the exports of the subject country. The average reduction is again measured only over those products on which the "before" applied tariff rate was cut.

The tables in Group R.2 are similar to those of Group R.1, except that they are summed over groups of exporting countries. Each numerator and denominator, as defined in table 7, is summed across the designated group of exporting countries — the group that makes up that particular World Bank analytical group. The makeup of these groups is listed in table 8.

Group R.3. Concessions Received: Product Category by Exporting Economy or Group

The information in the tables of Group R.3 is, on the whole, the same as the information in Group R.1 and R.2, but it has been rearranged to emphasize country comparisons. The definitions of the content of the columns are as given in table 7, except for columns 1, 2, 5 and 9.

The first two columns of the tables in Group R.3 provide measures of the percentage of a country's exports that were GATT bound, before and after the Uruguay Round. And in columns 5 and 9, parallel with the measure of average tariff reduction provided in Group G.3, zero reductions were included in the average. The content of these columns is precisely specified in table 9.

Notes

This volume would not have been possible without the excellent computer systems support provided by Tony Sihsobhon. Helpful comments from Christian Bach, Richard Blackhurst, Alice Enders, Han Herderschee, Bernhard Hoekman, Patrick Low, Sally Martin, Will Martin, Francis Ng, Alan Winters, and Alexander Yeats are gratefully acknowledged. We should like to thank Jeff Hayden for editing the volume.

1. "Market Access for Goods and Services: Overview of the Results," Geneva, November 1994, p.8.

2. Coverage of imports in "Agriculture exc. Fish: Estimate 2 "with AVEs for countries with less than 100% coverage: Switzerland, 38.7%; Austria, 42.3%; Sweden, 63.9%; Sri Lanka, 70.1%; European Union, 71.7%; Malaysia, 76.5%; Singapore, 85.5%; Canada, 84.7%; Thailand, 90.3%; Finland, 91.7%; Japan, 91.9%; Zimbabwe, 95.3%; United States, 96.6%; Norway, 97.5%; Australia, 98.8%; Peru, 98.8%; India, 99.1%; Brazil, 99.8%; New Zealand, 99.9%; World (all 40 IDB importers together), 84.8%.

3. Coverage of imports in "Petroleum Oils " with AVEs for countries with less than 100% coverage: Turkey, 0%; Brazil, 0.8%; Japan, 1.2%; Austria, 2.4%; Zimbabwe, 2.6%; Malaysia, 21.3%; India, 24.4%; Thailand, 64.6%; New Zealand, 87.8%; Singapore, 92.6%; Finland, 99.9%; World (all 40 IDB importers together), 72.2%.

4. GATT, "Market Access for Goods and Services: Overview of the Results," GATT, Geneva, November 1994; and GATT, "An Analysis of the Proposed Uruguay Round Agreement, with Particular Emphasis on Aspects of Interest to Developing Economies," GATT Secretariat, Geneva, 29 November 1993.

5. Argentina, Brazil, Chile, India, Mexico, Peru, Uruguay, and Venezuela.

6. A missing value in one of the series was treated as a value higher than the reported values for the other series.

7. C. A. Primo Braga and Alexander Yeats, "Minilateral and Managed Trade in the Post Uruguay Round World," *Minnesota Journal of Global Trade*, 3(2, Summer) 1994, have shown that bilateral and regional preferential arrangements cover almost 50 percent of world trade.

8. Once a country's submitted schedule of tariffed rates was accepted by other WTO members, the guidelines of the Uruguay Round Agreement become irrelevant. It was this acceptance, not the conversion guidelines, that established the WTO-legality of a country's schedule of rates.

9. Merlinda Ingco, "Agricultural Liberalization in the Uruguay Round," World Bank Working Paper No. 1500, World Bank, Washington DC, 1995. Ms. Ingco also explains some of the departures from these specifications that crept into several country's determinations.

10. The Uruguay Round guidelines stipulate that in some instances tariff equivalents be established at the four-digit or six-digit level of the Harmonized System.

11. Breakdown for countries with less than 100% AVE coverage in "Agriculture excluding Fish, Estimate 2:" Switzerland, 38.7%; Austria, 42.3%; Sweden, 63.9%; Sri Lanka, 70.1%; European Union, 71.7%; Malaysia, 76.5%; Singapore, 85.5%; Canada, 84.7%; Thailand, 90.3%; Finland, 91.7%; Japan, 91.9%; Zimbabwe, 95.3%; United States, 96.6%; Norway, 97.5%; Australia, 98.8%; Peru, 98.8%; India, 99.1%; Brazil, 99.8%; New Zealand, 99.9%; World (all 40 IDB importers together), 84.8%.

12. For a few countries, information on "before" rates is not complete. In these instances, the coverage figures in columns 3 through 5 will sum to less than the figure in column 2, (the percentages of bindings at, above, and below the "before" rates will sum to less than the figure for total bindings). It is impossible, of course, to determine which of the three sub-categories are understated. This problem occurs, for example, in the Austrian data.

13. This applies also to the aggregate figures in the bottom two lines to the tables. These aggregate figures are weighted rather than simple averages of the averages for the commodity categories given in the tables.

14. Operationally, the denominator is one plus the average of the "before" and the "after" rate.

15. If T is the ad valorem tariff rate, P is the domestic and P' the foreign price of an imported good, $P = (1+T)P'$ and $dP/P - dP'/P' = dT/(1+T)$. In words, when a tariff is reduced, the percentage decline of the domestic price plus the percentage increase of the foreign price will sum to $dT/(1+T)$.

16. For a country that has no free trade partners, the reduction shown in the commodity tables (G-3) is the product of column 5 and 7 in the country tables (G-1). The latter tables (G-1) report, for example, that the Republic of Korea reduced its tariff rates on 64.2% of all merchandise trade imports by 8.5%, while the commodity table on all merchandise trade shows that this reduction amounted to a 5.46% reduction. The reductions tabulated in the commodity tables are thus much smaller than those listed in the country tables (and fulfill the equation 8.5% x 64.2% = 5.46%).

2

Tables G.1

Concessions Given

Importing Economy or Group by Product Category

ARGENTINA Bindings and levels of MFN tariff rates before and after the Uruguay Round

Summary product category	Percentage of imports GATT bound					Levels and changes weighted by imports from: the World exc. FTA[1]			LMIEs exc. FTA[1]		Value of 1986 imports in $ million		
	Total pre-UR	Total post-UR	Above appl. rates	At appl. rates	Below appl. rates	Post-UR applied rate	Tariff reduction[3]	Post-UR bound rate	Post-UR applied rate	Tariff reduction[3]	from LMIEs exc. FTA[1]	from World exc. FTA[1]	from World inc. FTA
Agriculture, exc. Fish: Estimate 1	1.6	100.0	96.5	0.0	3.5	-0.7	31.8	34.6	7.9	31.8	120.1	133.0	241.5
Agriculture, exc. Fish: Estimate 2	7.3	100.0	99.7	0.3	0.1	4.9	0.8	31.9	5.3	..	153.1	213.2	350.2
Fish and Fish Products	0.0	100.0	100.0	0.0	0.0	5.1	..	35.0	5.1	..	5.6	5.7	10.8
Petroleum Oils	20.8	100.0	69.3	30.7	0.0	29.1	..	34.0	31.8	..	0.0	2.6	2.7
Wood, Pulp, Paper, and Furniture	23.0	100.0	99.8	0.0	0.2	9.9	11.0	30.5	10.9	11.0	42.8	111.4	179.9
Textiles and Clothing	1.1	100.0	99.9	0.0	0.1	12.1	2.2	35.0	13.6	..	16.8	44.8	76.6
Leather, Rubber, Footwear	0.0	100.0	100.0	0.0	0.0	8.4	2.2	35.0	12.7	..	5.6	64.3	74.6
Metals	4.2	100.0	100.0	0.0	0.0	9.3	2.2	34.9	5.8	..	115.1	349.8	501.2
Chemical & Photographic Suppl.	6.3	100.0	99.8	0.2	0.0	6.1	..	22.2	8.5	..	109.5	999.8	1,200.0
Transport Equipment	80.7	100.0	99.1	0.9	0.0	14.7	2.2	34.7	15.4	..	46.2	227.7	279.9
Non-Electric Machinery	24.8	100.0	100.0	0.0	0.0	13.7	..	34.8	15.4	..	48.3	637.7	703.8
Electric Machinery	35.0	100.0	100.0	0.0	0.0	15.2	..	34.8	15.5	..	36.4	441.8	494.8
Mineral Prod., Prec. Stones & Metal	2.1	100.0	99.9	0.0	0.1	9.6	2.2	33.7	9.9	..	375.3	530.0	550.1
Manufactured Articles nes.	19.6	100.0	99.7	0.3	0.0	14.2	..	33.5	9.4	..	25.8	259.4	294.7
Industrial goods (line 5-14)	**18.0**	**100.0**	**99.9**	**0.1**	**0.0**	**10.6**	**4.9**	**30.9**	**10.2**	**11.0**	**821.8**	**3,666.6**	**4,355.6**
All Merch. Trade (line 2-14)	**17.1**	**100.0**	**99.8**	**0.2**	**0.0**	**10.3**	**4.2**	**31.0**	**9.4**	**11.0**	**980.5**	**3,888.1**	**4,719.3**

Notes: 1. Value of imports from partner countries that do not participate in Free Trade Agreements with ARGENTINA

2. Pre-Uruguay Round applied MFN rates from 199 3. Weighted average tariff reduction measured by dT / (1 + T) in percent.

AUSTRALIA Bindings and levels of MFN tariff rates before and after the Uruguay Round

Summary product category	Percentage of imports GATT bound					Levels and changes weighted by imports from: the World exc. FTA[1]			LMIEs exc. FTA[1]		Value of 1988 imports in $ million		
	Total pre-UR	Total post-UR	Above appl. rates	At appl. rates	Below appl. rates	Post-UR applied rate	Tariff reduction[3]	Post-UR bound rate	Post-UR applied rate	Tariff reduction[3]	from LMIEs exc. FTA[1]	from World exc. FTA[1]	from World inc. FTA
Agriculture, exc. Fish: Estimate 1	54.8	100.0	53.1	37.0	9.9	0.1	15.0	1.3	0.5	10.9	282.5	489.1	531.5
Agriculture, exc. Fish: Estimate 2	44.0	100.0	39.5	27.3	32.0	3.3	2.5	4.3	3.8	2.6	501.9	1,202.7	1,443.2
Fish and Fish Products	60.4	100.0	40.9	55.1	4.0	0.4	4.4	1.5	1.3	4.4	143.9	270.2	318.8
Petroleum Oils	7.2	100.0	0.0	100.0	0.0	0.0	..	0.0	0.0	..	603.8	1,171.9	1,222.1
Wood, Pulp, Paper, and Furniture	26.7	100.0	9.3	50.1	40.6	5.6	8.4	5.9	16.0	9.8	272.9	2,036.3	2,338.7
Textiles and Clothing	3.8	89.5	17.5	17.9	54.1	21.6	16.6	24.5	46.4	19.0	924.8	2,099.7	2,245.7
Leather, Rubber, Footwear	7.7	96.4	9.3	17.3	69.7	16.0	7.1	16.7	22.3	7.6	338.5	926.6	991.0
Metals	21.2	96.5	11.7	11.2	73.6	6.4	8.2	6.8	11.9	9.5	378.4	1,672.2	1,772.3
Chemical & Photographic Suppl.	14.6	100.0	40.9	23.3	35.8	5.0	6.7	8.7	9.7	7.2	578.8	3,927.1	4,023.6
Transport Equipment	39.6	99.7	49.0	11.9	38.8	18.2	6.9	22.6	23.7	7.7	68.0	4,028.5	4,039.7
Non-Electric Machinery	67.7	97.2	49.9	8.2	39.2	6.4	7.8	9.6	12.8	9.9	243.2	6,322.3	6,440.3
Electric Machinery	26.4	90.7	8.0	2.6	80.2	13.2	7.0	14.6	21.2	5.4	327.7	2,615.1	2,687.0
Mineral Prod., Prec. Stones & Metal	32.1	97.0	32.4	28.7	36.0	4.8	5.5	6.9	5.1	5.3	385.5	1,389.7	1,449.1
Manufactured Articles nes.	27.9	97.0	24.7	38.5	33.8	4.7	7.6	5.7	10.7	5.8	316.7	2,880.1	2,981.1
Industrial goods (line 5-14)	**33.5**	**96.9**	**31.7**	**19.1**	**46.2**	**9.7**	**8.2**	**12.1**	**21.4**	**10.2**	**3,834.3**	**27,897.6**	**28,968.6**
All Merch. Trade (line 2-14)	**33.3**	**97.2**	**30.9**	**22.9**	**43.3**	**8.9**	**8.0**	**11.1**	**16.5**	**9.6**	**5,084.0**	**30,542.4**	**31,962.7**

Notes: 1. Value of imports from partner countries that do not participate in Free Trade Agreements with AUSTRALIA

2. Pre-Uruguay Round applied MFN rates from 198 3. Weighted average tariff reduction measured by dT / (1 + T) in percent.

AUSTRIA Bindings and levels of MFN tariff rates before and after the Uruguay Round

Summary product category	Percentage of imports GATT bound					Levels and changes weighted by imports from: the World exc. FTA[1]			LMIEs exc. FTA[1]		Value of 1988 imports in $ million		
	Total pre-UR	Total post-UR	Above appl. rates	At appl. rates	Below appl. rates	Post-UR applied rate	Tariff reduction[3]	Post-UR bound rate	Post-UR applied rate	Tariff reduction[3]	from LMIEs exc. FTA[1]	from World exc. FTA[1]	from World inc. FTA
Agriculture, exc. Fish: Estimate 1	58.0	100.0	69.4	8.5	21.1	20.0	67.9	50.3	17.6	67.8	521.8	1,003.8	1,003.8
Agriculture, exc. Fish: Estimate 2	49.9	100.0	11.1	20.5	10.7	3.2	4.2	4.8	1.7	3.8	680.6	1,959.4	1,959.4
Fish and Fish Products	88.0	100.0	21.2	38.2	7.5	2.8	5.8	6.3	10.2	5.8	18.8	29.4	100.8
Petroleum Oils	75.8	100.0	2.3	0.0	0.1	5.7	2.7	6.4	6.9	2.2	878.1	897.1	1,139.4
Wood, Pulp, Paper, and Furniture	100.0	100.0	35.6	55.7	6.9	0.3	5.5	3.8	4.9	5.7	280.1	379.6	2,605.4
Textiles and Clothing	77.4	100.0	74.5	6.3	17.0	11.0	7.8	14.3	22.9	7.5	409.4	550.1	3,015.2
Leather, Rubber, Footwear	100.0	100.0	79.1	6.8	14.1	7.4	5.2	10.1	13.6	5.3	133.6	174.9	1,046.0
Metals	100.0	100.0	49.5	41.7	4.9	0.5	5.0	3.7	3.4	5.6	279.1	385.9	2,997.9
Chemical & Photographic Suppl.	89.9	100.0	46.9	42.2	5.2	0.4	6.3	3.3	4.0	6.7	189.7	451.4	3,669.9
Transport Equipment	98.7	100.0	71.7	5.3	20.7	17.3	3.8	18.3	11.6	3.2	29.5	878.3	3,883.8
Non-Electric Machinery	100.0	100.0	62.5	30.4	6.9	0.8	2.6	3.3	6.3	2.8	67.9	884.7	4,855.1
Electric Machinery	94.9	100.0	66.6	12.9	17.8	6.7	4.8	8.5	17.4	6.2	159.3	593.8	2,488.8
Mineral Prod.,Prec. Stones & Metal	100.0	100.0	45.5	30.6	21.8	1.1	1.8	3.6	2.2	1.7	737.2	852.0	1,916.0
Manufactured Articles nes.	99.0	100.0	47.1	28.9	19.1	2.3	4.3	3.6	7.0	4.7	208.4	693.0	2,176.8
Industrial goods (line 5-14)	**95.6**	**100.0**	**57.9**	**27.0**	**12.5**	**3.3**	**4.5**	**7.4**	**8.5**	**4.9**	**2,494.1**	**5,843.7**	**28,654.8**
All Merch. Trade (line 2-14)	**92.1**	**100.0**	**52.9**	**25.7**	**12.0**	**3.3**	**4.5**	**7.3**	**7.3**	**4.9**	**4,071.5**	**8,729.6**	**31,854.5**

Notes: 1. Value of imports from partner countries that do not participate in Free Trade Agreements with AUSTRIA

2. Pre-Uruguay Round applied MFN rates from 198 3. Weighted average tariff reduction measured by dT / (1 + T) in percent.

BRAZIL Bindings and levels of MFN tariff rates before and after the Uruguay Round

Summary product category	Percentage of imports GATT bound					Levels and changes weighted by imports from: the World exc. FTA[1]			LMIEs exc. FTA[1]		Value of 1989 imports in $ million		
	Total pre-UR	Total post-UR	Above appl. rates	At appl. rates	Below appl. rates	Post-UR applied rate	Tariff reduction[3]	Post-UR bound rate	Post-UR applied rate	Tariff reduction[3]	from LMIEs exc. FTA[1]	from World exc. FTA[1]	from World inc. FTA
Agriculture, exc. Fish: Estimate 1	25.9	100.0	99.8	0.2	0.0	-21.4	..	35.9	-23.0	..	75.8	463.0	1,230.6
Agriculture, exc. Fish: Estimate 2	29.3	100.0	92.2	2.2	5.4	11.0	0.9	39.3	10.4	0.9	183.9	904.4	1,856.4
Fish and Fish Products	36.0	100.0	64.2	35.8	0.0	5.8	..	22.4	11.7	..	32.1	122.5	185.9
Petroleum Oils	0.0	100.0	0.8	0.0	0.0	0.0	..	35.0	17.9	..	3,435.3	4,155.3	4,171.2
Wood, Pulp, Paper, and Furniture	47.1	100.0	66.4	33.6	0.0	2.0	..	19.3	2.2	..	98.1	424.1	495.3
Textiles and Clothing	2.2	100.0	98.0	2.0	0.0	15.5	3.6	33.9	14.5	3.6	44.1	158.6	263.0
Leather, Rubber, Footwear	2.6	100.0	100.0	0.0	0.0	10.6	..	34.7	9.0	..	63.0	400.3	616.7
Metals	22.8	100.0	99.9	0.1	0.0	5.6	..	29.2	2.2	..	514.0	1,321.5	1,414.4
Chemical & Photographic Suppl.	7.0	100.0	90.9	9.1	0.0	11.5	..	21.8	9.6	..	374.3	2,608.6	2,851.3
Transport Equipment	0.4	100.0	98.8	1.2	0.0	11.7	..	33.8	18.5	..	14.1	666.1	718.3
Non-Electric Machinery	18.8	100.0	93.7	6.3	0.0	18.9	..	30.0	20.9	..	42.0	2,526.2	2,634.5
Electric Machinery	11.8	100.0	96.1	3.9	0.0	16.6	..	31.6	19.3	..	71.3	1,478.7	1,492.9
Mineral Prod.,Prec. Stones & Metal	54.7	100.0	70.8	19.6	0.0	1.2	..	18.4	1.9	..	476.1	1,601.8	1,674.2
Manufactured Articles nes.	13.6	100.0	95.6	3.4	0.9	15.2	2.9	35.0	8.6	3.6	112.5	1,133.1	1,384.0
Industrial goods (line 5-14)	**18.9**	**100.0**	**91.0**	**7.7**	**0.1**	**11.8**	**2.9**	**27.7**	**7.4**	**3.6**	**1,809.4**	**12,319.0**	**13,544.7**
All Merch. Trade (line 2-14)	**16.0**	**100.0**	**71.8**	**5.8**	**0.6**	**11.7**	**1.1**	**29.0**	**12.6**	**1.2**	**5,460.8**	**17,501.3**	**19,758.1**

Notes: 1. Value of imports from partner countries that do not participate in Free Trade Agreements with BRAZIL

2. Pre-Uruguay Round applied MFN rates from 199 3. Weighted average tariff reduction measured by dT / (1 + T) in percent.

CANADA Bindings and levels of MFN tariff rates before and after the Uruguay Round

Summary product category	Percentage of imports GATT bound					Levels and changes weighted by imports from: the World exc. FTA[1]			LMIEs exc. FTA[1]		Value of 1988 imports in $ million		
	Total pre-UR	Total post-UR	Above appl. rates	At appl. rates	Below appl. rates	Post-UR applied rate	Tariff reduc-tion[3]	Post-UR bound rate	Post-UR applied rate	Tariff reduc-tion[3]	from LMIEs exc. FTA[1]	from World exc. FTA[1]	from World inc. FTA
Agriculture, exc. Fish: Estimate 1	98.4	100.0	13.0	86.3	0.0	7.0	..	7.7	1.5	..	699.2	1,226.0	2,780.9
Agriculture, exc. Fish: Estimate 2	98.5	100.0	20.3	49.9	14.5	1.5	2.4	2.8	2.6	2.8	1,128.0	2,508.9	5,650.8
Fish and Fish Products	99.7	100.0	8.3	64.5	27.2	1.9	3.1	2.1	5.5	3.1	197.1	308.7	584.2
Petroleum Oils	2.3	2.3	2.1	0.0	0.2	0.0	3.2	6.5	0.1	3.2	878.8	2,732.3	3,222.3
Wood, Pulp, Paper, and Furniture	95.5	100.0	12.2	70.9	16.9	0.6	7.2	1.2	8.4	5.9	167.1	1,007.6	4,632.5
Textiles and Clothing	100.0	100.0	30.4	4.8	64.8	14.2	5.7	13.5	20.5	5.4	1,391.2	2,958.4	4,308.9
Leather, Rubber, Footwear	100.0	100.0	34.6	13.9	51.5	9.2	4.7	8.7	15.5	4.8	635.8	1,484.5	2,561.0
Metals	100.0	100.0	40.7	28.1	31.2	1.5	5.5	3.0	4.8	5.1	865.3	2,955.3	7,689.9
Chemical & Photographic Suppl.	99.9	100.0	55.0	21.0	24.0	2.6	5.9	4.7	6.7	6.7	347.6	2,451.8	7,649.7
Transport Equipment	99.6	99.8	71.7	13.2	14.9	3.2	3.0	5.3	9.0	2.9	330.4	5,543.6	27,637.6
Non-Electric Machinery	100.0	100.0	38.4	42.5	19.0	1.2	4.1	3.0	6.3	3.7	413.6	5,465.2	20,245.2
Electric Machinery	100.0	100.0	41.3	38.6	20.1	1.6	5.3	3.5	5.3	6.5	638.7	3,011.8	9,196.9
Mineral Prod.,Prec. Stones & Metal	97.9	97.9	8.7	75.7	13.5	0.8	5.3	1.3	2.9	6.1	382.7	1,146.3	4,405.0
Manufactured Articles nes.	98.2	98.5	21.8	49.2	27.5	1.5	5.1	2.5	9.6	7.1	423.6	2,802.1	6,545.2
Industrial goods (line 5-14)	**99.4**	**99.8**	**45.7**	**31.6**	**22.5**	**2.6**	**4.8**	**4.3**	**10.2**	**5.3**	**5,595.9**	**28,826.5**	**94,872.0**
All Merch. Trade (line 2-14)	**96.4**	**96.8**	**42.7**	**31.8**	**21.4**	**2.4**	**4.7**	**4.2**	**8.0**	**5.1**	**7,799.8**	**34,376.3**	**104,329.0**

Notes: 1. Value of imports from partner countries that do not participate in Free Trade Agreements with CANADA

2. Pre-Uruguay Round applied MFN rates from 198 3. Weighted average tariff reduction measured by dT / (1 + T) in percent.

CHILE Bindings and levels of MFN tariff rates before and after the Uruguay Round

Summary product category	Percentage of imports GATT bound					Levels and changes weighted by imports from: the World exc. FTA[1]			LMIEs exc. FTA[1]		Value of 1986 imports in $ million		
	Total pre-UR	Total post-UR	Above appl. rates	At appl. rates	Below appl. rates	Post-UR applied rate	Tariff reduc-tion[3]	Post-UR bound rate	Post-UR applied rate	Tariff reduc-tion[3]	from LMIEs exc. FTA[1]	from World exc. FTA[1]	from World inc. FTA
Agriculture, exc. Fish: Estimate 1	100.0	100.0	87.2	0.0	12.8	-8.4	15.9	25.0	-2.3	15.8	78.1	110.8	110.8
Agriculture, exc. Fish: Estimate 2	100.0	100.0	100.0	0.0	0.0	11.0	..	26.5	11.0	..	96.3	155.8	155.8
Fish and Fish Products	100.0	100.0	100.0	0.0	0.0	11.0	..	25.0	11.0	..	0.4	0.8	0.8
Petroleum Oils	100.0	100.0	100.0	0.0	0.0	11.0	..	25.0	11.0	..	319.2	348.6	348.6
Wood, Pulp, Paper, and Furniture	100.0	100.0	100.0	0.0	0.0	11.0	..	25.0	11.0	..	27.5	82.9	82.9
Textiles and Clothing	100.0	100.0	99.7	0.3	0.0	11.0	..	24.9	11.0	..	84.7	181.7	181.7
Leather, Rubber, Footwear	100.0	100.0	100.0	0.0	0.0	11.0	..	25.0	11.0	..	27.9	77.1	77.1
Metals	100.0	100.0	100.0	0.0	0.0	11.0	..	25.0	11.0	..	77.0	204.9	204.9
Chemical & Photographic Suppl.	100.0	100.0	100.0	0.0	0.0	11.0	..	25.0	11.0	..	121.8	462.5	462.5
Transport Equipment	100.0	100.0	97.0	3.0	0.0	10.8	..	24.3	11.0	..	76.9	226.5	226.5
Non-Electric Machinery	100.0	100.0	100.0	0.0	0.0	11.0	..	25.0	11.0	..	60.2	561.7	561.7
Electric Machinery	100.0	100.0	100.0	0.0	0.0	11.0	..	25.0	11.0	..	39.1	247.1	247.1
Mineral Prod.,Prec. Stones & Metal	100.0	100.0	100.0	0.0	0.0	11.0	..	25.0	11.0	..	27.1	156.7	156.7
Manufactured Articles nes.	100.0	100.0	100.0	0.0	0.0	11.0	..	25.0	11.0	..	48.2	155.5	155.5
Industrial goods (line 5-14)	**100.0**	**100.0**	**99.7**	**0.3**	**0.0**	**11.0**	**..**	**24.9**	**11.0**	**..**	**590.2**	**2,356.6**	**2,356.6**
All Merch. Trade (line 2-14)	**100.0**	**100.0**	**99.7**	**0.3**	**0.0**	**11.0**	**..**	**25.0**	**11.0**	**..**	**1,006.2**	**2,861.8**	**2,861.8**

Notes: 1. Value of imports from partner countries that do not participate in Free Trade Agreements with CHILE

2. Pre-Uruguay Round applied MFN rates from 199 3. Weighted average tariff reduction measured by dT / (1 + T) in percent.

COLOMBIA Bindings and levels of MFN tariff rates before and after the Uruguay Round

Summary product category	Percentage of imports GATT bound					Levels and changes weighted by imports from: the World exc. FTA[1]			LMIEs exc. FTA[1]		Value of 1991 imports in $ million		
	Total pre-UR	Total post-UR	Above appl. rates	At appl. rates	Below appl. rates	Post-UR applied rate	Tariff reduc-tion[3]	Post-UR bound rate	Post-UR applied rate	Tariff reduc-tion[3]	from LMIEs exc. FTA[1]	from World exc. FTA[1]	from World inc. FTA
Agriculture, exc. Fish: Estimate 1	5.7	100.0	100.0	0.0	0.0	-17.2	..	106.0	-17.0	..	63.1	178.0	178.0
Agriculture, exc. Fish: Estimate 2	7.9	100.0	95.0	5.0	0.0	14.5	..	98.3	15.9	..	138.1	356.5	356.5
Fish and Fish Products	0.0	100.0	100.0	0.0	0.0	20.0	..	54.6	20.0	..	0.1	0.1	0.1
Petroleum Oils	0.0	100.0	100.0	0.0	0.0	13.7	..	35.0	13.7	..	258.3	283.5	283.5
Wood, Pulp, Paper, and Furniture	0.0	100.0	100.0	0.0	0.0	8.6	..	35.0	8.2	..	50.0	248.1	248.1
Textiles and Clothing	10.3	100.0	100.0	0.0	0.0	15.9	..	36.0	15.0	..	39.2	153.6	153.6
Leather, Rubber, Footwear	22.9	100.0	100.0	0.0	0.0	9.5	..	33.9	8.0	..	38.7	113.9	113.9
Metals	0.2	100.0	100.0	0.0	0.0	10.4	..	35.0	10.0	..	285.1	524.1	524.1
Chemical & Photographic Suppl.	9.8	100.0	100.0	0.0	0.0	8.1	..	34.6	8.5	..	240.3	1,113.9	1,113.9
Transport Equipment	0.0	100.0	73.3	19.7	7.0	20.9	3.6	36.6	16.5	3.6	52.0	374.6	374.6
Non-Electric Machinery	3.0	100.0	100.0	0.0	0.0	8.5	..	35.0	8.5	..	79.0	791.5	791.5
Electric Machinery	3.2	100.0	100.0	0.0	0.0	10.6	..	35.0	12.0	..	57.4	444.4	444.4
Mineral Prod.,Prec. Stones & Metal	0.0	100.0	100.0	0.0	0.0	7.3	..	35.0	8.2	..	48.1	221.1	221.1
Manufactured Articles nes.	0.4	100.0	100.0	0.0	0.0	12.4	..	37.1	9.6	..	48.0	308.0	308.0
Industrial goods (line 5-14)	4.4	100.0	97.7	1.7	0.6	10.4	3.6	35.2	9.9	3.6	937.6	4,293.2	4,293.2
All Merch. Trade (line 2-14)	4.4	100.0	97.6	1.9	0.5	10.9	3.6	35.7	11.2	3.6	1,334.2	4,933.3	4,933.3

Notes: 1. Value of imports from partner countries that do not participate in Free Trade Agreements with COLOMBIA

2. Pre-Uruguay Round applied MFN rates from 199 3. Weighted average tariff reduction measured by dT / (1 + T) in percent.

CZECH & SLOVAK CU Bindings and levels of MFN tariff rates before and after the Uruguay Round

Summary product category	Percentage of imports GATT bound					Levels and changes weighted by imports from: the World exc. FTA[1]			LMIEs exc. FTA[1]		Value of 1990 imports in $ million		
	Total pre-UR	Total post-UR	Above appl. rates	At appl. rates	Below appl. rates	Post-UR applied rate	Tariff reduc-tion[3]	Post-UR bound rate	Post-UR applied rate	Tariff reduc-tion[3]	from LMIEs exc. FTA[1]	from World exc. FTA[1]	from World inc. FTA
Agriculture, exc. Fish: Estimate 1	90.3	100.0	92.0	0.0	8.0	-0.3	14.3	19.0	0.2	13.5	545.5	680.1	680.1
Agriculture, exc. Fish: Estimate 2	86.0	100.0	8.3	35.6	56.0	8.5	3.0	10.5	9.2	3.2	611.7	892.5	892.5
Fish and Fish Products	100.0	100.0	0.0	39.3	60.7	0.0	0.6	0.0	0.2	0.8	14.6	44.5	44.5
Petroleum Oils	100.0	100.0	0.0	88.7	11.3	0.5	1.1	0.5	0.2	1.1	785.3	856.2	856.2
Wood, Pulp, Paper, and Furniture	100.0	100.0	0.0	24.5	75.5	4.8	1.8	4.8	7.4	2.0	90.7	218.1	218.1
Textiles and Clothing	93.5	100.0	0.1	15.8	84.1	6.6	2.0	6.6	9.6	2.0	334.8	615.5	615.5
Leather, Rubber, Footwear	77.5	100.0	0.0	32.4	67.6	3.4	1.7	3.4	5.4	1.8	221.2	322.1	322.1
Metals	100.0	100.0	0.0	54.4	45.6	1.9	0.9	1.9	2.0	0.9	825.2	1,096.6	1,096.6
Chemical & Photographic Suppl.	100.0	100.0	0.0	71.6	28.4	4.1	2.5	4.1	4.3	2.8	216.2	1,094.3	1,094.3
Transport Equipment	100.0	100.0	0.0	0.0	100.0	6.9	1.3	6.9	8.1	1.2	216.7	355.1	3.5.1
Non-Electric Machinery	96.7	100.0	0.0	0.8	99.2	3.3	1.0	3.3	4.5	1.0	731.1	2,813.5	2,813.5
Electric Machinery	99.6	100.0	0.0	4.0	96.0	5.4	1.6	5.4	7.7	1.7	265.8	658.9	658.9
Mineral Prod.,Prec. Stones & Metal	96.0	100.0	0.0	68.0	32.0	1.8	1.5	1.8	1.6	1.7	335.9	493.0	493.0
Manufactured Articles nes.	96.0	100.0	0.4	34.5	65.1	2.5	1.2	2.8	2.8	1.4	356.8	889.0	889.0
Industrial goods (line 5-14)	96.9	100.0	0.1	27.2	72.8	3.7	1.3	3.7	4.5	1.4	3,594.4	8,556.0	8,556.0
All Merch. Trade (line 2-14)	96.2	100.0	0.8	33.1	66.2	3.8	1.4	4.0	4.4	1.6	5,006.0	10,349.2	10,349.2

Notes: 1. Value of imports from partner countries that do not participate in Free Trade Agreements with CZECH & SLOVAK CU

2. Pre-Uruguay Round applied MFN rates from 199 3. Weighted average tariff reduction measured by dT / (1 + T) in percent.

EL SALVADOR Bindings and levels of MFN tariff rates before and after the Uruguay Round

Summary product category	Percentage of imports GATT bound					Levels and changes weighted by imports from: the World exc. FTA[1]			LMIEs exc. FTA[1]		Value of 1989 imports in $ million		
	Total pre-UR	Total post-UR	Above appl. rates	At appl. rates	Below appl. rates	Post-UR applied rate	Tariff reduction[3]	Post-UR bound rate	Post-UR applied rate	Tariff reduction[3]	from LMIEs exc. FTA[1]	from World exc. FTA[1]	from World inc. FTA
Agriculture, exc. Fish: Estimate 1	100.0	100.0	99.5	0.0	0.5	-11.8	18.2	33.8	-5.4	18.2	12.5	90.5	90.5
Agriculture, exc. Fish: Estimate 2	100.0	100.0	99.0	0.2	0.8	12.9	3.9	42.8	21.8	3.9	47.2	154.8	154.8
Fish and Fish Products	100.0	100.0	100.0	0.0	0.0	26.9	..	48.7	27.5	..	3.5	3.7	3.7
Petroleum Oils	100.0	100.0	100.0	0.0	0.0	5.3	..	40.0	5.0	..	81.3	102.4	102.4
Wood, Pulp, Paper, and Furniture	100.0	100.0	99.9	0.1	0.0	10.6	..	27.8	17.2	..	21.4	71.3	71.3
Textiles and Clothing	100.0	100.0	82.4	8.9	8.7	18.3	3.8	39.0	20.9	3.8	17.6	33.8	33.8
Leather, Rubber, Footwear	100.0	100.0	97.0	0.0	3.0	13.3	3.8	33.7	16.1	3.8	18.4	29.4	29.4
Metals	100.0	100.0	100.0	0.0	0.0	9.8	..	36.0	12.5	..	49.7	116.1	116.1
Chemical & Photographic Suppl.	100.0	100.0	98.8	1.2	0.0	9.9	..	29.9	14.5	..	77.4	185.4	185.4
Transport Equipment	100.0	100.0	100.0	0.0	0.0	15.5	6.9	32.0	13.7	..	20.5	118.7	118.7
Non-Electric Machinery	100.0	100.0	100.0	0.0	0.0	7.5	..	30.1	12.7	..	14.2	104.6	104.6
Electric Machinery	100.0	100.0	100.0	0.0	0.0	10.5	..	32.1	16.0	..	14.0	58.0	58.0
Mineral Prod.,Prec. Stones & Metal	100.0	100.0	100.0	0.0	0.0	7.2	..	28.8	10.2	..	18.8	62.1	62.1
Manufactured Articles nes.	50.7	50.7	50.7	0.0	0.0	12.7	..	36.3	19.0	..	29.7	48.3	48.3
Industrial goods (line 5-14)	**97.1**	**97.1**	**96.0**	**0.7**	**0.5**	**10.9**	**3.8**	**31.7**	**14.6**	**3.8**	**281.7**	**827.9**	**827.9**
All Merch. Trade (line 2-14)	**97.8**	**97.8**	**96.8**	**0.5**	**0.5**	**10.7**	**3.8**	**34.2**	**13.6**	**3.8**	**413.7**	**1,088.8**	**1,088.8**

Notes: 1. Value of imports from partner countries that do not participate in Free Trade Agreements with EL SALVADOR

2. Pre-Uruguay Round applied MFN rates from 199 3. Weighted average tariff reduction measured by dT / (1 + T) in percent.

EUROPEAN UNION Bindings and levels of MFN tariff rates before and after the Uruguay Round

Summary product category	Percentage of imports GATT bound					Levels and changes weighted by imports from: the World exc. FTA[1]			LMIEs exc. FTA[1]		Value of 1988 imports in $ million		
	Total pre-UR	Total post-UR	Above appl. rates	At appl. rates	Below appl. rates	Post-UR applied rate	Tariff reduction[3]	Post-UR bound rate	Post-UR applied rate	Tariff reduction[3]	from LMIEs exc. FTA[1]	from World exc. FTA[1]	from World inc. FTA
Agriculture, exc. Fish: Estimate 1	86.1	100.0	0.0	94.8	5.2	15.7	5.9	15.7	11.2	5.9	21,772.9	29,105.4	29,105.4
Agriculture, exc. Fish: Estimate 2	85.6	100.0	0.0	30.3	41.4	3.7	4.4	3.8	8.4	4.6	28,109.0	40,393.6	40,393.6
Fish and Fish Products	99.6	100.0	30.4	41.6	28.0	11.0	5.3	11.6	14.7	5.3	3,104.4	4,593.5	6,213.3
Petroleum Oils	100.0	100.0	13.6	83.8	2.7	0.4	1.3	0.9	0.4	1.3	35,940.1	39,091.2	43,950.3
Wood, Pulp, Paper, and Furniture	100.0	100.0	3.5	79.8	16.7	0.3	5.5	0.5	3.2	5.0	7,269.5	14,766.6	34,027.4
Textiles and Clothing	99.9	100.0	15.6	13.9	70.5	8.7	2.0	8.5	10.9	1.9	16,874.1	25,658.0	30,487.1
Leather, Rubber, Footwear	93.9	100.0	11.1	29.2	59.7	4.9	1.9	4.9	6.1	1.9	6,612.5	9,361.9	10,676.2
Metals	99.9	100.0	19.6	58.8	21.6	1.0	3.3	1.7	2.3	3.6	14,958.1	22,874.1	35,672.8
Chemical & Photographic Suppl.	97.3	100.0	27.2	28.2	44.5	3.8	3.3	4.4	6.9	3.7	7,255.3	19,044.6	30,322.8
Transport Equipment	100.0	100.0	17.3	60.6	22.2	5.5	2.4	6.2	3.8	2.4	6,315.6	21,795.2	27,233.0
Non-Electric Machinery	99.9	100.0	24.3	9.4	66.3	1.4	3.0	1.6	4.9	2.5	3,488.5	34,085.8	48,303.1
Electric Machinery	100.0	100.0	21.5	12.6	65.9	5.4	3.5	5.2	9.3	3.2	5,479.0	24,318.1	31,063.1
Mineral Prod.,Prec. Stones & Metal	100.0	100.0	19.2	60.8	20.0	0.5	1.1	0.7	0.6	1.3	29,552.3	37,605.3	43,437.5
Manufactured Articles nes.	99.9	100.0	12.0	33.9	54.1	2.5	3.3	2.6	3.8	3.0	8,096.5	30,143.3	37,740.3
Industrial goods (line 5-14)	**99.5**	**100.0**	**17.7**	**39.0**	**43.3**	**2.9**	**2.9**	**3.2**	**4.5**	**2.6**	**105,901.0**	**239,653.0**	**328,963.0**
All Merch. Trade (line 2-14)	**98.2**	**100.0**	**15.8**	**42.9**	**38.6**	**2.8**	**3.1**	**3.2**	**4.3**	**3.1**	**173,055.0**	**323,731.0**	**419,521.0**

Notes: 1. Value of imports from partner countries that do not participate in Free Trade Agreements with EUROPEAN UNION

2. Pre-Uruguay Round applied MFN rates from 198 3. Weighted average tariff reduction measured by dT / (1 + T) in percent.

FINLAND Bindings and levels of MFN tariff rates before and after the Uruguay Round

	Percentage of imports GATT bound					Levels and changes weighted by imports from: the World exc. FTA[1]			LMIEs exc. FTA[1]		Value of 1988 imports in $ million		
Summary product category	Total pre-UR	Total post-UR	Above appl. rates	At appl. rates	Below appl. rates	Post-UR applied rate	Tariff reduc-tion[3]	Post-UR bound rate	Post-UR applied rate	Tariff reduc-tion[3]	from LMIEs exc. FTA[1]	from World exc. FTA[1]	from World inc. FTA
Agriculture, exc. Fish: Estimate 1	73.9	100.0	0.0	94.6	5.4	36.2	11.1	36.2	33.6	11.1	304.6	570.6	570.6
Agriculture, exc. Fish: Estimate 2	75.8	100.0	0.0	21.4	70.3	48.7	10.3	48.7	61.0	9.8	429.6	1,256.0	1,256.0
Fish and Fish Products	94.1	100.0	67.7	26.9	1.7	8.1	2.8	7.4	9.0	2.5	18.5	29.1	94.7
Petroleum Oils	100.0	100.0	2.4	97.5	0.0	0.0	..	0.1	0.0	..	1,393.9	1,397.5	1,437.1
Wood, Pulp, Paper, and Furniture	100.0	100.0	8.8	84.4	6.7	0.1	4.2	0.4	0.7	4.0	254.1	322.8	942.7
Textiles and Clothing	90.8	100.0	68.1	8.3	23.5	13.9	7.4	15.5	27.0	7.4	252.3	357.4	1,381.8
Leather, Rubber, Footwear	100.0	100.0	65.2	19.0	15.8	6.3	4.6	9.6	11.3	4.3	131.7	160.3	612.9
Metals	99.9	100.0	32.0	63.4	4.6	0.3	5.0	1.5	1.4	5.9	382.5	590.1	2,068.7
Chemical & Photographic Suppl.	99.5	100.0	28.6	69.0	2.4	0.2	6.8	1.6	1.4	7.8	150.4	370.9	2,350.6
Transport Equipment	100.0	100.0	52.3	38.3	9.4	3.7	1.8	5.0	5.6	1.8	302.8	1,183.9	2,829.7
Non-Electric Machinery	97.6	100.0	61.0	31.4	7.6	1.0	2.6	2.3	3.7	1.7	101.3	937.8	3,536.8
Electric Machinery	100.0	100.0	69.1	11.8	19.0	3.9	4.3	5.3	9.1	5.0	133.1	563.4	1,682.8
Mineral Prod.,Prec. Stones & Metal	100.0	100.0	21.5	75.3	3.3	0.4	4.2	1.9	0.7	4.3	449.8	558.0	1,079.9
Manufactured Articles nes.	99.1	100.0	34.6	52.8	12.3	1.2	3.8	2.4	2.3	4.5	302.1	770.9	1,671.7
Industrial goods (line 5-14)	98.7	100.0	46.1	44.3	9.5	1.9	4.3	4.0	5.5	4.6	2,460.2	5,815.4	18,157.7
All Merch. Trade (line 2-14)	97.4	100.0	40.4	46.5	12.5	5.9	6.3	6.2	9.2	6.1	4,302.2	8,498.0	20,945.5

Notes: 1. Value of imports from partner countries that do not participate in Free Trade Agreements with FINLAND

2. Pre-Uruguay Round applied MFN rates from 198 3. Weighted average tariff reduction measured by dT / (1 + T) in percent.

HONG KONG Bindings and levels of MFN tariff rates before and after the Uruguay Round

	Percentage of imports GATT bound					Levels and changes weighted by imports from: the World exc. FTA[1]			LMIEs exc. FTA[1]		Value of 1992 imports in $ million		
Summary product category	Total pre-UR	Total post-UR	Above appl. rates	At appl. rates	Below appl. rates	Post-UR applied rate	Tariff reduc-tion[3]	Post-UR bound rate	Post-UR applied rate	Tariff reduc-tion[3]	from LMIEs exc. FTA[1]	from World exc. FTA[1]	from World inc. FTA
Agriculture, exc. Fish: Estimate 1	5.3	100.0	0.0	100.0	0.0	0.0	..	0.0	0.0	..	1,295.8	2,465.1	2,465.1
Agriculture, exc. Fish: Estimate 2	3.2	100.0	0.0	100.0	0.0	0.0	..	0.0	0.0	..	3,355.9	7,600.9	7,600.9
Fish and Fish Products	0.0	100.0	0.0	100.0	0.0	0.0	..	0.0	0.0	..	863.5	1,402.0	1,402.0
Petroleum Oils	0.0	0.0	0.0	0.0	0.0	0.0	..	0.0	0.0	..	399.5	1,942.9	1,942.9
Wood, Pulp, Paper, and Furniture	0.0	96.9	0.0	96.9	0.0	0.0	..	0.0	0.0	..	1,596.4	3,649.4	3,649.4
Textiles and Clothing	0.9	6.2	0.0	6.2	0.0	0.0	..	0.0	0.0	..	18,774.9	25,368.1	25,368.1
Leather, Rubber, Footwear	0.0	35.6	0.0	35.6	0.0	0.0	..	0.0	0.0	..	5,253.8	6,827.2	6,827.2
Metals	0.0	63.7	0.0	63.7	0.0	0.0	..	0.0	0.0	..	2,638.0	5,867.9	5,867.9
Chemical & Photographic Suppl.	4.8	5.1	0.0	5.1	0.0	0.0	..	0.0	0.0	..	3,365.3	10,574.1	10,574.1
Transport Equipment	0.0	0.2	0.0	0.2	0.0	0.0	..	0.0	0.0	..	458.2	5,144.1	5,144.1
Non-Electric Machinery	0.0	30.0	0.0	30.0	0.0	0.0	..	0.0	0.0	..	2,619.4	11,220.5	11,220.5
Electric Machinery	0.0	25.7	0.0	25.7	0.0	0.0	..	0.0	0.0	..	8,857.6	20,215.1	20,215.1
Mineral Prod.,Prec. Stones & Metal	0.0	10.2	0.0	10.2	0.0	0.0	..	0.0	0.0	..	4,053.2	9,205.2	9,205.2
Manufactured Articles nes.	0.0	28.9	0.0	28.9	0.0	0.0	..	0.0	0.0	..	8,170.7	16,893.6	16,893.6
Industrial goods (line 5-14)	0.6	22.8	0.0	22.8	0.0	0.0	..	0.0	0.0	..	55,787.5	114,965.0	114,965.0
All Merch. Trade (line 2-14)	0.8	27.9	0.0	27.9	0.0	0.0	..	0.0	0.0	..	60,406.4	125,911.0	125,911.0

Notes: 1. Value of imports from partner countries that do not participate in Free Trade Agreements with HONG KONG

2. Pre-Uruguay Round applied MFN rates from 199 3. Weighted average tariff reduction measured by dT / (1 + T) in percent.

HUNGARY Bindings and levels of MFN tariff rates before and after the Uruguay Round

Summary product category	Total pre-UR	Total post-UR	Above appl. rates	At appl. rates	Below appl. rates	Post-UR applied rate	Tariff reduction[3]	Post-UR bound rate	Post-UR applied rate	Tariff reduction[3]	from LMIEs exc. FTA[1]	from World exc. FTA[1]	from World inc. FTA
Agriculture, exc. Fish: Estimate 1	26.6	100.0	29.6	70.3	0.0	-1.5	3.5	2.7	-3.0	3.5	276.4	422.5	422.5
Agriculture, exc. Fish: Estimate 2	34.2	100.0	26.0	46.9	27.0	16.5	4.4	21.6	17.0	3.5	345.9	672.8	672.8
Fish and Fish Products	80.9	81.1	25.4	55.6	0.2	17.3	1.3	19.3	19.2	..	4.6	11.6	11.6
Petroleum Oils	100.0	100.0	6.1	93.7	0.1	0.0	4.9	0.3	0.0	4.9	773.9	821.1	821.1
Wood, Pulp, Paper, and Furniture	96.8	100.0	1.1	64.4	34.5	3.3	2.7	3.3	2.5	3.2	167.4	607.9	607.9
Textiles and Clothing	96.5	98.5	0.1	17.7	80.6	8.5	4.2	8.6	12.2	4.6	162.9	1,162.9	1,162.9
Leather, Rubber, Footwear	97.5	100.0	5.0	22.3	72.7	6.5	3.4	6.6	8.5	3.9	67.0	340.1	340.1
Metals	95.9	100.0	9.0	29.2	61.7	3.9	2.0	4.5	2.5	1.4	377.7	868.7	868.7
Chemical & Photographic Suppl.	93.1	97.3	7.3	33.9	56.1	4.2	3.7	4.3	4.5	2.9	222.2	1,442.1	1,442.1
Transport Equipment	52.4	54.0	7.3	32.5	14.3	16.1	1.6	11.8	12.5	2.2	178.1	942.4	942.4
Non-Electric Machinery	92.6	98.3	1.5	13.6	83.2	7.5	1.8	7.5	8.3	2.3	120.8	1,527.8	1,527.8
Electric Machinery	85.0	92.9	0.0	32.8	60.1	8.8	2.7	8.9	9.0	2.5	88.4	786.6	786.6
Mineral Prod.,Prec. Stones & Metal	95.6	96.9	0.0	78.3	18.6	2.5	2.3	2.3	2.0	2.4	642.7	829.1	829.1
Manufactured Articles nes.	93.2	98.2	1.2	43.3	53.7	4.6	2.2	4.5	1.5	2.5	389.0	1,108.7	1,108.7
Industrial goods (line 5-14)	**89.7**	**93.6**	**3.3**	**34.5**	**55.8**	**6.7**	**2.8**	**6.1**	**4.5**	**2.8**	**2,416.2**	**9,616.3**	**9,616.3**
All Merch. Trade (line 2-14)	**87.1**	**94.4**	**4.9**	**39.6**	**49.9**	**6.8**	**2.8**	**6.6**	**4.7**	**2.9**	**3,540.6**	**11,121.7**	**11,121.7**

Notes: 1. Value of imports from partner countries that do not participate in Free Trade Agreements with HUNGARY

2. Pre-Uruguay Round applied MFN rates from 199 3. Weighted average tariff reduction measured by dT / (1 + T) in percent.

ICELAND Bindings and levels of MFN tariff rates before and after the Uruguay Round

Summary product category	Total pre-UR	Total post-UR	Above appl. rates	At appl. rates	Below appl. rates	Post-UR applied rate	Tariff reduction[3]	Post-UR bound rate	Post-UR applied rate	Tariff reduction[3]	from LMIEs exc. FTA[1]	from World exc. FTA[1]	from World inc. FTA
Agriculture, exc. Fish: Estimate 1	58.8	99.9	33.2	65.3	1.2	4.5	11.5	38.4	0.5	3.1	9.0	31.9	31.9
Agriculture, exc. Fish: Estimate 2	83.0	100.0	50.1	40.3	9.5	8.2	16.0	29.9	2.2	8.1	14.0	133.0	133.0
Fish and Fish Products	95.8	99.5	13.0	83.8	2.7	0.3	8.7	1.6	1.6	8.7	2.1	5.3	9.0
Petroleum Oils	100.0	100.0	22.3	77.7	0.0	5.8	..	12.0	10.4	..	42.5	42.6	89.6
Wood, Pulp, Paper, and Furniture	95.1	99.3	72.6	26.7	0.1	0.3	8.9	14.5	1.4	9.5	9.2	16.9	158.8
Textiles and Clothing	99.0	99.5	93.6	5.9	0.0	5.8	..	17.7	12.1	..	9.9	30.4	130.1
Leather, Rubber, Footwear	79.2	79.6	66.1	13.6	0.0	6.9	..	17.8	13.7	..	4.4	10.5	41.4
Metals	99.9	100.0	63.9	36.1	0.0	0.2	..	7.5	0.5	..	5.2	11.1	118.0
Chemical & Photographic Suppl.	98.9	99.3	44.4	55.0	0.0	0.4	11.2	4.4	5.3	..	0.8	40.1	182.1
Transport Equipment	30.1	32.1	3.4	28.7	0.0	4.8	..	2.0	2.7	..	25.0	112.2	247.2
Non-Electric Machinery	95.0	97.0	47.4	48.6	0.9	0.5	15.3	7.2	1.5	..	1.2	43.9	192.3
Electric Machinery	61.5	86.6	75.6	11.0	0.0	1.8	2.6	17.2	16.7	2.6	2.7	23.4	114.7
Mineral Prod.,Prec. Stones & Metal	91.1	92.1	45.1	47.0	0.0	0.4	..	12.9	2.6	..	2.1	7.4	53.2
Manufactured Articles nes.	62.3	96.8	60.6	36.3	0.0	1.8	..	14.5	8.2	..	3.0	34.2	123.5
Industrial goods (line 5-14)	**78.1**	**84.7**	**51.8**	**32.7**	**0.1**	**2.0**	**14.8**	**10.8**	**5.4**	**7.2**	**63.6**	**330.0**	**1,361.2**
All Merch. Trade (line 2-14)	**79.9**	**86.9**	**49.8**	**36.2**	**0.9**	**2.9**	**15.8**	**12.6**	**6.7**	**8.5**	**122.1**	**511.0**	**1,592.8**

Notes: 1. Value of imports from partner countries that do not participate in Free Trade Agreements with ICELAND

2. Pre-Uruguay Round applied MFN rates from 198 3. Weighted average tariff reduction measured by dT / (1 + T) in percent.

INDIA Bindings and levels of MFN tariff rates before and after the Uruguay Round

Summary product category	Percentage of imports GATT bound					Levels and changes weighted by imports from: the World exc. FTA[1]			LMIEs exc. FTA[1]		Value of 1988 imports in $ million		
	Total pre-UR	Total post-UR	Above appl. rates	At appl. rates	Below appl. rates	Post-UR applied rate	Tariff reduction[3]	Post-UR bound rate	Post-UR applied rate	Tariff reduction[3]	from LMIEs exc. FTA[1]	from World exc. FTA[1]	from World inc. FTA
Agriculture, exc. Fish: Estimate 1	39.3	100.0	100.0	0.0	0.0	13.4	..	106.5	15.2	..	720.0	1,126.7	1,126.7
Agriculture, exc. Fish: Estimate 2	33.5	100.0	63.9	35.0	0.2	60.1	42.7	144.7	76.0	12.1	928.9	1,481.6	1,481.6
Fish and Fish Products	0.0	2.0	2.0	0.0	0.0	52.4	..	100.0	0.0	..	0.0	0.2	0.2
Petroleum Oils	0.0	0.0	0.0	0.0	0.0	0.0	..	..	0.0	..	2,381.3	3,117.3	3,117.3
Wood, Pulp, Paper, and Furniture	22.3	98.2	65.5	0.6	10.7	14.9	29.2	27.9	16.1	21.6	254.9	636.4	636.4
Textiles and Clothing	30.8	74.7	32.2	2.0	37.1	42.4	20.0	33.8	62.5	17.1	40.8	298.5	298.5
Leather, Rubber, Footwear	0.2	76.9	7.9	3.6	65.4	39.9	23.1	32.3	66.0	27.4	60.3	146.2	146.2
Metals	0.5	52.7	0.2	0.9	40.2	38.3	19.5	38.8	58.0	14.9	611.4	2,022.0	2,022.0
Chemical & Photographic Suppl.	2.6	83.7	5.9	0.1	71.6	36.4	20.0	38.7	63.7	19.2	518.6	1,701.9	1,701.9
Transport Equipment	35.5	89.6	10.4	37.0	34.6	30.9	15.4	22.3	43.6	16.6	32.7	549.0	549.0
Non-Electric Machinery	22.7	99.8	14.2	19.6	62.4	31.0	9.2	32.3	42.2	11.8	117.9	2,052.2	2,052.2
Electric Machinery	8.9	72.1	8.0	14.6	49.5	48.5	17.4	36.6	63.0	16.0	74.4	890.9	890.9
Mineral Prod.,Prec. Stones & Metal	9.3	26.8	22.3	0.3	4.2	5.5	23.2	25.6	17.7	25.1	320.6	2,258.9	2,258.9
Manufactured Articles nes.	15.7	82.3	15.5	15.3	46.4	43.4	16.3	48.8	32.1	17.4	48.1	579.7	579.7
Industrial goods (line 5-14)	**11.9**	**69.3**	**14.8**	**7.8**	**41.1**	**29.0**	**16.5**	**34.2**	**45.4**	**17.8**	**2,079.7**	**11,135.7**	**11,135.7**
All Merch. Trade (line 2-14)	**11.6**	**58.5**	**16.5**	**8.8**	**29.1**	**30.9**	**16.5**	**52.2**	**29.3**	**17.8**	**5,389.9**	**15,734.7**	**15,734.7**

Notes: 1. Value of imports from partner countries that do not participate in Free Trade Agreements with INDIA

2. Pre-Uruguay Round applied MFN rates from 199 3. Weighted average tariff reduction measured by dT / (1 + T) in percent.

INDONESIA Bindings and levels of MFN tariff rates before and after the Uruguay Round

Summary product category	Percentage of imports GATT bound					Levels and changes weighted by imports from: the World exc. FTA[1]			LMIEs exc. FTA[1]		Value of 1989 imports in $ million		
	Total pre-UR	Total post-UR	Above appl. rates	At appl. rates	Below appl. rates	Post-UR applied rate	Tariff reduction[3]	Post-UR bound rate	Post-UR applied rate	Tariff reduction[3]	from LMIEs exc. FTA[1]	from World exc. FTA[1]	from World inc. FTA
Agriculture, exc. Fish: Estimate 1	64.7	100.0	65.6	8.3	26.2	23.2	10.7	61.2	43.3	10.7	763.5	1,356.5	1,356.5
Agriculture, exc. Fish: Estimate 2	41.8	100.0	99.5	0.3	0.2	8.3	13.3	51.4	8.7	13.3	620.9	1,264.0	1,264.0
Fish and Fish Products	0.0	100.0	79.2	0.0	20.8	31.0	13.3	40.0	28.8	13.3	0.8	5.5	5.5
Petroleum Oils	0.0	100.0	100.0	0.0	0.0	2.4	..	40.0	0.9	..	655.4	1,102.5	1,102.5
Wood, Pulp, Paper, and Furniture	52.1	99.9	96.9	1.3	1.7	8.2	6.9	35.6	17.9	6.9	30.6	532.5	532.5
Textiles and Clothing	0.0	99.7	61.4	8.0	30.4	21.9	12.5	40.0	29.9	12.1	176.9	644.6	644.6
Leather, Rubber, Footwear	4.2	100.0	92.7	1.3	1.8	10.6	7.1	39.6	7.4	7.1	49.8	183.6	183.6
Metals	37.2	94.9	91.9	2.8	0.2	9.6	12.9	37.0	6.0	13.1	593.0	1,869.0	1,869.0
Chemical & Photographic Suppl.	23.1	95.6	93.1	2.3	0.3	6.0	7.2	37.6	5.0	7.1	515.0	3,068.0	3,068.0
Transport Equipment	28.2	61.3	57.6	0.0	3.7	19.4	6.9	35.5	6.6	6.9	110.2	1,356.4	1,356.4
Non-Electric Machinery	44.4	96.8	94.5	2.2	0.1	12.1	13.3	36.3	13.0	13.3	311.6	3,711.1	3,711.1
Electric Machinery	6.3	92.5	76.4	8.5	7.6	21.5	12.7	38.8	23.7	12.8	100.2	1,032.1	1,032.1
Mineral Prod.,Prec. Stones & Metal	4.7	98.9	94.4	2.5	1.9	5.4	11.9	39.5	3.3	12.1	235.6	629.6	629.6
Manufactured Articles nes.	54.0	88.1	82.2	1.6	4.3	7.7	7.4	32.5	3.7	8.9	240.8	945.2	945.2
Industrial goods (line 5-14)	**31.0**	**92.3**	**86.6**	**2.7**	**2.9**	**11.5**	**11.0**	**36.9**	**8.9**	**11.8**	**2,363.6**	**13,972.0**	**13,972.0**
All Merch. Trade (line 2-14)	**29.7**	**93.4**	**88.5**	**2.4**	**2.5**	**10.7**	**11.1**	**38.4**	**7.5**	**11.8**	**3,640.6**	**16,344.0**	**16,344.0**

Notes: 1. Value of imports from partner countries that do not participate in Free Trade Agreements with INDONESIA

2. Pre-Uruguay Round applied MFN rates from 198 3. Weighted average tariff reduction measured by dT / (1 + T) in percent.

JAMAICA Bindings and levels of MFN tariff rates before and after the Uruguay Round

Summary product category	Percentage of imports GATT bound					Levels and changes weighted by imports from: the World exc. FTA[1]			LMIEs exc. FTA[1]		Value of 1991 imports in $ million		
	Total pre-UR	Total post-UR	Above appl. rates	At appl. rates	Below appl. rates	Post-UR applied rate	Tariff reduc-tion[3]	Post-UR bound rate	Post-UR applied rate	Tariff reduc-tion[3]	from LMIEs exc. FTA[1]	from World exc. FTA[1]	from World inc. FTA
Agriculture, exc. Fish: Estimate 1	0.0	100.0	100.0	0.0	0.0	-1.3	..	100.0	-3.6	..	20.8	144.8	144.8
Agriculture, exc. Fish: Estimate 2	0.0	100.0	100.0	0.0	0.0	14.7	..	94.2	24.9	..	45.7	238.7	238.7
Fish and Fish Products	0.0	100.0	100.0	0.0	0.0	10.0	..	50.0	..	..	0.0	0.0	0.0
Petroleum Oils	0.0	100.0	100.0	0.0	0.0	10.2	..	50.0	6.2	..	201.7	309.6	309.6
Wood, Pulp, Paper, and Furniture	0.0	100.0	100.0	0.0	0.0	13.3	..	50.0	20.6	..	16.1	114.8	114.8
Textiles and Clothing	0.0	100.0	100.0	0.0	0.0	26.5	..	50.0	17.9	..	12.4	141.3	141.3
Leather, Rubber, Footwear	0.0	100.0	100.0	0.0	0.0	15.7	..	50.0	19.6	..	4.5	27.2	27.2
Metals	0.0	100.0	100.0	0.0	0.0	13.2	..	50.0	14.9	..	32.6	123.0	123.0
Chemical & Photographic Suppl.	0.0	100.0	100.0	0.0	0.0	13.1	..	50.0	26.3	..	29.7	223.9	223.9
Transport Equipment	0.0	100.0	100.0	0.0	0.0	27.2	..	50.0	25.7	..	4.5	148.9	148.9
Non-Electric Machinery	0.0	100.0	100.0	0.0	0.0	11.3	..	50.0	26.3	..	8.5	154.2	154.2
Electric Machinery	0.0	100.0	100.0	0.0	0.0	13.3	..	50.0	25.7	..	4.4	89.7	89.7
Mineral Prod.,Prec. Stones & Metal	0.0	100.0	99.5	0.5	0.0	19.7	..	50.0	17.3	..	8.4	71.9	71.9
Manufactured Articles nes.	0.0	100.0	99.3	0.0	0.7	20.9	12.5	51.6	25.5	12.5	2.1	37.0	37.0
Industrial goods (line 5-14)	**0.0**	**100.0**	**99.9**	**0.0**	**0.0**	**17.2**	**12.5**	**50.1**	**20.8**	**12.5**	**123.2**	**1,131.9**	**1,131.9**
All Merch. Trade (line 2-14)	**0.0**	**100.0**	**100.0**	**0.0**	**0.0**	**15.5**	**12.5**	**56.3**	**13.3**	**12.5**	**370.6**	**1,680.2**	**1,680.2**

Notes: 1. Value of imports from partner countries that do not participate in Free Trade Agreements with JAMAICA
2. Pre-Uruguay Round applied MFN rates from 199 3. Weighted average tariff reduction measured by dT / (1 + T) in percent.

JAPAN Bindings and levels of MFN tariff rates before and after the Uruguay Round

Summary product category	Percentage of imports GATT bound					Levels and changes weighted by imports from: the World exc. FTA[1]			LMIEs exc. FTA[1]		Value of 1988 imports in $ million		
	Total pre-UR	Total post-UR	Above appl. rates	At appl. rates	Below appl. rates	Post-UR applied rate	Tariff reduc-tion[3]	Post-UR bound rate	Post-UR applied rate	Tariff reduc-tion[3]	from LMIEs exc. FTA[1]	from World exc. FTA[1]	from World inc. FTA
Agriculture, exc. Fish: Estimate 1	55.4	100.0	0.0	71.5	28.5	65.1	36.6	64.9	42.0	26.7	4,514.1	15,201.4	15,201.4
Agriculture, exc. Fish: Estimate 2	53.1	99.9	15.3	38.8	37.7	10.5	3.7	16.9	16.8	5.3	6,267.6	22,214.3	22,214.3
Fish and Fish Products	87.4	98.0	0.0	14.5	83.5	4.1	1.9	3.9	5.7	2.0	5,356.4	10,501.2	10,501.2
Petroleum Oils	0.4	0.4	0.0	0.0	0.3	1.3	0.9	4.4	0.2	1.3	16,926.7	25,471.3	25,471.3
Wood, Pulp, Paper, and Furniture	45.0	62.5	0.0	39.8	22.7	0.7	3.3	1.1	2.4	3.0	4,749.5	13,766.9	13,766.9
Textiles and Clothing	99.4	100.0	0.0	16.5	83.5	7.2	2.3	7.2	10.0	2.4	6,808.8	11,773.9	11,773.9
Leather, Rubber, Footwear	97.9	100.0	2.1	54.5	43.4	8.2	2.5	8.3	8.1	2.4	2,098.6	4,115.7	4,115.7
Metals	99.4	100.0	0.0	41.4	58.6	0.5	2.1	0.5	2.1	2.4	11,636.6	21,890.0	21,890.0
Chemical & Photographic Suppl.	93.4	100.0	0.3	16.2	83.6	1.9	2.5	1.9	4.7	2.3	2,207.7	14,269.6	14,269.6
Transport Equipment	100.0	100.0	0.0	62.5	37.5	0.0	3.9	0.0	1.2	3.7	102.9	6,103.5	6,103.5
Non-Electric Machinery	100.0	100.0	0.0	66.2	33.8	0.0	3.9	0.0	1.1	4.0	674.4	9,303.8	9,303.8
Electric Machinery	100.0	100.0	0.0	89.6	10.4	0.1	2.3	0.1	0.4	2.4	1,272.6	6,790.2	6,790.2
Mineral Prod.,Prec. Stones & Metal	83.2	100.0	0.0	83.5	16.5	0.2	3.1	0.2	0.7	3.5	10,192.8	25,996.0	25,996.0
Manufactured Articles nes.	98.0	100.0	0.1	72.7	26.7	0.6	2.6	0.6	1.8	1.9	2,596.4	12,659.6	12,659.6
Industrial goods (line 5-14)	**89.4**	**95.9**	**0.1**	**53.7**	**42.1**	**1.4**	**2.6**	**1.5**	**3.4**	**2.5**	**42,340.2**	**126,669.0**	**126,669.0**
All Merch. Trade (line 2-14)	**72.7**	**83.4**	**1.9**	**42.3**	**38.1**	**2.8**	**2.7**	**3.7**	**5.2**	**2.7**	**70,890.8**	**184,856.0**	**184,856.0**

Notes: 1. Value of imports from partner countries that do not participate in Free Trade Agreements with JAPAN
2. Pre-Uruguay Round applied MFN rates from 198 3. Weighted average tariff reduction measured by dT / (1 + T) in percent.

KOREA REPUBLIC OF Bindings and levels of MFN tariff rates before and after the Uruguay Round

Summary product category	Percentage of imports GATT bound					Levels and changes weighted by imports from: the World exc. FTA[1]			LMIEs exc. FTA[1]		Value of 1988 imports in $ million		
	Total pre-UR	Total post-UR	Above appl. rates	At appl. rates	Below appl. rates	Post-UR applied rate	Tariff reduc-tion[3]	Post-UR bound rate	Post-UR applied rate	Tariff reduc-tion[3]	from LMIEs exc. FTA[1]	from World exc. FTA[1]	from World inc. FTA
Agriculture, exc. Fish: Estimate 1	31.9	100.0	0.0	30.1	69.9	42.3	52.7	42.3	87.7	22.5	811.4	2,907.5	2,907.5
Agriculture, exc. Fish: Estimate 2	37.7	100.0	47.6	2.0	50.4	11.6	4.7	152.8	15.0	4.2	821.9	2,779.0	2,779.0
Fish and Fish Products	5.4	63.6	0.1	1.7	61.8	14.0	8.4	10.5	20.0	8.6	56.8	296.4	296.4
Petroleum Oils	0.0	4.4	2.7	0.0	1.6	5.1	5.7	7.6	4.9	5.0	2,968.3	4,239.3	4,239.3
Wood, Pulp, Paper, and Furniture	41.1	77.8	19.8	7.2	50.7	3.3	8.2	1.7	6.2	5.4	846.7	2,480.0	2,480.0
Textiles and Clothing	6.1	98.2	19.6	0.9	77.7	13.0	6.5	14.8	19.1	6.2	614.7	2,140.6	2,140.6
Leather, Rubber, Footwear	15.1	99.7	0.0	1.1	98.6	9.0	7.4	8.9	13.0	7.8	409.8	1,256.3	1,256.3
Metals	15.4	99.9	0.9	25.1	73.9	3.7	10.1	3.8	8.7	8.3	1,492.8	6,459.3	6,459.3
Chemical & Photographic Suppl.	1.3	96.9	0.0	0.4	96.1	6.0	10.2	5.6	16.0	9.4	608.9	6,375.1	6,375.1
Transport Equipment	64.1	93.0	0.0	65.2	27.8	5.5	6.3	4.0	0.7	13.1	170.7	2,255.8	2,255.8
Non-Electric Machinery	20.0	81.7	1.0	9.5	71.2	11.8	8.1	10.0	18.3	12.3	82.8	8,232.0	8,232.0
Electric Machinery	46.0	81.7	0.1	1.5	80.1	8.2	8.6	5.6	12.6	9.3	150.7	6,876.3	6,876.3
Mineral Prod.,Prec. Stones & Metal	36.3	88.9	2.5	58.1	28.4	5.5	7.5	4.9	5.1	7.7	906.2	2,957.7	2,957.7
Manufactured Articles nes.	3.6	90.6	6.8	15.6	68.2	8.7	7.6	10.6	8.4	6.5	470.3	5,372.3	5,372.3
Industrial goods (line 5-14)	**22.4**	**89.8**	**3.4**	**15.3**	**71.1**	**7.6**	**8.7**	**6.9**	**9.9**	**8.1**	**5,753.8**	**44,405.4**	**44,405.4**
All Merch. Trade (line 2-14)	**21.3**	**83.2**	**5.7**	**13.2**	**64.2**	**7.7**	**8.5**	**16.4**	**8.9**	**7.5**	**9,600.8**	**51,720.0**	**51,720.0**

Notes: 1. Value of imports from partner countries that do not participate in Free Trade Agreements with KOREA REPUBLIC OF

2. Pre-Uruguay Round applied MFN rates from 198 3. Weighted average tariff reduction measured by dT / (1 + T) in percent.

MACAU Bindings and levels of MFN tariff rates before and after the Uruguay Round

Summary product category	Percentage of imports GATT bound					Levels and changes weighted by imports from: the World exc. FTA[1]			LMIEs exc. FTA[1]		Value of 1991 imports in $ million		
	Total pre-UR	Total post-UR	Above appl. rates	At appl. rates	Below appl. rates	Post-UR applied rate	Tariff reduc-tion[3]	Post-UR bound rate	Post-UR applied rate	Tariff reduc-tion[3]	from LMIEs exc. FTA[1]	from World exc. FTA[1]	from World inc. FTA
Agriculture, exc. Fish: Estimate 1	0.0	100.0	0.0	100.0	0.0	0.0	..	0.0	0.0	..	26.0	51.3	51.3
Agriculture, exc. Fish: Estimate 2	0.0	100.0	0.0	100.0	0.0	0.0	..	0.0	0.0	..	61.8	177.0	177.0
Fish and Fish Products	0.0	100.0	0.0	100.0	0.0	0.0	..	0.0	0.0	..	9.6	15.8	15.8
Petroleum Oils	0.0	0.0	0.0	0.0	0.0	0.0	..	..	0.0	..	40.8	68.1	68.1
Wood, Pulp, Paper, and Furniture	0.0	7.5	0.0	7.5	0.0	0.0	..	0.0	0.0	..	18.1	60.7	60.7
Textiles and Clothing	0.0	11.4	0.0	11.4	0.0	0.0	..	0.0	0.0	..	173.0	731.7	731.7
Leather, Rubber, Footwear	0.0	18.4	0.0	18.4	0.0	0.0	..	0.0	0.0	..	16.7	30.6	30.6
Metals	0.0	13.0	0.0	13.0	0.0	0.0	..	0.0	0.0	..	24.6	62.1	62.1
Chemical & Photographic Suppl.	0.0	0.0	0.0	0.0	0.0	0.0	..	0.0	0.0	..	24.4	120.3	120.3
Transport Equipment	0.0	0.0	0.0	0.0	0.0	0.0	..	..	0.0	..	1.3	37.8	37.8
Non-Electric Machinery	0.0	0.0	0.0	0.0	0.0	0.0	..	..	0.0	..	10.3	136.9	136.9
Electric Machinery	0.0	6.4	0.0	6.4	0.0	0.0	..	0.0	0.0	..	8.4	128.8	128.8
Mineral Prod.,Prec. Stones & Metal	0.0	10.1	0.0	10.1	0.0	0.0	..	0.0	0.0	..	44.8	71.1	71.1
Manufactured Articles nes.	0.0	36.6	0.0	36.6	0.0	0.0	..	0.0	0.0	..	39.9	201.1	201.1
Industrial goods (line 5-14)	**0.0**	**12.0**	**0.0**	**12.0**	**0.0**	**0.0**	**..**	**0.0**	**0.0**	**..**	**361.6**	**1,581.1**	**1,581.1**
All Merch. Trade (line 2-14)	**0.0**	**20.8**	**0.0**	**20.8**	**0.0**	**0.0**	**..**	**0.0**	**0.0**	**..**	**473.8**	**1,842.0**	**1,842.0**

Notes: 1. Value of imports from partner countries that do not participate in Free Trade Agreements with MACAU

2. Pre-Uruguay Round applied MFN rates from 199 3. Weighted average tariff reduction measured by dT / (1 + T) in percent.

MALAYSIA Bindings and levels of MFN tariff rates before and after the Uruguay Round

Summary product category	Percentage of imports GATT bound					Levels and changes weighted by imports from: the World exc. FTA[1]			LMIEs exc. FTA[1]		Value of 1988 imports in $ million		
	Total pre-UR	Total post-UR	Above appl. rates	At appl. rates	Below appl. rates	Post-UR applied rate	Tariff reduc-tion[3]	Post-UR bound rate	Post-UR applied rate	Tariff reduc-tion[3]	from LMIEs exc. FTA[1]	from World exc. FTA[1]	from World inc. FTA
Agriculture, exc. Fish: Estimate 1	0.0	100.0	0.1	38.6	61.3	56.8	35.1	56.8	103.0	27.8	621.6	1,234.6	1,234.6
Agriculture, exc. Fish: Estimate 2	3.3	100.0	43.3	24.4	8.8	2.5	7.4	11.6	3.0	6.1	782.7	1,699.5	1,699.5
Fish and Fish Products	0.2	26.9	0.5	17.7	8.7	9.9	17.2	18.1	12.2	16.6	102.3	124.5	124.5
Petroleum Oils	0.0	1.3	1.0	0.3	0.0	0.2	..	5.0	0.0	..	116.1	784.9	784.9
Wood, Pulp, Paper, and Furniture	6.6	64.1	38.9	12.6	11.7	6.5	8.7	16.3	7.4	6.5	89.8	520.1	520.1
Textiles and Clothing	0.0	97.8	18.0	7.8	66.9	17.5	5.3	18.4	24.5	5.2	183.3	753.7	753.7
Leather, Rubber, Footwear	9.6	87.1	21.5	42.3	23.3	15.2	7.8	17.7	13.2	8.6	54.7	133.4	133.4
Metals	0.0	52.8	29.1	15.4	4.8	7.3	6.4	13.5	5.8	7.2	444.8	1,780.9	1,780.9
Chemical & Photographic Suppl.	1.6	78.8	59.9	7.3	8.5	5.9	10.9	13.0	5.9	6.2	164.0	1,772.2	1,772.2
Transport Equipment	0.9	43.3	14.0	29.1	0.2	22.0	15.0	7.5	20.3	21.2	21.9	823.7	823.7
Non-Electric Machinery	5.7	93.0	49.0	27.6	16.4	4.4	7.2	8.3	7.8	8.6	83.3	2,267.4	2,267.4
Electric Machinery	0.0	84.3	8.3	10.8	65.0	3.8	6.1	4.4	5.9	3.8	407.7	4,113.4	4,113.4
Mineral Prod.,Prec. Stones & Metal	0.0	88.9	66.5	15.3	3.7	4.5	3.9	8.0	4.8	1.7	184.3	861.0	861.0
Manufactured Articles nes.	0.0	92.1	25.9	38.9	26.6	5.3	21.7	6.8	9.3	19.1	90.1	883.8	883.8
Industrial goods (line 5-14)	**1.5**	**79.3**	**31.0**	**17.1**	**29.8**	**6.8**	**7.2**	**8.9**	**8.4**	**4.8**	**1,724.0**	**13,909.7**	**13,909.7**
All Merch. Trade (line 2-14)	**1.6**	**77.4**	**30.6**	**17.0**	**26.1**	**6.4**	**7.3**	**9.3**	**6.8**	**5.2**	**2,725.0**	**16,518.5**	**16,518.5**

Notes: 1. Value of imports from partner countries that do not participate in Free Trade Agreements with MALAYSIA

2. Pre-Uruguay Round applied MFN rates from 198 3. Weighted average tariff reduction measured by dT / (1 + T) in percent.

MEXICO Bindings and levels of MFN tariff rates before and after the Uruguay Round

Summary product category	Percentage of imports GATT bound					Levels and changes weighted by imports from: the World exc. FTA[1]			LMIEs exc. FTA[1]		Value of 1988 imports in $ million		
	Total pre-UR	Total post-UR	Above appl. rates	At appl. rates	Below appl. rates	Post-UR applied rate	Tariff reduc-tion[3]	Post-UR bound rate	Post-UR applied rate	Tariff reduc-tion[3]	from LMIEs exc. FTA[1]	from World exc. FTA[1]	from World inc. FTA
Agriculture, exc. Fish: Estimate 1	100.0	100.0	58.7	41.3	0.0	3.0	..	26.2	24.0	..	121.4	277.8	2,069.3
Agriculture, exc. Fish: Estimate 2	100.0	100.0	93.1	6.9	0.0	5.4	0.7	37.5	13.0	..	164.1	381.4	2,684.4
Fish and Fish Products	100.0	100.0	100.0	0.0	0.0	20.0	..	41.4	..	..	0.0	0.0	0.0
Petroleum Oils	100.0	100.0	100.0	0.0	0.0	8.6	..	35.0	8.6	..	64.2	73.5	340.6
Wood, Pulp, Paper, and Furniture	100.0	100.0	92.1	7.9	0.0	2.9	..	24.7	7.5	..	31.6	104.6	751.9
Textiles and Clothing	100.0	100.0	99.8	0.2	0.0	15.3	..	34.9	15.5	..	45.8	91.7	324.4
Leather, Rubber, Footwear	100.0	100.0	100.0	0.0	0.0	11.9	..	34.7	11.3	..	46.6	91.6	301.1
Metals	100.0	100.0	97.7	2.3	0.0	10.5	..	32.9	10.4	..	76.0	332.9	1,118.6
Chemical & Photographic Suppl.	100.0	100.0	98.4	1.6	0.0	10.4	..	33.9	11.4	..	86.9	684.4	2,052.6
Transport Equipment	100.0	100.0	99.8	0.2	0.0	12.9	..	36.7	14.6	..	28.2	294.7	1,009.0
Non-Electric Machinery	100.0	100.0	100.0	0.0	0.0	12.6	..	35.1	12.7	..	100.2	1,013.8	2,815.2
Electric Machinery	100.0	100.0	100.0	0.0	0.0	13.6	..	34.8	14.3	..	129.9	572.6	1,446.6
Mineral Prod.,Prec. Stones & Metal	100.0	100.0	93.0	7.0	0.0	6.8	..	28.7	7.4	..	64.7	130.9	567.2
Manufactured Articles nes.	100.0	100.0	98.2	0.0	1.8	12.5	0.9	30.6	12.4	0.9	101.0	340.8	1,044.3
Industrial goods (line 5-14)	**100.0**	**100.0**	**98.4**	**1.4**	**0.2**	**11.4**	**0.9**	**33.3**	**12.0**	**0.9**	**710.9**	**3,658.0**	**11,431.0**
All Merch. Trade (line 2-14)	**100.0**	**100.0**	**97.5**	**2.4**	**0.1**	**10.4**	**0.9**	**34.1**	**11.9**	**0.9**	**939.2**	**4,112.8**	**14,455.9**

Notes: 1. Value of imports from partner countries that do not participate in Free Trade Agreements with MEXICO

2. Pre-Uruguay Round applied MFN rates from 199 3. Weighted average tariff reduction measured by dT / (1 + T) in percent.

NEW ZEALAND Bindings and levels of MFN tariff rates before and after the Uruguay Round

Summary product category	Percentage of imports GATT bound					Levels and changes weighted by imports from: the World exc. FTA[1]			LMIEs exc. FTA[1]		Value of 1991 imports in $ million		
	Total pre-UR	Total post-UR	Above appl. rates	At appl. rates	Below appl. rates	Post-UR applied rate	Tariff reduction[3]	Post-UR bound rate	Post-UR applied rate	Tariff reduction[3]	from LMIEs exc. FTA[1]	from World exc. FTA[1]	from World inc. FTA
Agriculture, exc. Fish: Estimate 1	75.2	100.0	16.9	76.1	7.0	1.4	4.5	2.5	2.4	9.7	103.2	142.9	212.9
Agriculture, exc. Fish: Estimate 2	71.6	100.0	34.5	49.7	15.6	3.5	4.4	7.5	4.8	4.2	151.0	313.1	552.0
Fish and Fish Products	61.5	100.0	0.4	81.9	0.6	0.1	3.0	0.2	1.8	3.9	14.8	28.7	30.9
Petroleum Oils	78.0	100.0	1.3	86.6	0.0	0.0	..	0.1	0.0	..	279.6	431.7	546.8
Wood, Pulp, Paper, and Furniture	71.5	100.0	5.8	58.1	35.8	1.3	13.8	2.0	14.7	11.0	30.6	292.8	422.9
Textiles and Clothing	53.9	100.0	63.5	19.9	16.4	12.8	4.7	20.6	19.2	4.2	188.6	426.1	543.4
Leather, Rubber, Footwear	39.4	100.0	38.2	33.7	28.1	17.8	4.8	22.2	27.0	5.3	49.3	132.1	162.3
Metals	45.0	100.0	76.8	20.2	3.0	7.7	1.8	14.6	8.4	2.1	36.4	309.8	516.7
Chemical & Photographic Suppl.	62.9	100.0	40.4	47.4	11.9	3.3	13.2	7.1	4.4	11.2	50.2	796.3	1,184.7
Transport Equipment	87.0	100.0	40.0	59.0	0.7	10.0	2.3	13.4	18.6	4.1	14.1	895.1	1,020.9
Non-Electric Machinery	62.4	100.0	43.8	50.0	4.6	6.9	3.2	10.3	10.5	4.1	16.6	948.0	1,080.1
Electric Machinery	14.9	100.0	56.2	23.3	19.6	12.8	4.5	16.3	10.9	5.3	58.6	661.3	754.4
Mineral Prod.,Prec. Stones & Metal	66.7	100.0	37.4	55.3	3.6	5.1	4.5	8.3	5.4	5.2	48.3	212.9	258.3
Manufactured Articles nes.	60.3	100.0	56.1	34.9	5.3	6.7	5.1	11.4	11.7	2.3	47.4	514.7	603.3
Industrial goods (line 5-14)	**58.8**	**100.0**	**46.5**	**41.9**	**10.5**	**7.7**	**8.2**	**11.9**	**14.5**	**5.9**	**540.1**	**5,189.1**	**6,546.9**
All Merch. Trade (line 2-14)	**61.1**	**100.0**	**42.3**	**45.8**	**10.1**	**6.8**	**7.8**	**10.8**	**8.7**	**5.5**	**985.5**	**5,962.6**	**7,676.6**

Notes: 1. Value of imports from partner countries that do not participate in Free Trade Agreements with NEW ZEALAND

2. Pre-Uruguay Round applied MFN rates from 199 3. Weighted average tariff reduction measured by dT / (1 + T) in percent.

NORWAY Bindings and levels of MFN tariff rates before and after the Uruguay Round

Summary product category	Percentage of imports GATT bound					Levels and changes weighted by imports from: the World exc. FTA[1]			LMIEs exc. FTA[1]		Value of 1988 imports in $ million		
	Total pre-UR	Total post-UR	Above appl. rates	At appl. rates	Below appl. rates	Post-UR applied rate	Tariff reduction[3]	Post-UR bound rate	Post-UR applied rate	Tariff reduction[3]	from LMIEs exc. FTA[1]	from World exc. FTA[1]	from World inc. FTA
Agriculture, exc. Fish: Estimate 1	90.0	100.0	0.1	92.5	7.4	50.9	11.1	51.1	26.2	11.1	235.0	594.0	594.0
Agriculture, exc. Fish: Estimate 2	78.2	100.0	16.8	57.5	23.2	2.7	2.8	30.4	0.9	2.5	314.3	1,408.5	1,408.5
Fish and Fish Products	99.3	100.0	0.4	92.2	7.4	0.0	1.4	1.1	0.3	1.5	25.8	61.9	109.7
Petroleum Oils	100.0	100.0	0.0	100.0	0.0	0.0	..	0.0	0.0	..	54.7	58.7	469.5
Wood, Pulp, Paper, and Furniture	100.0	100.0	12.7	82.3	3.3	0.0	3.4	0.2	1.9	3.7	76.0	125.0	1,911.5
Textiles and Clothing	96.8	100.0	74.8	6.1	18.8	8.4	6.8	10.2	18.1	6.6	189.0	336.5	1,698.2
Leather, Rubber, Footwear	69.7	100.0	38.5	36.0	25.3	1.8	2.8	4.3	7.5	2.6	116.7	165.4	596.5
Metals	94.6	100.0	18.7	75.8	4.5	0.1	3.4	0.8	0.4	2.6	436.4	860.7	2,878.6
Chemical & Photographic Suppl.	100.0	100.0	50.6	44.6	4.4	0.4	4.5	3.4	1.7	5.3	156.6	376.4	2,322.6
Transport Equipment	100.0	100.0	50.1	46.0	3.9	2.1	3.1	3.8	2.0	1.7	27.9	659.3	1,927.1
Non-Electric Machinery	100.0	100.0	48.9	28.2	22.8	0.8	2.7	2.1	4.9	2.5	29.5	792.3	3,294.8
Electric Machinery	100.0	100.0	54.6	22.7	22.7	2.1	2.9	3.1	12.3	5.1	60.3	429.3	1,656.7
Mineral Prod.,Prec. Stones & Metal	98.9	100.0	11.2	81.9	3.9	0.1	2.3	0.6	1.7	2.8	54.7	146.5	953.6
Manufactured Articles nes.	100.0	100.0	16.0	75.1	8.9	0.3	2.8	1.0	0.3	2.7	1,199.1	2,207.5	3,615.7
Industrial goods (line 5-14)	**98.1**	**100.0**	**36.5**	**51.8**	**11.2**	**0.8**	**3.5**	**2.6**	**2.7**	**4.4**	**2,346.2**	**6,098.9**	**20,855.1**
All Merch. Trade (line 2-14)	**96.9**	**100.0**	**34.4**	**53.3**	**11.7**	**1.0**	**3.4**	**4.2**	**2.4**	**4.3**	**2,741.0**	**7,628.0**	**22,842.8**

Notes: 1. Value of imports from partner countries that do not participate in Free Trade Agreements with NORWAY

2. Pre-Uruguay Round applied MFN rates from 198 3. Weighted average tariff reduction measured by dT / (1 + T) in percent.

PERU Bindings and levels of MFN tariff rates before and after the Uruguay Round

Summary product category	Percentage of imports GATT bound					Levels and changes weighted by imports from: the World exc. FTA[1]			LMIEs exc. FTA[1]		Value of 1986 imports in $ million		
	Total pre-UR	Total post-UR	Above appl. rates	At appl. rates	Below appl. rates	Post-UR applied rate	Tariff reduc-tion[3]	Post-UR bound rate	Post-UR applied rate	Tariff reduc-tion[3]	from LMIEs exc. FTA[1]	from World exc. FTA[1]	from World inc. FTA
Agriculture, exc. Fish: Estimate 1	13.2	100.0	82.8	0.0	17.2	-4.7	5.6	35.5	-4.4	6.3	217.9	455.5	455.5
Agriculture, exc. Fish: Estimate 2	14.4	100.0	97.4	1.4	0.1	14.5	34.2	48.1	15.6	34.4	260.3	549.8	549.8
Fish and Fish Products	0.1	100.0	100.0	0.0	0.0	15.0	..	30.0	15.0	..	3.9	4.1	4.1
Petroleum Oils	5.7	100.0	100.0	0.0	0.0	13.0	..	30.0	15.0	..	21.8	47.6	47.6
Wood, Pulp, Paper, and Furniture	31.2	100.0	99.4	0.0	0.5	10.7	21.4	30.0	18.0	32.6	59.5	119.7	119.7
Textiles and Clothing	6.9	100.0	100.0	0.0	0.0	14.9	34.4	30.0	20.0	..	10.1	35.0	35.0
Leather, Rubber, Footwear	24.0	100.0	100.0	0.0	0.0	15.0	14.9	28.3	15.2	14.9	10.0	47.3	47.3
Metals	17.0	100.0	98.2	0.0	0.0	13.9	..	29.7	15.1	..	44.5	142.1	142.1
Chemical & Photographic Suppl.	24.1	100.0	97.4	2.0	0.5	15.4	1.6	29.5	16.5	1.6	113.2	476.9	476.9
Transport Equipment	5.1	100.0	100.0	0.0	0.0	13.8	..	29.5	15.1	..	44.9	174.7	174.7
Non-Electric Machinery	24.0	100.0	98.8	0.4	0.0	15.1	..	28.5	15.7	..	52.9	401.0	401.0
Electric Machinery	4.2	100.0	99.7	0.0	0.3	14.3	8.1	29.9	18.2	8.1	24.9	154.2	154.2
Mineral Prod.,Prec. Stones & Metal	5.1	100.0	99.6	0.0	0.0	15.9	..	30.0	15.1	..	27.2	134.1	134.1
Manufactured Articles nes.	16.8	100.0	94.9	0.1	0.9	14.7	28.7	29.7	18.6	31.9	23.8	101.2	101.2
Industrial goods (line 5-14)	**18.2**	**100.0**	**98.5**	**0.7**	**0.2**	**14.6**	**10.8**	**29.4**	**16.5**	**24.9**	**411.1**	**1,786.3**	**1,786.3**
All Merch. Trade (line 2-14)	**17.1**	**100.0**	**98.3**	**0.8**	**0.2**	**14.6**	**12.8**	**33.7**	**16.1**	**26.9**	**697.1**	**2,387.8**	**2,387.8**

Notes: 1. Value of imports from partner countries that do not participate in Free Trade Agreements with PERU

2. Pre-Uruguay Round applied MFN rates from 199 3. Weighted average tariff reduction measured by dT / (1 + T) in percent.

PHILIPPINES Bindings and levels of MFN tariff rates before and after the Uruguay Round

Summary product category	Percentage of imports GATT bound					Levels and changes weighted by imports from: the World exc. FTA[1]			LMIEs exc. FTA[1]		Value of 1991 imports in $ million		
	Total pre-UR	Total post-UR	Above appl. rates	At appl. rates	Below appl. rates	Post-UR applied rate	Tariff reduc-tion[3]	Post-UR bound rate	Post-UR applied rate	Tariff reduc-tion[3]	from LMIEs exc. FTA[1]	from World exc. FTA[1]	from World inc. FTA
Agriculture, exc. Fish: Estimate 1	31.8	99.9	0.0	47.3	52.6	46.2	56.1	46.2	42.3	1.4	186.7	824.3	824.3
Agriculture, exc. Fish: Estimate 2	23.0	99.9	56.0	5.1	38.8	18.0	5.0	25.4	22.3	4.2	209.0	1,047.7	1,047.7
Fish and Fish Products	0.0	0.4	0.4	0.0	0.0	16.3	30.8	39.6	16.8	30.8	33.2	72.0	72.0
Petroleum Oils	0.0	0.0	0.0	0.0	0.0	11.6	..	..	11.1	..	1,192.8	1,735.8	1,735.8
Wood, Pulp, Paper, and Furniture	5.6	61.1	9.9	33.1	18.1	25.8	14.1	22.7	17.8	10.9	38.0	355.8	355.8
Textiles and Clothing	0.0	98.0	5.4	3.2	89.5	27.1	8.3	27.2	35.8	8.1	223.4	1,193.2	1,193.2
Leather, Rubber, Footwear	0.4	39.2	8.7	29.9	0.5	32.6	8.5	31.4	31.9	8.7	44.3	182.9	182.9
Metals	0.2	20.2	11.7	8.2	0.3	16.0	6.9	21.9	13.3	6.9	533.1	1,317.9	1,317.9
Chemical & Photographic Suppl.	9.8	58.2	20.8	33.2	4.2	19.5	5.2	19.7	19.0	6.5	216.9	1,424.4	1,424.4
Transport Equipment	29.8	37.4	3.6	33.7	0.0	18.8	14.3	11.5	26.4	..	30.7	733.7	733.7
Non-Electric Machinery	19.2	87.5	31.9	35.1	20.5	17.2	8.3	20.2	20.7	8.2	69.7	1,281.3	1,281.3
Electric Machinery	9.1	87.5	12.3	68.6	6.5	21.4	8.3	21.5	24.2	7.9	184.3	2,446.4	2,446.4
Mineral Prod.,Prec. Stones & Metal	0.2	50.0	30.8	18.1	1.1	15.7	10.6	11.1	14.4	9.8	271.3	562.0	562.0
Manufactured Articles nes.	33.0	73.9	14.0	41.2	18.8	22.0	11.4	20.8	20.9	11.9	54.8	466.7	466.7
Industrial goods (line 5-14)	**10.1**	**67.4**	**15.5**	**34.7**	**17.2**	**20.4**	**8.6**	**21.3**	**19.8**	**8.2**	**1,666.5**	**9,964.3**	**9,964.3**
All Merch. Trade (line 2-14)	**9.7**	**60.6**	**16.6**	**27.4**	**16.5**	**19.0**	**7.9**	**21.9**	**16.6**	**6.6**	**3,101.5**	**12,819.7**	**12,819.7**

Notes: 1. Value of imports from partner countries that do not participate in Free Trade Agreements with PHILIPPINES

2. Pre-Uruguay Round applied MFN rates from 199 3. Weighted average tariff reduction measured by dT / (1 + T) in percent.

POLAND Bindings and levels of MFN tariff rates before and after the Uruguay Round

Summary product category	Percentage of imports GATT bound					Levels and changes weighted by imports from: the World exc. FTA[1]			LMIEs exc. FTA[1]		Value of 1989 imports in $ million		
	Total pre-UR	Total post-UR	Above appl. rates	At appl. rates	Below appl. rates	Post-UR applied rate	Tariff reduc-tion[3]	Post-UR bound rate	Post-UR applied rate	Tariff reduc-tion[3]	from LMIEs exc. FTA[1]	from World exc. FTA[1]	from World inc. FTA
Agriculture, exc. Fish: Estimate 1	0.0	100.0	51.9	48.1	0.0	1.3	..	45.7	-2.7	..	658.5	1,030.4	1,030.4
Agriculture, exc. Fish: Estimate 2	0.0	98.4	91.2	1.9	5.3	9.7	4.7	39.9	7.4	3.5	712.6	1,275.6	1,275.6
Fish and Fish Products	0.0	2.0	2.0	0.0	0.0	11.5	..	11.7	26.6	..	15.8	55.6	55.6
Petroleum Oils	0.0	75.7	0.0	75.7	0.0	2.9	..	0.0	1.7	..	821.8	941.6	941.6
Wood, Pulp, Paper, and Furniture	0.0	100.0	37.2	8.4	54.4	5.3	3.9	7.0	8.9	5.1	99.0	218.1	218.1
Textiles and Clothing	0.0	100.0	67.6	0.2	32.2	10.4	4.4	14.7	12.6	4.6	383.0	762.6	762.6
Leather, Rubber, Footwear	0.0	100.0	36.1	20.8	43.1	8.0	5.6	9.7	14.0	5.8	98.1	170.9	170.9
Metals	0.0	100.0	69.3	14.2	16.4	5.2	3.8	8.3	4.4	4.3	550.9	980.4	980.4
Chemical & Photographic Suppl.	0.0	99.0	20.4	0.0	78.5	7.3	4.2	7.6	11.8	4.8	274.2	1,138.8	1,138.8
Transport Equipment	0.0	17.7	10.9	0.0	6.8	10.7	5.4	9.2	10.7	5.4	402.2	591.9	591.9
Non-Electric Machinery	0.0	98.7	56.4	3.9	38.4	6.4	3.3	8.4	9.6	3.9	504.8	1,731.2	1,731.2
Electric Machinery	0.0	100.0	72.9	4.4	22.7	9.5	4.4	11.5	8.7	5.2	188.2	464.4	464.4
Mineral Prod.,Prec. Stones & Metal	0.0	100.0	11.1	61.8	27.2	2.2	4.6	2.6	2.3	4.6	481.6	647.9	647.9
Manufactured Articles nes.	0.0	98.5	39.3	31.7	27.4	5.8	6.2	7.7	6.2	6.0	267.3	644.6	644.6
Industrial goods (line 5-14)	**0.0**	**92.8**	**44.6**	**12.1**	**36.1**	**6.9**	**4.2**	**8.5**	**8.1**	**4.7**	**3,249.2**	**7,350.6**	**7,350.6**
All Merch. Trade (line 2-14)	**0.0**	**91.3**	**46.1**	**16.9**	**28.3**	**6.9**	**4.2**	**12.3**	**7.0**	**4.6**	**4,799.5**	**9,623.4**	**9,623.4**

Notes: 1. Value of imports from partner countries that do not participate in Free Trade Agreements with POLAND

2. Pre-Uruguay Round applied MFN rates from 198 3. Weighted average tariff reduction measured by dT / (1 + T) in percent.

ROMANIA Bindings and levels of MFN tariff rates before and after the Uruguay Round

Summary product category	Percentage of imports GATT bound					Levels and changes weighted by imports from: the World exc. FTA[1]			LMIEs exc. FTA[1]		Value of 1991 imports in $ million		
	Total pre-UR	Total post-UR	Above appl. rates	At appl. rates	Below appl. rates	Post-UR applied rate	Tariff reduc-tion[3]	Post-UR bound rate	Post-UR applied rate	Tariff reduc-tion[3]	from LMIEs exc. FTA[1]	from World exc. FTA[1]	from World inc. FTA
Agriculture, exc. Fish: Estimate 1	5.2	100.0	100.0	0.0	0.0	4.2	..	129.0	1.9	..	270.2	588.6	588.6
Agriculture, exc. Fish: Estimate 2	26.3	100.0	57.5	36.0	6.5	26.9	1.7	109.7	26.3	1.7	326.7	776.2	776.2
Fish and Fish Products	56.2	100.0	43.3	56.2	0.5	22.1	17.4	26.4	24.8	..	0.8	2.1	2.1
Petroleum Oils	0.0	100.0	100.0	0.0	0.0	3.0	..	35.0	3.0	..	1,131.4	1,214.0	1,214.0
Wood, Pulp, Paper, and Furniture	29.1	100.0	70.9	29.1	0.0	8.4	..	27.1	7.2	..	14.0	73.0	73.0
Textiles and Clothing	31.2	100.0	68.4	31.3	0.3	22.9	3.6	34.0	23.4	3.6	96.9	156.4	156.4
Leather, Rubber, Footwear	31.5	100.0	68.5	31.5	0.0	20.8	..	31.9	21.1	..	44.7	90.3	90.3
Metals	2.0	100.0	97.9	2.1	0.0	7.2	..	34.5	4.9	..	327.0	480.3	480.3
Chemical & Photographic Suppl.	11.7	100.0	88.3	11.7	0.0	15.8	..	32.2	16.0	..	142.1	435.5	435.5
Transport Equipment	0.0	100.0	99.9	0.0	0.1	28.3	3.6	35.0	27.9	3.6	57.3	121.0	121.0
Non-Electric Machinery	2.0	100.0	93.1	6.4	0.4	15.4	3.6	33.8	15.5	3.6	142.7	450.9	450.9
Electric Machinery	45.9	100.0	54.1	45.9	0.0	25.1	..	36.6	24.5	..	89.6	229.9	229.9
Mineral Prod.,Prec. Stones & Metal	1.4	100.0	98.6	1.4	0.0	2.9	..	34.7	2.9	..	661.5	908.9	908.9
Manufactured Articles nes.	8.9	100.0	91.1	8.9	0.0	8.8	0.9	36.5	7.0	..	335.0	602.7	602.7
Industrial goods (line 5-14)	**9.6**	**100.0**	**89.8**	**10.2**	**0.1**	**11.4**	**3.6**	**34.4**	**9.1**	**3.6**	**1,910.7**	**3,548.8**	**3,548.8**
All Merch. Trade (line 2-14)	**9.8**	**100.0**	**87.5**	**11.6**	**1.0**	**11.7**	**1.8**	**45.1**	**8.7**	**1.7**	**3,369.7**	**5,541.1**	**5,541.1**

Notes: 1. Value of imports from partner countries that do not participate in Free Trade Agreements with ROMANIA

2. Pre-Uruguay Round applied MFN rates from 199 3. Weighted average tariff reduction measured by dT / (1 + T) in percent.

SENEGAL Bindings and levels of MFN tariff rates before and after the Uruguay Round

Summary product category	Percentage of imports GATT bound					Levels and changes weighted by imports from: the World exc. FTA[1]			LMIEs exc. FTA[1]		Value of 1989 imports in $ million		
	Total pre-UR	Total post-UR	Above appl. rates	At appl. rates	Below appl. rates	Post-UR applied rate	Tariff reduc-tion[3]	Post-UR bound rate	Post-UR applied rate	Tariff reduc-tion[3]	from LMIEs exc. FTA[1]	from World exc. FTA[1]	from World inc. FTA
Agriculture, exc. Fish: Estimate 1	13.4	99.9	99.9	0.0	0.0	-0.3	..	30.0	0.6	..	116.0	259.9	259.9
Agriculture, exc. Fish: Estimate 2	13.2	100.0	90.9	9.1	0.0	13.1	..	28.7	15.0	..	129.5	312.6	312.6
Fish and Fish Products	15.2	52.1	37.0	15.2	0.0	13.8	..	23.2	13.4	..	0.8	1.6	1.6
Petroleum Oils	65.3	65.3	0.0	65.3	0.0	9.6	..	6.8	9.7	..	404.9	415.1	415.1
Wood, Pulp, Paper, and Furniture	0.0	4.8	4.8	0.0	0.0	15.0	..	30.0	15.0	..	14.9	54.5	54.5
Textiles and Clothing	37.0	41.1	30.0	11.1	0.0	14.8	..	19.2	14.7	..	16.7	37.8	37.8
Leather, Rubber, Footwear	57.2	57.2	51.4	5.8	0.0	14.7	..	23.5	14.3	..	2.5	16.6	16.6
Metals	0.0	0.1	0.1	0.0	0.0	15.0	..	30.0	15.0	..	13.2	71.7	71.7
Chemical & Photographic Suppl.	0.4	3.6	3.5	0.1	0.0	15.0	..	28.1	15.0	..	4.9	114.0	114.0
Transport Equipment	87.0	87.0	58.0	29.0	0.0	12.8	..	19.0	13.8	..	3.1	98.0	98.0
Non-Electric Machinery	70.0	70.0	0.9	69.1	0.0	8.1	..	5.3	5.1	..	4.0	117.8	117.8
Electric Machinery	99.5	99.5	0.0	99.5	0.0	7.0	..	7.0	7.0	..	3.9	63.6	63.6
Mineral Prod.,Prec. Stones & Metal	3.5	4.7	1.7	3.0	0.0	14.8	..	14.2	15.0	..	11.0	44.2	44.2
Manufactured Articles nes.	0.2	0.4	0.2	0.2	0.0	14.9	..	17.8	15.0	..	71.6	109.4	109.4
Industrial goods (line 5-14)	35.3	36.5	11.7	24.7	0.0	12.6	..	12.3	13.9	..	145.7	727.5	727.5
All Merch. Trade (line 2-14)	39.1	58.3	25.4	32.9	0.0	11.8	..	16.6	11.3	..	680.9	1,456.8	1,456.8

Notes: 1. Value of imports from partner countries that do not participate in Free Trade Agreements with SENEGAL

2. Pre-Uruguay Round applied MFN rates from 198 3. Weighted average tariff reduction measured by dT / (1 + T) in percent.

SINGAPORE Bindings and levels of MFN tariff rates before and after the Uruguay Round

Summary product category	Percentage of imports GATT bound					Levels and changes weighted by imports from: the World exc. FTA[1]			LMIEs exc. FTA[1]		Value of 1989 imports in $ million		
	Total pre-UR	Total post-UR	Above appl. rates	At appl. rates	Below appl. rates	Post-UR applied rate	Tariff reduc-tion[3]	Post-UR bound rate	Post-UR applied rate	Tariff reduc-tion[3]	from LMIEs exc. FTA[1]	from World exc. FTA[1]	from World inc. FTA
Agriculture, exc. Fish: Estimate 1	0.0	100.0	2.6	0.0	95.3	8.2	15.9	8.4	26.2	14.7	937.1	1,474.2	1,474.2
Agriculture, exc. Fish: Estimate 2	1.3	100.0	1.3	0.9	82.2	8.8	15.2	9.0	26.6	14.5	1,837.8	3,181.1	3,181.1
Fish and Fish Products	0.0	99.7	98.2	1.3	0.2	0.0	14.3	9.9	0.0	14.3	224.1	357.0	357.0
Petroleum Oils	0.0	0.0	0.0	0.0	0.0	3.5	..	..	3.6	..	4,842.7	6,834.3	6,834.3
Wood, Pulp, Paper, and Furniture	0.0	99.2	29.5	64.1	5.6	0.1	4.9	3.0	0.3	4.9	534.9	1,240.8	1,240.8
Textiles and Clothing	0.0	77.6	77.2	0.4	0.0	1.2	14.3	9.8	2.0	14.3	1,111.5	2,496.5	2,496.5
Leather, Rubber, Footwear	0.0	57.2	57.2	0.0	0.0	0.2	..	10.0	0.1	..	818.8	1,423.9	1,423.9
Metals	0.0	74.3	34.0	40.3	0.0	0.0	..	4.6	0.0	..	1,222.9	3,543.4	3,543.4
Chemical & Photographic Suppl.	0.8	99.8	88.5	11.2	0.0	0.0	14.3	5.7	0.0	14.3	652.8	4,209.9	4,209.9
Transport Equipment	0.0	4.5	3.8	0.7	0.0	3.9	..	8.4	6.0	..	100.2	2,530.5	2,530.5
Non-Electric Machinery	1.6	78.7	38.5	40.2	0.0	0.0	..	4.9	0.0	..	1,199.4	7,964.6	7,964.6
Electric Machinery	0.2	87.1	80.2	6.9	0.0	0.0	..	9.2	0.0	..	2,792.6	9,469.3	9,469.3
Mineral Prod.,Prec. Stones & Metal	0.0	26.0	26.0	0.0	0.0	0.1	..	9.5	0.0	..	262.5	1,053.1	1,053.1
Manufactured Articles nes.	0.0	66.0	44.0	20.7	1.3	0.1	14.3	6.9	1.3	14.3	942.3	4,595.5	4,595.5
Industrial goods (line 5-14)	0.5	74.7	54.8	19.5	0.3	0.4	9.3	6.9	0.4	10.5	9,638.0	38,527.6	38,527.6
All Merch. Trade (line 2-14)	0.4	66.0	43.9	15.5	5.6	1.3	14.9	7.1	4.2	14.3	16,542.5	48,900.0	48,900.0

Notes: 1. Value of imports from partner countries that do not participate in Free Trade Agreements with SINGAPORE

2. Pre-Uruguay Round applied MFN rates from 198 3. Weighted average tariff reduction measured by dT / (1 + T) in percent.

SRI LANKA Bindings and levels of MFN tariff rates before and after the Uruguay Round

Summary product category	Percentage of imports GATT bound					Levels and changes weighted by imports from: the World exc. FTA[1]			LMIEs exc. FTA[1]		Value of 1991 imports in $ million		
	Total pre-UR	Total post-UR	Above appl. rates	At appl. rates	Below appl. rates	Post-UR applied rate	Tariff reduc-tion[3]	Post-UR bound rate	Post-UR applied rate	Tariff reduc-tion[3]	from LMIEs exc. FTA[1]	from World exc. FTA[1]	from World inc. FTA
Agriculture, exc. Fish: Estimate 1	14.1	100.0	100.0	0.0	0.0	1.2	..	50.0	5.2	..	311.9	497.1	497.1
Agriculture, exc. Fish: Estimate 2	12.9	99.5	41.4	27.8	0.4	25.5	9.8	46.1	28.0	6.5	375.6	618.9	618.9
Fish and Fish Products	0.0	100.0	99.8	0.2	0.0	3.9	..	50.0	3.5	..	60.1	65.9	65.9
Petroleum Oils	23.3	23.3	0.0	23.3	0.0	44.0	..	40.9	44.9	..	322.2	424.3	424.3
Wood, Pulp, Paper, and Furniture	7.6	7.9	0.0	7.8	0.0	23.2	..	7.0	20.6	..	71.4	154.9	154.9
Textiles and Clothing	0.0	0.2	0.2	0.0	0.0	53.0	6.5	50.0	51.5	6.5	311.7	820.4	820.4
Leather, Rubber, Footwear	0.0	1.7	0.0	1.7	0.0	43.9	..	50.0	46.7	..	15.0	40.1	40.1
Metals	0.5	5.5	0.8	4.7	0.0	16.8	..	51.0	14.7	..	109.4	226.2	226.2
Chemical & Photographic Suppl.	18.4	18.5	0.2	18.3	0.0	12.8	..	5.6	11.1	..	78.9	305.9	305.9
Transport Equipment	8.2	8.2	0.0	8.2	0.0	12.0	..	22.1	9.7	..	89.6	307.4	307.4
Non-Electric Machinery	16.9	16.9	0.1	16.9	0.0	12.0	..	7.4	17.6	..	52.1	293.3	293.3
Electric Machinery	17.2	17.8	2.7	14.4	0.6	19.1	15.4	23.0	23.7	15.4	41.3	136.6	136.6
Mineral Prod.,Prec. Stones & Metal	5.7	6.5	0.2	5.9	0.4	10.5	14.4	6.2	12.0	15.1	117.9	273.5	273.5
Manufactured Articles nes.	11.2	26.6	15.0	11.6	0.0	27.5	..	33.7	13.8	..	46.4	202.7	202.7
Industrial goods (line 5-14)	7.4	9.2	1.4	7.7	0.1	27.2	14.8	17.9	27.4	15.2	933.8	2,761.1	2,761.1
All Merch. Trade (line 2-14)	9.9	26.7	9.3	12.5	0.1	28.6	11.8	38.9	30.2	13.4	1,691.8	3,870.2	3,870.2

Notes: 1. Value of imports from partner countries that do not participate in Free Trade Agreements with SRI LANKA

2. Pre-Uruguay Round applied MFN rates from 199 3. Weighted average tariff reduction measured by dT / (1 + T) in percent.

SWEDEN Bindings and levels of MFN tariff rates before and after the Uruguay Round

Summary product category	Percentage of imports GATT bound					Levels and changes weighted by imports from: the World exc. FTA[1]			LMIEs exc. FTA[1]		Value of 1990 imports in $ million		
	Total pre-UR	Total post-UR	Above appl. rates	At appl. rates	Below appl. rates	Post-UR applied rate	Tariff reduc-tion[3]	Post-UR bound rate	Post-UR applied rate	Tariff reduc-tion[3]	from LMIEs exc. FTA[1]	from World exc. FTA[1]	from World inc. FTA
Agriculture, exc. Fish: Estimate 1	73.2	100.0	0.0	98.3	1.4	37.8	11.1	37.8	27.2	11.1	592.6	1,226.3	1,226.3
Agriculture, exc. Fish: Estimate 2	75.4	99.9	0.4	42.6	20.8	1.5	1.9	1.5	1.1	2.4	827.3	2,903.2	2,903.2
Fish and Fish Products	43.6	43.9	15.3	28.1	0.6	0.1	1.4	1.4	0.7	1.2	34.3	116.1	387.3
Petroleum Oils	100.0	100.0	0.0	100.0	0.0	0.0	..	0.0	0.0	..	729.1	738.1	2,539.6
Wood, Pulp, Paper, and Furniture	100.0	100.0	32.8	58.2	9.0	0.1	2.2	0.6	1.1	2.6	418.1	543.0	2,430.0
Textiles and Clothing	76.6	100.0	71.0	3.8	25.1	8.3	2.4	9.6	11.8	2.4	612.2	960.0	3,329.9
Leather, Rubber, Footwear	95.7	100.0	66.5	10.2	23.3	4.2	3.6	4.8	8.0	3.5	271.0	410.0	1,432.6
Metals	100.0	100.0	34.0	59.8	6.2	0.2	2.0	0.9	1.3	2.5	351.2	759.9	4,612.6
Chemical & Photographic Suppl.	100.0	100.0	56.6	39.0	4.4	0.7	4.0	3.8	2.9	3.9	238.0	715.4	4,757.7
Transport Equipment	100.0	100.0	69.6	20.8	9.6	4.1	1.7	4.9	6.3	1.6	47.2	1,527.6	5,733.7
Non-Electric Machinery	100.0	100.0	56.2	18.8	25.1	0.8	2.3	1.6	3.6	1.7	82.9	2,109.1	7,596.1
Electric Machinery	100.0	100.0	63.1	11.1	25.8	3.2	1.5	3.1	4.7	1.4	200.1	1,477.1	4,134.1
Mineral Prod.,Prec. Stones & Metal	100.0	100.0	33.6	60.5	5.9	0.4	1.9	1.7	1.4	1.7	193.8	423.5	1,555.3
Manufactured Articles nes.	99.2	100.0	37.1	35.0	27.2	0.9	1.9	1.5	3.0	2.7	161.9	1,101.7	3,097.2
Industrial goods (line 5-14)	97.8	100.0	54.1	29.5	16.4	1.7	2.2	3.2	5.2	2.5	2,576.4	10,027.1	38,679.2
All Merch. Trade (line 2-14)	96.0	99.5	47.1	34.4	15.6	1.4	2.1	2.9	3.5	2.5	4,167.1	13,784.4	44,509.2

Notes: 1. Value of imports from partner countries that do not participate in Free Trade Agreements with SWEDEN

2. Pre-Uruguay Round applied MFN rates from 198 3. Weighted average tariff reduction measured by dT / (1 + T) in percent.

SWITZERLAND Bindings and levels of MFN tariff rates before and after the Uruguay Round

Summary product category	Percentage of imports GATT bound					Levels and changes weighted by imports from: the World exc. FTA[1]			LMIEs exc. FTA[1]		Value of 1988 imports in $ million		
	Total pre-UR	Total post-UR	Above appl. rates	At appl. rates	Below appl. rates	Post-UR applied rate	Tariff reduction[3]	Post-UR bound rate	Post-UR applied rate	Tariff reduction[3]	from LMIEs exc. FTA[1]	from World exc. FTA[1]	from World inc. FTA
Agriculture, exc. Fish: Estimate 1	62.7	100.0	0.0	96.4	1.8	51.3	11.1	51.3	29.6	11.1	654.6	1,710.2	1,710.2
Agriculture, exc. Fish: Estimate 2	68.8	100.0	0.4	5.8	32.6	5.1	2.8	5.1	8.1	3.0	852.4	3,948.4	3,948.4
Fish and Fish Products	92.0	100.0	28.0	62.5	9.1	0.2	1.1	0.6	1.2	1.0	47.6	95.0	334.1
Petroleum Oils	0.2	0.2	0.2	0.0	0.0	14.4	..	2.7	14.2	..	497.3	502.8	1,735.9
Wood, Pulp, Paper, and Furniture	100.0	100.0	60.1	35.2	4.7	0.2	2.8	2.0	6.3	4.9	80.5	233.0	4,253.2
Textiles and Clothing	100.0	100.0	78.1	2.5	19.3	4.6	2.6	5.4	7.1	2.3	497.3	913.2	4,558.3
Leather, Rubber, Footwear	100.0	100.0	81.5	0.6	17.9	3.1	1.3	3.4	4.3	1.2	182.0	292.8	1,591.3
Metals	100.0	100.0	91.0	3.7	5.3	0.9	0.8	1.8	2.6	1.1	91.9	265.7	4,388.8
Chemical & Photographic Suppl.	99.5	99.7	65.2	31.0	3.4	0.2	0.5	1.0	0.8	0.6	221.7	909.9	7,294.3
Transport Equipment	100.0	100.0	72.7	17.4	10.0	3.6	1.6	4.2	3.6	1.4	22.2	1,647.6	6,289.6
Non-Electric Machinery	100.0	100.0	72.7	12.2	15.1	0.3	0.5	0.6	1.1	0.4	51.4	1,281.8	7,483.0
Electric Machinery	100.0	100.0	74.9	5.2	19.9	0.7	0.4	0.9	1.9	0.7	113.7	972.1	4,027.4
Mineral Prod.,Prec. Stones & Metal	96.1	96.1	51.4	42.2	2.5	0.2	0.3	0.5	0.2	0.4	1,000.2	2,378.6	5,700.5
Manufactured Articles nes.	99.9	100.0	52.9	25.3	20.3	0.4	0.5	0.8	1.1	0.6	244.8	1,334.8	4,483.3
Industrial goods (line 5-14)	99.5	99.5	68.9	19.6	10.9	1.0	1.1	1.9	2.4	1.6	2,505.7	10,229.5	50,069.8
All Merch. Trade (line 2-14)	94.2	96.5	61.7	18.2	12.1	1.7	1.4	2.0	4.9	2.0	3,902.9	14,775.6	56,088.2

Notes: 1. Value of imports from partner countries that do not participate in Free Trade Agreements with SWITZERLAND

2. Pre-Uruguay Round applied MFN rates from 198 3. Weighted average tariff reduction measured by dT / (1 + T) in percent.

THAILAND Bindings and levels of MFN tariff rates before and after the Uruguay Round

Summary product category	Percentage of imports GATT bound					Levels and changes weighted by imports from: the World exc. FTA[1]			LMIEs exc. FTA[1]		Value of 1988 imports in $ million		
	Total pre-UR	Total post-UR	Above appl. rates	At appl. rates	Below appl. rates	Post-UR applied rate	Tariff reduction[3]	Post-UR bound rate	Post-UR applied rate	Tariff reduction[3]	from LMIEs exc. FTA[1]	from World exc. FTA[1]	from World inc. FTA
Agriculture, exc. Fish: Estimate 1	16.1	100.0	0.1	73.0	26.9	33.8	27.2	33.8	24.1	4.4	346.4	682.5	682.5
Agriculture, exc. Fish: Estimate 2	21.7	99.3	21.4	21.2	47.0	26.5	6.3	50.5	20.4	4.0	162.5	649.7	649.7
Fish and Fish Products	0.0	99.8	0.0	0.0	99.8	5.5	41.1	5.5	60.0	41.1	168.8	567.2	567.2
Petroleum Oils	0.0	0.0	0.0	0.0	0.0	25.5	..	..	25.3	..	379.7	1,485.7	1,485.7
Wood, Pulp, Paper, and Furniture	0.7	63.4	1.6	0.4	61.3	15.1	7.6	17.3	17.0	7.4	274.9	585.1	585.1
Textiles and Clothing	0.0	94.1	0.2	12.8	81.1	28.9	24.2	28.7	56.6	22.1	275.2	717.6	717.6
Leather, Rubber, Footwear	0.0	43.0	0.0	6.2	36.7	34.8	10.2	29.6	36.7	9.3	28.7	159.5	159.5
Metals	17.6	73.1	36.8	8.1	5.6	17.1	6.3	21.0	13.3	9.3	881.1	2,790.7	2,790.7
Chemical & Photographic Suppl.	2.8	52.1	0.1	22.5	29.2	30.0	11.8	29.0	32.9	11.1	354.9	2,406.3	2,406.3
Transport Equipment	14.9	63.6	14.9	29.0	19.8	46.7	35.9	58.9	62.4	29.4	22.7	2,009.7	2,009.7
Non-Electric Machinery	6.1	92.6	1.6	17.8	73.2	22.9	11.2	22.9	36.9	13.4	272.2	3,555.6	3,555.6
Electric Machinery	0.0	32.7	0.0	3.9	28.8	31.3	11.7	25.3	43.1	19.9	159.5	2,237.2	2,237.2
Mineral Prod.,Prec. Stones & Metal	17.9	51.4	5.6	4.0	41.5	14.9	14.6	8.0	21.6	13.4	410.1	1,116.8	1,116.8
Manufactured Articles nes.	3.5	87.0	1.9	0.8	84.0	20.4	6.3	23.1	14.6	2.3	339.3	1,120.8	1,120.8
Industrial goods (line 5-14)	7.9	67.4	8.9	13.3	41.4	26.8	13.1	27.3	26.2	11.4	3,018.6	16,699.3	16,699.3
All Merch. Trade (line 2-14)	7.5	64.3	8.3	12.2	40.1	26.1	14.9	27.5	27.4	14.4	3,729.5	19,401.8	19,401.8

Notes: 1. Value of imports from partner countries that do not participate in Free Trade Agreements with THAILAND

2. Pre-Uruguay Round applied MFN rates from 198 3. Weighted average tariff reduction measured by dT / (1 + T) in percent.

TUNISIA Bindings and levels of MFN tariff rates before and after the Uruguay Round

Summary product category	Percentage of imports GATT bound					Levels and changes weighted by imports from: the World exc. FTA[1]			LMIEs exc. FTA[1]		Value of 1989 imports in $ million		
	Total pre-UR	Total post-UR	Above appl. rates	At appl. rates	Below appl. rates	Post-UR applied rate	Tariff reduc-tion[3]	Post-UR bound rate	Post-UR applied rate	Tariff reduc-tion[3]	from LMIEs exc. FTA[1]	from World exc. FTA[1]	from World inc. FTA
Agriculture, exc. Fish: Estimate 1	0.0	100.0	0.1	99.9	0.0	23.9	..	24.1	21.5	..	214.4	554.1	554.1
Agriculture, exc. Fish: Estimate 2	0.0	100.0	92.1	5.4	2.5	20.2	6.9	87.2	21.3	6.9	204.7	593.3	593.3
Fish and Fish Products	0.0	0.3	0.3	0.0	0.0	42.9	..	180.0	43.0	..	0.1	1.6	1.6
Petroleum Oils	0.0	0.0	0.0	0.0	0.0	15.2	..	..	6.5	..	101.7	279.2	279.2
Wood, Pulp, Paper, and Furniture	0.0	69.5	6.7	62.8	0.0	23.8	..	23.5	21.1	..	97.4	217.9	217.9
Textiles and Clothing	0.0	97.8	89.1	8.7	0.0	38.4	..	57.2	33.7	..	66.9	806.4	806.4
Leather, Rubber, Footwear	0.0	59.0	58.3	0.6	0.0	26.4	..	40.9	24.2	..	8.5	78.1	78.1
Metals	0.0	40.2	19.6	20.6	0.0	21.9	..	26.4	20.3	..	61.7	328.6	328.6
Chemical & Photographic Suppl.	0.0	75.8	55.9	19.9	0.0	18.9	..	26.9	19.9	..	84.7	441.8	441.8
Transport Equipment	0.0	68.3	8.9	59.4	0.0	28.4	..	29.1	28.2	..	19.1	162.4	162.4
Non-Electric Machinery	0.0	54.8	17.0	37.8	0.0	22.9	..	25.2	24.3	..	21.6	493.1	493.1
Electric Machinery	0.0	69.2	25.6	43.5	0.0	29.4	..	31.5	32.8	..	11.2	237.5	237.5
Mineral Prod.,Prec. Stones & Metal	0.0	34.8	7.3	27.5	0.0	16.1	..	20.0	10.3	..	162.9	295.2	295.2
Manufactured Articles nes.	0.0	54.8	41.7	13.1	0.0	23.1	..	42.0	19.2	..	43.0	183.6	183.6
Industrial goods (line 5-14)	0.0	67.9	41.5	26.3	0.0	26.4	..	38.4	19.7	..	577.0	3,244.6	3,244.6
All Merch. Trade (line 2-14)	0.0	67.9	46.0	21.5	0.4	24.8	6.9	48.7	18.6	6.9	883.6	4,118.6	4,118.6

Notes: 1. Value of imports from partner countries that do not participate in Free Trade Agreements with TUNISIA

2. Pre-Uruguay Round applied MFN rates from 199 3. Weighted average tariff reduction measured by dT / (1 + T) in percent.

TURKEY Bindings and levels of MFN tariff rates before and after the Uruguay Round

Summary product category	Percentage of imports GATT bound					Levels and changes weighted by imports from: the World exc. FTA[1]			LMIEs exc. FTA[1]		Value of 1989 imports in $ million		
	Total pre-UR	Total post-UR	Above appl. rates	At appl. rates	Below appl. rates	Post-UR applied rate	Tariff reduc-tion[3]	Post-UR bound rate	Post-UR applied rate	Tariff reduc-tion[3]	from LMIEs exc. FTA[1]	from World exc. FTA[1]	from World inc. FTA
Agriculture, exc. Fish: Estimate 1	3.4	100.0	100.0	0.0	0.0	1.6	1.9	98.2	3.4	1.9	461.6	1,069.1	1,069.1
Agriculture, exc. Fish: Estimate 2	4.3	100.0	39.5	1.0	59.4	45.6	8.0	110.1	30.3	5.2	451.5	1,279.5	1,279.5
Fish and Fish Products	3.2	4.6	0.2	0.0	4.5	21.3	2.4	20.0	24.8	..	0.7	3.4	3.4
Petroleum Oils	0.5	0.5	0.0	0.0	0.0	..	..	..	..	..	2,553.8	2,659.1	2,659.1
Wood, Pulp, Paper, and Furniture	51.5	60.6	0.0	3.0	57.6	28.8	8.1	18.5	29.3	8.3	83.8	392.1	392.1
Textiles and Clothing	61.3	62.6	0.0	1.3	61.3	44.2	17.2	23.6	59.7	15.9	129.6	531.8	531.8
Leather, Rubber, Footwear	30.8	46.6	0.0	0.4	46.1	46.2	9.0	20.8	38.5	10.6	76.4	231.2	231.2
Metals	19.9	19.9	0.0	14.3	5.6	18.2	4.0	23.9	16.8	3.9	972.0	2,766.0	2,766.0
Chemical & Photographic Suppl.	65.7	65.8	0.0	9.7	56.1	25.0	5.9	17.7	25.8	6.4	329.9	2,131.5	2,131.5
Transport Equipment	64.8	64.8	0.0	1.7	63.1	20.0	4.2	12.2	31.1	3.7	21.6	670.7	670.7
Non-Electric Machinery	69.3	69.3	0.0	6.9	62.4	20.6	4.7	11.9	30.2	4.2	147.0	2,211.5	2,211.5
Electric Machinery	56.9	56.9	0.0	8.8	48.1	22.9	6.0	15.7	24.0	5.4	115.4	1,028.3	1,028.3
Mineral Prod.,Prec. Stones & Metal	16.9	16.9	0.0	0.2	16.8	28.9	3.5	13.3	23.6	2.1	536.5	1,078.3	1,078.3
Manufactured Articles nes.	32.5	58.8	0.1	1.8	56.9	29.5	6.6	16.6	41.6	10.5	122.7	756.4	756.4
Industrial goods (line 5-14)	46.9	49.3	0.0	7.6	41.7	24.2	6.3	16.3	25.1	7.3	2,534.9	11,797.9	11,797.9
All Merch. Trade (line 2-14)	35.6	45.1	3.2	5.7	36.1	26.3	6.5	33.3	25.9	6.7	5,541.0	15,739.9	15,739.9

Notes: 1. Value of imports from partner countries that do not participate in Free Trade Agreements with TURKEY

2. Pre-Uruguay Round applied MFN rates from 198 3. Weighted average tariff reduction measured by dT / (1 + T) in percent.

UNITED STATES Bindings and levels of MFN tariff rates before and after the Uruguay Round

Summary product category	Percentage of imports GATT bound					Levels and changes weighted by imports from: the World exc. FTA[1]			LMIEs exc. FTA[1]		Value of 1989 imports in $ million		
	Total pre-UR	Total post-UR	Above appl. rates	At appl. rates	Below appl. rates	Post-UR applied rate	Tariff reduc-tion[3]	Post-UR bound rate	Post-UR applied rate	Tariff reduc-tion[3]	from LMIEs exc. FTA[1]	from World exc. FTA[1]	from World inc. FTA
Agriculture, exc. Fish: Estimate 1	88.0	100.0	6.1	93.7	0.2	10.8	1.5	10.9	10.5	1.3	5,539.6	8,085.6	10,578.1
Agriculture, exc. Fish: Estimate 2	91.8	100.0	14.1	47.8	34.7	2.2	1.9	2.6	4.5	2.3	8,592.8	15,795.2	21,438.8
Fish and Fish Products	67.2	100.0	0.8	91.8	7.4	0.9	2.3	0.9	1.5	2.9	2,474.1	3,819.7	5,426.2
Petroleum Oils	27.5	27.5	11.7	15.8	0.0	0.7	..	1.1	0.7	..	31,579.8	37,528.4	46,350.9
Wood, Pulp, Paper, and Furniture	100.0	100.0	1.0	76.6	22.5	0.2	3.4	0.2	3.7	4.2	2,079.2	8,206.3	23,731.4
Textiles and Clothing	98.8	100.0	4.8	9.2	86.0	14.8	2.0	14.7	17.1	1.8	15,861.0	29,101.4	30,781.8
Leather, Rubber, Footwear	100.0	100.0	7.3	68.2	24.6	6.9	1.9	6.8	8.3	2.0	8,435.4	15,365.6	16,907.6
Metals	100.0	100.0	12.0	44.8	43.2	1.1	3.8	1.3	2.9	3.3	6,139.0	20,536.7	30,379.1
Chemical & Photographic Suppl.	99.9	100.0	11.3	51.9	36.8	2.5	4.9	2.8	4.8	5.5	2,303.6	19,756.4	24,544.3
Transport Equipment	99.8	100.0	36.0	54.6	9.4	3.4	1.1	4.6	3.1	0.9	3,162.4	49,116.4	79,699.4
Non-Electric Machinery	100.0	100.0	6.7	29.6	63.7	0.9	2.8	1.0	3.1	2.8	4,330.4	51,211.1	60,918.9
Electric Machinery	100.0	100.0	16.6	34.9	48.5	1.7	2.5	2.0	3.5	3.0	10,344.5	39,322.3	49,728.0
Mineral Prod.,Prec. Stones & Metal	100.0	100.0	3.5	69.1	27.4	1.7	2.7	1.8	2.7	2.9	5,484.5	14,348.8	22,654.7
Manufactured Articles nes.	98.5	100.0	3.7	27.2	69.1	1.4	4.0	1.5	5.8	5.1	6,768.4	33,182.9	36,505.4
Industrial goods (line 5-14)	99.7	100.0	14.0	43.5	42.5	3.1	2.9	3.5	6.8	2.9	64,908.4	280,148.0	375,851.0
All Merch. Trade (line 2-14)	91.5	92.5	13.6	41.4	37.4	2.8	2.9	3.3	4.9	2.8	107,555.0	337,291.0	449,067.0

Notes: 1. Value of imports from partner countries that do not participate in Free Trade Agreements with UNITED STATES

2. Pre-Uruguay Round applied MFN rates from 198 3. Weighted average tariff reduction measured by dT / (1 + T) in percent.

URUGUAY Bindings and levels of MFN tariff rates before and after the Uruguay Round

Summary product category	Percentage of imports GATT bound					Levels and changes weighted by imports from: the World exc. FTA[1]			LMIEs exc. FTA[1]		Value of 1987 imports in $ million		
	Total pre-UR	Total post-UR	Above appl. rates	At appl. rates	Below appl. rates	Post-UR applied rate	Tariff reduc-tion[3]	Post-UR bound rate	Post-UR applied rate	Tariff reduc-tion[3]	from LMIEs exc. FTA[1]	from World exc. FTA[1]	from World inc. FTA
Agriculture, exc. Fish: Estimate 1	2.5	100.0	99.9	0.0	0.1	-9.2	31.8	40.4	-1.8	31.8	3.8	27.3	51.9
Agriculture, exc. Fish: Estimate 2	9.5	100.0	99.2	0.7	0.0	9.5	13.7	34.0	8.2	15.4	7.2	55.1	107.0
Fish and Fish Products	0.0	100.0	100.0	0.0	0.0	11.9	..	35.0	12.6	..	1.8	2.9	3.1
Petroleum Oils	0.0	100.0	12.9	87.1	0.0	33.7	..	35.0	32.4	..	152.2	175.6	190.3
Wood, Pulp, Paper, and Furniture	21.8	100.0	100.0	0.0	0.0	7.2	..	25.4	9.5	..	5.8	17.3	44.6
Textiles and Clothing	6.4	100.0	100.0	0.0	0.0	6.4	..	33.7	4.7	..	6.6	27.8	54.2
Leather, Rubber, Footwear	1.0	100.0	99.2	0.0	0.8	10.9	10.5	34.9	10.9	..	4.6	20.5	53.3
Metals	23.9	100.0	99.9	0.0	0.1	8.2	6.0	29.0	7.9	7.1	13.9	31.5	97.8
Chemical & Photographic Suppl.	0.0	100.0	99.2	0.8	0.0	9.9	15.9	23.5	11.6	..	23.4	156.3	261.1
Transport Equipment	70.3	100.0	78.2	21.8	0.0	10.7	..	18.9	13.7	..	2.5	52.7	146.9
Non-Electric Machinery	17.2	100.0	98.9	0.9	0.2	8.3	7.9	32.3	8.5	..	4.4	98.1	142.7
Electric Machinery	1.4	100.0	100.0	0.0	0.0	8.9	10.5	34.9	8.5	..	7.4	67.4	117.1
Mineral Prod.,Prec. Stones & Metal	5.2	100.0	95.9	4.0	0.1	9.5	4.1	25.8	11.6	4.1	11.5	38.0	55.4
Manufactured Articles nes.	0.1	100.0	100.0	0.0	0.0	8.8	..	33.4	5.8	..	8.1	54.4	80.2
Industrial goods (line 5-14)	16.1	100.0	96.3	3.6	0.1	9.1	9.2	27.9	10.0	4.2	88.2	563.9	1,053.3
All Merch. Trade (line 2-14)	13.3	100.0	84.9	15.1	0.1	14.6	9.4	29.4	14.5	8.4	249.4	797.4	1,353.8

Notes: 1. Value of imports from partner countries that do not participate in Free Trade Agreements with URUGUAY

2. Pre-Uruguay Round applied MFN rates from 199 3. Weighted average tariff reduction measured by dT / (1 + T) in percent.

VENEZUELA Bindings and levels of MFN tariff rates before and after the Uruguay Round

	Percentage of imports GATT bound				Levels and changes weighted by imports from: the World exc. FTA[1]			LMIEs exc. FTA[1]		Value of 1990 imports in $ million		
Summary product category	Total pre-UR	Total post-UR	Above appl. rates	At appl. rates	Below appl. rates	Post-UR applied rate	Tariff reduc-tion[3]	Post-UR bound rate	Post-UR applied rate	Tariff reduc-tion[3]	from LMIEs exc. FTA[1]	from World exc. FTA[1]	from World inc. FTA
Agriculture, exc. Fish: Estimate 1	100.0	100.0	100.0	0.0	0.0	-16.3	..	71.9	-14.1	..	138.1	575.6	575.6
Agriculture, exc. Fish: Estimate 2	100.0	100.0	85.5	14.4	0.1	16.2	11.2	33.0	19.8	8.7	142.4	755.9	755.9
Fish and Fish Products	100.0	100.0	100.0	0.0	0.0	10.0	..	35.0	..	..	0.0	0.0	0.0
Petroleum Oils	100.0	100.0	100.0	0.0	0.0	10.0	..	35.0	10.0	..	85.7	140.2	140.2
Wood, Pulp, Paper, and Furniture	100.0	100.0	93.4	5.3	1.3	6.2	3.6	25.1	5.5	3.6	61.7	285.1	285.1
Textiles and Clothing	100.0	100.0	49.3	1.2	49.5	26.5	3.6	34.8	34.5	3.6	91.6	225.3	225.3
Leather, Rubber, Footwear	100.0	100.0	78.3	2.7	19.0	16.7	2.9	34.1	22.2	3.0	34.3	125.5	125.5
Metals	100.0	100.0	99.7	0.2	0.2	9.9	3.6	34.2	7.4	3.6	233.4	734.7	734.7
Chemical & Photographic Suppl.	100.0	100.0	99.1	0.1	0.8	8.9	3.1	30.6	9.3	3.0	140.0	1,026.3	1,026.3
Transport Equipment	100.0	100.0	63.2	1.8	34.9	23.3	1.8	34.2	25.6	1.8	64.9	520.0	520.0
Non-Electric Machinery	100.0	100.0	96.8	2.7	0.5	10.0	1.8	29.2	10.6	1.7	84.7	1,616.3	1,616.3
Electric Machinery	100.0	100.0	89.6	2.1	8.3	14.0	1.6	33.0	25.5	2.6	53.6	556.6	556.6
Mineral Prod.,Prec. Stones & Metal	100.0	100.0	77.1	0.2	3.9	9.7	3.6	32.7	10.9	3.6	46.8	248.7	248.7
Manufactured Articles nes.	100.0	100.0	93.6	0.7	5.7	9.8	3.5	31.5	14.7	3.6	60.9	362.1	362.1
Industrial goods (line 5-14)	**100.0**	**100.0**	**90.3**	**1.6**	**7.3**	**12.0**	**2.5**	**31.3**	**14.5**	**3.1**	**871.9**	**5,700.6**	**5,700.6**
All Merch. Trade (line 2-14)	**100.0**	**100.0**	**89.9**	**3.1**	**6.3**	**12.4**	**2.6**	**31.6**	**14.9**	**3.1**	**1,100.0**	**6,596.7**	**6,596.7**

Notes: 1. Value of imports from partner countries that do not participate in Free Trade Agreements with VENEZUELA

2. Pre-Uruguay Round applied MFN rates from 199 3. Weighted average tariff reduction measured by dT / (1 + T) in percent.

ZIMBABWE Bindings and levels of MFN tariff rates before and after the Uruguay Round

	Percentage of imports GATT bound				Levels and changes weighted by imports from: the World exc. FTA[1]			LMIEs exc. FTA[1]		Value of 1987 imports in $ million		
Summary product category	Total pre-UR	Total post-UR	Above appl. rates	At appl. rates	Below appl. rates	Post-UR applied rate	Tariff reduc-tion[3]	Post-UR bound rate	Post-UR applied rate	Tariff reduc-tion[3]	from LMIEs exc. FTA[1]	from World exc. FTA[1]	from World inc. FTA
Agriculture, exc. Fish: Estimate 1	3.5	99.8	99.8	0.0	0.0	-3.4	..	150.0	-5.8	..	5.3	12.5	12.5
Agriculture, exc. Fish: Estimate 2	35.9	100.0	85.2	1.3	8.8	4.4	4.2	83.2	6.3	4.0	18.8	31.8	31.8
Fish and Fish Products	42.5	42.5	0.0	42.5	0.0	1.7	..	3.9	2.1	..	1.6	2.0	2.0
Petroleum Oils	0.0	0.0	0.0	0.0	0.0	10.3	..	..	9.2	..	117.5	119.8	119.8
Wood, Pulp, Paper, and Furniture	23.5	23.5	0.9	22.5	0.0	7.0	..	2.1	6.8	..	14.3	29.5	29.5
Textiles and Clothing	0.7	19.5	0.7	0.7	18.1	17.6	7.0	31.0	21.8	7.5	37.1	66.2	66.2
Leather, Rubber, Footwear	59.7	59.7	54.0	5.7	0.0	6.4	..	5.0	3.7	..	11.4	20.7	20.7
Metals	4.5	10.2	4.5	0.0	5.6	5.2	3.9	16.2	4.3	3.9	77.1	101.9	101.9
Chemical & Photographic Suppl.	9.0	15.8	6.7	9.0	0.0	2.1	..	64.5	2.7	..	82.5	180.4	180.4
Transport Equipment	9.4	9.4	0.0	9.4	0.0	2.9	..	3.2	7.7	..	9.7	156.8	156.8
Non-Electric Machinery	15.0	15.0	3.2	11.7	0.0	1.2	..	3.7	1.1	..	30.4	147.3	147.3
Electric Machinery	3.6	3.6	0.0	3.6	0.0	5.6	..	12.4	7.5	..	10.5	67.6	67.6
Mineral Prod.,Prec. Stones & Metal	18.5	18.5	0.0	18.5	0.0	3.7	..	3.3	2.8	..	26.3	49.1	49.1
Manufactured Articles nes.	1.2	2.8	2.2	0.6	0.0	6.1	..	93.3	4.3	..	35.3	73.0	73.0
Industrial goods (line 5-14)	**10.1**	**13.6**	**3.9**	**7.7**	**2.0**	**4.5**	**6.0**	**23.6**	**5.8**	**6.3**	**334.6**	**892.5**	**892.5**
All Merch. Trade (line 2-14)	**9.8**	**14.7**	**5.9**	**6.7**	**2.0**	**4.5**	**5.8**	**35.3**	**5.8**	**5.8**	**472.5**	**1,046.2**	**1,046.2**

Notes: 1. Value of imports from partner countries that do not participate in Free Trade Agreements with ZIMBABWE

2. Pre-Uruguay Round applied MFN rates from 198 3. Weighted average tariff reduction measured by dT / (1 + T) in percent.

3

Tables G.2

Concessions Given

Importing Group by Product Category

(The economies from each regional group for which data were available
are listed in a footnote to each table.)

EAST ASIA & PACIFIC[4] Bindings and levels of MFN tariff rates before and after the Uruguay Round

Summary product category	Percentage of imports GATT bound					Levels and changes weighted by imports from:					Value of 1991 imports in $ million		
						the World exc. FTA[1]			LMIEs exc. FTA[1]				
	Total pre-UR	Total post-UR	Above appl. rates	At appl. rates	Below appl. rates	Post-UR applied rate	Tariff reduction[3]	Post-UR bound rate	Post-UR applied rate	Tariff reduction[3]	from LMIEs exc. FTA[1]	from World exc. FTA[1]	from World inc. FTA
Agriculture, exc. Fish: Estimate 1	30.9	100.0	12.6	34.0	53.3	40.5	44.3	47.8	66.9	18.6	2,756	7,057	7,057
Agriculture, exc. Fish: Estimate 2	26.4	99.9	53.1	11.1	29.7	11.2	5.2	77.6	10.7	4.3	2,659	7,617	7,617
Fish and Fish Products	1.5	74.9	0.5	4.0	70.4	9.1	32.9	7.3	35.2	36.3	371	1,081	1,081
Petroleum Oils	0.0	13.8	13.0	0.0	0.7	8.3	5.7	35.1	7.1	5.0	5,353	9,416	9,416
Wood, Pulp, Paper and Furniture	29.8	74.7	27.7	8.3	38.6	7.4	8.3	11.5	8.9	6.8	1,298	4,534	4,534
Textiles and Clothing	2.1	87.5	16.4	5.5	64.9	17.5	9.7	22.5	27.4	10.2	1,647	6,181	6,181
Leather, Rubber, Footwear	10.8	87.2	11.0	7.3	68.5	13.8	7.5	14.5	14.7	7.8	604	1,946	1,946
Metals	15.3	80.4	24.3	16.0	35.2	8.2	10.0	12.8	9.4	8.3	3,969	14,280	14,280
Chemical & Photographic Suppl.	6.7	83.0	27.8	8.1	46.5	11.0	10.3	17.1	15.4	9.5	1,884	15,166	15,166
Transport Equipment	32.6	67.1	16.9	35.2	14.9	22.8	17.3	24.6	9.8	17.3	358	7,217	7,217
Non-Electric Machinery	20.3	87.8	26.9	13.4	47.4	13.3	8.9	18.6	21.3	12.8	830	19,184	19 184
Electric Machinery	20.5	76.8	8.5	14.3	53.9	12.9	8.1	11.5	17.8	7.7	1,011	16,834	16,834
Mineral Prod.,Prec. Stones & Metal	21.1	78.7	23.8	32.6	21.8	7.9	9.9	10.5	9.3	10.5	2,052	6,198	6,198
Manufactured Articles nes.	10.0	88.0	16.2	16.4	55.3	10.2	8.1	14.4	9.5	3.6	1,235	8,990	8,990
Industrial Goods (line 5-14)	**16.7**	**81.5**	**20.8**	**15.3**	**44.5**	**12.3**	**9.2**	**15.8**	**13.6**	**8.7**	**14,888**	**100,532**	**100,532**
All Merch. Trade (line 2-14)	**15.9**	**77.3**	**22.1**	**13.7**	**40.3**	**11.9**	**9.4**	**21.0**	**12.1**	**9.1**	**23,271**	**118,646**	**118,646**

Notes: 1. Value of imports from partner countries that do not participate in Free Trade Agreements with EAST ASIA & PACIFIC

2. Pre-Uruguay Round applied MFN rates 3. Weighted average tariff reduction measured by dT / (1 + T) in percent.

4. Regional aggregate based on available information from Indonesia, Korea, Macau, Malaysia, Philippines and Thailand

EASTERN EUROPE[4] Bindings and levels of MFN tariff rates before and after the Uruguay Round

Summary product category	Percentage of imports GATT bound					Levels and changes weighted by imports from:					Value of 1988 imports in $ million		
						the World exc. FTA[1]			LMIEs exc. FTA[1]				
	Total pre-UR	Total post-UR	Above appl. rates	At appl. rates	Below appl. rates	Post-UR applied rate	Tariff reduction[3]	Post-UR bound rate	Post-UR applied rate	Tariff reduction[3]	from LMIEs exc. FTA[1]	from World exc. FTA[1]	from World inc. FTA
Agriculture, exc. Fish: Estimate 1	27.8	100.0	68.9	29.1	2.0	1.1	14.3	50.4	-1.1	13.5	1,750	2,722	2,722
Agriculture, exc. Fish: Estimate 2	33.2	99.4	51.4	25.9	22.1	14.4	3.3	44.3	12.7	3.2	1,997	3,617	3,617
Fish and Fish Products	48.4	50.2	4.4	22.0	23.8	7.8	0.6	4.4	14.9	0.8	36	114	114
Petroleum Oils	43.8	94.0	33.0	58.5	2.5	1.8	1.2	12.0	1.4	1.3	3,512	3,833	3,833
Wood, Pulp, Paper and Furniture	74.1	100.0	12.5	43.4	44.1	4.3	2.7	5.9	5.6	3.3	371	1,117	1,117
Textiles and Clothing	64.7	99.3	23.2	13.1	63.1	9.5	3.6	11.3	12.6	3.1	978	2,697	2,697
Leather, Rubber, Footwear	66.0	100.0	15.2	26.4	58.3	7.1	3.0	8.6	9.5	2.8	431	923	923
Metals	56.6	100.0	35.9	29.2	35.0	4.1	1.8	9.0	3.2	1.4	2,081	3,426	3,426
Chemical & Photographic Suppl.	60.5	98.8	17.6	32.2	49.0	6.3	3.8	8.2	8.7	4.0	855	4,111	4,111
Transport Equipment	42.3	54.2	12.6	15.2	26.4	13.6	1.7	12.5	11.6	1.9	854	2,010	2,010
Non-Electric Machinery	63.5	99.2	21.7	5.0	72.5	6.0	1.6	7.7	7.5	1.8	1,499	6,523	6,523
Electric Machinery	66.9	97.4	21.6	19.2	56.6	9.7	2.3	11.4	10.6	2.1	632	2,140	2,140
Mineral Prod.,Prec. Stones & Metal	44.4	99.1	33.6	48.6	17.0	2.4	2.9	12.6	2.3	3.1	2,122	2,879	2,879
Manufactured Articles nes.	59.8	99.1	25.3	32.2	41.6	5.1	2.3	10.7	4.1	2.7	1,348	3,245	3,245
Industrial Goods (line 5-14)	**59.4**	**96.0**	**23.3**	**23.7**	**49.0**	**6.4**	**2.4**	**9.5**	**6.3**	**2.4**	**11,171**	**29,072**	**29,072**
All Merch. Trade (line 2-14)	**55.1**	**96.0**	**27.0**	**27.6**	**41.4**	**6.7**	**2.4**	**13.3**	**6.1**	**2.5**	**16,716**	**36,635**	**36,635**

Notes: 1. Value of imports from partner countries that do not participate in Free Trade Agreements with EASTERN EUROPE

2. Pre-Uruguay Round applied MFN rates 3. Weighted average tariff reduction measured by dT / (1 + T) in percent.

4. Regional aggregate based on available information from Czech and Slovak CU, Hungary, Poland and Romania.

Tables G.2. Concessions Given: *Importing Group by Product Category*

HIGH-INCOME ECONOMIES[4] Bindings and levels of MFN tariff rates before and after the Uruguay Round

Summary product category	Percentage of imports GATT bound					Levels and changes weighted by imports from: the World exc. FTA[1]			LMIEs exc. FTA[1]		Value of 1988 imports in $ million		
	Total pre-UR	Total post-UR	Above appl. rates	At appl. rates	Below appl. rates	Post-UR applied rate	Tariff reduction[3]	Post-UR bound rate	Post-UR applied rate	Tariff reduction[3]	from LMIEs exc. FTA[1]	from World exc. FTA[1]	from World inc. FTA
Agriculture, exc. Fish: Estimate 1	73.6	100.0	3.1	85.4	11.4	26.9	26.9	27.1	15.3	16.5	37,462	63,326	67,486
Agriculture, exc. Fish: Estimate 2	71.0	100.0	7.8	39.6	34.9	5.2	4.5	7.2	8.7	5.2	53,062	104,818	114,083
Fish and Fish Products	79.5	98.4	10.5	44.7	43.0	4.2	2.4	4.9	6.4	2.8	12,525	21,618	25,869
Petroleum Oils	45.8	47.0	8.4	36.7	0.9	0.7	1.3	0.9	0.8	1.3	95,047	118,841	136,962
Wood, Pulp, Paper and Furniture	84.9	94.5	7.6	69.3	17.5	0.5	4.6	0.9	2.9	4.6	17,818	46,587	96,112
Textiles and Clothing	73.7	79.9	17.0	9.8	53.0	8.4	2.6	11.0	10.0	2.4	63,905	103,030	122,119
Leather, Rubber, Footwear	79.1	89.7	16.5	41.8	31.4	5.5	2.5	6.5	6.1	2.4	25,082	40,851	48,986
Metals	90.8	97.5	19.2	47.4	30.8	0.9	3.4	1.6	2.2	3.2	39,421	82,523	124,397
Chemical & Photographic Suppl.	82.7	91.4	27.5	30.8	33.0	2.2	3.7	3.6	4.6	3.8	17,718	77,894	117,356
Transport Equipment	93.8	95.5	39.9	42.0	13.7	4.2	2.6	5.6	3.7	2.2	11,006	101,166	174,320
Non-Electric Machinery	88.7	94.9	24.4	26.5	44.1	1.1	3.1	1.9	3.0	2.8	13,320	132,571	192,435
Electric Machinery	77.5	88.5	25.3	26.8	36.4	2.3	3.2	3.7	3.5	3.3	30,441	110,462	144,008
Mineral Prod.,Prec. Stones & Metal	86.6	92.1	12.6	61.9	17.6	0.7	2.2	1.0	0.9	2.2	52,800	95,323	119,717
Manufactured Articles nes.	81.3	89.7	12.1	36.5	40.8	1.4	3.7	2.0	3.1	4.1	29,481	109,814	133,692
Industrial Goods (line 5-14)	**84.7**	**91.7**	**21.7**	**37.7**	**32.3**	**2.5**	**3.1**	**3.5**	**4.4**	**3.0**	**300,992**	**900,221**	**1,273,140**
All Merch. Trade (line 2-14)	**80.2**	**88.5**	**19.3**	**37.9**	**29.9**	**2.6**	**3.2**	**3.7**	**4.3**	**3.3**	**461,626**	**1,145,500**	**1,550,060**

Notes: 1. Value of imports from partner countries that do not participate in Free Trade Agreements with HIGH INCOME ECONMS.

2. Pre-Uruguay Round applied MFN rates 3. Weighted average tariff reduction measured by dT / (1 + T) in percent.

4. Average based on available information from Ausralia, Austria, Canada, Switzerland, European Union, Finland, Hong Kong, Island, Japan, Norway, New Zealand, Singapore, Sweden, USA.

LATIN AMERICA[4] Bindings and levels of MFN tariff rates before and after the Uruguay Round

Summary product category	Percentage of imports GATT bound					Levels and changes weighted by imports from: the World exc. FTA[1]			LMIEs exc. FTA[1]		Value of 1991 imports in $ million		
	Total pre-UR	Total post-UR	Above appl. rates	At appl. rates	Below appl. rates	Post-UR applied rate	Tariff reduction[3]	Post-UR bound rate	Post-UR applied rate	Tariff reduction[3]	from LMIEs exc. FTA[1]	from World exc. FTA[1]	from World inc. FTA
Agriculture, exc. Fish: Estimate 1	62.9	100.0	81.4	16.6	2.0	-7.6	9.3	40.0	-10.8	11.7	851	2,456	5,148
Agriculture, exc. Fish: Estimate 2	61.6	100.0	93.4	5.0	1.4	11.7	1.1	42.8	11.9	1.4	1,238	3,766	7,209
Fish and Fish Products	34.3	100.0	68.1	31.9	0.0	6.7	..	23.9	11.7	..	48	140	209
Petroleum Oils	15.8	100.0	27.5	2.8	0.0	13.2	..	35.8	16.7	..	4,620	5,639	5,937
Wood, Pulp, Paper and Furniture	63.2	100.0	89.7	10.1	0.2	6.4	6.4	26.7	8.5	8.4	414	1,579	2,394
Textiles and Clothing	53.3	100.0	91.5	0.8	7.7	18.1	3.6	35.0	17.2	3.6	369	1,094	1,489
Leather, Rubber, Footwear	40.0	100.0	98.0	0.2	1.7	11.7	3.1	34.1	10.8	3.0	253	997	1,466
Metals	51.6	100.0	99.3	0.6	0.0	8.8	3.8	32.5	6.6	3.7	1,441	3,880	4,977
Chemical & Photographic Suppl.	42.9	100.0	96.8	3.1	0.1	10.1	2.8	28.1	10.5	2.7	1,316	7,938	9,854
Transport Equipment	59.6	100.0	90.8	3.6	5.6	16.5	2.1	34.2	16.1	2.1	355	2,805	3,718
Non-Electric Machinery	59.6	100.0	97.7	2.1	0.1	13.6	2.0	32.0	14.1	1.7	494	7,905	9,926
Electric Machinery	52.5	100.0	97.7	1.4	0.9	14.3	1.7	33.3	15.6	2.6	438	4,111	5,101
Mineral Prod.,Prec. Stones & Metal	52.7	100.0	84.2	9.9	0.3	5.8	3.6	26.1	6.3	3.6	1,104	3,195	3,741
Manufactured Articles nes.	48.5	99.4	96.5	1.3	1.4	13.5	2.9	33.1	10.2	4.3	460	2,800	3,815
Industrial Goods (line 5-14)	**52.3**	**99.9**	**95.4**	**3.1**	**1.0**	**11.7**	**2.7**	**31.1**	**10.4**	**3.3**	**6,646**	**36,304**	**46,481**
All Merch. Trade (line 2-14)	**49.7**	**100.0**	**88.3**	**3.4**	**1.0**	**11.7**	**2.4**	**32.7**	**12.4**	**3.0**	**12,552**	**45,848**	**59,836**

Notes: 1. Value of imports from partner countries that do not participate in Free Trade Agreements with LATIN AMERICA

2. Pre-Uruguay Round applied MFN rates 3. Weighted average tariff reduction measured by dT / (1 + T) in percent.

4. Regional aggregate based on available information from Argentina, Brazil, Chile, Colombia, Jamaica, Mexico, Peru, El Salvador, Uruguay, Venezuela.

NORTH AFRICA[4] Bindings and levels of MFN tariff rates before and after the Uruguay Round

Summary product category	Percentage of imports GATT bound					Levels and changes weighted by imports from: the World exc. FTA[1]			LMIEs exc. FTA[1]		Value of 1991 imports in $ million		
	Total pre-UR	Total post-UR	Above appl. rates	At appl. rates	Below appl. rates	Post-UR applied rate	Tariff reduction[3]	Post-UR bound rate	Post-UR applied rate	Tariff reduction[3]	from LMIEs exc. FTA[1]	from World exc. FTA[1]	from World inc. FTA
Agriculture, exc. Fish: Estimate 1	0.0	100.0	0.1	99.9	0.0	23.9	..	24.1	21.5	..	214	554	554
Agriculture, exc. Fish: Estimate 2	0.0	100.0	92.1	5.4	2.5	20.2	6.9	87.2	21.3	6.9	205	593	593
Fish and Fish Products	0.0	0.3	0.3	0.0	0.0	42.9	..	180.0	43.0	..		2	2
Petroleum Oils	0.0	0.0	0.0	0.0	0.0	15.2	..	..	6.5	..	102	279	279
Wood, Pulp, Paper and Furniture	0.0	69.5	6.7	62.8	0.0	23.8	..	23.5	21.1	..	97	218	218
Textiles and Clothing	0.0	97.8	89.1	8.7	0.0	38.4	..	57.2	33.7	..	67	806	806
Leather, Rubber, Footwear	0.0	59.0	58.3	0.6	0.0	26.4	..	40.9	24.2	..	9	78	78
Metals	0.0	40.2	19.6	20.6	0.0	21.9	..	26.4	20.3	..	62	329	329
Chemical & Photographic Suppl.	0.0	75.8	55.9	19.9	0.0	18.9	..	26.9	19.9	..	85	442	442
Transport Equipment	0.0	68.3	8.9	59.4	0.0	28.4	..	29.1	28.2	..	19	162	162
Non-Electric Machinery	0.0	54.8	17.0	37.8	0.0	22.9	..	25.2	24.3	..	22	493	493
Electric Machinery	0.0	69.2	25.6	43.5	0.0	29.4	..	31.5	32.8	..	11	237	237
Mineral Prod.,Prec. Stones & Metal	0.0	34.8	7.3	27.5	0.0	16.1	..	20.0	10.3	..	163	295	295
Manufactured Articles nes.	0.0	54.8	41.7	13.1	0.0	23.1	..	42.0	19.2	..	43	184	184
Industrial Goods (line 5-14)	**0.0**	**67.9**	**41.5**	**26.3**	**0.0**	**26.4**	**..**	**38.4**	**19.7**	**..**	**577**	**3,245**	**3,245**
All Merch. Trade (line 2-14)	**0.0**	**67.9**	**46.0**	**21.5**	**0.4**	**24.8**	**6.9**	**48.7**	**18.6**	**6.9**	**884**	**4,119**	**4,119**

Notes: 1. Value of imports from partner countries that do not participate in Free Trade Agreements with NORTH AFRICA

2. Pre-Uruguay Round applied MFN rates 3. Weighted average tariff reduction measured by dT / (1 + T) in percent.

4. Regional aggregate based on information from Tunisia only.

REST OF EUROPE[4] Bindings and levels of MFN tariff rates before and after the Uruguay Round

Summary product category	Percentage of imports GATT bound					Levels and changes weighted by imports from: the World exc. FTA[1]			LMIEs exc. FTA[1]		Value of 1988 imports in $ million		
	Total pre-UR	Total post-UR	Above appl. rates	At appl. rates	Below appl. rates	Post-UR applied rate	Tariff reduction[3]	Post-UR bound rate	Post-UR applied rate	Tariff reduction[3]	from LMIEs exc. FTA[1]	from World exc. FTA[1]	from World inc. FTA
Agriculture, exc. Fish: Estimate 1	3.4	100.0	100.0	0.0	0.0	1.6	1.9	98.2	3.4	1.9	462	1,069	1,069
Agriculture, exc. Fish: Estimate 2	4.3	100.0	39.5	1.0	59.4	45.6	8.0	110.1	30.3	5.2	452	1,280	1,280
Fish and Fish Products	3.2	4.6	0.2	0.0	4.5	21.3	2.4	20.0	24.8	..	1	3	3
Petroleum Oils	0.5	0.5	0.0	0.0	0.0	..	..	..	..	..	2,554	2,659	2,659
Wood, Pulp, Paper and Furniture	51.5	60.6	0.0	3.0	57.6	28.8	8.1	18.5	29.3	8.3	84	392	392
Textiles and Clothing	61.3	62.6	0.0	1.3	61.3	44.2	17.2	23.6	59.7	15.9	130	532	532
Leather, Rubber, Footwear	30.8	46.6	0.0	0.4	46.1	46.2	9.0	20.8	38.5	10.6	76	231	231
Metals	19.9	19.9	0.0	14.3	5.6	18.2	4.0	23.9	16.8	3.9	972	2,766	2,766
Chemical & Photographic Suppl.	65.7	65.8	0.0	9.7	56.1	25.0	5.9	17.7	25.8	6.4	330	2,132	2,132
Transport Equipment	64.8	64.8	0.0	1.7	63.1	20.0	4.2	12.2	31.1	3.7	22	671	671
Non-Electric Machinery	69.3	69.3	0.0	6.9	62.4	20.6	4.7	11.9	30.2	4.2	147	2,212	2,212
Electric Machinery	56.9	56.9	0.0	8.8	48.1	22.9	6.0	15.7	24.0	5.4	115	1,028	1,028
Mineral Prod.,Prec. Stones & Metal	16.9	16.9	0.0	0.2	16.8	28.9	3.5	13.3	23.6	2.1	537	1,078	1,078
Manufactured Articles nes.	32.5	58.8	0.1	1.8	56.9	29.5	6.6	16.6	41.6	10.5	123	756	756
Industrial Goods (line 5-14)	**46.9**	**49.3**	**0.0**	**7.6**	**41.7**	**24.2**	**6.3**	**16.3**	**25.1**	**7.3**	**2,535**	**11,798**	**11,798**
All Merch. Trade (line 2-14)	**35.6**	**45.1**	**3.2**	**5.7**	**36.1**	**26.3**	**6.5**	**33.3**	**25.9**	**6.7**	**5,541**	**15,740**	**15,740**

Notes: 1. Value of imports from partner countries that do not participate in Free Trade Agreements with REST OF EUROPE

2. Pre-Uruguay Round applied MFN rates 3. Weighted average tariff reduction measured by dT / (1 + T) in percent.

4. Regional aggregate based on information from Turkkey only.

SOUTH ASIA[4] Bindings and levels of MFN tariff rates before and after the Uruguay Round

Summary product category	Total pre-UR	Total post-UR	Above appl. rates	At appl. rates	Below appl. rates	Post-UR applied rate	Tariff reduc-tion[3]	Post-UR bound rate	Post-UR applied rate	Tariff reduc-tion[3]	from LMIEs exc. FTA[1]	from World exc. FTA[1]	from World inc. FTA
Agriculture, exc. Fish: Estimate 1	31.6	100.0	100.0	0.0	0.0	9.7	..	89.2	12.2	..	1,032	1,624	1,624
Agriculture, exc. Fish: Estimate 2	27.4	99.8	57.3	32.9	0.2	52.2	25.1	115.6	67.0	9.5	1,305	2,100	2,100
Fish and Fish Products	0.0	99.7	99.5	0.2	0.0	4.1	..	50.0	3.5	..	60	66	66
Petroleum Oils	2.8	2.8	0.0	2.8	0.0	15.8	..	40.9	5.4	..	2,703	3,542	3,542
Wood, Pulp, Paper and Furniture	19.4	80.5	52.7	2.0	8.6	16.8	29.2	27.5	17.3	21.6	326	791	791
Textiles and Clothing	8.2	20.1	8.7	0.5	9.9	50.3	20.0	33.9	52.5	17.1	353	1,119	1,119
Leather, Rubber, Footwear	0.1	60.7	6.2	3.2	51.4	40.8	23.1	32.4	62.2	27.4	75	186	186
Metals	0.5	48.0	0.3	1.3	36.1	35.4	19.5	39.0	48.4	14.9	721	2,248	2,248
Chemical & Photographic Suppl.	5.0	73.8	5.0	2.9	60.7	32.4	20.0	37.3	55.5	19.2	597	2,008	2,008
Transport Equipment	25.7	60.4	6.7	26.6	22.2	24.1	15.4	22.3	15.9	16.6	122	856	856
Non-Electric Machinery	22.0	89.5	12.5	19.2	54.6	28.5	9.2	31.7	34.1	11.8	170	2,345	2,345
Electric Machinery	10.0	64.9	7.3	14.6	43.0	44.6	17.4	36.1	49.0	16.0	116	1,028	1,028
Mineral Prod.,Prec. Stones & Metal	8.9	24.6	19.9	0.9	3.7	6.1	23.1	25.0	16.1	25.0	439	2,532	2,532
Manufactured Articles nes.	14.5	67.9	15.4	14.3	34.4	39.1	16.3	47.2	23.1	17.4	94	782	782
Industrial Goods (line 5-14)	**11.0**	**57.4**	**12.1**	**7.8**	**33.0**	**28.6**	**16.5**	**33.7**	**38.9**	**17.8**	**3,014**	**13,897**	**13,897**
All Merch. Trade (line 2-14)	**11.3**	**52.2**	**15.1**	**9.5**	**23.4**	**30.4**	**16.5**	**50.8**	**29.5**	**17.8**	**7,082**	**19,605**	**19,605**

Notes: 1. Value of imports from partner countries that do not participate in Free Trade Agreements with SOUTH ASIA

2. Pre-Uruguay Round applied MFN rates 3. Weighted average tariff reduction measured by dT / (1 + T) in percent.

4. Regional aggregate based on available information from India and Sri Lanka.

SUB-SAHARAN AFRICA[4] Bindings and levels of MFN tariff rates before and after the Uruguay Round

Summary product category	Total pre-UR	Total post-UR	Above appl. rates	At appl. rates	Below appl. rates	Post-UR applied rate	Tariff reduc-tion[3]	Post-UR bound rate	Post-UR applied rate	Tariff reduc-tion[3]	from LMIEs exc. FTA[1]	from World exc. FTA[1]	from World inc. FTA
Agriculture, exc. Fish: Estimate 1	12.9	99.9	99.9	0.0	0.0	-0.4	..	35.5	0.3	..	121	272	272
Agriculture, exc. Fish: Estimate 2	15.3	100.0	90.4	8.4	0.8	12.4	4.2	33.5	13.9	4.0	148	344	344
Fish and Fish Products	30.6	46.7	16.1	30.6	0.0	6.9	..	13.3	6.0	..	2	4	4
Petroleum Oils	50.7	50.7	0.0	50.7	0.0	9.6	..	6.8	9.7	..	522	535	535
Wood, Pulp, Paper and Furniture	8.2	11.3	3.4	7.9	0.0	12.2	..	9.8	11.0	..	29	84	84
Textiles and Clothing	13.9	27.4	11.4	4.5	11.5	16.6	7.0	24.6	19.6	7.5	54	104	104
Leather, Rubber, Footwear	58.6	58.6	52.9	5.8	0.0	10.2	..	13.0	5.6	..	14	37	37
Metals	2.7	6.0	2.7	0.0	3.3	9.3	3.9	16.2	5.8	3.9	90	174	174
Chemical & Photographic Suppl.	5.7	11.1	5.5	5.6	0.0	7.1	..	59.9	3.4	..	87	294	294
Transport Equipment	39.2	39.2	22.3	16.9	0.0	6.9	..	16.7	9.5	..	13	255	255
Non-Electric Machinery	39.4	39.4	2.2	37.2	0.0	4.3	..	5.0	1.6	..	34	265	265
Electric Machinery	50.0	50.0	0.0	50.0	0.0	6.3	..	7.2	7.4	..	14	131	131
Mineral Prod.,Prec. Stones & Metal	11.4	12.0	0.8	11.2	0.0	9.0	..	5.3	6.5	..	37	93	93
Manufactured Articles nes.	0.6	1.4	1.0	0.4	0.0	9.8	..	79.3	5.3	..	107	182	182
Industrial Goods (line 5-14)	**21.4**	**23.9**	**7.4**	**15.3**	**1.1**	**8.0**	**6.0**	**15.8**	**7.4**	**6.3**	**480**	**1,620**	**1,620**
All Merch. Trade (line 2-14)	**26.8**	**40.1**	**17.3**	**22.0**	**0.8**	**9.0**	**5.8**	**19.4**	**9.4**	**5.8**	**1,153**	**2,503**	**2,503**

Notes: 1. Value of imports from partner countries that do not participate in Free Trade Agreements with SUB-SAHARAN AFRICA

2. Pre-Uruguay Round applied MFN rates 3. Weighted average tariff reduction measured by dT / (1 + T) in percent.

4. Regional aggregate based on available information from Senegal and Zimbabwe only.

All IDB LMIES[4] Bindings and levels of MFN tariff rates before and after the Uruguay Round

Summary product category	Percentage of imports GATT bound					Levels and changes weighted by imports from: the World exc. FTA[1]			LMIEs exc. FTA[1]		Value of 1989 imports in $ million		
	Total pre-UR	Total post-UR	Above appl. rates	At appl. rates	Below appl. rates	Post-UR applied rate	Tariff reduction[3]	Post-UR bound rate	Post-UR applied rate	Tariff reduction[3]	from LMIEs exc. FTA[1]	from World exc. FTA[1]	from World inc. FTA
Agriculture, exc. Fish: Estimate 1	36.6	100.0	53.7	25.0	21.3	17.6	43.0	51.6	22.5	18.2	7,187	15,754	18,446
Agriculture, exc. Fish: Estimate 2	36.6	99.9	66.8	12.8	17.4	18.6	5.3	66.0	19.9	4.1	8,003	19,317	22,761
Fish and Fish Products	9.7	77.3	14.8	9.2	53.3	8.6	31.8	12.7	25.9	35.8	518	1,410	1,478
Petroleum Oils	11.4	42.8	15.7	10.6	0.6	7.9	3.1	22.5	8.4	1.9	19,367	25,903	26,200
Wood, Pulp, Paper and Furniture	42.6	83.2	41.7	13.4	26.7	8 9	7.8	17.0	10.3	6.4	2,620	8,716	9,530
Textiles and Clothing	24.0	84.7	29.6	6.2	48.6	21.2	8.5	24.2	25.5	8.0	3,596	12,533	12,929
Leather, Rubber, Footwear	30.8	89.9	38.4	8.2	43.1	14.9	7.1	20.7	15.4	7.4	1,463	4,400	4,869
Metals	25.7	76.8	34.5	13.5	25.5	10.8	9.5	18.5	10.4	6.7	9,336	27,103	28,199
Chemical & Photographic Suppl.	27.2	87.5	43.6	9.5	33.8	12.4	9.7	20.7	16.8	9.4	5,155	32,090	34,006
Transport Equipment	41.5	72.9	33.4	22.6	16.3	19.9	10.1	26.1	13.2	2.4	1,742	13,977	14,890
Non-Electric Machinery	39.3	91.0	40.7	9.8	40.3	13.5	6.5	20.8	14.5	4.7	3,197	38,928	40,948
Electric Machinery	31.4	81.5	26.5	12.5	42.5	14.6	7.7	17.6	17.2	6.0	2,338	25,509	26,500
Mineral Prod.,Prec. Stones & Metal	29.6	73.7	36.4	23.2	12.6	7.8	8.3	16.4	8.1	7.3	6,453	16,272	16,818
Manufactured Articles nes.	28.1	89.1	34.3	15.1	39.4	12.1	7.2	19.4	9.2	4.0	3,411	16,940	17,955
Industrial Goods (line 5-14)	**31.8**	**83.6**	**36.4**	**13.0**	**33.4**	**13.3**	**8.1**	**20.0**	**13.3**	**6.7**	**39,310**	**196,467**	**206,644**
All Merch. Trade (line 2-14)	**30.1**	**80.8**	**36.8**	**12.7**	**28.7**	**13.3**	**8.1**	**25.2**	**13.0**	**6.8**	**67,198**	**243,096**	**257,084**

Notes: 1. Value of imports from partner countries that do not participate in Free Trade Agreements with All IDB LMIES

2. Pre-Uruguay Round applied MFN rates 3. Weighted average tariff reduction measured by dT / (1 + T) in percent.

4. Average based the 26 LMICs in the IDB (see table 1).

WORLD[4] Bindings and levels of MFN tariff rates before and after the Uruguay Round

Summary product category	Percentage of imports GATT bound					Levels and changes weighted by imports from: the World exc. FTA[1]			LMIEs exc. FTA[1]		Value of 1989 imports in $ million		
	Total pre-UR	Total post-UR	Above appl. rates	At appl. rates	Below appl. rates	Post-UR applied rate	Tariff reduction[3]	Post-UR bound rate	Post-UR applied rate	Tariff reduction[3]	from LMIEs exc. FTA[1]	from World exc. FTA[1]	from World inc. FTA
Agriculture, exc. Fish: Estimate 1	65.6	100.0	14.0	72.4	13.5	25.0	32.4	32.4	16.5	17.2	44,649	79,080	85,932
Agriculture, exc. Fish: Estimate 2	65.3	100.0	17.6	35.2	32.0	7.6	4.5	18.5	10.4	5.1	61,065	124,135	136,844
Fish and Fish Products	75.8	97.2	10.7	42.8	43.6	4.4	4.4	5.2	7.2	3.8	13,044	23,027	27,348
Petroleum Oils	40.3	46.3	9.6	32.6	0.9	1.7	1.5	3.1	2.0	1.3	114,413	144,743	163,162
Wood, Pulp, Paper and Furniture	81.1	93.5	10.7	64.3	18.3	1.2	5.1	2.2	3.8	4.7	20,439	55,303	105,642
Textiles and Clothing	68.9	80.3	18.2	9.4	52.6	9.8	3.1	12.4	10.8	2.7	67,501	115,563	135,048
Leather, Rubber, Footwear	74.7	89.7	18.5	38.7	32.5	6.4	3.1	7.8	6.7	2.9	26,545	45,251	53,854
Metals	78.8	93.7	22.0	41.2	29.8	2.9	4.3	4.1	3.8	3.5	48,757	109,626	152,596
Chemical & Photographic Suppl.	70.2	90.5	31.1	26.0	33.2	4.8	5.1	7.3	7.5	4.7	22,873	109,984	151,362
Transport Equipment	89.7	93.7	39.4	40.4	13.9	6.0	3.3	6.9	4.9	2.2	12,749	115,142	189,209
Non-Electric Machinery	80.1	94.2	27.3	23.5	43.4	3.7	3.6	5.1	5.0	3.1	16,516	171,499	233,383
Electric Machinery	70.3	87.4	25.5	24.6	37.4	4.6	4.0	5.7	4.3	3.5	32,778	135,971	170,508
Mineral Prod.,Prec. Stones & Metal	79.6	89.9	15.5	57.2	17.0	1.6	2.8	2.6	1.7	2.5	59,253	111,595	136,535
Manufactured Articles nes.	75.0	89.6	14.7	34.0	40.7	2.8	4.1	4.1	3.7	4.1	32,892	126,753	151,647
Industrial Goods (line 5-14)	**77.3**	**90.6**	**23.8**	**34.2**	**32.4**	**4.2**	**3.9**	**5.7**	**5.4**	**3.3**	**340,302**	**1,096,690**	**1,479,790**
All Merch. Trade (line 2-14)	**73.1**	**87.4**	**21.8**	**34.3**	**29.7**	**4.3**	**3.9**	**6.5**	**5.4**	**3.6**	**528,824**	**1,388,590**	**1,807,140**

Notes: 1. Value of imports from partner countries that do not participate in Free Trade Agreements with the WORLD

2. Pre-Uruguay Round applied MFN rates 3. Weighted average tariff reduction measured by dT / (1 + T) in percent.

4. Average based the 40 IDB countries (see table 1).

4

Tables G.3

Concessions Given

Product Category by Importing Economy or Group

Agriculture, excluding Fish: Estimate 1[3] Levels and changes in protection before and after the UR

Import market	Simple average MFN tariff rates			Weighted by value of imports from: the World exc. FTA[1]			LMIEs exc. FTA[1]		Value of imports in $ million		
	Post-UR appl. rates	Tariff reduction[2]	Post-UR bound rates	Post-UR applied rate	Tariff reduction[2]	Post-UR bound rate	Post-UR applied rate	Tariff reduction[2]	from LMIEs exc. FTA[1]	from World exc. FTA[1]	from World inc. FTA
EUROPEAN UNION	20.0	0.384	20.0	15.7	0.304	15.7	11.2	0.180	21,772.9	29,105.4	29,105.4
JAPAN	31.9	3.265	29.7	65.1	10.427	64.9	42.0	3.973	4,514.1	15,201.4	15,201.4
UNITED STATES	8.1	0.039	9.0	10.8	0.003	10.9	10.5	0.000	5,539.6	8,085.6	10,578.1
KOREA, REPUBLIC OF	39.7	13.404	39.6	42.3	36.819	42.3	87.7	14.493	811.4	2,907.5	2,907.5
CANADA	6.9	0.000	8.8	7.0	..	7.7	1.5	..	699.2	1,226.0	2,780.9
HONG KONG	0.0	0.000	0.0	0.0	..	0.0	0.0	..	1,295.8	2,465.1	2,465.1
MEXICO	9.4	0.000	25.1	3.0	..	26.2	24.0		121.4	277.8	2,069.3
SWITZERLAND	46.9	0.169	46.9	51.3	0.202	51.3	29.6	0.026	654.6	1,710.2	1,710.2
SINGAPORE	8.8	14.223	9.3	8.2	15.132	8.4	26.2	14.013	937.1	1,474.2	1,474.2
INDONESIA	13.6	1.942	59.9	23.2	2.804	61.2	43.3	4.150	763.5	1,356.5	1,356.5
MALAYSIA	38.8	7.371	39.0	56.8	21.496	56.8	103.0	18.198	621.6	1,234.6	1,234.6
BRAZIL	-12.3	0.000	35.2	-21.4	..	35.9	-23.0	..	75.8	463.0	1,230.6
SWEDEN	41.1	0.106	41.1	37.8	0.160	37.8	27.2	0.324	592.6	1,226.3	1,226.3
INDIA	5.5	0.000	101.0	13.4	..	106.5	15.2	..	720.0	1,126.7	1,126.7
TURKEY	-1.9	0.022	74.3	1.6	0.000	98.2	3.4	0.000	461.6	1,069.1	1,069.1
POLAND	-0.4	0.000	38.3	1.3	..	45.7	-2.7	..	658.5	1,030.4	1,030.4
AUSTRIA	23.9	13.790	58.0	20.0	14.324	50.3	17.6	5.832	521.8	1,003.8	1,003.8
PHILIPPINES	46.7	6.476	46.9	46.2	29.526	46.2	42.3	0.789	186.7	824.3	824.3
THAILAND	42.6	10.074	43.2	33.8	7.303	33.8	24.1	1.502	346.4	682.5	682.5
CZECH & SLOVAK CU	0.1	1.309	18.9	-0.3	1.153	19.0	0.2	0.789	545.5	680.1	680.1
NORWAY	49.0	0.355	50.4	50.9	0.823	51.1	26.2	0.004	235.0	594.0	594.0
ROMANIA	3.6	0.000	130.2	4.2	..	129.0	1.9	..	270.2	588.6	588.6
VENEZUELA	-5.7	0.000	67.7	-16.3	..	71.9	-14.1	..	138.1	575.6	575.6
FINLAND	34.7	0.318	34.7	36.2	0.595	36.2	33.6	1.088	304.6	570.6	570.6
TUNISIA	13.7	0.000	15.1	23.9	..	24.1	21.5	..	214.4	554.1	554.1
AUSTRALIA	0.4	1.438	2.5	0.1	1.622	1.3	0.5	0.426	282.5	489.1	531.5
SRI LANKA	-0.9	0.000	50.0	1.2	..	50.0	5.2	..	311.9	497.1	497.1
PERU	-5.7	0.751	30.4	-4.7	0.964	35.5	-4.4	1.166	217.9	455.5	455.5
HUNGARY	0.8	0.023	6.7	-1.5	0.001	2.7	-3.0	0.002	276.4	422.5	422.5
SENEGAL	-3.4	0.000	30.0	-0.3	..	30.0	0.6	..	116.0	259.9	259.9
ARGENTINA	-8.6	0.952	32.5	-0.7	2.009	34.6	7.9	2.187	120.1	133.0	241.5
NEW ZEALAND	0.6	0.672	0.7	1.4	0.474	2.5	2.4	0.151	103.2	142.9	212.9
COLOMBIA	-6.7	0.000	105.6	-17.2	..	106.0	-17.0	..	63.1	178.0	178.0
JAMAICA	0.0	0.000	100.0	-1.3	..	100.0	-3.6	..	20.8	144.8	144.8
CHILE	-5.7	2.576	25.0	-8.4	2.033	25.0	-2.3	2.437	78.1	110.8	110.8
EL SALVADOR	-3.9	1.186	38.4	-11.8	0.088	33.8	-5.4	0.563	12.5	90.5	90.5
URUGUAY	-3.7	0.457	35.7	-9.2	0.038	40.4	-1.8	0.271	3.8	27.3	51.9
MACAU	0.0	0.000	0.0	0.0	..	0.0	0.0	..	26.0	51.3	51.3
ICELAND	7.3	0.162	72.1	4.5	0.143	38.4	0.5	0.003	9.0	31.9	31.9
ZIMBABWE	-9.6	0.000	150.0	-3.4	..	150.0	-5.8	..	5.3	12.5	12.5

Notes: 1. Value of imports from partner countries that do not participate in Free Trade Agreements.

2. Weighted average tariff reduction measured by dT / (1 + T) in percent.

3. Estimate based on Merlinda Ingco's tariff equivalents of non tariff barriers.

Agriculture, excluding Fish: Estimate 2[3] Levels and changes in protection before and after the UR

Import market	Simple average MFN tariff rates			Weighted by value of imports from: the World exc. FTA[1]			LMIEs exc. FTA[1]		Value of imports in $ million		
	Post-UR appl. rates	Tariff reduction[2]	Post-UR bound rates	Post-UR applied rate	Tariff reduction[2]	Post-UR bound rate	Post-UR applied rate	Tariff reduction[2]	from LMIEs exc. FTA[1]	from World exc. FTA[1]	from World inc. FTA
EUROPEAN UNION	7.4	3.600	7.6	3.7	1.825	3.8	8.4	2.166	28,109.0	40,393.6	40,393.6
JAPAN	9.3	2.213	10.4	10.5	1.400	16.9	16.8	2.372	6,267.6	22,214.3	22,214.3
UNITED STATES	4.3	1.780	4.6	2.2	0.896	2.6	4.5	0.816	8,592.8	15,795.2	21,438.8
HONG KONG	0.0	0.000	0.0	0.0	..	0.0	0.0	..	3,355.9	7,600.9	7,600.9
CANADA	3.0	1.648	3.6	1.5	0.777	2.8	2.6	0.527	1,128.0	2,508.9	5,650.8
SWITZERLAND	4.3	2.331	4.4	5.1	0.920	5.1	8.1	1.511	852.4	3,948.4	3,948.4
SINGAPORE	9.3	14.094	9.5	8.8	12.484	9.0	26.6	13.727	1,837.8	3,181.1	3,181.1
SWEDEN	1.9	0.799	2.1	1.5	0.403	1.5	1.1	0.188	827.3	2,903.2	2,903.2
KOREA, REPUBLIC OF	21.3	4.030	48.7	11.6	2.376	152.8	15.0	2.395	821.9	2,779.0	2,779.0
MEXICO	13.7	0.001	36.1	5.4	0.000	37.5	13.0	..	164.1	381.4	2,684.4
AUSTRIA	5.5	2.144	5.9	3.2	0.446	4.8	1.7	0.367	680.6	1,959.4	1,959.4
BRAZIL	10.9	0.011	34.5	11.0	0.102	39.3	10.4	0.122	183.9	904.4	1,856.4
MALAYSIA	7.7	3.576	12.6	2.5	0.652	11.6	3.0	0.503	782.7	1,699.5	1,699.5
INDIA	50.6	0.900	113.1	60.1	0.067	144.7	76.0	0.001	928.9	1,481.6	1,481.6
AUSTRALIA	3.4	0.803	4.7	3.3	0.947	4.3	3.8	0.780	501.9	1,202.7	1,443.2
NORWAY	3.2	0.780	44.3	2.7	0.652	30.4	0.9	0.312	314.3	1,408.5	1,408.5
TURKEY	37.0	7.379	57.5	45.6	4.747	1!0.1	30.3	3.076	451.5	1,279.5	1,279.5
POLAND	15.5	0.525	50.6	9.7	0.247	39.9	7.4	0.227	712.6	1,275.6	1,275.6
INDONESIA	23.0	0.649	49.0	8.3	0.031	51.4	8.7	0.012	620.9	1,264.0	1,264.0
FINLAND	53.4	9.165	53.4	48.7	7.254	48.7	61.0	8.189	429.6	1,256.0	1,256.0
PHILIPPINES	29.8	3.021	34.6	18.0	1.938	25.4	22.3	2.884	209.0	1,047.7	1,047.7
CZECH & SLOVAK CU	7.2	1.781	9.0	8.5	1.654	10.5	9.2	1.568	611.7	892.5	892.5
ROMANIA	24.5	0.175	88.8	26.9	0.109	109.7	26.3	0.104	326.7	776.2	776.2
VENEZUELA	20.1	0.057	36.4	16.2	0.009	33.0	19.8	0.001	142.4	755.9	755.9
HUNGARY	18.9	1.616	24.0	16.5	1.180	21.6	17.0	0.985	345.9	672.8	672.8
THAILAND	31.0	8.097	34.5	26.5	2.983	50.5	20.4	1.857	162.5	649.7	649.7
SRI LANKA	34.7	0.074	49.8	25.5	0.042	46.1	28.0	0.002	375.6	618.9	618.9
TUNISIA	30.8	0.091	113.5	20.2	0.172	87.2	21.3	0.098	204.7	593.3	593.3
NEW ZEALAND	5.5	0.780	7.8	3.5	1.208	7.5	4.8	1.119	151.0	313.1	552.0
PERU	17.4	0.278	31.3	14.5	0.024	48.1	15.6	0.048	260.3	549.8	549.8
COLOMBIA	14.2	0.000	89.3	14.5	..	98.3	15.9	..	138.1	356.5	356.5
ARGENTINA	4.5	0.002	30.4	4.9	0.001	31.9	5.3	..	153.1	213.2	350.2
SENEGAL	13.8	0.000	29.5	13.1	..	28.7	15.0	..	129.5	312.6	312.6
JAMAICA	29.7	0.000	95.6	14.7	..	94.2	24.9	..	45.7	238.7	238.7
MACAU	0.0	0.000	0.0	0.0	..	0.0	0.0	..	61.8	177.0	177.0
CHILE	11.0	0.000	25.6	11.0	..	26.5	11.0	..	96.3	155.8	155.8
EL SALVADOR	18.6	0.041	40.5	12.9	0.032	42.8	21.8	0.012	47.2	154.8	154.8
ICELAND	7.0	0.142	44.8	8.2	1.531	29.9	2.2	0.055	14.0	133.0	133.0
URUGUAY	11.9	0.048	33.8	9.5	0.008	34.0	8.2	0.062	7.2	55.1	107.0
ZIMBABWE	9.4	0.207	122.8	4.4	0.372	83.2	6.3	0.568	18.8	31.8	31.8

Notes: 1. Value of imports from partner countries that do not participate in Free Trade Agreements.

2. Weighted average tariff reduction measured by $dT / (1 + T)$ in percent.

3. Estimate based on available ad valorem tariff rates in the IDB. The available AVEs cover only 85% of all agricultural impor Coverage of imports with AVEs for countries with less than 100% coverage: SWITZERLAND: 38.7%, AUSTRIA: 42.3%, SWEDEN: 63.9%, SRI LANKA: 70.1%, EUROPEAN UNION: 71.7%, MALAYSIA: 76.5%, SINGAPORE: 85.5%, CANADA: 84.7%, THAILAND: 90.3%, FINLAND: 91.7%, JAPAN: 91.9%, ZIMBABWE: 95.3%, USA: 96.6%, NORWAY: 97.5%, AUSTRALIA: 98.8%, PERU: 98.8%, INDIA: 99.1%, BRAZIL: 99.8%, NEW ZEALAND: 99.9%,

Fish and Fish Products Levels and changes in protection before and after the UR

Import market	Simple average MFN tariff rates			Weighted by value of imports from: the World exc. FTA[1]			LMIEs exc. FTA[1]		Value of imports in $ million		
	Post-UR appl. rates	Tariff reduc-tion[2]	Post-UR bound rates	Post-UR applied rate	Tariff reduc-tion[2]	Post-UR bound rate	Post-UR applied rate	Tariff reduc-tion[2]	from LMIEs exc. FTA[1]	from World exc. FTA[1]	from World inc. FTA
JAPAN	5.1	1.345	4.8	4.1	1.562	3.9	5.7	1.734	5,356.4	10,501.2	10,501.2
EUROPEAN UNION	10.7	1.848	11.6	11.0	2.016	11.6	14.7	2.418	3,104.4	4,593.5	6,213.3
UNITED STATES	1.1	0.500	1.2	0.9	0.237	0.9	1.5	0.175	2,474.1	3,819.7	5,426.2
HONG KONG	0.0	0.000	0.0	0.0	..	0.0	0.0	..	863.5	1,402.0	1,402.0
CANADA	1.6	0.791	1.7	1.9	1.574	2.1	5.5	1.757	197.1	308.7	584.2
THAILAND	10.1	36.852	9.2	5.5	41.053	5.5	60.0	41.107	168.8	567.2	567.2
SWEDEN	0.4	0.044	1.4	0.1	0.026	1.4	0.7	0.024	34.3	116.1	387.3
SINGAPORE	0.1	0.199	9.9	0.0	0.024	9.9	0.0	0.005	224.1	357.0	357.0
SWITZERLAND	0.2	0.195	0.4	0.2	0.338	0.6	1.2	0.490	47.6	95.0	334.1
AUSTRALIA	0.1	0.059	0.8	0.4	0.210	1.5	1.3	0.378	143.9	270.2	318.8
KOREA, REPUBLIC OF	16.9	2.742	13.3	14.0	5.192	10.5	20.0	3.372	56.8	296.4	296.4
BRAZIL	12.4	0.000	32.2	5.8	..	22.4	11.7	..	32.1	122.5	185.9
MALAYSIA	15.7	3.099	13.7	9.9	1.496	18.1	12.2	1.601	102.3	124.5	124.5
NORWAY	0.1	0.232	5.1	0.0	0.186	1.1	0.3	0.233	25.8	61.9	109.7
AUSTRIA	5.9	2.685	8.0	2.8	1.493	6.3	10.2	1.691	18.8	29.4	100.8
FINLAND	6.6	0.371	6.7	8.1	0.160	7.4	9.0	0.181	18.5	29.1	94.7
PHILIPPINES	27.5	0.577	28.8	16.3	0.002	39.6	16.8	0.002	33.2	72.0	72.0
SRI LANKA	14.1	0.000	50.0	3.9	..	50.0	3.5	..	60.1	65.9	65.9
POLAND	10.2	0.000	11.7	11.5	..	11.7	26.6	..	15.8	55.6	55.6
CZECH & SLOVAK CU	0.2	0.274	0.2	0.0	0.344	0.0	0.2	0.162	14.6	44.5	44.5
NEW ZEALAND	1.1	0.246	1.3	0.1	0.018	0.2	1.8	0.008	14.8	28.7	30.9
MACAU	0.0	0.000	0.0	0.0	..	0.0	0.0	..	9.6	15.8	15.8
HUNGARY	17.5	0.040	20.8	17.3	0.002	19.3	19.2	..	4.6	11.6	11.6
ARGENTINA	5.5	0.000	34.1	5.1	..	35.0	5.1	..	5.6	5.7	10.8
ICELAND	3.0	2.647	5.6	0.3	0.395	1.6	1.6	0.681	2.1	5.3	9.0
INDONESIA	29.9	2.505	40.0	31.0	2.779	40.0	28.8	0.544	0.8	5.5	5.5
PERU	17.3	0.000	30.0	15.0	..	30.0	15.0	..	3.9	4.1	4.1
EL SALVADOR	22.5	0.000	49.6	26.9	..	48.7	27.5	..	3.5	3.7	3.7
TURKEY	24.0	0.594	39.9	21.3	0.106	20.0	24.8	..	0.7	3.4	3.4
URUGUAY	11.0	0.000	35.0	11.9	..	35.0	12.6	..	1.8	2.9	3.1
ROMANIA	22.4	0.828	30.7	22.1	0.084	26.4	24.8	..	0.8	2.1	2.1
ZIMBABWE	1.0	0.000	2.0	1.7	..	3.9	2.1	..	1.6	2.0	2.0
SENEGAL	12.0	0.000	15.5	13.8	..	23.2	13.4	..	0.8	1.6	1.6
TUNISIA	42.2	0.000	180.0	42.9	..	180.0	43.0	..	0.1	1.6	1.6
CHILE	11.0	0.000	25.0	11.0	..	25.0	11.0	..	0.4	0.8	0.8
INDIA	40.0	0.000	100.0	52.4	..	100.0	0.0	..	0.0	0.2	0.2
COLOMBIA	20.0	0.000	58.3	20.0	..	54.6	20.0	..	0.1	0.1	0.1
MEXICO	20.0	0.000	43.0	20.0	..	41.4	..	..	0.0	0.0	0.0
VENEZUELA	10.0	0.000	35.0	10.0	..	35.0	..	..	0.0	0.0	0.0
JAMAICA	10.0	0.000	50.0	10.0	..	50.0	..	..	0.0	0.0	0.0

Notes: 1. Value of imports from partner countries that do not participate in Free Trade Agreements.

2. Weighted average tariff reduction measured by dT / (1 + T) in percent.

Petroleum Oils[3] Levels and changes in protection before and after the UR

Import market	Simple average MFN tariff rates			Weighted by value of imports from: the World exc. FTA[1]			LMIEs exc. FTA[1]		Value of imports in $ million		
	Post-UR appl. rates	Tariff reduction[2]	Post-UR bound rates	Post-UR applied rate	Tariff reduction[2]	Post-UR bound rate	Post-UR applied rate	Tariff reduction[2]	from LMIEs exc. FTA[1]	from World exc. FTA[1]	from World inc. FTA
UNITED STATES	1.3	0.000	1.8	0.7	..	1.1	0.7	..	31,579.8	37,528.4	46,350.9
EUROPEAN UNION	2.4	0.620	3.8	0.4	0.039	0.9	0.4	0.032	35,940.1	39,091.2	43,950.3
JAPAN	4.1	0.769	4.5	1.3	0.003	4.4	0.2	0.000	16,926.7	25,471.3	25,471.3
SINGAPORE	6.6	0.000	..	3.5	..	..	3.6	..	4,842.7	6,834.3	6,834.3
KOREA, REPUBLIC OF	9.2	3.064	12.0	5.1	0.093	7.6	4.9	0.010	2,968.3	4,239.3	4,239.3
BRAZIL	0.0	0.000	35.0	0.0	..	35.0	17.9	..	3,435.3	4,155.3	4,171.2
CANADA	2.5	1.194	7.2	0.0	0.008	6.5	0.1	0.018	878.8	2,732.3	3,222.3
INDIA	0.0	0.000	..	0.0	..	..	0.0	..	2,381.3	3,117.3	3,117.3
TURKEY	..	..	..	..	..	..	..	..	2,553.8	2,659.1	2,659.1
SWEDEN	0.0	0.000	0.0	0.0	..	0.0	0.0	..	729.1	738.1	2,539.6
HONG KONG	0.0	0.000	..	0.0	..	..	0.0	..	399.5	1,942.9	1,942.9
SWITZERLAND	38.8	0.000	2.7	14.4	..	2.7	14.2	..	497.3	502.8	1,735.9
PHILIPPINES	20.7	0.000	..	11.6	..	..	11.1	..	1,192.8	1,735.8	1,735.8
THAILAND	29.0	0.000	..	25.5	..	..	25.3	..	379.7	1,485.7	1,485.7
FINLAND	1.6	0.000	2.1	0.0	..	0.1	0.0	..	1,393.9	1,397.5	1,437.1
AUSTRALIA	0.0	0.000	0.0	0.0	..	0.0	0.0	..	603.8	1,171.9	1,232.1
ROMANIA	3.0	0.000	35.0	3.0	..	35.0	3.0	..	1,131.4	1,214.0	1,214.0
AUSTRIA	5.9	2.831	6.1	5.7	0.002	6.4	6.9	0.001	878.1	897.1	1,139.4
INDONESIA	5.1	0.000	40.0	2.4	..	40.0	0.9	..	655.4	1,102.5	1,102.5
POLAND	10.2	0.000	0.0	2.9	..	0.0	1.7	..	821.8	941.6	941.6
CZECH & SLOVAK CU	3.4	0.813	3.4	0.5	0.128	0.5	0.2	0.037	785.3	856.2	856.2
HUNGARY	0.5	0.512	2.6	0.0	0.006	0.3	0.0	0.006	773.9	821.1	821.1
MALAYSIA	2.5	0.000	5.0	0.2	..	5.0	0.0	..	116.1	784.9	784.9
NEW ZEALAND	3.4	0.000	5.3	0.0	..	0.1	0.0	..	279.6	431.7	546.8
NORWAY	0.0	0.000	0.0	0.0	..	0.0	0.0	..	54.7	58.7	469.5
SRI LANKA	31.3	0.000	30.0	44.0	..	40.9	44.9	..	322.2	424.3	424.3
SENEGAL	8.1	0.000	7.6	9.6	..	6.8	9.7	..	404.9	415.1	415.1
CHILE	11.0	0.000	25.0	11.0	..	25.0	11.0	..	319.2	348.6	348.6
MEXICO	8.6	0.000	35.0	8.6	..	35.0	8.6	..	64.2	73.5	340.6
JAMAICA	15.2	0.000	50.0	10.2	..	50.0	6.2	..	201.7	309.6	309.6
COLOMBIA	10.3	0.000	35.0	13.7	..	35.0	13.7	..	258.3	283.5	283.5
TUNISIA	23.7	0.000	..	15.2	..	..	6.5	..	101.7	279.2	279.2
URUGUAY	14.4	0.000	35.0	33.7	..	35.0	32.4	..	152.2	175.6	190.3
VENEZUELA	10.0	0.000	35.0	10.0	..	35.0	10.0	..	85.7	140.2	140.2
ZIMBABWE	8.6	0.000	..	10.3	..	..	9.2	..	117.5	119.8	119.8
EL SALVADOR	5.1	0.000	40.0	5.3	..	40.0	5.0	..	81.3	102.4	102.4
ICELAND	1.8	0.000	8.9	5.8	..	12.0	10.4	..	42.5	42.6	89.6
MACAU	0.0	0.000	..	0.0	..	..	0.0	..	40.8	68.1	68.1
PERU	14.4	0.000	30.0	13.0	..	30.0	15.0	..	21.8	47.6	47.6
ARGENTINA	29.3	0.000	34.5	29.1	..	34.0	31.8	..	0.0	2.6	2.7

Notes: 1. Value of imports from partner countries that do not participate in Free Trade Agreements.

2. Weighted average tariff reduction measured by dT / (1 + T) in percent.

3. Estimate based on available ad valorem tariff rates in the IDB. The available AVEs cover only 72% of all petrol imports.

Coverage of imports with AVEs for countries with less than 100% coverage: TURKEY: 0%, BRAZIL: 0.8%, JAPAN: 1.2
AUSTRIA: 2.4%, ZIMBABWE: 2.6%, MALAYSIA: 21.3%, INDIA: 24.4%, THAILAND: 64.6%, NEW ZEALAND:87.8
SINGAPORE: 92.6%, FINLAND: 99.9%.

Wood, Pulp, Paper and Furniture Levels and changes in protection before and after the UR

Import market	Simple average MFN tariff rates			Weighted by value of imports from: the World exc. FTA[1]			LMIEs exc. FTA[1]		Value of imports in $ million		
	Post-UR appl. rates	Tariff reduc-tion[2]	Post-UR bound rates	Post-UR applied rate	Tariff reduc-tion[2]	Post-UR bound rate	Post-UR applied rate	Tariff reduc-tion[2]	from LMIEs exc. FTA[1]	from World exc. FTA[1]	from World inc. FTA
EUROPEAN UNION	0.6	4.036	0.8	0.3	2.129	0.5	3.2	2.124	7,269.5	14,766.6	34,027.4
UNITED STATES	0.6	2.195	0.7	0.2	2.190	0.2	3.7	2.221	2,079.2	8,206.3	23,731.4
JAPAN	1.0	2.034	1.1	0.7	0.740	1.1	2.4	0.825	4,749.5	13,766.9	13,766.9
CANADA	1.7	5.129	1.9	0.6	5.578	1.2	8.4	4.628	167.1	1,007.6	4,632.5
SWITZERLAND	1.7	2.457	2.1	0.2	2.460	2.0	6.3	4.493	80.5	233.0	4,253.2
HONG KONG	0.0	0.000	0.0	0.0	..	0.0	0.0	..	1,596.4	3,649.4	3,649.4
AUSTRIA	2.8	4.188	3.6	0.3	2.589	3.8	4.9	2.281	280.1	379.6	2,605.4
KOREA, REPUBLIC OF	4.1	10.599	2.9	3.3	4.165	1.7	6.2	0.640	846.7	2,480.0	2,480.0
SWEDEN	0.5	1.150	0.8	0.1	0.883	0.6	1.1	0.865	418.1	543.0	2,430.0
AUSTRALIA	8.3	6.873	8.5	5.6	3.908	5.9	16.0	6.759	272.9	2,036.3	2,338.7
NORWAY	0.2	1.677	0.4	0.0	1.747	0.2	1.9	1.757	76.0	125.0	1,911.5
SINGAPORE	0.1	0.427	2.1	0.1	0.273	3.0	0.3	0.287	534.9	1,240.8	1,240.8
FINLAND	0.4	1.797	0.6	0.1	0.819	0.4	0.7	0.474	254.1	322.8	942.7
MEXICO	10.4	0.000	33.0	2.9	..	24.7	7.5	..	31.6	104.6	751.9
INDIA	36.1	10.135	33.2	14.9	3.123	27.9	16.1	1.349	254.9	636.4	636.4
HUNGARY	5.4	1.877	5.4	3.3	0.929	3.3	2.5	0.597	167.4	607.9	607.9
THAILAND	23.4	9.543	26.0	15.1	4.670	17.3	17.0	5.870	274.9	585.1	585.1
INDONESIA	23.8	0.806	39.2	8.2	0.117	35.6	17.9	0.112	30.6	532.5	532.5
MALAYSIA	13.3	2.250	19.9	6.5	1.017	16.3	7.4	0.660	89.8	520.1	520.1
BRAZIL	7.7	0.000	27.4	2.0	..	19.3	2.2	..	98.1	424.1	495.3
NEW ZEALAND	4.6	7.051	5.7	1.3	7.150	2.0	14.7	8.491	30.6	292.8	422.9
TURKEY	42.1	3.094	22.0	28.8	4.655	18.5	29.3	5.729	83.8	392.1	392.1
PHILIPPINES	32.7	0.575	25.6	25.8	2.553	22.7	17.8	0.148	38.0	355.8	355.8
VENEZUELA	18.9	0.460	33.3	6.2	0.046	25.1	5.5	0.114	61.7	285.1	285.1
COLOMBIA	12.1	0.000	35.0	8.6	..	35.0	8.2	..	50.0	248.1	248.1
CZECH & SLOVAK CU	5.4	1.647	5.4	4.8	1.343	4.8	7.4	1.580	90.7	218.1	218.1
POLAND	6.5	2.479	7.7	5.3	2.109	7.0	8.9	2.534	99.0	218.1	218.1
TUNISIA	29.9	0.000	32.4	23.8	..	23.5	21.1	..	97.4	217.9	217.9
ARGENTINA	11.3	0.026	31.5	9.9	0.029	30.5	10.9	0.076	42.8	111.4	179.9
ICELAND	2.7	0.021	16.5	0.3	0.053	14.5	1.4	0.002	9.2	16.9	158.8
SRI LANKA	32.9	0.000	23.9	23.2	..	7.0	20.6	..	71.4	154.9	154.9
PERU	18.5	0.415	30.0	10.7	0.104	30.0	18.0	0.190	59.5	119.7	119.7
JAMAICA	22.7	0.000	50.0	13.3	..	50.0	20.6	..	16.1	114.8	114.8
CHILE	11.0	0.000	25.0	11.0	..	25.0	11.0	..	27.5	82.9	82.9
ROMANIA	12.8	0.000	31.4	8.4	..	27.1	7.2	..	14.0	73.0	73.0
EL SALVADOR	17.2	0.000	37.3	10.6	..	27.8	17.2	..	21.4	71.3	71.3
MACAU	0.0	0.000	0.0	0.0	..	0.0	0.0	..	18.1	60.7	60.7
SENEGAL	15.0	0.000	30.0	15.0	..	30.0	15.0	..	14.9	54.5	54.5
URUGUAY	9.3	0.000	31.4	7.2	..	25.4	9.5	..	5.8	17.3	44.6
ZIMBABWE	11.7	0.000	2.4	7.0	..	2.1	6.8	..	14.3	29.5	29.5

Notes: 1. Value of imports from partner countries that do not participate in Free Trade Agreements.

2. Weighted average tariff reduction measured by dT / (1 + T) in percent.

Textiles and Clothing[3] Levels and changes in protection before and after the UR

Import market	Simple average MFN tariff rates			Weighted by value of imports from: the World exc. FTA[1]			LMIEs exc. FTA[1]		Value of imports in $ million		
	Post-UR appl. rates	Tariff reduction[2]	Post-UR bound rates	Post-UR applied rate	Tariff reduction[2]	Post-UR bound rate	Post-UR applied rate	Tariff reduction[2]	from LMIEs exc. FTA[1]	from World exc. FTA[1]	from World inc. FTA
UNITED STATES	10.8	2.445	10.8	14.8	1.835	14.7	17.1	1.616	15,861.0	29,101.4	30,781.8
EUROPEAN UNION	8.8	1.928	8.8	8.7	1.635	8.5	10.9	1.627	16,874.1	25,658.0	30,487.1
HONG KONG	0.0	0.000	0.0	0.0	..	0.0	0.0	..	18,774.9	25,368.1	25,368.1
JAPAN	7.3	2.094	7.3	7.2	1.960	7.2	10.0	2.085	6,808.8	11,773.9	11,773.9
SWITZERLAND	5.8	2.892	5.6	4.6	2.539	5.4	7.1	2.217	497.3	913.2	4,558.3
CANADA	13.9	5.702	13.8	14.2	5.356	13.5	20.5	5.192	1,391.2	2,958.4	4,308.9
SWEDEN	9.2	2.150	9.3	8.3	2.064	9.6	11.8	2.086	612.2	960.0	3,329.9
AUSTRIA	15.3	7.318	15.2	11.0	7.267	14.3	22.9	7.105	409.4	550.1	3,015.2
SINGAPORE	1.8	0.023	9.9	1.2	0.004	9.8	2.0	0.006	1,111.5	2,496.5	2,496.5
AUSTRALIA	24.0	10.086	26.7	21.6	9.634	24.5	46.4	10.006	924.8	2,099.7	2,245.7
KOREA, REPUBLIC OF	15.9	5.091	17.6	13.0	5.087	14.8	19.1	4.791	614.7	2,140.6	2,140.6
NORWAY	9.3	5.433	9.6	8.4	6.395	10.2	18.1	6.400	189.0	336.5	1,698.2
FINLAND	16.1	7.472	15.5	13.9	6.740	15.5	27.0	7.140	252.3	357.4	1,381.8
PHILIPPINES	27.3	8.913	27.3	27.1	7.463	27.2	35.8	6.846	223.4	1,193.2	1,193.2
HUNGARY	8.9	3.026	8.9	8.5	3.396	8.6	12.2	3.271	162.9	1,162.9	1,162.9
SRI LANKA	49.1	0.002	50.0	53.0	0.000	50.0	51.5	0.000	311.7	820.4	820.4
TUNISIA	36.3	0.000	56.3	38.4	..	57.2	33.7	..	66.9	806.4	806.4
POLAND	11.6	2.039	14.8	10.4	1.405	14.7	12.6	1.690	383.0	762.6	762.6
MALAYSIA	19.9	4.346	20.6	17.5	3.569	18.4	24.5	3.612	183.3	753.7	753.7
MACAU	0.0	0.000	0.0	0.0	..	0.0	0.0	..	173.0	731.7	731.7
THAILAND	29.2	25.350	29.0	28.9	19.655	28.7	56.6	19.555	275.2	717.6	717.6
INDONESIA	30.2	5.897	40.0	21.9	3.799	40.0	29.9	3.780	176.9	644.6	644.6
CZECH & SLOVAK CU	7.5	1.779	7.5	6.6	1.657	6.6	9.6	1.822	334.8	615.5	615.5
NEW ZEALAND	16.3	0.857	22.6	12.8	0.971	20.6	19.2	1.129	188.6	426.1	543.4
TURKEY	75.7	3.677	24.5	44.2	10.570	23.6	59.7	8.584	129.6	531.8	531.8
MEXICO	16.6	0.000	35.0	15.3	..	34.9	15.5	..	45.8	91.7	324.4
INDIA	62.2	11.711	39.2	42.4	7.427	33.8	62.5	6.623	40.8	298.5	298.5
BRAZIL	18.4	0.007	34.4	15.5	0.001	33.9	14.5	0.000	44.1	158.6	263.0
VENEZUELA	27.4	1.778	34.9	26.5	1.801	34.8	34.5	2.680	91.6	225.3	225.3
CHILE	11.0	0.000	24.7	11.0	..	24.9	11.0	..	84.7	181.7	181.7
ROMANIA	26.5	0.027	33.0	22.9	0.011	34.0	23.4	0.005	96.9	156.4	156.4
COLOMBIA	18.2	0.000	36.8	15.9	..	36.0	15.0	..	39.2	153.6	153.6
JAMAICA	26.1	0.000	50.0	26.5	..	50.0	17.9	..	12.4	141.3	141.3
ICELAND	8.0	0.000	16.7	5.8	..	17.7	12.1	..	9.9	30.4	130.1
ARGENTINA	13.8	0.004	35.0	12.1	0.002	35.0	13.6	..	16.8	44.8	76.6
ZIMBABWE	20.1	0.909	29.0	17.6	1.268	31.0	21.8	1.312	37.1	66.2	66.2
URUGUAY	5.9	0.000	34.0	6.4	..	33.7	4.7	..	6.6	27.8	54.2
SENEGAL	14.8	0.000	17.0	14.8	..	19.2	14.7	..	16.7	37.8	37.8
PERU	19.2	0.067	30.0	14.9	0.015	30.0	20.0	..	10.1	35.0	35.0
EL SALVADOR	22.6	0.141	39.8	18.3	0.327	39.0	20.9	0.438	17.6	33.8	33.8

Notes: 1. Value of imports from partner countries that do not participate in Free Trade Agreements.

2. Weighted average tariff reduction measured by dT / (1 + T) in percent.

3. MFN tariff rates only. This table does not report any levels or changes in quota rents due to the abolishion of the MFA.

Leather, Rubber, Footwear Levels and changes in protection before and after the UR

Import market	Simple average MFN tariff rates			Weighted by value of imports from: the World exc. FTA[1]			LMIEs exc. FTA[1]		Value of imports in $ million		
	Post-UR appl. rates	Tariff reduc-tion[2]	Post-UR bound rates	Post-UR applied rate	Tariff reduc-tion[2]	Post-UR bound rate	Post-UR applied rate	Tariff reduc-tion[2]	from LMIEs exc. FTA[1]	from World exc. FTA[1]	from World inc. FTA
UNITED STATES	7.3	1.095	7.5	6.9	0.505	6.8	8.3	0.318	8,435.4	15,365.6	16,907.6
EUROPEAN UNION	5.1	1.311	5.2	4.9	1.295	4.9	6.1	1.276	6,612.5	9,361.9	10,676.2
HONG KONG	0.0	0.000	0.0	0.0	..	0.0	0.0	..	5,253.8	6,827.2	6,827.2
JAPAN	11.0	1.930	11.1	8.2	1.088	8.3	8.1	1.054	2,098.6	4,115.7	4,115.7
CANADA	9.2	3.659	9.4	9.2	4.139	8.7	15.5	3.996	635.8	1,484.5	2,561.0
SWITZERLAND	3.1	1.218	3.0	3.1	1.235	3.4	4.3	1.181	182.0	292.8	1,591.3
SWEDEN	4.4	2.483	4.7	4.2	2.917	4.8	8.0	2.735	271.0	410.0	1,432.6
SINGAPORE	0.4	0.000	10.0	0.2	..	10.0	0.1	..	818.8	1,423.9	1,423.9
KOREA, REPUBLIC OF	13.3	6.438	11.5	9.0	7.266	8.9	13.0	7.773	409.8	1,256.3	1,256.3
AUSTRIA	8.8	4.239	9.0	7.4	4.355	10.1	13.6	4.334	133.6	174.9	1,046.0
AUSTRALIA	15.6	4.980	17.1	16.0	5.292	16.7	22.3	4.768	338.5	926.6	991.0
BRAZIL	14.5	0.000	34.6	10.6	..	34.7	9.0	..	63.0	400.3	616.7
FINLAND	9.0	2.905	9.6	6.3	2.757	9.6	11.3	2.433	131.7	160.3	612.9
NORWAY	3.0	2.824	3.6	1.8	2.582	4.3	7.5	2.362	116.7	165.4	596.5
HUNGARY	6.6	2.689	6.7	6.5	2.460	6.6	8.5	1.966	67.0	340.1	340.1
CZECH & SLOVAK CU	4.4	1.410	4.4	3.4	1.131	3.4	5.4	1.315	221.2	322.1	322.1
MEXICO	15.2	0.000	34.9	11.9	..	34.7	11.3	..	46.6	91.6	301.1
TURKEY	54.1	4.998	22.4	46.2	4.142	20.8	38.5	2.224	76.4	231.2	231.2
INDONESIA	19.9	0.859	39.5	10.6	0.129	39.6	7.4	0.050	49.8	183.6	183.6
PHILIPPINES	32.8	0.122	32.1	32.6	0.040	31.4	31.9	0.002	44.3	182.9	182.9
POLAND	10.3	3.301	11.8	8.0	2.421	9.7	14.0	2.640	98.1	170.9	170.9
NEW ZEALAND	18.4	1.227	22.2	17.8	1.663	22.2	27.0	1.077	49.3	132.1	162.3
THAILAND	36.5	9.033	29.4	34.8	3.726	29.6	36.7	3.010	28.7	159.5	159.5
INDIA	46.9	9.802	34.4	39.9	15.117	32.3	66.0	21.206	60.3	146.2	146.2
MALAYSIA	22.6	2.689	23.5	15.2	1.827	17.7	13.2	1.137	54.7	133.4	133.4
VENEZUELA	22.7	1.003	34.3	16.7	0.556	34.1	22.2	1.200	34.3	125.5	125.5
COLOMBIA	13.9	0.000	35.2	9.5	..	33.9	8.0	..	38.7	113.9	113.9
ROMANIA	21.8	0.000	31.7	20.8	..	31.9	21.1	..	44.7	90.3	90.3
TUNISIA	29.8	0.000	42.3	26.4	..	40.9	24.2	..	8.5	78.1	78.1
CHILE	11.0	0.000	25.0	11.0	..	25.0	11.0	..	27.9	77.1	77.1
ARGENTINA	12.9	0.017	35.0	8.4	0.000	35.0	12.7	..	5.6	64.3	74.6
URUGUAY	12.1	0.125	33.8	10.9	0.231	34.9	10.9	..	4.6	20.5	53.3
PERU	15.7	0.111	29.9	15.0	0.007	28.3	15.2	0.001	10.0	47.3	47.3
ICELAND	8.7	0.000	18.8	6.9	..	17.8	13.7	..	4.4	10.5	41.4
SRI LANKA	40.2	0.000	50.0	43.9	..	50.0	46.7	..	15.0	40.1	40.1
MACAU	0.0	0.000	0.0	0.0	..	0.0	0.0	..	16.7	30.6	30.6
EL SALVADOR	15.1	0.072	39.1	13.3	0.114	33.7	16.1	0.181	18.4	29.4	29.4
JAMAICA	20.2	0.000	50.0	15.7	..	50.0	19.6	..	4.5	27.2	27.2
ZIMBABWE	10.3	0.000	5.0	6.4	..	5.0	3.7	..	11.4	20.7	20.7
SENEGAL	14.1	0.000	17.8	14.7	..	23.5	14.3	..	2.5	16.6	16.6

Notes: 1. Value of imports from partner countries that do not participate in Free Trade Agreements.

2. Weighted average tariff reduction measured by dT / (1 + T) in percent.

Metals Levels and changes in protection before and after the UR

Import market	Simple average MFN tariff rates			Weighted by value of imports from: the World exc. FTA[1]			LMIEs exc. FTA[1]		Value of imports in $ million		
	Post-UR appl. rates	Tariff reduction[2]	Post-UR bound rates	Post-UR applied rate	Tariff reduction[2]	Post-UR bound rate	Post-UR applied rate	Tariff reduction[2]	from LMIEs exc. FTA[1]	from World exc. FTA[1]	from World inc. FTA
EUROPEAN UNION	1.9	2.334	2.1	1.0	1.107	1.7	2.3	1.114	14,958.1	22,874.1	35,672.8
UNITED STATES	2.0	2.056	2.1	1.1	2.396	1.3	2.9	1.436	6,139.0	20,536.7	30,379.1
JAPAN	1.0	2.329	1.0	0.5	1.256	0.5	2.1	1.479	11,636.6	21,890.0	21,890.0
CANADA	3.5	4.052	3.7	1.5	4.481	3.0	4.8	3.142	865.3	2,955.3	7,689.9
KOREA, REPUBLIC OF	8.3	8.741	8.6	3.7	7.498	3.8	8.7	4.614	1,492.8	6,459.3	6,459.3
HONG KONG	0.0	0.000	0.0	0.0	..	0.0	0.0	..	2,638.0	5,867.9	5,867.9
SWEDEN	1.0	1.158	1.4	0.2	0.765	0.9	1.3	0.789	351.2	759.9	4,612.6
SWITZERLAND	1.4	0.688	1.4	0.9	0.671	1.8	2.6	1.024	91.9	265.7	4,388.8
SINGAPORE	0.0	0.000	5.0	0.0	..	4.6	0.0	..	1,222.9	3,543.4	3,543.4
AUSTRIA	3.7	2.756	4.5	0.5	1.921	3.7	3.4	1.899	279.1	385.9	2,997.9
NORWAY	1.3	1.088	1.8	0.1	0.521	0.8	0.4	0.151	436.4	860.7	2,878.6
THAILAND	25.8	1.959	24.0	17.1	0.359	21.0	13.3	0.068	881.1	2,790.7	2,790.7
TURKEY	35.0	0.483	18.5	18.2	0.223	23.9	16.8	0.082	972.0	2,766.0	2,766.0
FINLAND	1.9	1.342	2.6	0.3	0.803	1.5	1.4	0.944	382.5	590.1	2,068.7
INDIA	56.6	9.092	38.9	38.3	7.857	38.8	58.0	4.266	611.4	2,022.0	2,022.0
INDONESIA	15.5	0.095	38.0	9.6	0.023	37.0	6.0	0.021	593.0	1,869.0	1,869.0
MALAYSIA	12.3	1.079	21.7	7.3	0.306	13.5	5.8	0.180	444.8	1,780.9	1,780.9
AUSTRALIA	7.2	5.412	7.9	6.4	6.402	6.8	11.9	7.263	378.4	1,672.2	1,772.3
BRAZIL	13.4	0.000	32.4	5.6	..	29.2	2.2	..	514.0	1,321.5	1,414.4
PHILIPPINES	23.9	0.034	28.1	16.0	0.019	21.9	13.3	0.005	533.1	1,317.9	1,317.9
MEXICO	13.0	0.000	34.6	10.5	..	32.9	10.4	..	76.0	332.9	1,118.6
CZECH & SLOVAK CU	4.1	0.871	4.1	1.9	0.413	1.9	2.0	0.346	825.2	1,096.6	1,096.6
POLAND	7.7	2.238	9.7	5.2	0.616	8.3	4.4	0.489	550.9	980.4	980.4
HUNGARY	5.8	1.575	5.8	3.9	1.228	4.5	2.5	0.528	377.7	868.7	868.7
VENEZUELA	14.2	0.043	33.4	9.9	0.006	34.2	7.4	0.008	233.4	734.7	734.7
COLOMBIA	11.5	0.000	35.0	10.4	..	35.0	10.0	..	285.1	524.1	524.1
NEW ZEALAND	8.6	0.075	13.3	7.7	0.089	14.6	8.4	0.134	36.4	309.8	516.7
ARGENTINA	12.0	0.002	34.5	9.3	0.000	34.9	5.8	..	115.1	349.8	501.2
ROMANIA	15.4	0.000	32.6	7.2	..	34.5	4.9	..	327.0	480.3	480.3
TUNISIA	26.8	0.000	29.4	21.9	..	26.4	20.3	..	61.7	328.6	328.6
SRI LANKA	20.0	0.000	52.0	16.8	..	51.0	14.7	..	109.4	226.2	226.2
CHILE	11.0	0.000	25.0	11.0	..	25.0	11.0	..	77.0	204.9	204.9
PERU	15.2	0.000	30.0	13.9	..	29.7	15.1	..	44.5	142.1	142.1
JAMAICA	13.0	0.000	50.0	13.2	..	50.0	14.9	..	32.6	123.0	123.0
ICELAND	1.2	0.000	10.6	0.2	..	7.5	0.5	..	5.2	11.1	118.0
EL SALVADOR	12.6	0.000	38.4	9.8	..	36.0	12.5	..	49.7	116.1	116.1
ZIMBABWE	9.0	0.090	9.2	5.2	0.221	16.2	4.3	0.157	77.1	101.9	101.9
URUGUAY	9.5	0.047	33.9	8.2	0.019	29.0	7.9	0.001	13.9	31.5	97.8
SENEGAL	15.0	0.000	30.0	15.0	..	30.0	15.0	..	13.2	71.7	71.7
MACAU	0.0	0.000	0.0	0.0	..	0.0	0.0	..	24.6	62.1	62.1

Notes: 1. Value of imports from partner countries that do not participate in Free Trade Agreements.

2. Weighted average tariff reduction measured by dT / (1 + T) in percent.

Chemical & Photographic Suppl. Levels and changes in protection before and after the UR

Import market	Simple average MFN tariff rates			Weighted by value of imports from: the World exc. FTA[1]			LMIEs exc. FTA[1]		Value of imports in $ million		
	Post-UR appl. rates	Tariff reduction[2]	Post-UR bound rates	Post-UR applied rate	Tariff reduction[2]	Post-UR bound rate	Post-UR applied rate	Tariff reduction[2]	from LMIEs exc. FTA[1]	from World exc. FTA[1]	from World inc. FTA
EUROPEAN UNION	4.4	2.434	4.7	3.8	2.365	4.4	6.9	2.534	7,255.3	19,044.6	30,322.8
UNITED STATES	3.2	2.648	3.4	2.5	2.254	2.8	4.8	2.050	2,303.6	19,756.4	24,544.3
JAPAN	2.6	1.855	2.6	1.9	2.076	1.9	4.7	1.893	2,207.7	14,269.6	14,269.6
HONG KONG	0.0	0.000	0.0	0.0	..	0.0	0.0	..	3,365.3	10,574.1	10,574.1
CANADA	4.3	4.330	4.8	2.6	4.408	4.7	6.7	3.683	347.6	2,451.8	7,649.7
SWITZERLAND	1.0	0.225	1.0	0.2	0.134	1.0	0.8	0.173	221.7	909.9	7,294.3
KOREA, REPUBLIC OF	6.4	11.226	6.0	6.0	9.780	5.6	16.0	9.329	608.9	6,375.1	6,375.1
SWEDEN	2.1	1.213	3.5	0.7	1.193	3.8	2.9	1.008	238.0	715.4	4,757.7
SINGAPORE	0.0	0.017	5.3	0.0	0.003	5.7	0.0	0.010	652.8	4,209.9	4,209.9
AUSTRALIA	5.5	2.875	9.4	5.0	2.450	8.7	9.7	3.412	578.8	3,927.1	4,023.6
AUSTRIA	1.8	1.647	3.1	0.4	2.669	3.3	4.0	2.020	189.7	451.4	3,669.9
INDONESIA	12.1	0.135	38.0	6.0	0.024	37.6	5.0	0.030	515.0	3,068.0	3,068.0
BRAZIL	12.2	0.000	22.1	11.5	..	21.8	9.6	..	374.3	2,608.6	2,851.3
THAILAND	28.8	4.635	28.8	30.0	3.453	29.0	32.9	1.522	354.9	2,406.3	2,406.3
FINLAND	0.9	1.434	1.9	0.2	1.018	1.6	1.4	0.720	150.4	370.9	2,350.6
NORWAY	2.3	2.304	3.6	0.4	1.230	3.4	1.7	0.757	156.6	376.4	2,322.6
TURKEY	31.9	2.728	16.5	25.0	3.330	17.7	25.8	3.447	329.9	2,131.5	2,131.5
MEXICO	11.7	0.000	35.2	10.4	..	33.9	11.4	..	86.9	684.4	2,052.6
MALAYSIA	9.1	0.863	16.5	5.9	0.930	13.0	5.9	0.433	164.0	1,772.2	1,772.2
INDIA	41.9	16.199	39.9	36.4	14.295	38.7	63.7	10.444	518.6	1,701.9	1,701.9
HUNGARY	6.1	3.231	6.1	4.2	2.086	4.3	4.5	1.427	222.2	1,442.1	1,442.1
PHILIPPINES	19.6	0.216	20.1	19.5	0.219	19.7	19.0	0.101	216.9	1,424.4	1,424.4
ARGENTINA	6.0	0.000	22.7	6.1	..	22.2	8.5	..	109.5	999.8	1,200.0
NEW ZEALAND	5.4	0.362	8.6	3.3	2.337	7.1	4.4	0.432	50.2	796.3	1,184.7
POLAND	8.4	2.528	9.0	7.3	3.326	7.6	11.8	4.219	274.2	1,138.8	1,138.8
COLOMBIA	9.3	0.000	35.0	8.1	..	34.6	8.5	..	240.3	1,113.9	1,113.9
CZECH & SLOVAK CU	4.3	0.915	4.3	4.1	0.717	4.1	4.3	0.966	216.2	1,094.3	1,094.3
VENEZUELA	10.8	0.068	33.2	8.9	0.025	30.6	9.3	0.025	140.0	1,026.3	1,026.3
PERU	15.3	0.013	29.6	15.4	0.008	29.5	16.5	0.004	113.2	476.9	476.9
CHILE	11.1	0.000	25.0	11.0	..	25.0	11.0	..	121.8	462.5	462.5
TUNISIA	23.5	0.000	31.6	18.9	..	26.9	19.9	..	84.7	441.8	441.8
ROMANIA	16.3	0.000	29.3	15.8	..	32.2	16.0	..	142.1	435.5	435.5
SRI LANKA	17.0	0.000	8.8	12.8	..	5.6	11.1	..	78.9	305.9	305.9
URUGUAY	10.2	0.009	23.1	9.9	0.005	23.5	11.6	..	23.4	156.3	261.1
JAMAICA	16.9	0.000	50.0	13.1	..	50.0	26.3	..	29.7	223.9	223.9
EL SALVADOR	10.5	0.000	36.9	9.9	..	29.9	14.5	..	77.4	185.4	185.4
ICELAND	1.8	0.009	5.8	0.4	0.005	4.4	5.3	..	0.8	40.1	182.1
ZIMBABWE	4.9	0.000	57.7	2.1	..	64.5	2.7	..	82.5	180.4	180.4
MACAU	0.0	0.000	0.0	0.0	..	0.0	0.0	..	24.4	120.3	120.3
SENEGAL	15.0	0.000	26.3	15.0	..	28.1	15.0	..	4.9	114.0	114.0

Notes: 1. Value of imports from partner countries that do not participate in Free Trade Agreements.

2. Weighted average tariff reduction measured by dT / (1 + T) in percent.

Transport Equipment Levels and changes in protection before and after the UR

Import market	Simple average MFN tariff rates			Weighted by value of imports from: the World exc. FTA[1]			LMIEs exc. FTA[1]		Value of imports in $ million		
	Post-UR appl. rates	Tariff reduc-tion[2]	Post-UR bound rates	Post-UR applied rate	Tariff reduc-tion[2]	Post-UR bound rate	Post-UR applied rate	Tariff reduc-tion[2]	from LMIEs exc. FTA[1]	from World exc. FTA[1]	from World inc. FTA
UNITED STATES	2.0	1.171	2.2	3.4	0.173	4.6	3.1	0.139	3,162.4	49,116.4	79,699.4
CANADA	4.6	2.516	5.1	3.2	2.241	5.3	9.0	2.718	330.4	5,543.6	27,637.6
EUROPEAN UNION	5.2	1.792	5.3	5.5	0.670	6.2	3.8	0.680	6,315.6	21,795.2	27,233.0
SWITZERLAND	2.7	0.705	2.7	3.6	0.620	4.2	3.6	1.084	22.2	1,647.6	6,289.6
JAPAN	0.0	1.383	0.0	0.0	1.449	0.0	1.2	1.217	102.9	6,103.5	6,103.5
SWEDEN	3.3	1.091	3.5	4.1	0.614	4.9	6.3	1.454	47.2	1,527.6	5,733.7
HONG KONG	0.0	0.000	0.0	0.0	..	0.0	0.0	..	458.2	5,144.1	5,144.1
AUSTRALIA	11.2	4.458	13.2	18.2	2.694	22.6	23.7	2.330	68.0	4,028.5	4,039.7
AUSTRIA	7.1	3.373	7.9	17.3	3.462	18.3	11.6	3.063	29.5	878.3	3,883.8
FINLAND	3.9	0.343	4.3	3.7	0.399	5.0	5.6	1.330	302.8	1,183.9	2,829.7
SINGAPORE	3.9	0.000	6.7	3.9	..	8.4	6.0	..	100.2	2,530.5	2,530.5
KOREA, REPUBLIC OF	18.1	4.144	12.1	5.5	1.749	4.0	0.7	0.127	170.7	2,255.8	2,255.8
THAILAND	47.4	5.097	59.1	46.7	7.107	58.9	62.4	2.397	22.7	2,009.7	2,009.7
NORWAY	2.9	1.011	3.6	2.1	0.352	3.8	2.0	0.253	27.9	659.3	1,927.1
INDONESIA	31.5	0.721	39.3	19.4	0.256	35.5	6.6	0.094	110.2	1,356.4	1,356.4
NEW ZEALAND	12.6	0.169	18.0	10.0	0.020	13.4	18.6	0.062	14.1	895.1	1,020.9
MEXICO	13.8	0.000	35.5	12.9	..	36.7	14.6	..	28.2	294.7	1,009.0
HUNGARY	17.0	0.702	10.6	16.1	0.222	11.8	12.5	0.425	178.1	942.4	942.4
MALAYSIA	61.7	0.768	19.4	22.0	0.027	7.5	20.3	0.062	21.9	823.7	823.7
PHILIPPINES	25.1	0.190	20.4	18.8	0.002	11.5	26.4	..	30.7	733.7	733.7
BRAZIL	19.9	0.000	31.7	11.7	..	33.8	18.5	..	14.1	666.1	718.3
TURKEY	24.8	4.007	17.9	20.0	2.629	12.2	31.1	2.102	21.6	670.7	670.7
POLAND	10.2	0.885	9.0	10.7	0.370	9.2	10.7	0.523	402.2	591.9	591.9
INDIA	62.7	8.563	36.2	30.9	5.315	22.3	43.6	2.481	32.7	549.0	549.0
VENEZUELA	17.0	0.217	32.3	23.3	0.646	34.2	25.6	0.792	64.9	520.0	520.0
COLOMBIA	17.9	0.162	35.9	20.9	0.253	36.6	16.5	0.426	52.0	374.6	374.6
CZECH & SLOVAK CU	6.2	1.478	6.2	6.9	1.281	6.9	8.1	1.234	216.7	355.1	355.1
SRI LANKA	23.6	0.000	25.7	12.0	..	22.1	9.7	..	89.6	307.4	307.4
ARGENTINA	14.6	0.010	34.1	14.7	0.000	34.7	15.4	..	46.2	227.7	279.9
ICELAND	9.4	0.000	17.9	4.8	..	2.0	2.7	..	25.0	112.2	247.2
CHILE	10.9	0.000	24.8	10.8	..	24.3	11.0	..	76.9	226.5	226.5
PERU	14.9	0.000	29.6	13.8	..	29.5	15.1	..	44.9	174.7	174.7
TUNISIA	27.3	0.000	28.2	28.4	..	29.1	28.2	..	19.1	162.4	162.4
ZIMBABWE	11.6	0.000	19.8	2.9	..	3.2	7.7	..	9.7	156.8	156.8
JAMAICA	21.0	0.000	50.0	27.2	..	50.0	25.7	..	4.5	148.9	148.9
URUGUAY	12.2	0.000	31.6	10.7	..	18.9	13.7	..	2.5	52.7	146.9
ROMANIA	27.9	0.056	35.0	28.3	0.002	35.0	27.9	0.000	57.3	121.0	121.0
EL SALVADOR	14.0	0.045	35.0	15.5	0.000	32.0	13.7	..	20.5	118.7	118.7
SENEGAL	11.6	0.000	15.6	12.8	..	19.0	13.8	..	3.1	98.0	98.0
MACAU	0.0	0.000	..	0.0	..	..	0.0	..	1.3	37.8	37.8

Notes: 1. Value of imports from partner countries that do not participate in Free Trade Agreements.

2. Weighted average tariff reduction measured by dT / (1 + T) in percent.

Non-Electric Machinery Levels and changes in protection before and after the UR

Import market	Simple average MFN tariff rates			Weighted by value of imports from: the World exc. FTA¹			LMIEs exc. FTA¹		Value of imports in $ million		
	Post-UR appl. rates	Tariff reduction²	Post-UR bound rates	Post-UR applied rate	Tariff reduc-tion²	Post-UR bound rate	Post-UR applied rate	Tariff reduc-tion²	from LMIEs exc. FTA¹	from World exc. FTA¹	from World inc. FTA
UNITED STATES	1.3	1.775	1.4	0.9	2.102	1.0	3.1	2.036	4,330.4	51,211.1	60,918.9
EUROPEAN UNION	1.8	2.218	1.9	1.4	2.841	1.6	4.9	2.465	3,488.5	34,085.8	48,303.1
CANADA	3.2	2.423	3.6	1.2	2.925	3.0	6.3	2.729	413.6	5,465.2	20,245.2
HONG KONG	0.0	0.000	0.0	0.0	..	0.0	0.0	..	2,619.4	11,220.5	11,220.5
JAPAN	0.0	1.851	0.0	0.0	1.302	0.0	1.1	1.125	674.4	9,303.8	9,303.8
KOREA, REPUBLIC OF	11.5	6.954	10.6	11.8	5.752	10.0	18.3	8.943	82.8	8,232.0	8,232.0
SINGAPORE	0.0	0.000	6.9	0.0	..	4.9	0.0	..	1,199.4	7,964.6	7,964.6
SWEDEN	1.4	1.488	1.7	0.8	2.057	1.6	3.6	1.682	82.9	2,109.1	7,596.1
SWITZERLAND	0.6	0.322	0.7	0.3	0.410	0.6	1.1	0.372	51.4	1,281.8	7,483.0
AUSTRALIA	7.5	3.882	9.5	6.4	3.104	9.6	12.8	4.338	243.2	6,322.3	6,440.3
AUSTRIA	3.3	1.938	3.8	0.8	0.989	3.3	6.3	2.325	67.9	884.7	4,855.1
INDONESIA	14.1	0.067	37.4	12.1	0.007	36.3	13.0	0.012	311.6	3,711.1	3,711.1
THAILAND	23.4	7.148	22.5	22.9	8.178	22.9	36.9	11.645	272.2	3,555.6	3,555.6
FINLAND	1.9	1.482	2.6	1.0	0.742	2.3	3.7	1.062	101.3	937.8	3,536.8
NORWAY	2.0	1.602	2.7	0.8	2.551	2.1	4.9	2.333	29.5	792.3	3,294.8
MEXICO	13.2	0.000	35.1	12.6	..	35.1	12.7	..	100.2	1,013.8	2,815.2
CZECH & SLOVAK CU	3.7	1.160	3.7	3.3	1.015	3.3	4.5	1.025	731.1	2,813.5	2,813.5
BRAZIL	19.5	0.000	31.2	18.9	..	30.0	20.9	..	42.0	2,526.2	2,634.5
MALAYSIA	5.8	1.644	10.3	4.4	1.184	8.3	7.8	1.486	83.3	2,267.4	2,267.4
TURKEY	21.7	3.217	12.8	20.6	2.917	11.9	30.2	1.422	147.0	2,211.5	2,211.5
INDIA	30.7	6.420	31.6	31.0	5.755	32.3	42.2	7.495	117.9	2,052.2	2,052.2
POLAND	6.6	1.481	8.6	6.4	1.274	8.4	9.6	1.953	504.8	1,731.2	1,731.2
VENEZUELA	10.5	0.037	32.6	10.0	0.009	29.2	10.6	0.046	84.7	1,616.3	1,616.3
HUNGARY	8.1	1.291	8.0	7.5	1.502	7.5	8.3	1.537	120.8	1,527.8	1,527.8
PHILIPPINES	18.9	0.871	20.5	17.2	1.695	20.2	20.7	1.469	69.7	1,281.3	1,281.3
NEW ZEALAND	10.6	0.151	15.1	6.9	0.170	10.3	10.5	0.170	16.6	948.0	1,080.1
COLOMBIA	9.6	0.000	35.0	8.5	..	35.0	8.5	..	79.0	791.5	791.5
ARGENTINA	13.6	0.000	34.8	13.7	..	34.8	15.4	..	48.3	637.7	703.8
CHILE	11.0	0.000	25.0	11.0	..	25.0	11.0	..	60.2	561.7	561.7
TUNISIA	23.3	0.000	24.8	22.9	..	25.2	24.3	..	21.6	493.1	493.1
ROMANIA	15.1	0.039	33.7	15.4	0.016	33.8	15.5	0.003	142.7	450.9	450.9
PERU	15.4	0.000	29.2	15.1	..	28.5	15.7	..	52.9	401.0	401.0
SRI LANKA	12.8	0.000	8.4	12.0	..	7.4	17.6	..	52.1	293.3	293.3
ICELAND	0.6	0.138	8.2	0.5	0.622	7.2	1.5	..	1.2	43.9	192.3
JAMAICA	12.4	0.000	50.0	11.3	..	50.0	26.3	..	8.5	154.2	154.2
ZIMBABWE	3.8	0.000	8.1	1.2	..	3.7	1.1	..	30.4	147.3	147.3
URUGUAY	8.1	0.087	33.2	8.3	0.022	32.3	8.5	..	4.4	98.1	142.7
MACAU	0.0	0.000	..	0.0	..	..	0.0	..	10.3	136.9	136.9
SENEGAL	7.1	0.000	5.2	8.1	..	5.3	5.1	..	4.0	117.8	117.8
EL SALVADOR	8.1	0.000	35.0	7.5	..	30.1	12.7	..	14.2	104.6	104.6

Notes: 1. Value of imports from partner countries that do not participate in Free Trade Agreements.

2. Weighted average tariff reduction measured by dT / (1 + T) in percent.

Electric Machinery Levels and changes in protection before and after the UR

Import market	Simple average MFN tariff rates			Weighted by value of imports from: the World exc. FTA[1]			LMIEs exc. FTA[1]		Value of imports in $ million		
	Post-UR appl. rates	Tariff reduc-tion[2]	Post-UR bound rates	Post-UR applied rate	Tariff reduc-tion[2]	Post-UR bound rate	Post-UR applied rate	Tariff reduc-tion[2]	from LMIEs exc. FTA[1]	from World exc. FTA[1]	from World inc. FTA
UNITED STATES	2.5	1.713	2.6	1.7	1.552	2.0	3.5	1.344	10,344.5	39,322.3	49,728.0
EUROPEAN UNION	3.6	2.506	3.6	5.4	2.921	5.2	9.3	2.575	5,479.0	24,318.1	31,063.1
HONG KONG	0.0	0.000	0.0	0.0	..	0.0	0.0	..	8,857.6	20,215.1	20,215.1
SINGAPORE	0.0	0.000	9.4	0.0	..	9.2	0.0	..	2,792.6	9,469.3	9,469.3
CANADA	4.3	3.417	4.7	1.6	3.233	3.5	5.3	3.358	638.7	3,011.8	9,196.9
KOREA, REPUBLIC OF	14.2	5.017	11.0	8.2	6.875	5.6	12.6	9.060	150.7	6,876.3	6,876.3
JAPAN	0.2	0.666	0.2	0.1	0.236	0.1	0.4	0.244	1,272.6	6,790.2	6,790.2
SWEDEN	2.7	1.444	2.8	3.2	1.062	3.1	4.7	0.860	200.1	1,477.1	4,134.1
MALAYSIA	12.5	3.522	16.2	3.8	3.984	4.4	5.9	2.348	407.7	4,113.4	4,113.4
SWITZERLAND	0.8	0.312	0.8	0.7	0.364	0.9	1.9	0.647	113.7	972.1	4,027.4
AUSTRALIA	13.0	5.445	14.1	13.2	5.804	14.6	21.2	5.023	327.7	2,615.1	2,687.0
AUSTRIA	7.7	3.833	8.0	6.7	3.619	8.5	17.4	4.645	159.3	593.8	2,488.8
PHILIPPINES	24.9	1.472	23.9	21.4	0.544	21.5	24.2	0.541	184.3	2,446.4	2,446.4
THAILAND	30.7	5.835	27.4	31.3	3.365	25.3	43.1	7.024	159.5	2,237.2	2,237.2
FINLAND	4.8	2.771	5.3	3.9	2.451	5.3	9.1	3.003	133.1	563.4	1,682.8
NORWAY	2.5	1.760	2.9	2.1	2.549	3.1	12.3	4.648	60.3	429.3	1,656.7
BRAZIL	18.4	0.000	31.4	16.6	..	31.6	19.3	..	71.3	1,478.7	1,492.9
MEXICO	13.5	0.000	34.1	13.6	..	34.8	14.3	..	129.9	572.6	1,446.6
INDONESIA	21.2	1.160	39.7	21.5	0.969	38.8	23.7	1.600	100.2	1,032.1	1,032.1
TURKEY	24.3	3.109	15.6	22.9	2.907	15.7	24.0	2.428	115.4	1,028.3	1,028.3
INDIA	41.2	10.758	36.9	48.5	8.623	36.6	63.0	10.647	74.4	890.9	890.9
HUNGARY	9.6	1.919	9.4	8.8	1.599	8.9	9.0	1.201	88.4	786.6	786.6
NEW ZEALAND	12.8	0.445	16.9	12.8	1.003	16.3	10.9	1.485	58.6	661.3	754.4
CZECH & SLOVAK CU	4.2	1.312	4.2	5.4	1.574	5.4	7.7	1.608	265.8	658.9	658.9
VENEZUELA	14.5	0.073	33.7	14.0	0.137	33.0	25.5	0.765	53.6	556.6	556.6
ARGENTINA	14.9	0.000	34.6	15.2	..	34.8	15.5	..	36.4	441.8	494.8
POLAND	7.1	1.564	9.6	9.5	0.994	11.5	8.7	0.656	188.2	464.4	464.4
COLOMBIA	10.8	0.000	35.0	10.6	..	35.0	12.0	..	57.4	444.4	444.4
CHILE	11.0	0.000	25.0	11.0	..	25.0	11.0	..	39.1	247.1	247.1
TUNISIA	28.8	0.000	30.0	29.4	..	31.5	32.8	..	11.2	237.5	237.5
ROMANIA	15.1	0.000	33.9	25.1	..	36.6	24.5	..	89.6	229.9	229.9
PERU	16.1	0.024	29.9	14.3	0.024	29.9	18.2	0.001	24.9	154.2	154.2
SRI LANKA	21.2	0.303	29.5	19.1	0.090	23.0	23.7	0.048	41.3	136.6	136.6
MACAU	0.0	0.000	0.0	0.0	..	0.0	0.0	..	8.4	128.8	128.8
URUGUAY	9.8	0.010	34.7	8.9	0.000	34.9	8.5	..	7.4	67.4	117.1
ICELAND	4.2	0.005	18.3	1.8	0.001	17.2	16.7	0.001	2.7	23.4	114.7
JAMAICA	17.8	0.000	50.0	13.3	..	50.0	25.7	..	4.4	89.7	89.7
ZIMBABWE	10.5	0.000	10.8	5.6	..	12.4	7.5	..	10.5	67.6	67.6
SENEGAL	7.2	0.000	7.0	7.0	..	7.0	7.0	..	3.9	63.6	63.6
EL SALVADOR	14.5	0.000	35.9	10.5	..	32.1	16.0	..	14.0	58.0	58.0

Notes: 1. Value of imports from partner countries that do not participate in Free Trade Agreements.

2. Weighted average tariff reduction measured by dT / (1 + T) in percent.

Mineral Products, Prec. Stones & Metal Levels and changes in protection before and after the UR

Import market	Simple average MFN tariff rates			Weighted by value of imports from: the World exc. FTA[1]			LMIEs exc. FTA[1]		Value of imports in $ million		
	Post-UR appl. rates	Tariff reduc-tion[2]	Post-UR bound rates	Post-UR applied rate	Tariff reduc-tion[2]	Post-UR bound rate	Post-UR applied rate	Tariff reduc-tion[2]	from LMIEs exc. FTA[1]	from World exc. FTA[1]	from World inc. FTA
EUROPEAN UNION	2.7	1.389	2.9	0.5	0.263	0.7	0.6	0.179	29,552.3	37,605.3	43,437.5
JAPAN	1.4	1.102	1.4	0.2	0.511	0.2	0.7	0.614	10,192.8	25,996.0	25,996.0
UNITED STATES	4.1	1.877	4.3	1.7	1.157	1.8	2.7	0.784	5,484.5	14,348.8	22,654.7
HONG KONG	0.0	0.000	0.0	0.0	..	0.0	0.0	..	4,053.2	9,205.2	9,205.2
SWITZERLAND	1.1	0.333	1.2	0.2	0.021	0.5	0.2	0.023	1,000.2	2,378.6	5,700.5
CANADA	2.9	3.709	3.2	0.8	2.755	1.3	2.9	1.610	382.7	1,146.3	4,405.0
KOREA, REPUBLIC OF	11.5	7.090	10.2	5.5	2.122	4.9	5.1	0.834	906.2	2,957.7	2,957.7
INDIA	36.5	13.793	37.6	5.5	0.966	25.6	17.7	1.542	320.6	2,258.9	2,258.9
AUSTRIA	4.4	1.951	4.8	1.1	0.880	3.6	2.2	0.883	737.2	852.0	1,916.0
BRAZIL	9.1	0.000	33.2	1.2	..	18.4	1.9	..	476.1	1,601.8	1,674.2
SWEDEN	2.1	0.907	2.6	0.4	0.414	1.7	1.4	0.355	193.8	423.5	1,555.3
AUSTRALIA	7.7	2.497	9.9	4.8	2.077	6.9	5.1	1.356	385.5	1,389.7	1,449.1
THAILAND	22.0	6.771	21.2	14.9	6.074	8.0	21.6	4.326	410.1	1,116.8	1,116.8
FINLAND	3.6	2.050	4.5	0.4	0.267	1.9	0.7	0.201	449.8	558.0	1,079.9
TURKEY	38.2	2.441	18.3	28.9	0.581	13.3	23.6	0.342	536.5	1,078.3	1,078.3
SINGAPORE	0.1	0.000	8.9	0.1	..	9.5	0.0	..	262.5	1,053.1	1,053.1
NORWAY	1.0	0.981	1.4	0.1	0.587	0.6	1.7	0.694	54.7	146.5	953.6
ROMANIA	12.9	0.000	32.6	2.9	..	34.7	2.9	..	661.5	908.9	908.9
MALAYSIA	14.4	0.565	17.3	4.5	0.144	8.0	4.8	0.105	184.3	861.0	861.0
HUNGARY	5.5	1.840	5.4	2.5	0.420	2.3	2.0	0.110	642.7	829.1	829.1
POLAND	6.4	3.368	7.4	2.2	1.242	2.6	2.3	0.675	481.6	647.9	647.9
INDONESIA	16.8	2.354	39.7	5.4	0.232	39.5	3.3	0.133	235.6	629.6	629.6
MEXICO	13.7	0.000	34.7	6.8	..	28.7	7.4	..	64.7	130.9	567.2
PHILIPPINES	27.0	0.457	19.0	15.7	0.115	11.1	14.4	0.026	271.3	562.0	562.0
ARGENTINA	9.4	0.054	33.2	9.6	0.003	33.7	9.9	..	375.3	530.0	550.1
CZECH & SLOVAK CU	4.3	1.274	4.3	1.8	0.495	1.8	1.6	0.316	335.9	493.0	493.0
TUNISIA	27.3	0.000	32.4	16.1	..	20.0	10.3	..	162.9	295.2	295.2
SRI LANKA	23.9	0.375	43.9	10.5	0.054	6.2	12.0	0.029	117.9	273.5	273.5
NEW ZEALAND	7.6	0.315	11.1	5.1	0.195	8.3	5.4	0.305	48.3	212.9	258.3
VENEZUELA	18.0	0.620	33.9	9.7	0.142	32.7	10.9	0.256	46.8	248.7	248.7
COLOMBIA	11.9	0.000	35.0	7.3	..	35.0	8.2	..	48.1	221.1	221.1
CHILE	11.0	0.000	25.0	11.0	..	25.0	11.0	..	27.1	156.7	156.7
PERU	15.8	0.000	30.0	15.9	..	30.0	15.1	..	27.2	134.1	134.1
JAMAICA	19.5	0.000	50.0	19.7	..	50.0	17.3	..	8.4	71.9	71.9
MACAU	0.0	0.000	0.0	0.0	..	0.0	0.0	..	44.8	71.1	71.1
EL SALVADOR	12.9	0.000	38.7	7.2	..	28.8	10.2	..	18.8	62.1	62.1
URUGUAY	10.1	0.012	32.8	9.5	0.005	25.8	11.6	0.016	11.5	38.0	55.4
ICELAND	2.8	0.000	18.5	0.4	..	12.9	2.6	..	2.1	7.4	53.2
ZIMBABWE	8.6	0.000	12.9	3.7	..	3.3	2.8	..	26.3	49.1	49.1
SENEGAL	14.6	0.000	13.8	14.8	..	14.2	15.0	..	11.0	44.2	44.2

Notes: 1. Value of imports from partner countries that do not participate in Free Trade Agreements.

2. Weighted average tariff reduction measured by dT / (1 + T) in percent.

Manufactured Articles nes. Levels and changes in protection before and after the UR

Import market	Simple average MFN tariff rates			Weighted by value of imports from: the World exc. FTA[1]			LMIEs exc. FTA[1]		Value of imports in $ million		
	Post-UR appl. rates	Tariff reduc-tion[2]	Post-UR bound rates	Post-UR applied rate	Tariff reduc-tion[2]	Post-UR bound rate	Post-UR applied rate	Tariff reduc-tion[2]	from LMIEs exc. FTA[1]	from World exc. FTA[1]	from World inc. FTA
EUROPEAN UNION	2.4	2.602	2.5	2.5	2.258	2.6	3.8	1.629	8,096.5	30,143.3	37,740.3
UNITED STATES	2.4	2.476	2.5	1.4	3.003	1.5	5.8	4.052	6,768.4	33,182.9	36,505.4
HONG KONG	0.0	0.000	0.0	0.0	..	0.0	0.0	..	8,170.7	16,893.6	16,893.6
JAPAN	1.1	1.365	1.1	0.6	0.690	0.6	1.8	0.644	2,596.4	12,659.6	12,659.6
CANADA	3.7	3.108	4.1	1.5	3.284	2.5	9.6	6.153	423.6	2,802.1	6,545.2
KOREA, REPUBLIC OF	11.0	7.375	12.2	8.7	5.192	10.6	8.4	1.097	470.3	5,372.3	5,372.3
SINGAPORE	0.5	0.601	5.1	0.1	0.189	6.9	1.3	0.688	942.3	4,595.5	4,595.5
SWITZERLAND	1.2	0.500	1.2	0.4	0.341	0.8	1.1	0.293	244.8	1,334.8	4,483.3
NORWAY	1.9	1.692	3.0	0.3	0.407	1.0	0.3	0.114	1,199.1	2,207.5	3,615.7
SWEDEN	1.5	1.276	1.7	0.9	1.418	1.5	3.0	1.779	161.9	1,101.7	3,097.2
AUSTRALIA	6.0	3.073	7.5	4.7	2.676	5.7	10.7	2.823	316.7	2,880.1	2,981.1
AUSTRIA	4.0	3.214	4.4	2.3	2.593	3.6	7.0	2.401	208.4	693.0	2,176.8
FINLAND	2.2	1.626	2.9	1.2	1.012	2.4	2.3	0.758	302.1	770.9	1,671.7
BRAZIL	17.8	0.092	31.6	15.2	0.033	35.0	8.6	0.080	112.5	1,133.1	1,384.0
THAILAND	29.0	7.984	28.5	20.4	5.336	23.1	14.6	2.100	339.3	1,120.8	1,120.8
HUNGARY	7.5	2.236	7.3	4.6	1.202	4.5	1.5	0.365	389.0	1,108.7	1,108.7
MEXICO	14.3	0.005	34.1	12.5	0.049	30.6	12.4	0.032	101.0	340.8	1,044.3
INDONESIA	21.0	1.166	38.5	7.7	0.321	32.5	3.7	0.182	240.8	945.2	945.2
CZECH & SLOVAK CU	3.7	1.173	4.4	2.5	0.812	2.8	2.8	0.682	356.8	889.0	889.0
MALAYSIA	8.5	2.025	10.3	5.3	5.788	6.8	9.3	1.858	90.1	883.8	883.8
TURKEY	34.4	3.185	17.6	29.5	3.744	16.6	41.6	6.496	122.7	756.4	756.4
POLAND	7.2	3.045	9.9	5.8	1.693	7.7	6.2	1.673	267.3	644.6	644.6
NEW ZEALAND	8.5	0.159	13.2	6.7	0.321	11.4	11.7	0.181	47.4	514.7	603.3
ROMANIA	16.0	0.001	34.2	8.8	0.000	36.5	7.0	..	335.0	602.7	602.7
INDIA	54.8	7.004	47.2	43.4	7.580	48.8	32.1	1.679	48.1	579.7	579.7
PHILIPPINES	24.7	1.314	21.8	22.0	2.135	20.8	20.9	1.225	54.8	466.7	466.7
VENEZUELA	12.2	0.239	32.2	9.8	0.201	31.5	14.7	0.477	60.9	362.1	362.1
COLOMBIA	10.2	0.000	37.5	12.4	..	37.1	9.6	..	48.0	308.0	308.0
ARGENTINA	14.0	0.000	32.9	14.2	..	33.5	9.4	..	25.8	259.4	294.7
SRI LANKA	24.0	0.000	32.2	27.5	..	33.7	13.8	..	46.4	202.7	202.7
MACAU	0.0	0.000	0.0	0.0	..	0.0	0.0	..	39.9	201.1	201.1
TUNISIA	25.9	0.000	35.7	23.1	..	42.0	19.2	..	43.0	183.6	183.6
CHILE	11.0	0.000	24.9	11.0	..	25.0	11.0	..	48.2	155.5	155.5
ICELAND	4.7	0.000	21.7	1.8	..	14.5	8.2	..	3.0	34.2	123.5
SENEGAL	14.9	0.000	21.4	14.9	..	17.8	15.0	..	71.6	109.4	109.4
PERU	17.2	0.313	29.7	14.7	0.254	29.7	18.6	0.912	23.8	101.2	101.2
URUGUAY	9.3	0.000	33.2	8.8	..	33.4	5.8	..	8.1	54.4	80.2
ZIMBABWE	12.9	0.000	78.8	6.1	..	93.3	4.3	..	35.3	73.0	73.0
EL SALVADOR	16.3	0.000	38.4	12.7	..	36.3	19.0	..	29.7	48.3	48.3
JAMAICA	22.7	0.097	52.3	20.9	0.082	51.6	25.5	0.095	2.1	37.0	37.0

Notes: 1. Value of imports from partner countries that do not participate in Free Trade Agreements.

2. Weighted average tariff reduction measured by dT / (1 + T) in percent.

Industrial Goods   Levels and changes in protection before and after the UR

Import market	Simple average MFN tariff rates			Weighted by value of imports from: the World exc. FTA[1]			LMIEs exc. FTA[1]		Value of imports in $ million		
	Post-UR appl. rates	Tariff reduction[2]	Post-UR bound rates	Post-UR applied rate	Tariff reduction[2]	Post-UR bound rate	Post-UR applied rate	Tariff reduction[2]	from LMIEs exc. FTA[1]	from World exc. FTA[1]	from World inc. FTA
UNITED STATES	4.4	2.144	4.6	3.1	1.664	3.5	6.8	1.562	64,908.4	280,148.0	375,851.0
EUROPEAN UNION	3.9	2.301	4.1	2.9	1.737	3.2	4.5	1.245	105,901.0	239,653.0	328,963.0
JAPAN	2.9	1.767	3.0	1.4	1.101	1.5	3.4	1.201	42,340.2	126,669.0	126,669.0
HONG KONG	0.0	0.000	0.0	0.0	..	0.0	0.0	..	55,787.5	114,965.0	114,965.0
CANADA	6.1	4.043	6.4	2.6	3.544	4.3	10.2	3.919	5,595.9	28,826.5	94,872.0
SWITZERLAND	2.2	1.119	2.2	1.0	0.583	1.9	2.4	0.807	2,505.7	10,229.5	50,069.8
KOREA, REPUBLIC OF	10.7	7.748	10.3	7.6	6.167	6.9	9.9	3.935	5,753.8	44,405.4	44,405.4
SWEDEN	3.5	1.511	4.0	1.7	1.364	3.2	5.2	1.411	2,576.4	10,027.1	38,679.2
SINGAPORE	0.5	0.103	6.7	0.4	0.032	6.9	0.4	0.085	9,638.0	38,527.6	38,527.6
AUSTRALIA	11.2	5.320	13.0	9.7	3.931	12.1	21.4	5.662	3,834.3	27,897.6	28,968.6
AUSTRIA	6.4	3.730	7.0	3.3	2.789	7.4	8.5	2.878	2,494.1	5,843.7	28,654.8
NORWAY	3.1	2.334	4.1	0.8	1.318	2.6	2.7	0.995	2,346.2	6,098.9	20,855.1
FINLAND	4.8	2.680	5.8	1.9	1.280	4.0	5.5	1.602	2,460.2	5,815.4	18,157.7
THAILAND	27.6	8.134	26.5	26.8	5.413	27.3	26.2	4.808	3,018.6	16,699.3	16,699.3
INDONESIA	17.9	1.038	38.5	11.5	0.320	36.9	8.9	0.403	2,363.6	13,972.0	13,972.0
MALAYSIA	13.4	2.065	16.7	6.8	2.156	8.9	8.4	1.278	1,724.0	13,909.7	13,909.7
BRAZIL	15.6	0.015	29.5	11.8	0.003	27.7	7.4	0.005	1,809.4	12,319.0	13,544.7
TURKEY	34.8	2.839	16.6	24.2	2.609	16.3	25.1	1.773	2,534.9	11,797.9	11,797.9
MEXICO	13.4	0.001	34.7	11.4	0.005	33.3	12.0	0.005	710.9	3,658.0	11,431.0
INDIA	44.8	10.576	37.5	29.0	6.790	34.2	45.4	5.890	2,079.7	11,135.7	11,135.7
PHILIPPINES	24.0	1.756	23.2	20.4	1.478	21.3	19.8	1.102	1,666.5	9,964.3	9,964.3
HUNGARY	7.8	2.177	7.4	6.7	1.546	6.1	4.5	0.770	2,416.2	9,616.3	9,616.3
CZECH & SLOVAK CU	4.7	1.247	4.8	3.7	0.962	3.7	4.5	0.927	3,594.4	8,556.0	8,556.0
POLAND	7.9	2.208	9.8	6.9	1.513	8.5	8.1	1.439	3,249.2	7,350.6	7,350.6
NEW ZEALAND	10.5	0.821	14.9	7.7	1.091	11.9	14.5	1.234	540.1	5,189.1	6,546.9
VENEZUELA	15.3	0.385	33.3	12.0	0.185	31.3	14.5	0.500	871.9	5,700.6	5,700.6
ARGENTINA	11.3	0.003	30.9	10.6	0.001	30.9	10.2	0.004	821.8	3,666.6	4,355.6
COLOMBIA	11.4	0.009	35.5	10.4	0.022	35.2	9.9	0.024	937.6	4,293.2	4,293.2
ROMANIA	18.1	0.013	32.7	11.4	0.003	34.4	9.1	0.001	1,910.7	3,548.8	3,548.8
TUNISIA	27.4	0.000	36.8	26.4	..	38.4	19.7	..	577.0	3,244.6	3,244.6
SRI LANKA	25.5	0.050	26.8	27.2	0.010	17.9	27.4	0.006	933.8	2,761.1	2,761.1
CHILE	11.0	0.000	25.0	11.0	..	24.9	11.0	..	590.2	2,356.6	2,356.6
PERU	15.9	0.064	29.7	14.6	0.026	29.4	16.5	0.082	411.1	1,786.3	1,786.3
MACAU	0.0	0.000	0.0	0.0	..	0.0	0.0	..	361.6	1,581.1	1,581.1
ICELAND	3.9	0.023	14.4	2.0	0.086	10.8	5.4	0.000	63.6	330.0	1,361.2
JAMAICA	18.5	0.011	50.2	17.2	0.003	50.1	20.8	0.002	123.2	1,131.9	1,131.9
URUGUAY	9.4	0.027	30.7	9.1	0.015	27.9	10.0	0.002	88.2	563.9	1,053.3
ZIMBABWE	9.3	0.117	24.5	4.5	0.119	23.6	5.8	0.182	334.6	892.5	892.5
EL SALVADOR	13.5	0.016	37.4	10.9	0.017	31.7	14.6	0.039	281.7	827.9	827.9
SENEGAL	12.7	0.000	10.9	12.6	..	12.3	13.9	..	145.7	727.5	727.5

Notes: 1. Value of imports from partner countries that do not participate in Free Trade Agreements.

2. Weighted average tariff reduction measured by dT / (1 + T) in percent.

Tables G.3. Concessions Given: *Product Category by Importing Economy or Group*

All Merchandise Trade Levels and changes in protection before and after the UR

Import market	Simple average MFN tariff rates			Weighted by value of imports from: the World exc. FTA[1]			LMIEs exc. FTA[1]		Value of imports in $ million		
	Post-UR appl. rates	Tariff reduc-tion[2]	Post-UR bound rates	Post-UR applied rate	Tariff reduc-tion[2]	Post-UR bound rate	Post-UR applied rate	Tariff reduc-tion[2]	from LMIEs exc. FTA[1]	from World exc. FTA[1]	from World inc. FTA
UNITED STATES	4.3	2.062	4.5	2.8	1.427	3.3	4.9	1.012	107,555.0	337,291.0	449,067.0
EUROPEAN UNION	4.4	2.409	4.6	2.8	1.547	3.2	4.3	1.164	173,055.0	323,731.0	419,521.0
JAPAN	3.7	1.799	3.9	2.8	1.012	3.7	5.2	1.058	70,890.8	184,856.0	184,856.0
HONG KONG	0.0	0.000	0.0	0.0	..	0.0	0.0	..	60,406.4	125,911.0	125,911.0
CANADA	5.7	3.726	6.0	2.4	3.044	4.2	8.0	2.934	7,799.8	34,376.3	104,329.0
SWITZERLAND	2.4	1.186	2.3	1.7	0.651	2.0	4.9	0.854	3,902.9	14,775.6	56,088.2
KOREA, REPUBLIC OF	11.5	7.403	13.3	7.7	5.460	16.4	8.9	2.586	9,600.8	51,720.0	51,720.0
SINGAPORE	1.3	1.311	7.1	1.3	0.837	7.1	4.2	1.574	16,542.5	48,900.0	48,900.0
SWEDEN	3.3	1.410	3.8	1.4	1.077	2.9	3.5	0.910	4,167.1	13,784.4	44,509.2
AUSTRALIA	10.4	4.858	12.1	8.9	3.630	11.1	16.5	4.358	5,084.0	30,542.4	31,962.7
AUSTRIA	6.3	3.588	7.0	3.3	1.973	7.3	7.3	1.833	4,071.5	8,729.6	31,854.5
NORWAY	3.1	2.060	8.5	1.0	1.176	4.2	2.4	0.889	2,741.0	7,628.0	22,842.8
FINLAND	9.2	3.254	8.9	5.9	1.949	6.2	9.2	1.735	4,302.2	8,498.0	20,945.5
BRAZIL	15.4	0.014	29.8	11.7	0.007	29.0	12.6	0.006	5,460.8	17,501.3	19,758.1
THAILAND	27.6	8.448	26.8	26.1	5.959	27.5	27.4	5.833	3,729.5	19,401.8	19,401.8
MALAYSIA	13.0	2.187	16.3	6.4	1.894	9.3	6.8	1.013	2,725.0	16,518.5	16,518.5
INDONESIA	18.3	1.012	39.4	10.7	0.277	38.4	7.5	0.263	3,640.6	16,344.0	16,344.0
TURKEY	34.8	2.995	19.3	26.3	2.341	33.3	25.9	1.062	5,541.0	15,739.9	15,739.9
INDIA	45.0	10.157	41.4	30.9	4.812	52.2	29.3	2.273	5,389.9	15,734.7	15,734.7
MEXICO	13.4	0.001	34.7	10.4	0.004	34.1	11.9	0.003	939.2	4,112.8	14,455.9
PHILIPPINES	24.4	1.834	24.5	19.0	1.307	21.9	16.6	0.786	3,101.5	12,819.7	12,819.7
HUNGARY	8.5	2.130	8.5	6.8	1.409	6.6	4.7	0.623	3,540.6	11,121.7	11,121.7
CZECH & SLOVAK CU	4.8	1.285	5.1	3.8	0.950	4.0	4.4	0.864	5,006.0	10,349.2	10,349.2
POLAND	8.6	2.055	13.2	6.9	1.188	12.3	7.0	1.008	4,799.5	9,623.4	9,623.4
NEW ZEALAND	10.0	0.811	14.2	6.8	1.013	10.8	8.7	0.848	985.5	5,962.6	7,676.6
VENEZUELA	15.5	0.369	33.5	12.4	0.161	31.6	14.9	0.397	1,100.0	6,596.7	6,596.7
ROMANIA	18.8	0.034	39.4	11.7	0.017	45.1	8.7	0.010	3,369.7	5,541.1	5,541.1
COLOMBIA	11.5	0.008	38.1	10.9	0.019	39.7	11.2	0.017	1,334.2	4,933.3	4,933.3
ARGENTINA	11.1	0.003	30.9	10.3	0.001	31.0	9.4	0.003	980.5	3,888.1	4,719.3
TUNISIA	27.6	0.006	45.7	24.8	0.025	48.7	18.6	0.023	883.6	4,118.6	4,118.6
SRI LANKA	26.0	0.051	35.9	28.6	0.014	38.9	30.2	0.004	1,691.8	3,870.2	3,870.2
CHILE	11.0	0.000	25.0	11.0	..	25.0	11.0	..	1,006.2	2,861.8	2,861.8
PERU	16.0	0.075	29.8	14.6	0.025	33.7	16.1	0.066	697.1	2,387.8	2,387.8
MACAU	0.0	0.000	0.0	0.0	..	0.0	0.0	..	473.8	1,842.0	1,842.0
JAMAICA	19.6	0.009	54.9	15.5	0.002	56.3	13.3	0.001	370.6	1,680.2	1,680.2
ICELAND	4.2	0.046	17.1	2.9	0.458	12.6	6.7	0.018	122.1	511.0	1,592.8
SENEGAL	12.8	0.000	15.9	11.8	..	16.6	11.3	..	680.9	1,456.8	1,456.8
URUGUAY	9.6	0.028	30.9	14.6	0.011	29.4	14.5	0.003	249.4	797.4	1,353.8
EL SALVADOR	13.9	0.018	37.8	10.7	0.018	34.2	13.6	0.028	413.7	1,088.8	1,088.8
ZIMBABWE	9.2	0.120	48.6	4.5	0.113	35.3	5.8	0.151	472.5	1,046.2	1,046.2

Notes: 1. Value of imports from partner countries that do not participate in Free Trade Agreements.

2. Weighted average tariff reduction measured by dT / (1 + T) in percent.

5

Tables R.1

Concessions Received

Exporting Economy or Group by Product Category

AFGHANISTAN Extent of other countries' MFN tariff reductions on AFGHANISTAN's exports

Summary product category	Average levels and changes weighted by value of exports to: the World exc. FTA[1]				LMIEs exc. FTA[1]				Value of exports in $ million		
	% of exports affected	Post-UR applied rate	Tariff reduc-tion[2]	Post-UR bound rate	% of exports affected	Post-UR applied rate	Tariff reduc-tion[2]	Post-UR bound rate	To IDB LMIEs exc. FTA[1]	To all IDB Ctrys exc. FTA[1]	To all IDB Ctrys inc. FTA
Agriculture, exc. Fish: Estimate 1	0.0	2.8	..	56.9	0.0	1.8	..	86.6	3.9	6.1	6.1
Agriculture, exc. Fish: Estimate 2	30.7	17.1	0.8	46.9	2.6	33.3	1.8	92.1	17.5	33.0	33.0
Fish and Fish Products	0.0	0.0	..	0.0	..	..	..	..	.0	.0	.0
Petroleum Oils	0.0	3.5	..	3.5	..	..	..	..	.0	.2	.2
Wood, Pulp, Paper and Furniture	89.7	2.5	4.2	2.5	..	..	..	..	.0	.0	.0
Textiles and Clothing	35.2	3.7	2.1	3.7	21.3	5.1	5.2	2.6	.9	42.5	42.5
Leather, Rubber, Footwear	99.0	3.3	1.5	3.4	92.2	10.5	8.7	12.0	.1	1.6	1.6
Metals	34.2	8.8	2.1	16.4	2.5	15.4	2.2	34.1	.2	.3	.3
Chemical & Photographic Suppl.	6.7	3.5	6.5	22.4	7.3	3.9	6.5	22.4	.1	.1	.1
Transport Equipment	16.7	0.7	1.3	0.7	..	..	..	..	.0	.0	.0
Non-Electric Machinery	74.3	1.4	2.6	2.0	0.0	12.7	..	35.0	.0	.2	.2
Electric Machinery	39.3	1.3	3.0	1.9	0.0	8.0	..	8.0	.0	.2	.2
Mineral Prod.,Prec. Stones & Metal	32.7	0.5	2.9	1.0	4.0	1.6	19.4	21.8	.0	1.1	1.1
Manufactured Articles nes.	4.2	0.1	0.9	0.1	2.7	1.0	13.3	1.2	2.2	48.3	48.3
Industrial Goods (line 5-14)	**20.5**	**1.8**	**2.0**	**1.9**	**10.6**	**3.1**	**7.6**	**3.6**	**3.4**	**94.3**	**94.3**
All Merch. Trade (line 2-14)	**23.1**	**5.4**	**1.6**	**12.8**	**3.9**	**27.6**	**4.4**	**76.3**	**20.9**	**127.5**	**127.5**

Notes: 1. Value of exports from reporter countries that do not participate in Free Trade Agreements with AFGHANISTAN

2. Weighted average tariff reduction measured by dT / (1 + T) in percent.

ALBANIA Extent of other countries' MFN tariff reductions on ALBANIA's exports

Summary product category	Average levels and changes weighted by value of exports to: the World exc. FTA[1]				LMIEs exc. FTA[1]				Value of exports in $ million		
	% of exports affected	Post-UR applied rate	Tariff reduc-tion[2]	Post-UR bound rate	% of exports affected	Post-UR applied rate	Tariff reduc-tion[2]	Post-UR bound rate	To IDB LMIEs exc. FTA[1]	To all IDB Ctrys exc. FTA[1]	To all IDB Ctrys inc. FTA
Agriculture, exc. Fish: Estimate 1	0.0	6.5	..	24.0	0.0	8.8	..	20.5	21.7	29.7	29.7
Agriculture, exc. Fish: Estimate 2	30.9	12.1	3.0	30.9	42.1	17.2	3.0	44.9	29.4	48.9	48.9
Fish and Fish Products	40.1	7.8	2.9	4.7	0.0	37.3	..	24.0	.2	1.6	1.6
Petroleum Oils	0.1	0.0	2.2	4.7	..	..	..	..	.0	9.8	9.8
Wood, Pulp, Paper and Furniture	73.2	1.8	4.6	1.8	97.9	7.2	3.4	7.3	.4	2.8	2.8
Textiles and Clothing	56.4	8.3	2.5	8.3	75.7	14.3	4.9	14.3	1.4	9.7	9.7
Leather, Rubber, Footwear	45.7	3.1	2.0	3.2	85.5	5.7	2.2	6.1	.3	1.0	1.0
Metals	37.7	1.7	3.0	2.0	10.9	1.0	2.1	1.9	17.6	71.3	71.3
Chemical & Photographic Suppl.	54.8	9.7	5.6	9.8	53.5	17.0	8.6	17.8	.9	1.9	1.9
Transport Equipment	100.0	9.5	0.5	9.5	100.0	9.5	0.5	9.5	.0	.0	.0
Non-Electric Machinery	96.6	4.4	2.2	4.7	94.6	6.0	1.6	6.4	.5	.8	.8
Electric Machinery	10.7	11.7	1.1	24.8	5.7	12.1	0.2	26.0	.6	.6	.6
Mineral Prod.,Prec. Stones & Metal	12.7	6.4	3.3	10.0	9.7	8.3	2.7	13.7	4.2	5.8	5.8
Manufactured Articles nes.	56.7	3.7	2.3	10.4	25.2	5.8	1.7	27.3	1.1	3.7	3.7
Industrial Goods (line 5-14)	**40.6**	**3.0**	**3.0**	**3.7**	**19.8**	**4.1**	**3.3**	**6.6**	**27.1**	**97.7**	**97.7**
All Merch. Trade (line 2-14)	**35.1**	**5.5**	**3.0**	**11.6**	**31.3**	**11.0**	**3.1**	**26.7**	**56.7**	**158.0**	**158.0**

Notes: 1. Value of exports from reporter countries that do not participate in Free Trade Agreements with ALBANIA

2. Weighted average tariff reduction measured by dT / (1 + T) in percent.

ALGERIA Extent of other countries' MFN tariff reductions on ALGERIA's exports

| Summary product category | Average levels and changes weighted by value of exports to: | | | | | | | | Value of exports in $ million | | |
| | the World exc. FTA[1] | | | | LMIEs exc. FTA[1] | | | | | | |
	% of exports affected	Post-UR applied rate	Tariff reduc-tion[2]	Post-UR bound rate	% of exports affected	Post-UR applied rate	Tariff reduc-tion[2]	Post-UR bound rate	To IDB LMIEs exc. FTA[1]	To all IDB Ctrys exc. FTA[1]	To all IDB Ctrys inc. FTA
Agriculture, exc. Fish: Estimate 1	0.1	4.3	14.3	4.4	0.0	0.0	..	54.2	.0	13.0	13.0
Agriculture, exc. Fish: Estimate 2	40.0	5.7	4.8	6.0	0.0	32.5	..	113.0	.1	30.2	30.2
Fish and Fish Products	61.2	5.2	2.3	5.2	..	..	..	..	.0	1.3	1.3
Petroleum Oils	4.8	0.7	1.2	1.2	0.0	1.6	..	4.9	518.3	5,687.4	5,687.4
Wood, Pulp, Paper and Furniture	18.7	0.9	3.4	0.7	0.0	26.3	..	43.0	.1	13.2	13.2
Textiles and Clothing	96.2	7.7	2.5	7.7	100.0	40.0	13.3	40.0	.0	1.5	1.5
Leather, Rubber, Footwear	82.6	5.2	1.7	3.3	0.0	26.1	..	..	.1	.7	.7
Metals	55.5	4.1	4.1	6.3	9.0	12.5	9.5	24.1	49.7	163.0	163.0
Chemical & Photographic Suppl.	58.3	4.8	6.4	4.5	3.2	20.0	13.0	22.1	2.4	31.8	31.8
Transport Equipment	40.5	15.1	4.5	15.1	0.0	28.5	..	28.5	2.8	9.4	9.4
Non-Electric Machinery	95.0	1.3	3.6	1.4	0.0	11.0	..	15.4	.4	18.6	18.6
Electric Machinery	68.3	11.6	3.1	13.1	0.1	34.8	2.9	43.7	.7	2.4	2.4
Mineral Prod.,Prec. Stones & Metal	16.2	0.3	1.6	0.8	0.0	2.8	5.4	15.2	145.4	1,820.4	1,820.4
Manufactured Articles nes.	3.5	0.2	3.9	0.1	2.2	26.4	0.3	0.9	.2	37.9	37.9
Industrial Goods (line 5-14)	**20.6**	**0.8**	**2.5**	**1.3**	**2.3**	**6.7**	**9.6**	**22.2**	**201.7**	**2,099.1**	**2,099.1**
All Merch. Trade (line 2-14)	**9.2**	**0.8**	**2.0**	**1.2**	**0.6**	**3.7**	**9.6**	**9.5**	**720.2**	**7,818.0**	**7,818.0**

Notes: 1. Value of exports from reporter countries that do not participate in Free Trade Agreements with ALGERIA

2. Weighted average tariff reduction measured by dT / (1 + T) in percent.

ANGOLA Extent of other countries' MFN tariff reductions on ANGOLA's exports

| Summary product category | Average levels and changes weighted by value of exports to: | | | | | | | | Value of exports in $ million | | |
| | the World exc. FTA[1] | | | | LMIEs exc. FTA[1] | | | | | | |
	% of exports affected	Post-UR applied rate	Tariff reduc-tion[2]	Post-UR bound rate	% of exports affected	Post-UR applied rate	Tariff reduc-tion[2]	Post-UR bound rate	To IDB LMIEs exc. FTA[1]	To all IDB Ctrys exc. FTA[1]	To all IDB Ctrys inc. FTA
Agriculture, exc. Fish: Estimate 1	0.0	0.0	..	0.3	..	..	..	..	.0	30.7	30.7
Agriculture, exc. Fish: Estimate 2	95.6	0.7	4.7	0.9	..	..	..	..	.0	30.9	30.9
Fish and Fish Products	80.1	11.3	5.6	11.3	..	..	..	..	.0	30.1	30.1
Petroleum Oils	0.0	0.6	..	0.3	0.0	5.9	..	3.5	117.1	2,496.7	2,496.7
Wood, Pulp, Paper and Furniture	18.6	0.3	4.4	0.4	0.0	0.0	..	30.0	.0	.3	.3
Textiles and Clothing	80.2	8.6	1.8	10.8	100.0	6.0	2.7	6.0	.0	.2	.2
Leather, Rubber, Footwear	94.1	4.2	2.8	4.2	..	..	..	..	.0	.0	.0
Metals	100.0	2.3	2.5	2.3	..	..	..	..	.0	.2	.2
Chemical & Photographic Suppl.	54.1	5.5	5.8	12.8	50.0	6.3	6.1	15.3	.1	.1	.1
Transport Equipment	28.0	0.8	1.0	0.8	..	..	..	..	.0	.4	.4
Non-Electric Machinery	52.1	0.9	2.5	0.9	..	..	..	..	.0	1.9	1.9
Electric Machinery	96.4	2.8	2.0	2.8	..	..	..	..	.0	.2	.2
Mineral Prod.,Prec. Stones & Metal	0.0	0.0	1.0	0.0	0.0	..	..	..	17.0	203.6	203.6
Manufactured Articles nes.	88.3	2.6	3.0	2.6	0.0	..	..	..	.0	.2	.2
Industrial Goods (line 5-14)	**1.0**	**0.0**	**2.5**	**0.0**	**0.2**	**6.2**	**5.6**	**14.9**	**17.1**	**207.1**	**207.1**
All Merch. Trade (line 2-14)	**2.0**	**0.7**	**5.0**	**0.6**	**0.0**	**5.9**	**5.6**	**3.5**	**134.2**	**2,764.9**	**2,764.9**

Notes: 1. Value of exports from reporter countries that do not participate in Free Trade Agreements with ANGOLA

2. Weighted average tariff reduction measured by dT / (1 + T) in percent.

ANTIGUA & BARBUDA Extent of other countries' MFN tariff reductions on ANTIGUA & BARBUDA's exports

Summary product category	Average levels and changes weighted by value of exports to: the World exc. FTA[1]				LMIEs exc. FTA[1]				Value of exports in $ million		
	% of exports affected	Post-UR applied rate	Tariff reduc- tion[2]	Post-UR bound rate	% of exports affected	Post-UR applied rate	Tariff reduc- tion[2]	Post-UR bound rate	To IDB LMIEs exc. FTA[1]	To all IDB Ctrys exc. FTA[1]	To all IDB Ctrys inc. FTA
Agriculture, exc. Fish: Estimate 1	0.0	7.0	..	7.0	..	..	..	..	.0	.7	.7
Agriculture, exc. Fish: Estimate 2	87.8	8.9	2.7	8.9	0.0	50.0	..	50.0	.0	3.5	3.5
Fish and Fish Products	16.2	0.0	0.6	0.0	..	..	..	..	.0	.5	.5
Petroleum Oils	0.0	7.4	..	35.0	0.0	15.0	..	35.0	6.8	14.3	14.3
Wood, Pulp, Paper and Furniture	71.4	15.0	3.2	16.2	0.0	45.0	..	50.0	.0	.1	.1
Textiles and Clothing	99.7	4.5	2.8	4.5	0.0	44.0	..	55.0	.0	1.5	1.5
Leather, Rubber, Footwear	81.2	10.6	6.3	10.6	..	..	..	..	.0	.1	.1
Metals	31.4	2.1	3.2	2.1	..	..	..	..	.0	.4	.4
Chemical & Photographic Suppl.	26.5	3.4	1.2	3.9	..	..	..	..	.0	.2	.2
Transport Equipment	1.4	1.3	2.3	1.3	..	..	..	..	.0	1.3	1.3
Non-Electric Machinery	20.2	0.4	2.5	0.5	0.0	15.4	..	31.4	.0	1.0	1.0
Electric Machinery	75.7	2.5	2.7	3.0	0.0	12.5	..	42.5	.0	.1	.1
Mineral Prod.,Prec. Stones & Metal	48.0	1.3	1.0	1.3	..	..	..	..	.0	.2	.2
Manufactured Articles nes.	10.3	0.4	2.7	0.4	..	..	..	..	.0	2.3	2.3
Industrial Goods (line 5-14)	**34.6**	**2.1**	**2.9**	**2.1**	**0.0**	**38.3**	**..**	**46.7**	**.0**	**7.3**	**7.3**
All Merch. Trade (line 2-14)	**22.3**	**5.9**	**2.7**	**15.7**	**0.0**	**15.3**	**..**	**35.1**	**6.8**	**25.6**	**25.6**

Notes: 1. Value of exports from reporter countries that do not participate in Free Trade Agreements with Antigua.&Barbuda

2. Weighted average tariff reduction measured by dT / (1 + T) in percent.

ARGENTINA Extent of other countries' MFN tariff reductions on ARGENTINA's exports

Summary product category	Average levels and changes weighted by value of exports to: the World exc. FTA[1]				LMIEs exc. FTA[1]				Value of exports in $ million		
	% of exports affected	Post-UR applied rate	Tariff reduc- tion[2]	Post-UR bound rate	% of exports affected	Post-UR applied rate	Tariff reduc- tion[2]	Post-UR bound rate	To IDB LMIEs exc. FTA[1]	To all IDB Ctrys exc. FTA[1]	To all IDB Ctrys inc. FTA
Agriculture, exc. Fish: Estimate 1	14.4	22.9	22.0	34.4	8.0	4.8	41.6	50.4	611.3	3,062.5	3,409.1
Agriculture, exc. Fish: Estimate 2	17.6	5.2	4.0	15.0	7.8	16.3	3.0	37.7	634.6	3,542.6	4,213.2
Fish and Fish Products	45.0	6.5	4.3	9.7	3.1	16.3	4.3	33.9	6.6	328.1	371.0
Petroleum Oils	5.7	3.7	1.3	10.5	0.5	14.5	4.7	34.6	42.3	224.0	246.4
Wood, Pulp, Paper and Furniture	16.2	1.0	3.2	7.0	0.4	2.1	18.6	16.1	19.0	119.7	174.0
Textiles and Clothing	49.5	6.7	2.6	12.2	5.2	12.9	7.0	30.5	21.9	247.9	296.4
Leather, Rubber, Footwear	41.2	4.2	2.9	8.4	37.5	9.3	6.7	23.8	71.9	594.0	649.0
Metals	48.7	4.3	3.9	10.9	5.5	14.4	11.5	29.6	146.0	620.0	743.3
Chemical & Photographic Suppl.	27.6	5.1	5.7	14.0	4.5	10.9	9.1	23.2	96.7	345.4	547.2
Transport Equipment	24.9	7.5	1.5	20.9	2.4	14.0	5.9	27.6	21.8	58.7	130.6
Non-Electric Machinery	23.9	4.4	3.9	19.1	4.7	11.2	12.5	30.6	59.2	180.2	297.5
Electric Machinery	23.1	7.9	2.3	24.4	0.2	12.0	7.2	31.6	6.7	13.6	26.3
Mineral Prod.,Prec. Stones & Metal	20.1	3.6	3.3	21.9	0.0	3.6	3.6	33.5	16.9	57.7	119.0
Manufactured Articles nes.	16.2	1.8	3.2	7.4	18.8	6.3	1.6	23.8	51.1	233.4	258.0
Industrial Goods (line 5-14)	**34.9**	**4.3**	**3.6**	**12.3**	**8.2**	**10.1**	**7.5**	**26.6**	**511.3**	**2,470.4**	**3,241.3**
All Merch. Trade (line 2-14)	**25.4**	**4.8**	**3.8**	**13.5**	**7.7**	**13.4**	**5.3**	**32.4**	**1,194.8**	**6,565.2**	**8,071.9**

Notes: 1. Value of exports from reporter countries that do not participate in Free Trade Agreements with ARGENTINA

2. Weighted average tariff reduction measured by dT / (1 + T) in percent.

ARUBA Extent of other countries' MFN tariff reductions on ARUBA's exports

Summary product category	Average levels and changes weighted by value of exports to: the World exc. FTA[1]				LMIEs exc. FTA[1]				Value of exports in $ million		
	% of exports affected	Post-UR applied rate	Tariff reduc-tion[2]	Post-UR bound rate	% of exports affected	Post-UR applied rate	Tariff reduc-tion[2]	Post-UR bound rate	To IDB LMIEs exc. FTA[1]	To all IDB Ctrys exc. FTA[1]	To all IDB Ctrys inc. FTA
Agriculture, exc. Fish: Estimate 1	0.0	0.0	..	0.0	..	..	..	..	.0	1.8	1.8
Agriculture, exc. Fish: Estimate 2	96.5	1.3	4.5	1.3	..	..	..	..	.0	2.1	2.1
Fish and Fish Products	0.0	0.0	..	0.0	..	..	..	..	.0	.0	.0
Petroleum Oils	0.0	0.4	..	2.4	..	..	..	..	.0	2.0	2.0
Wood, Pulp, Paper and Furniture	55.0	2.8	5.4	5.2	0.0	18.4	..	35.0	.0	.0	.0
Textiles and Clothing	99.8	34.4	3.6	34.4	99.8	35.0	3.6	35.0	.6	.6	.6
Leather, Rubber, Footwear	66.7	19.0	3.1	19.0	100.0	35.0	3.6	35.0	.0	.0	.0
Metals	11.2	3.9	3.1	13.4	0.0	14.2	..	35.0	.4	1.3	1.3
Chemical & Photographic Suppl.	65.0	4.8	8.3	12.9	0.0	9.5	..	35.0	.1	.2	.2
Transport Equipment	33.3	8.7	1.2	18.5	0.0	12.0	..	35.0	.0	.0	.0
Non-Electric Machinery	55.5	5.7	3.7	14.9	0.0	12.1	..	32.9	.1	.2	.2
Electric Machinery	83.5	3.9	2.5	4.9	0.0	10.2	..	35.0	.0	.1	.1
Mineral Prod.,Prec. Stones & Metal	1.8	7.2	2.5	26.2	0.0	9.5	..	35.0	.3	.4	.4
Manufactured Articles nes.	85.8	8.9	12.5	11.3	0.0	8.9	..	32.0	.2	1.4	1.4
Industrial Goods (line 5-14)	**53.9**	**10.3**	**8.4**	**16.9**	**37.4**	**20.2**	**3.6**	**34.6**	**1.6**	**4.3**	**4.3**
All Merch. Trade (line 2-14)	**51.7**	**5.8**	**6.6**	**11.4**	**37.4**	**20.2**	**3.6**	**34.6**	**1.6**	**8.3**	**8.3**

Notes: 1. Value of exports from reporter countries that do not participate in Free Trade Agreements with ARUBA

2. Weighted average tariff reduction measured by dT / (1 + T) in percent.

AUSTRALIA Extent of other countries' MFN tariff reductions on AUSTRALIA's exports

Summary product category	Average levels and changes weighted by value of exports to: the World exc. FTA[1]				LMIEs exc. FTA[1]				Value of exports in $ million		
	% of exports affected	Post-UR applied rate	Tariff reduc-tion[2]	Post-UR bound rate	% of exports affected	Post-UR applied rate	Tariff reduc-tion[2]	Post-UR bound rate	To IDB LMIEs exc. FTA[1]	To all IDB Ctrys exc. FTA[1]	To all IDB Ctrys inc. FTA
Agriculture, exc. Fish: Estimate 1	30.9	45.8	26.9	48.1	46.3	43.2	37.8	54.1	868.2	3,708.8	3,778.8
Agriculture, exc. Fish: Estimate 2	21.3	13.0	6.5	26.3	23.0	8.8	3.6	33.0	963.8	4,564.3	4,803.2
Fish and Fish Products	50.4	2.3	2.6	2.5	45.2	12.7	40.7	5.9	6.9	566.5	568.8
Petroleum Oils	0.6	1.6	2.7	11.1	1.3	7.3	6.0	38.9	94.7	501.1	616.2
Wood, Pulp, Paper and Furniture	7.2	0.8	5.1	4.4	26.5	8.8	6.3	22.9	62.0	567.4	697.5
Textiles and Clothing	17.9	1.4	4.0	3.3	50.7	5.0	6.7	8.6	492.9	2,587.0	2,704.3
Leather, Rubber, Footwear	34.4	3.8	3.0	8.6	60.3	15.1	8.7	19.0	18.7	145.8	176.0
Metals	25.9	1.3	2.5	2.4	25.1	6.1	6.3	9.7	1,407.1	7,037.5	7,244.3
Chemical & Photographic Suppl.	9.2	1.9	6.2	7.2	16.1	8.0	12.0	29.4	577.5	2,453.4	2,841.8
Transport Equipment	17.4	3.4	3.6	11.9	16.9	25.3	29.5	39.7	31.8	273.5	399.3
Non-Electric Machinery	55.0	3.6	3.4	6.9	39.8	14.7	8.4	21.9	134.6	711.1	843.1
Electric Machinery	27.1	5.5	3.2	14.6	17.1	18.4	8.7	28.5	52.1	203.2	296.3
Mineral Prod.,Prec. Stones & Metal	16.1	0.8	2.2	2.1	8.1	5.2	12.2	12.7	990.5	6,259.6	6,305.1
Manufactured Articles nes.	18.6	1.3	4.8	3.1	41.0	4.8	6.9	10.8	406.2	1,817.6	1,906.1
Industrial Goods (line 5-14)	**20.2**	**1.4**	**3.1**	**3.6**	**24.9**	**6.5**	**7.8**	**14.1**	**4,173.3**	**22,056.0**	**23,413.8**
All Merch. Trade (line 2-14)	**20.5**	**3.1**	**3.7**	**7.2**	**24.1**	**7.0**	**7.1**	**18.0**	**5,238.6**	**27,687.9**	**29,402.0**

Notes: 1. Value of exports from reporter countries that do not participate in Free Trade Agreements with AUSTRALIA

2. Weighted average tariff reduction measured by dT / (1 + T) in percent.

Tables R.1. Concessions Received: *Exporting Economy or Group by Product Category*

AUSTRIA Extent of other countries' MFN tariff reductions on AUSTRIA's exports

Summary product category	Average levels and changes weighted by value of exports to: the World exc. FTA[1]				LMIEs exc. FTA[1]				Value of exports in $ million		
	% of exports affected	Post-UR applied rate	Tariff reduction[2]	Post-UR bound rate	% of exports affected	Post-UR applied rate	Tariff reduction[2]	Post-UR bound rate	To IDB LMIEs exc. FTA[1]	To all IDB Ctrys exc. FTA[1]	To all IDB Ctrys inc. FTA
Agriculture, exc. Fish: Estimate 1	35.1	61.2	6.8	72.8	7.4	0.9	19.8	43.5	119.8	438.8	438.8
Agriculture, exc. Fish: Estimate 2	22.9	9.8	4.5	24.6	26.4	18.2	3.3	55.9	181.1	971.2	971.2
Fish and Fish Products	2.4	13.3	1.9	9.0	3.2	17.1	1.6	15.1	1.8	1.9	4.0
Petroleum Oils	37.5	6.8	1.1	5.5	55.8	6.9	1.1	6.0	90.7	90.7	134.9
Wood, Pulp, Paper and Furniture	4.3	0.8	3.6	1.4	42.6	9.9	3.0	8.2	247.6	357.1	3,721.3
Textiles and Clothing	10.3	10.2	4.0	8.3	66.5	11.8	4.2	12.0	299.8	420.1	2,822.2
Leather, Rubber, Footwear	6.7	3.3	3.8	5.4	69.6	8.8	3.7	9.9	63.5	176.1	988.1
Metals	10.3	1.8	3.6	2.9	55.7	9.4	3.3	11.6	346.9	618.1	3,904.6
Chemical & Photographic Suppl.	11.9	4.1	4.5	5.7	47.6	7.9	4.5	11.2	481.9	690.8	2,686.2
Transport Equipment	6.4	7.9	2.1	6.0	38.3	14.5	2.2	16.5	121.1	170.3	1,260.5
Non-Electric Machinery	21.8	4.2	2.1	3.7	73.7	7.1	1.8	9.0	1,030.7	1,491.7	5,090.5
Electric Machinery	9.7	8.0	2.8	6.6	64.5	10.8	2.6	11.5	361.4	483.0	2,915.4
Mineral Prod.,Prec. Stones & Metal	13.4	2.8	3.4	3.7	49.0	10.5	4.0	13.1	167.2	398.9	1,384.7
Manufactured Articles nes.	22.9	2.8	3.3	3.9	67.7	7.9	3.2	10.8	385.2	849.4	2,631.5
Industrial Goods (line 5-14)	**12.8**	**3.1**	**3.1**	**4.4**	**61.4**	**8.9**	**2.9**	**10.6**	**3,505.1**	**5,655.6**	**27,405.0**
All Merch. Trade (line 2-14)	**13.2**	**3.4**	**3.1**	**4.8**	**59.6**	**9.3**	**2.9**	**12.8**	**3,778.7**	**6,719.4**	**28,515.0**

Notes: 1. Value of exports from reporter countries that do not participate in Free Trade Agreements with AUSTRIA

2. Weighted average tariff reduction measured by dT / (1 + T) in percent.

BAHAMAS, THE Extent of other countries' MFN tariff reductions on the BAHAMAS's exports

Summary product category	Average levels and changes weighted by value of exports to: the World exc. FTA[1]				LMIEs exc. FTA[1]				Value of exports in $ million		
	% of exports affected	Post-UR applied rate	Tariff reduction[2]	Post-UR bound rate	% of exports affected	Post-UR applied rate	Tariff reduction[2]	Post-UR bound rate	To IDB LMIEs exc. FTA[1]	To all IDB Ctrys exc. FTA[1]	To all IDB Ctrys inc. FTA
Agriculture, exc. Fish: Estimate 1	7.3	5.1	5.9	7.8	0.0	-9.0	..	19.0	.0	.4	.4
Agriculture, exc. Fish: Estimate 2	89.5	13.1	7.5	13.1	0.0	21.8	..	33.9	.2	29.0	29.0
Fish and Fish Products	31.2	3.7	9.8	3.7	..	..	..	..	.0	34.9	34.9
Petroleum Oils	0.0	0.4	2.2	0.7	..	..	..	..	.0	118.1	118.1
Wood, Pulp, Paper and Furniture	7.5	0.1	4.8	0.1	0.0	0.3	..	1.2	.0	1.5	1.5
Textiles and Clothing	87.6	17.3	5.4	17.3	100.0	40.0	13.3	40.0	.0	.4	.4
Leather, Rubber, Footwear	100.0	4.6	1.5	4.6	..	..	..	..	.0	.0	.0
Metals	3.9	0.3	6.8	8.6	1.5	0.2	4.7	9.4	12.0	13.2	13.2
Chemical & Photographic Suppl.	97.0	5.6	1.1	5.9	8.4	9.4	7.8	27.2	5.8	381.7	381.7
Transport Equipment	59.5	1.9	0.9	2.3	0.0	2.7	..	50.0	.0	.1	.1
Non-Electric Machinery	60.8	5.9	2.6	14.1	0.3	12.7	0.5	34.8	2.2	5.9	5.9
Electric Machinery	26.9	9.5	3.1	27.2	0.0	12.0	..	36.6	.8	1.1	1.1
Mineral Prod.,Prec. Stones & Metal	1.4	0.2	1.6	0.3	2.0	12.2	13.3	36.1	.1	20.3	20.3
Manufactured Articles nes.	0.9	0.1	1.9	0.9	0.3	7.5	3.3	13.5	2.2	263.8	263.8
Industrial Goods (line 5-14)	**54.9**	**3.2**	**1.1**	**4.0**	**3.1**	**4.9**	**7.3**	**17.7**	**23.3**	**688.0**	**688.0**
All Merch. Trade (line 2-14)	**47.7**	**3.2**	**1.7**	**3.9**	**3.1**	**5.1**	**7.3**	**17.9**	**23.5**	**870.0**	**870.0**

Notes: 1. Value of exports from reporter countries that do not participate in Free Trade Agreements with the BAHAMAS

2. Weighted average tariff reduction measured by dT / (1 + T) in percent.

BAHRAIN Extent of other countries' MFN tariff reductions on BAHRAIN's exports

Summary product category	Average levels and changes weighted by value of exports to: the World exc. FTA[1]				LMIEs exc. FTA[1]				Value of exports in $ million		
	% of exports affected	Post-UR applied rate	Tariff reduc-tion[2]	Post-UR bound rate	% of exports affected	Post-UR applied rate	Tariff reduc-tion[2]	Post-UR bound rate	To IDB LMIEs exc. FTA[1]	To all IDB Ctrys exc. FTA[1]	To all IDB Ctrys inc. FTA
Agriculture, exc. Fish: Estimate 1	0.9	0.8	5.9	0.8	..	..	..	..	.0	.2	.2
Agriculture, exc. Fish: Estimate 2	30.4	5.3	3.7	9.1	74.9	10.1	2.9	21.2	.3	1.0	1.0
Fish and Fish Products	82.0	8.5	4.6	8.6	0.0	5.0	..	50.0	.0	1.2	1.2
Petroleum Oils	0.0	4.2	..	1.5	0.0	2.0	..	5.0	14.9	448.8	448.8
Wood, Pulp, Paper and Furniture	6.5	3.6	6.1	8.2	0.4	16.2	7.4	39.9	.2	1.1	1.1
Textiles and Clothing	94.8	16.5	1.1	16.6	0.8	16.0	13.3	48.2	.6	13.4	13.4
Leather, Rubber, Footwear	78.2	3.9	1.6	5.2	..	..	..	..	.0	.3	.3
Metals	51.9	6.9	2.3	3.8	49.2	21.0	6.1	7.5	63.8	263.5	263.5
Chemical & Photographic Suppl.	87.1	7.3	9.1	8.1	82.1	12.6	11.9	15.3	13.9	44.9	44.9
Transport Equipment	3.0	2.0	2.8	5.1	0.0	115.3	..	3.0	.0	2.5	2.5
Non-Electric Machinery	33.9	0.9	2.1	1.0	5.9	39.2	11.4	16.0	.0	14.8	14.8
Electric Machinery	88.2	3.6	2.1	3.6	2.8	7.8	12.3	7.7	.2	1.6	1.6
Mineral Prod.,Prec. Stones & Metal	28.8	0.2	4.4	1.1	0.0	0.4	13.3	13.2	5.1	41.7	41.7
Manufactured Articles nes.	46.9	3.5	5.2	4.9	88.5	32.6	14.3	30.6	.4	5.1	5.1
Industrial Goods (line 5-14)	**53.9**	**6.2**	**3.6**	**4.4**	**51.2**	**18.3**	**7.7**	**10.0**	**84.3**	**388.8**	**388.8**
All Merch. Trade (line 2-14)	**25.1**	**5.5**	**3.6**	**4.1**	**43.6**	**16.1**	**7.7**	**9.1**	**99.4**	**839.8**	**839.8**

Notes: 1. Value of exports from reporter countries that do not participate in Free Trade Agreements with BAHRAIN

2. Weighted average tariff reduction measured by dT / (1 + T) in percent.

BANGLADESH Extent of other countries' MFN tariff reductions on BANGLADESH's exports

Summary product category	Average levels and changes weighted by value of exports to: the World exc. FTA[1]				LMIEs exc. FTA[1]				Value of exports in $ million		
	% of exports affected	Post-UR applied rate	Tariff reduc-tion[2]	Post-UR bound rate	% of exports affected	Post-UR applied rate	Tariff reduc-tion[2]	Post-UR bound rate	To IDB LMIEs exc. FTA[1]	To all IDB Ctrys exc. FTA[1]	To all IDB Ctrys inc. FTA
Agriculture, exc. Fish: Estimate 1	0.7	-0.4	14.0	8.2	0.1	-1.4	1.2	22.2	12.7	34.8	34.8
Agriculture, exc. Fish: Estimate 2	14.3	3.9	4.6	7.0	3.7	17.0	6.2	38.4	4.1	30.9	30.9
Fish and Fish Products	63.1	4.3	3.6	4.5	4.8	0.2	41.5	5.0	3.4	188.0	188.0
Petroleum Oils	0.0	1.2	..	4.2	0.0	2.0	..	5.0	4.0	32.9	32.9
Wood, Pulp, Paper and Furniture	4.1	1.1	6.0	23.4	0.4	5.1	13.4	24.9	6.9	7.4	7.4
Textiles and Clothing	87.9	12.1	2.0	12.5	48.3	10.3	6.3	18.6	33.6	707.8	707.8
Leather, Rubber, Footwear	36.7	2.8	1.5	7.7	4.1	6.6	8.2	33.3	19.8	158.3	158.3
Metals	11.0	0.8	2.8	1.5	0.0	8.9	..	..	.0	1.0	1.0
Chemical & Photographic Suppl.	12.9	3.9	2.8	21.1	1.4	6.2	4.3	31.1	1.2	2.2	2.2
Transport Equipment	40.8	2.7	2.3	0.8	0.0	50.0	..	..	.0	.1	.1
Non-Electric Machinery	18.7	1.9	3.2	2.1	23.5	26.5	16.7	15.5	.1	1.5	1.5
Electric Machinery	63.6	2.3	2.3	5.3	6.9	19.3	6.0	32.6	.1	1.6	1.6
Mineral Prod.,Prec. Stones & Metal	8.9	10.0	1.4	5.8	0.0	10.1	..	5.0	10.2	11.9	11.9
Manufactured Articles nes.	40.1	3.2	4.0	48.1	5.8	5.1	5.7	135.5	2.1	6.3	6.3
Industrial Goods (line 5-14)	**76.4**	**10.3**	**2.0**	**12.1**	**23.3**	**9.0**	**6.4**	**26.7**	**73.9**	**898.0**	**898.0**
All Merch. Trade (line 2-14)	**70.4**	**9.0**	**2.2**	**10.6**	**20.5**	**8.7**	**6.7**	**26.0**	**85.5**	**1,149.9**	**1,149.9**

Notes: 1. Value of exports from reporter countries that do not participate in Free Trade Agreements with BANGLADESH

2. Weighted average tariff reduction measured by dT / (1 + T) in percent.

BARBADOS Extent of other countries' MFN tariff reductions on BARBADOS's exports

Summary product category	Average levels and changes weighted by value of exports to: the World exc. FTA[1]				LMIEs exc. FTA[1]				Value of exports in $ million		
	% of exports affected	Post-UR applied rate	Tariff reduc-tion[2]	Post-UR bound rate	% of exports affected	Post-UR applied rate	Tariff reduc-tion[2]	Post-UR bound rate	To IDB LMIEs exc. FTA[1]	To all IDB Ctrys exc. FTA[1]	To all IDB Ctrys inc. FTA
Agriculture, exc. Fish: Estimate 1	0.0	139.4	33.9	139.5	0.0	0.0	..	100.0	.0	29.7	29.7
Agriculture, exc. Fish: Estimate 2	19.7	9.9	3.3	20.8	0.0	31.6	..	100.0	1.6	38.9	38.9
Fish and Fish Products	9.5	0.6	4.1	0.6	..	..	..	..	.0	.8	.8
Petroleum Oils	0.0	0.0	..	..	..	..	..	..	.0	.7	.7
Wood, Pulp, Paper and Furniture	6.0	16.4	4.8	43.7	0.0	18.1	..	48.3	1.8	2.0	2.0
Textiles and Clothing	85.0	12.0	5.7	12.0	0.0	45.0	..	50.0	.0	7.5	7.5
Leather, Rubber, Footwear	40.0	11.3	2.9	11.8	0.0	45.0	..	50.0	.0	.0	.0
Metals	36.3	9.7	2.8	24.1	0.0	18.0	..	50.0	2.6	5.8	5.8
Chemical & Photographic Suppl.	11.6	28.8	6.8	39.8	0.0	35.6	..	49.8	2.1	2.7	2.7
Transport Equipment	93.8	11.7	2.2	13.2	84.5	33.8	1.8	39.4	.1	.4	.4
Non-Electric Machinery	67.6	2.2	2.5	2.5	0.0	13.2		37.3	.0	.8	.8
Electric Machinery	73.8	3.6	2.6	3.6	..	..	..	..	.0	24.4	24.4
Mineral Prod.,Prec. Stones & Metal	0.0	1.6	6.8	3.3	0.0	15.0	..	30.0	.3	2.5	2.5
Manufactured Articles nes.	65.8	1.6	3.0	1.7	0.0	45.0		50.0	.0	3.5	3.5
Industrial Goods (line 5-14)	**60.9**	**7.2**	**3.4**	**10.7**	**1.4**	**23.6**	**1.8**	**48.5**	**6.9**	**49.6**	**49.6**
All Merch. Trade (line 2-14)	**42.2**	**7.5**	**3.3**	**12.2**	**1.2**	**25.1**	**1.8**	**58.2**	**8.5**	**90.0**	**90.0**

Notes: 1. Value of exports from reporter countries that do not participate in Free Trade Agreements with BARBADOS

2. Weighted average tariff reduction measured by dT / (1 + T) in percent.

BELIZE Extent of other countries' MFN tariff reductions on BELIZE's exports

Summary product category	Average levels and changes weighted by value of exports to: the World exc. FTA[1]				LMIEs exc. FTA[1]				Value of exports in $ million		
	% of exports affected	Post-UR applied rate	Tariff reduc-tion[2]	Post-UR bound rate	% of exports affected	Post-UR applied rate	Tariff reduc-tion[2]	Post-UR bound rate	To IDB LMIEs exc. FTA[1]	To all IDB Ctrys exc. FTA[1]	To all IDB Ctrys inc. FTA
Agriculture, exc. Fish: Estimate 1	0.0	77.3	..	83.1	0.0	-1.6	..	48.6	6.4	54.6	54.6
Agriculture, exc. Fish: Estimate 2	17.4	15.4	3.5	20.8	0.0	24.3	..	47.1	9.5	78.9	78.9
Fish and Fish Products	15.6	1.9	10.0	1.9	..	..	..	..	.0	8.0	8.0
Petroleum Oils	0.0	0.4	..	0.7	..	..	..	..	.0	.0	.0
Wood, Pulp, Paper and Furniture	3.6	9.4	4.4	26.9	0.0	13.3	..	38.4	2.5	3.6	3.6
Textiles and Clothing	99.4	16.0	1.1	16.1	0.0	24.0	..	37.4	.1	15.7	15.7
Leather, Rubber, Footwear	20.7	7.1	5.3	11.2	0.0	19.0	..	35.0	.1	.3	.3
Metals	23.0	2.3	6.1	4.1	3.2	16.9	7.4	34.2	.3	1.6	1.6
Chemical & Photographic Suppl.	39.6	11.0	3.4	23.6	0.0	15.4	..	36.3	.2	.3	.3
Transport Equipment	52.2	12.2	2.8	21.0	0.0	19.3	..	38.0	.1	.3	.3
Non-Electric Machinery	16.7	13.2	3.5	28.4	0.2	15.6	8.0	34.2	.6	.7	.7
Electric Machinery	0.1	11.7	2.5	25.6	0.0	16.0	..	35.0	2.8	3.8	3.8
Mineral Prod.,Prec. Stones & Metal	36.7	6.6	1.8	4.2	0.0	12.3	..	9.8	.2	.4	.4
Manufactured Articles nes.	14.2	11.8	3.1	25.0	0.7	13.7	0.9	30.2	1.8	2.2	2.2
Industrial Goods (line 5-14)	**58.7**	**13.2**	**1.3**	**19.0**	**0.2**	**14.8**	**3.7**	**34.8**	**8.6**	**29.0**	**29.0**
All Merch. Trade (line 2-14)	**27.6**	**13.2**	**2.6**	**18.2**	**0.1**	**19.8**	**3.7**	**41.3**	**18.2**	**115.9**	**115.9**

Notes: 1. Value of exports from reporter countries that do not participate in Free Trade Agreements with BELIZE

2. Weighted average tariff reduction measured by dT / (1 + T) in percent.

BENIN Extent of other countries' MFN tariff reductions on BENIN's exports

Summary product category	Average levels and changes weighted by value of exports to: the World exc. FTA[1]				LMIEs exc. FTA[1]				Value of exports in $ million		
	% of exports affected	Post-UR applied rate	Tariff reduc-tion[2]	Post-UR bound rate	% of exports affected	Post-UR applied rate	Tariff reduc-tion[2]	Post-UR bound rate	To IDB LMIEs exc. FTA[1]	To all IDB Ctrys exc. FTA[1]	To all IDB Ctrys inc. FTA
Agriculture, exc. Fish: Estimate 1	0.6	0.2	14.3	0.6	0.0	0.0	..	2.6	4.6	31.2	31.2
Agriculture, exc. Fish: Estimate 2	67.7	4.2	3.9	4.8	57.0	19.0	11.1	49.6	.2	11.4	11.4
Fish and Fish Products	99.2	12.0	5.2	12.0	..	..	..	..	.0	.9	.9
Petroleum Oils	0.0	0.4	..	..	..	..	..	..	.0	6.5	6.5
Wood, Pulp, Paper and Furniture	6.5	0.8	3.8	0.2	0.0	15.0	..	..	.0	.3	.3
Textiles and Clothing	59.8	10.6	1.9	6.2	30.1	16.5	2.2	10.5	.3	.5	.5
Leather, Rubber, Footwear	86.5	3.8	1.3	3.8	..	..	..	..	.0	.0	.0
Metals	35.1	1.1	2.9	1.1	..	..	..	..	.0	.3	.3
Chemical & Photographic Suppl.	86.9	2.5	4.9	2.3	0.0	15.0	..	..	.0	.2	.2
Transport Equipment	1.0	0.2	1.9	0.2	0.0	16.5	..	50.0	.0	6.9	6.9
Non-Electric Machinery	48.3	1.7	3.2	4.7	0.0	10.0	..	40.0	.0	.4	.4
Electric Machinery	5.4	7.4	2.9	14.2	0.0	15.5	..	35.1	.3	.8	.8
Mineral Prod.,Prec. Stones & Metal	99.3	4.1	3.7	4.0	0.0	15.0	..	..	.0	.1	.1
Manufactured Articles nes.	6.8	2.8	2.3	8.8	26.1	12.7	0.5	41.3	4.6	21.6	21.6
Industrial Goods (line 5-14)	**8.2**	**2.4**	**2.6**	**6.7**	**24.6**	**13.0**	**0.6**	**40.1**	**5.2**	**31.2**	**31.2**
All Merch. Trade (line 2-14)	**22.5**	**2.7**	**3.7**	**6.3**	**25.9**	**13.2**	**1.5**	**40.5**	**5.4**	**50.0**	**50.0**

Notes: 1. Value of exports from reporter countries that do not participate in Free Trade Agreements with BENIN

2. Weighted average tariff reduction measured by dT / (1 + T) in percent.

BERMUDA Extent of other countries' MFN tariff reductions on BERMUDA's exports

Summary product category	Average levels and changes weighted by value of exports to: the World exc. FTA[1]				LMIEs exc. FTA[1]				Value of exports in $ million		
	% of exports affected	Post-UR applied rate	Tariff reduc-tion[2]	Post-UR bound rate	% of exports affected	Post-UR applied rate	Tariff reduc-tion[2]	Post-UR bound rate	To IDB LMIEs exc. FTA[1]	To all IDB Ctrys exc. FTA[1]	To all IDB Ctrys inc. FTA
Agriculture, exc. Fish: Estimate 1	0.8	0.5	43.6	94.4	0.0	..	..	106.0	6.3	7.2	7.2
Agriculture, exc. Fish: Estimate 2	13.9	12.9	3.1	106.2	0.0	15.7	..	144.0	6.4	8.9	8.9
Fish and Fish Products	..	..	..	..	..	..	..	..	.0	.0	.0
Petroleum Oils	0.0	2.0	..	10.2	0.0	10.0	..	35.0	.3	1.5	1.5
Wood, Pulp, Paper and Furniture	21.8	0.0	6.1	0.0	..	..	..	..	.0	.6	.6
Textiles and Clothing	86.8	8.5	3.1	9.1	..	..	..	..	.0	.1	.1
Leather, Rubber, Footwear	100.0	5.9	0.8	5.9	..	..	..	..	.0	.0	.0
Metals	61.0	2.4	5.2	3.2	0.0	20.0	..	35.0	.0	.2	.2
Chemical & Photographic Suppl.	41.0	7.4	2.3	16.1	0.0	9.7	..	28.1	3.9	8.3	8.3
Transport Equipment	34.2	0.1	0.2	0.1	..	..	..	..	.0	29.6	29.6
Non-Electric Machinery	88.3	5.5	4.7	5.3	95.5	13.4	6.2	13.1	.1	.3	.3
Electric Machinery	89.0	4.7	2.3	5.9	48.1	17.6	9.7	25.4	.0	.2	.2
Mineral Prod.,Prec. Stones & Metal	0.0	0.1	1.2	0.1	0.6	10.1	6.0	34.9	.3	607.6	607.6
Manufactured Articles nes.	6.0	0.3	3.6	0.3	65.3	12.1	6.0	20.6	.0	10.8	10.8
Industrial Goods (line 5-14)	**2.3**	**0.2**	**1.0**	**0.3**	**3.9**	**10.0**	**6.4**	**28.1**	**4.5**	**657.6**	**657.6**
All Merch. Trade (line 2-14)	**2.4**	**0.4**	**1.2**	**1.8**	**1.5**	**13.2**	**6.4**	**94.8**	**11.2**	**668.1**	**668.1**

Notes: 1. Value of exports from reporter countries that do not participate in Free Trade Agreements with BERMUDA

2. Weighted average tariff reduction measured by dT / (1 + T) in percent.

BHUTAN Extent of other countries' MFN tariff reductions on BHUTAN's exports

| Summary product category | Average levels and changes weighted by value of exports to: | | | | | | | | Value of exports in $ million | | |
| | the World exc. FTA[1] | | | | LMIEs exc. FTA[1] | | | | | | |
	% of exports affected	Post-UR applied rate	Tariff reduc-tion[2]	Post-UR bound rate	% of exports affected	Post-UR applied rate	Tariff reduc-tion[2]	Post-UR bound rate	To IDB LMIEs exc. FTA[1]	To all IDB Ctrys exc. FTA[1]	To all IDB Ctrys inc. FTA
Agriculture, exc. Fish: Estimate 1	0.0	0.0	..	54.6	..	..	..	..	.0	.0	.0
Agriculture, exc. Fish: Estimate 2	92.4	9.7	14.2	9.7	0.0	5.0	..	5.0	.0	.3	.3
Fish and Fish Products	100.0	10.0	4.4	10.0	..	..	..	..	.0	.1	.1
Petroleum Oils	..	..	..	..	..	..	..	..	.0	.0	.0
Wood, Pulp, Paper and Furniture	37.4	0.1	5.7	0.1	..	..	..	..	.0	.4	.4
Textiles and Clothing	94.9	12.3	2.5	12.4	..	..	..	..	.0	.2	.2
Leather, Rubber, Footwear	100.0	15.5	3.6	15.5	..	..	..	..	.0	.1	.1
Metals	100.0	0.3	4.5	0.3	..	..	..	..	.0	.0	.0
Chemical & Photographic Suppl.	0.0	0.0	..	5.0	0.0	0.0	..	5.0	.0	.0	.0
Transport Equipment	..	..	..	..	..	..	..	..	.0	.0	.0
Non-Electric Machinery	75.0	17.2	6.0	17.2	75.0	17.2	6.0	17.2	.0	.0	.0
Electric Machinery	0.0	14.0	..	14.0	..	..	..	..	.0	.0	.0
Mineral Prod.,Prec. Stones & Metal	100.0	2.3	0.7	2.3	..	..	..	..	.0	.0	.0
Manufactured Articles nes.	72.6	4.1	5.9	4.9	56.3	16.1	6.0	20.4	.0	.1	.1
Industrial Goods (line 5-14)	**66.4**	**5.5**	**4.0**	**5.6**	**42.9**	**11.6**	**6.0**	**16.0**	**.0**	**.8**	**.8**
All Merch. Trade (line 2-14)	**74.9**	**6.8**	**7.3**	**6.9**	**40.0**	**11.2**	**6.0**	**15.2**	**.0**	**1.2**	**1.2**

Notes: 1. Value of exports from reporter countries that do not participate in Free Trade Agreements with BHUTAN

2. Weighted average tariff reduction measured by dT / (1 + T) in percent.

BOLIVIA Extent of other countries' MFN tariff reductions on BOLIVIA's exports

| Summary product category | Average levels and changes weighted by value of exports to: | | | | | | | | Value of exports in $ million | | |
| | the World exc. FTA[1] | | | | LMIEs exc. FTA[1] | | | | | | |
	% of exports affected	Post-UR applied rate	Tariff reduc-tion[2]	Post-UR bound rate	% of exports affected	Post-UR applied rate	Tariff reduc-tion[2]	Post-UR bound rate	To IDB LMIEs exc. FTA[1]	To all IDB Ctrys exc. FTA[1]	To all IDB Ctrys inc. FTA
Agriculture, exc. Fish: Estimate 1	1.6	-10.3	10.8	48.7	1.4	-24.6	6.8	83.8	34.1	63.5	63.5
Agriculture, exc. Fish: Estimate 2	12.7	7.6	5.4	45.9	0.0	13.8	..	84.3	36.4	68.2	68.2
Fish and Fish Products	56.6	6.7	5.1	6.7	..	..	..	..	.0	.3	.3
Petroleum Oils	0.0	11.0	..	25.0	0.0	11.0	..	25.0	.0	.0	.0
Wood, Pulp, Paper and Furniture	8.0	4.7	5.7	12.0	8.6	9.5	8.0	25.0	13.5	28.9	28.9
Textiles and Clothing	34.4	11.2	2.4	26.6	0.2	10.2	3.6	35.0	7.2	11.7	11.7
Leather, Rubber, Footwear	23.4	4.9	1.6	15.9	0.0	9.3	0.4	34.4	8.2	18.7	18.7
Metals	2.9	0.8	3.0	3.1	0.0	4.2	..	17.4	30.1	169.7	169.7
Chemical & Photographic Suppl.	18.7	3.2	1.4	3.4	0.0	11.1	..	14.7	.7	2.5	2.5
Transport Equipment	0.0	3.1	..	18.2	0.0	6.0	..	35.0	.9	1.7	1.7
Non-Electric Machinery	10.6	4.8	2.3	11.3	0.0	13.1	..	31.7	.2	.6	.6
Electric Machinery	7.5	9.1	2.1	27.9	0.0	14.7	..	32.2	.1	.2	.2
Mineral Prod.,Prec. Stones & Metal	2.5	8.3	1.3	28.7	0.0	10.0	..	35.0	345.0	422.4	422.4
Manufactured Articles nes.	3.0	2.6	5.4	14.8	0.0	4.8	..	28.9	2.7	5.2	5.2
Industrial Goods (line 5-14)	**4.1**	**6.1**	**2.2**	**20.8**	**0.3**	**9.5**	**7.9**	**33.3**	**408.6**	**661.6**	**661.6**
All Merch. Trade (line 2-14)	**4.9**	**6.2**	**3.0**	**23.1**	**0.3**	**9.9**	**7.9**	**37.5**	**445.0**	**730.1**	**730.1**

Notes: 1. Value of exports from reporter countries that do not participate in Free Trade Agreements with BOLIVIA

2. Weighted average tariff reduction measured by dT / (1 + T) in percent.

BOTSWANA Extent of other countries' MFN tariff reductions on BOTSWANA's exports

Summary product category	Average levels and changes weighted by value of exports to: the World exc. FTA[1]				LMIEs exc. FTA[1]				Value of exports in $ million		
	% of exports affected	Post-UR applied rate	Tariff reduction[2]	Post-UR bound rate	% of exports affected	Post-UR applied rate	Tariff reduction[2]	Post-UR bound rate	To IDB LMIEs exc. FTA[1]	To all IDB Ctrys exc. FTA[1]	To all IDB Ctrys inc. FTA
Agriculture, exc. Fish: Estimate 1	95.4	60.8	8.5	61.0	0.0	0.0	..	150.0	.0	29.6	29.6
Agriculture, exc. Fish: Estimate 2	23.0	4.8	14.3	22.2	2.3	1.3	7.4	24.7	9.6	40.7	40.7
Fish and Fish Products	55.2	9.1	6.7	9.9	0.0	3.3	..	7.5	1.0	6.6	6.6
Petroleum Oils	0.0	0.0	..	..	0.0	0.0	..	..	.0	.0	.0
Wood, Pulp, Paper and Furniture	10.5	11.3	5.6	1.8	0.0	12.9	..	4.0	1.4	1.6	1.6
Textiles and Clothing	42.2	26.9	5.3	24.6	28.1	30.9	8.4	36.7	16.2	20.2	20.2
Leather, Rubber, Footwear	61.7	2.7	1.6	2.2	0.0	19.2	..	..	.3	9.9	9.9
Metals	0.1	0.1	1.1	0.0	0.0	0.7	..	0.0	34.1	209.1	209.1
Chemical & Photographic Suppl.	0.3	17.4	4.4	45.9	0.0	17.7	..	86.9	3.7	3.8	3.8
Transport Equipment	8.9	10.4	1.8	24.7	0.0	14.0	..	34.9	.1	.1	.1
Non-Electric Machinery	31.1	1.9	2.6	4.9	0.0	1.2	..	30.4	.4	.7	.7
Electric Machinery	71.9	5.1	2.9	3.2	0.0	21.9	..	..	.0	.3	.3
Mineral Prod.,Prec. Stones & Metal	0.1	1.1	4.5	0.3	0.0	4.6	..	1.9	3.5	13.9	13.9
Manufactured Articles nes.	7.6	12.2	2.6	22.8	1.9	22.0	0.7	110.3	2.4	4.2	4.2
Industrial Goods (line 5-14)	**6.0**	**2.8**	**3.7**	**1.4**	**7.4**	**11.0**	**8.3**	**15.4**	**62.1**	**263.7**	**263.7**
All Merch. Trade (line 2-14)	**9.2**	**3.1**	**7.5**	**3.3**	**6.6**	**9.6**	**8.2**	**18.8**	**72.6**	**311.0**	**311.0**

Notes: 1. Value of exports from reporter countries that do not participate in Free Trade Agreements with BOTSWANA

2. Weighted average tariff reduction measured by dT / (1 + T) in percent.

BRAZIL Extent of other countries' MFN tariff reductions on BRAZIL's exports

Summary product category	Average levels and changes weighted by value of exports to: the World exc. FTA[1]				LMIEs exc. FTA[1]				Value of exports in $ million		
	% of exports affected	Post-UR applied rate	Tariff reduction[2]	Post-UR bound rate	% of exports affected	Post-UR applied rate	Tariff reduction[2]	Post-UR bound rate	To IDB LMIEs exc. FTA[1]	To all IDB Ctrys exc. FTA[1]	To all IDB Ctrys inc. FTA
Agriculture, exc. Fish: Estimate 1	3.3	5.1	8.9	11.5	5.9	4.6	8.0	54.9	771.1	6,898.4	6,996.9
Agriculture, exc. Fish: Estimate 2	36.8	5.7	4.3	7.8	10.5	15.8	5.1	32.7	781.7	8,732.9	8,869.3
Fish and Fish Products	28.8	1.9	3.3	3.3	0.1	15.4	20.7	35.0	.4	222.5	227.4
Petroleum Oils	0.9	2.5	1.6	2.4	0.0	10.1	..	35.1	2.2	700.9	709.3
Wood, Pulp, Paper and Furniture	35.5	1.5	5.5	3.3	10.9	11.0	7.6	26.7	81.0	1,492.3	1,554.2
Textiles and Clothing	75.9	8.3	2.6	9.9	15.8	11.5	4.3	25.0	76.4	1,099.7	1,130.7
Leather, Rubber, Footwear	28.5	7.9	2.7	8.6	40.1	11.1	8.1	22.9	61.6	1,947.3	1,961.4
Metals	33.3	2.0	3.8	4.1	11.4	7.9	9.5	21.3	1,478.9	6,960.9	7,133.6
Chemical & Photographic Suppl.	38.1	4.7	4.6	10.7	7.6	11.4	10.6	25.4	265.0	1,269.9	1,507.5
Transport Equipment	33.3	5.7	1.4	8.4	9.3	16.7	1.9	29.3	195.8	1,802.1	1,920.6
Non-Electric Machinery	64.6	3.1	2.5	7.0	5.4	12.0	6.1	29.8	231.4	1,628.3	1,723.0
Electric Machinery	68.6	5.7	2.3	11.4	5.0	14.2	11.5	32.7	79.0	641.4	736.5
Mineral Prod.,Prec. Stones & Metal	22.7	2.6	3.6	5.3	10.5	12.2	7.6	28.8	77.1	841.6	870.3
Manufactured Articles nes.	52.6	3.2	3.5	9.4	14.5	6.7	1.6	29.9	110.9	483.8	502.1
Industrial Goods (line 5-14)	**40.1**	**3.8**	**3.2**	**6.6**	**10.6**	**9.8**	**8.0**	**25.4**	**2,657.1**	**18,167.3**	**19,039.8**
All Merch. Trade (line 2-14)	**38.0**	**4.3**	**3.6**	**6.8**	**10.6**	**11.2**	**7.4**	**27.1**	**3,441.5**	**27,823.6**	**28,845.8**

Notes: 1. Value of exports from reporter countries that do not participate in Free Trade Agreements with BRAZIL

2. Weighted average tariff reduction measured by dT / (1 + T) in percent.

BRUNEI Extent of other countries' MFN tariff reductions on BRUNEI's exports

| | Average levels and changes weighted by value of exports to: | | | | | | | | Value of exports in $ million | | |
| | the World exc. FTA[1] | | | | LMIEs exc. FTA[1] | | | | | | |
Summary product category	% of exports affected	Post-UR applied rate	Tariff reduc-tion[2]	Post-UR bound rate	% of exports affected	Post-UR applied rate	Tariff reduc-tion[2]	Post-UR bound rate	To IDB LMIEs exc. FTA[1]	To all IDB Ctrys exc. FTA[1]	To all IDB Ctrys inc. FTA
Agriculture, exc. Fish: Estimate 1	10.9	3.4	13.1	3.7	10.7	5.3	10.0	5.3	.2	.3	.3
Agriculture, exc. Fish: Estimate 2	73.6	8.4	13.4	9.6	68.9	17.5	8.4	28.6	.2	1.5	1.5
Fish and Fish Products	0.0	10.2	..	14.7	0.0	18.6	..	19.3	.0	.1	.1
Petroleum Oils	0.0	10.1	..	0.4	0.0	13.6	..	..	443.6	882.2	882.2
Wood, Pulp, Paper and Furniture	12.5	3.2	8.7	3.9	28.0	18.2	18.1	22.4	.3	1.7	1.7
Textiles and Clothing	89.2	17.0	2.9	18.4	7.5	12.0	13.6	46.9	.1	6.0	6.0
Leather, Rubber, Footwear	29.0	7.1	2.0	20.2	0.9	11.0	8.0	34.8	.2	.4	.4
Metals	4.7	0.3	3.0	21.3	0.1	0.5	3.8	34.5	1.8	4.5	4.5
Chemical & Photographic Suppl.	23.4	4.3	2.7	11.0	0.0	10.1	..	28.6	.0	.1	.1
Transport Equipment	5.8	17.7	3.1	8.7	4.8	21.4	21.3	31.1	.0	.6	.6
Non-Electric Machinery	21.9	0.3	4.2	2.2	15.3	7.5	4.9	8.1	.1	3.0	3.0
Electric Machinery	47.7	4.2	3.1	8.8	2.3	19.9	14.3	34.2	.0	.6	.6
Mineral Prod.,Prec. Stones & Metal	20.0	0.5	1.0	0.5	0.0	16.5	..	28.6	.1	1,102.7	1,102.7
Manufactured Articles nes.	64.5	3.0	1.4	3.4	87.7	9.7	15.8	9.9	.5	25.4	25.4
Industrial Goods (line 5-14)	**21.3**	**0.7**	**1.1**	**0.7**	**17.8**	**5.9**	**15.9**	**28.9**	**3.2**	**1,145.0**	**1,145.0**
All Merch. Trade (line 2-14)	**12.1**	**3.9**	**1.1**	**0.7**	**0.2**	**13.6**	**14.7**	**28.8**	**447.0**	**2,028.7**	**2,028.7**

Notes: 1. Value of exports from reporter countries that do not participate in Free Trade Agreements with BRUNEI

2. Weighted average tariff reduction measured by dT / (1 + T) in percent.

BULGARIA Extent of other countries' MFN tariff reductions on BULGARIA's exports

| | Average levels and changes weighted by value of exports to: | | | | | | | | Value of exports in $ million | | |
| | the World exc. FTA[1] | | | | LMIEs exc. FTA[1] | | | | | | |
Summary product category	% of exports affected	Post-UR applied rate	Tariff reduc-tion[2]	Post-UR bound rate	% of exports affected	Post-UR applied rate	Tariff reduc-tion[2]	Post-UR bound rate	To IDB LMIEs exc. FTA[1]	To all IDB Ctrys exc. FTA[1]	To all IDB Ctrys inc. FTA
Agriculture, exc. Fish: Estimate 1	5.4	22.1	10.6	32.2	0.0	-0.9	..	60.7	8.7	88.5	88.5
Agriculture, exc. Fish: Estimate 2	39.9	16.3	4.4	27.5	20.2	31.1	4.4	61.9	58.4	238.6	238.6
Fish and Fish Products	25.6	6.0	5.0	6.0	60.2	7.2	40.3	7.4	.7	21.3	21.3
Petroleum Oils	0.5	1.5	1.3	4.0	0.0	11.3	..	29.3	7.1	64.4	64.4
Wood, Pulp, Paper and Furniture	53.2	2.4	5.5	2.1	31.9	16.7	4.9	14.3	3.9	37.2	37.2
Textiles and Clothing	88.6	12.3	3.3	12.3	61.4	16.3	5.2	16.0	6.9	64.2	64.2
Leather, Rubber, Footwear	42.2	4.6	2.3	5.8	52.6	11.9	2.9	18.3	3.3	17.1	17.1
Metals	47.1	4.9	3.6	8.1	9.8	11.1	1.8	21.2	64.6	145.8	145.8
Chemical & Photographic Suppl.	64.0	6.5	5.7	7.7	52.2	10.9	8.8	13.8	46.5	117.8	117.8
Transport Equipment	92.5	5.1	1.1	4.9	93.1	5.1	1.1	4.8	26.6	27.8	27.8
Non-Electric Machinery	68.1	7.1	2.1	8.2	61.4	8.4	2.2	10.1	143.1	189.8	189.8
Electric Machinery	67.2	6.7	2.2	8.8	55.0	8.4	2.2	11.3	39.0	57.1	57.1
Mineral Prod.,Prec. Stones & Metal	44.8	4.0	2.4	3.9	30.6	7.8	2.5	7.9	14.5	54.3	54.3
Manufactured Articles nes.	43.3	3.9	3.5	11.7	27.1	7.5	3.1	26.9	16.6	41.0	41.0
Industrial Goods (line 5-14)	**61.6**	**6.2**	**3.2**	**7.9**	**49.6**	**9.1**	**3.0**	**13.0**	**364.8**	**752.1**	**752.1**
All Merch. Trade (line 2-14)	**52.4**	**7.6**	**3.4**	**11.0**	**44.8**	**12.2**	**3.2**	**20.5**	**431.0**	**1,076.4**	**1,076.4**

Notes: 1. Value of exports from reporter countries that do not participate in Free Trade Agreements with BULGARIA

2. Weighted average tariff reduction measured by dT / (1 + T) in percent.

BURKINA FASO Extent of other countries' MFN tariff reductions on BURKINA FASO's exports

Summary product category	Average levels and changes weighted by value of exports to: the World exc. FTA[1]				LMIEs exc. FTA[1]				Value of exports in $ million		
	% of exports affected	Post-UR applied rate	Tariff reduc-tion[2]	Post-UR bound rate	% of exports affected	Post-UR applied rate	Tariff reduc-tion[2]	Post-UR bound rate	To IDB LMIEs exc. FTA[1]	To all IDB Ctrys exc. FTA[1]	To all IDB Ctrys inc. FTA
Agriculture, exc. Fish: Estimate 1	0.2	0.0	14.3	0.5	0.0	0.0	..	5.6	4.4	49.2	49.2
Agriculture, exc. Fish: Estimate 2	63.7	5.4	3.1	5.4	0.0	15.0	..	30.0	.0	13.2	13.2
Fish and Fish Products	..	..	..	..	..	..	..	..	.0	.0	.0
Petroleum Oils	..	..	..	..	..	..	..	..	.0	.0	.0
Wood, Pulp, Paper and Furniture	80.8	2.1	5.0	2.1	..	..	..	..	.0	.2	.2
Textiles and Clothing	97.7	5.4	0.2	5.4	100.0	5.0	0.1	5.0	.7	.7	.7
Leather, Rubber, Footwear	97.0	2.3	0.9	2.3	..	..	..	..	.0	1.6	1.6
Metals	38.3	2.2	2.2	2.2	..	..	..	..	.0	.2	.2
Chemical & Photographic Suppl.	73.0	3.0	4.7	3.0	..	..	..	..	.0	.2	.2
Transport Equipment	18.8	9.5	3.3	9.5	0.0	5.0	..	5.0	.0	.1	.1
Non-Electric Machinery	98.9	1.5	2.6	1.5	..	..	..	..	.0	.4	.4
Electric Machinery	100.0	3.0	2.3	3.0	..	..	..	..	.0	.0	.0
Mineral Prod.,Prec. Stones & Metal	0.1	0.0	2.7	0.0	..	..	..	..	.0	43.0	43.0
Manufactured Articles nes.	3.0	1.4	2.3	4.9	16.7	13.0	0.5	47.8	4.5	43.9	43.9
Industrial Goods (line 5-14)	**5.0**	**0.8**	**1.7**	**2.5**	**27.4**	**11.9**	**0.3**	**42.2**	**5.1**	**90.4**	**90.4**
All Merch. Trade (line 2-14)	**12.4**	**1.4**	**2.6**	**2.8**	**27.4**	**11.9**	**0.3**	**42.2**	**5.1**	**103.5**	**103.5**

Notes: 1. Value of exports from reporter countries that do not participate in Free Trade Agreements with BURKINA FASO

2. Weighted average tariff reduction measured by dT / (1 + T) in percent.

BURUNDI Extent of other countries' MFN tariff reductions on BURUNDI's exports

Summary product category	Average levels and changes weighted by value of exports to: the World exc. FTA[1]				LMIEs exc. FTA[1]				Value of exports in $ million		
	% of exports affected	Post-UR applied rate	Tariff reduc-tion[2]	Post-UR bound rate	% of exports affected	Post-UR applied rate	Tariff reduc-tion[2]	Post-UR bound rate	To IDB LMIEs exc. FTA[1]	To all IDB Ctrys exc. FTA[1]	To all IDB Ctrys inc. FTA
Agriculture, exc. Fish: Estimate 1	0.0	0.0	14.3	0.2	0.0	1.7	..	15.1	.9	104.0	104.0
Agriculture, exc. Fish: Estimate 2	83.8	0.2	4.7	0.3	69.1	5.0	3.9	15.3	.9	103.0	103.0
Fish and Fish Products	0.0	0.0	..	0.0	..	..	..	..	.0	.3	.3
Petroleum Oils	..	..	..	..	..	..	..	..	.0	.0	.0
Wood, Pulp, Paper and Furniture	45.8	0.2	6.2	3.5	..	..	..	..	.0	.0	.0
Textiles and Clothing	79.8	5.1	2.0	6.1	..	..	..	..	.0	.2	.2
Leather, Rubber, Footwear	100.0	8.7	2.3	8.7	..	..	..	..	.0	.1	.1
Metals	25.7	0.2	6.1	0.2	..	..	..	..	.0	.1	.1
Chemical & Photographic Suppl.	100.0	5.7	2.5	5.7	..	..	..	..	.0	.0	.0
Transport Equipment	5.7	9.8	2.4	10.2	0.0	11.0	..	25.0	.0	.1	.1
Non-Electric Machinery	97.7	0.7	3.7	0.8	28.6	11.0	3.6	17.0	.0	.2	.2
Electric Machinery	35.8	8.2	3.1	17.2	0.0	11.0	..	25.0	.1	.1	.1
Mineral Prod.,Prec. Stones & Metal	2.2	0.3	0.5	0.6	0.0	9.3	..	19.0	1.6	48.1	48.1
Manufactured Articles nes.	2.9	0.1	3.4	0.1	0.0	..	..	..	.0	4.9	4.9
Industrial Goods (line 5-14)	**3.2**	**0.4**	**1.6**	**0.7**	**0.1**	**9.4**	**3.6**	**19.3**	**1.8**	**53.9**	**53.9**
All Merch. Trade (line 2-14)	**56.0**	**0.3**	**4.7**	**0.5**	**24.1**	**7.9**	**3.9**	**17.9**	**2.7**	**157.2**	**157.2**

Notes: 1. Value of exports from reporter countries that do not participate in Free Trade Agreements with BURUNDI

2. Weighted average tariff reduction measured by dT / (1 + T) in percent.

CAMEROON Extent of other countries' MFN tariff reductions on CAMEROON's exports

Summary product category	Average levels and changes weighted by value of exports to: the World exc. FTA[1]				Average levels and changes weighted by value of exports to: LMIEs exc. FTA[1]				Value of exports in $ million		
	% of exports affected	Post-UR applied rate	Tariff reduc-tion[2]	Post-UR bound rate	% of exports affected	Post-UR applied rate	Tariff reduc-tion[2]	Post-UR bound rate	To IDB LMIEs exc. FTA[1]	To all IDB Ctrys exc. FTA[1]	To all IDB Ctrys inc. FTA
Agriculture, exc. Fish: Estimate 1	0.3	-0.1	14.3	0.3	0.0	-3.2	..	7.2	14.9	485.7	485.7
Agriculture, exc. Fish: Estimate 2	86.0	1.0	3.8	1.2	58.8	7.6	4.6	21.7	6.5	483.6	483.6
Fish and Fish Products	99.4	11.7	5.2	11.7	..	..	..	..	.0	9.3	9.3
Petroleum Oils	0.0	0.3	..	0.1	0.0	1.8	..	0.0	25.5	777.0	777.0
Wood, Pulp, Paper and Furniture	13.5	0.9	3.4	0.8	46.9	9.6	8.2	8.9	10.7	219.2	219.2
Textiles and Clothing	97.6	8.6	1.7	8.9	9.6	40.2	11.2	55.5	.2	20.0	20.0
Leather, Rubber, Footwear	7.6	0.5	0.8	1.5	0.0	8.9	..	35.0	1.6	42.5	42.5
Metals	0.8	5.9	5.1	5.8	14.3	14.6	13.6	20.0	1.0	122.0	122.0
Chemical & Photographic Suppl.	97.1	5.4	2.3	5.4	0.0	5.0	..	5.0	.0	.9	.9
Transport Equipment	20.2	9.0	3.5	9.0	19.0	24.3	4.7	29.3	.0	2.5	2.5
Non-Electric Machinery	97.3	1.3	3.0	1.4	97.2	4.1	1.1	4.4	.4	2.9	2.9
Electric Machinery	91.2	2.9	2.7	2.9	30.0	8.8	6.0	8.8	.0	.7	.7
Mineral Prod.,Prec. Stones & Metal	8.4	2.3	3.0	0.4	0.0	15.0	..	..	.2	1.5	1.5
Manufactured Articles nes.	17.2	2.5	6.0	7.5	46.2	8.8	3.8	29.0	9.8	39.6	39.6
Industrial Goods (line 5-14)	**14.4**	**2.8**	**3.0**	**3.2**	**42.4**	**9.6**	**6.0**	**20.4**	**24.0**	**451.8**	**451.8**
All Merch. Trade (line 2-14)	**28.5**	**1.2**	**3.7**	**1.5**	**25.0**	**5.8**	**5.6**	**13.1**	**56.0**	**1,721.6**	**1,721.6**

Notes: 1. Value of exports from reporter countries that do not participate in Free Trade Agreements with CAMEROON

2. Weighted average tariff reduction measured by $dT / (1 + T)$ in percent.

CANADA Extent of other countries' MFN tariff reductions on CANADA's exports

Summary product category	Average levels and changes weighted by value of exports to: the World exc. FTA[1]				Average levels and changes weighted by value of exports to: LMIEs exc. FTA[1]				Value of exports in $ million		
	% of exports affected	Post-UR applied rate	Tariff reduc-tion[2]	Post-UR bound rate	% of exports affected	Post-UR applied rate	Tariff reduc-tion[2]	Post-UR bound rate	To IDB LMIEs exc. FTA[1]	To all IDB Ctrys exc. FTA[1]	To all IDB Ctrys inc. FTA
Agriculture, exc. Fish: Estimate 1	15.8	41.2	40.7	40.9	17.0	1.9	74.1	53.8	340.2	1,963.2	3,301.5
Agriculture, exc. Fish: Estimate 2	8.9	2.6	3.0	6.8	6.7	9.7	4.1	42.8	455.1	2,780.1	6,119.2
Fish and Fish Products	28.3	2.7	2.5	2.8	30.3	11.5	15.1	16.2	16.2	1,147.8	2,361.2
Petroleum Oils	0.1	6.7	1.3	1.3	0.1	11.9	6.0	38.0	18.0	90.3	4,778.9
Wood, Pulp, Paper and Furniture	5.9	0.2	5.7	0.7	26.8	4.6	6.5	18.4	616.8	6,045.3	20,427.4
Textiles and Clothing	16.5	7.1	5.3	9.4	38.8	14.7	8.3	21.7	76.0	254.2	913.5
Leather, Rubber, Footwear	5.2	2.4	3.6	4.1	42.9	12.4	6.2	24.2	46.7	150.5	1,330.6
Metals	6.6	0.6	2.8	1.2	21.9	6.9	7.7	14.1	682.6	4,762.3	13,365.9
Chemical & Photographic Suppl.	14.6	1.8	5.3	3.9	53.0	7.5	9.2	17.4	434.6	1,370.6	5,253.1
Transport Equipment	0.7	1.0	4.1	6.7	3.5	13.1	9.7	28.8	71.1	440.2	27,980.4
Non-Electric Machinery	7.9	0.8	3.7	2.0	29.0	12.4	7.6	26.3	266.4	1,237.9	8,531.6
Electric Machinery	8.4	2.4	4.0	2.9	27.9	17.8	9.3	22.3	164.2	645.8	4,188.8
Mineral Prod.,Prec. Stones & Metal	2.3	0.4	1.8	1.1	7.0	3.5	4.3	8.9	880.4	4,102.2	9,628.7
Manufactured Articles nes.	12.8	0.9	3.7	1.6	57.6	9.0	5.5	15.3	103.4	741.2	2,570.2
Industrial Goods (line 5-14)	**5.1**	**0.6**	**4.3**	**3.2**	**25.0**	**7.1**	**7.5**	**16.0**	**3,342.1**	**19,750.3**	**94,190.2**
All Merch. Trade (line 2-14)	**5.6**	**0.8**	**4.0**	**3.3**	**22.4**	**7.5**	**7.4**	**20.1**	**3,831.4**	**23,768.5**	**107,450.0**

Notes: 1. Value of exports from reporter countries that do not participate in Free Trade Agreements with CANADA

2. Weighted average tariff reduction measured by $dT / (1 + T)$ in percent.

CENTRAL AFRICAN REPUBLIC Extent of other countries' MFN tariff reductions on CENTRAL AFRICAN REPUBLIC's exports

Summary product category	Average levels and changes weighted by value of exports to: the World exc. FTA[1]				Average levels and changes weighted by value of exports to: LMIEs exc. FTA[1]				Value of exports in $ million		
	% of exports affected	Post-UR applied rate	Tariff reduc-tion[2]	Post-UR bound rate	% of exports affected	Post-UR applied rate	Tariff reduc-tion[2]	Post-UR bound rate	To IDB LMIEs exc. FTA[1]	To all IDB Ctrys exc. FTA[1]	To all IDB Ctrys inc. FTA
Agriculture, exc. Fish: Estimate 1	0.0	0.0	..	0.1	0.0	0.0	..	8.7	.4	36.7	36.7
Agriculture, exc. Fish: Estimate 2	91.1	1.1	4.9	1.2	..	..	..	..	.0	34.4	34.4
Fish and Fish Products	..	..	..	..	..	..	..	..	.0	.0	.0
Petroleum Oils	..	..	..	..	..	..	..	..	.0	.0	.0
Wood, Pulp, Paper and Furniture	5.8	0.2	3.1	0.2	1.6	2.0	2.9	3.3	.2	8.7	8.7
Textiles and Clothing	88.5	2.5	0.7	2.5	..	..	..	..	.0	.7	.7
Leather, Rubber, Footwear	100.0	6.9	4.8	6.9	100.0	10.0	8.7	10.0	.0	.1	.1
Metals	10.5	0.5	4.0	2.0	0.0	5.0	..	30.0	.0	.6	.6
Chemical & Photographic Suppl.	89.1	3.1	6.3	3.1	100.0	6.6	9.6	6.6	.0	.1	.1
Transport Equipment	1.3	4.0	1.1	4.0	..	..	..	..	.0	.8	.8
Non-Electric Machinery	86.7	3.4	2.6	4.6	0.0	15.2	..	25.0	.0	.2	.2
Electric Machinery	88.3	3.0	2.8	3.0	..	..	..	..	.0	.2	.2
Mineral Prod.,Prec. Stones & Metal	3.1	0.0	0.5	0.0	..	..	..	..	.0	51.2	51.2
Manufactured Articles nes.	3.6	0.7	1.1	2.5	28.4	7.5	0.5	27.6	.5	5.7	5.7
Industrial Goods (line 5-14)	**5.0**	**0.2**	**1.5**	**0.3**	**23.5**	**6.3**	**2.5**	**20.5**	**.8**	**68.2**	**68.2**
All Merch. Trade (line 2-14)	**33.9**	**0.5**	**4.6**	**0.6**	**23.5**	**6.3**	**2.5**	**20.5**	**.8**	**102.6**	**102.6**

Notes: 1. Value of exports from reporter countries that do not participate in Free Trade Agreements with Cen. African. Rep

2. Weighted average tariff reduction measured by dT / (1 + T) in percent.

CHAD Extent of other countries' MFN tariff reductions on CHAD's exports

Summary product category	Average levels and changes weighted by value of exports to: the World exc. FTA[1]				Average levels and changes weighted by value of exports to: LMIEs exc. FTA[1]				Value of exports in $ million		
	% of exports affected	Post-UR applied rate	Tariff reduc-tion[2]	Post-UR bound rate	% of exports affected	Post-UR applied rate	Tariff reduc-tion[2]	Post-UR bound rate	To IDB LMIEs exc. FTA[1]	To all IDB Ctrys exc. FTA[1]	To all IDB Ctrys inc. FTA
Agriculture, exc. Fish: Estimate 1	0.0	0.0	..	0.9	0.0	0.0	..	20.6	2.4	53.8	53.8
Agriculture, exc. Fish: Estimate 2	32.8	2.1	3.4	2.1	..	..	..	..	.0	4.8	4.8
Fish and Fish Products	95.4	3.3	1.4	3.3	..	..	..	..	.0	.1	.1
Petroleum Oils	..	..	..	..	..	..	..	..	.0	.0	.0
Wood, Pulp, Paper and Furniture	81.0	6.3	3.0	6.3	..	..	..	..	.0	.3	.3
Textiles and Clothing	62.0	15.0	5.0	21.4	0.0	14.0	..	35.0	.0	.1	.1
Leather, Rubber, Footwear	58.3	11.1	3.9	17.4	0.0	15.0	..	30.0	.0	.0	.0
Metals	15.6	2.9	0.9	5.2	0.0	15.0	..	30.0	.0	.0	.0
Chemical & Photographic Suppl.	31.1	8.8	4.7	20.6	0.0	15.0	..	44.4	.0	.0	.0
Transport Equipment	1.4	9.8	3.2	9.8	..	..	..	..	.0	.1	.1
Non-Electric Machinery	70.6	1.1	2.5	1.1	..	..	..	..	.0	.1	.1
Electric Machinery	95.7	3.7	3.6	4.7	0.0	13.1	..	35.0	.0	.0	.0
Mineral Prod.,Prec. Stones & Metal	96.7	9.9	1.1	9.9	..	..	..	..	.0	.1	.1
Manufactured Articles nes.	2.1	0.3	1.2	1.2	35.8	6.1	0.5	27.3	2.4	54.3	54.3
Industrial Goods (line 5-14)	**2.9**	**0.4**	**1.7**	**1.3**	**35.0**	**6.3**	**0.5**	**27.5**	**2.5**	**54.9**	**54.9**
All Merch. Trade (line 2-14)	**5.4**	**0.5**	**2.5**	**1.4**	**35.0**	**6.3**	**0.5**	**27.5**	**2.5**	**59.8**	**59.8**

Notes: 1. Value of exports from reporter countries that do not participate in Free Trade Agreements with CHAD

2. Weighted average tariff reduction measured by dT / (1 + T) in percent.

CHILE Extent of other countries' MFN tariff reductions on CHILE's exports

Summary product category	Average levels and changes weighted by value of exports to: the World exc. FTA[1]				LMIEs exc. FTA[1]				Value of exports in $ million		
	% of exports affected	Post-UR applied rate	Tariff reduc-tion[2]	Post-UR bound rate	% of exports affected	Post-UR applied rate	Tariff reduc-tion[2]	Post-UR bound rate	To IDB LMIEs exc. FTA[1]	To all IDB Ctrys exc. FTA[1]	To all IDB Ctrys inc. FTA
Agriculture, exc. Fish: Estimate 1	1.6	2.4	12.7	10.4	0.3	0.1	28.6	46.5	48.7	304.7	304.7
Agriculture, exc. Fish: Estimate 2	28.2	3.9	2.0	6.7	9.9	11.7	2.0	29.4	197.0	1,478.6	1,478.6
Fish and Fish Products	27.8	8.2	3.4	9.7	5.6	12.3	8.7	37.9	20.9	357.1	357.1
Petroleum Oils	0.0	3.7	..	12.0	0.0	10.3	..	34.7	2.4	7.3	7.3
Wood, Pulp, Paper and Furniture	10.3	2.8	4.0	8.7	7.2	6.4	6.0	21.5	257.0	659.3	659.3
Textiles and Clothing	62.2	10.1	1.8	12.4	12.2	11.6	5.8	31.9	6.5	83.6	83.6
Leather, Rubber, Footwear	17.4	6.8	1.6	9.6	4.7	14.7	3.9	32.8	1.9	35.9	35.9
Metals	13.4	1.0	2.9	4.7	13.4	3.4	8.4	22.1	703.7	3,410.5	3,410.5
Chemical & Photographic Suppl.	26.2	4.1	7.0	8.3	8.2	9.3	16.8	23.8	45.5	157.3	157.3
Transport Equipment	2.9	13.9	1.4	32.0	0.0	15.0	..	34.6	16.4	17.9	17.9
Non-Electric Machinery	31.5	7.5	2.8	18.0	0.1	12.4	8.0	30.6	4.8	8.4	8.4
Electric Machinery	25.8	9.5	2.1	24.3	1.9	14.9	0.8	34.1	5.4	9.2	9.2
Mineral Prod.,Prec. Stones & Metal	7.4	0.4	2.9	5.7	2.9	1.2	11.3	27.1	66.8	331.9	331.9
Manufactured Articles nes.	10.6	2.4	4.9	6.5	6.0	10.0	9.9	30.8	10.1	48.2	48.2
Industrial Goods (line 5-14)	**13.9**	**1.6**	**3.2**	**5.7**	**10.8**	**4.6**	**8.3**	**22.9**	**1,118.2**	**4,762.2**	**4,762.2**
All Merch. Trade (line 2-14)	**17.8**	**2.4**	**2.8**	**6.1**	**10.5**	**5.8**	**7.5**	**24.2**	**1,338.5**	**6,605.2**	**6,605.2**

Notes: 1. Value of exports from reporter countries that do not participate in Free Trade Agreements with CHILE

2. Weighted average tariff reduction measured by $dT / (1 + T)$ in percent.

CHINA Extent of other countries' MFN tariff reductions on CHINA's exports

Summary product category	Average levels and changes weighted by value of exports to: the World exc. FTA[1]				LMIEs exc. FTA[1]				Value of exports in $ million		
	% of exports affected	Post-UR applied rate	Tariff reduc-tion[2]	Post-UR bound rate	% of exports affected	Post-UR applied rate	Tariff reduc-tion[2]	Post-UR bound rate	To IDB LMIEs exc. FTA[1]	To all IDB Ctrys exc. FTA[1]	To all IDB Ctrys inc. FTA
Agriculture, exc. Fish: Estimate 1	21.4	19.6	19.4	23.1	50.5	32.6	8.0	48.2	752.0	3,385.6	3,385.6
Agriculture, exc. Fish: Estimate 2	28.2	4.3	5.4	7.9	21.3	8.9	4.0	34.6	866.3	6,599.3	6,599.3
Fish and Fish Products	46.1	1.9	2.6	2.0	40.7	7.4	37.5	4.7	19.0	1,290.8	1,290.8
Petroleum Oils	0.1	7.6	1.5	7.4	0.0	12.3	..	28.3	255.2	3,369.7	3,369.7
Wood, Pulp, Paper and Furniture	29.9	0.9	4.6	1.0	23.2	11.3	3.9	21.4	56.3	1,430.4	1,430.4
Textiles and Clothing	31.7	4.6	2.9	11.2	48.8	16.2	9.0	20.8	864.7	26,173.2	26,173.2
Leather, Rubber, Footwear	16.5	3.4	2.5	6.2	64.2	9.1	2.7	11.4	164.7	6,490.7	6,490.7
Metals	34.8	2.1	2.7	3.4	9.6	11.1	6.5	19.4	405.0	3,744.2	3,744.2
Chemical & Photographic Suppl.	27.3	2.5	3.2	5.8	20.4	14.6	9.3	24.2	323.2	4,400.2	4,400.2
Transport Equipment	11.3	2.6	2.3	12.3	1.3	16.9	8.7	29.2	29.8	514.5	514.5
Non-Electric Machinery	16.5	1.8	3.1	5.2	27.4	13.7	4.7	26.6	216.9	2,601.2	2,601.2
Electric Machinery	15.7	1.1	3.7	4.0	27.4	18.1	12.5	28.2	96.5	8,800.7	8,800.7
Mineral Prod.,Prec. Stones & Metal	19.5	1.9	2.9	3.9	11.5	8.4	5.8	23.7	225.7	2,563.6	2,563.6
Manufactured Articles nes.	31.1	1.2	4.9	3.1	39.7	11.0	3.6	26.9	409.5	13,461.1	13,461.1
Industrial Goods (line 5-14)	**26.9**	**2.9**	**3.4**	**6.4**	**33.0**	**13.3**	**6.9**	**22.5**	**2,792.4**	**70,179.7**	**70,179.7**
All Merch. Trade (line 2-14)	**26.2**	**3.0**	**3.6**	**6.5**	**28.3**	**12.2**	**6.6**	**25.8**	**3,933.0**	**81,439.4**	**81,439.4**

Notes: 1. Value of exports from reporter countries that do not participate in Free Trade Agreements with CHINA

2. Weighted average tariff reduction measured by $dT / (1 + T)$ in percent.

TAIWAN (CHINA) Extent of other countries' MFN tariff reductions on TAIWAN (CHINA)'s exports

Summary product category	Average levels and changes weighted by value of exports to: the World exc. FTA[1]				LMIEs exc. FTA[1]				Value of exports in $ million		
	% of exports affected	Post-UR applied rate	Tariff reduc-tion[2]	Post-UR bound rate	% of exports affected	Post-UR applied rate	Tariff reduc-tion[2]	Post-UR bound rate	To IDB LMIEs exc. FTA[1]	To all IDB Ctrys exc. FTA[1]	To all IDB Ctrys inc. FTA
Agriculture, exc. Fish: Estimate 1	3.1	32.2	10.0	32.8	16.9	8.3	5.6	21.3	41.6	784.6	784.6
Agriculture, exc. Fish: Estimate 2	70.7	7.3	3.2	9.1	28.6	16.5	4.7	36.5	173.0	1,891.1	1,891.1
Fish and Fish Products	50.0	4.5	5.0	4.7	78.3	8.3	41.5	5.9	82.4	1,533.0	1,533.0
Petroleum Oils	7.2	5.6	4.1	10.4	26.0	13.5	6.0	14.6	22.7	134.1	134.1
Wood, Pulp, Paper and Furniture	77.1	1.5	4.0	1.8	32.7	11.5	7.7	20.1	154.5	3,364.6	3,364.6
Textiles and Clothing	58.1	11.4	3.5	15.8	60.3	27.9	10.5	26.9	1,423.5	12,239.0	12,239.0
Leather, Rubber, Footwear	52.7	8.7	2.6	9.5	45.1	18.6	8.3	23.0	191.2	4,556.2	4,556.2
Metals	58.2	3.9	3.2	4.5	37.8	13.5	9.3	17.9	475.2	4,468.9	4,468.9
Chemical & Photographic Suppl.	36.4	4.0	3.5	7.2	28.7	16.9	12.7	25.5	479.1	4,614.0	4,614.0
Transport Equipment	45.3	5.5	2.5	6.7	28.9	19.1	6.3	26.1	98.0	1,828.7	1,828.7
Non-Electric Machinery	59.6	2.4	3.5	3.9	32.8	12.1	8.5	22.3	1,091.0	10,348.0	10,348.0
Electric Machinery	44.0	3.4	3.6	4.6	41.7	16.3	9.3	19.4	833.6	10,555.1	10,555.1
Mineral Prod.,Prec. Stones & Metal	70.5	4.7	3.2	5.4	18.0	14.9	10.7	23.3	95.3	1,512.0	1,512.0
Manufactured Articles nes.	58.1	3.4	4.1	4.0	40.0	21.1	11.3	24.7	333.5	7,966.6	7,966.6
Industrial Goods (line 5-14)	**54.9**	**5.3**	**3.5**	**6.7**	**42.4**	**18.7**	**9.9**	**23.2**	**5,175.0**	**61,453.2**	**61,453.2**
All Merch. Trade (line 2-14)	**55.1**	**5.3**	**3.5**	**6.7**	**42.5**	**18.4**	**10.6**	**23.4**	**5,453.0**	**65,011.4**	**65,011.4**

Notes: 1. Value of exports from reporter countries that do not participate in Free Trade Agreements with Taiwan (China)

2. Weighted average tariff reduction measured by dT / (1 + T) in percent.

FORMER USSR Extent of other countries' MFN tariff reductions on FORMER USSR's exports

Summary product category	Average levels and changes weighted by value of exports to: the World exc. FTA[1]				LMIEs exc. FTA[1]				Value of exports in $ million		
	% of exports affected	Post-UR applied rate	Tariff reduc-tion[2]	Post-UR bound rate	% of exports affected	Post-UR applied rate	Tariff reduc-tion[2]	Post-UR bound rate	To IDB LMIEs exc. FTA[1]	To all IDB Ctrys exc. FTA[1]	To all IDB Ctrys inc. FTA
Agriculture, exc. Fish: Estimate 1	0.1	0.9	21.7	15.7	0.0	0.1	2.9	36.1	200.0	485.9	485.9
Agriculture, exc. Fish: Estimate 2	46.3	15.8	5.2	29.8	43.4	21.6	3.2	56.3	107.8	295.7	295.7
Fish and Fish Products	49.7	6.3	4.3	6.5	24.0	12.7	34.6	10.9	48.6	458.5	458.5
Petroleum Oils	1.3	0.8	1.3	1.1	0.6	1.0	1.4	0.5	2,545.0	11,406.3	11,406.3
Wood, Pulp, Paper and Furniture	10.3	0.9	3.7	2.0	16.3	6.2	2.9	10.6	287.1	2,414.2	2,414.2
Textiles and Clothing	54.9	10.6	4.4	9.7	53.6	21.6	7.1	15.1	48.4	162.6	162.6
Leather, Rubber, Footwear	20.9	2.1	3.4	2.6	23.1	3.6	4.8	4.8	45.2	124.5	124.5
Metals	23.2	1.4	2.2	3.3	13.9	3.5	1.9	8.9	1,024.6	3,058.1	3,058.1
Chemical & Photographic Suppl.	30.3	4.3	5.8	4.6	51.7	12.6	7.2	13.6	337.9	1,224.7	1,224.7
Transport Equipment	35.6	9.0	2.1	9.1	26.2	12.5	2.1	15.7	356.9	971.1	971.1
Non-Electric Machinery	70.3	8.3	3.2	10.2	65.6	10.3	3.8	12.9	535.4	732.2	732.2
Electric Machinery	52.4	9.5	4.0	11.1	48.1	11.8	2.9	14.1	159.1	238.2	238.2
Mineral Prod.,Prec. Stones & Metal	9.2	1.5	1.9	3.8	3.0	4.4	6.7	12.8	1,862.4	6,007.0	6,007.0
Manufactured Articles nes.	8.3	1.4	3.6	5.1	8.9	2.7	4.0	10.4	730.1	1,568.6	1,568.6
Industrial Goods (line 5-14)	**18.9**	**2.6**	**3.0**	**4.4**	**19.4**	**6.1**	**4.1**	**11.8**	**5,387.2**	**16,501.0**	**16,501.0**
All Merch. Trade (line 2-14)	**12.6**	**2.1**	**3.1**	**3.4**	**13.8**	**5.1**	**4.3**	**9.5**	**8,088.6**	**28,661.5**	**28,661.5**

Notes: 1. Value of exports from reporter countries that do not participate in Free Trade Agreements with FORMER USSR

2. Weighted average tariff reduction measured by dT / (1 + T) in percent.

COLOMBIA Extent of other countries' MFN tariff reductions on COLOMBIA's exports

Summary product category	Average levels and changes weighted by value of exports to: the World exc. FTA[1]				LMIEs exc. FTA[1]				Value of exports in $ million		
	% of exports affected	Post-UR applied rate	Tariff reduction[2]	Post-UR bound rate	% of exports affected	Post-UR applied rate	Tariff reduction[2]	Post-UR bound rate	To IDB LMIEs exc. FTA[1]	To all IDB Ctrys exc. FTA[1]	To all IDB Ctrys inc. FTA
Agriculture, exc. Fish: Estimate 1	0.1	4.9	8.6	7.8	0.7	1.2	6.8	30.7	204.6	2,296.4	2,296.4
Agriculture, exc. Fish: Estimate 2	48.3	2.3	4.3	3.7	11.5	10.6	4.3	27.3	190.2	2,551.5	2,551.5
Fish and Fish Products	32.4	1.3	2.7	2.3	..	..	..	..	.0	59.6	59.6
Petroleum Oils	0.0	0.8	..	4.2	0.0	9.5	..	33.9	37.0	1,177.0	1,177.0
Wood, Pulp, Paper and Furniture	28.2	2.6	4.5	12.8	2.4	6.4	6.0	32.7	19.4	50.1	50.1
Textiles and Clothing	77.2	14.7	1.8	15.5	35.1	24.1	3.7	32.3	24.7	249.5	249.5
Leather, Rubber, Footwear	27.0	7.4	2.2	8.5	36.1	20.5	2.7	31.7	7.5	77.3	77.3
Metals	13.4	1.8	2.5	3.6	0.4	8.9	3.6	27.9	25.4	163.9	163.9
Chemical & Photographic Suppl.	16.3	10.2	5.5	22.2	0.8	13.0	7.1	29.1	83.5	113.3	113.3
Transport Equipment	15.0	11.3	2.1	23.6	5.3	13.3	1.8	28.5	1.8	2.2	2.2
Non-Electric Machinery	51.7	10.7	2.4	18.8	17.2	18.1	1.7	33.3	11.7	22.1	22.1
Electric Machinery	30.2	18.0	1.9	27.0	13.7	22.3	0.5	33.4	7.7	9.9	9.9
Mineral Prod.,Prec. Stones & Metal	22.4	0.6	1.3	1.5	7.5	9.6	5.3	29.1	24.7	512.8	512.8
Manufactured Articles nes.	17.2	6.7	6.3	17.8	3.6	11.8	13.2	33.8	47.6	94.2	94.2
Industrial Goods (line 5-14)	**32.0**	**5.6**	**2.2**	**9.0**	**7.6**	**13.4**	**4.3**	**30.9**	**254.1**	**1,295.1**	**1,295.1**
All Merch. Trade (line 2-14)	**32.8**	**2.8**	**3.8**	**5.4**	**8.5**	**12.0**	**4.3**	**29.7**	**481.3**	**5,083.2**	**5,083.2**

Notes: 1. Value of exports from reporter countries that do not participate in Free Trade Agreements with COLOMBIA

2. Weighted average tariff reduction measured by dT / (1 + T) in percent.

CONGO Extent of other countries' MFN tariff reductions on CONGO's exports

Summary product category	Average levels and changes weighted by value of exports to: the World exc. FTA[1]				LMIEs exc. FTA[1]				Value of exports in $ million		
	% of exports affected	Post-UR applied rate	Tariff reduction[2]	Post-UR bound rate	% of exports affected	Post-UR applied rate	Tariff reduction[2]	Post-UR bound rate	To IDB LMIEs exc. FTA[1]	To all IDB Ctrys exc. FTA[1]	To all IDB Ctrys inc. FTA
Agriculture, exc. Fish: Estimate 1	0.0	101.9	..	101.9	..	..	..	..	.0	9.4	9.4
Agriculture, exc. Fish: Estimate 2	20.5	0.4	4.4	0.4	100.0	30.0	3.8	30.0	.0	16.1	16.1
Fish and Fish Products	80.1	9.6	5.2	9.6	0.0	0.0	..	0.0	.0	2.7	2.7
Petroleum Oils	0.0	0.4	2.2	0.1	0.0	5.0	..	..	21.7	328.4	328.4
Wood, Pulp, Paper and Furniture	17.9	1.0	3.0	1.0	15.5	5.5	7.9	6.3	12.3	141.5	141.5
Textiles and Clothing	40.9	8.1	2.9	8.3	21.3	10.0	3.5	10.2	.1	.2	.2
Leather, Rubber, Footwear	100.0	6.0	0.7	6.0	..	..	..	..	.0	.6	.6
Metals	2.8	0.0	5.7	0.0	..	..	..	..	.0	13.2	13.2
Chemical & Photographic Suppl.	45.2	11.6	2.4	7.7	2.0	18.4	9.7	12.2	.0	.1	.1
Transport Equipment	18.7	7.7	1.6	7.7	0.0	15.0	..	15.0	.0	.8	.8
Non-Electric Machinery	96.5	1.8	2.8	1.8	89.8	4.5	0.7	3.6	.0	1.2	1.2
Electric Machinery	98.7	2.7	2.3	2.7	0.0	15.6	..	35.0	.0	2.4	2.4
Mineral Prod.,Prec. Stones & Metal	0.2	0.0	8.0	0.0	3.3	0.0	12.9	1.1	2.7	74.9	74.9
Manufactured Articles nes.	47.1	1.5	3.1	1.6	21.4	11.0	1.1	5.0	.0	2.0	2.0
Industrial Goods (line 5-14)	**13.1**	**0.7**	**2.9**	**0.7**	**13.5**	**4.6**	**7.9**	**6.3**	**15.2**	**236.8**	**236.8**
All Merch. Trade (line 2-14)	**6.3**	**0.6**	**3.2**	**0.4**	**5.6**	**4.8**	**7.9**	**6.3**	**36.9**	**584.0**	**584.0**

Notes: 1. Value of exports from reporter countries that do not participate in Free Trade Agreements with CONGO

2. Weighted average tariff reduction measured by dT / (1 + T) in percent.

COSTA RICA Extent of other countries' MFN tariff reductions on COSTA RICA's exports

Summary product category	Average levels and changes weighted by value of exports to: the World exc. FTA[1]				Average levels and changes weighted by value of exports to: LMIEs exc. FTA[1]				Value of exports in $ million		
	% of exports affected	Post-UR applied rate	Tariff reduc-tion[2]	Post-UR bound rate	% of exports affected	Post-UR applied rate	Tariff reduc-tion[2]	Post-UR bound rate	To IDB LMIEs exc. FTA[1]	To all IDB Ctrys exc. FTA[1]	To all IDB Ctrys inc. FTA
Agriculture, exc. Fish: Estimate 1	0.3	1.9	7.7	4.1	5.5	0.9	7.2	16.1	48.5	918.4	918.4
Agriculture, exc. Fish: Estimate 2	34.0	2.5	4.7	4.2	9.8	12.7	9.1	35.0	57.7	1,029.7	1,029.7
Fish and Fish Products	50.8	2.2	1.0	3.4	0.0	30.0	..	50.0	3.0	55.4	55.4
Petroleum Oils	0.0	0.8	..	9.6	0.0	5.0	..	40.0	.0	.1	.1
Wood, Pulp, Paper and Furniture	70.9	4.6	3.3	8.0	0.0	20.6	..	38.8	6.8	36.3	36.3
Textiles and Clothing	98.8	17.7	2.2	17.8	0.3	23.5	3.8	37.5	2.5	347.6	347.6
Leather, Rubber, Footwear	34.4	8.6	1.3	16.2	4.3	12.7	3.8	32.3	6.8	17.7	17.7
Metals	23.4	9.1	4.7	15.4	12.3	17.1	9.3	32.0	8.0	19.0	19.0
Chemical & Photographic Suppl.	25.2	8.3	3.8	16.2	0.0	16.0	3.2	34.9	14.9	35.4	35.4
Transport Equipment	7.9	4.7	1.3	6.6	0.0	32.2	..	46.0	.6	4.8	4.8
Non-Electric Machinery	56.6	8.2	2.3	14.1	0.0	19.9	..	36.5	2.7	7.8	7.8
Electric Machinery	78.0	4.1	2.7	5.5	10.8	20.6	8.0	36.8	5.0	61.8	61.8
Mineral Prod.,Prec. Stones & Metal	72.2	6.4	2.0	7.7	0.0	18.1	6.0	34.8	3.3	29.8	29.8
Manufactured Articles nes.	79.3	2.3	4.3	2.9	0.0	26.4	..	39.1	.9	15.7	15.7
Industrial Goods (line 5-14)	**82.6**	**13.1**	**2.4**	**14.6**	**3.6**	**17.8**	**8.0**	**35.2**	**51.5**	**575.9**	**575.9**
All Merch. Trade (line 2-14)	**51.4**	**6.7**	**3.3**	**8.2**	**6.7**	**15.5**	**8.9**	**35.5**	**112.2**	**1,661.1**	**1,661.1**

Notes: 1. Value of exports from reporter countries that do not participate in Free Trade Agreements with COSTA RICA

2. Weighted average tariff reduction measured by dT / (1 + T) in percent.

CÔTE d'IVOIRE Extent of other countries' MFN tariff reductions on CÔTE d'IVOIRE's export

Summary product category	Average levels and changes weighted by value of exports to: the World exc. FTA[1]				Average levels and changes weighted by value of exports to: LMIEs exc. FTA[1]				Value of exports in $ million		
	% of exports affected	Post-UR applied rate	Tariff reduc-tion[2]	Post-UR bound rate	% of exports affected	Post-UR applied rate	Tariff reduc-tion[2]	Post-UR bound rate	To IDB LMIEs exc. FTA[1]	To all IDB Ctrys exc. FTA[1]	To all IDB Ctrys inc. FTA
Agriculture, exc. Fish: Estimate 1	0.1	0.9	14.2	2.6	0.0	-0.4	..	21.5	109.0	1,470.4	1,470.4
Agriculture, exc. Fish: Estimate 2	73.9	2.0	3.9	2.8	21.7	9.1	3.6	23.6	74.8	1,484.0	1,484.0
Fish and Fish Products	5.5	17.4	5.0	22.3	0.0	15.0	..	..	.0	138.3	138.3
Petroleum Oils	0.1	0.7	1.3	0.9	0.0	4.0	..	4.0	.1	53.5	53.5
Wood, Pulp, Paper and Furniture	18.7	1.9	2.9	1.5	3.6	17.7	8.4	24.2	26.8	335.7	335.7
Textiles and Clothing	92.8	8.6	1.8	9.0	3.6	11.5	5.7	20.9	2.8	47.4	47.4
Leather, Rubber, Footwear	0.7	0.1	1.8	0.3	0.0	9.9	..	33.7	.4	69.2	69.2
Metals	6.7	7.6	4.3	3.0	2.4	14.0	8.9	26.0	5.0	9.4	9.4
Chemical & Photographic Suppl.	34.3	7.5	4.2	4.8	0.0	14.8	..	24.5	.6	1.6	1.6
Transport Equipment	6.7	1.1	4.3	1.1	0.0	5.5	..	5.5	.0	17.0	17.0
Non-Electric Machinery	98.9	1.6	2.7	1.8	27.3	12.1	4.1	26.0	.1	5.1	5.1
Electric Machinery	81.9	2.4	3.8	2.3	13.9	8.4	28.5	7.9	.2	1.5	1.5
Mineral Prod.,Prec. Stones & Metal	0.7	0.0	1.6	0.1	0.0	0.4	..	40.0	1.3	85.5	85.5
Manufactured Articles nes.	18.9	1.9	2.3	6.6	37.3	4.2	0.5	17.0	41.5	112.2	112.2
Industrial Goods (line 5-14)	**20.1**	**2.0**	**2.5**	**2.6**	**21.3**	**9.8**	**1.1**	**19.0**	**78.7**	**684.5**	**684.5**
All Merch. Trade (line 2-14)	**52.7**	**2.9**	**3.8**	**3.9**	**21.5**	**9.4**	**2.3**	**21.6**	**153.6**	**2,360.4**	**2,360.4**

Notes: 1. Value of exports from reporter countries that do not participate in Free Trade Agreements with CÔTE d'IVOIRE

2. Weighted average tariff reduction measured by dT / (1 + T) in percent.

CUBA Extent of other countries' MFN tariff reductions on CUBA's exports

Summary product category	Average levels and changes weighted by value of exports to: the World exc. FTA[1]				LMIEs exc. FTA[1]				Value of exports in $ million		
	% of exports affected	Post-UR applied rate	Tariff reduc-tion[2]	Post-UR bound rate	% of exports affected	Post-UR applied rate	Tariff reduc-tion[2]	Post-UR bound rate	To IDB LMIEs exc. FTA[1]	To all IDB Ctrys exc. FTA[1]	To all IDB Ctrys inc. FTA
Agriculture, exc. Fish: Estimate 1	41.1	49.5	6.7	60.8	37.9	27.2	10.2	61.6	87.6	266.4	266.4
Agriculture, exc. Fish: Estimate 2	35.3	44.2	8.9	79.7	22.5	23.9	4.5	72.1	114.7	372.9	372.9
Fish and Fish Products	75.9	9.6	4.7	9.7	0.0	15.0	..	30.0	1.5	148.0	148.0
Petroleum Oils	33.9	1.6	1.2	3.9	..	..	..	..	.0	51.3	51.3
Wood, Pulp, Paper and Furniture	53.7	1.9	7.7	7.0	10.6	6.2	2.8	28.4	.8	3.4	3.4
Textiles and Clothing	82.0	12.5	4.1	13.2	36.8	12.1	2.0	17.4	1.2	8.6	8.6
Leather, Rubber, Footwear	94.7	5.5	2.5	5.9	90.1	10.3	4.0	11.6	.2	.5	.5
Metals	16.3	1.0	3.5	3.4	0.0	2.2	1.6	10.6	21.6	64.8	64.8
Chemical & Photographic Suppl.	0.9	7.8	4.3	32.3	0.4	8.0	4.9	33.5	30.3	31.5	31.5
Transport Equipment	19.8	6.1	2.4	6.1	50.0	17.0	1.2	27.0	.0	.2	.2
Non-Electric Machinery	73.9	2.6	0.5	4.1	73.6	2.8	0.2	4.4	3.6	3.9	3.9
Electric Machinery	28.3	7.2	2.9	16.3	0.7	10.0	1.9	21.9	.1	.2	.2
Mineral Prod.,Prec. Stones & Metal	0.6	0.1	2.6	0.2	25.5	5.1	2.5	14.4	.9	62.1	62.1
Manufactured Articles nes.	14.1	1.7	3.0	4.3	29.5	7.9	2.8	23.5	.7	4.4	4.4
Industrial Goods (line 5-14)	**13.5**	**2.5**	**3.6**	**8.1**	**6.4**	**5.6**	**1.0**	**23.3**	**59.3**	**179.7**	**179.7**
All Merch. Trade (line 2-14)	**37.9**	**23.8**	**6.3**	**42.5**	**16.9**	**17.6**	**4.0**	**55.9**	**175.5**	**751.8**	**751.8**

Notes: 1. Value of exports from reporter countries that do not participate in Free Trade Agreements with CUBA

2. Weighted average tariff reduction measured by dT / (1 + T) in percent.

CYPRUS Extent of other countries' MFN tariff reductions on CYPRUS's exports

Summary product category	Average levels and changes weighted by value of exports to: the World exc. FTA[1]				LMIEs exc. FTA[1]				Value of exports in $ million		
	% of exports affected	Post-UR applied rate	Tariff reduc-tion[2]	Post-UR bound rate	% of exports affected	Post-UR applied rate	Tariff reduc-tion[2]	Post-UR bound rate	To IDB LMIEs exc. FTA[1]	To all IDB Ctrys exc. FTA[1]	To all IDB Ctrys inc. FTA
Agriculture, exc. Fish: Estimate 1	2.4	6.2	18.3	14.7	31.7	29.6	18.4	134.9	4.6	62.5	62.5
Agriculture, exc. Fish: Estimate 2	49.9	12.1	3.9	27.0	14.8	32.8	5.3	95.1	20.5	204.7	204.7
Fish and Fish Products	6.1	6.1	3.6	6.1	..	..	..	..	.0	2.7	2.7
Petroleum Oils	0.0	24.6	2.2	24.6	0.0	45.0	..	45.0	7.5	13.7	13.7
Wood, Pulp, Paper and Furniture	72.9	8.0	7.1	1.4	28.0	52.8	8.2	21.6	1.6	11.1	11.1
Textiles and Clothing	94.8	11.6	1.9	11.4	61.9	18.6	4.2	14.1	5.7	127.3	127.3
Leather, Rubber, Footwear	57.0	7.3	2.8	6.9	14.0	18.5	0.7	12.7	.8	10.4	10.4
Metals	54.3	3.6	3.7	1.6	56.9	13.3	8.1	2.5	3.4	18.3	18.3
Chemical & Photographic Suppl.	37.7	6.4	4.5	5.8	19.3	20.0	6.8	16.0	4.0	15.0	15.0
Transport Equipment	19.4	7.8	1.9	7.8	0.0	17.7	..	22.4	.1	7.7	7.7
Non-Electric Machinery	67.6	8.7	3.0	3.2	28.7	26.3	3.7	14.1	3.1	10.4	10.4
Electric Machinery	60.2	7.3	2.7	9.8	4.7	23.3	10.5	32.8	.5	3.4	3.4
Mineral Prod.,Prec. Stones & Metal	69.1	4.7	0.7	7.3	2.2	8.3	13.1	29.9	5.4	32.9	32.9
Manufactured Articles nes.	5.4	0.5	4.3	2.3	33.0	24.5	14.1	27.6	1.8	129.9	129.9
Industrial Goods (line 5-14)	**52.0**	**6.0**	**2.3**	**6.4**	**31.8**	**19.5**	**6.3**	**18.3**	**26.3**	**366.3**	**366.3**
All Merch. Trade (line 2-14)	**49.9**	**8.0**	**2.9**	**12.2**	**21.0**	**28.0**	**6.0**	**55.9**	**54.3**	**587.3**	**587.3**

Notes: 1. Value of exports from reporter countries that do not participate in Free Trade Agreements with CYPRUS

2. Weighted average tariff reduction measured by dT / (1 + T) in percent.

CZECH & SLOVAK CU Extent of other countries' MFN tariff reductions on CZECH & SLOVAK CU's exports

Summary product category	Average levels and changes weighted by value of exports to: the World exc. FTA[1]				LMIEs exc. FTA[1]				Value of exports in $ million		
	% of exports affected	Post-UR applied rate	Tariff reduction[2]	Post-UR bound rate	% of exports affected	Post-UR applied rate	Tariff reduction[2]	Post-UR bound rate	To IDB LMIEs exc. FTA[1]	To all IDB Ctrys exc. FTA[1]	To all IDB Ctrys inc. FTA
Agriculture, exc. Fish: Estimate 1	24.8	67.3	17.7	78.7	0.1	35.2	3.5	64.3	35.3	146.1	146.1
Agriculture, exc. Fish: Estimate 2	33.4	9.9	4.8	21.6	9.6	18.5	4.0	42.6	82.5	338.4	338.4
Fish and Fish Products	2.7	7.9	5.5	7.7	0.0	16.5	..	24.0	.5	7.3	7.3
Petroleum Oils	7.7	8.2	1.2	3.8	0.0	8.8	..	4.5	9.9	199.5	199.5
Wood, Pulp, Paper and Furniture	35.0	1.0	5.0	1.1	38.2	5.2	4.9	3.7	53.4	594.2	594.2
Textiles and Clothing	84.2	10.6	3.6	10.7	60.6	13.3	5.9	11.8	73.3	452.5	452.5
Leather, Rubber, Footwear	57.1	7.9	3.2	8.1	55.4	9.9	5.8	11.2	23.7	191.3	191.3
Metals	70.6	3.7	4.3	4.1	39.0	10.8	3.2	12.7	259.1	783.4	783.4
Chemical & Photographic Suppl.	56.2	4.9	4.0	6.0	45.4	8.3	4.3	11.7	136.3	471.5	471.5
Transport Equipment	35.4	8.6	5.7	7.2	17.7	11.9	5.4	13.9	199.6	343.9	343.9
Non-Electric Machinery	54.3	8.4	2.7	10.6	31.3	12.1	3.7	15.9	321.7	516.3	516.3
Electric Machinery	62.4	6.7	2.7	8.2	35.4	10.8	3.8	13.5	75.2	163.8	163.8
Mineral Prod.,Prec. Stones & Metal	49.4	3.7	2.7	4.3	29.9	6.7	5.0	8.6	127.9	584.9	584.9
Manufactured Articles nes.	74.0	4.4	3.4	5.2	48.3	8.6	4.0	11.4	49.8	178.2	178.2
Industrial Goods (line 5-14)	**57.0**	**5.5**	**3.7**	**6.0**	**35.3**	**10.4**	**4.3**	**12.6**	**1,319.9**	**4,280.1**	**4,280.1**
All Merch. Trade (line 2-14)	**53.3**	**5.8**	**3.8**	**6.7**	**33.5**	**10.9**	**4.3**	**14.7**	**1,412.8**	**4,825.2**	**4,825.2**

Notes: 1. Value of exports from reporter countries that do not participate in Free Trade Agreements with Czech&Slovak CU

2. Weighted average tariff reduction measured by dT / (1 + T) in percent.

DJIBOUTI Extent of other countries' MFN tariff reductions on DJIBOUTI's exports

Summary product category	Average levels and changes weighted by value of exports to: the World exc. FTA[1]				LMIEs exc. FTA[1]				Value of exports in $ million		
	% of exports affected	Post-UR applied rate	Tariff reduction[2]	Post-UR bound rate	% of exports affected	Post-UR applied rate	Tariff reduction[2]	Post-UR bound rate	To IDB LMIEs exc. FTA[1]	To all IDB Ctrys exc. FTA[1]	To all IDB Ctrys inc. FTA
Agriculture, exc. Fish: Estimate 1	0.0	51.6	..	71.5	0.0	0.0	..	0.0	.0	.0	.0
Agriculture, exc. Fish: Estimate 2	4.9	1.9	1.9	2.3	87.0	27.3	2.3	33.0	.0	.8	.8
Fish and Fish Products	1.2	0.1	41.5	9.6	100.0	5.0	41.5	5.0	.0	.1	.1
Petroleum Oils	..	..	..	..	..	..	..	..	.0	.0	.0
Wood, Pulp, Paper and Furniture	19.1	0.0	7.7	0.0	..	..	..	..	.0	.0	.0
Textiles and Clothing	99.7	12.5	2.0	12.5	..	..	..	..	.0	.7	.7
Leather, Rubber, Footwear	0.0	8.0	..	8.0	..	..	..	..	.0	.0	.0
Metals	18.5	0.3	4.2	0.3	..	..	..	..	.0	.5	.5
Chemical & Photographic Suppl.	19.4	2.4	1.8	2.4	..	..	..	..	.0	.0	.0
Transport Equipment	0.2	0.1	3.5	0.1	..	..	..	..	.0	8.8	8.8
Non-Electric Machinery	100.0	2.4	2.6	2.4	..	..	..	..	.0	.1	.1
Electric Machinery	100.0	4.1	1.6	4.1	..	..	..	..	.0	.2	.2
Mineral Prod.,Prec. Stones & Metal	100.0	0.8	0.3	0.8	..	..	..	..	.0	.0	.0
Manufactured Articles nes.	7.4	0.4	3.0	0.4	0.0	..	..	..	.0	2.9	2.9
Industrial Goods (line 5-14)	**10.0**	**0.9**	**2.4**	**0.9**	**0.0**	**..**	**..**	**..**	**.0**	**13.3**	**13.3**
All Merch. Trade (line 2-14)	**9.7**	**0.9**	**2.4**	**1.0**	**43.8**	**26.3**	**4.2**	**31.9**	**.0**	**14.2**	**14.2**

Notes: 1. Value of exports from reporter countries that do not participate in Free Trade Agreements with DJIBOUTI

2. Weighted average tariff reduction measured by dT / (1 + T) in percent.

DOMINICA Extent of other countries' MFN tariff reductions on DOMINICA's exports

| Summary product category | Average levels and changes weighted by value of exports to: | | | | | | | | Value of exports in $ million | | |
| | the World exc. FTA[1] | | | | LMIEs exc. FTA[1] | | | | | | |
	% of exports affected	Post-UR applied rate	Tariff reduc-tion[2]	Post-UR bound rate	% of exports affected	Post-UR applied rate	Tariff reduc-tion[2]	Post-UR bound rate	To IDB LMIEs exc. FTA[1]	To all IDB Ctrys exc. FTA[1]	To all IDB Ctrys inc. FTA
Agriculture, exc. Fish: Estimate 1	0.0	0.0	..	0.0	..	..	..	..	.0	63.2	63.2
Agriculture, exc. Fish: Estimate 2	1.7	4.0	2.8	5.3	0.0	38.6	..	88.3	.1	64.4	64.4
Fish and Fish Products	..	..	..	..	..	..	..	..	.0	.0	.0
Petroleum Oils	0.0	0.0	..	3.5	..	..	..	..	.0	.2	.2
Wood, Pulp, Paper and Furniture	79.4	1.8	5.9	2.1	0.0	10.0	..	35.0	.0	.4	.4
Textiles and Clothing	98.4	16.6	3.6	16.6	..	..	..	..	.0	3.0	3.0
Leather, Rubber, Footwear	48.1	8.7	1.7	21.8	0.0	14.2	..	39.3	.1	.1	.1
Metals	44.5	3.4	2.7	3.5	0.0	4.8	..	5.1	2.3	5.5	5.5
Chemical & Photographic Suppl.	14.2	36.3	4.7	40.9	0.0	43.9	..	49.5	6.6	8.1	8.1
Transport Equipment	90.7	3.7	0.8	6.9	0.0	12.8	..	50.0	.0	.2	.2
Non-Electric Machinery	76.0	3.5	3.7	5.2	4.6	12.4	0.9	25.6	.3	2.0	2.0
Electric Machinery	71.8	6.0	2.7	7.0	0.0	15.4	..	34.5	.0	.7	.7
Mineral Prod.,Prec. Stones & Metal	11.4	1.8	2.9	16.9	0.0	0.0	..	50.0	.1	.5	.5
Manufactured Articles nes.	71.5	1.9	4.4	1.9	64.7	21.0	4.4	29.4	.0	1.9	1.9
Industrial Goods (line 5-14)	**47.2**	**16.9**	**3.6**	**19.4**	**0.4**	**32.1**	**2.9**	**38.1**	**9.6**	**22.4**	**22.4**
All Merch. Trade (line 2-14)	**13.4**	**15.7**	**3.5**	**18.0**	**0.4**	**32.1**	**2.9**	**38.4**	**9.6**	**87.0**	**87.0**

Notes: 1. Value of exports from reporter countries that do not participate in Free Trade Agreements with DOMINICA

2. Weighted average tariff reduction measured by dT / (1 + T) in percent.

DOMINICAN REPUBLIC Extent of other countries' MFN tariff reductions on DOMINICAN REPUBLIC's exports

| Summary product category | Average levels and changes weighted by value of exports to: | | | | | | | | Value of exports in $ million | | |
| | the World exc. FTA[1] | | | | LMIEs exc. FTA[1] | | | | | | |
	% of exports affected	Post-UR applied rate	Tariff reduc-tion[2]	Post-UR bound rate	% of exports affected	Post-UR applied rate	Tariff reduc-tion[2]	Post-UR bound rate	To IDB LMIEs exc. FTA[1]	To all IDB Ctrys exc. FTA[1]	To all IDB Ctrys inc. FTA
Agriculture, exc. Fish: Estimate 1	1.0	46.3	11.1	46.9	0.1	2.1	15.6	73.2	2.5	305.4	305.4
Agriculture, exc. Fish: Estimate 2	29.8	5.8	3.9	6.3	0.8	18.7	15.3	86.2	2.6	393.4	393.4
Fish and Fish Products	27.2	0.2	0.8	0.2	..	..	..	..	.0	1.2	1.2
Petroleum Oils	0.0	0.5	..	0.5	..	..	..	..	.0	1.0	1.0
Wood, Pulp, Paper and Furniture	86.7	0.6	5.1	0.6	35.7	34.9	4.3	42.0	.1	24.5	24.5
Textiles and Clothing	96.3	16.6	1.7	16.6	56.5	18.9	4.4	37.0	.1	754.8	754.8
Leather, Rubber, Footwear	51.8	5.4	1.8	5.4	0.0	20.4	..	35.0	.0	32.2	32.2
Metals	23.5	0.9	2.7	1.3	0.0	0.5	..	35.4	7.3	275.7	275.7
Chemical & Photographic Suppl.	27.2	2.6	2.8	4.3	0.0	7.5	..	36.7	.9	16.6	16.6
Transport Equipment	4.7	8.1	0.6	24.3	0.0	11.6	..	35.2	.2	.3	.3
Non-Electric Machinery	86.1	0.4	3.5	0.7	0.0	7.8	..	31.8	.1	7.1	7.1
Electric Machinery	97.3	3.3	1.9	3.3	33.3	13.1	6.0	22.7	.0	83.7	83.7
Mineral Prod.,Prec. Stones & Metal	41.5	3.2	1.1	3.3	0.0	15.2	..	41.0	.5	184.7	184.7
Manufactured Articles nes.	94.9	0.2	6.8	0.2	48.0	14.5	0.9	20.2	.2	75.3	75.3
Industrial Goods (line 5-14)	**73.5**	**9.6**	**2.2**	**9.7**	**2.0**	**3.0**	**2.2**	**35.5**	**9.4**	**1,454.8**	**1,454.8**
All Merch. Trade (line 2-14)	**64.2**	**8.8**	**2.3**	**9.0**	**1.8**	**6.4**	**3.6**	**54.1**	**12.0**	**1,850.4**	**1,850.4**

Notes: 1. Value of exports from reporter countries that do not participate in Free Trade Agreements with Domenican Rep.

2. Weighted average tariff reduction measured by dT / (1 + T) in percent.

EAST TIMOR Extent of other countries' MFN tariff reductions on EAST TIMOR's exports

| | Average levels and changes weighted by value of exports to: | | | | | | | | Value of exports in $ million | | |
| | the World exc. FTA[1] | | | | LMIEs exc. FTA[1] | | | | | | |
Summary product category	% of exports affected	Post-UR applied rate	Tariff reduc-tion[2]	Post-UR bound rate	% of exports affected	Post-UR applied rate	Tariff reduc-tion[2]	Post-UR bound rate	To IDB LMIEs exc. FTA[1]	To all IDB Ctrys exc. FTA[1]	To all IDB Ctrys inc. FTA
Agriculture, exc. Fish: Estimate 1	100.0	10.0	14.3	10.0	..	..	..	..	.0	.7	.7
Agriculture, exc. Fish: Estimate 2	100.0	10.0	14.3	10.0	..	..	..	..	.0	.7	.7
Fish and Fish Products	0.0	0.0	..	10.0	..	..	..	..	.0	.0	.0
Petroleum Oils	..	..	..	..	..	..	..	..	.0	.0	.0
Wood, Pulp, Paper and Furniture	..	..	..	..	..	..	..	..	.0	.0	.0
Textiles and Clothing	100.0	9.1	1.9	9.1	..	..	..	..	.0	.0	.0
Leather, Rubber, Footwear	80.0	3.2	4.7	4.0	..	..	..	..	.0	.0	.0
Metals	28.6	0.0	2.5	7.1	..	..	..	..	.0	.0	.0
Chemical & Photographic Suppl.	50.0	3.2	5.0	6.5	..	..	..	..	.0	.0	.0
Transport Equipment	..	..	..	..	..	..	..	..	.0	.0	.0
Non-Electric Machinery	84.9	1.5	2.0	2.0	..	..	..	..	.0	.1	.1
Electric Machinery	0.0	0.0	..	10.0	..	..	..	..	.0	.1	.1
Mineral Prod.,Prec. Stones & Metal	100.0	3.7	0.1	3.7	..	..	..	..	.0	.0	.0
Manufactured Articles nes.	1.6	0.0	0.8	9.9	..	..	..	..	.0	.3	.3
Industrial Goods (line 5-14)	**19.1**	**0.6**	**1.8**	**8.5**	..	..	..	..	**.0**	**.4**	**.4**
All Merch. Trade (line 2-14)	**69.6**	**6.5**	**13.1**	**9.5**	..	..	..	..	**.0**	**1.1**	**1.1**

Notes: 1. Value of exports from reporter countries that do not participate in Free Trade Agreements with EAST TIMOR

2. Weighted average tariff reduction measured by dT / (1 + T) in percent.

ECUADOR Extent of other countries' MFN tariff reductions on ECUADOR's exports

| | Average levels and changes weighted by value of exports to: | | | | | | | | Value of exports in $ million | | |
| | the World exc. FTA[1] | | | | LMIEs exc. FTA[1] | | | | | | |
Summary product category	% of exports affected	Post-UR applied rate	Tariff reduc-tion[2]	Post-UR bound rate	% of exports affected	Post-UR applied rate	Tariff reduc-tion[2]	Post-UR bound rate	To IDB LMIEs exc. FTA[1]	To all IDB Ctrys exc. FTA[1]	To all IDB Ctrys inc. FTA
Agriculture, exc. Fish: Estimate 1	0.6	0.9	30.9	3.6	6.8	1.1	32.9	31.9	62.1	821.9	821.9
Agriculture, exc. Fish: Estimate 2	13.6	3.3	8.1	7.5	6.1	12.7	3.2	44.1	98.2	937.7	937.7
Fish and Fish Products	12.3	1.4	3.5	2.3	0.0	13.5	..	34.3	7.2	429.0	429.0
Petroleum Oils	0.0	2.3	0.3	13.0	0.0	5.9	..	27.8	308.8	972.4	972.4
Wood, Pulp, Paper and Furniture	42.6	2.8	3.4	4.8	2.7	9.3	7.8	31.8	2.4	24.8	24.8
Textiles and Clothing	30.8	8.8	2.2	14.2	1.4	18.2	9.6	36.6	6.8	23.7	23.7
Leather, Rubber, Footwear	11.8	7.8	2.2	5.4	0.0	40.9	..	32.1	.2	1.4	1.4
Metals	33.1	4.8	3.4	13.5	0.0	11.8	..	33.8	1.8	4.5	4.5
Chemical & Photographic Suppl.	14.7	10.5	3.3	31.9	0.5	13.2	3.9	42.2	5.6	7.6	7.6
Transport Equipment	7.4	15.0	2.4	30.5	0.0	16.6	..	35.1	1.4	1.6	1.6
Non-Electric Machinery	40.8	7.1	2.5	19.3	0.1	11.1	6.0	32.1	1.8	3.2	3.2
Electric Machinery	10.2	14.7	2.5	28.7	0.0	16.4	..	31.9	4.1	4.7	4.7
Mineral Prod.,Prec. Stones & Metal	5.7	0.5	2.2	1.6	2.7	8.0	3.6	36.4	2.6	67.5	67.5
Manufactured Articles nes.	40.4	4.3	3.2	16.2	0.7	6.7	1.2	31.8	4.3	9.1	9.1
Industrial Goods (line 5-14)	**20.3**	**3.9**	**2.9**	**8.5**	**0.9**	**13.2**	**6.3**	**35.4**	**30.9**	**148.0**	**148.0**
All Merch. Trade (line 2-14)	**8.5**	**2.6**	**6.2**	**6.5**	**1.4**	**8.0**	**3.4**	**37.7**	**445.1**	**2,487.1**	**2,487.1**

Notes: 1. Value of exports from reporter countries that do not participate in Free Trade Agreements with ECUADOR

2. Weighted average tariff reduction measured by dT / (1 + T) in percent.

EGYPT, ARAB REP. Extent of other countries' MFN tariff reductions on EGYPT, ARAB REP.'s exports

Summary product category	Average levels and changes weighted by value of exports to: the World exc. FTA[1]				LMIEs exc. FTA[1]				Value of exports in $ million		
	% of exports affected	Post-UR applied rate	Tariff reduc-tion[2]	Post-UR bound rate	% of exports affected	Post-UR applied rate	Tariff reduc-tion[2]	Post-UR bound rate	To IDB LMIEs exc. FTA[1]	To all IDB Ctrys exc. FTA[1]	To all IDB Ctrys inc. FTA
Agriculture, exc. Fish: Estimate 1	0.1	0.2	7.8	5.8	0.0	-1.3	..	26.5	62.4	315.5	315.5
Agriculture, exc. Fish: Estimate 2	51.8	9.0	3.5	15.1	40.7	17.8	2.3	42.5	28.8	136.9	136.9
Fish and Fish Products	88.3	12.0	1.5	12.1	0.0	21.7	..	28.3	.0	12.3	12.3
Petroleum Oils	2.7	2.5	1.2	7.0	0.0	8.1	..	32.4	503.8	1,740.2	1,740.2
Wood, Pulp, Paper and Furniture	70.8	1.4	3.7	3.1	2.4	5.9	12.8	32.9	1.3	6.4	6.4
Textiles and Clothing	76.7	10.3	2.1	9.9	21.2	24.2	4.9	24.0	62.4	368.8	368.8
Leather, Rubber, Footwear	32.3	7.6	1.8	8.2	13.0	14.6	1.5	15.8	8.2	19.4	19.4
Metals	24.7	5.8	3.3	5.8	23.4	20.5	9.0	24.0	12.2	260.0	260.0
Chemical & Photographic Suppl.	10.5	9.5	5.7	15.4	2.1	11.0	19.1	19.2	35.2	48.8	48.8
Transport Equipment	3.9	21.0	2.7	24.4	0.0	30.0	..	35.0	14.1	20.7	20.7
Non-Electric Machinery	35.4	6.9	2.5	12.6	2.2	17.5	1.8	32.5	9.0	24.6	24.6
Electric Machinery	16.8	11.8	3.0	26.1	0.0	14.5	..	31.6	12.8	16.5	16.5
Mineral Prod.,Prec. Stones & Metal	28.4	3.7	2.6	10.2	0.3	7.1	6.0	29.3	16.5	41.3	41.3
Manufactured Articles nes.	5.0	0.5	3.7	0.8	13.0	2.1	4.3	3.9	55.2	285.5	285.5
Industrial Goods (line 5-14)	**36.7**	**6.4**	**2.4**	**7.2**	**11.2**	**14.4**	**5.5**	**19.4**	**226.8**	**1,091.9**	**1,091.9**
All Merch. Trade (line 2-14)	**17.8**	**4.3**	**2.5**	**7.5**	**4.9**	**10.6**	**4.5**	**27.5**	**759.4**	**2,981.3**	**2,981.3**

Notes: 1. Value of exports from reporter countries that do not participate in Free Trade Agreements with Egypt

2. Weighted average tariff reduction measured by dT / (1 + T) in percent.

EL SALVADOR Extent of other countries' MFN tariff reductions on EL SALVADOR's exports

Summary product category	Average levels and changes weighted by value of exports to: the World exc. FTA[1]				LMIEs exc. FTA[1]				Value of exports in $ million		
	% of exports affected	Post-UR applied rate	Tariff reduc-tion[2]	Post-UR bound rate	% of exports affected	Post-UR applied rate	Tariff reduc-tion[2]	Post-UR bound rate	To IDB LMIEs exc. FTA[1]	To all IDB Ctrys exc. FTA[1]	To all IDB Ctrys inc. FTA
Agriculture, exc. Fish: Estimate 1	1.3	5.3	11.7	5.8	0.0	3.4	..	53.8	1.4	371.2	371.2
Agriculture, exc. Fish: Estimate 2	46.7	0.5	4.9	0.9	32.7	10.8	3.5	68.7	1.3	380.1	380.1
Fish and Fish Products	3.5	0.0	0.8	0.0	..	..	..	..	.0	19.1	19.1
Petroleum Oils	..	..	..	..	..	..	..	..	.0	.0	.0
Wood, Pulp, Paper and Furniture	97.4	0.3	4.6	0.5	5.1	2.6	2.9	11.4	.1	5.8	5.8
Textiles and Clothing	86.8	13.4	1.7	13.5	15.8	18.6	14.1	35.4	.4	66.3	66.3
Leather, Rubber, Footwear	10.4	8.2	2.0	9.1	0.0	10.8	..	25.7	.2	4.0	4.0
Metals	17.4	3.6	1.5	8.2	1.5	11.5	0.6	30.1	1.1	4.6	4.6
Chemical & Photographic Suppl.	42.0	5.3	3.8	12.5	10.4	10.4	1.0	26.8	.6	1.5	1.5
Transport Equipment	15.1	11.0	1.4	15.6	0.7	18.3	0.5	30.5	.1	.3	.3
Non-Electric Machinery	37.9	4.2	3.6	16.5	10.2	10.3	1.6	32.0	.1	.2	.2
Electric Machinery	98.6	8.6	1.3	8.7	19.4	10.6	1.9	20.5	.2	26.9	26.9
Mineral Prod.,Prec. Stones & Metal	21.3	6.6	3.0	7.1	0.0	7.3	..	10.6	.1	.4	.4
Manufactured Articles nes.	8.1	4.5	4.6	8.2	0.7	15.3	14.3	38.8	24.4	27.4	27.4
Industrial Goods (line 5-14)	**68.4**	**10.6**	**1.8**	**11.2**	**1.3**	**12.5**	**9.6**	**29.9**	**27.4**	**137.5**	**137.5**
All Merch. Trade (line 2-14)	**50.7**	**2.8**	**3.8**	**3.2**	**2.8**	**12.0**	**6.3**	**40.4**	**28.7**	**536.6**	**536.6**

Notes: 1. Value of exports from reporter countries that do not participate in Free Trade Agreements with EL SALVADOR

2. Weighted average tariff reduction measured by dT / (1 + T) in percent.

EQUATORIAL GUINEA **Extent of other countries' MFN tariff reductions on EQUATORIAL GUINEA's exports**

Summary product category	Average levels and changes weighted by value of exports to: the World exc. FTA[1]				LMIEs exc. FTA[1]				Value of exports in $ million		
	% of exports affected	Post-UR applied rate	Tariff reduc-tion[2]	Post-UR bound rate	% of exports affected	Post-UR applied rate	Tariff reduc-tion[2]	Post-UR bound rate	To IDB LMIEs exc. FTA[1]	To all IDB Ctrys exc. FTA[1]	To all IDB Ctrys inc. FTA
Agriculture, exc. Fish: Estimate 1	0.0	0.0	..	0.0	0.0	0.0	..	0.0	.0	15.1	15.1
Agriculture, exc. Fish: Estimate 2	98.8	0.0	3.1	0.0	..	..	..	..	.0	15.1	15.1
Fish and Fish Products	100.0	12.0	5.2	12.0	..	..	..	..	.0	4.2	4.2
Petroleum Oils	..	..	..	..	..	..	..	..	.0	.0	.0
Wood, Pulp, Paper and Furniture	8.9	0.3	2.5	0.3	0.0	0.0	..	0.0	.0	28.8	28.8
Textiles and Clothing	100.0	6.8	1.9	6.8	..	..	..	..	.0	.1	.1
Leather, Rubber, Footwear	60.4	3.8	1.4	3.8	..	..	..	..	.0	.0	.0
Metals	62.0	0.8	3.7	0.8	..	..	..	..	.0	.1	.1
Chemical & Photographic Suppl.	100.0	6.5	4.6	6.5	..	..	..	..	.0	.1	.1
Transport Equipment	48.4	6.4	5.7	6.4	..	..	..	..	.0	.1	.1
Non-Electric Machinery	80.5	0.3	4.8	0.3	..	..	..	..	.0	.0	.0
Electric Machinery	42.0	11.0	2.6	21.5	0.0	16.8	..	35.0	.1	.1	.1
Mineral Prod.,Prec. Stones & Metal	0.0	0.0	..	0.0	..	..	..	..	.0	.1	.1
Manufactured Articles nes.	7.4	5.5	6.1	19.1	0.0	16.9	..	58.2	.0	.1	.1
Industrial Goods (line 5-14)	**10.0**	**0.4**	**2.6**	**0.5**	**0.0**	**12.1**	**..**	**32.2**	**.1**	**29.5**	**29.5**
All Merch. Trade (line 2-14)	**45.2**	**1.3**	**3.4**	**1.3**	**0.0**	**12.1**	**..**	**32.2**	**.1**	**48.8**	**48.8**

Notes: 1. Value of exports from reporter countries that do not participate in Free Trade Agreements with Equat. Guinea

2. Weighted average tariff reduction measured by dT / (1 + T) in percent.

ETHIOPIA **Extent of other countries' MFN tariff reductions on ETHIOPIA's exports**

Summary product category	Average levels and changes weighted by value of exports to: the World exc. FTA[1]				LMIEs exc. FTA[1]				Value of exports in $ million		
	% of exports affected	Post-UR applied rate	Tariff reduc-tion[2]	Post-UR bound rate	% of exports affected	Post-UR applied rate	Tariff reduc-tion[2]	Post-UR bound rate	To IDB LMIEs exc. FTA[1]	To all IDB Ctrys exc. FTA[1]	To all IDB Ctrys inc. FTA
Agriculture, exc. Fish: Estimate 1	0.1	0.0	23.2	0.1	0.5	-0.4	15.6	6.8	1.0	236.0	236.0
Agriculture, exc. Fish: Estimate 2	52.2	0.5	4.8	0.8	0.4	10.4	7.4	52.4	1.2	244.6	244.6
Fish and Fish Products	6.3	0.8	10.5	0.8	..	..	..	..	.0	.0	.0
Petroleum Oils	..	..	..	..	..	..	..	..	.0	.0	.0
Wood, Pulp, Paper and Furniture	12.6	15.3	5.4	20.4	0.0	22.4	..	30.2	.1	.2	.2
Textiles and Clothing	97.6	9.8	1.5	9.8	100.0	2.5	3.0	2.5	.7	6.0	6.0
Leather, Rubber, Footwear	83.8	2.5	1.1	2.6	100.0	9.8	8.4	9.8	.7	28.0	28.0
Metals	7.1	1.5	2.7	3.4	0.0	9.5	..	28.3	.1	.5	.5
Chemical & Photographic Suppl.	91.4	0.2	4.1	4.1	0.0	1.3	..	48.8	.2	2.2	2.2
Transport Equipment	31.8	3.9	0.5	2.5	1.5	13.6	6.0	13.0	.1	.5	.5
Non-Electric Machinery	32.7	2.4	2.4	5.2	0.0	14.7	..	36.1	.1	.9	.9
Electric Machinery	11.5	7.9	2.2	16.3	0.0	17.4	..	37.3	.0	.1	.1
Mineral Prod.,Prec. Stones & Metal	3.9	2.9	2.0	1.0	0.0	5.1	..	25.0	.4	.7	.7
Manufactured Articles nes.	8.5	0.4	2.1	4.9	0.0	1.2	..	41.9	4.0	36.9	36.9
Industrial Goods (line 5-14)	**46.1**	**2.1**	**1.5**	**4.4**	**21.7**	**3.4**	**5.8**	**33.2**	**6.3**	**76.0**	**76.0**
All Merch. Trade (line 2-14)	**50.8**	**0.9**	**4.1**	**1.6**	**18.3**	**4.6**	**5.8**	**36.5**	**7.5**	**320.6**	**320.6**

Notes: 1. Value of exports from reporter countries that do not participate in Free Trade Agreements with ETHIOPIA

2. Weighted average tariff reduction measured by dT / (1 + T) in percent.

EUROPEAN UNION Extent of other countries' MFN tariff reductions on EUROPEAN UNION's exports

Summary product category	Average levels and changes weighted by value of exports to: the World exc. FTA[1]				LMIEs exc. FTA[1]				Value of exports in $ million		
	% of exports affected	Post-UR applied rate	Tariff reduc-tion[2]	Post-UR bound rate	% of exports affected	Post-UR applied rate	Tariff reduc-tion[2]	Post-UR bound rate	To IDB LMIEs exc. FTA[1]	To all IDB Ctrys exc. FTA[1]	To all IDB Ctrys inc. FTA
Agriculture, exc. Fish: Estimate 1	9.6	33.6	52.6	55.9	9.9	12.8	78.8	66.6	2,522.1	6,872.5	6,872.5
Agriculture, exc. Fish: Estimate 2	42.5	9.2	3.1	19.9	21.7	19.4	5.3	54.7	4,140.4	20,420.0	20,420.0
Fish and Fish Products	31.9	2.7	6.7	2.8	59.8	6.6	27.1	6.7	115.9	755.7	1,177.1
Petroleum Oils	0.5	1.7	1.5	2.5	3.9	14.0	1.8	28.8	608.9	5,814.9	8,420.4
Wood, Pulp, Paper and Furniture	23.8	2.2	4.9	3.2	28.6	13.5	8.0	19.5	1,255.8	6,184.5	13,285.2
Textiles and Clothing	34.7	11.4	4.3	12.2	44.0	23.4	6.7	27.9	2,665.7	10,493.3	19,919.0
Leather, Rubber, Footwear	25.1	8.0	3.9	8.0	49.0	18.0	6.4	18.0	1,143.8	6,451.4	10,078.7
Metals	30.7	5.2	5.3	5.4	26.0	16.2	10.0	23.1	5,527.8	15,072.8	25,945.7
Chemical & Photographic Suppl.	31.3	5.2	5.5	6.6	35.5	13.5	8.8	19.7	10,882.0	31,276.8	46,415.5
Transport Equipment	12.5	5.0	3.2	6.1	18.4	18.7	8.8	21.5	3,953.6	23,531.5	36,357.1
Non-Electric Machinery	38.5	5.4	3.5	6.1	41.5	13.9	4.7	19.9	12,616.5	36,304.0	53,832.3
Electric Machinery	27.1	7.9	3.9	7.6	29.6	17.7	6.6	22.5	5,135.5	13,448.7	21,556.8
Mineral Prod.,Prec. Stones & Metal	22.5	3.1	3.3	4.0	16.4	7.2	7.9	18.2	3,566.4	14,682.7	20,756.2
Manufactured Articles nes.	32.0	3.1	4.1	4.1	41.1	13.6	6.2	21.7	3,269.4	16,296.2	23,774.5
Industrial Goods (line 5-14)	**28.9**	**5.3**	**4.3**	**6.3**	**33.6**	**14.9**	**6.9**	**21.0**	**50,016.5**	**173,742.0**	**271,921.0**
All Merch. Trade (line 2-14)	**29.0**	**5.5**	**4.2**	**7.0**	**32.4**	**15.2**	**6.9**	**24.0**	**54,881.7**	**200,732.0**	**301,939.0**

Notes: 1. Value of exports from reporter countries that do not participate in Free Trade Agreements with European Union

2. Weighted average tariff reduction measured by dT / (1 + T) in percent.

FIJI Extent of other countries' MFN tariff reductions on FIJI's exports

Summary product category	Average levels and changes weighted by value of exports to: the World exc. FTA[1]				LMIEs exc. FTA[1]				Value of exports in $ million		
	% of exports affected	Post-UR applied rate	Tariff reduc-tion[2]	Post-UR bound rate	% of exports affected	Post-UR applied rate	Tariff reduc-tion[2]	Post-UR bound rate	To IDB LMIEs exc. FTA[1]	To all IDB Ctrys exc. FTA[1]	To all IDB Ctrys inc. FTA
Agriculture, exc. Fish: Estimate 1	18.6	128.0	5.1	128.0	100.0	82.0	5.3	82.0	16.9	139.6	139.6
Agriculture, exc. Fish: Estimate 2	3.8	27.6	5.7	52.1	2.9	0.3	7.8	14.9	17.4	156.2	156.2
Fish and Fish Products	32.0	14.6	3.8	14.7	100.0	5.0	41.5	5.0	.0	33.0	33.0
Petroleum Oils	..	..	..	..	..	..	..	..	.0	.0	.0
Wood, Pulp, Paper and Furniture	25.8	3.0	10.9	5.4	4.6	4.0	3.7	12.2	1.9	20.0	20.0
Textiles and Clothing	56.4	36.2	3.9	45.0	100.0	7.0	3.1	7.0	.0	41.5	41.5
Leather, Rubber, Footwear	20.9	36.6	7.9	38.4	..	..	..	..	.0	2.3	2.3
Metals	14.0	3.2	5.8	3.9	100.0	3.0	6.6	3.0	.0	.8	.8
Chemical & Photographic Suppl.	23.4	12.5	6.3	16.0	20.0	27.6	9.7	35.6	.1	.4	.4
Transport Equipment	2.5	4.9	7.6	5.8	..	..	..	..	.0	.7	.7
Non-Electric Machinery	11.2	3.1	2.1	5.2	0.0	22.0	..	22.0	.0	.3	.3
Electric Machinery	12.8	5.1	2.6	6.4	0.0	17.5	..	25.0	.0	.1	.1
Mineral Prod.,Prec. Stones & Metal	0.1	0.0	5.7	0.1	..	..	..	..	.0	28.7	28.7
Manufactured Articles nes.	22.2	4.2	3.9	4.6	100.0	13.0	6.0	13.0	.0	1.2	1.2
Industrial Goods (line 5-14)	**30.8**	**17.3**	**5.2**	**23.0**	**10.9**	**5.3**	**5.0**	**13.2**	**2.1**	**96.0**	**96.0**
All Merch. Trade (line 2-14)	**16.2**	**20.0**	**4.9**	**30.8**	**3.8**	**0.9**	**7.0**	**14.7**	**19.5**	**285.2**	**285.2**

Notes: 1. Value of exports from reporter countries that do not participate in Free Trade Agreements with FIJI

2. Weighted average tariff reduction measured by dT / (1 + T) in percent.

FINLAND Extent of other countries' MFN tariff reductions on FINLAND's exports

Summary product category	Average levels and changes weighted by value of exports to: the World exc. FTA[1]				Average levels and changes weighted by value of exports to: LMIEs exc. FTA[1]				Value of exports in $ million		
	% of exports affected	Post-UR applied rate	Tariff reduc-tion[2]	Post-UR bound rate	% of exports affected	Post-UR applied rate	Tariff reduc-tion[2]	Post-UR bound rate	To IDB LMIEs exc. FTA[1]	To all IDB Ctrys exc. FTA[1]	To all IDB Ctrys inc. FTA
Agriculture, exc. Fish: Estimate 1	4.0	77.0	4.4	82.7	0.0	10.8	..	56.5	12.8	118.2	118.2
Agriculture, exc. Fish: Estimate 2	22.2	6.7	2.6	19.0	15.4	17.3	2.6	54.8	30.7	332.8	332.8
Fish and Fish Products	25.9	1.3	1.8	4.6	0.0	6.1	..	47.3	.1	6.1	21.8
Petroleum Oils	0.0	0.0	..	1.7	0.0	10.2	..	13.0	.0	.0	373.6
Wood, Pulp, Paper and Furniture	7.1	0.5	4.8	1.2	23.8	10.3	9.2	18.3	321.0	1,282.8	8,551.8
Textiles and Clothing	5.4	9.3	7.2	9.8	70.2	18.8	13.7	21.1	21.3	50.1	731.6
Leather, Rubber, Footwear	11.2	4.6	4.5	5.4	79.7	13.9	8.2	15.6	11.6	46.4	225.0
Metals	11.4	0.9	7.2	1.8	45.9	11.0	16.2	12.9	102.2	405.1	1,984.0
Chemical & Photographic Suppl.	8.4	3.6	5.4	5.7	34.5	13.9	10.0	22.3	74.0	192.8	1,064.9
Transport Equipment	1.6	1.6	4.3	5.8	25.6	9.1	1.7	15.7	13.3	30.0	768.5
Non-Electric Machinery	21.0	2.3	3.7	2.6	49.8	11.0	3.8	16.4	153.3	823.9	2,143.9
Electric Machinery	9.5	8.5	5.8	6.2	63.7	19.6	9.3	21.0	60.1	158.9	961.8
Mineral Prod.,Prec. Stones & Metal	4.3	0.9	2.8	2.5	21.8	11.9	4.2	16.5	12.4	39.0	371.9
Manufactured Articles nes.	14.2	1.9	3.2	4.2	15.6	9.8	4.1	29.6	88.3	308.8	892.2
Industrial Goods (line 5-14)	**9.5**	**1.1**	**4.8**	**2.8**	**35.9**	**11.7**	**8.8**	**19.2**	**857.4**	**3,337.7**	**17,695.5**
All Merch. Trade (line 2-14)	**9.6**	**1.2**	**4.7**	**2.9**	**35.2**	**11.9**	**8.7**	**20.5**	**888.2**	**3,676.6**	**18,423.5**

Notes: 1. Value of exports from reporter countries that do not participate in Free Trade Agreements with FINLAND

2. Weighted average tariff reduction measured by dT / (1 + T) in percent.

FORMER YUGOSLAVIA Extent of other countries' MFN tariff reductions on YUGOSLAVIA's exports

Summary product category	Average levels and changes weighted by value of exports to: the World exc. FTA[1]				Average levels and changes weighted by value of exports to: LMIEs exc. FTA[1]				Value of exports in $ million		
	% of exports affected	Post-UR applied rate	Tariff reduc-tion[2]	Post-UR bound rate	% of exports affected	Post-UR applied rate	Tariff reduc-tion[2]	Post-UR bound rate	To IDB LMIEs exc. FTA[1]	To all IDB Ctrys exc. FTA[1]	To all IDB Ctrys inc. FTA
Agriculture, exc. Fish: Estimate 1	25.9	33.9	6.5	62.0	0.0	11.0	3.8	96.0	121.4	375.9	375.9
Agriculture, exc. Fish: Estimate 2	40.0	10.9	3.3	34.9	24.8	21.2	2.9	102.7	179.4	975.1	975.1
Fish and Fish Products	30.2	10.9	3.1	9.8	0.0	15.3	..	6.8	6.2	31.8	31.8
Petroleum Oils	4.3	1.6	1.1	4.2	79.5	4.8	1.1	4.7	6.0	173.5	173.5
Wood, Pulp, Paper and Furniture	72.2	1.9	5.6	1.9	68.0	13.4	7.8	13.7	74.9	1,036.1	1,036.1
Textiles and Clothing	92.9	10.5	2.5	10.6	72.8	12.3	5.2	12.9	120.9	1,204.8	1,204.8
Leather, Rubber, Footwear	70.2	7.1	2.3	6.4	76.1	18.6	2.7	8.0	35.9	524.2	524.2
Metals	51.4	6.2	3.8	4.8	27.3	15.9	4.3	13.8	570.1	1,995.9	1,995.9
Chemical & Photographic Suppl.	61.4	7.0	4.1	7.8	45.6	11.4	5.1	14.4	272.3	721.4	721.4
Transport Equipment	49.0	7.6	2.2	7.8	23.1	7.4	1.8	10.6	83.6	671.8	671.8
Non-Electric Machinery	92.0	3.4	2.3	3.8	81.5	6.1	2.2	7.4	136.4	576.5	576.5
Electric Machinery	81.5	5.2	2.7	5.5	41.0	10.2	4.3	11.5	145.2	586.2	586.2
Mineral Prod.,Prec. Stones & Metal	68.8	4.8	1.6	5.5	41.2	10.5	2.2	17.3	92.8	497.0	497.0
Manufactured Articles nes.	52.0	3.4	3.5	6.9	25.4	8.6	6.0	25.2	79.1	361.8	361.8
Industrial Goods (line 5-14)	**68.1**	**6.1**	**3.2**	**6.0**	**43.1**	**12.4**	**4.3**	**13.5**	**1,611.1**	**8,175.5**	**8,175.5**
All Merch. Trade (line 2-14)	**63.9**	**6.4**	**3.2**	**8.1**	**41.3**	**13.3**	**4.2**	**24.6**	**1,802.7**	**9,356.0**	**9,356.0**

Notes: 1. Value of exports from reporter countries that do not participate in Free Trade Agreements with F.Yugoslavia

2. Weighted average tariff reduction measured by dT / (1 + T) in percent.

GABON Extent of other countries' MFN tariff reductions on GABON's exports

Summary product category	Average levels and changes weighted by value of exports to: the World exc. FTA[1]				LMIEs exc. FTA[1]				Value of exports in $ million		
	% of exports affected	Post-UR applied rate	Tariff reduction[2]	Post-UR bound rate	% of exports affected	Post-UR applied rate	Tariff reduc-tion[2]	Post-UR bound rate	To IDB LMIEs exc. FTA[1]	To all IDB Ctrys exc. FTA[1]	To all IDB Ctrys inc. FTA
Agriculture, exc. Fish: Estimate 1	0.0	2.9	..	4.0	0.0	0.0	..	59.0	.1	7.4	7.4
Agriculture, exc. Fish: Estimate 2	63.6	0.6	3.7	0.6	0.0	16.4	..	35.2	.0	11.4	11.4
Fish and Fish Products	98.6	11.9	5.1	12.0	0.0	15.0	..	30.0	.0	19.8	19.8
Petroleum Oils	0.0	1.7	2.2	0.4	0.0	11.3	..	7.0	151.2	903.4	903.4
Wood, Pulp, Paper and Furniture	15.9	1.4	3.6	1.6	40.8	10.4	8.3	18.9	8.4	181.1	181.1
Textiles and Clothing	91.0	11.3	1.7	11.3	0.0	15.0	..	..	.0	.1	.1
Leather, Rubber, Footwear	60.0	3.3	2.4	2.5	0.0	15.0	..	..	.0	.0	.0
Metals	0.4	0.1	6.1	0.0	4.4	2.1	14.8	1.8	3.8	162.4	162.4
Chemical & Photographic Suppl.	0.1	0.1	2.8	0.0	0.0	13.8	..	41.0	.5	80.5	80.5
Transport Equipment	0.1	0.1	1.8	0.1	..	..	..	..	.0	270.1	270.1
Non-Electric Machinery	93.4	1.2	4.1	2.1	0.0	13.8	..	35.1	.1	2.5	2.5
Electric Machinery	79.6	2.9	2.5	3.1	0.0	17.1	..	31.4	.0	.7	.7
Mineral Prod.,Prec. Stones & Metal	57.6	2.5	1.7	2.3	60.0	22.5	13.3	27.7	.2	4.3	4.3
Manufactured Articles nes.	62.8	1.1	4.5	2.5	0.0	1.4	..	27.6	.3	3.0	3.0
Industrial Goods (line 5-14)	**5.2**	**0.4**	**3.6**	**0.5**	**27.8**	**8.2**	**8.8**	**13.7**	**13.3**	**704.6**	**704.6**
All Merch. Trade (line 2-14)	**3.9**	**1.2**	**4.0**	**0.7**	**2.3**	**11.0**	**8.8**	**9.3**	**164.6**	**1,639.1**	**1,639.1**

Notes: 1. Value of exports from reporter countries that do not participate in Free Trade Agreements with GABON

2. Weighted average tariff reduction measured by dT / (1 + T) in percent.

GAMBIA, THE Extent of other countries' MFN tariff reductions on GAMBIA's exports

Summary product category	Average levels and changes weighted by value of exports to: the World exc. FTA[1]				LMIEs exc. FTA[1]				Value of exports in $ million		
	% of exports affected	Post-UR applied rate	Tariff reduc-tion[2]	Post-UR bound rate	% of exports affected	Post-UR applied rate	Tariff reduc-tion[2]	Post-UR bound rate	To IDB LMIEs exc. FTA[1]	To all IDB Ctrys exc. FTA[1]	To all IDB Ctrys inc. FTA
Agriculture, exc. Fish: Estimate 1	0.0	39.4	..	39.4	0.0	0.0	..	30.0	.0	14.9	14.9
Agriculture, exc. Fish: Estimate 2	43.7	4.7	3.6	4.7	0.0	12.6	..	23.3	.0	15.0	15.0
Fish and Fish Products	87.3	5.8	2.6	5.8	0.0	15.0	..	30.0	.0	56.3	56.3
Petroleum Oils	0.0	7.0	..	7.0	0.0	7.0	..	7.0	.0	.0	.0
Wood, Pulp, Paper and Furniture	31.0	0.5	4.5	0.5	..	..	..	..	.0	.3	.3
Textiles and Clothing	78.4	9.3	2.0	9.3	..	..	..	..	.0	.0	.0
Leather, Rubber, Footwear	14.1	0.9	1.0	2.9	0.0	5.5	..	35.0	.0	.5	.5
Metals	0.3	4.8	2.4	5.0	0.0	10.0	..	35.0	.0	1.3	1.3
Chemical & Photographic Suppl.	97.9	5.4	5.1	5.4	100.0	30.0	3.8	30.0	.0	.3	.3
Transport Equipment	95.0	3.9	2.4	4.0	..	..	..	..	.0	.3	.3
Non-Electric Machinery	95.1	0.2	5.1	0.7	0.0	15.0	..	30.0	.0	.9	.9
Electric Machinery	31.3	0.9	2.4	0.9	..	..	..	..	.0	.0	.0
Mineral Prod.,Prec. Stones & Metal	0.2	0.0	0.7	0.0	..	..	..	..	.0	26.9	26.9
Manufactured Articles nes.	14.0	0.3	5.8	0.3	0.0	..	..	..	.0	.6	.6
Industrial Goods (line 5-14)	**6.0**	**0.3**	**4.3**	**0.4**	**4.5**	**7.9**	**3.8**	**34.5**	**.0**	**31.2**	**31.2**
All Merch. Trade (line 2-14)	**56.1**	**3.9**	**2.8**	**4.0**	**2.3**	**10.7**	**3.8**	**30.1**	**.1**	**102.5**	**102.5**

Notes: 1. Value of exports from reporter countries that do not participate in Free Trade Agreements with GAMBIA

2. Weighted average tariff reduction measured by dT / (1 + T) in percent.

GHANA Extent of other countries' MFN tariff reductions on GHANA's exports

Summary product category	Average levels and changes weighted by value of exports to: the World exc. FTA[1]				LMIEs exc. FTA[1]				Value of exports in $ million		
	% of exports affected	Post-UR applied rate	Tariff reduc-tion[2]	Post-UR bound rate	% of exports affected	Post-UR applied rate	Tariff reduc-tion[2]	Post-UR bound rate	To IDB LMIEs exc. FTA[1]	To all IDB Ctrys exc. FTA[1]	To all IDB Ctrys inc. FTA
Agriculture, exc. Fish: Estimate 1	1.1	0.5	14.3	0.8	0.0	0.0	..	7.9	11.3	313.2	313.2
Agriculture, exc. Fish: Estimate 2	64.4	1.4	3.5	1.4	67.1	10.5	6.1	11.6	11.3	345.2	345.2
Fish and Fish Products	46.0	2.9	1.8	2.9	0.0	15.0	..	..	.0	30.1	30.1
Petroleum Oils	0.0	0.9	..	1.2	..	..	..	..	.0	11.5	11.5
Wood, Pulp, Paper and Furniture	13.1	0.4	2.7	0.4	20.0	0.2	6.0	0.2	1.2	143.1	143.1
Textiles and Clothing	19.9	13.5	2.0	28.6	0.0	15.1	..	35.1	.3	.5	.5
Leather, Rubber, Footwear	1.3	3.7	1.4	0.7	0.0	15.0	..	..	.1	.5	.5
Metals	0.4	4.8	5.1	5.0	15.4	6.3	8.2	29.7	2.9	250.6	250.6
Chemical & Photographic Suppl.	25.6	6.1	5.3	12.1	1.7	7.7	2.7	34.4	.1	.3	.3
Transport Equipment	84.5	3.7	1.9	3.7	0.0	27.5	..	27.5	.0	.3	.3
Non-Electric Machinery	96.5	2.2	4.4	2.9	6.7	12.6	7.0	33.8	.1	1.9	1.9
Electric Machinery	94.8	4.1	2.9	4.4	0.0	18.4	..	35.0	.0	.6	.6
Mineral Prod.,Prec. Stones & Metal	0.3	0.1	12.3	0.5	1.0	0.2	12.9	29.2	26.5	84.5	84.5
Manufactured Articles nes.	47.0	2.7	3.5	5.6	0.9	6.0	20.7	30.7	.1	.9	.9
Industrial Goods (line 5-14)	**4.8**	**2.6**	**3.1**	**3.0**	**3.1**	**1.0**	**9.0**	**23.0**	**31.2**	**483.0**	**483.0**
All Merch. Trade (line 2-14)	**29.8**	**2.1**	**3.3**	**2.3**	**20.1**	**3.6**	**6.4**	**15.0**	**42.5**	**869.9**	**869.9**

Notes: 1. Value of exports from reporter countries that do not participate in Free Trade Agreements with GHANA

2. Weighted average tariff reduction measured by dT / (1 + T) in percent.

GIBRALTAR Extent of other countries' MFN tariff reductions on GIBRALTAR's exports

Summary product category	Average levels and changes weighted by value of exports to: the World exc. FTA[1]				LMIEs exc. FTA[1]				Value of exports in $ million		
	% of exports affected	Post-UR applied rate	Tariff reduc-tion[2]	Post-UR bound rate	% of exports affected	Post-UR applied rate	Tariff reduc-tion[2]	Post-UR bound rate	To IDB LMIEs exc. FTA[1]	To all IDB Ctrys exc. FTA[1]	To all IDB Ctrys inc. FTA
Agriculture, exc. Fish: Estimate 1	0.0	13.3	..	13.3	..	..	..	..	.0	.4	.4
Agriculture, exc. Fish: Estimate 2	18.4	3.9	3.6	5.1	0.0	5.0	..	50.0	.0	.6	.6
Fish and Fish Products	0.0	0.5	..	21.4	..	..	..	..	.0	.0	.0
Petroleum Oils	..	..	..	..	..	..	..	..	.0	.0	.0
Wood, Pulp, Paper and Furniture	71.5	3.3	6.4	3.4	0.0	0.0	..	0.0	.0	.5	.5
Textiles and Clothing	82.1	12.1	2.0	12.7	0.0	30.0	..	35.0	.0	.1	.1
Leather, Rubber, Footwear	58.6	7.1	1.7	7.5	0.0	14.8	..	16.0	.0	.1	.1
Metals	53.3	2.5	3.3	2.5	0.0	30.0	..	30.0	.0	1.2	1.2
Chemical & Photographic Suppl.	55.5	3.3	3.9	3.5	0.0	8.9	..	15.2	.1	1.5	1.5
Transport Equipment	19.2	3.8	2.2	3.8	0.0	30.0	..	..	.0	3.1	3.1
Non-Electric Machinery	97.8	2.1	2.7	2.2	0.0	2.5	..	5.0	.0	2.2	2.2
Electric Machinery	95.6	2.9	2.2	3.0	0.0	10.0	..	10.0	.0	.9	.9
Mineral Prod.,Prec. Stones & Metal	44.0	3.0	2.5	3.2	0.0	37.5	..	41.0	.0	.3	.3
Manufactured Articles nes.	11.0	0.6	3.0	0.6	0.0	0.0	..	0.0	.0	16.0	16.0
Industrial Goods (line 5-14)	**29.0**	**1.6**	**3.0**	**1.6**	**0.0**	**16.3**	**..**	**21.1**	**.2**	**25.9**	**25.9**
All Merch. Trade (line 2-14)	**28.7**	**1.6**	**3.0**	**1.7**	**0.0**	**15.9**	**..**	**22.2**	**.2**	**26.6**	**26.6**

Notes: 1. Value of exports from reporter countries that do not participate in Free Trade Agreements with GIBRALTAR

2. Weighted average tariff reduction measured by dT / (1 + T) in percent.

GREENLAND Extent of other countries' MFN tariff reductions on GREENLAND's exports

Summary product category	Average levels and changes weighted by value of exports to: the World exc. FTA[1]				Average levels and changes weighted by value of exports to: LMIEs exc. FTA[1]				Value of exports in $ million		
	% of exports affected	Post-UR applied rate	Tariff reduc-tion[2]	Post-UR bound rate	% of exports affected	Post-UR applied rate	Tariff reduc-tion[2]	Post-UR bound rate	To IDB LMIEs exc. FTA[1]	To all IDB Ctrys exc. FTA[1]	To all IDB Ctrys inc. FTA
Agriculture, exc. Fish: Estimate 1	0.0	10.4	..	10.4	..	..	..	..	.0	.3	.3
Agriculture, exc. Fish: Estimate 2	21.3	8.0	6.5	10.7	..	..	..	..	.0	.9	.9
Fish and Fish Products	34.6	9.6	2.6	10.0	0.0	20.0	..	..	.0	473.8	473.8
Petroleum Oils	0.0	0.0	..	3.5	..	..	..	..	.0	.0	.0
Wood, Pulp, Paper and Furniture	19.0	0.0	5.2	0.0	..	..	..	..	.0	.1	.1
Textiles and Clothing	78.6	9.7	2.0	9.7	..	..	..	..	.0	.1	.1
Leather, Rubber, Footwear	98.1	4.0	1.8	4.0	..	..	..	..	.0	.4	.4
Metals	0.2	0.0	2.1	0.0	0.0	29.8	..	30.0	.1	60.5	60.5
Chemical & Photographic Suppl.	49.1	3.6	4.5	7.7	14.3	8.8	2.0	42.9	.0	.3	.3
Transport Equipment	2.9	6.1	1.4	6.3	..	..	..	..	.0	.5	.5
Non-Electric Machinery	96.4	1.9	3.2	1.9	..	..	..	..	.0	1.1	1.1
Electric Machinery	95.3	3.7	5.5	3.7	..	..	..	..	.0	.4	.4
Mineral Prod.,Prec. Stones & Metal	2.2	0.3	2.4	0.7	0.0	15.0	..	35.0	.0	1.1	1.1
Manufactured Articles nes.	23.4	1.0	2.2	1.5	0.0	10.0	..	36.0	.0	.9	.9
Industrial Goods (line 5-14)	**3.7**	**0.2**	**3.2**	**0.2**	**4.1**	**18.7**	**2.0**	**38.9**	**.1**	**65.3**	**65.3**
All Merch. Trade (line 2-14)	**30.9**	**8.4**	**2.6**	**8.7**	**3.8**	**18.8**	**2.0**	**38.9**	**.1**	**540.0**	**540.0**

Notes: 1. Value of exports from reporter countries that do not participate in Free Trade Agreements with GREENLAND

2. Weighted average tariff reduction measured by dT / (1 + T) in percent.

GRENADA Extent of other countries' MFN tariff reductions on GRENADA's exports

Summary product category	Average levels and changes weighted by value of exports to: the World exc. FTA[1]				Average levels and changes weighted by value of exports to: LMIEs exc. FTA[1]				Value of exports in $ million		
	% of exports affected	Post-UR applied rate	Tariff reduc-tion[2]	Post-UR bound rate	% of exports affected	Post-UR applied rate	Tariff reduc-tion[2]	Post-UR bound rate	To IDB LMIEs exc. FTA[1]	To all IDB Ctrys exc. FTA[1]	To all IDB Ctrys inc. FTA
Agriculture, exc. Fish: Estimate 1	0.0	0.0	..	0.0	..	..	..	..	.0	11.7	11.7
Agriculture, exc. Fish: Estimate 2	39.5	0.4	8.2	1.3	28.4	8.1	4.7	32.7	.5	23.6	23.6
Fish and Fish Products	8.9	0.2	0.5	0.2	..	..	..	..	.0	.4	.4
Petroleum Oils	..	..	..	..	..	..	..	..	.0	.0	.0
Wood, Pulp, Paper and Furniture	38.2	26.3	4.8	29.3	0.0	45.0	..	50.0	.1	.2	.2
Textiles and Clothing	87.0	12.4	1.5	12.5	0.0	35.8	..	60.0	.0	3.0	3.0
Leather, Rubber, Footwear	100.0	15.5	2.8	15.5	..	..	..	..	.0	.0	.0
Metals	14.3	2.3	4.3	14.7	0.0	5.0	..	35.0	.1	.2	.2
Chemical & Photographic Suppl.	73.8	1.2	4.8	1.2	..	..	..	..	.0	.7	.7
Transport Equipment	6.7	14.4	2.8	33.1	0.0	15.0	..	35.0	.0	.0	.0
Non-Electric Machinery	100.0	0.2	2.9	0.2	100.0	6.0	3.1	6.0	.0	2.2	2.2
Electric Machinery	37.0	5.1	2.0	5.6	0.0	12.6	..	35.0	.0	.2	.2
Mineral Prod.,Prec. Stones & Metal	0.9	0.1	3.1	0.1	..	..	..	..	.0	.3	.3
Manufactured Articles nes.	27.8	0.3	5.7	0.3	..	..	..	..	.0	1.8	1.8
Industrial Goods (line 5-14)	**69.6**	**5.2**	**2.7**	**5.6**	**13.6**	**21.5**	**3.1**	**37.4**	**.3**	**8.6**	**8.6**
All Merch. Trade (line 2-14)	**47.1**	**2.1**	**6.1**	**2.8**	**23.6**	**12.4**	**4.4**	**34.2**	**.8**	**32.7**	**32.7**

Notes: 1. Value of exports from reporter countries that do not participate in Free Trade Agreements with GRENADA

2. Weighted average tariff reduction measured by dT / (1 + T) in percent.

GUADELOUPE Extent of other countries' MFN tariff reductions on GUADELOUPE's exports

Summary product category	Average levels and changes weighted by value of exports to: the World exc. FTA[1]				Average levels and changes weighted by value of exports to: LMIEs exc. FTA[1]				Value of exports in $ million		
	% of exports affected	Post-UR applied rate	Tariff reduc-tion[2]	Post-UR bound rate	% of exports affected	Post-UR applied rate	Tariff reduc-tion[2]	Post-UR bound rate	To IDB LMIEs exc. FTA[1]	To all IDB Ctrys exc. FTA[1]	To all IDB Ctrys inc. FTA
Agriculture, exc. Fish: Estimate 1	0.0	43.0	..	43.0	0.0	0.0	..	0.0	.0	134.1	134.1
Agriculture, exc. Fish: Estimate 2	6.7	14.4	7.1	14.7	0.0	10.0	..	15.0	.0	144.8	144.8
Fish and Fish Products	83.5	7.4	6.7	7.4	..	..	..	..	.0	.2	.2
Petroleum Oils	..	..	..	..	..	..	..	..	.0	.0	.0
Wood, Pulp, Paper and Furniture	50.7	1.2	5.9	7.9	0.0	5.0	..	35.0	.1	.4	.4
Textiles and Clothing	87.1	10.7	2.2	10.7	..	..	..	..	.0	.3	.3
Leather, Rubber, Footwear	61.4	10.9	3.2	10.9	..	..	..	..	.0	.1	.1
Metals	37.1	1.0	3.2	1.0	..	..	..	..	.0	1.6	1.6
Chemical & Photographic Suppl.	81.3	5.4	1.7	5.4	..	..	..	..	.0	.7	.7
Transport Equipment	18.8	1.4	2.1	1.4	..	..	..	..	.0	2.9	2.9
Non-Electric Machinery	74.5	1.2	3.0	1.3	..	..	..	..	.0	2.6	2.6
Electric Machinery	91.9	4.1	2.7	4.1	..	..	..	..	.0	2.7	2.7
Mineral Prod.,Prec. Stones & Metal	90.4	2.4	1.6	2.4	..	..	..	..	.0	.8	.8
Manufactured Articles nes.	54.6	1.5	3.8	1.5	..	..	..	..	.0	1.2	1.2
Industrial Goods (line 5-14)	**60.1**	**2.4**	**2.8**	**2.6**	**0.0**	**5.0**	**..**	**35.0**	**.1**	**13.2**	**13.2**
All Merch. Trade (line 2-14)	**11.3**	**7.6**	**5.2**	**7.8**	**0.0**	**5.2**	**..**	**34.0**	**.1**	**158.2**	**158.2**

Notes: 1. Value of exports from reporter countries that do not participate in Free Trade Agreements with GUADELOUPE

2. Weighted average tariff reduction measured by dT / (1 + T) in percent.

GUINEA Extent of other countries' MFN tariff reductions on GUINEA's exports

Summary product category	Average levels and changes weighted by value of exports to: the World exc. FTA[1]				Average levels and changes weighted by value of exports to: LMIEs exc. FTA[1]				Value of exports in $ million		
	% of exports affected	Post-UR applied rate	Tariff reduc-tion[2]	Post-UR bound rate	% of exports affected	Post-UR applied rate	Tariff reduc-tion[2]	Post-UR bound rate	To IDB LMIEs exc. FTA[1]	To all IDB Ctrys exc. FTA[1]	To all IDB Ctrys inc. FTA
Agriculture, exc. Fish: Estimate 1	0.2	1.9	8.5	2.8	0.0	-6.1	..	19.0	.7	24.3	24.3
Agriculture, exc. Fish: Estimate 2	56.9	0.8	4.5	1.3	14.7	9.8	8.4	18.1	.9	24.2	24.2
Fish and Fish Products	35.3	2.0	1.7	2.0	..	..	..	..	.0	3.7	3.7
Petroleum Oils	..	..	..	..	..	..	..	..	.0	.0	.0
Wood, Pulp, Paper and Furniture	9.2	6.7	2.8	16.4	0.0	9.7	..	24.3	1.4	2.1	2.1
Textiles and Clothing	69.5	9.4	3.5	10.4	0.0	15.0	..	19.5	.0	.1	.1
Leather, Rubber, Footwear	12.2	0.3	0.9	0.3	..	..	..	..	.0	.3	.3
Metals	0.3	0.0	4.8	0.6	0.0	2.8	..	32.9	5.3	300.0	300.0
Chemical & Photographic Suppl.	78.5	3.1	1.5	3.8	0.0	0.0	..	17.5	2.0	52.9	52.9
Transport Equipment	67.3	19.9	3.4	20.3	100.0	35.0	3.6	35.0	.2	.4	.4
Non-Electric Machinery	60.5	1.1	3.4	1.2	0.0	15.0	..	..	.0	.7	.7
Electric Machinery	60.5	2.5	3.0	5.9	..	..	..	..	.0	.4	.4
Mineral Prod.,Prec. Stones & Metal	0.1	0.0	2.9	0.0	0.0	0.0	..	40.0	1.6	67.5	67.5
Manufactured Articles nes.	45.2	0.9	2.7	0.9	0.0	..	..	..	.0	5.5	5.5
Industrial Goods (line 5-14)	**10.7**	**0.5**	**1.6**	**1.0**	**1.8**	**3.4**	**3.6**	**28.1**	**10.5**	**430.0**	**430.0**
All Merch. Trade (line 2-14)	**13.4**	**0.5**	**2.3**	**1.0**	**2.8**	**3.9**	**5.7**	**27.2**	**11.4**	**457.8**	**457.8**

Notes: 1. Value of exports from reporter countries that do not participate in Free Trade Agreements with GUINEA

2. Weighted average tariff reduction measured by dT / (1 + T) in percent.

GUINEA-BISSAU Extent of other countries' MFN tariff reductions on GUINEA-BISSAU's exports

Summary product category	Average levels and changes weighted by value of exports to: the World exc. FTA[1]				LMIEs exc. FTA[1]				Value of exports in $ million		
	% of exports affected	Post-UR applied rate	Tariff reduc-tion[2]	Post-UR bound rate	% of exports affected	Post-UR applied rate	Tariff reduc-tion[2]	Post-UR bound rate	To IDB LMIEs exc. FTA[1]	To all IDB Ctrys exc. FTA[1]	To all IDB Ctrys inc. FTA
Agriculture, exc. Fish: Estimate 1	0.0	0.0	..	76.6	0.0	0.0	..	99.8	9.7	12.7	12.7
Agriculture, exc. Fish: Estimate 2	0.8	0.0	4.9	84.9	0.0	0.0	..	99.8	9.7	11.5	11.5
Fish and Fish Products	74.7	11.1	5.0	11.1	0.0	15.0	..	30.0	.0	3.1	3.1
Petroleum Oils	100.0	3.7	2.2	3.7	..	..	..	..	.0	.0	.0
Wood, Pulp, Paper and Furniture	13.4	0.6	3.4	0.2	0.0	11.0	..	0.0	.0	.8	.8
Textiles and Clothing	23.1	11.6	3.7	11.6	0.0	12.1	..	12.1	.0	.1	.1
Leather, Rubber, Footwear	..	..	..	..	..	..	..	..	.0	.0	.0
Metals	2.7	0.0	4.3	0.0	..	..	..	..	.0	.3	.3
Chemical & Photographic Suppl.	100.0	6.2	0.8	6.2	100.0	6.0	0.2	6.0	.0	.0	.0
Transport Equipment	0.0	10.0	..	10.0	..	..	..	..	.0	.0	.0
Non-Electric Machinery	100.0	2.8	2.1	2.8	100.0	8.0	0.8	8.0	.0	.0	.0
Electric Machinery	22.5	14.5	2.9	28.0	0.0	17.7	..	35.0	.1	.2	.2
Mineral Prod.,Prec. Stones & Metal	0.0	0.0	..	0.0	0.0	0.0	..	..	.1	.3	.3
Manufactured Articles nes.	1.1	0.1	5.3	0.1	0.0	12.0	..	..	.0	1.4	1.4
Industrial Goods (line 5-14)	**8.6**	**1.4**	**2.9**	**2.2**	**10.7**	**10.6**	**0.4**	**25.2**	**.4**	**3.2**	**3.2**
All Merch. Trade (line 2-14)	**15.1**	**2.2**	**4.8**	**57.5**	**0.4**	**0.4**	**0.4**	**98.0**	**10.1**	**17.8**	**17.8**

Notes: 1. Value of exports from reporter countries that do not participate in Free Trade Agreements with GUINEA-BISSAU

2. Weighted average tariff reduction measured by dT / (1 + T) in percent.

GUYANA Extent of other countries' MFN tariff reductions on GUYANA's exports

Summary product category	Average levels and changes weighted by value of exports to: the World exc. FTA[1]				LMIEs exc. FTA[1]				Value of exports in $ million		
	% of exports affected	Post-UR applied rate	Tariff reduc-tion[2]	Post-UR bound rate	% of exports affected	Post-UR applied rate	Tariff reduc-tion[2]	Post-UR bound rate	To IDB LMIEs exc. FTA[1]	To all IDB Ctrys exc. FTA[1]	To all IDB Ctrys inc. FTA
Agriculture, exc. Fish: Estimate 1	0.1	132.5	14.3	133.0	0.0	36.4	..	94.2	.9	83.1	83.1
Agriculture, exc. Fish: Estimate 2	15.0	13.2	6.6	16.4	0.8	38.5	10.9	68.4	2.2	103.5	103.5
Fish and Fish Products	19.6	0.7	2.7	0.7	..	..	..	..	.0	17.8	17.8
Petroleum Oils	..	..	..	..	..	..	..	..	.0	.0	.0
Wood, Pulp, Paper and Furniture	1.6	3.0	3.5	6.2	0.0	23.9	..	49.4	.4	3.5	3.5
Textiles and Clothing	99.7	16.1	1.3	16.1	75.0	12.5	6.0	16.0	.0	1.6	1.6
Leather, Rubber, Footwear	60.5	2.3	1.6	2.3	..	..	..	..	.0	.3	.3
Metals	0.0	1.0	2.1	6.2	0.0	4.9	..	31.9	15.1	78.1	78.1
Chemical & Photographic Suppl.	86.2	7.2	1.3	10.0	0.0	19.3	..	48.7	.4	3.9	3.9
Transport Equipment	9.5	18.9	0.7	18.9	..	..	..	..	.0	.2	.2
Non-Electric Machinery	73.4	11.6	6.2	13.1	0.8	44.0	3.6	49.3	.7	2.5	2.5
Electric Machinery	92.8	2.6	2.3	2.6	..	..	..	..	.0	.1	.1
Mineral Prod.,Prec. Stones & Metal	0.0	0.0	1.9	0.2	0.0	0.0	..	40.0	.3	11.3	11.3
Manufactured Articles nes.	84.5	4.7	6.0	4.9	0.0	42.5	..	48.9	.1	4.1	4.1
Industrial Goods (line 5-14)	**10.0**	**1.8**	**3.7**	**6.0**	**0.1**	**7.4**	**5.2**	**33.5**	**17.0**	**105.4**	**105.4**
All Merch. Trade (line 2-14)	**13.1**	**3.3**	**5.1**	**6.8**	**0.2**	**11.0**	**8.4**	**37.6**	**19.2**	**226.7**	**226.7**

Notes: 1. Value of exports from reporter countries that do not participate in Free Trade Agreements with GUYANA

2. Weighted average tariff reduction measured by dT / (1 + T) in percent.

HAITI Extent of other countries' MFN tariff reductions on HAITI's exports

Summary product category	Average levels and changes weighted by value of exports to: the World exc. FTA[1]				LMIEs exc. FTA[1]				Value of exports in $ million		
	% of exports affected	Post-UR applied rate	Tariff reduction[2]	Post-UR bound rate	% of exports affected	Post-UR applied rate	Tariff reduction[2]	Post-UR bound rate	To IDB LMIEs exc. FTA[1]	To all IDB Ctrys exc. FTA[1]	To all IDB Ctrys inc. FTA
Agriculture, exc. Fish: Estimate 1	0.0	0.0	..	0.1	0.0	0.0	..	40.0	.0	51.1	51.1
Agriculture, exc. Fish: Estimate 2	87.7	1.2	4.2	1.3	0.0	12.1	..	35.4	.0	56.2	56.2
Fish and Fish Products	7.8	0.9	8.2	1.0	..	..	..	..	.0	3.1	3.1
Petroleum Oils	0.0	0.6	..	..	..	..	..	..	.0	.0	.0
Wood, Pulp, Paper and Furniture	99.6	0.4	5.0	0.4	..	..	..	..	.0	7.9	7.9
Textiles and Clothing	92.9	16.9	1.8	16.9	0.0	5.0	..	40.0	.0	202.3	202.3
Leather, Rubber, Footwear	67.9	6.1	2.3	6.1	..	..	..	..	.0	17.1	17.1
Metals	31.8	3.4	2.9	3.6	0.0	10.0	..	35.0	.0	3.5	3.5
Chemical & Photographic Suppl.	74.7	3.9	2.3	4.1	0.0	13.7	..	39.6	.0	3.1	3.1
Transport Equipment	79.6	5.8	1.6	5.8	0.0	40.0	..	40.0	.0	.4	.4
Non-Electric Machinery	59.4	1.6	2.6	2.7	0.0	14.1	..	35.0	.0	.6	.6
Electric Machinery	67.5	3.3	2.6	3.3	100.0	4.6	1.6	4.6	.1	58.4	58.4
Mineral Prod.,Prec. Stones & Metal	87.5	4.7	1.5	4.7	..	..	..	..	.0	16.5	16.5
Manufactured Articles nes.	80.0	1.5	3.3	1.5	86.4	9.3	1.1	9.7	.4	55.7	55.7
Industrial Goods (line 5-14)	**84.8**	**10.7**	**2.2**	**10.7**	**65.7**	**10.6**	**1.2**	**16.7**	**.6**	**365.4**	**365.4**
All Merch. Trade (line 2-14)	**84.6**	**9.4**	**2.5**	**9.4**	**65.0**	**10.6**	**1.2**	**17.0**	**.6**	**424.7**	**424.7**

Notes: 1. Value of exports from reporter countries that do not participate in Free Trade Agreements with HAITI

2. Weighted average tariff reduction measured by dT / (1 + T) in percent.

HONDURAS Extent of other countries' MFN tariff reductions on HONDURAS's exports

Summary product category	Average levels and changes weighted by value of exports to: the World exc. FTA[1]				LMIEs exc. FTA[1]				Value of exports in $ million		
	% of exports affected	Post-UR applied rate	Tariff reduction[2]	Post-UR bound rate	% of exports affected	Post-UR applied rate	Tariff reduction[2]	Post-UR bound rate	To IDB LMIEs exc. FTA[1]	To all IDB Ctrys exc. FTA[1]	To all IDB Ctrys inc. FTA
Agriculture, exc. Fish: Estimate 1	0.5	2.6	5.7	3.6	11.4	8.7	5.7	20.3	26.7	561.2	561.2
Agriculture, exc. Fish: Estimate 2	25.1	2.5	4.3	3.1	54.2	11.4	3.4	19.5	30.1	612.9	612.9
Fish and Fish Products	31.5	1.8	2.5	1.9	..	..	..	..	.0	89.3	89.3
Petroleum Oils	0.0	0.4	..	0.7	..	..	..	..	.0	.6	.6
Wood, Pulp, Paper and Furniture	35.1	1.9	3.2	4.1	0.0	16.2	..	35.9	2.7	26.4	26.4
Textiles and Clothing	95.5	18.6	1.7	18.7	0.0	25.4	..	43.0	.6	91.1	91.1
Leather, Rubber, Footwear	13.5	14.1	2.5	28.6	6.8	18.6	3.8	38.3	.5	.6	.6
Metals	3.2	0.8	1.0	1.3	0.0	22.8	..	41.4	.6	21.0	21.0
Chemical & Photographic Suppl.	3.2	9.1	4.4	19.0	0.0	14.7	..	32.4	4.2	8.5	8.5
Transport Equipment	0.5	2.8	1.8	12.3	0.2	2.8	3.6	33.2	6.2	6.4	6.4
Non-Electric Machinery	9.4	17.1	2.7	25.6	2.3	25.0	6.0	37.4	.8	1.2	1.2
Electric Machinery	8.7	6.0	2.7	11.3	0.0	16.1	..	36.3	.1	.4	.4
Mineral Prod.,Prec. Stones & Metal	19.0	2.1	3.0	4.9	0.0	10.7	..	36.8	.3	2.8	2.8
Manufactured Articles nes.	59.7	2.3	2.9	6.7	0.0	6.6	..	37.8	1.2	8.6	8.6
Industrial Goods (line 5-14)	**61.8**	**11.5**	**1.9**	**13.3**	**0.4**	**11.3**	**4.4**	**35.6**	**17.2**	**167.0**	**167.0**
All Merch. Trade (line 2-14)	**32.8**	**4.4**	**3.3**	**5.1**	**34.6**	**11.3**	**3.4**	**23.9**	**47.4**	**869.8**	**869.8**

Notes: 1. Value of exports from reporter countries that do not participate in Free Trade Agreements with HONDURAS

2. Weighted average tariff reduction measured by dT / (1 + T) in percent.

HONG KONG Extent of other countries' MFN tariff reductions on HONG KONG's exports

Summary product category	Average levels and changes weighted by value of exports to: the World exc. FTA[1]				LMIEs exc. FTA[1]				Value of exports in $ million		
	% of exports affected	Post-UR applied rate	Tariff reduc-tion[2]	Post-UR bound rate	% of exports affected	Post-UR applied rate	Tariff reduc-tion[2]	Post-UR bound rate	To IDB LMIEs exc. FTA[1]	To all IDB Ctrys exc. FTA[1]	To all IDB Ctrys inc. FTA
Agriculture, exc. Fish: Estimate 1	17.3	8.2	12.8	9.7	20.5	16.2	12.1	19.6	22.2	54.6	54.6
Agriculture, exc. Fish: Estimate 2	44.0	7.7	5.5	9.8	27.0	12.1	6.1	18.4	88.6	355.7	355.7
Fish and Fish Products	60.5	2.7	3.2	2.9	44.1	7.1	35.8	4.9	12.0	189.2	189.2
Petroleum Oils	4.0	3.8	2.0	11.8	1.1	5.5	6.0	21.0	2.3	3.8	3.8
Wood, Pulp, Paper and Furniture	31.8	2.1	6.4	2.1	12.6	8.7	11.7	14.7	123.5	629.1	629.1
Textiles and Clothing	84.6	14.7	2.7	14.7	42.0	22.9	10.4	24.7	1,319.6	10,302.1	10,302.1
Leather, Rubber, Footwear	45.4	11.8	2.6	12.1	22.3	20.6	8.8	26.2	32.3	848.3	848.3
Metals	56.3	4.1	3.4	4.8	31.6	10.6	7.9	14.7	172.4	858.0	858.0
Chemical & Photographic Suppl.	45.1	7.5	5.1	8.5	20.0	16.3	13.4	22.8	235.0	836.8	836.8
Transport Equipment	18.4	6.2	2.1	4.8	2.3	13.1	5.8	17.8	19.9	62.8	62.8
Non-Electric Machinery	67.0	2.2	3.6	3.2	28.5	12.7	9.1	21.4	258.0	2,420.2	2,420.2
Electric Machinery	62.6	4.6	4.2	5.2	55.7	11.6	8.8	11.9	567.7	3,890.7	3,890.7
Mineral Prod.,Prec. Stones & Metal	56.5	3.3	2.5	3.5	42.9	10.3	11.5	14.5	91.1	1,655.6	1,655.6
Manufactured Articles nes.	67.3	4.7	3.6	4.3	26.7	23.5	10.7	23.3	406.2	4,187.8	4,187.8
Industrial Goods (line 5-14)	**70.0**	**8.6**	**3.2**	**8.8**	**37.7**	**18.0**	**10.0**	**20.0**	**3,225.9**	**25,691.3**	**25,691.3**
All Merch. Trade (line 2-14)	**69.6**	**8.6**	**3.3**	**8.8**	**37.4**	**17.8**	**10.0**	**19.9**	**3,328.7**	**26,240.1**	**26,240.1**

Notes: 1. Value of exports from reporter countries that do not participate in Free Trade Agreements with HONG KONG

2. Weighted average tariff reduction measured by dT / (1 + T) in percent.

HUNGARY Extent of other countries' MFN tariff reductions on HUNGARY's exports

Summary product category	Average levels and changes weighted by value of exports to: the World exc. FTA[1]				LMIEs exc. FTA[1]				Value of exports in $ million		
	% of exports affected	Post-UR applied rate	Tariff reduc-tion[2]	Post-UR bound rate	% of exports affected	Post-UR applied rate	Tariff reduc-tion[2]	Post-UR bound rate	To IDB LMIEs exc. FTA[1]	To all IDB Ctrys exc. FTA[1]	To all IDB Ctrys inc. FTA
Agriculture, exc. Fish: Estimate 1	5.5	27.9	44.0	38.8	2.9	-6.9	1.8	44.4	98.5	540.7	540.7
Agriculture, exc. Fish: Estimate 2	38.6	7.8	3.6	14.9	18.9	12.9	2.8	45.2	180.7	1,207.5	1,207.5
Fish and Fish Products	26.4	5.4	3.3	4.2	1.7	6.5	2.7	0.3	1.6	6.5	6.5
Petroleum Oils	6.9	25.1	1.3	4.8	0.2	10.2	1.1	34.8	6.6	187.3	187.3
Wood, Pulp, Paper and Furniture	57.3	1.7	4.5	2.0	66.2	9.3	3.5	11.7	19.8	238.1	238.1
Textiles and Clothing	85.1	10.9	3.2	12.2	55.4	9.7	3.5	20.2	39.6	317.5	317.5
Leather, Rubber, Footwear	68.8	6.6	2.4	6.8	61.0	14.4	2.9	15.6	21.9	151.4	151.4
Metals	62.8	3.1	3.7	2.8	20.0	8.8	3.3	8.3	136.5	585.3	585.3
Chemical & Photographic Suppl.	56.1	6.7	4.3	7.4	44.3	14.7	6.3	18.1	161.7	505.4	505.4
Transport Equipment	58.1	8.6	1.4	8.5	46.7	12.5	1.2	14.3	110.4	186.7	186.7
Non-Electric Machinery	83.0	5.5	1.8	4.9	73.4	7.9	1.2	7.1	208.2	377.0	377.0
Electric Machinery	75.5	9.4	2.9	8.6	61.8	18.4	3.8	17.0	83.6	227.9	227.9
Mineral Prod.,Prec. Stones & Metal	67.7	4.8	1.9	4.6	42.1	11.5	2.3	14.2	30.9	239.8	239.8
Manufactured Articles nes.	66.3	5.8	2.7	7.3	59.5	9.3	1.8	12.4	76.1	155.8	155.8
Industrial Goods (line 5-14)	**67.7**	**6.0**	**3.0**	**6.2**	**51.9**	**11.4**	**2.7**	**12.6**	**888.7**	**2,984.9**	**2,984.9**
All Merch. Trade (line 2-14)	**57.0**	**6.8**	**3.1**	**8.1**	**46.0**	**11.6**	**2.7**	**18.9**	**1,077.5**	**4,386.1**	**4,386.1**

Notes: 1. Value of exports from reporter countries that do not participate in Free Trade Agreements with HUNGARY

2. Weighted average tariff reduction measured by dT / (1 + T) in percent.

ICELAND Extent of other countries' MFN tariff reductions on ICELAND's exports

Summary product category	Average levels and changes weighted by value of exports to: the World exc. FTA[1]				LMIEs exc. FTA[1]				Value of exports in $ million		
	% of exports affected	Post-UR applied rate	Tariff reduction[2]	Post-UR bound rate	% of exports affected	Post-UR applied rate	Tariff reduction[2]	Post-UR bound rate	To IDB LMIEs exc. FTA[1]	To all IDB Ctrys exc. FTA[1]	To all IDB Ctrys inc. FTA
Agriculture, exc. Fish: Estimate 1	0.5	110.6	5.9	110.7	0.0	0.0	..	0.8	.4	6.0	6.0
Agriculture, exc. Fish: Estimate 2	7.6	4.8	4.3	15.7	1.9	2.3	1.4	65.1	10.9	115.7	115.7
Fish and Fish Products	24.1	1.2	1.4	8.3	14.7	4.5	6.4	6.0	10.6	291.2	929.5
Petroleum Oils	3.1	0.3	3.9	0.4	..	..	..	..	.0	.0	.1
Wood, Pulp, Paper and Furniture	9.8	0.4	5.2	1.7	5.5	2.3	14.6	3.1	.1	.7	2.3
Textiles and Clothing	31.2	8.8	4.0	9.3	75.4	8.7	1.2	9.7	.2	6.8	20.7
Leather, Rubber, Footwear	3.3	1.1	2.2	2.8	98.1	9.9	3.3	9.6	.1	.7	11.8
Metals	10.5	0.5	3.0	4.1	4.6	1.5	7.5	1.4	2.7	31.3	202.0
Chemical & Photographic Suppl.	8.6	3.8	5.6	4.8	33.6	9.4	10.2	9.0	.3	1.4	10.7
Transport Equipment	2.8	0.4	2.9	5.4	..	..	..	..	.0	.4	5.5
Non-Electric Machinery	16.7	2.1	2.7	2.1	95.4	4.0	0.6	3.6	.4	2.5	11.7
Electric Machinery	17.7	2.9	6.4	3.6	87.3	16.3	12.1	16.6	.1	.5	1.7
Mineral Prod.,Prec. Stones & Metal	1.2	0.1	3.4	0.4	25.0	11.6	6.2	10.1	.1	3.8	15.8
Manufactured Articles nes.	5.8	1.2	11.3	1.6	79.8	29.2	15.7	34.3	.9	2.7	26.4
Industrial Goods (line 5-14)	**10.8**	**1.6**	**3.7**	**3.9**	**33.5**	**8.1**	**8.9**	**8.9**	**4.8**	**50.9**	**308.6**
All Merch. Trade (line 2-14)	**19.6**	**2.0**	**1.8**	**7.8**	**12.8**	**4.2**	**7.3**	**11.7**	**26.2**	**457.8**	**1,353.9**

Notes: 1. Value of exports from reporter countries that do not participate in Free Trade Agreements with ICELAND

2. Weighted average tariff reduction measured by dT / (1 + T) in percent.

INDIA Extent of other countries' MFN tariff reductions on INDIA's exports

Summary product category	Average levels and changes weighted by value of exports to: the World exc. FTA[1]				LMIEs exc. FTA[1]				Value of exports in $ million		
	% of exports affected	Post-UR applied rate	Tariff reduction[2]	Post-UR bound rate	% of exports affected	Post-UR applied rate	Tariff reduction[2]	Post-UR bound rate	To IDB LMIEs exc. FTA[1]	To all IDB Ctrys exc. FTA[1]	To all IDB Ctrys inc. FTA
Agriculture, exc. Fish: Estimate 1	14.1	9.6	11.6	22.5	32.4	16.7	10.7	55.5	306.2	928.0	928.0
Agriculture, exc. Fish: Estimate 2	26.4	3.1	5.5	8.4	24.8	8.0	4.5	26.8	331.7	1,273.3	1,273.3
Fish and Fish Products	66.8	2.3	2.3	2.8	6.4	2.5	31.8	41.5	9.1	494.0	494.0
Petroleum Oils	1.5	0.6	1.2	0.6	0.0	2.2	..	5.0	4.8	390.8	390.8
Wood, Pulp, Paper and Furniture	53.2	7.3	4.5	2.3	29.3	22.1	3.6	8.6	17.6	60.1	60.1
Textiles and Clothing	79.4	10.3	2.4	10.4	56.1	21.5	6.3	17.5	172.8	3,087.5	3,087.5
Leather, Rubber, Footwear	66.9	5.7	1.9	6.0	64.4	17.4	6.8	13.4	31.5	881.9	881.9
Metals	27.0	1.6	3.0	2.5	2.0	4.8	5.4	11.0	182.2	1,123.1	1,123.1
Chemical & Photographic Suppl.	49.7	5.0	4.5	8.2	18.5	9.0	5.4	18.7	138.3	478.5	478.5
Transport Equipment	22.0	10.9	2.7	11.1	2.1	14.7	6.3	25.5	92.2	137.0	137.0
Non-Electric Machinery	50.1	3.9	4.0	6.2	29.9	11.1	11.9	19.7	61.0	228.3	228.3
Electric Machinery	52.3	6.9	3.1	8.6	34.9	15.6	4.6	20.2	21.3	68.9	68.9
Mineral Prod.,Prec. Stones & Metal	7.6	0.4	6.2	0.4	71.1	4.4	12.3	3.2	148.5	3,438.7	3,438.7
Manufactured Articles nes.	34.3	2.9	4.3	5.6	16.7	5.9	4.6	20.6	36.3	196.3	196.3
Industrial Goods (line 5-14)	**42.5**	**4.8**	**2.8**	**5.4**	**32.2**	**11.1**	**8.7**	**13.7**	**901.6**	**9,700.3**	**9,700.3**
All Merch. Trade (line 2-14)	**40.4**	**4.4**	**3.0**	**5.5**	**30.0**	**10.2**	**7.8**	**18.1**	**1,247.1**	**11,858.3**	**11,858.3**

Notes: 1. Value of exports from reporter countries that do not participate in Free Trade Agreements with INDIA

2. Weighted average tariff reduction measured by dT / (1 + T) in percent.

INDONESIA Extent of other countries' MFN tariff reductions on INDONESIA's exports

Summary product category	Average levels and changes weighted by value of exports to: the World exc. FTA[1]				LMIEs exc. FTA[1]				Value of exports in $ million		
	% of exports affected	Post-UR applied rate	Tariff reduc-tion[2]	Post-UR bound rate	% of exports affected	Post-UR applied rate	Tariff reduc-tion[2]	Post-UR bound rate	To IDB LMIEs exc. FTA[1]	To all IDB Ctrys exc. FTA[1]	To all IDB Ctrys inc. FTA
Agriculture, exc. Fish: Estimate 1	6.1	5.2	5.1	8.1	39.0	28.2	3.7	46.7	184.9	1,214.0	1,214.0
Agriculture, exc. Fish: Estimate 2	37.4	6.7	4.2	12.5	24.2	25.6	4.6	60.2	256.0	1,758.8	1,758.8
Fish and Fish Products	75.0	2.9	4.4	2.9	67.1	6.0	38.4	7.7	52.5	767.9	767.9
Petroleum Oils	0.0	1.2	1.6	0.4	0.0	5.7	..	..	238.7	5,179.9	5,179.9
Wood, Pulp, Paper and Furniture	49.5	5.6	3.4	5.1	16.8	13.8	8.8	11.0	268.3	2,540.6	2,540.6
Textiles and Clothing	80.1	14.4	2.6	16.2	65.0	22.9	7.8	19.6	119.4	1,517.5	1,517.5
Leather, Rubber, Footwear	14.7	2.1	3.6	2.3	47.8	7.4	7.7	10.4	98.3	1,234.2	1,234.2
Metals	32.8	1.3	2.1	0.8	15.4	11.1	7.8	12.7	154.6	1,420.4	1,420.4
Chemical & Photographic Suppl.	29.0	7.0	8.4	8.9	33.9	15.7	12.4	16.3	66.9	175.5	175.5
Transport Equipment	15.9	1.9	2.9	4.6	8.1	14.1	16.7	12.6	1.7	36.4	36.4
Non-Electric Machinery	67.1	4.4	3.2	4.8	38.3	19.0	8.6	18.7	4.0	24.0	24.0
Electric Machinery	46.3	2.8	4.2	3.5	76.1	6.3	4.3	4.0	18.5	84.4	84.4
Mineral Prod.,Prec. Stones & Metal	5.5	1.1	4.0	0.8	3.2	7.4	7.6	5.8	485.0	3,654.5	3,654.5
Manufactured Articles nes.	56.4	3.4	2.1	4.0	42.9	23.4	7.3	30.7	12.5	183.2	183.2
Industrial Goods (line 5-14)	**32.5**	**4.3**	**3.0**	**4.2**	**20.5**	**11.4**	**8.2**	**9.9**	**1,229.2**	**10,870.7**	**10,870.7**
All Merch. Trade (line 2-14)	**25.7**	**4.1**	**3.4**	**4.9**	**19.7**	**12.5**	**10.6**	**21.0**	**1,776.3**	**18,577.3**	**18,577.3**

Notes: 1. Value of exports from reporter countries that do not participate in Free Trade Agreements with INDONESIA

2. Weighted average tariff reduction measured by $dT / (1 + T)$ in percent.

IRAN ISLAMIC REP. Extent of other countries' MFN tariff reductions on IRAN's exports

Summary product category	Average levels and changes weighted by value of exports to: the World exc. FTA[1]				LMIEs exc. FTA[1]				Value of exports in $ million		
	% of exports affected	Post-UR applied rate	Tariff reduc-tion[2]	Post-UR bound rate	% of exports affected	Post-UR applied rate	Tariff reduc-tion[2]	Post-UR bound rate	To IDB LMIEs exc. FTA[1]	To all IDB Ctrys exc. FTA[1]	To all IDB Ctrys inc. FTA
Agriculture, exc. Fish: Estimate 1	0.5	0.1	15.9	1.6	0.1	0.1	1.2	60.4	3.1	199.6	199.6
Agriculture, exc. Fish: Estimate 2	64.2	2.5	1.2	4.9	15.7	20.1	2.6	60.0	16.4	272.8	272.8
Fish and Fish Products	55.5	10.0	7.0	10.4	100.0	0.0	0.5	0.0	.0	26.1	26.1
Petroleum Oils	0.0	2.6	2.2	6.1	0.0	11.2	..	33.1	1,776.7	6,440.6	6,440.6
Wood, Pulp, Paper and Furniture	61.5	0.5	5.0	1.0	0.0	1.9	..	30.0	.0	.4	.4
Textiles and Clothing	28.6	4.4	2.7	4.5	74.4	23.9	13.7	23.9	.6	435.1	435.1
Leather, Rubber, Footwear	65.1	6.7	2.5	5.5	17.1	36.7	2.6	28.4	.2	2.1	2.1
Metals	3.4	0.3	4.1	14.5	0.1	0.6	0.5	32.7	27.2	69.8	69.8
Chemical & Photographic Suppl.	63.3	4.4	2.3	5.7	17.6	13.7	6.7	11.0	.4	6.8	6.8
Transport Equipment	0.8	0.8	4.9	0.9	18.3	27.1	5.9	31.6	2.2	77.1	77.1
Non-Electric Machinery	31.7	0.7	1.8	0.6	89.7	9.4	3.8	5.8	.2	7.5	7.5
Electric Machinery	52.8	6.2	2.9	7.1	13.2	14.0	2.6	14.2	.4	1.4	1.4
Mineral Prod.,Prec. Stones & Metal	4.9	12.5	2.2	19.3	0.0	14.3	10.7	22.1	16.9	19.6	19.6
Manufactured Articles nes.	3.6	0.4	4.8	0.4	89.4	20.9	8.5	21.7	1.5	96.5	96.5
Industrial Goods (line 5-14)	**19.6**	**3.2**	**2.7**	**4.9**	**5.2**	**7.8**	**8.3**	**28.1**	**49.6**	**716.2**	**716.2**
All Merch. Trade (line 2-14)	**4.4**	**2.7**	**2.1**	**5.9**	**0.3**	**11.2**	**5.4**	**33.3**	**1,842.7**	**7,455.8**	**7,455.8**

Notes: 1. Value of exports from reporter countries that do not participate in Free Trade Agreements with IRAN

2. Weighted average tariff reduction measured by $dT / (1 + T)$ in percent.

IRAQ Extent of other countries' MFN tariff reductions on IRAQ's exports

Summary product category	Average levels and changes weighted by value of exports to: the World exc. FTA[1]				LMIEs exc. FTA[1]				Value of exports in $ million		
	% of exports affected	Post-UR applied rate	Tariff reduc-tion[2]	Post-UR bound rate	% of exports affected	Post-UR applied rate	Tariff reduc-tion[2]	Post-UR bound rate	To IDB LMIEs exc. FTA[1]	To all IDB Ctrys exc. FTA[1]	To all IDB Ctrys inc. FTA
Agriculture, exc. Fish: Estimate 1	1.8	15.4	14.3	60.5	0.0	17.7	..	70.1	30.6	35.9	35.9
Agriculture, exc. Fish: Estimate 2	24.0	45.2	4.7	73.9	11.4	53.3	5.6	87.8	33.1	39.9	39.9
Fish and Fish Products	42.9	13.2	6.4	13.4	..	..	..	..	.0	.0	.0
Petroleum Oils	0.2	0.4	1.1	3.6	0.0	0.0	..	25.6	4,178.6	10,521.9	10,521.9
Wood, Pulp, Paper and Furniture	48.4	0.5	5.7	0.5	100.0	30.0	7.4	30.0	.0	.4	.4
Textiles and Clothing	27.8	2.7	6.2	2.8	95.5	8.6	10.6	9.4	.6	5.3	5.3
Leather, Rubber, Footwear	5.2	86.8	2.5	6.9	0.0	94.8	..	31.7	1.9	2.0	2.0
Metals	9.3	0.6	4.8	3.9	0.0	4.2	..	38.9	.9	7.3	7.3
Chemical & Photographic Suppl.	75.0	13.8	4.7	16.0	79.0	14.5	4.7	17.0	23.6	25.0	25.0
Transport Equipment	50.1	5.3	5.5	6.4	0.0	15.3	..	30.4	.1	1.0	1.0
Non-Electric Machinery	55.8	1.0	4.1	1.6	26.9	14.9	5.7	30.6	.2	5.2	5.2
Electric Machinery	98.1	3.8	2.7	4.0	57.6	23.7	6.1	31.8	.1	2.5	2.5
Mineral Prod.,Prec. Stones & Metal	11.1	18.6	1.3	19.9	5.6	22.1	1.4	30.5	86.9	105.9	105.9
Manufactured Articles nes.	37.8	10.4	12.2	10.4	94.4	31.2	14.0	31.3	7.0	21.4	21.4
Industrial Goods (line 5-14)	**26.6**	**15.7**	**5.0**	**14.2**	**25.5**	**22.0**	**6.3**	**25.8**	**121.2**	**175.9**	**175.9**
All Merch. Trade (line 2-14)	**0.7**	**1.1**	**3.9**	**4.7**	**0.8**	**7.0**	**6.2**	**29.6**	**4,332.9**	**10,737.7**	**10,737.7**

Notes: 1. Value of exports from reporter countries that do not participate in Free Trade Agreements with IRAQ

2. Weighted average tariff reduction measured by dT / (1 + T) in percent.

ISRAEL Extent of other countries' MFN tariff reductions on ISRAEL's exports

Summary product category	Average levels and changes weighted by value of exports to: the World exc. FTA[1]				LMIEs exc. FTA[1]				Value of exports in $ million		
	% of exports affected	Post-UR applied rate	Tariff reduc-tion[2]	Post-UR bound rate	% of exports affected	Post-UR applied rate	Tariff reduc-tion[2]	Post-UR bound rate	To IDB LMIEs exc. FTA[1]	To all IDB Ctrys exc. FTA[1]	To all IDB Ctrys inc. FTA
Agriculture, exc. Fish: Estimate 1	0.6	7.6	14.7	16.1	3.4	0.3	15.4	59.1	27.6	241.8	251.4
Agriculture, exc. Fish: Estimate 2	48.0	8.7	4.2	10.0	14.5	12.4	3.5	39.6	14.7	961.7	1,033.2
Fish and Fish Products	6.6	4.1	2.1	4.5	0.0	9.5	..	14.4	.0	5.3	5.6
Petroleum Oils	7.5	2.9	2.0	2.1	0.0	10.2	..	35.0	4.3	16.2	29.8
Wood, Pulp, Paper and Furniture	60.5	1.9	5.8	1.9	12.8	23.5	3.4	24.3	1.6	60.2	89.1
Textiles and Clothing	67.0	9.6	2.1	10.9	10.9	23.8	16.1	32.0	11.7	485.5	639.4
Leather, Rubber, Footwear	62.9	5.9	2.4	5.7	72.4	24.1	9.1	25.4	2.9	66.8	101.0
Metals	46.0	3.1	2.6	2.9	33.0	22.0	5.0	16.8	8.2	156.3	252.8
Chemical & Photographic Suppl.	52.6	5.6	3.6	6.1	21.6	14.6	6.6	20.6	92.8	673.1	881.7
Transport Equipment	10.2	0.9	2.5	1.1	1.5	9.5	0.4	11.6	4.0	20.0	120.8
Non-Electric Machinery	42.1	1.7	2.8	2.3	53.9	11.7	3.4	18.2	25.5	285.1	512.8
Electric Machinery	28.5	4.3	3.2	4.3	3.3	18.0	9.8	21.7	60.8	268.0	659.5
Mineral Prod.,Prec. Stones & Metal	2.9	0.3	5.1	0.8	18.0	3.9	14.0	11.6	161.7	2,136.3	3,664.7
Manufactured Articles nes.	29.5	2.4	3.9	4.0	19.0	11.4	3.0	25.5	77.5	358.7	590.3
Industrial Goods (line 5-14)	**24.3**	**2.3**	**3.2**	**3.3**	**19.2**	**10.9**	**8.2**	**19.4**	**446.7**	**4,510.0**	**7,512.1**
All Merch. Trade (line 2-14)	**27.0**	**2.9**	**3.4**	**4.0**	**18.9**	**11.0**	**8.1**	**20.2**	**465.8**	**5,493.1**	**8,580.8**

Notes: 1. Value of exports from reporter countries that do not participate in Free Trade Agreements with ISRAEL

2. Weighted average tariff reduction measured by dT / (1 + T) in percent.

JAMAICA Extent of other countries' MFN tariff reductions on JAMAICA's exports

| Summary product category | *Average levels and changes weighted by value of exports to:* | | | | | | | | *Value of exports in $ million* | | |
| | *the World exc. FTA[1]* | | | | *LMIEs exc. FTA[1]* | | | | | | |
	% of exports affected	Post-UR applied rate	Tariff reduction[2]	Post-UR bound rate	% of exports affected	Post-UR applied rate	Tariff reduction[2]	Post-UR bound rate	To IDB LMIEs exc. FTA[1]	To all IDB Ctrys exc. FTA[1]	To all IDB Ctrys inc. FTA
Agriculture, exc. Fish: Estimate 1	0.0	85.9	..	86.1	0.0	-0.4	..	50.4	.5	137.9	137.9
Agriculture, exc. Fish: Estimate 2	35.8	5.2	3.1	6.9	0.0	4.7	..	83.7	2.3	221.8	221.8
Fish and Fish Products	1.4	0.4	1.9	0.4	..	..	..	..	.0	1.7	1.7
Petroleum Oils	0.0	0.0	..	..	..	..	..	..	.0	.0	.0
Wood, Pulp, Paper and Furniture	81.6	0.1	3.7	0.2	25.0	13.7	3.9	32.9	.0	2.3	2.3
Textiles and Clothing	98.9	18.8	1.6	18.8	9.6	22.3	3.6	47.8	.6	241.1	241.1
Leather, Rubber, Footwear	2.1	6.0	1.4	6.6	16.5	15.1	1.4	31.3	.1	2.8	2.8
Metals	0.6	0.0	5.6	0.0	0.0	18.4	..	38.2	.0	112.2	112.2
Chemical & Photographic Suppl.	30.4	1.3	1.5	2.2	0.2	1.4	3.3	21.7	15.9	353.1	353.1
Transport Equipment	9.8	15.0	5.2	18.7	1.8	22.0	0.5	36.5	.1	.1	.1
Non-Electric Machinery	61.2	2.7	2.5	8.2	19.6	7.7	1.0	24.8	.6	1.9	1.9
Electric Machinery	80.4	3.7	2.3	4.7	0.6	15.1	0.2	21.1	.3	2.7	2.7
Mineral Prod.,Prec. Stones & Metal	28.8	10.0	3.2	25.4	34.4	15.3	3.6	39.7	.5	.8	.8
Manufactured Articles nes.	49.1	2.5	3.6	2.7	19.8	11.5	1.9	27.8	.1	5.7	5.7
Industrial Goods (line 5-14)	**49.1**	**7.0**	**1.6**	**7.5**	**2.2**	**3.2**	**2.7**	**23.3**	**18.3**	**722.5**	**722.5**
All Merch. Trade (line 2-14)	**45.9**	**6.7**	**1.9**	**7.4**	**2.0**	**3.4**	**2.7**	**30.0**	**20.6**	**946.0**	**946.0**

Notes: 1. Value of exports from reporter countries that do not participate in Free Trade Agreements with JAMAICA

2. Weighted average tariff reduction measured by dT / (1 + T) in percent.

JAPAN Extent of other countries' MFN tariff reductions on JAPAN's exports

| Summary product category | *Average levels and changes weighted by value of exports to:* | | | | | | | | *Value of exports in $ million* | | |
| | *the World exc. FTA[1]* | | | | *LMIEs exc. FTA[1]* | | | | | | |
	% of exports affected	Post-UR applied rate	Tariff reduction[2]	Post-UR bound rate	% of exports affected	Post-UR applied rate	Tariff reduction[2]	Post-UR bound rate	To IDB LMIEs exc. FTA[1]	To all IDB Ctrys exc. FTA[1]	To all IDB Ctrys inc. FTA
Agriculture, exc. Fish: Estimate 1	14.0	6.6	13.8	11.7	10.9	25.5	19.5	54.5	21.5	121.8	121.8
Agriculture, exc. Fish: Estimate 2	31.1	4.4	5.6	8.2	45.2	17.1	6.0	34.6	160.8	1,010.7	1,010.7
Fish and Fish Products	34.6	4.2	24.0	4.5	77.0	7.9	38.6	8.0	199.2	773.9	773.9
Petroleum Oils	12.0	10.3	5.5	11.6	27.8	14.9	5.7	15.0	122.9	304.7	304.7
Wood, Pulp, Paper and Furniture	45.9	2.5	7.3	2.6	51.6	12.8	14.6	15.4	357.8	2,269.9	2,269.9
Textiles and Clothing	52.2	8.6	5.9	12.2	63.8	19.6	9.0	22.1	1,388.8	5,620.7	5,620.7
Leather, Rubber, Footwear	57.3	6.3	3.2	7.4	55.7	18.4	7.5	19.9	613.5	3,355.1	3,355.1
Metals	56.1	4.8	6.8	6.2	44.4	10.9	12.7	15.8	5,263.7	14,047.5	14,047.5
Chemical & Photographic Suppl.	44.2	5.9	6.6	8.1	54.4	11.8	10.7	15.6	4,650.0	14,490.4	14,490.4
Transport Equipment	21.9	8.3	3.4	8.5	22.3	34.2	15.4	43.4	4,315.3	58,524.4	58,524.4
Non-Electric Machinery	65.1	3.9	3.7	5.2	48.7	14.5	8.2	19.3	9,806.6	51,002.3	51,002.3
Electric Machinery	55.2	4.7	3.8	5.6	53.6	14.0	8.5	14.8	7,778.8	45,087.0	45,087.0
Mineral Prod.,Prec. Stones & Metal	47.4	5.2	4.3	7.4	42.2	13.0	8.9	20.3	883.2	3,407.8	3,407.8
Manufactured Articles nes.	61.8	3.5	3.9	4.2	54.0	15.9	9.8	17.8	3,525.2	34,468.7	34,468.7
Industrial Goods (line 5-14)	**49.0**	**5.4**	**4.2**	**6.4**	**47.9**	**16.2**	**9.8**	**19.5**	**38,582.7**	**232,274.0**	**232,274.0**
All Merch. Trade (line 2-14)	**48.9**	**5.4**	**4.2**	**6.4**	**47.9**	**16.1**	**10.0**	**19.5**	**39,065.7**	**234,363.0**	**234,363.0**

Notes: 1. Value of exports from reporter countries that do not participate in Free Trade Agreements with JAPAN

2. Weighted average tariff reduction measured by dT / (1 + T) in percent.

JORDAN Extent of other countries' MFN tariff reductions on JORDAN's exports

Summary product category	Average levels and changes weighted by value of exports to: the World exc. FTA[1]				LMIEs exc. FTA[1]				Value of exports in $ million		
	% of exports affected	Post-UR applied rate	Tariff reduction[2]	Post-UR bound rate	% of exports affected	Post-UR applied rate	Tariff reduction[2]	Post-UR bound rate	To IDB LMIEs exc. FTA[1]	To all IDB Ctrys exc. FTA[1]	To all IDB Ctrys inc. FTA
Agriculture, exc. Fish: Estimate 1	0.0	0.0	..	19.5	0.0	-0.1	..	26.8	5.6	7.9	7.9
Agriculture, exc. Fish: Estimate 2	80.6	27.0	3.3	27.9	96.5	34.9	3.4	36.1	5.8	8.9	8.9
Fish and Fish Products	84.6	11.0	2.7	12.5	..	..	..	..	.0	.0	.0
Petroleum Oils	1.9	3.7	2.2	3.7	..	..	..	..	.0	9.5	9.5
Wood, Pulp, Paper and Furniture	34.1	7.9	9.7	7.5	83.6	29.5	12.9	30.6	.5	1.9	1.9
Textiles and Clothing	93.6	12.0	2.9	12.2	89.4	10.4	10.6	10.1	.7	3.7	3.7
Leather, Rubber, Footwear	73.9	10.3	1.7	7.2	23.7	31.6	7.0	22.5	.3	1.6	1.6
Metals	26.8	3.2	5.0	1.1	37.7	29.3	10.5	11.5	2.5	14.9	14.9
Chemical & Photographic Suppl.	7.3	2.1	2.7	30.8	0.2	1.7	13.2	38.2	9.8	12.3	12.3
Transport Equipment	18.9	8.9	4.7	8.5	0.5	11.3	1.6	11.0	1.7	3.9	3.9
Non-Electric Machinery	83.9	3.7	3.0	2.8	57.9	12.4	14.8	5.8	2.4	16.2	16.2
Electric Machinery	50.5	3.8	3.0	3.8	0.3	19.9	0.6	2.2	.3	3.2	3.2
Mineral Prod.,Prec. Stones & Metal	12.9	7.1	1.1	9.5	1.7	8.8	8.5	13.7	252.6	352.2	352.2
Manufactured Articles nes.	55.1	11.7	8.9	11.9	69.5	24.0	13.1	23.7	1.8	4.0	4.0
Industrial Goods (line 5-14)	**17.8**	**6.8**	**2.1**	**9.5**	**3.3**	**8.9**	**10.7**	**15.0**	**272.6**	**413.9**	**413.9**
All Merch. Trade (line 2-14)	**18.7**	**7.2**	**2.2**	**10.0**	**5.2**	**9.4**	**7.9**	**15.7**	**278.4**	**432.3**	**432.3**

Notes: 1. Value of exports from reporter countries that do not participate in Free Trade Agreements with JORDAN

2. Weighted average tariff reduction measured by dT / (1 + T) in percent.

CAMBODIA Extent of other countries' MFN tariff reductions on CAMBODIA's exports

Summary product category	Average levels and changes weighted by value of exports to: the World exc. FTA[1]				LMIEs exc. FTA[1]				Value of exports in $ million		
	% of exports affected	Post-UR applied rate	Tariff reduction[2]	Post-UR bound rate	% of exports affected	Post-UR applied rate	Tariff reduction[2]	Post-UR bound rate	To IDB LMIEs exc. FTA[1]	To all IDB Ctrys exc. FTA[1]	To all IDB Ctrys inc. FTA
Agriculture, exc. Fish: Estimate 1	95.8	58.4	1.2	58.4	100.0	61.0	1.2	61.0	1.9	2.0	2.0
Agriculture, exc. Fish: Estimate 2	0.1	0.4	4.9	8.1	0.0	0.5	..	10.5	1.9	2.5	2.5
Fish and Fish Products	0.0	7.8	..	35.1	0.0	10.0	..	50.0	.0	.0	.0
Petroleum Oils	..	..	..	..	..	..	..	..	.0	.0	.0
Wood, Pulp, Paper and Furniture	0.8	0.0	5.2	0.1	0.0	0.0	..	0.5	.1	1.3	1.3
Textiles and Clothing	23.4	4.0	1.4	11.4	0.0	19.4	..	19.3	.1	.7	.7
Leather, Rubber, Footwear	17.5	3.8	0.8	3.9	17.3	4.0	0.8	4.0	1.4	1.5	1.5
Metals	92.3	3.7	2.9	3.7	..	..	..	..	.0	.0	.0
Chemical & Photographic Suppl.	0.0	2.6	..	2.6	..	..	..	..	.0	.0	.0
Transport Equipment	..	..	..	..	..	..	..	..	.0	.0	.0
Non-Electric Machinery	0.0	8.9	..	30.8	0.0	20.2	..	30.8	.0	.0	.0
Electric Machinery	17.4	0.6	2.3	1.0	..	..	..	..	.0	.1	.1
Mineral Prod.,Prec. Stones & Metal	22.6	0.5	2.3	0.5	..	..	..	..	.0	.1	.1
Manufactured Articles nes.	40.7	3.0	4.1	3.0	100.0	27.0	2.3	27.0	.0	.5	.5
Industrial Goods (line 5-14)	**16.6**	**2.5**	**2.1**	**2.9**	**16.1**	**4.7**	**0.9**	**4.6**	**1.7**	**4.3**	**4.3**
All Merch. Trade (line 2-14)	**10.5**	**1.8**	**2.1**	**5.2**	**7.5**	**2.5**	**0.9**	**8.1**	**3.6**	**6.8**	**6.8**

Notes: 1. Value of exports from reporter countries that do not participate in Free Trade Agreements with CAMBODIA

2. Weighted average tariff reduction measured by dT / (1 + T) in percent.

KENYA Extent of other countries' MFN tariff reductions on KENYA's exports

Summary product category	Average levels and changes weighted by value of exports to: the World exc. FTA[1]				LMIEs exc. FTA[1]				Value of exports in $ million		
	% of exports affected	Post-UR applied rate	Tariff reduction[2]	Post-UR bound rate	% of exports affected	Post-UR applied rate	Tariff reduction[2]	Post-UR bound rate	To IDB LMIEs exc. FTA[1]	To all IDB Ctrys exc. FTA[1]	To all IDB Ctrys inc. FTA
Agriculture, exc. Fish: Estimate 1	0.8	0.8	30.8	1.1	0.0	-0.6	..	10.8	9.6	529.4	529.4
Agriculture, exc. Fish: Estimate 2	49.1	3.1	4.6	3.8	18.2	19.0	3.8	45.7	8.2	637.5	637.5
Fish and Fish Products	36.4	4.5	5.0	5.9	0.0	0.0	..	0.0	.1	16.3	16.3
Petroleum Oils	0.0	0.0	..	..	0.0	0.0	..	..	.4	3.2	3.2
Wood, Pulp, Paper and Furniture	74.9	7.4	3.4	1.7	1.1	41.5	3.3	6.3	.4	3.0	3.0
Textiles and Clothing	40.7	4.8	3.5	4.3	59.6	11.3	6.7	10.9	4.2	20.8	20.8
Leather, Rubber, Footwear	56.5	2.5	0.8	2.5	8.5	16.0	7.1	27.4	1.4	50.6	50.6
Metals	20.9	4.2	7.3	3.6	30.0	16.6	13.3	24.8	1.0	3.7	3.7
Chemical & Photographic Suppl.	5.6	9.1	5.1	17.9	1.3	10.5	10.0	21.8	15.7	18.3	18.3
Transport Equipment	29.1	8.9	3.0	4.3	0.0	73.5	..	..	.2	1.8	1.8
Non-Electric Machinery	42.5	0.9	3.5	1.4	55.7	6.6	6.6	17.1	.3	4.2	4.2
Electric Machinery	62.2	4.9	5.1	2.6	9.7	23.8	14.7	28.8	.8	4.7	4.7
Mineral Prod.,Prec. Stones & Metal	9.3	1.4	3.0	0.5	4.4	14.0	12.4	6.7	2.7	32.1	32.1
Manufactured Articles nes.	35.4	2.4	3.1	6.9	14.1	12.7	15.4	116.7	1.2	17.9	17.9
Industrial Goods (line 5-14)	**35.4**	**3.6**	**2.2**	**4.3**	**13.1**	**12.7**	**8.2**	**23.2**	**27.9**	**157.1**	**157.1**
All Merch. Trade (line 2-14)	**46.0**	**3.2**	**4.3**	**3.9**	**14.1**	**14.1**	**6.9**	**30.3**	**36.7**	**814.0**	**814.0**

Notes: 1. Value of exports from reporter countries that do not participate in Free Trade Agreements with KENYA

2. Weighted average tariff reduction measured by dT / (1 + T) in percent.

KIRIBATI Extent of other countries' MFN tariff reductions on KIRIBATI's exports

Summary product category	Average levels and changes weighted by value of exports to: the World exc. FTA[1]				LMIEs exc. FTA[1]				Value of exports in $ million		
	% of exports affected	Post-UR applied rate	Tariff reduction[2]	Post-UR bound rate	% of exports affected	Post-UR applied rate	Tariff reduction[2]	Post-UR bound rate	To IDB LMIEs exc. FTA[1]	To all IDB Ctrys exc. FTA[1]	To all IDB Ctrys inc. FTA
Agriculture, exc. Fish: Estimate 1	0.0	10.3	..	10.3	..	..	..	..	.0	4.0	4.0
Agriculture, exc. Fish: Estimate 2	4.0	0.3	2.3	0.3	0.0	20.4	..	27.0	.0	4.2	4.2
Fish and Fish Products	1.6	0.0	0.5	0.0	..	..	..	..	.0	.2	.2
Petroleum Oils	0.0	0.0	..	3.5	..	..	..	..	.0	3.2	3.2
Wood, Pulp, Paper and Furniture	100.0	1.0	2.8	1.0	100.0	6.0	2.7	6.0	.0	.1	.1
Textiles and Clothing	86.4	17.2	1.6	22.4	0.0	10.0	..	50.0	.0	.2	.2
Leather, Rubber, Footwear	96.5	10.2	2.5	10.3	100.0	6.0	2.7	6.0	.0	.1	.1
Metals	5.9	0.6	3.3	0.6	66.7	6.3	3.3	6.3	.0	.1	.1
Chemical & Photographic Suppl.	81.9	6.2	5.5	6.2	..	..	..	..	.0	.1	.1
Transport Equipment	51.1	2.7	2.5	5.3	100.0	9.5	0.5	9.5	.0	.0	.0
Non-Electric Machinery	83.3	1.5	2.0	1.5	..	..	..	..	.0	.0	.0
Electric Machinery	100.0	5.3	7.8	5.3	..	..	..	..	.0	.6	.6
Mineral Prod.,Prec. Stones & Metal	77.4	5.0	4.0	5.0	100.0	7.0	2.6	7.0	.0	.3	.3
Manufactured Articles nes.	92.6	1.7	2.4	1.7	..	..	..	..	.0	.4	.4
Industrial Goods (line 5-14)	**87.5**	**5.3**	**4.8**	**5.8**	**78.0**	**7.3**	**2.6**	**15.3**	**.1**	**1.9**	**1.9**
All Merch. Trade (line 2-14)	**19.3**	**1.2**	**4.6**	**2.6**	**75.0**	**7.8**	**2.6**	**15.8**	**.1**	**9.4**	**9.4**

Notes: 1. Value of exports from reporter countries that do not participate in Free Trade Agreements with KIRIBATI

2. Weighted average tariff reduction measured by dT / (1 + T) in percent.

KOREA REP. OF Extent of other countries' MFN tariff reductions on KOREA's exports

Summary product category	Average levels and changes weighted by value of exports to: the World exc. FTA[1]				LMIEs exc. FTA[1]				Value of exports in $ million		
	% of exports affected	Post-UR applied rate	Tariff reduc-tion[2]	Post-UR bound rate	% of exports affected	Post-UR applied rate	Tariff reduc-tion[2]	Post-UR bound rate	To IDB LMIEs exc. FTA[1]	To all IDB Ctrys exc. FTA[1]	To all IDB Ctrys inc. FTA
Agriculture, exc. Fish: Estimate 1	1.7	11.4	11.9	20.6	3.1	25.1	11.7	76.9	47.3	264.9	264.9
Agriculture, exc. Fish: Estimate 2	57.4	7.3	4.3	10.3	9.4	23.9	7.7	68.8	58.8	1,007.9	1,007.9
Fish and Fish Products	71.4	5.6	3.2	5.5	90.8	7.0	41.1	6.5	34.0	1,731.5	1,731.5
Petroleum Oils	0.5	4.5	1.3	4.6	0.0	19.5	..	39.7	81.5	645.8	645.8
Wood, Pulp, Paper and Furniture	50.8	1.8	4.8	1.4	12.5	26.3	10.7	31.4	33.8	769.3	769.3
Textiles and Clothing	71.7	11.3	3.1	13.3	47.1	31.9	12.0	29.4	599.5	12,250.8	12,250.8
Leather, Rubber, Footwear	38.4	9.3	2.8	9.7	12.6	21.4	7.4	31.0	136.0	7,118.4	7,118.4
Metals	71.3	3.0	3.9	3.2	6.4	17.5	11.3	32.4	591.0	4,667.2	4,667.2
Chemical & Photographic Suppl.	38.9	4.7	3.8	8.3	15.1	18.5	14.9	30.9	335.5	2,145.2	2,145.2
Transport Equipment	13.0	4.3	2.4	4.0	1.5	23.3	6.9	48.9	79.7	2,416.2	2,416.2
Non-Electric Machinery	67.1	2.0	3.2	3.0	21.3	15.2	8.9	28.2	308.5	4,269.0	4,269.0
Electric Machinery	41.2	4.1	3.4	4.7	28.6	20.0	9.1	23.1	738.5	9,896.2	9,896.2
Mineral Prod.,Prec. Stones & Metal	47.2	4.3	3.5	3.5	9.1	21.0	21.2	24.6	163.2	1,471.3	1,471.3
Manufactured Articles nes.	66.7	3.0	3.7	3.3	29.7	24.1	9.6	30.9	189.6	5,700.1	5,700.1
Industrial Goods (line 5-14)	**54.9**	**6.2**	**3.3**	**6.9**	**23.3**	**21.7**	**10.9**	**28.3**	**3,175.5**	**50,703.7**	**50,703.7**
All Merch. Trade (line 2-14)	**54.8**	**6.1**	**3.4**	**6.9**	**23.2**	**21.6**	**12.1**	**29.1**	**3,349.8**	**54,088.9**	**54,088.9**

Notes: 1. Value of exports from reporter countries that do not participate in Free Trade Agreements with KOREA

2. Weighted average tariff reduction measured by dT / (1 + T) in percent.

KUWAIT Extent of other countries' MFN tariff reductions on KUWAIT's exports

Summary product category	Average levels and changes weighted by value of exports to: the World exc. FTA[1]				LMIEs exc. FTA[1]				Value of exports in $ million		
	% of exports affected	Post-UR applied rate	Tariff reduc-tion[2]	Post-UR bound rate	% of exports affected	Post-UR applied rate	Tariff reduc-tion[2]	Post-UR bound rate	To IDB LMIEs exc. FTA[1]	To all IDB Ctrys exc. FTA[1]	To all IDB Ctrys inc. FTA
Agriculture, exc. Fish: Estimate 1	0.0	23.0	..	23.0	..	..	..	..	.0	.2	.2
Agriculture, exc. Fish: Estimate 2	69.4	10.5	3.4	11.2	90.7	12.6	2.9	13.8	.6	1.1	1.1
Fish and Fish Products	93.2	1.0	2.0	1.0	..	..	..	..	.0	9.7	9.7
Petroleum Oils	2.2	1.7	1.2	2.4	0.0	8.6	..	40.0	741.3	5,900.4	5,900.4
Wood, Pulp, Paper and Furniture	7.6	3.3	6.9	8.5	0.3	13.4	7.4	39.2	.7	2.9	2.9
Textiles and Clothing	58.2	10.2	2.6	8.9	48.6	30.7	8.2	17.5	.3	3.4	3.4
Leather, Rubber, Footwear	39.0	29.4	1.6	3.2	16.5	126.4	4.8	7.2	.1	.4	.4
Metals	26.0	1.5	7.6	1.4	50.8	3.8	8.7	3.5	17.5	43.8	43.8
Chemical & Photographic Suppl.	47.7	9.4	24.5	9.4	99.6	25.0	30.5	24.9	6.6	18.0	18.0
Transport Equipment	48.6	8.5	2.5	6.7	7.4	54.8	6.9	31.3	.2	3.7	3.7
Non-Electric Machinery	75.9	1.3	3.8	1.6	95.9	16.6	5.1	16.5	.3	7.8	7.8
Electric Machinery	96.9	3.2	2.8	3.2	0.0	20.0	..	10.0	.0	3.6	3.6
Mineral Prod.,Prec. Stones & Metal	61.1	3.7	4.0	1.8	0.0	10.3	11.4	8.1	142.4	405.4	405.4
Manufactured Articles nes.	32.6	3.2	5.9	3.2	96.2	29.1	13.1	28.9	1.0	10.4	10.4
Industrial Goods (line 5-14)	**57.0**	**3.8**	**4.8**	**2.3**	**10.0**	**10.5**	**17.4**	**9.0**	**169.1**	**499.4**	**499.4**
All Merch. Trade (line 2-14)	**6.7**	**1.9**	**3.6**	**2.3**	**1.9**	**9.3**	**17.0**	**18.3**	**911.0**	**6,410.5**	**6,410.5**

Notes: 1. Value of exports from reporter countries that do not participate in Free Trade Agreements with KUWAIT

2. Weighted average tariff reduction measured by dT / (1 + T) in percent.

LAO PDR Extent of other countries' MFN tariff reductions on LAO's exports

Summary product category	Average levels and changes weighted by value of exports to: the World exc. FTA [1]				LMIEs exc. FTA [1]				Value of exports in $ million		
	% of exports affected	Post-UR applied rate	Tariff reduc-tion [2]	Post-UR bound rate	% of exports affected	Post-UR applied rate	Tariff reduc-tion [2]	Post-UR bound rate	To IDB LMIEs exc. FTA [1]	To all IDB Ctrys exc. FTA [1]	To all IDB Ctrys inc. FTA
Agriculture, exc. Fish: Estimate 1	4.7	2.9	1.2	3.5	98.6	60.2	1.2	60.2	.1	1.6	1.6
Agriculture, exc. Fish: Estimate 2	53.2	13.2	3.8	13.8	89.9	28.3	3.6	29.3	1.4	3.0	3.0
Fish and Fish Products	16.0	0.0	0.6	0.0	..	..	..	..	.0	.0	.0
Petroleum Oils	..	..	..	..	..	..	..	..	.0	.0	.0
Wood, Pulp, Paper and Furniture	56.0	4.6	7.2	5.6	99.9	8.2	7.2	8.2	9.7	17.4	17.4
Textiles and Clothing	93.9	12.8	2.6	13.6					.0	1.8	1.8
Leather, Rubber, Footwear	100.0	1.3	0.3	1.3	..	..	..	..	.0	.0	.0
Metals	0.0	6.0	..	7.9	0.0	6.1	..	8.0	11.0	11.1	11.1
Chemical & Photographic Suppl.	70.0	8.4	5.2	11.5	26.7	16.8	2.5	32.1	.0	.1	.1
Transport Equipment	1.1	0.5	1.9	1.4	..	..	..	..	.0	.2	.2
Non-Electric Machinery	14.3	2.3	6.1	2.3	100.0	26.7	7.6	26.7	.0	.0	.0
Electric Machinery	0.0	0.0	..	..	..	..	..	..	.0	.2	.2
Mineral Prod.,Prec. Stones & Metal	30.6	3.2	5.4	3.7	23.1	8.8	15.7	11.3	.0	.1	.1
Manufactured Articles nes.	83.5	21.9	2.4	23.9	100.0	27.0	2.3	27.0	.5	.6	.6
Industrial Goods (line 5-14)	38.1	5.8	6.3	7.3	47.9	7.5	7.0	8.5	21.2	31.5	31.5
All Merch. Trade (line 2-14)	39.4	6.5	6.0	7.9	50.5	8.8	6.6	9.8	22.6	34.6	34.6

Notes: 1. Value of exports from reporter countries that do not participate in Free Trade Agreements with LAO PDR

2. Weighted average tariff reduction measured by $dT / (1 + T)$ in percent.

LEBANON Extent of other countries' MFN tariff reductions on LEBANON's exports

Summary product category	Average levels and changes weighted by value of exports to: the World exc. FTA [1]				LMIEs exc. FTA [1]				Value of exports in $ million		
	% of exports affected	Post-UR applied rate	Tariff reduc-tion [2]	Post-UR bound rate	% of exports affected	Post-UR applied rate	Tariff reduc-tion [2]	Post-UR bound rate	To IDB LMIEs exc. FTA [1]	To all IDB Ctrys exc. FTA [1]	To all IDB Ctrys inc. FTA
Agriculture, exc. Fish: Estimate 1	1.1	2.4	11.8	41.3	0.0	-1.6	..	130.2	3.4	11.5	11.5
Agriculture, exc. Fish: Estimate 2	26.8	19.8	3.6	34.1	1.3	40.8	1.8	72.4	16.7	39.9	39.9
Fish and Fish Products	0.0	15.1	..	37.3	0.0	15.2	..	37.6	.1	.1	.1
Petroleum Oils	0.0	3.0	..	35.0	0.0	3.0	..	35.0	.1	.1	.1
Wood, Pulp, Paper and Furniture	41.3	4.8	6.5	3.6	9.1	10.6	11.8	28.2	4.5	10.6	10.6
Textiles and Clothing	83.6	12.2	1.7	12.3	43.8	20.0	2.2	21.3	3.3	34.5	34.5
Leather, Rubber, Footwear	75.0	6.4	2.2	6.8	13.8	22.5	3.7	27.4	.5	7.3	7.3
Metals	46.2	2.3	3.9	2.2	84.8	1.9	9.2	1.4	3.5	33.0	33.0
Chemical & Photographic Suppl.	78.8	6.6	3.7	6.5	9.9	19.2	4.0	18.8	1.4	8.8	8.8
Transport Equipment	39.3	7.3	1.9	7.6	0.0	16.4	..	25.7	.0	1.7	1.7
Non-Electric Machinery	87.9	2.8	2.8	4.5	5.8	13.1	5.0	31.0	.3	3.5	3.5
Electric Machinery	73.7	7.5	2.3	11.2	0.0	20.7	..	35.9	1.3	5.5	5.5
Mineral Prod.,Prec. Stones & Metal	25.8	1.4	1.2	1.3	1.0	49.5	6.2	34.5	.3	101.7	101.7
Manufactured Articles nes.	7.3	2.8	8.8	4.4	27.9	19.6	14.4	30.8	5.0	36.3	36.3
Industrial Goods (line 5-14)	40.1	3.9	2.5	4.2	32.0	15.1	8.7	22.3	20.3	242.9	242.9
All Merch. Trade (line 2-14)	38.2	6.0	2.6	8.3	18.1	26.6	8.5	47.8	37.2	283.0	283.0

Notes: 1. Value of exports from reporter countries that do not participate in Free Trade Agreements with LEBANON

2. Weighted average tariff reduction measured by $dT / (1 + T)$ in percent.

LESOTHO Extent of other countries' MFN tariff reductions on LESOTHO's exports

Summary product category	Average levels and changes weighted by value of exports to: the World exc. FTA[1]				LMIEs exc. FTA[1]				Value of exports in $ million		
	% of exports affected	Post-UR applied rate	Tariff reduc-tion[2]	Post-UR bound rate	% of exports affected	Post-UR applied rate	Tariff reduc-tion[2]	Post-UR bound rate	To IDB LMIEs exc. FTA[1]	To all IDB Ctrys exc. FTA[1]	To all IDB Ctrys inc. FTA
Agriculture, exc. Fish: Estimate 1	0.0	0.0	..	1.1	0.0	0.0	..	0.0	.0	.1	.1
Agriculture, exc. Fish: Estimate 2	26.6	13.6	3.6	30.7	0.1	12.5	2.7	36.2	3.6	5.0	5.0
Fish and Fish Products	0.0	0.0	..	0.0	..	..	..	..	.0	.0	.0
Petroleum Oils	..	..	..	..	..	..	..	..	.0	.0	.0
Wood, Pulp, Paper and Furniture	37.5	5.6	11.3	0.0	0.0	30.0	..	..	.0	.0	.0
Textiles and Clothing	98.6	15.5	1.7	15.6	0.0	10.4	..	25.0	.2	24.0	24.0
Leather, Rubber, Footwear	78.7	8.4	0.7	7.5	0.0	15.9	..	..	.1	.5	.5
Metals	13.2	6.6	7.7	9.6	0.0	8.0	..	12.0	.1	.1	.1
Chemical & Photographic Suppl.	0.0	1.8	..	2.1	0.0	11.0	..	25.0	.0	.1	.1
Transport Equipment	78.1	1.7	2.6	1.7	..	..	..	..	.0	.0	.0
Non-Electric Machinery	95.8	3.6	1.8	4.1	0.0	5.4	..	30.0	.0	.3	.3
Electric Machinery	52.4	7.9	1.7	17.6	0.0	13.6	..	34.0	.0	.0	.0
Mineral Prod.,Prec. Stones & Metal	0.2	0.0	1.4	0.0	..	..	..	..	.0	17.5	17.5
Manufactured Articles nes.	20.8	42.3	1.6	70.2	0.0	59.9	..	100.1	.9	1.4	1.4
Industrial Goods (line 5-14)	**56.3**	**9.9**	**1.7**	**10.9**	**0.0**	**46.2**	**..**	**81.8**	**1.3**	**43.9**	**43.9**
All Merch. Trade (line 2-14)	**53.3**	**10.3**	**1.8**	**12.9**	**0.1**	**21.5**	**2.7**	**47.8**	**4.9**	**48.9**	**48.9**

Notes: 1. Value of exports from reporter countries that do not participate in Free Trade Agreements with LESOTHO

2. Weighted average tariff reduction measured by dT / (1 + T) in percent.

LIBERIA Extent of other countries' MFN tariff reductions on LIBERIA's exports

Summary product category	Average levels and changes weighted by value of exports to: the World exc. FTA[1]				LMIEs exc. FTA[1]				Value of exports in $ million		
	% of exports affected	Post-UR applied rate	Tariff reduc-tion[2]	Post-UR bound rate	% of exports affected	Post-UR applied rate	Tariff reduc-tion[2]	Post-UR bound rate	To IDB LMIEs exc. FTA[1]	To all IDB Ctrys exc. FTA[1]	To all IDB Ctrys inc. FTA
Agriculture, exc. Fish: Estimate 1	1.4	1.3	74.6	1.4	100.0	95.0	74.6	95.0	.2	15.1	15.1
Agriculture, exc. Fish: Estimate 2	92.7	0.9	3.7	5.4	1.0	19.4	20.7	191.9	.4	15.7	15.7
Fish and Fish Products	17.2	1.8	3.1	5.4	..	..	..	..	.0	.2	.2
Petroleum Oils	3.6	3.5	2.2	3.5	..	..	..	..	.0	3.4	3.4
Wood, Pulp, Paper and Furniture	6.2	0.9	6.8	0.8	72.5	12.0	7.4	12.3	10.3	137.0	137.0
Textiles and Clothing	59.6	13.0	2.9	14.9	0.0	23.7	..	28.1	.1	.3	.3
Leather, Rubber, Footwear	0.2	0.7	2.6	3.6	0.3	7.9	6.0	33.5	10.6	119.2	119.2
Metals	0.0	0.0	7.8	0.5	1.0	1.8	9.3	34.5	7.8	355.6	355.6
Chemical & Photographic Suppl.	8.4	1.4	6.8	2.3	88.2	11.9	8.9	14.8	.1	2.0	2.0
Transport Equipment	3.2	5.2	2.9	5.7	0.0	35.3	..	39.2	.1	.7	.7
Non-Electric Machinery	62.1	7.5	5.3	13.4	0.0	19.3	..	35.0	.5	1.5	1.5
Electric Machinery	94.3	3.6	2.5	4.1	0.0	20.0	..	..	.0	.4	.4
Mineral Prod.,Prec. Stones & Metal	1.7	0.0	0.4	0.0	61.1	8.9	4.7	5.0	.6	316.5	316.5
Manufactured Articles nes.	0.0	0.1	1.7	0.7	0.0	2.9	..	35.0	25.7	679.1	679.1
Industrial Goods (line 5-14)	**1.0**	**0.2**	**4.3**	**0.7**	**14.4**	**5.7**	**7.3**	**27.5**	**55.7**	**1,612.2**	**1,612.2**
All Merch. Trade (line 2-14)	**1.9**	**0.2**	**4.0**	**0.8**	**14.3**	**5.8**	**7.3**	**29.7**	**56.1**	**1,631.5**	**1,631.5**

Notes: 1. Value of exports from reporter countries that do not participate in Free Trade Agreements with LIBERIA

2. Weighted average tariff reduction measured by dT / (1 + T) in percent.

LIBYA Extent of other countries' MFN tariff reductions on LIBYA's exports

Summary product category	Average levels and changes weighted by value of exports to: the World exc. FTA[1]				LMIEs exc. FTA[1]				Value of exports in $ million		
	% of exports affected	Post-UR applied rate	Tariff reduc-tion[2]	Post-UR bound rate	% of exports affected	Post-UR applied rate	Tariff reduc-tion[2]	Post-UR bound rate	To IDB LMIEs exc. FTA[1]	To all IDB Ctrys exc. FTA[1]	To all IDB Ctrys inc. FTA
Agriculture, exc. Fish: Estimate 1	2.5	10.8	5.9	29.4	0.0	10.5	..	33.1	.3	.4	.4
Agriculture, exc. Fish: Estimate 2	39.7	15.5	2.2	63.2	29.0	16.4	1.8	73.0	.9	1.1	1.1
Fish and Fish Products	88.7	6.8	2.2	6.8	..	..	..	..	.0	1.7	1.7
Petroleum Oils	1.1	0.3	1.2	1.3	0.0	2.0	..	22.0	458.6	6,037.7	6,037.7
Wood, Pulp, Paper and Furniture	55.1	3.6	5.1	1.0	40.4	8.4	0.7	3.6	.1	.3	.3
Textiles and Clothing	9.4	5.3	1.2	8.3	0.0	25.9	..	45.2	.4	2.3	2.3
Leather, Rubber, Footwear	8.5	25.0	0.6	33.7	0.0	28.3	..	43.0	.4	.5	.5
Metals	21.8	4.4	2.6	2.0	0.0	7.8	..	30.7	1.6	3.2	3.2
Chemical & Photographic Suppl.	50.5	3.4	7.6	2.8	72.3	7.2	9.5	5.2	69.4	270.0	270.0
Transport Equipment	2.8	0.4	0.6	0.1	0.0	10.0	..	25.0	.3	10.0	10.0
Non-Electric Machinery	81.5	5.1	3.4	3.6	50.3	21.6	5.9	16.0	.3	1.8	1.8
Electric Machinery	81.1	3.4	1.5	3.9	0.0	13.3	..	18.0	.0	.2	.2
Mineral Prod.,Prec. Stones & Metal	14.5	1.5	1.2	1.9	97.9	13.6	1.4	13.4	16.8	154.1	154.1
Manufactured Articles nes.	94.8	2.4	1.0	5.7	3.5	17.6	16.2	96.0	.5	10.6	10.6
Industrial Goods (line 5-14)	**37.9**	**2.7**	**6.3**	**2.5**	**74.5**	**8.7**	**7.5**	**7.8**	**89.7**	**452.9**	**452.9**
All Merch. Trade (line 2-14)	**3.7**	**0.5**	**4.9**	**1.5**	**12.2**	**4.2**	**7.5**	**18.0**	**549.2**	**6,493.3**	**6,493.3**

Notes: 1. Value of exports from reporter countries that do not participate in Free Trade Agreements with LIBYA

2. Weighted average tariff reduction measured by $dT / (1 + T)$ in percent.

MACAU Extent of other countries' MFN tariff reductions on MACAU's exports

Summary product category	Average levels and changes weighted by value of exports to: the World exc. FTA[1]				LMIEs exc. FTA[1]				Value of exports in $ million		
	% of exports affected	Post-UR applied rate	Tariff reduc-tion[2]	Post-UR bound rate	% of exports affected	Post-UR applied rate	Tariff reduc-tion[2]	Post-UR bound rate	To IDB LMIEs exc. FTA[1]	To all IDB Ctrys exc. FTA[1]	To all IDB Ctrys inc. FTA
Agriculture, exc. Fish: Estimate 1	0.0	0.9	..	0.9	..	..	..	..	.0	1.2	1.2
Agriculture, exc. Fish: Estimate 2	12.8	0.8	6.2	0.8	11.5	41.8	14.1	41.8	.0	5.9	5.9
Fish and Fish Products	39.9	0.7	2.2	0.7	..	..	..	..	.0	39.6	39.6
Petroleum Oils	..	..	..	..	..	..	..	..	.0	.0	.0
Wood, Pulp, Paper and Furniture	63.0	1.0	4.6	1.0	52.4	22.0	15.0	21.7	.1	7.5	7.5
Textiles and Clothing	85.4	14.3	2.3	15.5	97.6	20.8	6.7	20.9	.8	1,120.3	1,120.3
Leather, Rubber, Footwear	46.6	7.2	2.1	9.3	100.0	8.2	3.4	8.2	.1	25.5	25.5
Metals	22.8	0.4	1.5	0.6	100.0	10.0	8.7	10.0	.0	2.3	2.3
Chemical & Photographic Suppl.	35.1	2.6	3.0	4.1	0.0	4.7	..	6.6	.4	24.1	24.1
Transport Equipment	93.9	3.4	2.3	3.7	0.0	25.0	..	30.0	.0	.6	.6
Non-Electric Machinery	61.7	0.7	3.2	1.0	90.9	3.6	4.0	3.6	.0	5.4	5.4
Electric Machinery	56.4	3.6	3.7	5.3	34.0	19.9	20.7	27.4	.1	24.9	24.9
Mineral Prod.,Prec. Stones & Metal	61.1	3.1	4.1	3.4	0.0	20.0	..	30.0	.0	13.1	13.1
Manufactured Articles nes.	73.6	3.1	5.5	3.3	11.6	15.1	17.7	28.4	1.2	315.8	315.8
Industrial Goods (line 5-14)	**80.6**	**11.3**	**2.9**	**12.3**	**39.8**	**15.3**	**8.7**	**21.5**	**2.7**	**1,539.4**	**1,539.4**
All Merch. Trade (line 2-14)	**79.3**	**11.0**	**2.9**	**11.9**	**39.5**	**15.6**	**8.7**	**21.7**	**2.7**	**1,585.0**	**1,585.0**

Notes: 1. Value of exports from reporter countries that do not participate in Free Trade Agreements with MACAU

2. Weighted average tariff reduction measured by $dT / (1 + T)$ in percent.

MADAGASCAR Extent of other countries' MFN tariff reductions on MADAGASCAR's exports

Summary product category	Average levels and changes weighted by value of exports to: the World exc. FTA[1]				Average levels and changes weighted by value of exports to: LMIEs exc. FTA[1]				Value of exports in $ million		
	% of exports affected	Post-UR applied rate	Tariff reduction[2]	Post-UR bound rate	% of exports affected	Post-UR applied rate	Tariff reduction[2]	Post-UR bound rate	To IDB LMIEs exc. FTA[1]	To all IDB Ctrys exc. FTA[1]	To all IDB Ctrys inc. FTA
Agriculture, exc. Fish: Estimate 1	0.2	14.2	14.3	15.8	0.0	0.0	..	48.5	2.7	107.3	107.3
Agriculture, exc. Fish: Estimate 2	68.0	2.3	6.2	3.3	44.5	17.0	4.0	63.0	3.7	196.4	196.4
Fish and Fish Products	90.1	5.4	3.6	5.9	..	..	..	..	.0	49.5	49.5
Petroleum Oils	..	..	..	...	..	..	..	..	.0	.0	.0
Wood, Pulp, Paper and Furniture	28.7	0.2	5.2	1.3	0.0	15.0	..	..	.0	.7	.7
Textiles and Clothing	79.0	7.1	2.0	7.2	4.1	37.6	5.6	52.3	.1	24.3	24.3
Leather, Rubber, Footwear	90.2	5.8	0.7	5.9	0.0	15.0	..	30.0	.0	2.5	2.5
Metals	3.3	0.1	1.0	0.1	0.0	32.0	..	..	.0	9.7	9.7
Chemical & Photographic Suppl.	92.0	4.7	2.6	4.7	..	..	..	..	.0	.0	.0
Transport Equipment	6.0	9.5	2.5	9.5	..	..	..	..	.0	.1	.1
Non-Electric Machinery	99.3	2.2	2.3	2.2	..	..	..	..	.0	.3	.3
Electric Machinery	95.2	3.1	1.8	3.1	..	..	..	..	.0	.3	.3
Mineral Prod.,Prec. Stones & Metal	4.7	0.1	2.6	0.1	58.5	2.5	6.8	8.5	.1	15.3	15.3
Manufactured Articles nes.	64.0	1.3	2.6	1.7	0.0	69.3	..	111.3	.1	8.0	8.0
Industrial Goods (line 5-14)	**46.4**	**3.3**	**2.0**	**3.5**	**27.2**	**29.7**	**6.7**	**47.8**	**.3**	**61.3**	**61.3**
All Merch. Trade (line 2-14)	**67.3**	**3.0**	**5.1**	**3.8**	**43.2**	**18.0**	**4.1**	**61.8**	**4.0**	**307.3**	**307.3**

Notes: 1. Value of exports from reporter countries that do not participate in Free Trade Agreements with MADAGASCAR

2. Weighted average tariff reduction measured by dT / (1 + T) in percent.

MALAWI Extent of other countries' MFN tariff reductions on MALAWI's exports

Summary product category	Average levels and changes weighted by value of exports to: the World exc. FTA[1]				Average levels and changes weighted by value of exports to: LMIEs exc. FTA[1]				Value of exports in $ million		
	% of exports affected	Post-UR applied rate	Tariff reduction[2]	Post-UR bound rate	% of exports affected	Post-UR applied rate	Tariff reduction[2]	Post-UR bound rate	To IDB LMIEs exc. FTA[1]	To all IDB Ctrys exc. FTA[1]	To all IDB Ctrys inc. FTA
Agriculture, exc. Fish: Estimate 1	0.0	14.1	56.2	15.1	0.1	-0.3	1.2	98.3	2.2	209.7	209.7
Agriculture, exc. Fish: Estimate 2	41.6	6.8	3.4	7.9	13.8	10.1	3.9	88.1	2.7	214.0	214.0
Fish and Fish Products	16.7	0.6	1.9	0.7	0.0	0.0	..	0.0	.1	.4	.4
Petroleum Oils	..	..	..	..	..	..	..	..	.0	.0	.0
Wood, Pulp, Paper and Furniture	75.7	0.4	5.3	0.5	0.0	0.0	..	0.0	.0	.4	.4
Textiles and Clothing	93.3	10.9	1.9	10.6	0.0	17.5	..	50.0	.6	11.9	11.9
Leather, Rubber, Footwear	6.6	1.3	2.5	5.8	0.0	0.3	..	5.0	.7	.8	.8
Metals	9.2	16.1	5.0	2.9	3.5	20.5	3.9	25.0	.2	.2	.2
Chemical & Photographic Suppl.	6.3	9.6	6.7	19.8	0.0	14.6	..	40.0	.1	.1	.1
Transport Equipment	..	..	..	..	..	..	..	..	.0	.0	.0
Non-Electric Machinery	21.8	1.7	2.6	6.9	9.7	6.6	3.6	43.9	.1	.6	.6
Electric Machinery	85.1	2.6	2.3	2.6	..	..	..	..	.0	.2	.2
Mineral Prod.,Prec. Stones & Metal	5.4	0.8	3.0	2.3	0.0	0.0	..	..	.1	.1	.1
Manufactured Articles nes.	12.1	1.1	3.4	18.5	0.0	2.0	..	74.0	.5	1.9	1.9
Industrial Goods (line 5-14)	**74.5**	**8.6**	**2.0**	**10.8**	**0.8**	**7.4**	**3.7**	**33.6**	**2.2**	**16.2**	**16.2**
All Merch. Trade (line 2-14)	**43.9**	**7.0**	**3.2**	**8.1**	**7.8**	**8.7**	**3.9**	**69.3**	**5.0**	**230.6**	**230.6**

Notes: 1. Value of exports from reporter countries that do not participate in Free Trade Agreements with MALAWI

2. Weighted average tariff reduction measured by dT / (1 + T) in percent.

MALAYSIA Extent of other countries' MFN tariff reductions on MALAYSIA's exports

Summary product category	Average levels and changes weighted by value of exports to: the World exc. FTA[1]				Average levels and changes weighted by value of exports to: LMIEs exc. FTA[1]				Value of exports in $ million		
	% of exports affected	Post-UR applied rate	Tariff reduc-tion[2]	Post-UR bound rate	% of exports affected	Post-UR applied rate	Tariff reduc-tion[2]	Post-UR bound rate	To IDB LMIEs exc. FTA[1]	To all IDB Ctrys exc. FTA[1]	To all IDB Ctrys inc. FTA
Agriculture, exc. Fish: Estimate 1	34.8	14.2	12.6	33.8	27.6	28.3	7.5	77.4	737.9	1,852.5	1,852.5
Agriculture, exc. Fish: Estimate 2	54.5	26.4	10.6	55.8	10.9	73.8	6.4	170.6	777.3	2,705.2	2,705.2
Fish and Fish Products	40.9	3.8	6.3	5.7	69.4	9.7	39.1	12.2	13.1	251.7	251.7
Petroleum Oils	0.0	5.9	0.8	16.4	0.0	13.1	6.0	36.0	946.2	2,836.0	2,836.0
Wood, Pulp, Paper and Furniture	12.7	1.6	5.6	2.9	17.3	5.9	7.8	8.7	754.4	3,863.8	3,863.8
Textiles and Clothing	55.0	11.4	2.5	14.0	40.1	33.2	14.4	29.1	57.5	1,416.5	1,416.5
Leather, Rubber, Footwear	24.1	1.8	6.7	3.9	70.2	7.9	10.7	9.3	392.6	2,379.5	2,379.5
Metals	11.1	2.3	7.1	4.1	34.2	13.7	10.5	16.7	146.5	917.4	917.4
Chemical & Photographic Suppl.	27.5	2.8	4.6	6.3	32.0	13.7	8.8	23.9	89.1	647.8	647.8
Transport Equipment	6.8	7.3	7.8	13.2	17.6	41.5	27.9	45.7	3.5	45.7	45.7
Non-Electric Machinery	26.7	1.3	3.3	4.5	19.6	18.1	10.0	31.0	63.8	1,043.8	1,043.8
Electric Machinery	24.0	1.5	4.2	4.5	60.0	11.8	10.1	10.5	197.1	6,341.7	6,341.7
Mineral Prod.,Prec. Stones & Metal	7.3	0.9	3.6	0.8	6.8	17.0	7.4	20.6	54.6	1,343.1	1,343.1
Manufactured Articles nes.	42.6	1.0	4.9	3.8	36.8	17.6	8.2	20.4	12.8	990.2	990.2
Industrial Goods (line 5-14)	**23.4**	**2.3**	**4.4**	**4.5**	**36.6**	**9.8**	**10.0**	**11.9**	**1,771.9**	**18,989.5**	**18,989.5**
All Merch. Trade (line 2-14)	**24.3**	**5.2**	**6.0**	**11.2**	**21.2**	**24.7**	**10.0**	**62.8**	**3,508.5**	**24,782.4**	**24,782.4**

Notes: 1. Value of exports from reporter countries that do not participate in Free Trade Agreements with MALAYSIA

2. Weighted average tariff reduction measured by dT / (1 + T) in percent.

MALI Extent of other countries' MFN tariff reductions on MALI's exports

Summary product category	Average levels and changes weighted by value of exports to: the World exc. FTA[1]				Average levels and changes weighted by value of exports to: LMIEs exc. FTA[1]				Value of exports in $ million		
	% of exports affected	Post-UR applied rate	Tariff reduc-tion[2]	Post-UR bound rate	% of exports affected	Post-UR applied rate	Tariff reduc-tion[2]	Post-UR bound rate	To IDB LMIEs exc. FTA[1]	To all IDB Ctrys exc. FTA[1]	To all IDB Ctrys inc. FTA
Agriculture, exc. Fish: Estimate 1	1.1	0.0	14.3	1.6	0.0	-0.3	..	5.1	19.5	67.5	67.5
Agriculture, exc. Fish: Estimate 2	59.7	3.8	5.1	7.1	0.8	18.8	0.6	48.5	.8	7.7	7.7
Fish and Fish Products	89.9	9.3	3.7	10.9	0.0	5.0	..	50.0	.0	.4	.4
Petroleum Oils	100.0	3.7	2.2	3.7	..	..	..	..	.0	.0	.0
Wood, Pulp, Paper and Furniture	55.4	1.3	3.5	1.0	58.3	11.9	2.2	9.6	.0	.3	.3
Textiles and Clothing	50.2	13.7	2.5	16.1	0.0	15.0	..	20.0	.7	1.4	1.4
Leather, Rubber, Footwear	31.3	1.4	2.7	0.5	0.0	90.0	..	..	.0	.4	.4
Metals	32.5	0.7	4.3	5.2	..	..	..	..	.0	.2	.2
Chemical & Photographic Suppl.	42.9	4.3	2.7	4.3	66.7	9.5	4.5	9.5	.0	.7	.7
Transport Equipment	9.8	10.1	3.1	10.1	..	..	..	..	.0	.2	.2
Non-Electric Machinery	51.0	0.1	2.2	0.1	0.0	5.0	..	5.0	.0	10.8	10.8
Electric Machinery	71.6	3.8	3.4	3.8	0.0	7.0	..	7.0	.0	1.2	1.2
Mineral Prod.,Prec. Stones & Metal	3.6	0.0	0.9	0.0	..	..	..	..	.0	15.2	15.2
Manufactured Articles nes.	11.2	2.4	1.9	7.3	34.7	8.1	0.5	25.7	19.2	68.4	68.4
Industrial Goods (line 5-14)	**16.1**	**2.0**	**2.1**	**5.4**	**33.5**	**8.4**	**0.5**	**25.5**	**19.9**	**99.0**	**99.0**
All Merch. Trade (line 2-14)	**19.5**	**2.1**	**2.8**	**5.6**	**32.2**	**8.8**	**0.5**	**26.4**	**20.8**	**107.0**	**107.0**

Notes: 1. Value of exports from reporter countries that do not participate in Free Trade Agreements with MALI

2. Weighted average tariff reduction measured by dT / (1 + T) in percent.

MALTA Extent of other countries' MFN tariff reductions on MALTA's exports

Summary product category	Average levels and changes weighted by value of exports to: the World exc. FTA[1]				Average levels and changes weighted by value of exports to: LMIEs exc. FTA[1]				Value of exports in $ million		
	% of exports affected	Post-UR applied rate	Tariff reduc-tion[2]	Post-UR bound rate	% of exports affected	Post-UR applied rate	Tariff reduc-tion[2]	Post-UR bound rate	To IDB LMIEs exc. FTA[1]	To all IDB Ctrys exc. FTA[1]	To all IDB Ctrys inc. FTA
Agriculture, exc. Fish: Estimate 1	6.4	5.5	7.4	10.3	..	..	..	..	.0	2.1	2.1
Agriculture, exc. Fish: Estimate 2	60.4	9.6	4.8	10.9	21.5	39.5	3.9	61.1	.2	5.4	5.4
Fish and Fish Products	21.1	13.8	1.3	13.8	..	..	..	..	.0	.1	.1
Petroleum Oils	1.6	0.6	2.2	3.5	..	..	..	..	.0	.4	.4
Wood, Pulp, Paper and Furniture	44.8	0.3	5.2	7.4	2.8	0.7	8.6	39.8	2.1	11.6	11.6
Textiles and Clothing	93.5	10.3	2.0	10.3	97.6	17.0	2.5	17.0	.2	139.6	139.6
Leather, Rubber, Footwear	96.6	2.9	1.7	2.9	50.0	18.7	5.4	9.0	.0	27.4	27.4
Metals	83.5	3.1	2.5	3.1	68.7	9.5	9.5	11.3	.1	24.0	24.0
Chemical & Photographic Suppl.	88.3	3.8	3.5	4.0	74.5	8.6	3.6	6.9	.3	14.0	14.0
Transport Equipment	17.9	1.1	1.5	1.0	0.0	6.9	..	..	.2	9.3	9.3
Non-Electric Machinery	95.3	2.1	2.0	2.1	97.4	4.5	1.4	4.3	1.3	6.6	6.6
Electric Machinery	45.8	3.7	4.4	5.0	19.4	16.3	3.7	29.7	.3	227.5	227.5
Mineral Prod.,Prec. Stones & Metal	72.3	3.9	1.4	3.9	42.9	21.7	3.5	8.0	.0	10.3	10.3
Manufactured Articles nes.	34.3	1.6	3.7	1.1	57.7	20.7	1.1	6.1	3.1	115.6	115.6
Industrial Goods (line 5-14)	**60.4**	**4.7**	**3.0**	**5.2**	**48.2**	**11.2**	**1.8**	**18.7**	**7.6**	**585.9**	**585.9**
All Merch. Trade (line 2-14)	**60.3**	**4.7**	**3.0**	**5.3**	**47.4**	**12.0**	**1.8**	**20.1**	**7.8**	**591.9**	**591.9**

Notes: 1. Value of exports from reporter countries that do not participate in Free Trade Agreements with MALTA

2. Weighted average tariff reduction measured by dT / (1 + T) in percent.

MARTINIQUE Extent of other countries' MFN tariff reductions on MARTINIQUE's exports

Summary product category	Average levels and changes weighted by value of exports to: the World exc. FTA[1]				Average levels and changes weighted by value of exports to: LMIEs exc. FTA[1]				Value of exports in $ million		
	% of exports affected	Post-UR applied rate	Tariff reduc-tion[2]	Post-UR bound rate	% of exports affected	Post-UR applied rate	Tariff reduc-tion[2]	Post-UR bound rate	To IDB LMIEs exc. FTA[1]	To all IDB Ctrys exc. FTA[1]	To all IDB Ctrys inc. FTA
Agriculture, exc. Fish: Estimate 1	0.0	0.1	5.9	0.1	..	..	..	..	.0	146.3	146.3
Agriculture, exc. Fish: Estimate 2	21.3	13.2	6.5	13.2	..	..	..	..	.0	184.5	184.5
Fish and Fish Products	94.6	7.8	5.8	7.8	..	..	..	..	.0	.0	.0
Petroleum Oils	0.0	2.4	..	2.4	..	..	..	..	.0	9.0	9.0
Wood, Pulp, Paper and Furniture	34.4	0.3	5.4	0.3	..	..	..	..	.0	.4	.4
Textiles and Clothing	91.4	10.9	1.8	11.5	0.0	10.0	..	50.0	.0	.5	.5
Leather, Rubber, Footwear	94.4	7.3	0.9	7.3	..	..	..	..	.0	.1	.1
Metals	38.7	1.3	1.9	1.3	..	..	..	..	.0	.7	.7
Chemical & Photographic Suppl.	63.2	2.8	3.5	2.8	..	..	..	..	.0	.4	.4
Transport Equipment	85.4	1.8	1.3	1.8	..	..	..	..	.0	3.2	3.2
Non-Electric Machinery	87.6	1.2	3.0	1.3	..	..	..	..	.0	2.8	2.8
Electric Machinery	90.6	3.7	2.9	3.9	0.0	10.0	..	50.0	.0	1.1	1.1
Mineral Prod.,Prec. Stones & Metal	80.6	2.7	1.6	2.7	0.0	0.0	..	0.0	.0	.4	.4
Manufactured Articles nes.	56.1	1.8	4.3	1.8	..	..	..	..	.0	1.8	1.8
Industrial Goods (line 5-14)	**76.5**	**2.3**	**2.5**	**2.3**	**0.0**	**2.5**	**..**	**12.7**	**.1**	**11.5**	**11.5**
All Merch. Trade (line 2-14)	**23.4**	**9.5**	**5.8**	**9.5**	**0.0**	**2.5**	**..**	**12.7**	**.1**	**205.0**	**205.0**

Notes: 1. Value of exports from reporter countries that do not participate in Free Trade Agreements with MARTINIQUE

2. Weighted average tariff reduction measured by dT / (1 + T) in percent.

MAURITANIA Extent of other countries' MFN tariff reductions on MAURITANIA's exports

Summary product category	Average levels and changes weighted by value of exports to: the World exc. FTA[1]				LMIEs exc. FTA[1]				Value of exports in $ million		
	% of exports affected	Post-UR applied rate	Tariff reduction[2]	Post-UR bound rate	% of exports affected	Post-UR applied rate	Tariff reduction[2]	Post-UR bound rate	To IDB LMIEs exc. FTA[1]	To all IDB Ctrys exc. FTA[1]	To all IDB Ctrys inc. FTA
Agriculture, exc. Fish: Estimate 1	0.0	-6.2	..	13.8	0.0	-8.5	..	19.0	.4	.5	.5
Agriculture, exc. Fish: Estimate 2	2.9	1.5	5.3	2.4	0.0	3.0	..	5.4	.4	1.6	1.6
Fish and Fish Products	90.8	7.0	2.8	7.1	0.0	15.0	..	30.0	.4	222.0	222.0
Petroleum Oils	48.6	2.3	1.2	4.7	..	..	..	..	.0	7.9	7.9
Wood, Pulp, Paper and Furniture	50.0	0.0	5.6	0.0	..	..	..	..	.0	.0	.0
Textiles and Clothing	86.6	10.1	1.9	10.2	93.5	6.5	2.1	7.1	.0	.3	.3
Leather, Rubber, Footwear	75.0	10.6	1.6	9.1	20.0	13.9	2.2	9.6	.0	.1	.1
Metals	0.0	0.0	2.1	0.0	0.0	15.0	..	25.0	.3	176.8	176.8
Chemical & Photographic Suppl.	87.8	5.6	5.0	5.6	0.0	11.0	..	25.0	.0	1.3	1.3
Transport Equipment	54.5	5.5	1.1	9.5	4.5	10.6	1.0	24.0	.1	.4	.4
Non-Electric Machinery	99.4	2.4	1.6	2.5	83.3	6.1	1.3	8.5	.0	.9	.9
Electric Machinery	95.1	3.8	2.3	3.8	94.8	5.7	1.8	5.9	.1	.2	.2
Mineral Prod.,Prec. Stones & Metal	13.9	12.9	1.5	5.7	0.0	14.6	..	0.0	.1	.2	.2
Manufactured Articles nes.	29.8	3.1	2.0	1.5	83.5	10.1	1.6	4.9	.4	1.4	1.4
Industrial Goods (line 5-14)	**1.8**	**0.2**	**2.9**	**0.1**	**40.2**	**11.8**	**1.7**	**9.3**	**1.1**	**181.5**	**181.5**
All Merch. Trade (line 2-14)	**50.5**	**3.9**	**2.8**	**4.0**	**22.0**	**10.5**	**1.7**	**13.1**	**2.0**	**412.9**	**412.9**

Notes: 1. Value of exports from reporter countries that do not participate in Free Trade Agreements with MAURITANIA

2. Weighted average tariff reduction measured by dT / (1 + T) in percent.

MAURITIUS Extent of other countries' MFN tariff reductions on MAURITIUS's exports

Summary product category	Average levels and changes weighted by value of exports to: the World exc. FTA[1]				LMIEs exc. FTA[1]				Value of exports in $ million		
	% of exports affected	Post-UR applied rate	Tariff reduction[2]	Post-UR bound rate	% of exports affected	Post-UR applied rate	Tariff reduction[2]	Post-UR bound rate	To IDB LMIEs exc. FTA[1]	To all IDB Ctrys exc. FTA[1]	To all IDB Ctrys inc. FTA
Agriculture, exc. Fish: Estimate 1	2.1	140.2	11.5	140.2	0.0	2.0	..	150.0	.0	304.4	304.4
Agriculture, exc. Fish: Estimate 2	4.0	48.8	19.1	49.1	2.3	3.9	3.9	18.2	.1	320.4	320.4
Fish and Fish Products	8.5	13.3	2.4	13.9	0.0	1.7	..	7.5	.0	23.7	23.7
Petroleum Oils	0.2	0.6	6.0	0.3	33.3	7.7	6.0	13.0	.0	.4	.4
Wood, Pulp, Paper and Furniture	89.4	0.3	5.6	0.3	25.0	25.0	3.9	25.0	.0	2.1	2.1
Textiles and Clothing	95.8	12.8	1.6	13.0	42.5	12.3	5.6	13.0	.3	502.2	502.2
Leather, Rubber, Footwear	88.5	6.1	1.8	6.2	0.0	30.0	..	30.0	.0	3.6	3.6
Metals	79.6	2.5	2.6	2.6	97.4	23.8	10.4	24.4	.2	3.7	3.7
Chemical & Photographic Suppl.	52.0	5.9	1.6	4.3	8.3	18.9	2.1	6.5	.2	1.4	1.4
Transport Equipment	70.5	2.4	2.0	11.1	0.0	0.0	..	50.0	.1	.8	.8
Non-Electric Machinery	63.8	1.7	2.9	0.8	28.7	0.8	3.3	2.6	.1	3.5	3.5
Electric Machinery	40.0	2.8	2.5	6.0	1.0	19.3	6.0	13.0	.1	2.2	2.2
Mineral Prod.,Prec. Stones & Metal	17.9	0.7	1.1	0.7	..	..	..	..	.0	20.9	20.9
Manufactured Articles nes.	82.7	3.6	3.1	3.6	0.0	11.9	..	30.0	.1	29.9	29.9
Industrial Goods (line 5-14)	**91.5**	**11.6**	**1.7**	**11.8**	**29.1**	**13.3**	**7.5**	**26.4**	**1.1**	**570.2**	**570.2**
All Merch. Trade (line 2-14)	**58.7**	**14.2**	**2.1**	**14.4**	**26.5**	**12.6**	**7.5**	**25.4**	**1.2**	**914.8**	**914.8**

Notes: 1. Value of exports from reporter countries that do not participate in Free Trade Agreements with MAURITIUS

2. Weighted average tariff reduction measured by dT / (1 + T) in percent.

MEXICO Extent of other countries' MFN tariff reductions on MEXICO's exports

Summary product category	Average levels and changes weighted by value of exports to: the World exc. FTA[1]				Average levels and changes weighted by value of exports to: LMIEs exc. FTA[1]				Value of exports in $ million		
	% of exports affected	Post-UR applied rate	Tariff reduc-tion[2]	Post-UR bound rate	% of exports affected	Post-UR applied rate	Tariff reduc-tion[2]	Post-UR bound rate	To IDB LMIEs exc. FTA[1]	To all IDB Ctrys exc. FTA[1]	To all IDB Ctrys inc. FTA
Agriculture, exc. Fish: Estimate 1	0.5	3.0	11.4	6.4	0.0	15.8	45.7	29.5	90.9	395.5	1,716.8
Agriculture, exc. Fish: Estimate 2	8.8	4.4	5.1	7.6	12.7	14.1	5.1	60.0	76.1	484.6	2,936.4
Fish and Fish Products	11.0	0.8	2.2	2.0	74.5	8.1	39.5	10.3	1.0	137.2	533.1
Petroleum Oils	0.0	1.7	1.3	4.1	0.0	11.8	..	41.4	242.9	2,655.2	6,824.2
Wood, Pulp, Paper and Furniture	2.7	0.1	6.6	0.7	38.2	2.2	5.0	15.3	36.3	63.5	1,214.4
Textiles and Clothing	7.5	3.9	4.5	13.5	11.6	12.8	13.4	32.4	37.7	114.6	1,016.2
Leather, Rubber, Footwear	5.8	3.6	2.2	8.9	8.4	8.1	7.4	30.0	18.0	80.7	419.7
Metals	7.2	1.9	5.9	4.3	17.3	9.3	11.0	26.8	204.8	533.4	1,795.0
Chemical & Photographic Suppl.	17.3	6.0	4.1	9.0	13.6	10.8	7.6	22.6	453.5	711.2	1,427.9
Transport Equipment	0.9	3.4	2.2	3.8	5.1	12.0	4.3	30.2	43.3	99.2	3,201.3
Non-Electric Machinery	10.0	1.0	2.3	2.3	8.7	13.5	7.6	29.3	62.6	424.5	2,948.1
Electric Machinery	0.7	0.8	4.0	3.5	14.6	14.3	8.1	30.3	43.8	125.4	6,802.3
Mineral Prod.,Prec. Stones & Metal	7.6	0.3	2.7	1.9	21.4	6.1	12.7	26.2	43.2	419.6	1,812.6
Manufactured Articles nes.	3.5	0.9	3.7	2.6	9.3	9.0	1.3	21.9	68.4	183.6	1,467.9
Industrial Goods (line 5-14)	**4.9**	**1.6**	**3.6**	**4.0**	**14.5**	**10.3**	**8.4**	**25.0**	**1,011.7**	**2,755.6**	**22,105.4**
All Merch. Trade (line 2-14)	**4.3**	**1.9**	**3.8**	**4.3**	**11.8**	**10.8**	**8.3**	**29.5**	**1,331.7**	**6,032.6**	**32,399.1**

Notes: 1. Value of exports from reporter countries that do not participate in Free Trade Agreements with MEXICO

2. Weighted average tariff reduction measured by dT / (1 + T) in percent.

MONGOLIA Extent of other countries' MFN tariff reductions on MONGOLIA's exports

Summary product category	Average levels and changes weighted by value of exports to: the World exc. FTA[1]				Average levels and changes weighted by value of exports to: LMIEs exc. FTA[1]				Value of exports in $ million		
	% of exports affected	Post-UR applied rate	Tariff reduc-tion[2]	Post-UR bound rate	% of exports affected	Post-UR applied rate	Tariff reduc-tion[2]	Post-UR bound rate	To IDB LMIEs exc. FTA[1]	To all IDB Ctrys exc. FTA[1]	To all IDB Ctrys inc. FTA
Agriculture, exc. Fish: Estimate 1	0.0	0.8	..	4.6	0.0	-1.2	..	92.1	.0	.4	.4
Agriculture, exc. Fish: Estimate 2	14.2	2.2	1.3	3.4	45.8	7.1	1.1	11.2	.5	1.9	1.9
Fish and Fish Products	97.1	0.4	0.6	0.7	..	..	..	..	.0	.0	.0
Petroleum Oils	..	..	..	..	..	..	..	..	.0	.0	.0
Wood, Pulp, Paper and Furniture	53.8	4.1	3.5	7.4	34.0	9.1	2.5	21.8	.0	.2	.2
Textiles and Clothing	50.0	4.3	3.2	5.0	55.6	7.4	5.5	9.1	5.1	12.3	12.3
Leather, Rubber, Footwear	89.5	4.9	1.6	6.2	90.0	5.0	1.8	6.6	5.1	6.0	6.0
Metals	0.0	0.0	1.4	0.0	0.0	0.0	..	0.0	1.6	6.1	6.1
Chemical & Photographic Suppl.	83.1	3.6	2.6	3.6	87.5	3.7	2.7	3.7	.3	.4	.4
Transport Equipment	0.0	10.0	..	10.0	..	..	..	..	.0	.0	.0
Non-Electric Machinery	37.7	1.5	1.9	2.1	0.0	5.0	..	9.0	.0	.2	.2
Electric Machinery	75.0	2.3	3.2	3.0	100.0	3.2	1.0	3.2	.0	.0	.0
Mineral Prod.,Prec. Stones & Metal	2.0	4.2	1.4	4.4	0.0	4.2	..	4.4	1.2	1.3	1.3
Manufactured Articles nes.	1.7	0.2	0.9	0.8	3.2	1.9	1.1	9.4	3.8	43.5	43.5
Industrial Goods (line 5-14)	**18.3**	**1.4**	**2.4**	**2.1**	**45.4**	**4.5**	**3.2**	**7.2**	**17.3**	**69.9**	**69.9**
All Merch. Trade (line 2-14)	**18.2**	**1.4**	**2.3**	**2.1**	**45.4**	**4.6**	**3.1**	**7.3**	**17.8**	**71.9**	**71.9**

Notes: 1. Value of exports from reporter countries that do not participate in Free Trade Agreements with MONGOLIA

2. Weighted average tariff reduction measured by dT / (1 + T) in percent.

MOROCCO Extent of other countries' MFN tariff reductions on MOROCCO's exports

Summary product category	Average levels and changes weighted by value of exports to: the World exc. FTA[1]				LMIEs exc. FTA[1]				Value of exports in $ million		
	% of exports affected	Post-UR applied rate	Tariff reduc-tion[2]	Post-UR bound rate	% of exports affected	Post-UR applied rate	Tariff reduc-tion[2]	Post-UR bound rate	To IDB LMIEs exc. FTA[1]	To all IDB Ctrys exc. FTA[1]	To all IDB Ctrys inc. FTA
Agriculture, exc. Fish: Estimate 1	0.0	1.5	5.7	3.1	0.1	4.8	1.2	6.8	.9	137.6	137.6
Agriculture, exc. Fish: Estimate 2	37.3	8.2	3.5	9.8	1.4	30.7	2.4	82.8	10.2	652.7	652.7
Fish and Fish Products	67.0	9.3	3.7	10.1	0.1	10.4	28.6	34.5	10.7	403.7	403.7
Petroleum Oils	39.7	4.9	1.5	4.5	0.0	36.0	..	..	5.8	54.1	54.1
Wood, Pulp, Paper and Furniture	21.6	5.2	4.5	5.4	22.8	17.4	5.4	18.6	19.7	71.8	71.8
Textiles and Clothing	89.3	10.9	1.7	11.2	2.7	20.3	3.5	43.2	10.8	794.0	794.0
Leather, Rubber, Footwear	66.9	6.3	2.4	6.3	17.9	20.8	0.7	30.1	1.0	103.5	103.5
Metals	26.5	1.7	1.4	1.8	3.6	15.9	8.8	26.6	7.8	123.6	123.6
Chemical & Photographic Suppl.	73.5	18.1	12.3	22.1	64.5	27.8	19.4	35.6	180.1	312.6	312.6
Transport Equipment	35.0	3.0	2.1	3.1	0.0	25.8	..	28.6	2.5	50.2	50.2
Non-Electric Machinery	53.0	4.0	2.9	3.8	0.2	21.9	6.8	24.8	3.1	21.1	21.1
Electric Machinery	72.2	4.5	4.8	5.9	0.9	17.2	6.0	13.7	.7	92.6	92.6
Mineral Prod.,Prec. Stones & Metal	15.3	1.6	0.3	4.5	2.2	3.0	2.0	21.6	114.7	698.6	698.6
Manufactured Articles nes.	35.2	1.8	3.1	1.5	5.3	25.7	0.4	21.2	.7	45.7	45.7
Industrial Goods (line 5-14)	**55.1**	**7.5**	**3.7**	**9.0**	**36.3**	**18.3**	**18.4**	**29.7**	**341.1**	**2,313.5**	**2,313.5**
All Merch. Trade (line 2-14)	**52.8**	**7.8**	**3.7**	**9.2**	**33.7**	**18.6**	**18.4**	**31.5**	**367.8**	**3,424.0**	**3,424.0**

Notes: 1. Value of exports from reporter countries that do not participate in Free Trade Agreements with MOROCCO

2. Weighted average tariff reduction measured by dT / (1 + T) in percent.

MOZAMBIQUE Extent of other countries' MFN tariff reductions on MOZAMBIQUE's exports

Summary product category	Average levels and changes weighted by value of exports to: the World exc. FTA[1]				LMIEs exc. FTA[1]				Value of exports in $ million		
	% of exports affected	Post-UR applied rate	Tariff reduc-tion[2]	Post-UR bound rate	% of exports affected	Post-UR applied rate	Tariff reduc-tion[2]	Post-UR bound rate	To IDB LMIEs exc. FTA[1]	To all IDB Ctrys exc. FTA[1]	To all IDB Ctrys inc. FTA
Agriculture, exc. Fish: Estimate 1	12.6	27.3	14.3	31.8	0.0	24.4	..	67.2	3.4	31.9	31.9
Agriculture, exc. Fish: Estimate 2	17.2	3.7	10.5	6.9	12.3	14.1	3.3	45.8	3.8	42.4	42.4
Fish and Fish Products	96.0	7.9	7.7	8.0	81.7	4.2	41.5	4.1	7.6	68.0	68.0
Petroleum Oils	0.0	36.0	..	..	0.0	36.0	..	..	.1	.1	.1
Wood, Pulp, Paper and Furniture	10.9	9.1	7.2	10.9	4.4	12.4	13.4	15.0	5.7	7.7	7.7
Textiles and Clothing	65.4	4.9	2.1	4.9	83.3	37.8	26.5	43.3	.0	2.2	2.2
Leather, Rubber, Footwear	68.4	4.0	2.1	4.0	..	..	..	..	.0	.2	.2
Metals	2.1	1.2	4.9	11.6	0.7	4.0	16.4	37.2	26.4	90.0	90.0
Chemical & Photographic Suppl.	7.3	2.3	7.8	5.7	25.5	8.8	8.7	19.7	2.3	9.5	9.5
Transport Equipment	7.0	14.1	1.2	16.8	0.0	11.0	..	27.5	.0	.3	.3
Non-Electric Machinery	16.1	0.5	3.6	0.6	0.0	15.5	..	29.7	.0	1.7	1.7
Electric Machinery	29.8	6.3	2.7	4.8	0.0	27.0	..	..	.0	.4	.4
Mineral Prod.,Prec. Stones & Metal	0.5	5.8	1.2	19.6	0.0	6.9	..	20.4	14.1	16.7	16.7
Manufactured Articles nes.	8.4	1.0	6.0	5.6	6.8	4.0	14.8	27.5	1.0	4.5	4.5
Industrial Goods (line 5-14)	**4.4**	**2.4**	**4.7**	**11.5**	**2.2**	**6.0**	**11.5**	**29.2**	**49.5**	**133.1**	**133.1**
All Merch. Trade (line 2-14)	**32.2**	**4.2**	**7.8**	**9.7**	**12.7**	**6.3**	**35.0**	**27.0**	**61.0**	**243.7**	**243.7**

Notes: 1. Value of exports from reporter countries that do not participate in Free Trade Agreements with MOZAMBIQUE

2. Weighted average tariff reduction measured by dT / (1 + T) in percent.

MYANMAR Extent of other countries' MFN tariff reductions on MYANMAR's exports

Summary product category	Average levels and changes weighted by value of exports to: the World exc. FTA[1]				Average levels and changes weighted by value of exports to: LMIEs exc. FTA[1]				Value of exports in $ million		
	% of exports affected	Post-UR applied rate	Tariff reduc-tion[2]	Post-UR bound rate	% of exports affected	Post-UR applied rate	Tariff reduc-tion[2]	Post-UR bound rate	To IDB LMIEs exc. FTA[1]	To all IDB Ctrys exc. FTA[1]	To all IDB Ctrys inc. FTA
Agriculture, exc. Fish: Estimate 1	16.4	18.3	13.4	39.7	12.3	14.3	11.5	64.7	5.0	11.0	11.0
Agriculture, exc. Fish: Estimate 2	14.8	8.3	9.0	52.3	10.6	10.9	4.2	81.9	20.5	35.7	35.7
Fish and Fish Products	16.2	0.7	7.9	3.5	47.1	2.8	40.8	5.9	1.6	33.1	33.1
Petroleum Oils	..	..	..	..	..	..	..	..	.0	.0	.0
Wood, Pulp, Paper and Furniture	33.2	4.6	5.5	8.1	66.2	9.4	5.5	13.6	82.5	167.0	167.0
Textiles and Clothing	88.0	16.6	1.7	17.9	28.7	19.4	20.8	36.0	.4	9.1	9.1
Leather, Rubber, Footwear	0.3	3.3	3.8	6.8	0.2	4.6	6.8	5.3	8.6	12.1	12.1
Metals	4.1	3.2	8.2	8.4	4.8	7.5	13.1	17.5	6.9	15.6	15.6
Chemical & Photographic Suppl.	76.7	2.5	4.0	2.3	16.1	20.3	4.8	29.8	.1	1.5	1.5
Transport Equipment	4.9	25.5	9.3	6.1	1.0	29.4	50.0	80.0	.2	.2	.2
Non-Electric Machinery	53.9	1.5	3.6	2.9	0.0	5.0	..	17.7	.0	.5	.5
Electric Machinery	62.9	12.5	1.2	15.5	9.5	28.1	1.9	37.1	.0	.1	.1
Mineral Prod.,Prec. Stones & Metal	7.7	0.3	5.3	0.6	78.9	5.1	9.5	5.4	1.3	31.7	31.7
Manufactured Articles nes.	7.1	2.3	3.2	1.5	22.4	15.5	2.5	28.5	.1	.8	.8
Industrial Goods (line 5-14)	**28.5**	**4.4**	**5.0**	**7.9**	**56.1**	**8.9**	**5.6**	**13.2**	**100.2**	**238.5**	**238.5**
All Merch. Trade (line 2-14)	**25.6**	**4.4**	**5.5**	**12.5**	**48.3**	**9.2**	**6.0**	**24.7**	**122.3**	**307.3**	**307.3**

Notes: 1. Value of exports from reporter countries that do not participate in Free Trade Agreements with MYANMAR

2. Weighted average tariff reduction measured by dT / (1 + T) in percent.

NAMIBIA Extent of other countries' MFN tariff reductions on NAMIBIA's exports

Summary product category	Average levels and changes weighted by value of exports to: the World exc. FTA[1]				Average levels and changes weighted by value of exports to: LMIEs exc. FTA[1]				Value of exports in $ million		
	% of exports affected	Post-UR applied rate	Tariff reduc-tion[2]	Post-UR bound rate	% of exports affected	Post-UR applied rate	Tariff reduc-tion[2]	Post-UR bound rate	To IDB LMIEs exc. FTA[1]	To all IDB Ctrys exc. FTA[1]	To all IDB Ctrys inc. FTA
Agriculture, exc. Fish: Estimate 1	26.5	0.8	20.9	0.8	..	..	..	..	.0	.3	.3
Agriculture, exc. Fish: Estimate 2	11.9	6.3	11.9	11.4	0.9	10.3	5.9	17.5	1.0	1.7	1.7
Fish and Fish Products	99.5	1.0	2.0	1.0	..	..	..	..	.0	22.3	22.3
Petroleum Oils	0.0	0.4	..	0.7	..	..	..	..	.0	9.1	9.1
Wood, Pulp, Paper and Furniture	0.0	0.0	..	0.0	..	..	..	..	.0	.1	.1
Textiles and Clothing	0.0	0.0	..	0.2	..	..	..	..	.0	.0	.0
Leather, Rubber, Footwear	75.0	2.5	1.4	3.3	..	..	..	..	.0	.0	.0
Metals	9.0	0.2	1.3	0.2	..	..	..	..	.0	1.8	1.8
Chemical & Photographic Suppl.	0.0	0.2	11.8	5.8	0.0	11.1	..	25.0	.1	7.8	7.8
Transport Equipment	0.0	25.0	..	25.0	0.0	25.0	..	25.0	.0	.0	.0
Non-Electric Machinery	98.3	0.0	4.1	0.0	..	..	..	..	.0	.1	.1
Electric Machinery	0.0	0.0	..	7.7	..	..	..	..	.0	.1	.1
Mineral Prod.,Prec. Stones & Metal	27.1	0.9	2.0	0.9	100.0	5.0	4.7	5.0	.1	.5	.5
Manufactured Articles nes.	0.4	0.0	1.6	0.0	0.0	..	..	..	.0	.6	.6
Industrial Goods (line 5-14)	**3.4**	**0.2**	**2.0**	**4.3**	**27.4**	**9.5**	**4.7**	**19.5**	**.2**	**11.0**	**11.0**
All Merch. Trade (line 2-14)	**51.7**	**0.9**	**2.0**	**2.2**	**5.1**	**10.2**	**4.8**	**17.8**	**1.2**	**44.1**	**44.1**

Notes: 1. Value of exports from reporter countries that do not participate in Free Trade Agreements with NAMIBIA

2. Weighted average tariff reduction measured by dT / (1 + T) in percent.

119

NAURU Extent of other countries' MFN tariff reductions on NAURU's exports

Summary product category	Average levels and changes weighted by value of exports to: the World exc. FTA[1]				LMIEs exc. FTA[1]				Value of exports in $ million		
	% of exports affected	Post-UR applied rate	Tariff reduc-tion[2]	Post-UR bound rate	% of exports affected	Post-UR applied rate	Tariff reduc-tion[2]	Post-UR bound rate	To IDB LMIEs exc. FTA[1]	To all IDB Ctrys exc. FTA[1]	To all IDB Ctrys inc. FTA
Agriculture, exc. Fish: Estimate 1	5.4	4.5	5.9	4.5	..	..	..	..	.0	.2	.2
Agriculture, exc. Fish: Estimate 2	92.2	2.4	2.9	2.4	..	..	..	..	.0	.3	.3
Fish and Fish Products	..	..	..	..	..	..	..	..	.0	.0	.0
Petroleum Oils	0.0	2.4	..	2.4	..	..	..	..	.0	4.9	4.9
Wood, Pulp, Paper and Furniture	0.9	0.0	2.6	0.0	..	..	..	..	.0	2.3	2.3
Textiles and Clothing	86.1	7.7	0.8	10.5	0.0	15.0	..	35.0	.0	.1	.1
Leather, Rubber, Footwear	1.1	8.5	1.2	8.5	..	..	..	..	.0	.1	.1
Metals	50.9	1.6	1.9	1.6	..	..	..	..	.0	.2	.2
Chemical & Photographic Suppl.	21.6	1.4	2.5	9.4	0.0	2.5	..	35.0	.0	.2	.2
Transport Equipment	0.0	4.6	..	4.6	..	..	..	..	.0	.0	.0
Non-Electric Machinery	91.4	1.7	1.9	2.5	0.0	27.0	..	..	.0	.3	.3
Electric Machinery	30.0	8.7	2.1	17.8	0.0	11.0	..	25.0	.0	.0	.0
Mineral Prod.,Prec. Stones & Metal	0.1	0.6	1.5	0.6	0.0	6.4	..	6.4	7.0	79.3	79.3
Manufactured Articles nes.	39.8	1.3	2.5	2.9	100.0	0.0	11.4	0.0	.0	.1	.1
Industrial Goods (line 5-14)	**0.8**	**0.6**	**1.8**	**0.6**	**0.1**	**6.4**	**11.4**	**6.5**	**7.0**	**82.7**	**82.7**
All Merch. Trade (line 2-14)	**1.1**	**0.7**	**2.1**	**0.7**	**0.1**	**6.4**	**11.4**	**6.5**	**7.0**	**87.8**	**87.8**

Notes: 1. Value of exports from reporter countries that do not participate in Free Trade Agreements with NAURU

2. Weighted average tariff reduction measured by dT / (1 + T) in percent.

NEPAL Extent of other countries' MFN tariff reductions on NEPAL's exports

Summary product category	Average levels and changes weighted by value of exports to: the World exc. FTA[1]				LMIEs exc. FTA[1]				Value of exports in $ million		
	% of exports affected	Post-UR applied rate	Tariff reduc-tion[2]	Post-UR bound rate	% of exports affected	Post-UR applied rate	Tariff reduc-tion[2]	Post-UR bound rate	To IDB LMIEs exc. FTA[1]	To all IDB Ctrys exc. FTA[1]	To all IDB Ctrys inc. FTA
Agriculture, exc. Fish: Estimate 1	0.3	12.0	14.9	79.4	0.2	14.7	1.2	98.9	9.2	11.5	11.5
Agriculture, exc. Fish: Estimate 2	5.8	47.5	8.2	94.9	0.6	52.7	5.5	105.6	28.9	32.3	32.3
Fish and Fish Products	0.0	0.0	..	0.0	0.0	0.0	..	..	.0	.0	.0
Petroleum Oils	..	..	..	..	..	..	..	..	.0	.0	.0
Wood, Pulp, Paper and Furniture	61.4	10.4	7.5	11.9	24.5	23.5	15.1	29.3	.3	.7	.7
Textiles and Clothing	42.0	12.1	1.9	10.1	9.6	68.8	26.6	40.0	7.0	144.0	144.0
Leather, Rubber, Footwear	96.3	3.7	1.5	4.3	92.9	4.9	3.3	6.6	1.6	5.2	5.2
Metals	45.7	1.0	2.9	1.5	0.0	2.0	..	..	.0	1.0	1.0
Chemical & Photographic Suppl.	97.1	38.3	16.3	38.9	97.7	38.8	16.4	39.5	5.3	5.4	5.4
Transport Equipment	2.1	0.1	2.9	0.2	..	..	..	..	.0	.0	.0
Non-Electric Machinery	25.1	0.9	1.6	1.4	75.0	3.8	3.6	5.0	.0	.8	.8
Electric Machinery	5.5	2.8	4.4	4.4	66.7	10.3	6.0	13.0	.0	.3	.3
Mineral Prod.,Prec. Stones & Metal	87.9	8.8	4.7	9.8	96.4	38.6	19.4	39.5	.2	1.5	1.5
Manufactured Articles nes.	11.3	1.3	9.0	8.1	2.3	2.7	34.2	19.5	.6	2.0	2.0
Industrial Goods (line 5-14)	**45.6**	**12.4**	**3.0**	**10.8**	**51.1**	**47.4**	**14.8**	**32.9**	**15.0**	**161.1**	**161.1**
All Merch. Trade (line 2-14)	**39.0**	**18.2**	**3.1**	**25.1**	**17.8**	**50.9**	**14.6**	**86.8**	**44.0**	**193.4**	**193.4**

Notes: 1. Value of exports from reporter countries that do not participate in Free Trade Agreements with NEPAL

2. Weighted average tariff reduction measured by dT / (1 + T) in percent.

NETHERLANDS ANTILLES Extent of other countries' MFN tariff reductions on NETHERLANDS ANTILLES's exports

Summary product category	Average levels and changes weighted by value of exports to: the World exc. FTA[1]				LMIEs exc. FTA[1]				Value of exports in $ million		
	% of exports affected	Post-UR applied rate	Tariff reduc-tion[2]	Post-UR bound rate	% of exports affected	Post-UR applied rate	Tariff reduc-tion[2]	Post-UR bound rate	To IDB LMIEs exc. FTA[1]	To all IDB Ctrys exc. FTA[1]	To all IDB Ctrys inc. FTA
Agriculture, exc. Fish: Estimate 1	0.0	19.5	..	47.3	0.0	0.0	..	83.7	.3	.8	.8
Agriculture, exc. Fish: Estimate 2	58.8	7.9	4.0	16.1	0.0	18.6	..	67.4	.5	3.3	3.3
Fish and Fish Products	4.1	0.4	4.6	0.5	..	..	..	..	.0	13.9	13.9
Petroleum Oils	2.4	5.5	2.2	13.5	0.0	14.1	..	37.1	192.7	592.7	592.7
Wood, Pulp, Paper and Furniture	79.6	3.0	5.2	6.5	4.0	16.4	2.8	35.0	.4	1.9	1.9
Textiles and Clothing	94.1	34.2	3.6	34.9	94.2	34.4	3.6	35.1	10.3	10.4	10.4
Leather, Rubber, Footwear	75.0	28.7	3.0	32.9	73.4	30.2	3.1	34.7	4.6	5.0	5.0
Metals	11.9	0.8	1.9	22.6	0.1	0.6	3.6	35.0	4.0	6.3	6.3
Chemical & Photographic Suppl.	22.5	5.7	4.3	14.5	0.7	9.5	1.5	31.8	2.3	5.7	5.7
Transport Equipment	7.8	3.3	2.5	31.3	3.9	3.3	3.6	34.9	4.6	5.1	5.1
Non-Electric Machinery	23.6	9.4	2.8	24.5	1.3	12.2	1.5	32.5	1.4	1.8	1.8
Electric Machinery	52.1	9.4	1.8	15.4	17.2	18.6	1.6	34.9	1.2	3.3	3.3
Mineral Prod.,Prec. Stones & Metal	4.2	0.6	1.8	1.6	1.0	11.5	3.6	35.5	.8	19.2	19.2
Manufactured Articles nes.	19.3	2.7	2.8	4.8	10.7	17.4	3.5	33.0	.8	5.5	5.5
Industrial Goods (line 5-14)	**33.4**	**9.8**	**3.3**	**16.8**	**45.1**	**19.8**	**3.5**	**34.6**	**30.3**	**64.2**	**64.2**
All Merch. Trade (line 2-14)	**5.7**	**5.9**	**2.9**	**13.6**	**6.1**	**14.9**	**3.5**	**36.8**	**223.4**	**674.1**	**674.1**

Notes: 1. Value of exports from reporter countries that do not participate in Free Trade Agreements with Nthlds Antilles

2. Weighted average tariff reduction measured by dT / (1 + T) in percent.

NEW ZEALAND Extent of other countries' MFN tariff reductions on NEW ZEALAND's exports

Summary product category	Average levels and changes weighted by value of exports to: the World exc. FTA[1]				LMIEs exc. FTA[1]				Value of exports in $ million		
	% of exports affected	Post-UR applied rate	Tariff reduc-tion[2]	Post-UR bound rate	% of exports affected	Post-UR applied rate	Tariff reduc-tion[2]	Post-UR bound rate	To IDB LMIEs exc. FTA[1]	To all IDB Ctrys exc. FTA[1]	To all IDB Ctrys inc. FTA
Agriculture, exc. Fish: Estimate 1	21.3	51.9	8.9	56.2	6.2	47.7	30.4	76.3	392.3	2,318.1	2,360.5
Agriculture, exc. Fish: Estimate 2	20.7	5.6	4.2	10.4	10.4	13.3	3.7	33.6	486.3	3,096.3	3,336.8
Fish and Fish Products	30.5	1.3	4.7	1.6	88.6	7.8	28.7	7.0	14.7	334.0	382.6
Petroleum Oils	0.0	0.0	1.5	0.0	0.0	..	..	..	.0	35.0	95.2
Wood, Pulp, Paper and Furniture	9.1	1.3	3.3	5.7	20.7	4.9	4.9	18.4	145.0	439.3	741.7
Textiles and Clothing	16.4	1.5	3.6	6.4	53.1	5.2	5.8	8.2	52.1	306.0	452.1
Leather, Rubber, Footwear	19.0	2.4	3.1	7.5	96.2	11.3	8.7	10.6	6.8	103.4	167.7
Metals	72.3	0.6	1.7	1.5	23.6	10.9	6.7	13.0	25.5	596.5	696.6
Chemical & Photographic Suppl.	33.5	2.0	5.2	6.7	48.5	7.4	5.8	16.1	14.9	97.3	193.8
Transport Equipment	52.4	2.1	0.9	5.1	0.2	8.7	6.0	23.9	.7	29.5	40.7
Non-Electric Machinery	21.0	1.8	2.9	9.6	19.8	10.7	7.1	22.6	11.0	80.2	198.3
Electric Machinery	13.4	4.2	3.3	15.2	23.3	17.8	8.3	23.9	3.5	22.5	94.4
Mineral Prod.,Prec. Stones & Metal	7.8	0.7	2.8	5.3	42.8	8.7	5.1	11.5	3.3	49.4	108.9
Manufactured Articles nes.	22.0	1.5	4.5	2.3	82.3	9.0	6.2	12.6	132.7	934.7	1,035.8
Industrial Goods (line 5-14)	**28.2**	**1.4**	**2.8**	**4.5**	**48.3**	**7.3**	**6.1**	**14.2**	**395.5**	**2,658.7**	**3,729.7**
All Merch. Trade (line 2-14)	**24.7**	**3.0**	**3.4**	**6.4**	**28.4**	**10.3**	**6.8**	**24.4**	**896.5**	**6,124.0**	**7,544.3**

Notes: 1. Value of exports from reporter countries that do not participate in Free Trade Agreements with NEW ZEALAND

2. Weighted average tariff reduction measured by dT / (1 + T) in percent.

NICARAGUA Extent of other countries' MFN tariff reductions on NICARAGUA's exports

| Summary product category | *Average levels and changes weighted by value of exports to:* | | | | | | | | *Value of exports in $ million* | | |
| | *the World exc. FTA[1]* | | | | *LMIEs exc. FTA[1]* | | | | | | |
	% of exports affected	Post-UR applied rate	Tariff reduc-tion[2]	Post-UR bound rate	% of exports affected	Post-UR applied rate	Tariff reduc-tion[2]	Post-UR bound rate	To IDB LMIEs exc. FTA[1]	To all IDB Ctrys exc. FTA[1]	To all IDB Ctrys inc. FTA
Agriculture, exc. Fish: Estimate 1	0.1	2.0	37.2	5.0	0.6	2.0	18.2	14.3	9.1	192.6	192.6
Agriculture, exc. Fish: Estimate 2	57.9	2.1	5.0	3.1	6.7	16.9	1.3	27.2	7.5	148.7	148.7
Fish and Fish Products	58.8	5.2	3.9	5.4	0.0	20.5	..	40.9	.1	9.2	9.2
Petroleum Oils	0.0	0.0	..	40.0	0.0	5.0	..	40.0	.0	12.5	12.5
Wood, Pulp, Paper and Furniture	8.7	10.6	6.7	26.8	0.0	12.1	..	30.5	1.0	1.1	1.1
Textiles and Clothing	76.1	7.6	1.5	7.6	..	..	..	..	.0	.2	.2
Leather, Rubber, Footwear	5.1	7.6	3.0	37.7	0.2	7.8	2.7	39.9	.5	.6	.6
Metals	3.0	12.5	4.7	39.6	0.0	14.2	..	45.1	5.4	6.2	6.2
Chemical & Photographic Suppl.	17.0	9.6	5.1	28.3	0.5	11.6	11.9	36.7	1.5	2.0	2.0
Transport Equipment	66.4	10.8	2.7	12.3	0.0	35.0	..	43.9	.0	.1	.1
Non-Electric Machinery	73.1	3.8	2.1	6.4	0.0	7.3	..	17.7	.2	.7	.7
Electric Machinery	21.7	1.5	2.3	2.6	0.0	12.2	..	35.0	.1	1.2	1.2
Mineral Prod.,Prec. Stones & Metal	0.1	0.5	1.3	0.8	0.0	21.9	..	34.0	.3	14.2	14.2
Manufactured Articles nes.	2.8	0.2	3.2	0.8	0.0	1.8	..	12.3	2.9	47.6	47.6
Industrial Goods (line 5-14)	**4.0**	**1.8**	**3.3**	**5.6**	**0.1**	**10.6**	**10.9**	**34.0**	**11.9**	**73.9**	**73.9**
All Merch. Trade (line 2-14)	**38.7**	**2.0**	**4.9**	**4.2**	**2.6**	**13.0**	**1.4**	**31.4**	**19.4**	**244.2**	**244.2**

Notes: 1. Value of exports from reporter countries that do not participate in Free Trade Agreements with NICARAGUA

2. Weighted average tariff reduction measured by dT / (1 + T) in percent.

NIGER Extent of other countries' MFN tariff reductions on NIGER's exports

| Summary product category | *Average levels and changes weighted by value of exports to:* | | | | | | | | *Value of exports in $ million* | | |
| | *the World exc. FTA[1]* | | | | *LMIEs exc. FTA[1]* | | | | | | |
	% of exports affected	Post-UR applied rate	Tariff reduc-tion[2]	Post-UR bound rate	% of exports affected	Post-UR applied rate	Tariff reduc-tion[2]	Post-UR bound rate	To IDB LMIEs exc. FTA[1]	To all IDB Ctrys exc. FTA[1]	To all IDB Ctrys inc. FTA
Agriculture, exc. Fish: Estimate 1	0.4	0.1	68.0	0.3	..	..	..	..	.0	1.5	1.5
Agriculture, exc. Fish: Estimate 2	58.7	4.4	2.7	5.9	0.0	15.0	..	30.0	.2	1.9	1.9
Fish and Fish Products	15.7	10.2	5.0	10.2	..	..	..	..	.0	.5	.5
Petroleum Oils	..	..	..	..	..	..	..	..	.0	.0	.0
Wood, Pulp, Paper and Furniture	28.6	3.1	6.6	0.0	0.0	10.0	..	..	.1	.4	.4
Textiles and Clothing	36.9	12.7	4.0	15.8	0.9	15.2	13.3	20.2	1.0	1.6	1.6
Leather, Rubber, Footwear	80.3	3.6	0.8	2.5	21.1	12.5	0.8	3.0	.1	.9	.9
Metals	5.7	0.8	3.6	0.8	..	..	..	..	.0	3.6	3.6
Chemical & Photographic Suppl.	0.2	0.0	2.5	0.2	2.3	34.0	2.8	28.2	.0	285.2	285.2
Transport Equipment	34.6	8.1	3.2	8.1	..	..	..	..	.0	.2	.2
Non-Electric Machinery	98.9	3.7	3.0	3.7	..	..	..	..	.0	1.3	1.3
Electric Machinery	85.0	3.7	3.2	3.7	100.0	13.9	5.2	13.9	.0	.3	.3
Mineral Prod.,Prec. Stones & Metal	30.9	1.7	1.3	1.7	..	..	..	..	.0	1.5	1.5
Manufactured Articles nes.	15.3	0.4	3.2	0.4	0.0	..	..	..	.0	4.5	4.5
Industrial Goods (line 5-14)	**1.6**	**0.1**	**2.7**	**0.3**	**5.1**	**15.1**	**4.9**	**19.7**	**1.3**	**299.4**	**299.4**
All Merch. Trade (line 2-14)	**2.0**	**0.2**	**2.7**	**0.4**	**4.5**	**15.1**	**4.9**	**21.2**	**1.5**	**301.8**	**301.8**

Notes: 1. Value of exports from reporter countries that do not participate in Free Trade Agreements with NIGER

2. Weighted average tariff reduction measured by dT / (1 + T) in percent.

NIGERIA Extent of other countries' MFN tariff reductions on NIGERIA's exports

Summary product category	Average levels and changes weighted by value of exports to: the World exc. FTA[1]				LMIEs exc. FTA[1]				Value of exports in $ million		
	% of exports affected	Post-UR applied rate	Tariff reduc-tion[2]	Post-UR bound rate	% of exports affected	Post-UR applied rate	Tariff reduc-tion[2]	Post-UR bound rate	To IDB LMIEs exc. FTA[1]	To all IDB Ctrys exc. FTA[1]	To all IDB Ctrys inc. FTA
Agriculture, exc. Fish: Estimate 1	0.5	0.2	14.3	2.0	0.0	4.7	..	48.6	14.7	382.7	382.7
Agriculture, exc. Fish: Estimate 2	69.5	0.6	3.1	2.4	21.6	3.8	4.0	49.6	15.7	413.7	413.7
Fish and Fish Products	45.5	3.2	3.3	3.2	0.0	0.0	..	..	.0	15.9	15.9
Petroleum Oils	0.0	0.8	2.2	1.1	0.0	19.9	..	29.8	307.0	8,419.6	8,419.6
Wood, Pulp, Paper and Furniture	16.7	1.0	5.3	2.3	0.2	9.4	6.0	23.4	.6	5.8	5.8
Textiles and Clothing	13.7	9.1	2.9	9.2	85.3	35.9	13.2	37.3	.1	4.2	4.2
Leather, Rubber, Footwear	32.6	1.3	0.8	3.6	1.5	9.6	7.0	5.1	8.6	133.9	133.9
Metals	4.3	1.1	4.5	1.0	7.4	4.8	8.1	4.4	3.9	19.1	19.1
Chemical & Photographic Suppl.	88.1	6.1	5.1	5.5	12.1	17.8	15.5	37.8	.4	6.2	6.2
Transport Equipment	1.8	0.1	2.9	0.1	0.0	64.1	..	22.1	.0	58.1	58.1
Non-Electric Machinery	87.5	1.1	4.2	1.1	33.1	12.2	8.0	15.2	.1	3.7	3.7
Electric Machinery	85.7	4.6	2.0	4.9	0.0	9.9	..	9.9	.1	1.8	1.8
Mineral Prod.,Prec. Stones & Metal	35.0	2.5	4.6	2.9	24.4	4.5	11.2	7.9	7.4	74.0	74.0
Manufactured Articles nes.	2.8	0.2	4.6	2.0	12.8	9.1	14.7	153.9	.5	35.9	35.9
Industrial Goods (line 5-14)	**24.6**	**1.4**	**2.6**	**2.6**	**11.2**	**7.3**	**10.8**	**10.6**	**21.7**	**342.8**	**342.8**
All Merch. Trade (line 2-14)	**4.1**	**0.8**	**3.0**	**1.4**	**1.7**	**17.4**	**6.8**	**29.6**	**344.4**	**9,192.0**	**9,192.0**

Notes: 1. Value of exports from reporter countries that do not participate in Free Trade Agreements with NIGERIA

2. Weighted average tariff reduction measured by dT / (1 + T) in percent.

NORWAY Extent of other countries' MFN tariff reductions on NORWAY's exports

Summary product category	Average levels and changes weighted by value of exports to: the World exc. FTA[1]				LMIEs exc. FTA[1]				Value of exports in $ million		
	% of exports affected	Post-UR applied rate	Tariff reduc-tion[2]	Post-UR bound rate	% of exports affected	Post-UR applied rate	Tariff reduc-tion[2]	Post-UR bound rate	To IDB LMIEs exc. FTA[1]	To all IDB Ctrys exc. FTA[1]	To all IDB Ctrys inc. FTA
Agriculture, exc. Fish: Estimate 1	3.7	90.9	16.3	92.6	0.6	12.2	15.6	57.6	3.5	120.4	120.4
Agriculture, exc. Fish: Estimate 2	16.3	7.7	5.0	12.3	9.5	12.8	3.2	47.6	17.2	311.8	311.8
Fish and Fish Products	9.0	1.9	2.3	6.0	6.6	3.0	12.4	7.5	95.3	398.9	1,538.9
Petroleum Oils	0.0	0.2	0.8	0.3	0.0	9.5	6.0	0.0	38.2	1,108.6	5,939.3
Wood, Pulp, Paper and Furniture	3.8	0.6	6.7	1.1	14.5	14.1	16.0	22.3	67.8	187.8	1,554.0
Textiles and Clothing	5.2	6.3	3.7	8.3	22.7	19.3	4.2	23.4	3.1	14.7	185.8
Leather, Rubber, Footwear	4.1	3.5	2.5	5.2	7.7	17.0	7.1	38.5	2.4	19.6	112.5
Metals	5.8	1.5	3.2	3.6	16.4	16.1	9.8	10.6	132.3	874.9	4,465.0
Chemical & Photographic Suppl.	10.2	3.9	4.5	5.3	27.8	14.4	8.9	19.2	102.7	334.3	1,546.0
Transport Equipment	3.2	0.9	4.9	2.9	4.3	8.4	5.5	29.0	24.7	188.1	705.7
Non-Electric Machinery	12.9	2.0	4.7	2.3	56.2	12.8	8.0	17.1	71.9	259.3	1,113.2
Electric Machinery	7.7	10.7	4.0	5.6	16.9	19.4	6.8	26.1	41.8	117.0	533.8
Mineral Prod.,Prec. Stones & Metal	0.3	0.5	2.9	1.3	4.4	17.0	3.3	26.9	67.5	117.1	2,456.3
Manufactured Articles nes.	10.5	5.8	4.2	2.6	17.7	35.4	9.8	23.5	72.0	185.2	704.5
Industrial Goods (line 5-14)	**5.8**	**1.7**	**4.2**	**3.1**	**21.4**	**17.7**	**9.1**	**19.1**	**586.2**	**2,298.1**	**13,376.8**
All Merch. Trade (line 2-14)	**4.6**	**1.1**	**4.0**	**2.7**	**18.1**	**15.2**	**9.2**	**17.7**	**736.9**	**4,117.4**	**21,166.7**

Notes: 1. Value of exports from reporter countries that do not participate in Free Trade Agreements with NORWAY

2. Weighted average tariff reduction measured by dT / (1 + T) in percent.

OMAN Extent of other countries' MFN tariff reductions on OMAN's exports

Summary product category	Average levels and changes weighted by value of exports to: the World exc. FTA[1]				LMIEs exc. FTA[1]				Value of exports in $ million		
	% of exports affected	Post-UR applied rate	Tariff reduc-tion[2]	Post-UR bound rate	% of exports affected	Post-UR applied rate	Tariff reduc-tion[2]	Post-UR bound rate	To IDB LMIEs exc. FTA[1]	To all IDB Ctrys exc. FTA[1]	To all IDB Ctrys inc. FTA
Agriculture, exc. Fish: Estimate 1	2.8	4.4	21.7	69.8	0.0	0.0	..	98.8	.9	1.3	1.3
Agriculture, exc. Fish: Estimate 2	36.4	61.4	6.0	61.6	2.7	96.2	3.6	96.5	.9	1.6	1.6
Fish and Fish Products	17.4	1.9	10.0	5.7	96.1	4.8	41.5	5.0	.5	22.4	22.4
Petroleum Oils	0.0	5.3	..	0.1	0.0	7.8	..	15.0	799.6	2,836.6	2,836.6
Wood, Pulp, Paper and Furniture	13.4	2.8	4.9	6.8	0.0	15.8	..	40.0	.2	.9	.9
Textiles and Clothing	98.4	17.0	1.2	17.1	100.0	29.9	10.6	29.9	.0	6.7	6.7
Leather, Rubber, Footwear	84.7	4.3	1.9	4.3	100.0	5.0	4.7	5.0	.0	.2	.2
Metals	51.4	3.1	4.1	3.4	51.1	8.4	8.7	9.3	6.5	18.3	18.3
Chemical & Photographic Suppl.	11.4	0.8	4.7	2.4	0.0	48.9	..	30.0	.0	.9	.9
Transport Equipment	14.3	1.6	2.4	1.8	0.0	69.0	..	10.0	.0	6.4	6.4
Non-Electric Machinery	51.4	0.6	3.2	2.4	16.7	9.0	12.7	13.5	.0	6.0	6.0
Electric Machinery	96.2	3.1	2.3	3.1	..	..	..	..	.0	1.3	1.3
Mineral Prod.,Prec. Stones & Metal	82.7	7.3	1.0	2.4	0.0	40.0	..	..	3.6	27.0	27.0
Manufactured Articles nes.	79.3	2.4	1.9	2.4	0.0	80.0	..	..	.0	9.0	9.0
Industrial Goods (line 5-14)	**66.7**	**5.5**	**1.9**	**4.1**	**32.6**	**22.8**	**8.7**	**10.4**	**10.3**	**76.6**	**76.6**
All Merch. Trade (line 2-14)	**1.9**	**5.3**	**2.5**	**2.5**	**0.5**	**8.0**	**13.0**	**22.9**	**811.3**	**2,937.2**	**2,937.2**

Notes: 1. Value of exports from reporter countries that do not participate in Free Trade Agreements with OMAN

2. Weighted average tariff reduction measured by dT / (1 + T) in percent.

PAKISTAN Extent of other countries' MFN tariff reductions on PAKISTAN's exports

Summary product category	Average levels and changes weighted by value of exports to: the World exc. FTA[1]				LMIEs exc. FTA[1]				Value of exports in $ million		
	% of exports affected	Post-UR applied rate	Tariff reduc-tion[2]	Post-UR bound rate	% of exports affected	Post-UR applied rate	Tariff reduc-tion[2]	Post-UR bound rate	To IDB LMIEs exc. FTA[1]	To all IDB Ctrys exc. FTA[1]	To all IDB Ctrys inc. FTA
Agriculture, exc. Fish: Estimate 1	0.8	0.0	12.9	10.8	0.2	-1.1	1.4	28.5	260.7	711.5	711.5
Agriculture, exc. Fish: Estimate 2	12.2	12.1	3.7	17.6	6.5	31.1	3.1	46.3	63.3	251.9	251.9
Fish and Fish Products	50.6	2.9	3.7	13.1	3.1	0.2	41.5	48.6	21.1	100.3	100.3
Petroleum Oils	0.0	1.9	2.2	5.0	0.0	6.6	..	5.0	5.8	26.4	26.4
Wood, Pulp, Paper and Furniture	71.4	2.2	5.1	1.4	39.9	17.1	14.0	12.2	.3	3.5	3.5
Textiles and Clothing	67.7	8.4	2.8	9.6	69.5	23.6	8.8	16.7	184.8	2,204.5	2,204.5
Leather, Rubber, Footwear	75.7	5.5	1.9	5.7	71.9	14.8	8.0	13.0	26.4	459.6	459.6
Metals	40.1	3.4	5.6	5.6	35.0	6.6	9.7	21.6	4.1	24.2	24.2
Chemical & Photographic Suppl.	25.0	7.4	4.7	6.5	8.2	10.5	11.4	9.2	5.0	10.4	10.4
Transport Equipment	11.1	1.8	2.7	1.7	0.0	19.3	..	21.5	.1	5.7	5.7
Non-Electric Machinery	62.0	2.9	2.8	2.3	13.4	7.6	6.5	13.4	.8	3.0	3.0
Electric Machinery	50.6	9.9	3.3	18.1	5.8	14.0	6.0	33.8	1.3	2.6	2.6
Mineral Prod.,Prec. Stones & Metal	33.6	4.2	4.5	3.8	64.3	36.2	17.9	36.3	2.1	25.2	25.2
Manufactured Articles nes.	23.6	1.2	3.2	4.9	34.4	3.1	0.6	16.3	212.5	760.7	760.7
Industrial Goods (line 5-14)	**58.5**	**6.3**	**2.7**	**7.7**	**51.2**	**12.8**	**6.1**	**16.3**	**437.3**	**3,499.3**	**3,499.3**
All Merch. Trade (line 2-14)	**54.9**	**6.5**	**2.7**	**8.4**	**43.4**	**14.4**	**6.2**	**21.6**	**527.6**	**3,878.0**	**3,878.0**

Notes: 1. Value of exports from reporter countries that do not participate in Free Trade Agreements with PAKISTAN

2. Weighted average tariff reduction measured by dT / (1 + T) in percent.

PANAMA Extent of other countries' MFN tariff reductions on PANAMA's exports

Summary product category	Average levels and changes weighted by value of exports to: the World exc. FTA[1]				LMIEs exc. FTA[1]				Value of exports in $ million		
	% of exports affected	Post-UR applied rate	Tariff reduc-tion[2]	Post-UR bound rate	% of exports affected	Post-UR applied rate	Tariff reduc-tion[2]	Post-UR bound rate	To IDB LMIEs exc. FTA[1]	To all IDB Ctrys exc. FTA[1]	To all IDB Ctrys inc. FTA
Agriculture, exc. Fish: Estimate 1	0.6	0.5	22.4	3.4	22.3	19.8	22.4	33.8	10.8	399.5	399.5
Agriculture, exc. Fish: Estimate 2	12.6	4.3	7.1	7.2	11.4	17.8	4.0	49.7	18.2	424.2	424.2
Fish and Fish Products	32.4	2.4	1.9	5.3	10.6	18.9	41.5	20.4	.4	217.4	217.4
Petroleum Oils	0.0	12.1	..	28.7	0.0	16.1	..	38.7	7.6	10.3	10.3
Wood, Pulp, Paper and Furniture	22.5	2.7	5.0	19.4	3.2	3.8	8.3	29.5	6.1	9.2	9.2
Textiles and Clothing	76.3	23.2	2.4	26.7	58.0	29.0	3.6	35.3	62.8	114.4	114.4
Leather, Rubber, Footwear	41.8	18.0	2.7	24.9	42.6	24.8	3.4	34.7	18.4	26.3	26.3
Metals	11.0	5.0	6.8	12.6	17.1	11.3	9.1	28.9	7.4	17.1	17.1
Chemical & Photographic Suppl.	20.5	7.7	4.7	24.1	4.5	9.3	6.3	30.3	60.3	77.2	77.2
Transport Equipment	4.6	6.8	3.0	16.7	4.9	11.4	3.9	29.3	18.2	27.9	27.9
Non-Electric Machinery	8.0	10.9	2.1	31.2	1.0	11.7	0.7	33.6	27.8	30.1	30.1
Electric Machinery	4.8	17.9	2.0	33.9	3.8	18.2	1.9	34.4	95.4	96.9	96.9
Mineral Prod.,Prec. Stones & Metal	1.9	0.6	3.1	1.4	6.2	6.5	3.7	15.5	12.7	148.4	148.4
Manufactured Articles nes.	2.0	3.8	3.6	6.1	4.5	15.4	3.6	33.0	199.8	806.5	806.5
Industrial Goods (line 5-14)	**10.8**	**6.9**	**2.9**	**12.0**	**12.4**	**16.5**	**3.7**	**32.6**	**508.9**	**1,354.0**	**1,354.0**
All Merch. Trade (line 2-14)	**13.5**	**6.1**	**3.5**	**10.7**	**12.2**	**16.5**	**3.8**	**33.4**	**535.1**	**2,005.9**	**2,005.9**

Notes: 1. Value of exports from reporter countries that do not participate in Free Trade Agreements with PANAMA

2. Weighted average tariff reduction measured by dT / (1 + T) in percent.

PAPUA N. GUINEA Extent of other countries' MFN tariff reductions on PAPUA N. GUINEA's exports

Summary product category	Average levels and changes weighted by value of exports to: the World exc. FTA[1]				LMIEs exc. FTA[1]				Value of exports in $ million		
	% of exports affected	Post-UR applied rate	Tariff reduc-tion[2]	Post-UR bound rate	% of exports affected	Post-UR applied rate	Tariff reduc-tion[2]	Post-UR bound rate	To IDB LMIEs exc. FTA[1]	To all IDB Ctrys exc. FTA[1]	To all IDB Ctrys inc. FTA
Agriculture, exc. Fish: Estimate 1	1.1	4.5	10.0	5.0	6.4	3.2	1.3	8.7	17.5	312.2	312.2
Agriculture, exc. Fish: Estimate 2	61.4	1.5	3.8	2.1	26.4	10.0	5.0	17.6	19.0	317.6	317.6
Fish and Fish Products	30.2	11.5	2.1	2.1	0.0	19.7	..	..	18.4	32.9	32.9
Petroleum Oils	..	..	..	..	..	..	..	..	.0	.0	.0
Wood, Pulp, Paper and Furniture	1.1	0.8	5.1	1.5	1.7	2.1	4.7	3.5	59.7	159.3	159.3
Textiles and Clothing	16.4	36.3	2.9	38.3	2.3	5.8	13.3	40.0	.1	1.6	1.6
Leather, Rubber, Footwear	7.8	0.5	0.8	0.6	100.0	10.0	8.7	10.0	.0	3.5	3.5
Metals	0.0	0.8	5.9	0.1	0.0	4.3	..	1.0	139.8	750.0	750.0
Chemical & Photographic Suppl.	11.8	4.1	4.3	12.8	41.6	15.0	4.3	23.6	.2	.6	.6
Transport Equipment	4.7	6.9	6.9	8.1	0.3	10.1	6.9	10.1	.3	.6	.6
Non-Electric Machinery	9.4	1.9	5.7	5.1	23.0	12.0	8.8	31.2	.3	3.1	3.1
Electric Machinery	43.4	10.0	3.5	19.1	0.0	17.1	..	35.0	.4	.9	.9
Mineral Prod.,Prec. Stones & Metal	6.4	0.3	13.3	0.4	99.6	5.0	13.3	5.1	6.9	108.5	108.5
Manufactured Articles nes.	9.5	0.6	4.5	0.9	0.4	3.8	8.7	33.7	.2	7.4	7.4
Industrial Goods (line 5-14)	**1.0**	**0.8**	**10.2**	**0.5**	**3.9**	**3.7**	**12.1**	**2.4**	**208.0**	**1,035.4**	**1,035.4**
All Merch. Trade (line 2-14)	**15.6**	**1.2**	**4.1**	**0.9**	**5.3**	**5.4**	**9.4**	**4.0**	**245.4**	**1,385.9**	**1,385.9**

Notes: 1. Value of exports from reporter countries that do not participate in Free Trade Agreements with Papua N. Guinea

2. Weighted average tariff reduction measured by dT / (1 + T) in percent.

PARAGUAY Extent of other countries' MFN tariff reductions on PARAGUAY's exports

| Summary product category | Average levels and changes weighted by value of exports to: | | | | | | | | Value of exports in $ million | | |
| | the World exc. FTA[1] | | | | LMIEs exc. FTA[1] | | | | | | |
	% of exports affected	Post-UR applied rate	Tariff reduc-tion[2]	Post-UR bound rate	% of exports affected	Post-UR applied rate	Tariff reduc-tion[2]	Post-UR bound rate	To IDB LMIEs exc. FTA[1]	To all IDB Ctrys exc. FTA[1]	To all IDB Ctrys inc. FTA
Agriculture, exc. Fish: Estimate 1	0.5	1.4	10.0	15.8	0.0	-7.7	..	32.9	49.8	517.4	830.5
Agriculture, exc. Fish: Estimate 2	10.1	1.1	4.7	13.0	0.7	12.0	15.4	45.9	32.2	441.8	565.3
Fish and Fish Products	47.6	6.1	2.8	9.2	0.0	11.0	..	25.0	.1	.3	.3
Petroleum Oils	0.0	3.5	..	24.5	0.0	..	..	35.0	.0	.0	.0
Wood, Pulp, Paper and Furniture	21.9	0.5	3.5	13.3	0.2	0.0	4.6	19.9	.1	19.5	54.7
Textiles and Clothing	80.1	13.8	1.2	17.8	0.8	6.2	7.5	34.7	.0	18.3	22.5
Leather, Rubber, Footwear	61.4	5.1	1.5	7.2	30.9	10.6	8.7	23.2	3.0	31.8	33.0
Metals	47.4	2.3	5.1	12.4	0.0	12.5	..	35.0	.0	.2	.3
Chemical & Photographic Suppl.	1.8	2.8	7.4	15.9	0.8	9.8	12.1	20.8	1.3	5.3	16.5
Transport Equipment	14.2	8.9	3.2	12.9	0.0	13.2	..	31.6	.0	.1	.1
Non-Electric Machinery	28.6	8.6	3.9	23.2	0.0	14.4	..	33.3	.3	.5	.7
Electric Machinery	25.3	12.0	3.8	20.8	0.0	18.9	..	31.6	.1	.1	.2
Mineral Prod.,Prec. Stones & Metal	34.5	3.3	3.8	21.5	12.3	2.1	4.7	30.0	.0	.1	.3
Manufactured Articles nes.	0.7	0.8	13.2	36.9	0.0	0.9	4.7	45.8	32.2	100.6	347.5
Industrial Goods (line 5-14)	**11.3**	**1.7**	**2.5**	**30.5**	**0.5**	**1.0**	**8.6**	**41.7**	**37.0**	**176.6**	**475.7**
All Merch. Trade (line 2-14)	**10.6**	**1.4**	**3.6**	**21.0**	**0.5**	**2.3**	**11.4**	**43.0**	**69.3**	**618.7**	**1,041.3**

Notes: 1. Value of exports from reporter countries that do not participate in Free Trade Agreements with PARAGUAY

2. Weighted average tariff reduction measured by dT / (1 + T) in percent.

PERU Extent of other countries' MFN tariff reductions on PERU's exports

| Summary product category | Average levels and changes weighted by value of exports to: | | | | | | | | Value of exports in $ million | | |
| | the World exc. FTA[1] | | | | LMIEs exc. FTA[1] | | | | | | |
	% of exports affected	Post-UR applied rate	Tariff reduc-tion[2]	Post-UR bound rate	% of exports affected	Post-UR applied rate	Tariff reduc-tion[2]	Post-UR bound rate	To IDB LMIEs exc. FTA[1]	To all IDB Ctrys exc. FTA[1]	To all IDB Ctrys inc. FTA
Agriculture, exc. Fish: Estimate 1	3.1	9.5	33.7	22.2	10.0	0.8	32.4	51.5	57.1	229.8	229.8
Agriculture, exc. Fish: Estimate 2	20.2	4.2	3.6	12.8	12.7	7.8	2.8	36.7	135.4	449.2	449.2
Fish and Fish Products	20.6	6.6	4.3	9.9	1.5	17.9	0.6	32.7	14.2	65.0	65.0
Petroleum Oils	0.0	2.0	0.6	6.6	0.0	9.1	..	33.0	38.3	218.3	218.3
Wood, Pulp, Paper and Furniture	26.4	4.6	3.9	9.6	9.5	12.2	2.4	25.9	2.6	7.0	7.0
Textiles and Clothing	68.7	9.0	2.2	11.9	6.8	13.9	6.0	30.5	45.7	265.9	265.9
Leather, Rubber, Footwear	50.5	6.0	1.9	11.1	5.8	9.6	1.1	21.6	3.5	8.1	8.1
Metals	13.8	1.3	2.6	5.6	3.0	3.7	8.0	22.8	311.2	1,398.1	1,398.1
Chemical & Photographic Suppl.	18.2	4.4	4.0	13.3	2.6	7.9	12.2	26.7	23.6	49.9	49.9
Transport Equipment	15.7	9.8	0.7	22.0	0.5	11.2	0.7	25.7	12.2	14.6	14.6
Non-Electric Machinery	56.0	5.6	1.8	13.8	2.6	11.4	2.0	31.4	2.2	5.3	5.3
Electric Machinery	8.9	6.6	1.8	10.2	0.9	11.5	1.1	24.9	5.2	20.1	20.1
Mineral Prod.,Prec. Stones & Metal	48.6	3.2	1.6	10.5	0.6	2.1	3.6	34.9	58.0	261.2	261.2
Manufactured Articles nes.	8.3	2.9	3.5	14.6	0.2	5.1	2.5	27.2	34.1	64.5	64.5
Industrial Goods (line 5-14)	**25.3**	**2.8**	**2.3**	**7.7**	**2.8**	**5.1**	**7.3**	**25.6**	**498.1**	**2,094.7**	**2,094.7**
All Merch. Trade (line 2-14)	**22.4**	**3.0**	**2.5**	**8.5**	**4.6**	**6.2**	**4.8**	**28.3**	**686.0**	**2,827.1**	**2,827.1**

Notes: 1. Value of exports from reporter countries that do not participate in Free Trade Agreements with PERU

2. Weighted average tariff reduction measured by dT / (1 + T) in percent.

PHILIPPINES Extent of other countries' MFN tariff reductions on PHILIPPINES's exports

Summary product category	Average levels and changes weighted by value of exports to: the World exc. FTA[1]				LMIEs exc. FTA[1]				Value of exports in $ million		
	% of exports affected	Post-UR applied rate	Tariff reduc-tion[2]	Post-UR bound rate	% of exports affected	Post-UR applied rate	Tariff reduc-tion[2]	Post-UR bound rate	To IDB LMIEs exc. FTA[1]	To all IDB Ctrys exc. FTA[1]	To all IDB Ctrys inc. FTA
Agriculture, exc. Fish: Estimate 1	3.7	11.9	12.5	13.0	56.6	34.6	5.7	60.7	47.9	1,155.9	1,155.9
Agriculture, exc. Fish: Estimate 2	56.7	9.2	8.6	10.4	44.4	14.9	4.0	39.5	72.9	1,550.9	1,550.9
Fish and Fish Products	59.7	3.8	2.4	3.9	71.9	10.3	41.0	12.0	3.7	461.3	461.3
Petroleum Oils	0.2	12.4	5.4	4.9	0.9	3.2	5.4	5.2	15.7	57.7	57.7
Wood, Pulp, Paper and Furniture	66.4	2.0	5.0	2.1	61.9	13.0	8.1	12.1	4.0	639.1	639.1
Textiles and Clothing	89.3	14.1	2.0	14.5	69.3	19.8	8.9	18.8	17.6	1,404.5	1,404.5
Leather, Rubber, Footwear	56.8	10.9	3.3	11.3	58.8	6.8	9.9	9.4	5.5	181.1	181.1
Metals	27.4	1.7	3.8	2.8	61.0	7.3	8.7	12.5	122.0	917.5	917.5
Chemical & Photographic Suppl.	31.9	3.1	3.5	12.6	19.6	4.0	9.9	31.0	47.5	168.4	168.4
Transport Equipment	22.7	11.2	9.3	11.0	25.7	68.9	47.5	78.9	2.6	17.4	17.4
Non-Electric Machinery	64.6	7.9	10.7	9.1	95.1	18.7	15.4	19.7	159.4	383.3	383.3
Electric Machinery	25.6	1.3	3.7	2.2	55.8	1.5	3.5	0.8	109.8	1,326.7	1,326.7
Mineral Prod.,Prec. Stones & Metal	16.4	1.5	3.8	1.6	32.0	22.1	4.5	12.3	30.1	634.0	634.0
Manufactured Articles nes.	64.6	3.3	4.2	4.0	53.7	15.2	10.7	18.5	9.7	407.4	407.4
Industrial Goods (line 5-14)	**50.1**	**5.3**	**3.8**	**6.5**	**64.9**	**11.2**	**10.9**	**16.1**	**508.2**	**6,079.2**	**6,079.2**
All Merch. Trade (line 2-14)	**51.5**	**6.0**	**4.7**	**7.1**	**60.8**	**11.4**	**10.5**	**19.0**	**600.4**	**8,149.1**	**8,149.1**

Notes: 1. Value of exports from reporter countries that do not participate in Free Trade Agreements with PHILIPPINES

2. Weighted average tariff reduction measured by dT / (1 + T) in percent.

POLAND Extent of other countries' MFN tariff reductions on POLAND's exports

Summary product category	Average levels and changes weighted by value of exports to: the World exc. FTA[1]				LMIEs exc. FTA[1]				Value of exports in $ million		
	% of exports affected	Post-UR applied rate	Tariff reduc-tion[2]	Post-UR bound rate	% of exports affected	Post-UR applied rate	Tariff reduc-tion[2]	Post-UR bound rate	To IDB LMIEs exc. FTA[1]	To all IDB Ctrys exc. FTA[1]	To all IDB Ctrys inc. FTA
Agriculture, exc. Fish: Estimate 1	4.2	25.3	16.4	35.9	11.9	9.2	17.5	63.0	81.0	442.0	442.0
Agriculture, exc. Fish: Estimate 2	46.3	8.8	2.7	17.8	29.5	22.4	2.1	72.0	109.5	973.4	973.4
Fish and Fish Products	40.9	7.0	4.7	7.0	94.1	5.2	41.5	5.0	.0	157.0	157.0
Petroleum Oils	4.3	1.4	1.0	2.0	0.6	4.3	1.1	16.4	.8	60.3	60.3
Wood, Pulp, Paper and Furniture	50.8	1.6	4.8	1.7	31.7	11.2	3.6	12.6	33.0	461.5	461.5
Textiles and Clothing	90.9	12.2	3.1	11.6	61.9	22.5	7.1	13.2	28.0	334.8	334.8
Leather, Rubber, Footwear	56.2	7.0	2.8	7.0	77.2	9.6	2.2	9.6	27.4	188.8	188.8
Metals	43.3	1.7	3.1	2.0	38.7	5.3	1.2	6.4	264.6	1,078.8	1,078.8
Chemical & Photographic Suppl.	43.9	5.2	3.9	6.6	32.6	8.7	4.9	11.2	140.1	382.6	382.6
Transport Equipment	33.2	6.7	2.5	7.3	71.2	9.1	1.1	10.9	55.8	326.9	326.9
Non-Electric Machinery	82.9	6.7	1.8	6.1	80.1	8.8	1.5	8.0	302.9	461.5	461.5
Electric Machinery	90.1	5.6	2.5	5.7	85.5	8.7	2.6	8.8	99.5	244.6	244.6
Mineral Prod.,Prec. Stones & Metal	36.8	1.5	1.2	3.8	5.7	3.0	2.2	11.1	403.3	1,419.7	1,419.7
Manufactured Articles nes.	43.8	2.7	2.6	4.6	77.9	6.3	1.6	11.1	68.6	365.6	365.6
Industrial Goods (line 5-14)	**50.8**	**3.8**	**2.6**	**4.6**	**45.0**	**6.7**	**2.1**	**9.5**	**1,423.4**	**5,264.7**	**5,264.7**
All Merch. Trade (line 2-14)	**49.4**	**4.4**	**2.7**	**6.1**	**43.9**	**7.8**	**2.1**	**14.2**	**1,533.7**	**6,455.3**	**6,455.3**

Notes: 1. Value of exports from reporter countries that do not participate in Free Trade Agreements with POLAND

2. Weighted average tariff reduction measured by dT / (1 + T) in percent.

PUERTO RICO Extent of other countries' MFN tariff reductions on PUERTO RICO's exports

| Summary product category | Average levels and changes weighted by value of exports to: | | | | | | | | Value of exports in $ million | | |
| | the World exc. FTA[1] | | | | LMIEs exc. FTA[1] | | | | | | |
	% of exports affected	Post-UR applied rate	Tariff reduc-tion[2]	Post-UR bound rate	% of exports affected	Post-UR applied rate	Tariff reduc-tion[2]	Post-UR bound rate	To IDB LMIEs exc. FTA[1]	To all IDB Ctrys exc. FTA[1]	To all IDB Ctrys inc. FTA
Agriculture, exc. Fish: Estimate 1	19.3	33.3	11.1	35.9	0.0	0.0	..	0.2	.5	1.5	1.5
Agriculture, exc. Fish: Estimate 2	81.5	5.6	2.3	7.0	22.5	16.5	28.5	50.0	4.0	100.9	100.9
Fish and Fish Products	0.0	0.0	..	0.0	..	..	..	..	.0	.0	.0
Petroleum Oils	0.0	10.8	..	36.2	0.0	10.8	..	36.2	76.8	76.8	76.8
Wood, Pulp, Paper and Furniture	4.7	5.4	6.8	33.8	0.1	5.7	3.6	35.7	9.0	9.6	9.6
Textiles and Clothing	64.5	17.4	4.6	21.6	23.2	22.5	3.4	32.5	.7	1.6	1.6
Leather, Rubber, Footwear	95.9	7.7	2.2	8.3	3.0	18.0	3.4	39.4	.3	10.6	10.6
Metals	17.3	4.2	6.8	17.9	8.7	7.3	7.9	34.3	6.3	12.5	12.5
Chemical & Photographic Suppl.	70.7	3.8	4.1	7.7	2.6	9.9	9.5	26.5	95.0	418.3	418.3
Transport Equipment	54.1	14.3	3.0	19.0	2.4	25.5	1.8	36.5	.0	.1	.1
Non-Electric Machinery	71.2	2.7	3.4	4.1	1.7	8.4	4.6	30.0	3.3	59.6	59.6
Electric Machinery	66.8	6.3	4.4	9.3	2.4	14.7	4.6	31.3	2.4	16.9	16.9
Mineral Prod.,Prec. Stones & Metal	21.8	5.0	3.0	21.4	11.7	9.5	3.7	46.5	1.5	3.5	3.5
Manufactured Articles nes.	14.7	0.8	4.4	2.2	16.4	10.6	3.1	30.4	2.9	43.4	43.4
Industrial Goods (line 5-14)	**64.3**	**3.7**	**4.0**	**7.7**	**3.3**	**9.6**	**7.9**	**28.2**	**121.4**	**576.0**	**576.0**
All Merch. Trade (line 2-14)	**60.1**	**4.7**	**3.7**	**10.5**	**2.4**	**10.2**	**11.7**	**31.7**	**202.3**	**753.7**	**753.7**

Notes: 1. Value of exports from reporter countries that do not participate in Free Trade Agreements with PUERTO RICO

2. Weighted average tariff reduction measured by dT / (1 + T) in percent.

QATAR Extent of other countries' MFN tariff reductions on QATAR's exports

| Summary product category | Average levels and changes weighted by value of exports to: | | | | | | | | Value of exports in $ million | | |
| | the World exc. FTA[1] | | | | LMIEs exc. FTA[1] | | | | | | |
	% of exports affected	Post-UR applied rate	Tariff reduc-tion[2]	Post-UR bound rate	% of exports affected	Post-UR applied rate	Tariff reduc-tion[2]	Post-UR bound rate	To IDB LMIEs exc. FTA[1]	To all IDB Ctrys exc. FTA[1]	To all IDB Ctrys inc. FTA
Agriculture, exc. Fish: Estimate 1	0.0	14.7	..	14.7	..	..	..	..	.0	.2	.2
Agriculture, exc. Fish: Estimate 2	52.1	4.1	4.7	4.1	100.0	11.7	2.9	11.7	.0	.4	.4
Fish and Fish Products	100.0	12.0	5.2	12.0	..	..	..	..	.0	.1	.1
Petroleum Oils	0.0	6.5	..	0.0	0.0	13.5	..	..	319.4	1,570.5	1,570.5
Wood, Pulp, Paper and Furniture	69.8	0.7	4.5	0.2	10.0	13.5	18.2	8.0	.0	.2	.2
Textiles and Clothing	96.2	15.5	1.3	15.7	100.0	8.0	10.5	8.0	.0	5.0	5.0
Leather, Rubber, Footwear	63.5	4.9	1.2	4.9	..	..	..	..	.0	.2	.2
Metals	80.4	3.5	3.5	7.2	0.0	5.0	..	40.0	.2	2.0	2.0
Chemical & Photographic Suppl.	32.1	14.6	11.6	12.0	25.4	18.7	15.0	16.6	94.5	121.3	121.3
Transport Equipment	56.6	5.7	2.1	5.7	..	..	..	..	.0	.4	.4
Non-Electric Machinery	97.3	1.8	2.7	2.5	10.0	4.5	18.2	36.0	.0	.4	.4
Electric Machinery	93.4	2.3	4.7	2.1	0.0	41.7	..	..	.0	.6	.6
Mineral Prod.,Prec. Stones & Metal	55.5	3.2	4.3	1.4	0.0	14.0	..	8.7	35.8	153.9	153.9
Manufactured Articles nes.	43.9	11.6	12.3	12.3	99.9	35.9	16.2	35.9	1.2	3.7	3.7
Industrial Goods (line 5-14)	**46.5**	**7.9**	**6.4**	**5.0**	**19.1**	**17.4**	**15.1**	**14.2**	**131.7**	**287.6**	**287.6**
All Merch. Trade (line 2-14)	**7.2**	**7.1**	**6.4**	**3.5**	**5.6**	**15.1**	**15.1**	**14.2**	**451.1**	**1,858.5**	**1,858.5**

Notes: 1. Value of exports from reporter countries that do not participate in Free Trade Agreements with QATAR

2. Weighted average tariff reduction measured by dT / (1 + T) in percent.

ROMANIA Extent of other countries' MFN tariff reductions on ROMANIA's exports

Summary product category	Average levels and changes weighted by value of exports to: the World exc. FTA[1]				LMIEs exc. FTA[1]				Value of exports in $ million		
	% of exports affected	Post-UR applied rate	Tariff reduc-tion[2]	Post-UR bound rate	% of exports affected	Post-UR applied rate	Tariff reduc-tion[2]	Post-UR bound rate	To IDB LMIEs exc. FTA[1]	To all IDB Ctrys exc. FTA[1]	To all IDB Ctrys inc. FTA
Agriculture, exc. Fish: Estimate 1	3.0	36.1	15.3	47.2	0.5	3.7	2.6	60.8	13.6	115.8	115.8
Agriculture, exc. Fish: Estimate 2	34.9	8.4	4.1	21.6	14.0	13.8	2.6	74.8	21.0	177.3	177.3
Fish and Fish Products	14.1	10.8	1.7	11.0	0.0	24.9	..	25.0	.6	2.7	2.7
Petroleum Oils	6.7	3.0	1.3	3.4	24.0	9.6	1.1	4.7	26.5	960.3	960.3
Wood, Pulp, Paper and Furniture	88.0	1.8	5.4	1.9	47.6	13.6	5.8	13.7	32.5	442.4	442.4
Textiles and Clothing	94.4	12.9	3.3	12.6	80.4	23.4	13.5	20.1	33.9	398.3	398.3
Leather, Rubber, Footwear	41.4	7.1	2.6	7.2	41.3	11.1	4.2	9.8	3.0	117.4	117.4
Metals	48.1	6.1	4.2	3.1	8.6	19.1	7.0	18.0	208.2	712.1	712.1
Chemical & Photographic Suppl.	53.5	7.9	4.4	8.6	30.0	17.3	7.0	18.9	78.6	225.8	225.8
Transport Equipment	59.3	8.8	3.3	8.9	66.2	12.9	2.6	14.2	55.1	129.2	129.2
Non-Electric Machinery	72.1	6.1	2.3	8.0	57.0	8.7	2.7	11.7	85.1	161.3	161.3
Electric Machinery	80.8	6.5	3.6	4.8	36.1	16.1	1.8	11.4	18.2	64.9	64.9
Mineral Prod.,Prec. Stones & Metal	47.7	11.8	2.1	9.9	12.3	17.5	1.8	20.3	154.4	302.7	302.7
Manufactured Articles nes.	92.5	3.9	3.5	3.9	94.7	8.1	4.8	8.0	8.7	48.0	48.0
Industrial Goods (line 5-14)	**65.8**	**7.4**	**3.9**	**6.4**	**30.1**	**16.5**	**5.2**	**16.1**	**677.7**	**2,602.1**	**2,602.1**
All Merch. Trade (line 2-14)	**49.1**	**6.3**	**3.8**	**6.0**	**29.4**	**16.1**	**5.1**	**18.6**	**725.7**	**3,742.3**	**3,742.3**

Notes: 1. Value of exports from reporter countries that do not participate in Free Trade Agreements with ROMANIA

2. Weighted average tariff reduction measured by dT / (1 + T) in percent.

RWANDA Extent of other countries' MFN tariff reductions on RWANDA's exports

Summary product category	Average levels and changes weighted by value of exports to: the World exc. FTA[1]				LMIEs exc. FTA[1]				Value of exports in $ million		
	% of exports affected	Post-UR applied rate	Tariff reduc-tion[2]	Post-UR bound rate	% of exports affected	Post-UR applied rate	Tariff reduc-tion[2]	Post-UR bound rate	To IDB LMIEs exc. FTA[1]	To all IDB Ctrys exc. FTA[1]	To all IDB Ctrys inc. FTA
Agriculture, exc. Fish: Estimate 1	0.0	0.0	5.9	0.0	..	..	..	..	.0	121.8	121.8
Agriculture, exc. Fish: Estimate 2	86.1	0.2	4.8	0.2	..	..	..	..	.0	125.5	125.5
Fish and Fish Products	..	..	..	..	..	..	..	..	.0	.0	.0
Petroleum Oils	..	..	..	..	..	..	..	..	.0	.0	.0
Wood, Pulp, Paper and Furniture	15.6	0.1	7.1	0.1	100.0	13.0	6.0	13.0	.0	.3	.3
Textiles and Clothing	39.3	4.2	3.8	4.2	..	..	..	..	.0	.1	.1
Leather, Rubber, Footwear	100.0	18.1	1.8	18.1	..	..	..	..	.0	.1	.1
Metals	5.2	0.2	2.4	0.2	..	..	..	..	.0	.2	.2
Chemical & Photographic Suppl.	19.4	2.7	4.1	4.7	..	..	..	..	.0	.3	.3
Transport Equipment	100.0	2.8	1.5	2.8	..	..	..	..	.0	.0	.0
Non-Electric Machinery	89.7	2.3	2.1	2.3	..	..	..	..	.0	.1	.1
Electric Machinery	70.2	2.4	3.4	3.8	..	..	..	..	.0	.1	.1
Mineral Prod.,Prec. Stones & Metal	28.3	1.5	1.9	1.5	..	..	..	..	.0	.4	.4
Manufactured Articles nes.	1.2	0.1	3.1	0.1	22.2	16.0	11.4	16.0	.0	6.2	6.2
Industrial Goods (line 5-14)	**7.9**	**0.6**	**3.0**	**0.7**	**30.0**	**15.0**	**9.6**	**15.0**	**.0**	**7.9**	**'7.9**
All Merch. Trade (line 2-14)	**81.5**	**0.3**	**4.8**	**0.3**	**30.0**	**15.0**	**9.6**	**15.0**	**.0**	**133.4**	**133.4**

Notes: 1. Value of exports from reporter countries that do not participate in Free Trade Agreements with RWANDA

2. Weighted average tariff reduction measured by dT / (1 + T) in percent.

SAUDI ARABIA Extent of other countries' MFN tariff reductions on SAUDI ARABIA's exports

Summary product category	Average levels and changes weighted by value of exports to: the World exc. FTA[1]				LMIEs exc. FTA[1]				Value of exports in $ million		
	% of exports affected	Post-UR applied rate	Tariff reduc-tion[2]	Post-UR bound rate	% of exports affected	Post-UR applied rate	Tariff reduc-tion[2]	Post-UR bound rate	To IDB LMIEs exc. FTA[1]	To all IDB Ctrys exc. FTA[1]	To all IDB Ctrys inc. FTA
Agriculture, exc. Fish: Estimate 1	18.2	30.7	97.3	78.7	28.5	9.0	105.5	91.2	81.0	138.9	138.9
Agriculture, exc. Fish: Estimate 2	36.5	5.4	1.7	47.0	15.1	7.8	4.5	83.5	86.8	206.9	206.9
Fish and Fish Products	70.9	12.4	5.3	14.3	0.0	5.0	..	50.0	.2	4.6	4.6
Petroleum Oils	0.6	1.5	1.3	2.9	0.1	7.4	4.7	31.5	2,825.4	22,534.4	22,534.4
Wood, Pulp, Paper and Furniture	6.9	5.5	7.4	28.9	0.9	6.9	12.0	36.7	7.4	9.4	9.4
Textiles and Clothing	42.3	7.4	4.7	6.4	70.2	22.5	10.4	17.1	1.4	7.0	7.0
Leather, Rubber, Footwear	56.6	36.6	3.4	4.5	39.7	57.4	6.8	8.1	6.7	10.6	10.6
Metals	30.9	3.9	5.5	1.6	59.4	13.3	8.2	5.4	44.1	160.9	160.9
Chemical & Photographic Suppl.	66.2	6.5	5.6	8.1	43.8	11.4	9.8	16.3	614.5	1,757.8	1,757.8
Transport Equipment	4.8	0.4	0.8	0.2	0.1	0.3	6.5	0.1	157.6	204.5	204.5
Non-Electric Machinery	54.5	1.8	3.8	1.7	18.5	8.5	8.7	8.2	6.3	43.7	43.7
Electric Machinery	77.6	3.4	2.6	3.3	31.6	12.0	7.2	10.5	.5	7.7	7.7
Mineral Prod.,Prec. Stones & Metal	68.3	1.2	4.3	1.4	0.6	6.6	5.7	9.7	280.8	1,435.5	1,435.5
Manufactured Articles nes.	41.8	11.3	12.7	11.7	92.8	32.6	15.6	33.6	18.2	52.7	52.7
Industrial Goods (line 5-14)	**61.4**	**4.1**	**5.0**	**4.6**	**28.0**	**9.4**	**9.9**	**11.8**	**1,137.4**	**3,689.8**	**3,689.8**
All Merch. Trade (line 2-14)	**9.4**	**2.0**	**4.7**	**4.2**	**8.3**	**8.2**	**9.7**	**23.0**	**4,049.7**	**26,435.8**	**26,435.8**

Notes: 1. Value of exports from reporter countries that do not participate in Free Trade Agreements with SAUDI ARABIA

2. Weighted average tariff reduction measured by dT / (1 + T) in percent.

SENEGAL Extent of other countries' MFN tariff reductions on SENEGAL's exports

Summary product category	Average levels and changes weighted by value of exports to: the World exc. FTA[1]				LMIEs exc. FTA[1]				Value of exports in $ million		
	% of exports affected	Post-UR applied rate	Tariff reduc-tion[2]	Post-UR bound rate	% of exports affected	Post-UR applied rate	Tariff reduc-tion[2]	Post-UR bound rate	To IDB LMIEs exc. FTA[1]	To all IDB Ctrys exc. FTA[1]	To all IDB Ctrys inc. FTA
Agriculture, exc. Fish: Estimate 1	0.0	0.0	15.6	0.9	0.0	-1.4	15.6	18.1	7.0	153.8	153.8
Agriculture, exc. Fish: Estimate 2	56.3	3.8	3.2	4.3	0.2	0.0	7.4	40.5	1.9	158.1	158.1
Fish and Fish Products	52.1	12.9	4.0	15.1	..	..	..	..	.0	216.1	216.1
Petroleum Oils	..	..	..	..	..	..	..	..	.0	.0	.0
Wood, Pulp, Paper and Furniture	40.2	0.1	5.6	0.1	..	..	..	..	.0	.9	.9
Textiles and Clothing	95.3	6.1	1.8	6.1	0.0	40.0	..	40.0	.0	2.8	2.8
Leather, Rubber, Footwear	51.8	5.9	1.5	6.0	..	..	..	..	.0	.8	.8
Metals	4.3	0.1	3.1	0.1	100.0	3.0	6.6	3.0	.0	4.2	4.2
Chemical & Photographic Suppl.	99.0	38.8	19.0	39.0	99.4	39.8	19.4	40.0	9.0	9.3	9.3
Transport Equipment	15.2	7.6	2.6	7.6	100.0	9.5	0.5	9.5	.0	1.9	1.9
Non-Electric Machinery	53.0	1.4	2.3	1.7	22.2	15.1	3.6	31.7	.0	2.1	2.1
Electric Machinery	49.5	2.6	3.2	2.7	0.0	13.1	..	35.0	.0	1.5	1.5
Mineral Prod.,Prec. Stones & Metal	10.5	1.9	0.1	2.6	0.0	5.6	..	8.8	22.6	104.3	104.3
Manufactured Articles nes.	1.7	4.9	2.4	17.7	0.4	13.7	0.5	51.1	72.4	82.3	82.3
Industrial Goods (line 5-14)	**13.0**	**4.7**	**7.1**	**6.6**	**9.0**	**15.1**	**18.6**	**22.7**	**104.1**	**210.1**	**210.1**
All Merch. Trade (line 2-14)	**39.2**	**7.9**	**4.1**	**9.5**	**8.8**	**14.4**	**18.6**	**23.6**	**106.0**	**584.3**	**584.3**

Notes: 1. Value of exports from reporter countries that do not participate in Free Trade Agreements with SENEGAL

2. Weighted average tariff reduction measured by dT / (1 + T) in percent.

SEYCHELLES Extent of other countries' MFN tariff reductions on SEYCHELLES's exports

| Summary product category | Average levels and changes weighted by value of exports to: | | | | | | | | Value of exports in $ million | | |
| | the World exc. FTA[1] | | | | LMIEs exc. FTA[1] | | | | | | |
	% of exports affected	Post-UR applied rate	Tariff reduc-tion[2]	Post-UR bound rate	% of exports affected	Post-UR applied rate	Tariff reduc-tion[2]	Post-UR bound rate	To IDB LMIEs exc. FTA[1]	To all IDB Ctrys exc. FTA[1]	To all IDB Ctrys inc. FTA
Agriculture, exc. Fish: Estimate 1	40.0	4.0	14.3	4.0	..	..	..	..	.0	.0	.0
Agriculture, exc. Fish: Estimate 2	20.4	4.6	7.7	11.4	0.0	7.3	..	27.4	.4	.7	.7
Fish and Fish Products	17.8	4.9	40.3	18.4	100.0	5.0	41.5	5.0	24.8	144.4	144.4
Petroleum Oils	0.0	..	..	..	..	..	..	..	.0	.0	.0
Wood, Pulp, Paper and Furniture	27.2	8.2	6.4	3.1	0.0	14.7	..	..	.1	.2	.2
Textiles and Clothing	77.9	4.1	4.2	5.8	..	..	..	..	.0	.1	.1
Leather, Rubber, Footwear	38.0	4.4	0.7	4.4	..	..	..	..	.0	.1	.1
Metals	63.3	2.0	2.3	2.4	..	..	..	..	.0	.2	.2
Chemical & Photographic Suppl.	42.4	2.7	3.1	5.5	..	..	..	..	.0	.2	.2
Transport Equipment	18.5	2.3	1.0	1.3	0.0	78.0	..	..	.0	.1	.1
Non-Electric Machinery	83.7	1.1	2.9	1.2	..	..	..	..	.0	1.6	1.6
Electric Machinery	75.7	2.8	2.9	2.9	..	..	..	..	.0	.7	.7
Mineral Prod.,Prec. Stones & Metal	55.9	2.2	1.2	2.2	..	..	..	..	.0	.0	.0
Manufactured Articles nes.	97.3	2.7	4.2	2.7	..	..	..	..	.0	1.0	1.0
Industrial Goods (line 5-14)	**78.4**	**2.3**	**3.3**	**2.4**	**0.0**	**15.4**	**..**	**..**	**.1**	**4.2**	**4.2**
All Merch. Trade (line 2-14)	**19.5**	**4.8**	**35.9**	**17.9**	**98.1**	**5.1**	**41.5**	**5.2**	**25.3**	**149.3**	**149.3**

Notes: 1. Value of exports from reporter countries that do not participate in Free Trade Agreements with SEYCHELLES

2. Weighted average tariff reduction measured by dT / (1 + T) in percent.

SIERRA LEONE Extent of other countries' MFN tariff reductions on SIERRA LEONE's exports

| Summary product category | Average levels and changes weighted by value of exports to: | | | | | | | | Value of exports in $ million | | |
| | the World exc. FTA[1] | | | | LMIEs exc. FTA[1] | | | | | | |
	% of exports affected	Post-UR applied rate	Tariff reduc-tion[2]	Post-UR bound rate	% of exports affected	Post-UR applied rate	Tariff reduc-tion[2]	Post-UR bound rate	To IDB LMIEs exc. FTA[1]	To all IDB Ctrys exc. FTA[1]	To all IDB Ctrys inc. FTA
Agriculture, exc. Fish: Estimate 1	0.0	0.0	..	0.1	..	..	..	..	.0	26.5	26.5
Agriculture, exc. Fish: Estimate 2	77.5	0.1	3.9	0.3	32.5	41.2	3.8	73.3	.0	27.3	27.3
Fish and Fish Products	91.1	10.9	4.9	10.9	0.0	15.0	..	30.0	.0	13.5	13.5
Petroleum Oils	..	..	..	..	..	..	..	..	.0	.0	.0
Wood, Pulp, Paper and Furniture	12.8	0.0	3.9	0.0	0.0	0.0	..	0.0	.0	.4	.4
Textiles and Clothing	97.2	12.5	3.6	12.5	..	..	..	..	.0	.4	.4
Leather, Rubber, Footwear	11.1	0.4	4.1	0.4	0.0	0.0	..	0.0	.0	.0	.0
Metals	0.0	0.7	3.7	2.5	0.0	0.9	..	35.1	5.1	97.5	97.5
Chemical & Photographic Suppl.	13.8	1.4	8.9	1.3	0.0	4.1	..	3.9	.0	.1	.1
Transport Equipment	92.2	2.5	1.9	2.5	..	..	..	..	.0	.1	.1
Non-Electric Machinery	15.0	0.1	4.4	0.1	..	..	..	..	.0	.2	.2
Electric Machinery	99.4	9.3	1.7	9.3	..	..	..	..	.0	.3	.3
Mineral Prod.,Prec. Stones & Metal	0.1	0.0	3.1	0.0	0.0	0.0	..	..	.6	67.2	67.2
Manufactured Articles nes.	31.2	1.3	1.9	1.6	76.7	8.2	3.3	12.3	.0	.4	.4
Industrial Goods (line 5-14)	**0.7**	**0.4**	**2.8**	**1.5**	**0.4**	**0.8**	**3.3**	**34.8**	**5.7**	**166.7**	**166.7**
All Merch. Trade (line 2-14)	**16.7**	**1.1**	**4.2**	**2.0**	**0.6**	**1.1**	**3.4**	**35.1**	**5.8**	**207.5**	**207.5**

Notes: 1. Value of exports from reporter countries that do not participate in Free Trade Agreements with SIERRA LEONE

2. Weighted average tariff reduction measured by dT / (1 + T) in percent.

SINGAPORE Extent of other countries' MFN tariff reductions on SINGAPORE's exports

Summary product category	Average levels and changes weighted by value of exports to: the World exc. FTA[1]				LMIEs exc. FTA[1]				Value of exports in $ million		
	% of exports affected	Post-UR applied rate	Tariff reduc-tion[2]	Post-UR bound rate	% of exports affected	Post-UR applied rate	Tariff reduc-tion[2]	Post-UR bound rate	To IDB LMIEs exc. FTA[1]	To all IDB Ctrys exc. FTA[1]	To all IDB Ctrys inc. FTA
Agriculture, exc. Fish: Estimate 1	26.6	19.1	5.3	27.2	58.0	38.6	5.3	56.0	58.6	129.0	129.0
Agriculture, exc. Fish: Estimate 2	23.7	6.4	4.5	11.3	22.5	16.7	5.4	35.1	152.5	618.0	618.0
Fish and Fish Products	31.9	2.7	22.6	2.7	87.6	7.3	37.8	6.9	52.9	253.9	253.9
Petroleum Oils	0.4	2.6	2.6	19.6	0.4	10.4	5.8	36.8	1,624.5	4,222.5	4,222.5
Wood, Pulp, Paper and Furniture	37.4	3.7	5.6	5.9	21.9	11.0	9.7	23.0	187.2	768.6	768.6
Textiles and Clothing	92.9	18.9	2.1	19.2	64.7	25.3	8.6	22.6	89.1	1,064.9	1,064.9
Leather, Rubber, Footwear	18.6	7.6	3.9	19.9	6.0	11.3	10.1	32.7	168.0	293.3	293.3
Metals	32.7	8.3	4.9	10.8	16.0	15.1	9.4	23.0	387.4	762.8	762.8
Chemical & Photographic Suppl.	31.9	8.4	6.8	15.5	21.7	13.9	12.6	26.6	905.0	1,759.9	1,759.9
Transport Equipment	14.9	2.7	3.4	4.9	8.4	10.1	10.0	25.6	70.9	356.5	356.5
Non-Electric Machinery	53.1	2.7	5.1	3.4	58.2	15.6	13.5	20.5	999.8	6,898.7	6,898.7
Electric Machinery	45.0	5.2	4.8	5.3	42.2	14.7	10.6	14.9	1,336.0	6,483.1	6,483.1
Mineral Prod.,Prec. Stones & Metal	34.2	3.2	3.9	7.8	5.2	6.1	19.2	15.7	335.3	668.1	668.1
Manufactured Articles nes.	50.7	4.2	5.8	4.2	45.5	18.4	15.4	17.7	271.2	1,604.5	1,604.5
Industrial Goods (line 5-14)	**47.5**	**5.2**	**4.8**	**6.5**	**34.9**	**14.3**	**12.2**	**20.4**	**4,749.9**	**20,660.4**	**20,660.4**
All Merch. Trade (line 2-14)	**39.1**	**5.0**	**5.0**	**7.1**	**26.5**	**13.9**	**12.7**	**22.3**	**6,579.9**	**25,754.8**	**25,754.8**

Notes: 1. Value of exports from reporter countries that do not participate in Free Trade Agreements with SINGAPORE

2. Weighted average tariff reduction measured by dT / (1 + T) in percent.

SOMALIA Extent of other countries' MFN tariff reductions on SOMALIA's exports

Summary product category	Average levels and changes weighted by value of exports to: the World exc. FTA[1]				LMIEs exc. FTA[1]				Value of exports in $ million		
	% of exports affected	Post-UR applied rate	Tariff reduc-tion[2]	Post-UR bound rate	% of exports affected	Post-UR applied rate	Tariff reduc-tion[2]	Post-UR bound rate	To IDB LMIEs exc. FTA[1]	To all IDB Ctrys exc. FTA[1]	To all IDB Ctrys inc. FTA
Agriculture, exc. Fish: Estimate 1	0.0	0.0	..	0.1	0.0	0.0	..	43.7	.1	29.4	29.4
Agriculture, exc. Fish: Estimate 2	1.5	1.7	4.3	2.0	45.7	21.3	10.8	37.8	.1	34.7	34.7
Fish and Fish Products	65.4	8.3	7.1	8.7	0.0	5.0		..	.0	9.6	9.6
Petroleum Oils	..	..	..	..	..	..	..	..	.0	.0	.0
Wood, Pulp, Paper and Furniture	8.4	0.0	5.5	0.0	..	..	..	..	.0	.2	.2
Textiles and Clothing	100.0	11.9	2.1	11.9	..	..	..	..	.0	.0	.0
Leather, Rubber, Footwear	20.6	0.4	0.7	0.4	..	..	..	..	.0	1.5	1.5
Metals	100.0	0.1	4.2	0.1	..	..	..	..	.0	.0	.0
Chemical & Photographic Suppl.	97.3	4.7	3.1	4.7	100.0	5.5	2.1	5.5	.0	.0	.0
Transport Equipment	0.7	18.6	2.2	18.6	..	..	..	..	.0	.4	.4
Non-Electric Machinery	87.5	0.8	2.8	0.9	83.3	8.2	5.3	9.5	.0	.6	.6
Electric Machinery	12.9	5.8	3.6	9.8	6.7	15.9	0.6	32.8	.0	.1	.1
Mineral Prod.,Prec. Stones & Metal	52.5	2.7	0.7	2.7	..	..	..	..	.0	.1	.1
Manufactured Articles nes.	6.6	0.5	4.6	0.5	98.1	35.5	16.2	36.0	.1	6.0	6.0
Industrial Goods (line 5-14)	**15.8**	**1.4**	**2.8**	**1.5**	**82.6**	**21.1**	**10.5**	**23.9**	**.1**	**8.9**	**8.9**
All Merch. Trade (line 2-14)	**15.5**	**4.5**	**6.2**	**4.7**	**64.4**	**20.5**	**10.6**	**29.6**	**.2**	**53.3**	**53.3**

Notes: 1. Value of exports from reporter countries that do not participate in Free Trade Agreements with SOMALIA

2. Weighted average tariff reduction measured by dT / (1 + T) in percent.

SOUTH AFRICA Extent of other countries' MFN tariff reductions on SOUTH AFRICA's exports

Summary product category	Average levels and changes weighted by value of exports to: the World exc. FTA[1]				LMIEs exc. FTA[1]				Value of exports in $ million		
	% of exports affected	Post-UR applied rate	Tariff reduc-tion[2]	Post-UR bound rate	% of exports affected	Post-UR applied rate	Tariff reduc-tion[2]	Post-UR bound rate	To IDB LMIEs exc. FTA[1]	To all IDB Ctrys exc. FTA[1]	To all IDB Ctrys inc. FTA
Agriculture, exc. Fish: Estimate 1	20.5	30.3	16.1	59.5	0.0	12.1	..	157.2	117.9	602.1	602.1
Agriculture, exc. Fish: Estimate 2	25.6	23.8	3.5	62.8	0.6	14.8	2.9	150.1	128.0	1,131.1	1,131.1
Fish and Fish Products	28.8	7.9	5.0	8.5	0.0	0.1	..	3.1	.2	130.8	130.8
Petroleum Oils	1.4	6.6	2.2	6.8	0.0	32.4	..	42.1	18.4	46.5	46.5
Wood, Pulp, Paper and Furniture	33.5	1.9	5.6	3.3	6.2	9.2	8.1	22.5	76.3	470.9	470.9
Textiles and Clothing	29.6	2.4	2.2	2.7	39.5	15.7	11.6	21.7	15.5	454.5	454.5
Leather, Rubber, Footwear	47.9	3.2	1.7	3.2	21.6	15.2	10.1	17.7	4.7	85.2	85.2
Metals	30.9	2.4	2.7	2.4	0.8	9.5	4.4	31.3	380.9	3,111.5	3,111.5
Chemical & Photographic Suppl.	15.0	4.2	3.2	6.7	0.5	9.4	5.3	33.6	204.9	617.8	617.8
Transport Equipment	28.3	2.3	2.5	2.2	0.6	8.8	20.3	20.0	7.8	69.5	69.5
Non-Electric Machinery	66.3	2.2	3.3	2.9	0.4	3.5	4.0	16.1	25.6	134.2	134.2
Electric Machinery	54.8	4.2	3.0	5.5	2.0	7.5	3.0	15.1	12.3	41.8	41.8
Mineral Prod.,Prec. Stones & Metal	5.1	0.3	1.0	0.2	1.2	28.1	9.7	28.5	138.5	14,566.6	14,566.6
Manufactured Articles nes.	8.2	1.1	5.2	1.7	16.6	13.7	12.3	28.1	29.2	314.4	314.4
Industrial Goods (line 5-14)	**11.5**	**0.9**	**2.4**	**0.9**	**2.6**	**12.4**	**9.4**	**28.6**	**895.7**	**19,866.4**	**19,866.4**
All Merch. Trade (line 2-14)	**12.4**	**1.7**	**2.5**	**3.3**	**2.3**	**12.8**	**9.2**	**64.0**	**1,042.3**	**21,174.8**	**21,174.8**

Notes: 1. Value of exports from reporter countries that do not participate in Free Trade Agreements with SOUTH AFRICA

2. Weighted average tariff reduction measured by $dT / (1 + T)$ in percent.

SRI LANKA Extent of other countries' MFN tariff reductions on SRI LANKA's exports

Summary product category	Average levels and changes weighted by value of exports to: the World exc. FTA[1]				LMIEs exc. FTA[1]				Value of exports in $ million		
	% of exports affected	Post-UR applied rate	Tariff reduc-tion[2]	Post-UR bound rate	% of exports affected	Post-UR applied rate	Tariff reduc-tion[2]	Post-UR bound rate	To IDB LMIEs exc. FTA[1]	To all IDB Ctrys exc. FTA[1]	To all IDB Ctrys inc. FTA
Agriculture, exc. Fish: Estimate 1	2.6	0.5	14.0	2.0	6.0	4.2	11.3	29.2	8.2	153.8	153.8
Agriculture, exc. Fish: Estimate 2	31.5	4.1	4.0	7.9	24.3	18.2	2.4	39.1	37.3	208.5	208.5
Fish and Fish Products	62.3	1.9	2.5	3.0	27.5	2.1	40.4	6.3	.4	29.4	29.4
Petroleum Oils	0.0	0.0	..	0.0	..	..	..	..	.0	15.2	15.2
Wood, Pulp, Paper and Furniture	36.0	1.1	4.8	1.4	12.1	14.6	5.5	21.5	.4	8.2	8.2
Textiles and Clothing	92.9	14.9	1.7	15.0	85.6	10.1	5.9	8.8	3.1	576.7	576.7
Leather, Rubber, Footwear	33.5	3.2	2.8	6.1	17.0	4.4	6.3	17.5	17.8	100.8	100.8
Metals	34.6	2.9	3.4	3.6	29.8	16.5	13.5	23.9	2.6	30.2	30.2
Chemical & Photographic Suppl.	27.2	4.1	4.0	6.1	31.0	17.4	14.5	27.5	.9	11.6	11.6
Transport Equipment	47.3	4.0	0.6	17.5	26.4	4.7	0.3	31.5	.5	1.2	1.2
Non-Electric Machinery	25.4	1.1	2.9	2.7	17.9	12.4	8.6	19.0	.2	4.0	4.0
Electric Machinery	24.4	10.8	1.5	5.7	0.2	22.4	14.7	10.6	3.1	6.9	6.9
Mineral Prod.,Prec. Stones & Metal	19.6	1.0	4.9	1.5	31.6	1.8	9.8	5.1	23.1	162.8	162.8
Manufactured Articles nes.	77.1	3.6	3.5	3.9	47.5	24.4	3.6	36.0	.5	25.5	25.5
Industrial Goods (line 5-14)	**69.1**	**10.1**	**2.0**	**10.8**	**27.8**	**5.8**	**8.5**	**11.7**	**52.1**	**928.0**	**928.0**
All Merch. Trade (line 2-14)	**61.4**	**8.8**	**2.2**	**10.1**	**26.3**	**10.8**	**6.3**	**23.4**	**89.7**	**1,181.1**	**1,181.1**

Notes: 1. Value of exports from reporter countries that do not participate in Free Trade Agreements with SRI LANKA

2. Weighted average tariff reduction measured by $dT / (1 + T)$ in percent.

SUDAN Extent of other countries' MFN tariff reductions on SUDAN's exports

| Summary product category | Average levels and changes weighted by value of exports to: | | | | | | | | Value of exports in $ million | | |
| | the World exc. FTA[1] | | | | LMIEs exc. FTA[1] | | | | | | |
	% of exports affected	Post-UR applied rate	Tariff reduc-tion[2]	Post-UR bound rate	% of exports affected	Post-UR applied rate	Tariff reduc-tion[2]	Post-UR bound rate	To IDB LMIEs exc. FTA[1]	To all IDB Ctrys exc. FTA[1]	To all IDB Ctrys inc. FTA
Agriculture, exc. Fish: Estimate 1	0.1	7.6	35.1	9.1	0.0	0.9	..	5.7	101.5	323.4	323.4
Agriculture, exc. Fish: Estimate 2	15.9	3.1	4.1	5.4	71.7	23.3	5.3	47.0	15.7	203.3	203.3
Fish and Fish Products	0.0	0.0	..	0.0	..	..	..	..	.0	.0	.0
Petroleum Oils	..	..	..	..	..	..	..	..	.0	.0	.0
Wood, Pulp, Paper and Furniture	16.2	0.1	5.0	0.1	0.0	0.0	..	0.0	.0	.1	.1
Textiles and Clothing	96.9	4.3	1.9	4.4	0.0	0.3	..	5.0	.1	2.5	2.5
Leather, Rubber, Footwear	27.7	27.6	4.8	2.2	28.3	67.4	8.7	10.0	.7	1.7	1.7
Metals	2.8	2.6	2.5	0.9	0.1	5.0	6.0	23.0	1.2	2.3	2.3
Chemical & Photographic Suppl.	40.0	3.2	4.5	3.2	100.0	9.0	2.4	9.0	.0	.1	.1
Transport Equipment	0.4	0.1	0.1	0.1	..	..	..	..	.0	3.6	3.6
Non-Electric Machinery	5.3	0.1	2.8	0.3	..	..	..	..	.0	2.7	2.7
Electric Machinery	92.9	5.4	2.5	5.4	..	..	..	..	.0	.0	.0
Mineral Prod.,Prec. Stones & Metal	16.7	1.1	0.2	1.1	..	..	..	..	.0	5.4	5.4
Manufactured Articles nes.	30.1	1.8	0.8	2.2	71.6	4.2	0.7	5.2	89.7	214.9	214.9
Industrial Goods (line 5-14)	**29.5**	**1.9**	**0.9**	**2.1**	**70.3**	**4.7**	**0.8**	**5.2**	**91.7**	**233.5**	**233.5**
All Merch. Trade (line 2-14)	**23.2**	**2.4**	**1.9**	**3.5**	**70.5**	**7.4**	**1.4**	**11.4**	**107.4**	**436.8**	**436.8**

Notes: 1. Value of exports from reporter countries that do not participate in Free Trade Agreements with SUDAN

2. Weighted average tariff reduction measured by dT / (1 + T) in percent.

SURINAME Extent of other countries' MFN tariff reductions on SURINAME's exports

| Summary product category | Average levels and changes weighted by value of exports to: | | | | | | | | Value of exports in $ million | | |
| | the World exc. FTA[1] | | | | LMIEs exc. FTA[1] | | | | | | |
	% of exports affected	Post-UR applied rate	Tariff reduc-tion[2]	Post-UR bound rate	% of exports affected	Post-UR applied rate	Tariff reduc-tion[2]	Post-UR bound rate	To IDB LMIEs exc. FTA[1]	To all IDB Ctrys exc. FTA[1]	To all IDB Ctrys inc. FTA
Agriculture, exc. Fish: Estimate 1	0.0	54.7	..	54.8	0.0	2.0	..	30.0	.2	62.9	62.9
Agriculture, exc. Fish: Estimate 2	3.2	8.4	3.1	9.3	0.0	15.0	..	30.0	.2	63.9	63.9
Fish and Fish Products	87.6	2.5	2.4	2.5	..	..	..	..	.0	27.7	27.7
Petroleum Oils	100.0	3.7	2.2	3.7	..	..	..	..	.0	.0	.0
Wood, Pulp, Paper and Furniture	3.8	0.5	3.4	0.8	0.0	30.0	..	50.0	.0	3.5	3.5
Textiles and Clothing	97.6	15.3	1.7	15.3	50.0	25.0	13.3	28.3	.0	.4	.4
Leather, Rubber, Footwear	14.3	8.8	0.9	13.8	0.0	5.6	..	47.5	.0	.1	.1
Metals	5.1	3.8	2.8	3.8	0.0	27.4	..	46.4	.0	15.4	15.4
Chemical & Photographic Suppl.	37.9	1.7	1.4	3.6	18.3	1.8	0.9	16.0	34.7	262.4	262.4
Transport Equipment	14.8	13.7	0.6	8.8	0.0	30.0	..	50.0	.0	.1	.1
Non-Electric Machinery	95.3	0.5	3.6	1.4	0.0	10.1	..	47.7	.0	.5	.5
Electric Machinery	84.8	3.1	1.7	3.0	0.0	40.0	..	50.0	.0	.7	.7
Mineral Prod.,Prec. Stones & Metal	9.6	0.6	2.3	0.6	..	..	..	..	.0	.3	.3
Manufactured Articles nes.	11.9	1.3	2.0	1.4	0.0	10.0	..	50.0	.0	1.4	1.4
Industrial Goods (line 5-14)	**35.8**	**1.8**	**1.4**	**3.6**	**18.3**	**1.8**	**0.9**	**16.1**	**34.8**	**284.7**	**284.7**
All Merch. Trade (line 2-14)	**34.1**	**2.0**	**1.6**	**3.5**	**18.2**	**1.9**	**0.9**	**16.2**	**34.9**	**376.3**	**376.3**

Notes: 1. Value of exports from reporter countries that do not participate in Free Trade Agreements with SURINAME

2. Weighted average tariff reduction measured by dT / (1 + T) in percent.

SWAZILAND Extent of other countries' MFN tariff reductions on SWAZILAND's exports

Summary product category	Average levels and changes weighted by value of exports to: the World exc. FTA[1]				Average levels and changes weighted by value of exports to: LMIEs exc. FTA[1]				Value of exports in $ million		
	% of exports affected	Post-UR applied rate	Tariff reduction[2]	Post-UR bound rate	% of exports affected	Post-UR applied rate	Tariff reduction[2]	Post-UR bound rate	To IDB LMIEs exc. FTA[1]	To all IDB Ctrys exc. FTA[1]	To all IDB Ctrys inc. FTA
Agriculture, exc. Fish: Estimate 1	5.0	110.2	17.7	110.2	99.9	70.6	22.0	70.6	4.0	130.5	130.5
Agriculture, exc. Fish: Estimate 2	18.4	15.9	5.7	16.6	18.0	0.8	3.1	13.1	4.1	180.6	180.6
Fish and Fish Products	..	..	..	..	..	..	..	..	.0	.0	.0
Petroleum Oils	..	..	..	..	..	..	..	..	.0	.0	.0
Wood, Pulp, Paper and Furniture	33.1	4.4	4.7	1.8	27.1	6.1	4.8	3.5	37.6	51.4	51.4
Textiles and Clothing	85.8	14.4	3.9	16.5	6.4	21.4	6.5	29.6	.5	9.2	9.2
Leather, Rubber, Footwear	49.2	6.6	5.9	6.5	99.3	13.3	6.0	13.1	.1	.3	.3
Metals	91.9	4.1	2.8	4.0	54.0	15.6	6.0	19.7	.2	2.6	2.6
Chemical & Photographic Suppl.	37.8	12.8	9.5	11.3	45.2	15.4	9.8	14.1	2.6	3.3	3.3
Transport Equipment	0.0	0.2	0.8	0.0	0.0	9.9	..	..	.2	6.4	6.4
Non-Electric Machinery	85.0	5.1	12.1	5.0	91.2	5.9	13.5	5.9	2.9	3.5	3.5
Electric Machinery	47.2	10.8	2.6	5.7	43.2	15.4	2.7	10.7	.4	.6	.6
Mineral Prod.,Prec. Stones & Metal	35.1	1.0	0.5	0.5	0.1	11.0	11.9	10.0	1.5	17.1	17.1
Manufactured Articles nes.	67.2	3.6	5.0	3.8	76.6	7.0	10.4	8.4	.4	2.9	2.9
Industrial Goods (line 5-14)	**41.0**	**4.8**	**4.5**	**4.1**	**31.8**	**7.3**	**6.9**	**6.5**	**46.4**	**97.4**	**97.4**
All Merch. Trade (line 2-14)	**26.3**	**10.4**	**5.0**	**11.3**	**30.7**	**6.7**	**6.7**	**7.7**	**50.5**	**278.0**	**278.0**

Notes: 1. Value of exports from reporter countries that do not participate in Free Trade Agreements with SWAZILAND

2. Weighted average tariff reduction measured by dT / (1 + T) in percent.

SWEDEN Extent of other countries' MFN tariff reductions on SWEDEN's exports

Summary product category	Average levels and changes weighted by value of exports to: the World exc. FTA[1]				Average levels and changes weighted by value of exports to: LMIEs exc. FTA[1]				Value of exports in $ million		
	% of exports affected	Post-UR applied rate	Tariff reduction[2]	Post-UR bound rate	% of exports affected	Post-UR applied rate	Tariff reduction[2]	Post-UR bound rate	To IDB LMIEs exc. FTA[1]	To all IDB Ctrys exc. FTA[1]	To all IDB Ctrys inc. FTA
Agriculture, exc. Fish: Estimate 1	7.1	33.3	19.6	36.0	7.6	28.5	96.7	52.6	16.9	166.0	166.0
Agriculture, exc. Fish: Estimate 2	43.8	15.2	4.9	27.4	31.5	11.0	2.5	33.8	34.2	751.7	751.7
Fish and Fish Products	25.5	1.9	1.6	6.7	64.5	6.3	6.9	7.9	.5	34.6	127.0
Petroleum Oils	0.0	0.5	1.4	2.7	0.0	12.0	6.0	31.3	12.1	139.7	896.3
Wood, Pulp, Paper and Furniture	3.2	0.4	6.0	0.8	27.3	10.4	8.8	18.0	315.4	934.8	10,229.1
Textiles and Clothing	7.2	9.4	4.1	9.1	41.1	22.7	6.2	22.3	34.5	88.8	776.7
Leather, Rubber, Footwear	13.3	3.9	3.3	4.9	37.6	17.5	7.4	23.3	17.7	81.9	447.9
Metals	11.2	1.0	6.1	2.4	26.7	12.1	10.0	24.7	263.9	1,112.6	5,917.4
Chemical & Photographic Suppl.	10.1	2.0	5.2	4.4	34.8	13.5	8.0	19.6	182.2	713.6	3,438.3
Transport Equipment	4.1	4.8	6.3	7.6	20.9	29.7	26.6	35.6	154.8	2,480.3	6,721.2
Non-Electric Machinery	17.4	2.8	3.6	3.4	40.4	12.8	4.7	19.7	621.5	2,277.7	7,848.6
Electric Machinery	16.3	8.4	5.0	6.4	28.4	15.3	7.7	23.7	375.2	1,029.5	3,351.6
Mineral Prod.,Prec. Stones & Metal	3.8	0.8	3.6	2.4	27.7	13.7	5.7	18.4	13.6	81.9	868.2
Manufactured Articles nes.	14.8	1.2	4.0	2.2	43.7	8.9	5.4	14.2	108.7	530.5	2,130.0
Industrial Goods (line 5-14)	**9.6**	**1.9**	**4.8**	**3.7**	**32.7**	**14.1**	**7.7**	**21.4**	**2,087.5**	**9,331.5**	**41,729.0**
All Merch. Trade (line 2-14)	**10.0**	**2.2**	**4.8**	**4.0**	**32.5**	**14.1**	**7.6**	**21.6**	**2,134.3**	**10,257.5**	**43,504.0**

Notes: 1. Value of exports from reporter countries that do not participate in Free Trade Agreements with SWEDEN

2. Weighted average tariff reduction measured by dT / (1 + T) in percent.

SWITZERLAND Extent of other countries' MFN tariff reductions on SWITZERLAND's exports

Summary product category	Average levels and changes weighted by value of exports to: the World exc. FTA[1]				Average levels and changes weighted by value of exports to: LMIEs exc. FTA[1]				Value of exports in $ million		
	% of exports affected	Post-UR applied rate	Tariff reduc- tion[2]	Post-UR bound rate	% of exports affected	Post-UR applied rate	Tariff reduc- tion[2]	Post-UR bound rate	To IDB LMIEs exc. FTA[1]	To all IDB Ctrys exc. FTA[1]	To all IDB Ctrys inc. FTA
Agriculture, exc. Fish: Estimate 1	2.2	74.7	69.3	86.2	5.9	-1.8	95.2	49.3	133.2	621.4	621.4
Agriculture, exc. Fish: Estimate 2	25.6	13.2	5.4	20.5	22.8	27.6	8.2	47.5	194.9	1,410.3	1,410.3
Fish and Fish Products	12.5	4.4	39.1	10.0	86.3	6.8	41.1	6.4	1.9	5.0	13.8
Petroleum Oils	0.4	0.8	1.4	7.9	0.4	1.0	1.5	10.5	54.1	62.3	84.9
Wood, Pulp, Paper and Furniture	4.0	0.5	5.2	1.5	38.1	10.5	6.3	17.6	66.1	161.6	1,707.7
Textiles and Clothing	8.9	8.1	3.8	7.7	52.4	15.2	5.0	17.6	141.7	386.2	2,798.9
Leather, Rubber, Footwear	10.9	6.1	4.6	6.4	41.3	15.8	4.9	19.6	22.7	120.5	453.7
Metals	6.1	2.2	3.6	3.9	32.5	16.8	4.8	20.3	118.0	437.0	3,123.0
Chemical & Photographic Suppl.	18.4	3.2	5.0	5.8	24.7	11.4	6.9	20.9	1,413.0	3,808.3	10,847.8
Transport Equipment	5.5	2.3	1.8	6.3	25.0	22.9	1.9	20.3	43.7	122.3	1,044.4
Non-Electric Machinery	17.5	5.3	3.5	4.0	45.8	13.0	4.3	18.9	1,143.3	2,810.6	9,055.4
Electric Machinery	15.3	7.5	3.1	4.6	35.5	17.9	6.8	22.5	298.1	930.0	3,637.1
Mineral Prod.,Prec. Stones & Metal	2.2	0.4	5.4	1.0	23.9	9.8	11.2	21.2	148.2	2,842.9	5,038.0
Manufactured Articles nes.	8.2	1.6	4.7	2.8	49.9	16.4	6.5	20.9	394.5	3,256.3	7,893.3
Industrial Goods (line 5-14)	**12.1**	**2.7**	**4.2**	**4.2**	**36.1**	**13.3**	**5.7**	**20.2**	**3,789.3**	**14,875.7**	**45,599.4**
All Merch. Trade (line 2-14)	**12.5**	**3.0**	**4.3**	**4.4**	**35.0**	**13.9**	**5.9**	**21.5**	**4,040.2**	**16,353.2**	**47,108.4**

Notes: 1. Value of exports from reporter countries that do not participate in Free Trade Agreements with SWITZERLAND

2. Weighted average tariff reduction measured by $dT / (1 + T)$ in percent.

SYRIA Extent of other countries' MFN tariff reductions on SYRIA's exports

Summary product category	Average levels and changes weighted by value of exports to: the World exc. FTA[1]				Average levels and changes weighted by value of exports to: LMIEs exc. FTA[1]				Value of exports in $ million		
	% of exports affected	Post-UR applied rate	Tariff reduc- tion[2]	Post-UR bound rate	% of exports affected	Post-UR applied rate	Tariff reduc- tion[2]	Post-UR bound rate	To IDB LMIEs exc. FTA[1]	To all IDB Ctrys exc. FTA[1]	To all IDB Ctrys inc. FTA
Agriculture, exc. Fish: Estimate 1	0.0	1.8	5.9	33.9	0.0	2.9	..	62.9	21.6	40.4	40.4
Agriculture, exc. Fish: Estimate 2	11.1	21.6	3.5	48.1	11.3	33.5	3.5	75.1	32.7	51.5	51.5
Fish and Fish Products	0.3	5.7	6.7	5.7	..	..	..	..	.0	.4	.4
Petroleum Oils	3.5	0.8	1.2	2.2	0.0	1.3	..	35.0	23.9	504.4	504.4
Wood, Pulp, Paper and Furniture	72.8	2.0	3.9	3.1	0.0	2.5	..	26.2	.0	.3	.3
Textiles and Clothing	42.0	18.7	2.0	15.3	2.2	36.5	5.0	30.7	8.7	20.2	20.2
Leather, Rubber, Footwear	1.8	22.7	2.3	25.2	0.1	24.4	3.1	27.1	4.7	5.1	5.1
Metals	47.0	1.5	4.7	0.9	88.7	4.3	9.5	1.1	.2	.8	.8
Chemical & Photographic Suppl.	17.8	10.5	7.6	11.0	21.3	17.9	8.6	19.1	1.6	3.0	3.0
Transport Equipment	0.3	0.1	2.4	0.1	20.0	24.6	1.0	28.6	.0	45.8	45.8
Non-Electric Machinery	73.2	2.5	2.8	3.6	9.9	5.9	4.3	9.9	.4	1.5	1.5
Electric Machinery	83.0	6.8	2.8	7.9	23.3	21.5	0.6	27.0	.2	1.1	1.1
Mineral Prod.,Prec. Stones & Metal	5.7	4.0	1.6	5.8	0.0	11.3	..	35.0	10.6	31.0	31.0
Manufactured Articles nes.	9.0	1.4	3.9	3.6	30.4	5.3	3.8	14.3	10.0	40.6	40.6
Industrial Goods (line 5-14)	**11.6**	**4.8**	**2.7**	**5.4**	**10.4**	**17.6**	**4.5**	**23.9**	**36.5**	**149.4**	**149.4**
All Merch. Trade (line 2-14)	**5.8**	**3.2**	**2.2**	**6.7**	**8.1**	**19.0**	**4.0**	**48.9**	**93.1**	**705.7**	**705.7**

Notes: 1. Value of exports from reporter countries that do not participate in Free Trade Agreements with SYRIA

2. Weighted average tariff reduction measured by $dT / (1 + T)$ in percent.

TANZANIA Extent of other countries' MFN tariff reductions on TANZANIA's exports

Summary product category	Average levels and changes weighted by value of exports to: the World exc. FTA[1]				LMIEs exc. FTA[1]				Value of exports in $ million		
	% of exports affected	Post-UR applied rate	Tariff reduction[2]	Post-UR bound rate	% of exports affected	Post-UR applied rate	Tariff reduction[2]	Post-UR bound rate	To IDB LMIEs exc. FTA[1]	To all IDB Ctrys exc. FTA[1]	To all IDB Ctrys inc. FTA
Agriculture, exc. Fish: Estimate 1	5.1	5.7	9.1	13.4	14.7	8.9	1.2	64.4	30.2	220.2	220.2
Agriculture, exc. Fish: Estimate 2	61.8	2.6	6.0	13.6	14.5	4.9	4.0	73.1	32.3	210.2	210.2
Fish and Fish Products	38.3	3.0	4.2	3.8	0.0	0.0	..	0.0	.0	9.9	9.9
Petroleum Oils	0.0	0.6	..	..	..	..	..	..	.0	22.1	22.1
Wood, Pulp, Paper and Furniture	9.4	1.4	4.4	5.6	1.9	8.4	10.2	26.4	1.5	6.9	6.9
Textiles and Clothing	73.4	6.4	4.0	6.7	35.0	6.4	7.4	17.5	.9	23.8	23.8
Leather, Rubber, Footwear	6.5	0.2	1.0	0.3	..	..	..	..	.0	2.1	2.1
Metals	14.3	0.8	1.3	0.3	6.9	20.3	12.4	28.0	1.1	26.6	26.6
Chemical & Photographic Suppl.	3.6	9.1	6.2	11.9	1.8	13.3	11.0	29.2	1.7	2.5	2.5
Transport Equipment	72.0	5.8	9.9	2.1	0.0	150.0	..	..	.0	.2	.2
Non-Electric Machinery	65.5	0.8	3.5	0.8	..	..	..	..	.0	1.0	1.0
Electric Machinery	71.5	7.5	2.1	7.5	0.0	20.0	..	20.0	.1	.2	.2
Mineral Prod.,Prec. Stones & Metal	1.0	6.1	3.4	1.5	0.0	16.3	..	37.1	12.6	33.8	33.8
Manufactured Articles nes.	12.5	1.2	13.4	2.4	0.0	0.2	..	12.9	5.4	56.7	56.7
Industrial Goods (line 5-14)	**19.8**	**3.2**	**5.8**	**2.8**	**1.9**	**11.7**	**8.6**	**18.8**	**23.3**	**153.9**	**153.9**
All Merch. Trade (line 2-14)	**41.5**	**2.7**	**5.9**	**9.1**	**9.2**	**7.7**	**4.5**	**61.2**	**55.7**	**396.1**	**396.1**

Notes: 1. Value of exports from reporter countries that do not participate in Free Trade Agreements with TANZANIA

2. Weighted average tariff reduction measured by dT / (1 + T) in percent.

THAILAND Extent of other countries' MFN tariff reductions on THAILAND's exports

Summary product category	Average levels and changes weighted by value of exports to: the World exc. FTA[1]				LMIEs exc. FTA[1]				Value of exports in $ million		
	% of exports affected	Post-UR applied rate	Tariff reduction[2]	Post-UR bound rate	% of exports affected	Post-UR applied rate	Tariff reduction[2]	Post-UR bound rate	To IDB LMIEs exc. FTA[1]	To all IDB Ctrys exc. FTA[1]	To all IDB Ctrys inc. FTA
Agriculture, exc. Fish: Estimate 1	19.2	24.0	20.9	30.8	33.6	44.0	35.4	73.6	577.0	2,269.2	2,269.2
Agriculture, exc. Fish: Estimate 2	29.4	13.6	4.7	44.6	15.1	8.6	2.6	96.2	729.3	3,374.5	3,374.5
Fish and Fish Products	38.7	6.6	2.7	7.0	7.3	9.7	15.9	34.5	79.6	1,869.2	1,869.2
Petroleum Oils	0.0	0.8	2.2	1.0	0.3	10.8	6.0	39.2	1.9	96.0	96.0
Wood, Pulp, Paper and Furniture	72.0	1.6	4.0	1.7	27.4	12.8	6.7	16.1	24.2	495.3	495.3
Textiles and Clothing	76.7	11.8	2.8	12.8	37.9	26.6	6.8	21.4	103.7	2,080.0	2,080.0
Leather, Rubber, Footwear	25.5	3.3	3.1	4.2	56.6	7.6	9.2	7.0	68.8	1,600.9	1,600.9
Metals	28.5	2.1	3.4	3.7	14.4	10.1	9.3	21.5	45.6	437.4	437.4
Chemical & Photographic Suppl.	35.0	5.7	4.3	9.3	19.5	17.6	11.3	23.5	53.6	367.1	367.1
Transport Equipment	67.7	6.5	2.6	7.2	2.9	17.3	11.2	26.9	8.6	117.3	117.3
Non-Electric Machinery	22.8	0.9	4.3	1.3	29.6	11.3	13.3	15.5	67.5	1,413.0	1,413.0
Electric Machinery	31.4	2.0	3.2	2.9	71.8	6.1	3.4	4.6	146.6	1,321.7	1,321.7
Mineral Prod.,Prec. Stones & Metal	43.8	2.8	2.2	3.6	13.9	11.8	11.0	25.0	52.4	1,311.2	1,311.2
Manufactured Articles nes.	51.4	3.0	3.9	3.5	24.9	16.6	7.1	22.2	17.0	995.5	995.5
Industrial Goods (line 5-14)	**44.5**	**4.4**	**3.2**	**5.3**	**40.6**	**13.0**	**6.6**	**14.3**	**587.8**	**10,139.2**	**10,139.2**
All Merch. Trade (line 2-14)	**40.3**	**6.2**	**3.3**	**12.5**	**25.4**	**10.6**	**5.6**	**63.4**	**1,398.6**	**15,478.9**	**15,478.9**

Notes: 1. Value of exports from reporter countries that do not participate in Free Trade Agreements with THAILAND

2. Weighted average tariff reduction measured by dT / (1 + T) in percent.

TOGO Extent of other countries' MFN tariff reductions on TOGO's exports

Summary product category	Average levels and changes weighted by value of exports to: the World exc. FTA[1]				LMIEs exc. FTA[1]				Value of exports in $ million		
	% of exports affected	Post-UR applied rate	Tariff reduc-tion[2]	Post-UR bound rate	% of exports affected	Post-UR applied rate	Tariff reduc-tion[2]	Post-UR bound rate	To IDB LMIEs exc. FTA[1]	To all IDB Ctrys exc. FTA[1]	To all IDB Ctrys inc. FTA
Agriculture, exc. Fish: Estimate 1	0.0	-0.1	5.9	2.1	0.0	-1.2	..	31.8	5.2	81.2	81.2
Agriculture, exc. Fish: Estimate 2	78.9	0.9	4.2	3.9	5.6	1.5	11.3	95.1	1.4	43.6	43.6
Fish and Fish Products	78.2	9.4	5.3	9.4	..	..	..	..	.0	6.9	6.9
Petroleum Oils	0.0	0.0	..	0.1	..	..	..	..	.0	6.5	6.5
Wood, Pulp, Paper and Furniture	83.9	1.4	3.9	1.9	0.0	10.8	..	35.0	.0	.5	.5
Textiles and Clothing	66.5	9.9	2.0	12.4	0.0	43.0	..	60.0	.0	.3	.3
Leather, Rubber, Footwear	96.0	4.4	1.5	4.4	..	..	..	..	.0	.7	.7
Metals	16.9	0.8	3.9	0.9	0.0	10.0	..	50.0	.0	.6	.6
Chemical & Photographic Suppl.	87.9	6.9	3.6	7.1	0.0	30.8	..	36.4	.0	.1	.1
Transport Equipment	27.0	9.8	2.6	9.8	..	..	..	..	.0	.1	.1
Non-Electric Machinery	68.8	0.7	3.2	0.8	0.0	20.0	..	40.0	.0	1.7	1.7
Electric Machinery	50.7	7.0	3.1	12.8	0.0	13.6	..	29.8	.2	.6	.6
Mineral Prod.,Prec. Stones & Metal	0.1	0.9	1.8	1.5	0.0	3.6	..	6.3	33.5	134.8	134.8
Manufactured Articles nes.	4.6	0.8	2.1	2.4	46.8	8.7	2.0	25.7	3.9	41.1	41.1
Industrial Goods (line 5-14)	**2.8**	**0.9**	**2.5**	**1.8**	**4.9**	**4.2**	**2.0**	**8.5**	**37.7**	**180.5**	**180.5**
All Merch. Trade (line 2-14)	**18.9**	**1.2**	**4.1**	**2.3**	**4.9**	**4.1**	**2.4**	**11.8**	**39.1**	**237.6**	**237.6**

Notes: 1. Value of exports from reporter countries that do not participate in Free Trade Agreements with TOGO

2. Weighted average tariff reduction measured by dT / (1 + T) in percent.

TONGA Extent of other countries' MFN tariff reductions on TONGA's exports

Summary product category	Average levels and changes weighted by value of exports to: the World exc. FTA[1]				LMIEs exc. FTA[1]				Value of exports in $ million		
	% of exports affected	Post-UR applied rate	Tariff reduc-tion[2]	Post-UR bound rate	% of exports affected	Post-UR applied rate	Tariff reduc-tion[2]	Post-UR bound rate	To IDB LMIEs exc. FTA[1]	To all IDB Ctrys exc. FTA[1]	To all IDB Ctrys inc. FTA
Agriculture, exc. Fish: Estimate 1	0.0	0.0	..	0.2	..	..	..	..	.0	1.6	1.6
Agriculture, exc. Fish: Estimate 2	24.4	1.5	2.7	1.6	100.0	11.0	7.8	11.0	.0	3.7	3.7
Fish and Fish Products	84.1	0.2	0.5	0.2	..	..	..	..	.0	.3	.3
Petroleum Oils	..	..	..	..	..	..	..	..	.0	.0	.0
Wood, Pulp, Paper and Furniture	0.0	0.7	..	0.9	0.0	1.5	..	2.0	.0	.1	.1
Textiles and Clothing	99.4	38.0	10.6	38.0	..	..	..	..	.0	.7	.7
Leather, Rubber, Footwear	88.2	34.4	8.3	34.4	..	..	..	..	.0	.8	.8
Metals	11.3	12.3	0.8	28.3	0.0	15.0	..	35.0	.1	.1	.1
Chemical & Photographic Suppl.	0.0	5.0	..	5.0	..	..	..	..	.0	.0	.0
Transport Equipment	37.0	5.6	8.3	5.6	..	..	..	..	.0	.0	.0
Non-Electric Machinery	98.0	1.3	2.8	1.3	..	..	..	..	.0	.1	.1
Electric Machinery	97.0	3.8	4.2	3.8	..	..	..	..	.0	.2	.2
Mineral Prod.,Prec. Stones & Metal	7.1	0.3	1.9	0.3	100.0	3.9	1.6	3.9	.0	.2	.2
Manufactured Articles nes.	45.4	5.2	5.6	5.5	..	..	..	..	.0	.1	.1
Industrial Goods (line 5-14)	**75.7**	**24.4**	**8.3**	**25.4**	**6.7**	**10.9**	**1.6**	**24.7**	**.2**	**2.4**	**2.4**
All Merch. Trade (line 2-14)	**46.4**	**9.8**	**5.8**	**10.2**	**7.8**	**10.9**	**2.5**	**24.6**	**.2**	**6.4**	**6.4**

Notes: 1. Value of exports from reporter countries that do not participate in Free Trade Agreements with TONGA

2. Weighted average tariff reduction measured by dT / (1 + T) in percent.

TRINIDAD&TOBAGO Extent of other countries' MFN tariff reductions on TRINIDAD&TOBAGO's exports

Summary product category	Average levels and changes weighted by value of exports to: the World exc. FTA[1]				Average levels and changes weighted by value of exports to: LMIEs exc. FTA[1]				Value of exports in $ million		
	% of exports affected	Post-UR applied rate	Tariff reduc-tion[2]	Post-UR bound rate	% of exports affected	Post-UR applied rate	Tariff reduc-tion[2]	Post-UR bound rate	To IDB LMIEs exc. FTA[1]	To all IDB Ctrys exc. FTA[1]	To all IDB Ctrys inc. FTA
Agriculture, exc. Fish: Estimate 1	0.0	90.6	..	108.7	0.0	-26.6	..	81.9	7.3	43.5	43.5
Agriculture, exc. Fish: Estimate 2	41.5	19.4	8.3	33.7	0.0	35.3	..	84.6	19.0	92.7	92.7
Fish and Fish Products	7.3	0.7	3.0	0.7	0.0	43.0	..	..	.0	8.9	8.9
Petroleum Oils	0.0	1.7	1.2	9.6	0.0	15.6	..	36.1	45.8	666.5	666.5
Wood, Pulp, Paper and Furniture	5.4	30.2	4.5	44.7	0.0	33.1	3.7	49.1	5.2	5.7	5.7
Textiles and Clothing	56.8	20.1	1.2	28.4	0.0	31.6	..	51.8	1.4	3.4	3.4
Leather, Rubber, Footwear	1.3	25.9	1.9	42.9	0.0	30.1	..	50.0	.7	.9	.9
Metals	39.2	2.8	4.6	19.1	0.0	5.5	9.5	37.8	63.7	126.1	126.1
Chemical & Photographic Suppl.	48.9	4.4	7.2	5.4	0.1	19.2	2.7	32.0	16.8	191.5	191.5
Transport Equipment	3.8	6.6	0.9	34.5	0.2	6.6	6.9	40.3	1.3	1.5	1.5
Non-Electric Machinery	18.5	25.8	3.2	35.9	0.9	31.4	0.5	43.8	3.4	4.2	4.2
Electric Machinery	7.4	24.2	4.7	34.7	0.0	33.2	..	48.5	1.8	2.6	2.6
Mineral Prod.,Prec. Stones & Metal	23.3	3.0	3.5	5.9	0.0	12.6	..	36.4	6.3	50.5	50.5
Manufactured Articles nes.	82.0	2.3	4.5	4.1	13.6	18.1	0.4	33.0	.5	4.6	4.6
Industrial Goods (line 5-14)	**41.4**	**4.6**	**6.0**	**11.4**	**0.1**	**11.6**	**1.5**	**38.1**	**101.1**	**391.0**	**391.0**
All Merch. Trade (line 2-14)	**17.3**	**3.7**	**6.4**	**12.9**	**0.1**	**15.4**	**1.5**	**42.9**	**166.0**	**1,159.1**	**1,159.1**

Notes: 1. Value of exports from reporter countries that do not participate in Free Trade Agreements with Trinidad&Tobago

2. Weighted average tariff reduction measured by dT / (1 + T) in percent.

TUNISIA Extent of other countries' MFN tariff reductions on TUNISIA's exports

Summary product category	Average levels and changes weighted by value of exports to: the World exc. FTA[1]				Average levels and changes weighted by value of exports to: LMIEs exc. FTA[1]				Value of exports in $ million		
	% of exports affected	Post-UR applied rate	Tariff reduc-tion[2]	Post-UR bound rate	% of exports affected	Post-UR applied rate	Tariff reduc-tion[2]	Post-UR bound rate	To IDB LMIEs exc. FTA[1]	To all IDB Ctrys exc. FTA[1]	To all IDB Ctrys inc. FTA
Agriculture, exc. Fish: Estimate 1	0.0	0.2	5.9	0.6	0.0	-0.2	..	40.9	.9	130.0	130.0
Agriculture, exc. Fish: Estimate 2	32.1	7.6	4.3	7.8	52.6	7.2	2.3	13.8	1.7	163.4	163.4
Fish and Fish Products	61.6	9.4	4.4	9.4	0.0	17.9	..	17.9	.3	108.4	108.4
Petroleum Oils	1.6	0.3	1.2	0.6	..	..	..	..	.0	323.0	323.0
Wood, Pulp, Paper and Furniture	44.5	1.1	5.4	1.6	8.4	7.8	3.7	36.5	.4	17.0	17.0
Textiles and Clothing	92.7	10.9	1.8	10.9	33.5	21.2	3.0	18.0	.4	620.9	620.9
Leather, Rubber, Footwear	85.8	11.7	1.7	5.9	13.4	75.7	0.3	6.2	2.3	27.8	27.8
Metals	37.8	1.0	3.8	1.0	51.8	6.1	9.2	7.5	1.0	33.8	33.8
Chemical & Photographic Suppl.	60.3	7.6	7.0	19.2	23.4	10.4	17.2	36.8	41.6	92.6	92.6
Transport Equipment	95.7	4.5	2.7	4.5	97.3	9.8	16.7	10.4	.1	13.4	13.4
Non-Electric Machinery	92.7	2.7	2.5	2.7	15.3	6.0	4.1	7.0	.1	11.6	11.6
Electric Machinery	94.6	3.6	2.5	3.6	15.3	9.4	11.6	9.6	.3	75.4	75.4
Mineral Prod.,Prec. Stones & Metal	49.7	3.8	0.7	8.5	0.0	2.1	..	33.0	48.6	265.3	265.3
Manufactured Articles nes.	84.8	1.5	5.2	1.4	43.5	12.7	5.0	10.7	.3	20.4	20.4
Industrial Goods (line 5-14)	**78.1**	**7.9**	**2.1**	**9.7**	**11.6**	**7.7**	**15.9**	**34.3**	**95.1**	**1,178.2**	**1,178.2**
All Merch. Trade (line 2-14)	**58.9**	**6.5**	**2.4**	**8.1**	**12.3**	**7.8**	**14.9**	**33.8**	**97.1**	**1,773.1**	**1,773.1**

Notes: 1. Value of exports from reporter countries that do not participate in Free Trade Agreements with TUNISIA

2. Weighted average tariff reduction measured by dT / (1 + T) in percent.

TURKEY Extent of other countries' MFN tariff reductions on TURKEY's exports

Summary product category	Average levels and changes weighted by value of exports to: the World exc. FTA[1]				LMIEs exc. FTA[1]				Value of exports in $ million		
	% of exports affected	Post-UR applied rate	Tariff reduc-tion[2]	Post-UR bound rate	% of exports affected	Post-UR applied rate	Tariff reduc-tion[2]	Post-UR bound rate	To IDB LMIEs exc. FTA[1]	To all IDB Ctrys exc. FTA[1]	To all IDB Ctrys inc. FTA
Agriculture, exc. Fish: Estimate 1	1.1	1.9	104.2	8.1	8.0	5.3	106.5	35.6	122.5	899.5	899.5
Agriculture, exc. Fish: Estimate 2	70.0	6.2	2.3	13.5	20.8	14.3	2.1	60.3	230.2	1,578.2	1,578.2
Fish and Fish Products	34.8	9.1	3.3	9.1	0.0	24.7	..	25.0	.1	71.9	71.9
Petroleum Oils	1.5	1.0	1.2	3.5	0.0	7.1	..	35.2	10.0	623.5	623.5
Wood, Pulp, Paper and Furniture	67.5	4.2	4.4	4.8	22.3	17.3	1.7	20.8	3.2	17.7	17.7
Textiles and Clothing	94.0	10.4	2.0	10.6	31.6	12.2	3.2	18.8	69.1	2,813.1	2,813.1
Leather, Rubber, Footwear	92.4	4.5	2.6	4.5	27.9	17.3	4.5	18.7	9.9	542.0	542.0
Metals	64.8	2.5	4.3	2.9	34.1	17.9	13.4	25.5	55.6	644.8	644.8
Chemical & Photographic Suppl.	56.7	5.7	5.2	6.7	45.9	11.5	9.1	16.7	51.4	221.2	221.2
Transport Equipment	51.1	9.1	2.5	8.7	2.4	20.7	7.8	33.1	16.3	52.8	52.8
Non-Electric Machinery	86.2	3.8	2.5	4.8	7.7	19.1	2.6	29.6	10.3	96.3	96.3
Electric Machinery	56.9	10.1	2.6	10.6	17.4	26.6	4.8	33.4	7.2	84.1	84.1
Mineral Prod.,Prec. Stones & Metal	39.9	3.0	2.0	3.5	19.0	8.8	6.9	20.6	30.9	496.6	496.6
Manufactured Articles nes.	20.8	2.0	2.5	7.1	1.9	3.1	1.8	15.0	77.5	181.3	181.3
Industrial Goods (line 5-14)	**79.5**	**7.4**	**2.5**	**7.9**	**23.4**	**11.7**	**7.8**	**19.8**	**331.4**	**5,150.0**	**5,150.0**
All Merch. Trade (line 2-14)	**70.5**	**6.6**	**2.4**	**8.9**	**22.0**	**12.7**	**5.6**	**37.4**	**571.6**	**7,423.6**	**7,423.6**

Notes: 1. Value of exports from reporter countries that do not participate in Free Trade Agreements with TURKEY

2. Weighted average tariff reduction measured by dT / (1 + T) in percent.

UGANDA Extent of other countries' MFN tariff reductions on UGANDA's exports

Summary product category	Average levels and changes weighted by value of exports to: the World exc. FTA[1]				LMIEs exc. FTA[1]				Value of exports in $ million		
	% of exports affected	Post-UR applied rate	Tariff reduc-tion[2]	Post-UR bound rate	% of exports affected	Post-UR applied rate	Tariff reduc-tion[2]	Post-UR bound rate	To IDB LMIEs exc. FTA[1]	To all IDB Ctrys exc. FTA[1]	To all IDB Ctrys inc. FTA
Agriculture, exc. Fish: Estimate 1	0.0	0.0	..	0.2	0.0	0.0	..	16.8	3.7	280.8	280.8
Agriculture, exc. Fish: Estimate 2	79.6	0.1	4.8	0.2	98.0	4.8	3.9	4.9	3.7	277.6	277.6
Fish and Fish Products	0.7	0.1	2.1	0.1	..	..	..	..	.0	2.2	2.2
Petroleum Oils	..	..	..	..	..	..	..	..	.0	.0	.0
Wood, Pulp, Paper and Furniture	91.1	0.0	5.5	0.0	..	..	..	..	.0	.0	.0
Textiles and Clothing	89.6	13.2	1.7	17.4	0.0	20.0	..	60.0	.0	.1	.1
Leather, Rubber, Footwear	16.9	16.0	2.7	20.8	0.0	43.0	..	52.0	.0	.1	.1
Metals	5.0	11.2	2.1	5.1	0.0	13.5	..	5.0	.1	.1	.1
Chemical & Photographic Suppl.	74.5	9.1	6.6	11.3	65.7	11.0	8.7	14.3	.1	.1	.1
Transport Equipment	8.7	3.6	2.2	3.6	..	..	..	..	.1	.2	.2
Non-Electric Machinery	83.9	1.1	3.8	3.9	0.0	6.0	..	37.0	.0	.1	.1
Electric Machinery	31.8	1.0	3.4	2.2	..	..	..	..	.0	.1	.1
Mineral Prod.,Prec. Stones & Metal	6.7	0.6	7.3	0.6	100.0	16.0	11.4	16.0	.0	.0	.0
Manufactured Articles nes.	0.6	0.0	3.6	0.0	100.0	16.0	11.4	16.0	.0	.8	.8
Industrial Goods (line 5-14)	**2.3**	**0.3**	**4.7**	**0.3**	**32.1**	**16.6**	**8.8**	**20.4**	**.3**	**22.1**	**22.1**
All Merch. Trade (line 2-14)	**73.3**	**0.2**	**4.8**	**0.2**	**93.3**	**5.6**	**4.0**	**5.8**	**4.0**	**301.9**	**301.9**

Notes: 1. Value of exports from reporter countries that do not participate in Free Trade Agreements with UGANDA

2. Weighted average tariff reduction measured by dT / (1 + T) in percent.

UNITED STATES Extent of other countries' MFN tariff reductions on UNITED STATES's exports

Summary product category	Average levels and changes weighted by value of exports to: the World exc. FTA[1]				Average levels and changes weighted by value of exports to: LMIEs exc. FTA[1]				Value of exports in $ million		
	% of exports affected	Post-UR applied rate	Tariff reduc-tion[2]	Post-UR bound rate	% of exports affected	Post-UR applied rate	Tariff reduc-tion[2]	Post-UR bound rate	To IDB LMIEs exc. FTA[1]	To all IDB Ctrys exc. FTA[1]	To all IDB Ctrys inc. FTA
Agriculture, exc. Fish: Estimate 1	23.0	37.6	46.7	43.3	27.5	15.8	62.8	40.6	3,973.5	16,685.0	19,854.7
Agriculture, exc. Fish: Estimate 2	19.5	6.9	4.5	27.7	14.6	18.8	7.6	91.5	4,179.6	23,176.5	28,402.6
Fish and Fish Products	63.2	4.5	3.8	4.3	76.7	10.5	21.4	8.4	279.8	2,847.9	3,120.2
Petroleum Oils	8.2	4.8	1.7	22.4	1.8	11.6	5.8	37.1	422.2	1,357.9	2,066.4
Wood, Pulp, Paper and Furniture	16.7	1.3	5.8	4.0	29.2	6.8	7.6	18.6	2,162.2	11,580.4	15,815.9
Textiles and Clothing	40.7	9.7	4.8	14.1	26.8	21.5	12.8	32.7	907.4	3,485.9	5,034.8
Leather, Rubber, Footwear	26.3	6.0	3.7	10.2	29.6	15.0	7.2	28.0	583.1	2,257.0	3,531.6
Metals	25.7	3.1	3.3	6.4	18.0	9.0	8.2	22.3	2,777.1	9,137.0	14,538.2
Chemical & Photographic Suppl.	39.9	4.9	4.4	9.0	27.1	11.4	10.8	23.5	6,257.0	23,196.1	29,742.2
Transport Equipment	10.7	2.3	3.7	5.9	6.3	7.2	4.2	19.1	3,310.1	14,283.9	36,932.2
Non-Electric Machinery	38.5	3.0	3.7	6.0	23.2	13.6	8.2	25.5	7,492.1	37,975.2	54,219.6
Electric Machinery	35.8	4.9	4.9	6.6	41.2	12.8	7.3	16.9	6,100.1	19,845.8	26,699.1
Mineral Prod.,Prec. Stones & Metal	21.4	1.8	1.7	4.1	10.4	9.7	9.0	20.6	2,114.7	10,963.4	14,516.4
Manufactured Articles nes.	37.8	2.5	4.5	4.6	37.8	9.5	6.4	17.6	3,942.2	19,847.3	24,271.3
Industrial Goods (line 5-14)	**30.1**	**3.3**	**4.1**	**6.3**	**26.2**	**11.2**	**8.2**	**21.7**	**35,646.0**	**152,572.0**	**225,301.0**
All Merch. Trade (line 2-14)	**29.2**	**3.8**	**4.1**	**8.7**	**24.7**	**12.0**	**8.3**	**31.5**	**40,527.5**	**179,954.0**	**258,890.0**

Notes: 1. Value of exports from reporter countries that do not participate in Free Trade Agreements with UNITED STATES

2. Weighted average tariff reduction measured by dT / (1 + T) in percent.

UNITED ARAB EMIRATES Extent of other countries' MFN tariff reductions on UNITED ARAB EMIRATES's exports

Summary product category	Average levels and changes weighted by value of exports to: the World exc. FTA[1]				Average levels and changes weighted by value of exports to: LMIEs exc. FTA[1]				Value of exports in $ million		
	% of exports affected	Post-UR applied rate	Tariff reduc-tion[2]	Post-UR bound rate	% of exports affected	Post-UR applied rate	Tariff reduc-tion[2]	Post-UR bound rate	To IDB LMIEs exc. FTA[1]	To all IDB Ctrys exc. FTA[1]	To all IDB Ctrys inc. FTA
Agriculture, exc. Fish: Estimate 1	8.0	1.7	14.3	16.2	0.0	0.0	..	47.5	1.3	4.2	4.2
Agriculture, exc. Fish: Estimate 2	46.3	11.4	5.5	15.1	27.0	40.5	4.9	56.8	1.8	9.1	9.1
Fish and Fish Products	33.8	3.3	5.4	9.5	14.8	4.4	41.5	43.3	1.2	9.2	9.2
Petroleum Oils	0.1	4.9	1.2	2.0	0.0	11.8	..	33.6	1,908.2	7,955.3	7,955.3
Wood, Pulp, Paper and Furniture	15.9	12.1	4.8	31.5	1.5	14.8	11.3	38.6	7.5	9.2	9.2
Textiles and Clothing	93.2	14.6	1.4	14.9	11.6	27.9	7.4	29.6	3.0	101.1	101.1
Leather, Rubber, Footwear	91.9	4.5	1.5	4.8	67.4	13.7	4.8	14.3	.4	9.8	9.8
Metals	74.4	1.2	1.4	0.9	48.2	10.3	5.8	8.0	37.4	343.5	343.5
Chemical & Photographic Suppl.	74.1	16.4	22.3	18.0	79.7	23.3	28.7	26.0	20.1	29.3	29.3
Transport Equipment	48.5	9.0	3.8	6.0	49.1	51.0	12.7	23.7	.5	4.5	4.5
Non-Electric Machinery	72.6	2.4	3.9	4.1	82.3	17.2	8.1	18.9	1.7	17.8	17.8
Electric Machinery	67.4	3.8	2.1	5.8	20.8	13.1	3.5	26.4	.9	8.3	8.3
Mineral Prod.,Prec. Stones & Metal	51.0	1.4	4.4	0.5	11.5	13.9	13.1	9.4	102.1	1,056.0	1,056.0
Manufactured Articles nes.	41.5	6.2	5.4	7.5	44.6	23.2	13.2	26.0	4.8	21.4	21.4
Industrial Goods (line 5-14)	**59.4**	**2.6**	**3.7**	**2.2**	**28.3**	**14.9**	**15.2**	**15.2**	**178.3**	**1,601.0**	**1,601.0**
All Merch. Trade (line 2-14)	**10.1**	**4.1**	**3.7**	**2.2**	**2.4**	**12.2**	**15.2**	**21.6**	**2,089.5**	**9,574.6**	**9,574.6**

Notes: 1. Value of exports from reporter countries that do not participate in Free Trade Agreements with UAE

2. Weighted average tariff reduction measured by dT / (1 + T) in percent.

URUGUAY Extent of other countries' MFN tariff reductions on URUGUAY's exports

Summary product category	Average levels and changes weighted by value of exports to: the World exc. FTA[1]				LMIEs exc. FTA[1]				Value of exports in $ million		
	% of exports affected	Post-UR applied rate	Tariff reduction[2]	Post-UR bound rate	% of exports affected	Post-UR applied rate	Tariff reduction[2]	Post-UR bound rate	To IDB LMIEs exc. FTA[1]	To all IDB Ctrys exc. FTA[1]	To all IDB Ctrys inc. FTA
Agriculture, exc. Fish: Estimate 1	18.0	51.3	9.2	52.5	0.1	-4.4	10.6	44.0	21.5	148.4	290.9
Agriculture, exc. Fish: Estimate 2	8.2	4.5	7.5	34.2	0.8	6.9	2.1	44.6	32.7	213.3	423.7
Fish and Fish Products	26.3	3.7	4.8	12.8	0.3	16.2	15.3	34.9	.4	52.0	72.9
Petroleum Oils	33.3	3.3	0.6	3.3	..	..	..	..	.0	.0	.0
Wood, Pulp, Paper and Furniture	14.6	2.3	2.8	19.4	0.0	5.4	3.6	29.7	1.7	11.4	27.0
Textiles and Clothing	45.8	6.2	2.8	15.5	6.8	4.6	8.6	29.0	29.2	250.8	329.9
Leather, Rubber, Footwear	30.8	4.5	2.2	20.5	2.1	14.4	5.7	34.4	6.3	178.0	367.2
Metals	10.3	2.7	2.8	29.8	0.0	3.9	..	34.5	3.4	6.4	21.0
Chemical & Photographic Suppl.	5.4	3.7	7.0	21.3	0.1	4.8	1.4	22.6	3.9	10.3	107.4
Transport Equipment	10.3	3.9	1.4	29.8	0.7	10.1	0.3	34.6	.2	1.7	9.8
Non-Electric Machinery	5.5	8.7	2.7	31.4	0.6	10.8	1.1	33.0	1.3	1.7	8.6
Electric Machinery	15.8	3.0	2.7	26.8	0.0	12.1	..	31.8	.1	2.0	11.1
Mineral Prod.,Prec. Stones & Metal	1.5	0.1	3.8	0.8	0.2	2.3	8.5	25.5	1.0	702.7	722.4
Manufactured Articles nes.	13.4	1.6	1.3	16.5	4.9	3.7	1.6	36.1	11.7	52.8	75.0
Industrial Goods (line 5-14)	**17.9**	**2.2**	**2.6**	**11.1**	**2.6**	**5.0**	**6.8**	**30.5**	**58.8**	**1,218.0**	**1,679.5**
All Merch. Trade (line 2-14)	**16.3**	**2.5**	**3.2**	**14.8**	**2.0**	**5.8**	**6.2**	**35.0**	**91.9**	**1,483.3**	**2,176.1**

Notes: 1. Value of exports from reporter countries that do not participate in Free Trade Agreements with URUGUAY
2. Weighted average tariff reduction measured by dT / (1 + T) in percent.

VANUATU Extent of other countries' MFN tariff reductions on VANUATU's exports

Summary product category	Average levels and changes weighted by value of exports to: the World exc. FTA[1]				LMIEs exc. FTA[1]				Value of exports in $ million		
	% of exports affected	Post-UR applied rate	Tariff reduction[2]	Post-UR bound rate	% of exports affected	Post-UR applied rate	Tariff reduction[2]	Post-UR bound rate	To IDB LMIEs exc. FTA[1]	To all IDB Ctrys exc. FTA[1]	To all IDB Ctrys inc. FTA
Agriculture, exc. Fish: Estimate 1	0.0	9.2	..	9.2	0.0	0.0	..	0.0	.0	13.5	13.5
Agriculture, exc. Fish: Estimate 2	7.3	4.5	3.9	8.9	91.3	12.2	7.8	12.6	.2	13.7	13.7
Fish and Fish Products	2.4	0.3	5.2	0.3	..	..	..	..	.0	13.9	13.9
Petroleum Oils	..	..	..	..	..	..	..	..	.0	.0	.0
Wood, Pulp, Paper and Furniture	2.4	2.4	8.7	3.1	0.0	1.5	..	2.0	.4	.7	.7
Textiles and Clothing	61.3	13.3	5.2	28.8	0.0	10.0	..	50.0	.0	.0	.0
Leather, Rubber, Footwear	..	..	..	..	..	..	..	..	.0	.0	.0
Metals	0.0	0.0	..	0.0	..	..	..	..	.0	.0	.0
Chemical & Photographic Suppl.	0.0	10.0	..	10.0	..	..	..	..	.0	.0	.0
Transport Equipment	0.0	8.3	..	8.5	..	..	..	..	.0	.0	.0
Non-Electric Machinery	13.3	4.1	2.9	8.8	..	..	..	..	.0	.0	.0
Electric Machinery	98.2	10.0	4.4	10.3	0.0	10.0	..	35.0	.0	.3	.3
Mineral Prod.,Prec. Stones & Metal	39.1	5.3	1.0	7.2	..	..	..	..	.0	.0	.0
Manufactured Articles nes.	43.3	4.2	5.3	4.3	100.0	13.0	6.0	13.0	.2	.6	.6
Industrial Goods (line 5-14)	**34.2**	**4.6**	**4.9**	**5.3**	**28.6**	**5.0**	**6.0**	**6.3**	**.6**	**1.7**	**1.7**
All Merch. Trade (line 2-14)	**6.5**	**2.5**	**4.4**	**4.6**	**45.0**	**6.9**	**6.9**	**7.9**	**.8**	**29.3**	**29.3**

Notes: 1. Value of exports from reporter countries that do not participate in Free Trade Agreements with VANUATU
2. Weighted average tariff reduction measured by dT / (1 + T) in percent.

VENEZUELA Extent of other countries' MFN tariff reductions on VENEZUELA's exports

Summary product category	Average levels and changes weighted by value of exports to: the World exc. FTA[1]				Average levels and changes weighted by value of exports to: LMIEs exc. FTA[1]				Value of exports in $ million		
	% of exports affected	Post-UR applied rate	Tariff reduc-tion[2]	Post-UR bound rate	% of exports affected	Post-UR applied rate	Tariff reduc-tion[2]	Post-UR bound rate	To IDB LMIEs exc. FTA[1]	To all IDB Ctrys exc. FTA[1]	To all IDB Ctrys inc. FTA
Agriculture, exc. Fish: Estimate 1	0.6	-0.6	1.2	6.9	7.3	-6.7	1.2	77.7	5.5	63.1	63.1
Agriculture, exc. Fish: Estimate 2	41.4	4.0	3.8	14.7	1.5	13.7	5.9	76.2	15.9	96.6	96.6
Fish and Fish Products	13.4	0.9	1.6	5.3	..	..	..	..	.0	129.2	129.2
Petroleum Oils	0.1	1.0	2.1	3.9	0.0	8.4	..	35.0	514.3	7,494.2	7,494.2
Wood, Pulp, Paper and Furniture	65.6	1.7	6.0	4.9	1.6	11.8	34.4	34.4	4.3	30.4	30.4
Textiles and Clothing	54.4	13.2	1.9	20.5	0.3	14.3	7.0	33.5	8.1	21.6	21.6
Leather, Rubber, Footwear	27.0	4.9	1.8	9.1	0.0	12.8	..	34.8	4.1	22.2	22.2
Metals	42.7	3.3	2.4	6.4	8.9	13.3	10.5	32.5	263.6	1,359.7	1,359.7
Chemical & Photographic Suppl.	11.8	7.6	3.9	19.7	0.0	10.9	7.6	30.3	108.7	174.6	174.6
Transport Equipment	70.8	6.1	1.1	11.4	0.4	14.8	3.6	36.3	12.3	50.6	50.6
Non-Electric Machinery	39.5	7.3	2.0	18.4	0.3	11.9	1.1	31.4	15.4	27.0	27.0
Electric Machinery	53.5	5.7	1.6	9.6	0.4	13.3	8.0	36.6	4.2	24.1	24.1
Mineral Prod., Prec. Stones & Metal	13.9	1.4	3.1	4.2	0.0	8.0	..	33.2	67.6	354.8	354.8
Manufactured Articles nes.	30.3	5.1	3.0	8.3	29.2	15.2	2.3	25.9	6.1	20.8	20.8
Industrial Goods (line 5-14)	**36.1**	**3.6**	**2.5**	**7.7**	**5.2**	**12.3**	**9.9**	**32.1**	**494.4**	**2,085.7**	**2,085.7**
All Merch. Trade (line 2-14)	**8.4**	**1.6**	**2.5**	**5.3**	**2.5**	**10.7**	**9.9**	**34.2**	**1,024.7**	**9,805.7**	**9,805.7**

Notes: 1. Value of exports from reporter countries that do not participate in Free Trade Agreements with VENEZUELA

2. Weighted average tariff reduction measured by dT / (1 + T) in percent.

VIETNAM Extent of other countries' MFN tariff reductions on VIETNAM's exports

Summary product category	Average levels and changes weighted by value of exports to: the World exc. FTA[1]				Average levels and changes weighted by value of exports to: LMIEs exc. FTA[1]				Value of exports in $ million		
	% of exports affected	Post-UR applied rate	Tariff reduc-tion[2]	Post-UR bound rate	% of exports affected	Post-UR applied rate	Tariff reduc-tion[2]	Post-UR bound rate	To IDB LMIEs exc. FTA[1]	To all IDB Ctrys exc. FTA[1]	To all IDB Ctrys inc. FTA
Agriculture, exc. Fish: Estimate 1	20.1	19.3	18.0	36.1	28.2	27.1	17.5	50.8	92.6	131.3	131.3
Agriculture, exc. Fish: Estimate 2	9.9	8.3	4.5	23.0	4.7	13.7	3.7	38.4	103.9	176.1	176.1
Fish and Fish Products	46.8	1.8	2.3	1.3	16.8	13.8	36.4	8.4	.6	212.2	212.2
Petroleum Oils	0.0	..	..	..	..	..	..	..	.0	50.5	50.5
Wood, Pulp, Paper and Furniture	37.1	2.7	4.7	3.7	69.8	5.5	4.5	7.9	9.9	23.4	23.4
Textiles and Clothing	74.3	11.3	2.8	13.3	83.2	13.7	3.0	14.4	33.9	50.2	50.2
Leather, Rubber, Footwear	21.1	7.9	3.3	11.5	21.8	8.9	3.6	11.7	6.3	7.6	7.6
Metals	7.0	0.9	3.8	18.3	12.1	1.6	3.8	33.0	20.9	37.2	37.2
Chemical & Photographic Suppl.	60.0	7.8	5.8	12.6	78.5	10.5	5.8	13.1	2.1	2.9	2.9
Transport Equipment	9.2	14.0	2.5	11.2	0.0	42.0	..	33.3	.0	.1	.1
Non-Electric Machinery	45.6	1.2	0.4	7.4	79.8	2.1	0.2	8.0	1.1	2.2	2.2
Electric Machinery	25.5	11.2	0.9	15.1	32.5	14.4	0.9	15.1	3.9	5.1	5.1
Mineral Prod., Prec. Stones & Metal	4.1	15.2	3.5	1.9	3.3	19.5	4.1	7.8	46.4	59.9	59.9
Manufactured Articles nes.	54.5	6.5	3.9	15.9	74.5	9.8	4.1	24.7	13.8	22.0	22.0
Industrial Goods (line 5-14)	**32.6**	**8.8**	**3.3**	**12.7**	**39.5**	**12.5**	**3.5**	**19.0**	**138.4**	**210.5**	**210.5**
All Merch. Trade (line 2-14)	**28.6**	**6.1**	**2.9**	**11.5**	**24.6**	**13.0**	**3.6**	**29.1**	**242.9**	**649.4**	**649.4**

Notes: 1. Value of exports from reporter countries that do not participate in Free Trade Agreements with VIETNAM

2. Weighted average tariff reduction measured by dT / (1 + T) in percent.

YEMEN Extent of other countries' MFN tariff reductions on YEMEN's exports

Summary product category	Average levels and changes weighted by value of exports to: the World exc. FTA[1]				LMIEs exc. FTA[1]				Value of exports in $ million		
	% of exports affected	Post-UR applied rate	Tariff reduc-tion[2]	Post-UR bound rate	% of exports affected	Post-UR applied rate	Tariff reduc-tion[2]	Post-UR bound rate	To IDB LMIEs exc. FTA[1]	To all IDB Ctrys exc. FTA[1]	To all IDB Ctrys inc. FTA
Agriculture, exc. Fish: Estimate 1	0.0	0.0	..	0.0	..	..	..	..	.0	3.3	3.3
Agriculture, exc. Fish: Estimate 2	3.1	0.4	1.4	1.2	0.0	21.6	..	71.5	.1	3.7	3.7
Fish and Fish Products	85.1	7.5	5.5	8.8	0.0	0.0	..	50.0	.0	14.6	14.6
Petroleum Oils	0.0	1.6	..	1.1	0.0	7.1	..	45.0	140.7	795.5	795.5
Wood, Pulp, Paper and Furniture	40.4	9.6	6.4	24.1	0.0	15.0	..	40.0	.1	.1	.1
Textiles and Clothing	86.3	11.2	3.6	13.2	0.0	36.2	..	56.7	.0	.2	.2
Leather, Rubber, Footwear	95.0	2.2	1.1	2.2	100.0	0.4	0.1	0.4	.0	.4	.4
Metals	25.8	5.0	3.7	0.9	2.1	73.8	6.6	9.8	.3	1.2	1.2
Chemical & Photographic Suppl.	25.3	1.4	12.4	7.3	77.9	3.2	12.7	12.0	.1	.2	.2
Transport Equipment	6.6	6.9	2.7	2.2	0.0	90.2	..	25.0	.0	.3	.3
Non-Electric Machinery	54.5	0.6	4.1	6.8	1.3	0.9	2.2	38.9	.2	1.1	1.1
Electric Machinery	41.6	1.2	3.0	1.8	0.0	5.0	..	25.0	.0	.3	.3
Mineral Prod.,Prec. Stones & Metal	0.8	9.1	0.8	2.6	0.0	9.2	..	..	2.4	2.5	2.5
Manufactured Articles nes.	9.3	0.9	10.9	0.9	17.7	6.8	15.9	7.9	.5	11.0	11.0
Industrial Goods (line 5-14)	**16.1**	**2.6**	**6.3**	**2.0**	**4.6**	**10.2**	**13.0**	**18.8**	**3.6**	**17.3**	**17.3**
All Merch. Trade (line 2-14)	**1.8**	**1.7**	**5.6**	**1.4**	**0.1**	**7.2**	**13.0**	**42.6**	**144.3**	**831.1**	**831.1**

Notes: 1. Value of exports from reporter countries that do not participate in Free Trade Agreements with YEMEN

2. Weighted average tariff reduction measured by dT / (1 + T) in percent.

ZAIRE Extent of other countries' MFN tariff reductions on ZAIRE's exports

Summary product category	Average levels and changes weighted by value of exports to: the World exc. FTA[1]				LMIEs exc. FTA[1]				Value of exports in $ million		
	% of exports affected	Post-UR applied rate	Tariff reduc-tion[2]	Post-UR bound rate	% of exports affected	Post-UR applied rate	Tariff reduc-tion[2]	Post-UR bound rate	To IDB LMIEs exc. FTA[1]	To all IDB Ctrys exc. FTA[1]	To all IDB Ctrys inc. FTA
Agriculture, exc. Fish: Estimate 1	0.1	0.0	1.2	0.3	4.0	1.9	1.2	15.5	2.6	183.5	183.5
Agriculture, exc. Fish: Estimate 2	91.0	0.5	4.7	1.4	15.3	15.5	3.6	73.5	2.7	192.5	192.5
Fish and Fish Products	0.4	0.1	6.7	0.1	..	..	..	..	.0	1.3	1.3
Petroleum Oils	0.0	0.6	..	0.7	..	..	..	..	.0	147.5	147.5
Wood, Pulp, Paper and Furniture	13.8	0.6	2.8	0.6	40.2	9.0	8.4	6.2	.4	51.4	51.4
Textiles and Clothing	93.9	13.0	3.4	13.0	100.0	8.5	3.7	8.5	.0	1.2	1.2
Leather, Rubber, Footwear	0.3	0.0	1.0	0.2	0.0	8.9	..	35.0	.1	12.4	12.4
Metals	8.1	0.8	3.2	0.7	11.7	7.6	10.4	6.8	115.3	803.5	803.5
Chemical & Photographic Suppl.	63.4	1.9	8.6	1.9	0.0	20.0	..	20.0	.1	11.7	11.7
Transport Equipment	52.0	6.6	1.0	6.6	93.8	10.6	0.5	10.6	.0	.5	.5
Non-Electric Machinery	76.3	1.6	2.6	1.6	0.0	5.0	..	5.0	.0	.5	.5
Electric Machinery	83.1	3.8	0.8	3.8	0.0	10.5	..	35.0	.0	.8	.8
Mineral Prod.,Prec. Stones & Metal	0.4	0.1	4.5	0.0	1.9	6.5	3.7	24.9	7.8	425.8	425.8
Manufactured Articles nes.	24.9	1.7	2.8	1.9	0.0	1.0	..	25.0	.1	5.3	5.3
Industrial Goods (line 5-14)	**6.5**	**0.6**	**3.6**	**0.5**	**11.2**	**7.5**	**10.3**	**7.1**	**123.7**	**1,313.2**	**1,313.2**
All Merch. Trade (line 2-14)	**15.7**	**0.6**	**4.4**	**0.6**	**11.3**	**7.8**	**10.1**	**11.3**	**126.4**	**1,654.5**	**1,654.5**

Notes: 1. Value of exports from reporter countries that do not participate in Free Trade Agreements with ZAIRE

2. Weighted average tariff reduction measured by dT / (1 + T) in percent.

ZAMBIA Extent of other countries' MFN tariff reductions on ZAMBIA's exports

Summary product category	Average levels and changes weighted by value of exports to: the World exc. FTA[1]				Average levels and changes weighted by value of exports to: LMIEs exc. FTA[1]				Value of exports in $ million		
	% of exports affected	Post-UR applied rate	Tariff reduc-tion[2]	Post-UR bound rate	% of exports affected	Post-UR applied rate	Tariff reduc-tion[2]	Post-UR bound rate	To IDB LMIEs exc. FTA[1]	To all IDB Ctrys exc. FTA[1]	To all IDB Ctrys inc. FTA
Agriculture, exc. Fish: Estimate 1	0.0	-0.1	..	5.5	0.0	-6.5	..	128.9	.7	18.0	18.0
Agriculture, exc. Fish: Estimate 2	65.0	7.8	3.3	14.6	0.2	3.1	4.9	129.0	.9	18.1	18.1
Fish and Fish Products	17.1	2.2	6.7	2.2	0.0	0.0	..	0.0	.0	.2	.2
Petroleum Oils	0.0	..	..	..	0.0	..	..	..	.1	.1	.1
Wood, Pulp, Paper and Furniture	19.9	6.6	4.0	2.7	0.0	15.9	..	15.0	.1	.2	.2
Textiles and Clothing	82.5	7.5	1.9	8.5	17.7	12.7	3.9	25.0	.6	8.7	8.7
Leather, Rubber, Footwear	20.3	0.4	0.9	0.8	0.0	0.0	..	25.0	.0	1.6	1.6
Metals	39.4	2.0	1.7	4.9	4.2	4.3	8.1	22.1	240.2	1,000.8	1,000.8
Chemical & Photographic Suppl.	0.0	3.4	..	2.6	0.0	3.8	..	150.0	1.0	1.1	1.1
Transport Equipment	18.6	0.7	1.0	0.6	0.0	21.8	..	33.5	.0	1.2	1.2
Non-Electric Machinery	73.8	2.1	4.1	2.1	0.0	19.1	..	20.0	.0	.6	.6
Electric Machinery	54.1	3.2	3.7	3.2	..	..	..	..	.0	.4	.4
Mineral Prod.,Prec. Stones & Metal	1.7	1.0	6.6	2.3	5.3	7.1	9.2	30.4	3.8	28.0	28.0
Manufactured Articles nes.	1.3	0.0	2.9	0.1	0.0	0.0	..	32.3	10.1	15.8	15.8
Industrial Goods (line 5-14)	**38.1**	**1.9**	**1.7**	**4.8**	**4.1**	**4.2**	**8.1**	**22.2**	**255.7**	**1,058.5**	**1,058.5**
All Merch. Trade (line 2-14)	**38.5**	**2.0**	**1.8**	**4.9**	**4.1**	**4.1**	**8.0**	**22.8**	**256.7**	**1,076.9**	**1,076.9**

Notes: 1. Value of exports from reporter countries that do not participate in Free Trade Agreements with ZAMBIA

2. Weighted average tariff reduction measured by dT / (1 + T) in percent.

ZIMBABWE Extent of other countries' MFN tariff reductions on ZIMBABWE's exports

Summary product category	Average levels and changes weighted by value of exports to: the World exc. FTA[1]				Average levels and changes weighted by value of exports to: LMIEs exc. FTA[1]				Value of exports in $ million		
	% of exports affected	Post-UR applied rate	Tariff reduc-tion[2]	Post-UR bound rate	% of exports affected	Post-UR applied rate	Tariff reduc-tion[2]	Post-UR bound rate	To IDB LMIEs exc. FTA[1]	To all IDB Ctrys exc. FTA[1]	To all IDB Ctrys inc. FTA
Agriculture, exc. Fish: Estimate 1	11.7	21.7	19.1	22.6	21.9	3.5	106.8	15.9	28.0	397.9	397.9
Agriculture, exc. Fish: Estimate 2	54.1	12.4	4.0	13.2	53.6	22.5	3.4	30.2	28.7	348.8	348.8
Fish and Fish Products	0.0	0.0	..	0.0	..	..	..	..	.0	.0	.0
Petroleum Oils	0.0	0.0	..	0.0	..	..	..	..	.0	7.3	7.3
Wood, Pulp, Paper and Furniture	75.1	1.7	4.0	7.7	0.0	0.0	..	30.0	.8	4.0	4.0
Textiles and Clothing	97.5	9.8	1.8	9.8	..	..	..	..	.0	37.6	37.6
Leather, Rubber, Footwear	26.2	1.5	1.3	1.5	100.0	10.0	8.7	10.0	.0	13.3	13.3
Metals	47.1	2.2	2.6	2.5	7.5	6.4	13.4	13.3	14.4	455.2	455.2
Chemical & Photographic Suppl.	33.4	8.4	1.6	6.7	1.2	10.1	14.4	32.0	2.7	4.4	4.4
Transport Equipment	65.1	9.4	3.0	5.6	0.0	150.0	..	..	.0	.2	.2
Non-Electric Machinery	70.2	3.5	3.8	4.2	6.1	10.7	2.1	23.9	.1	1.2	1.2
Electric Machinery	93.4	3.1	3.0	3.2	..	..	..	..	.0	.6	.6
Mineral Prod.,Prec. Stones & Metal	5.3	1.6	3.4	2.6	13.1	12.4	9.5	23.6	17.4	142.5	142.5
Manufactured Articles nes.	1.3	0.0	3.5	0.2	0.0	0.7	..	27.0	2.3	72.8	72.8
Industrial Goods (line 5-14)	**36.8**	**2.3**	**2.5**	**2.7**	**9.0**	**9.5**	**10.8**	**19.0**	**37.9**	**731.8**	**731.8**
All Merch. Trade (line 2-14)	**42.1**	**5.0**	**3.1**	**5.5**	**28.3**	**15.3**	**4.8**	**24.5**	**66.5**	**1,087.8**	**1,087.8**

Notes: 1. Value of exports from reporter countries that do not participate in Free Trade Agreements with ZIMBABWE

2. Weighted average tariff reduction measured by dT / (1 + T) in percent.

6

Tables R.2

Concessions Received

Exporting Group by Product Category

CENTRAL ASIA Extent of other countries' MFN tariff reductions on CENTRAL ASIA's exports

Summary product category	Average levels and changes weighted by value of exports to: the World exc. FTA[1]				LMIEs exc. FTA[1]				Value of exports in $ million		
	% of exports affected	Post-UR applied rate	Tariff reduc-tion[2]	Post-UR bound rate	% of exports affected	Post-UR applied rate	Tariff reduc-tion[2]	Post-UR bound rate	To IDB LMIEs exc. FTA[1]	To all IDB Ctrys exc. FTA[1]	To all IDB Ctrys inc. FTA
Agriculture, exc. Fish: Estimate 1	0.1	1.3	21.7	16.2	0.0	1.0	2.9	34.5	222	516	516
Agriculture, exc. Fish: Estimate 2	44.1	15.3	5.0	29.9	43.1	20.7	3.2	53.9	137	345	345
Fish and Fish Products	49.7	6.3	4.3	6.5	23.9	12.8	34.6	10.9	49	460	460
Petroleum Oils	1.3	0.8	1.3	1.1	0.6	1.0	1.4	0.5	2,545	11,416	11,416
Wood, Pulp, Paper and Furniture	10.4	0.9	3.7	2.0	16.5	6.2	2.9	10.6	288	2,417	2,417
Textiles and Clothing	55.0	10.5	4.3	9.6	54.3	21.3	7.0	15.1	50	172	172
Leather, Rubber, Footwear	21.1	2.1	3.4	2.6	23.6	3.6	4.7	4.8	46	126	126
Metals	23.5	1.4	2.2	3.3	13.9	3.4	1.9	8.8	1,042	3,129	3,129
Chemical & Photographic Suppl.	30.3	4.3	5.8	4.6	51.7	12.7	7.2	13.7	339	1,227	1,227
Transport Equipment	35.6	9.0	2.1	9.1	26.2	12.5	2.1	15.7	357	971	971
Non-Electric Machinery	70.3	8.3	3.2	10.2	65.6	10.3	3.8	12.9	536	733	733
Electric Machinery	52.3	9.5	4.0	11.1	47.9	11.8	2.9	14.2	160	239	239
Mineral Prod.,Prec. Stones & Metal	9.2	1.5	1.9	3.8	3.0	4.4	6.6	12.8	1,867	6,013	6,013
Manufactured Articles nes.	8.4	1.4	3.6	5.2	8.9	2.7	4.0	10.5	731	1,572	1,572
Industrial Goods (line 5-14)	19.0	2.6	3.0	4.4	19.4	6.1	4.1	11.7	5,414	16,599	16,599
All Merch. Trade (line 2-14)	12.8	2.1	3.1	3.5	13.9	5.1	4.3	9.7	8,145	28,820	28,820

Notes: 1. Value of exports from reporter countries that do not participate in Free Trade Agreements with CENTRAL ASIA

2. Weighted average tariff reduction measured by dT / (1 + T) in percent.

EAST ASIA & PACIFIC Extent of other countries' MFN tariff reductions on E. ASIA&PACIFIC's exports

Summary product category	Average levels and changes weighted by value of exports to: the World exc. FTA[1]				LMIEs exc. FTA[1]				Value of exports in $ million		
	% of exports affected	Post-UR applied rate	Tariff reduc-tion[2]	Post-UR bound rate	% of exports affected	Post-UR applied rate	Tariff reduc-tion[2]	Post-UR bound rate	To IDB LMIEs exc. FTA[1]	To all IDB Ctrys exc. FTA[1]	To all IDB Ctrys inc. FTA
Agriculture, exc. Fish: Estimate 1	18.4	17.8	16.6	24.7	37.2	33.4	13.4	63.5	2,482	10,808	10,808
Agriculture, exc. Fish: Estimate 2	37.7	10.2	6.6	22.2	16.9	28.7	4.2	90.0	2,927	17,801	17,801
Fish and Fish Products	54.4	4.5	3.3	4.7	45.0	8.8	38.4	12.7	238	6,844	6,844
Petroleum Oils	0.0	4.7	1.5	4.7	0.0	12.0	5.4	32.9	1,539	12,248	12,248
Wood, Pulp, Paper and Furniture	33.8	2.6	4.4	3.0	21.0	8.5	7.2	9.8	1,313	10,166	10,166
Textiles and Clothing	49.8	7.8	2.9	12.8	49.3	23.0	9.7	23.5	1,813	46,137	46,137
Leather, Rubber, Footwear	26.7	5.4	3.3	7.0	55.6	10.0	8.3	12.1	889	19,068	19,068
Metals	42.3	2.2	3.5	2.9	13.9	12.3	9.0	20.2	1,703	13,638	13,638
Chemical & Photographic Suppl.	31.0	3.4	3.7	7.1	20.6	15.6	11.2	26.4	926	7,952	7,952
Transport Equipment	14.8	4.2	2.5	4.7	2.7	22.8	19.6	38.8	127	3,157	3,157
Non-Electric Machinery	42.7	2.0	3.7	3.6	37.8	15.3	11.5	25.2	835	9,765	9,765
Electric Machinery	28.0	2.3	3.6	4.3	40.2	15.3	7.6	17.7	1,354	27,857	27,857
Mineral Prod.,Prec. Stones & Metal	19.4	1.9	3.1	2.1	8.9	11.2	9.0	12.7	1,088	11,398	11,398
Manufactured Articles nes.	43.1	1.8	4.4	3.3	36.7	15.2	5.4	28.2	686	22,170	22,170
Industrial Goods (line 5-14)	37.3	4.1	3.4	6.1	30.8	14.5	8.8	19.2	10,735	171,307	171,307
All Merch. Trade (line 2-14)	35.7	4.6	3.7	7.8	25.3	16.8	9.0	37.5	15,439	208,199	208,199

Notes: 1. Value of exports from reporter countries that do not participate in Free Trade Agreements with E. ASIA&PACIFIC

2. Weighted average tariff reduction measured by dT / (1 + T) in percent.

EASTERN EUROPE Extent of other countries' MFN tariff reductions on EASTERN EUROPE's exports

Summary product category	Average levels and changes weighted by value of exports to: the World exc. FTA[1]				LMIEs exc. FTA[1]				Value of exports in $ million		
	% of exports affected	Post-UR applied rate	Tariff reduc-tion[2]	Post-UR bound rate	% of exports affected	Post-UR applied rate	Tariff reduc-tion[2]	Post-UR bound rate	To IDB LMIEs exc. FTA[1]	To all IDB Ctrys exc. FTA[1]	To all IDB Ctrys inc. FTA
Agriculture, exc. Fish: Estimate 1	11.1	32.1	15.7	46.7	3.5	7.5	13.8	69.1	359	1,709	1,709
Agriculture, exc. Fish: Estimate 2	40.3	9.5	3.4	22.1	21.2	19.3	2.9	68.3	632	3,910	3,910
Fish and Fish Products	36.0	7.4	4.5	7.3	4.7	13.9	38.2	7.8	9	226	226
Petroleum Oils	6.2	4.5	1.2	3.5	19.6	9.1	1.1	8.4	57	1,645	1,645
Wood, Pulp, Paper and Furniture	61.8	1.7	5.3	1.7	51.3	10.7	6.1	10.9	218	2,810	2,810
Textiles and Clothing	90.5	11.1	2.9	11.2	67.1	14.5	6.4	14.5	303	2,772	2,772
Leather, Rubber, Footwear	62.4	7.1	2.5	6.9	67.7	13.5	3.1	10.9	115	1,190	1,190
Metals	53.3	4.5	3.8	3.7	27.3	12.8	3.3	12.0	1,503	5,301	5,301
Chemical & Photographic Suppl.	55.9	6.3	4.2	7.2	42.0	11.6	5.5	14.3	835	2,425	2,425
Transport Equipment	45.7	7.8	2.8	7.7	39.0	10.9	2.2	12.4	531	1,686	1,686
Non-Electric Machinery	76.7	6.1	2.1	6.6	62.1	9.2	2.0	10.4	1,197	2,282	2,282
Electric Machinery	79.1	6.3	2.7	6.5	54.4	11.5	3.3	12.2	461	1,344	1,344
Mineral Prod.,Prec. Stones & Metal	47.9	3.7	1.8	4.6	16.5	7.5	3.0	12.1	824	3,098	3,098
Manufactured Articles nes.	56.1	3.7	3.1	6.0	52.1	8.2	2.8	16.0	299	1,150	1,150
Industrial Goods (line 5-14)	**61.9**	**5.6**	**3.2**	**5.8**	**42.1**	**10.8**	**3.5**	**12.3**	**6,285**	**24,059**	**24,059**
All Merch. Trade (line 2-14)	**55.8**	**5.9**	**3.3**	**7.3**	**40.0**	**11.6**	**3.4**	**18.4**	**6,983**	**29,841**	**29,841**

Notes: 1. Value of exports from reporter countries that do not participate in Free Trade Agreements with EASTERN EUROP

2. Weighted average tariff reduction measured by dT / (1 + T) in percent.

HIGH INCOME ECONOMIES Extent of other countries' MFN tariff reductions on High Inc. Econ's exports

Summary product category	Average levels and changes weighted by value of exports to: the World exc. FTA[1]				LMIEs exc. FTA[1]				Value of exports in $ million		
	% of exports affected	Post-UR applied rate	Tariff reduc-tion[2]	Post-UR bound rate	% of exports affected	Post-UR applied rate	Tariff reduc-tion[2]	Post-UR bound rate	To IDB LMIEs exc. FTA[1]	To all IDB Ctrys exc. FTA[1]	To all IDB Ctrys inc. FTA
Agriculture, exc. Fish: Estimate 1	19.9	39.5	40.0	47.3	23.0	18.1	58.9	50.7	8,491	34,060	38,690
Agriculture, exc. Fish: Estimate 2	27.4	7.9	3.9	21.7	17.8	17.5	6.0	68.8	11,200	61,842	70,958
Fish and Fish Products	39.1	3.8	5.1	4.6	65.5	8.1	30.3	7.7	893	10,303	13,737
Petroleum Oils	1.2	4.7	1.9	3.7	2.3	11.5	3.0	32.5	6,508	31,322	42,935
Wood, Pulp, Paper and Furniture	21.1	1.1	5.3	2.0	29.5	9.2	8.1	18.3	6,072	41,461	83,381
Textiles and Clothing	58.2	10.9	3.9	12.4	48.7	21.4	8.7	24.8	8,972	55,705	64,699
Leather, Rubber, Footwear	43.5	7.3	3.3	8.2	43.1	16.8	6.9	22.1	2,933	21,645	26,022
Metals	36.0	3.2	4.3	4.3	30.4	11.9	10.3	18.7	17,844	70,809	101,334
Chemical & Photographic Suppl.	36.4	4.8	5.0	7.2	35.2	12.4	9.7	20.4	26,994	101,278	126,252
Transport Equipment	16.5	6.5	3.3	7.1	16.7	20.9	11.0	26.6	12,379	113,164	171,104
Non-Electric Machinery	50.1	3.6	3.4	5.2	40.4	13.6	6.5	20.8	36,184	170,852	212,465
Electric Machinery	45.3	5.0	3.8	6.0	43.2	14.6	7.8	17.4	23,323	110,998	130,633
Mineral Prod.,Prec. Stones & Metal	22.5	1.9	2.8	3.0	15.8	8.1	8.5	16.7	9,975	58,161	75,525
Manufactured Articles nes.	46.7	3.0	3.8	4.0	44.2	13.2	7.5	18.5	13,584	100,493	116,312
Industrial Goods (line 5-14)	**37.4**	**4.4**	**3.9**	**5.7**	**35.8**	**13.9**	**8.2**	**20.2**	**158,261**	**844,564**	**1,107,730**
All Merch. Trade (line 2-14)	**35.6**	**4.5**	**3.9**	**6.5**	**33.4**	**14.0**	**8.3**	**24.4**	**176,861**	**948,031**	**1,235,360**

Notes: 1. Value of exports from reporter countries that do not participate in Free Trade Agreements with High Inc. Econ

2. Weighted average tariff reduction measured by dT / (1 + T) in percent.

LATIN AMERICA Extent of other countries' MFN tariff reductions on LATIN AMERICA's exports

Summary product category	Average levels and changes weighted by value of exports to: the World exc. FTA[1]				LMIEs exc. FTA[1]				Value of exports in $ million		
	% of exports affected	Post-UR applied rate	Tariff reduc-tion[2]	Post-UR bound rate	% of exports affected	Post-UR applied rate	Tariff reduc-tion[2]	Post-UR bound rate	To IDB LMIEs exc. FTA[1]	To all IDB Ctrys exc. FTA[1]	To all IDB Ctrys inc. FTA
Agriculture, exc. Fish: Estimate 1	4.3	10.4	16.0	16.7	5.9	4.4	24.1	46.6	2,187	19,462	21,684
Agriculture, exc. Fish: Estimate 2	28.4	5.2	4.4	9.7	8.9	14.8	4.0	38.9	2,543	24,441	28,034
Fish and Fish Products	27.9	3.5	3.4	5.3	3.0	15.4	13.3	34.9	56	2,454	2,918
Petroleum Oils	0.3	1.6	1.6	5.3	0.0	10.0	4.7	36.1	1,518	14,914	19,114
Wood, Pulp, Paper and Furniture	20.8	1.5	5.1	4.2	7.7	7.1	6.4	23.8	490	2,683	4,001
Textiles and Clothing	66.3	12.5	2.2	14.5	18.3	16.5	4.8	30.5	354	4,447	5,511
Leather, Rubber, Footwear	29.1	6.8	2.6	10.2	20.2	12.4	6.6	29.6	237	3,144	3,742
Metals	25.1	1.9	3.5	5.0	10.1	7.3	9.4	24.2	3,326	15,423	16,996
Chemical & Photographic Suppl.	30.7	5.0	4.4	10.6	6.6	11.0	8.6	25.3	1,420	4,327	5,592
Transport Equipment	13.8	5.7	1.5	6.2	6.5	14.8	2.4	29.6	339	2,112	5,413
Non-Electric Machinery	30.6	2.5	2.6	5.3	5.6	12.5	7.0	30.3	441	2,444	5,187
Electric Machinery	10.4	3.9	2.4	4.8	5.4	16.1	7.9	32.9	270	1,262	8,056
Mineral Prod.,Prec. Stones & Metal	13.8	1.7	2.4	5.3	3.1	8.1	9.3	32.2	742	4,541	6,044
Manufactured Articles nes.	14.6	2.3	4.0	8.4	6.1	7.7	2.4	34.9	631	2,475	4,071
Industrial Goods (line 5-14)	**25.0**	**3.8**	**3.0**	**6.9**	**8.6**	**9.4**	**7.5**	**27.6**	**8,250**	**42,860**	**64,613**
All Merch. Trade (line 2-14)	**21.8**	**3.8**	**3.5**	**7.4**	**7.8**	**10.6**	**6.6**	**31.2**	**12,367**	**84,668**	**114,679**

Notes: 1. Value of exports from reporter countries that do not participate in Free Trade Agreements with Latin America

2. Weighted average tariff reduction measured by dT / (1 + T) in percent.

MIDDLE EAST Extent of other countries' MFN tariff reductions on MIDDLE EAST's exports

Summary product category	Average levels and changes weighted by value of exports to: the World exc. FTA[1]				LMIEs exc. FTA[1]				Value of exports in $ million		
	% of exports affected	Post-UR applied rate	Tariff reduc-tion[2]	Post-UR bound rate	% of exports affected	Post-UR applied rate	Tariff reduc-tion[2]	Post-UR bound rate	To IDB LMIEs exc. FTA[1]	To all IDB Ctrys exc. FTA[1]	To all IDB Ctrys inc. FTA
Agriculture, exc. Fish: Estimate 1	6.2	11.3	91.8	35.3	15.8	9.1	105.5	80.4	146	439	439
Agriculture, exc. Fish: Estimate 2	45.5	9.7	1.7	27.7	15.1	25.4	4.1	78.5	193	626	626
Fish and Fish Products	50.5	7.0	6.6	8.8	59.9	5.9	38.8	20.2	1	70	70
Petroleum Oils	0.4	1.6	1.3	3.8	0.0	7.5	4.7	30.5	9,760	44,092	44,092
Wood, Pulp, Paper and Furniture	26.1	5.0	6.7	15.3	6.8	9.3	12.3	35.8	13	25	25
Textiles and Clothing	35.9	6.0	2.4	6.0	26.4	28.5	7.7	25.3	16	526	526
Leather, Rubber, Footwear	50.6	25.7	2.7	10.0	20.1	49.0	6.6	20.9	14	30	30
Metals	38.4	4.7	3.3	4.3	43.6	14.0	7.3	12.8	149	570	570
Chemical & Photographic Suppl.	66.4	6.6	5.6	8.3	45.1	11.4	9.6	16.7	665	1,860	1,860
Transport Equipment	3.9	0.6	1.5	0.5	0.3	0.8	5.9	0.6	162	343	343
Non-Electric Machinery	55.8	1.8	3.3	1.9	28.6	9.6	11.1	9.7	10	99	99
Electric Machinery	75.3	4.7	2.6	5.7	9.8	17.8	5.1	26.1	3	25	25
Mineral Prod.,Prec. Stones & Metal	52.0	3.3	4.0	3.3	1.6	10.2	4.9	13.7	659	2,117	2,117
Manufactured Articles nes.	19.0	4.0	9.3	4.7	69.8	23.7	13.6	27.4	44	277	277
Industrial Goods (line 5-14)	**49.5**	**4.7**	**4.6**	**5.1**	**24.1**	**10.9**	**9.4**	**13.9**	**1,736**	**5,871**	**5,871**
All Merch. Trade (line 2-14)	**6.7**	**2.2**	**4.2**	**4.8**	**3.9**	**9.1**	**9.0**	**26.9**	**11,689**	**50,658**	**50,658**

Notes: 1. Value of exports from reporter countries that do not participate in Free Trade Agreements with MIDDLE EAST

2. Weighted average tariff reduction measured by dT / (1 + T) in percent.

NORTH AFRICA Extent of other countries' MFN tariff reductions on NORTH AFRICA's exports

| Summary product category | *Average levels and changes weighted by value of exports to:* | | | | | | | | *Value of exports in $ million* | | |
| | *the World exc. FTA[1]* | | | | *LMIEs exc. FTA[1]* | | | | | | |
	% of exports affected	*Post-UR applied rate*	*Tariff reduction[2]*	*Post-UR bound rate*	*% of exports affected*	*Post-UR applied rate*	*Tariff reduction[2]*	*Post-UR bound rate*	*To IDB LMIEs exc. FTA[1]*	*To all IDB Ctrys exc. FTA[1]*	*To all IDB Ctrys inc. FTA*
Agriculture, exc. Fish: Estimate 1	0.1	0.6	7.8	4.1	0.0	-1.1	1.2	26.4	65	597	597
Agriculture, exc. Fish: Estimate 2	38.6	8.3	3.7	10.7	31.2	20.6	2.3	52.0	42	984	984
Fish and Fish Products	66.4	9.4	3.7	9.9	0.1	10.6	28.6	34.1	11	527	527
Petroleum Oils	3.0	0.8	1.2	1.9	0.0	5.2	..	21.9	1,486	13,843	13,843
Wood, Pulp, Paper and Furniture	27.8	3.8	4.5	4.1	21.2	16.5	5.3	19.2	22	109	109
Textiles and Clothing	87.8	10.8	1.8	10.9	18.5	23.7	4.9	27.5	74	1,788	1,788
Leather, Rubber, Footwear	65.8	7.5	2.1	6.5	13.0	27.5	1.1	16.9	12	152	152
Metals	34.4	4.2	3.4	4.7	11.3	14.1	9.3	24.1	72	584	584
Chemical & Photographic Suppl.	59.0	10.4	9.9	13.6	53.8	19.4	16.4	27.6	329	756	756
Transport Equipment	34.0	7.7	2.6	8.4	0.4	28.9	16.7	33.2	20	104	104
Non-Electric Machinery	64.1	4.1	3.0	5.8	3.1	18.4	3.8	29.8	13	78	78
Electric Machinery	76.3	4.8	3.6	6.8	0.4	15.5	10.7	30.9	15	187	187
Mineral Prod.,Prec. Stones & Metal	19.0	1.0	1.2	2.6	5.6	3.6	1.5	23.2	342	2,980	2,980
Manufactured Articles nes.	14.7	0.7	3.5	1.0	13.0	2.6	4.3	4.7	57	400	400
Industrial Goods (line 5-14)	**44.8**	**5.1**	**3.1**	**6.3**	**24.3**	**13.3**	**13.6**	**24.3**	**955**	**7,136**	**7,136**
All Merch. Trade (line 2-14)	**19.3**	**2.7**	**3.0**	**3.9**	**9.8**	**9.6**	**13.0**	**24.2**	**2,494**	**22,490**	**22,490**

Notes: 1. Value of exports from reporter countries that do not participate in Free Trade Agreements with NORTH AFRICA

2. Weighted average tariff reduction measured by dT / (1 + T) in percent.

REST OF EUROPE Extent of other countries' MFN tariff reductions on REST of EUROPE's exports

| Summary product category | *Average levels and changes weighted by value of exports to:* | | | | | | | | *Value of exports in $ million* | | |
| | *the World exc. FTA[1]* | | | | *LMIEs exc. FTA[1]* | | | | | | |
	% of exports affected	*Post-UR applied rate*	*Tariff reduction[2]*	*Post-UR bound rate*	*% of exports affected*	*Post-UR applied rate*	*Tariff reduction[2]*	*Post-UR bound rate*	*To IDB LMIEs exc. FTA[1]*	*To all IDB Ctrys exc. FTA[1]*	*To all IDB Ctrys inc. FTA*
Agriculture, exc. Fish: Estimate 1	2.0	2.8	84.4	10.0	7.3	2.2	105.3	26.1	239	1,141	1,141
Agriculture, exc. Fish: Estimate 2	64.8	7.5	2.5	14.8	21.4	16.9	2.3	51.1	408	2,101	2,101
Fish and Fish Products	43.0	6.8	2.5	7.1	23.3	9.9	14.9	13.4	3	136	136
Petroleum Oils	1.0	2.1	1.2	3.3	0.0	16.2	..	32.4	86	904	904
Wood, Pulp, Paper and Furniture	57.2	2.4	3.0	3.5	45.8	9.2	5.0	14.9	59	328	328
Textiles and Clothing	94.6	11.3	2.9	11.5	37.1	16.2	4.6	19.5	89	4,314	4,314
Leather, Rubber, Footwear	86.4	5.6	3.0	5.7	27.3	18.1	5.4	17.2	18	891	891
Metals	61.7	3.1	3.9	3.9	21.6	15.7	10.1	24.5	129	924	924
Chemical & Photographic Suppl.	53.5	5.8	5.3	6.3	44.4	13.3	9.1	16.9	109	404	404
Transport Equipment	50.9	7.6	2.3	6.9	5.4	19.5	6.5	30.9	22	93	93
Non-Electric Machinery	84.3	3.6	2.4	4.1	17.9	17.7	3.5	24.4	26	237	237
Electric Machinery	49.4	5.7	3.8	7.3	11.6	17.3	13.1	30.1	33	420	420
Mineral Prod.,Prec. Stones & Metal	44.0	3.2	2.1	3.7	22.8	10.9	6.7	21.1	58	794	794
Manufactured Articles nes.	19.5	1.7	3.8	3.9	19.6	5.2	5.8	13.4	148	669	669
Industrial Goods (line 5-14)	**74.5**	**7.5**	**3.1**	**8.0**	**28.0**	**12.5**	**7.1**	**19.0**	**689**	**9,074**	**9,074**
All Merch. Trade (line 2-14)	**67.1**	**7.1**	**3.0**	**8.9**	**23.7**	**14.2**	**5.6**	**32.0**	**1,187**	**12,215**	**12,215**

Notes: 1. Value of exports from reporter countries that do not participate in Free Trade Agreements with REST OF EUROPE

2. Weighted average tariff reduction measured by dT / (1 + T) in percent.

SUB-SAHARAN AFRICA Extent of other countries' MFN tariff reductions on SUB-SHRN. AFRICA's exports

Summary product category	Average levels and changes weighted by value of exports to: the World exc. FTA[1]				LMIEs exc. FTA[1]				Value of exports in $ million		
	% of exports affected	Post-UR applied rate	Tariff reduc-tion[2]	Post-UR bound rate	% of exports affected	Post-UR applied rate	Tariff reduc-tion[2]	Post-UR bound rate	To IDB LMIEs exc. FTA[1]	To all IDB Ctrys exc. FTA[1]	To all IDB Ctrys inc. FTA
Agriculture, exc. Fish: Estimate 1	3.3	16.1	15.6	19.7	2.9	4.3	51.2	53.5	513	7,285	7,285
Agriculture, exc. Fish: Estimate 2	54.7	5.2	4.2	10.6	19.4	11.7	4.3	77.7	376	7,868	7,868
Fish and Fish Products	54.7	9.0	5.3	11.6	89.1	4.9	41.5	5.5	35	1,274	1,274
Petroleum Oils	0.0	0.8	1.5	0.8	0.0	13.4	6.0	18.5	642	13,251	13,251
Wood, Pulp, Paper and Furniture	20.5	1.5	4.3	1.7	17.5	10.0	7.0	17.0	197	1,810	1,810
Textiles and Clothing	68.1	8.4	1.9	8.8	33.4	20.0	8.7	22.5	46	1,233	1,233
Leather, Rubber, Footwear	27.7	1.6	1.2	2.7	7.8	11.3	8.8	22.7	31	587	587
Metals	22.9	1.8	2.5	2.5	3.5	7.4	9.1	23.5	852	7,245	7,245
Chemical & Photographic Suppl.	15.0	3.2	4.0	4.4	5.0	10.7	16.2	31.6	248	1,128	1,128
Transport Equipment	5.8	0.7	2.6	0.7	3.1	12.2	5.9	24.2	9	457	457
Non-Electric Machinery	67.0	2.0	3.4	2.5	11.3	4.3	10.8	15.0	31	201	201
Electric Machinery	60.6	4.2	3.0	5.1	4.2	9.3	5.3	17.3	15	70	70
Mineral Prod.,Prec. Stones & Metal	4.9	0.3	1.1	0.2	2.3	16.2	9.8	18.2	319	16,745	16,745
Manufactured Articles nes.	10.1	1.0	2.9	2.5	30.6	6.0	1.5	18.6	334	2,048	2,048
Industrial Goods (line 5-14)	**14.1**	**1.3**	**2.3**	**1.5**	**10.0**	**9.7**	**5.4**	**21.4**	**2,082**	**31,524**	**31,524**
All Merch. Trade (line 2-14)	**17.5**	**1.8**	**3.4**	**3.2**	**10.0**	**10.5**	**8.7**	**33.9**	**3,135**	**53,916**	**53,916**

Notes: 1. Value of exports from reporter countries that do not participate in Free Trade Agreements with S. Saharn. Africa

2. Weighted average tariff reduction measured by dT / (1 + T) in percent.

SOUTH ASIA Extent of other countries' MFN tariff reductions on SOUTH ASIA's exports

Summary product category	Average levels and changes weighted by value of exports to: the World exc. FTA[1]				LMIEs exc. FTA[1]				Value of exports in $ million		
	% of exports affected	Post-UR applied rate	Tariff reduc-tion[2]	Post-UR bound rate	% of exports affected	Post-UR applied rate	Tariff reduc-tion[2]	Post-UR bound rate	To IDB LMIEs exc. FTA[1]	To all IDB Ctrys exc. FTA[1]	To all IDB Ctrys inc. FTA
Agriculture, exc. Fish: Estimate 1	7.6	4.9	11.7	16.4	16.7	8.3	10.6	43.6	601	1,846	1,846
Agriculture, exc. Fish: Estimate 2	24.6	5.3	5.1	11.5	19.9	16.0	4.2	37.1	484	1,833	1,833
Fish and Fish Products	63.4	3.1	4.8	5.4	40.2	2.8	41.3	29.1	74	864	864
Petroleum Oils	1.2	0.7	1.2	0.7	0.0	3.9	..	5.0	15	466	466
Wood, Pulp, Paper and Furniture	47.8	6.4	4.6	4.5	21.2	21.9	4.0	17.0	26	80	80
Textiles and Clothing	76.6	10.3	2.4	10.8	60.9	22.3	7.7	17.2	402	6,777	6,777
Leather, Rubber, Footwear	64.4	5.2	1.9	6.0	46.0	11.9	7.2	18.4	97	1,608	1,608
Metals	27.4	1.7	3.1	2.6	3.1	5.0	7.5	11.4	189	1,180	1,180
Chemical & Photographic Suppl.	49.0	5.4	4.8	8.6	20.9	10.2	7.4	19.4	151	508	508
Transport Equipment	21.8	10.5	2.6	10.2	2.2	14.6	5.9	25.7	93	144	144
Non-Electric Machinery	49.6	3.8	3.9	6.0	29.6	11.0	11.9	19.7	62	238	238
Electric Machinery	49.9	7.2	3.1	8.6	29.2	16.4	4.6	20.1	26	81	81
Mineral Prod.,Prec. Stones & Metal	8.4	0.5	6.0	0.5	62.1	4.8	12.3	3.9	184	3,641	3,641
Manufactured Articles nes.	26.1	1.5	3.5	5.0	31.4	3.6	1.0	17.7	254	1,040	1,040
Industrial Goods (line 5-14)	**49.7**	**5.8**	**2.7**	**6.8**	**37.4**	**11.7**	**7.6**	**15.3**	**1,484**	**15,297**	**15,297**
All Merch. Trade (line 2-14)	**46.6**	**5.6**	**2.9**	**7.1**	**33.1**	**12.2**	**8.6**	**21.8**	**2,057**	**18,460**	**18,460**

Notes: 1. Value of exports from reporter countries that do not participate in Free Trade Agreements with SOUTH ASIA

2. Weighted average tariff reduction measured by dT / (1 + T) in percent.

ALL LMIES Extent of other countries' MFN tariff reductions on ALL LMIES' exports

Summary product category	Average levels and changes weighted by value of exports to: the World exc. FTA[1]				LMIEs exc. FTA[1]				Value of exports in $ million		
	% of exports affected	Post-UR applied rate	Tariff reduc-tion[2]	Post-UR bound rate	% of exports affected	Post-UR applied rate	Tariff reduc-tion[2]	Post-UR bound rate	To IDB LMIEs exc. FTA[1]	To all IDB Ctrys exc. FTA[1]	To all IDB Ctrys inc. FTA
Agriculture, exc. Fish: Estimate 1	7.7	13.3	17.1	20.0	16.5	15.1	18.1	52.8	6,813	43,802	46,024
Agriculture, exc. Fish: Estimate 2	36.5	7.1	4.8	14.6	14.8	20.7	3.8	60.9	7,742	59,909	63,501
Fish and Fish Products	49.1	5.0	3.8	5.9	34.0	8.9	38.6	21.5	476	12,855	13,320
Petroleum Oils	0.8	1.5	1.3	2.8	0.2	7.3	1.7	20.3	17,648	112,777	116,977
Wood, Pulp, Paper and Furniture	31.7	2.0	4.6	2.9	20.0	8.4	6.4	14.2	2,624	20,428	21,746
Textiles and Clothing	59.4	8.8	2.7	12.3	46.2	21.1	8.4	23.0	3,146	68,166	69,230
Leather, Rubber, Footwear	33.0	5.6	2.9	7.2	43.0	11.3	7.4	18.0	1,459	26,794	27,393
Metals	33.4	2.3	3.4	3.7	14.0	9.0	6.5	19.0	8,967	47,995	49,567
Chemical & Photographic Suppl.	37.6	4.8	4.7	8.3	25.4	12.7	9.2	22.1	5,022	20,586	21,851
Transport Equipment	20.1	5.6	2.2	5.9	18.5	12.5	2.4	20.0	1,659	9,067	12,368
Non-Electric Machinery	45.6	2.9	3.1	4.8	43.8	11.6	4.7	18.8	3,151	16,078	18,820
Electric Machinery	26.9	2.7	3.4	4.7	36.9	14.4	6.0	19.4	2,335	31,484	38,278
Mineral Prod.,Prec. Stones & Metal	15.6	1.4	2.6	2.3	7.8	7.7	7.4	16.4	6,082	51,327	52,830
Manufactured Articles nes.	34.8	1.9	4.2	4.3	22.3	7.7	3.9	22.1	3,183	31,801	33,398
Industrial Goods (line 5-14)	35.6	4.0	3.3	5.8	23.8	10.9	6.6	19.3	37,629	323,726	345,480
All Merch. Trade (line 2-14)	28.5	3.9	3.5	6.6	16.5	11.6	6.8	27.3	63,496	509,266	539,277

Notes: 1. Value of exports from reporter countries that do not participate in Free Trade Agreements with ALL LMIES

2. Weighted average tariff reduction measured by dT / (1 + T) in percent.

WORLD Extent of other countries' MFN tariff reductions on WORLD's exports

Summary product category	Average levels and changes weighted by value of exports to: the World exc. FTA[1]				LMIEs exc. FTA[1]				Value of exports in $ million		
	% of exports affected	Post-UR applied rate	Tariff reduc-tion[2]	Post-UR bound rate	% of exports affected	Post-UR applied rate	Tariff reduc-tion[2]	Post-UR bound rate	To IDB LMIEs exc. FTA[1]	To all IDB Ctrys exc. FTA[1]	To all IDB Ctrys inc. FTA
Agriculture, exc. Fish: Estimate 1	13.3	25.0	32.8	32.5	20.2	16.8	44.6	51.6	15,303	77,862	84,714
Agriculture, exc. Fish: Estimate 2	31.7	7.5	4.4	18.3	16.6	18.8	5.3	65.7	18,943	121,751	134,459
Fish and Fish Products	44.0	4.4	4.4	5.2	53.6	8.4	32.3	12.7	1,368	23,158	27,057
Petroleum Oils	0.9	2.2	1.5	3.0	0.8	8.5	2.8	22.9	24,156	144,099	159,912
Wood, Pulp, Paper and Furniture	23.3	1.3	5.1	2.2	26.7	9.0	7.8	17.1	8,696	61,889	105,127
Textiles and Clothing	58.8	9.8	3.3	12.3	48.1	21.3	8.6	24.3	12,118	123,870	133,929
Leather, Rubber, Footwear	38.1	6.4	3.1	7.7	43.1	14.9	7.1	20.7	4,393	48,439	53,415
Metals	35.2	2.9	4.0	4.1	25.0	10.9	9.6	18.8	26,810	118,804	150,901
Chemical & Photographic Suppl.	36.6	4.8	5.0	7.3	33.6	12.4	9.7	20.7	32,016	121,864	148,103
Transport Equipment	16.7	6.4	3.2	7.0	16.9	19.9	9.8	25.9	14,038	122,231	183,472
Non-Electric Machinery	49.7	3.6	3.4	5.1	40.7	13.4	6.4	20.6	39,336	186,930	231,286
Electric Machinery	41.1	4.5	3.8	5.7	42.6	14.6	7.7	17.6	25,658	142,482	168,911
Mineral Prod.,Prec. Stones & Metal	19.6	1.7	2.7	2.7	12.8	8.0	8.2	16.6	16,058	109,488	128,355
Manufactured Articles nes.	44.0	2.8	3.9	4.1	39.9	12.1	7.1	19.2	16,767	132,295	149,710
Industrial Goods (line 5-14)	37.0	4.3	3.7	5.7	33.4	13.3	8.0	20.0	195,890	1,168,290	1,453,210
All Merch. Trade (line 2-14)	33.4	4.4	3.8	6.5	28.9	13.4	8.1	25.1	240,357	1,457,300	1,774,640

Notes: 1. Value of exports from reporter countries that do not participate in Free Trade Agreements with WORLD

2. Weighted average tariff reduction measured by dT / (1 + T) in percent.

7

Tables R.3

Concessions Received

Product Category by Exporting Economy or Group

Agriculture, exc. Fish: Estimate 1[3] Extent of other countries' MFN tariff reductions on exports from:

| Export market | % of exports GATT bount | | Average levels and changes weighted by value of exports to: | | | | | | | | Value of exports in $ million | | |
| | Total pre-UR | Total post-UR | the World exc. FTA[1] | | | | LMIEs exc. FTA[1] | | | | To IDB LMIEs exc. FTA[1] | To all IDB Ctrys exc. FTA[1] | To all IDB Ctrys inc. FTA |
			% of exports affected	Post-UR applied rate	Tariff reduction[2]	Post-UR bound rate	% of exports affected	Post-UR applied rate	Tariff reduction[2]	Post-UR bound rate			
UNITED STATES	67.3	100.0	23.0	37.6	12.762	43.3	27.5	15.8	24.568	40.6	3,973.5	16,685.0	19,854.7
BRAZIL	85.8	100.0	3.3	5.1	0.300	11.5	5.9	4.6	0.534	54.9	771.1	6,898.4	6,996.9
EUROPEAN UNION	47.6	100.0	9.6	33.6	5.040	55.9	9.9	12.8	7.803	66.6	2,522.1	6,872.5	6,872.5
AUSTRALIA	45.5	100.0	30.9	45.8	8.491	48.1	46.3	43.2	17.491	54.1	868.2	3,708.8	3,778.8
ARGENTINA	75.5	100.0	14.4	22.9	3.543	34.4	8.0	4.8	5.224	50.4	611.3	3,062.5	3,409.1
CHINA	54.0	100.0	21.4	19.6	4.156	23.1	50.5	32.6	4.018	48.2	752.0	3,385.6	3,385.6
CANADA	69.9	100.0	15.8	41.2	10.844	40.9	17.0	1.9	16.899	53.8	340.2	1,963.2	3,301.5
NEW ZEALAND	68.8	100.0	21.3	51.9	1.929	56.2	6.2	47.7	1.876	76.3	392.3	2,318.1	2,360.5
COLOMBIA	89.5	100.0	0.1	4.9	0.006	7.8	0.7	1.2	0.045	30.7	204.6	2,296.4	2,296.4
THAILAND	46.5	99.8	19.2	24.0	4.026	30.8	33.6	44.0	11.878	73.6	577.0	2,269.2	2,269.2
MALAYSIA	35.4	100.0	34.8	14.2	4.367	33.8	27.6	28.3	2.062	77.4	737.9	1,852.5	1,852.5
MEXICO	63.1	100.0	0.5	3.0	0.246	6.4	0.0	15.8	0.007	29.5	90.9	395.5	1,716.8
COTE D'IVOIRE	93.5	100.0	0.1	0.9	0.019	2.6	0.0	-0.4	..	21.5	109.0	1,470.4	1,470.4
INDONESIA	80.5	100.0	6.1	5.2	0.314	8.1	39.0	28.2	1.441	46.7	184.9	1,214.0	1,214.0
PHILIPPINES	49.3	100.0	3.7	11.9	0.464	13.0	56.6	34.6	3.227	60.7	47.9	1,155.9	1,155.9
INDIA	64.6	100.0	14.1	9.6	1.637	22.5	32.4	16.7	3.464	55.5	306.2	928.0	928.0
COSTA RICA	91.5	100.0	0.3	1.9	0.024	4.1	5.5	0.9	0.394	16.1	48.5	918.4	918.4
TURKEY	54.2	100.0	1.1	1.9	1.182	8.1	8.0	5.3	8.515	35.6	122.5	899.5	899.5
PARAGUAY	57.3	100.0	0.5	1.4	0.076	15.8	0.0	-7.7	..	32.9	49.8	517.4	830.5
ECUADOR	90.3	100.0	0.6	0.9	0.177	3.6	6.8	1.1	2.225	31.9	62.1	821.9	821.9
TAIWAN (CHINA)	11.7	100.0	3.1	32.2	0.310	32.8	16.9	8.3	0.945	21.3	41.6	784.6	784.6
PAKISTAN	52.3	100.0	0.8	0.0	0.102	10.8	0.2	-1.1	0.002	28.5	260.7	711.5	711.5
SWITZERLAND	85.6	100.0	2.2	74.7	1.543	86.2	5.9	-1.8	5.645	49.3	133.2	621.4	621.4
SOUTH AFRICA	54.1	100.0	20.5	30.3	3.309	59.5	0.0	12.1	..	157.2	117.9	602.1	602.1
HONDURAS	95.3	100.0	0.5	2.6	0.031	3.6	11.4	8.7	0.648	20.3	26.7	561.2	561.2
HUNGARY	48.7	100.0	5.5	27.9	2.405	38.8	2.9	-6.9	0.050	44.4	98.5	540.7	540.7
KENYA	91.3	100.0	0.8	0.8	0.238	1.1	0.0	-0.6	..	10.8	9.6	529.4	529.4
FORMER USSR	76.8	100.0	0.1	0.9	0.026	15.7	0.0	0.1	0.001	36.1	200.0	485.9	485.9
CAMEROON	96.6	100.0	0.3	-0.1	0.038	0.3	0.0	-3.2	..	7.2	14.9	485.7	485.7
POLAND	67.1	100.0	4.2	25.3	0.695	35.9	11.9	9.2	2.081	63.0	81.0	442.0	442.0
AUSTRIA	66.1	100.0	35.1	61.2	2.376	72.8	7.4	0.9	1.470	43.5	119.8	438.8	438.8
PANAMA	99.2	100.0	0.6	0.5	0.136	3.4	22.3	19.8	5.015	33.8	10.8	399.5	399.5
ZIMBABWE	82.3	100.0	11.7	21.7	2.240	22.6	21.9	3.5	23.340	15.9	28.0	397.9	397.9
NIGERIA	96.2	100.0	0.5	0.2	0.073	2.0	0.0	4.7	..	48.6	14.7	382.7	382.7
FORMER YUGOSLAVIA	61.4	100.0	25.9	33.9	1.697	62.0	0.0	11.0	0.001	96.0	121.4	375.9	375.9
EL SALVADOR	95.9	100.0	1.3	5.3	0.148	5.8	0.0	3.4	..	53.8	1.4	371.2	371.2
SUDAN	58.2	100.0	0.1	7.6	0.037	9.1	0.0	0.9	..	5.7	101.5	323.4	323.4
EGYPT, ARAB REP.	79.2	100.0	0.1	0.2	0.009	5.8	0.0	-1.3	..	26.5	62.4	315.5	315.5
GHANA	95.5	100.0	1.1	0.5	0.160	0.8	0.0	0.0	..	7.9	11.3	313.2	313.2
PAPUA NEW GUINEA	78.9	100.0	1.1	4.5	0.111	5.0	6.4	3.2	0.086	8.7	17.5	312.2	312.2
DOMINICAN REPUBLIC	61.4	100.0	1.0	46.3	0.115	46.9	0.1	2.1	0.019	73.2	2.5	305.4	305.4
CHILE	85.5	100.0	1.6	2.4	0.201	10.4	0.3	0.1	0.074	46.5	48.7	304.7	304.7
MAURITIUS	6.4	100.0	2.1	140.2	0.244	140.2	0.0	2.0	..	150.0	.0	304.4	304.4
URUGUAY	31.6	100.0	18.0	51.3	3.248	52.5	0.1	-4.4	0.118	44.0	21.5	148.4	290.9
UGANDA	99.6	100.0	0.0	0.0	..	0.2	0.0	0.0	..	16.8	3.7	280.8	280.8

Notes: 1. Value of exports from reporter countries that do not participate in Free Trade Agreements.

2. Weighted average tariff reduction measured by dT / (1 + T) in percent.

3. Estimate based on Merlinda Ingco's tarrif equivalents of non tariff barriers.

Agriculture, exc. Fish: Estimate 1[3] (continued)

| Export market | % of exports GATT bound | | Average levels and changes weighted by value of exports to: | | | | | | | | Value of exports in $ million | | |
| | | | the World exc. FTA[1] | | | | LMIEs exc. FTA[1] | | | | | | |
	Total pre-UR	Total post-UR	% of exports affected	Post-UR applied rate	Tariff reduc-tion[2]	Post-UR bound rate	% of exports affected	Post-UR applied rate	Tariff reduc-tion[2]	Post-UR bound rate	To IDB LMIEs exc. FTA[1]	To all IDB Ctrys exc. FTA[1]	To all IDB Ctrys inc. FTA
CUBA	36.3	100.0	41.1	49.5	2.752	60.8	37.9	27.2	3.854	61.6	87.6	266.4	266.4
KOREA, REPUBLIC OF	45.0	100.0	1.7	11.4	0.199	20.6	3.1	25.1	0.359	76.9	47.3	264.9	264.9
ISRAEL	64.2	100.0	0.6	7.6	0.090	16.1	3.4	0.3	0.526	59.1	27.6	241.8	251.4
ETHIOPIA	98.5	100.0	0.1	0.0	0.013	0.1	0.5	-0.4	0.079	6.8	1.0	236.0	236.0
PERU	76.7	100.0	3.1	9.5	1.032	22.2	10.0	0.8	3.223	51.5	57.1	229.8	229.8
TANZANIA	80.8	100.0	5.1	5.7	0.461	13.4	14.7	8.9	0.182	64.4	30.2	220.2	220.2
MALAWI	67.8	100.0	0.0	14.1	0.005	15.1	0.1	-0.3	0.002	98.3	2.2	209.7	209.7
IRAN, ISLAMIC REP.	6.7	100.0	0.5	0.1	0.080	1.6	0.1	0.1	0.001	60.4	3.1	199.6	199.6
NICARAGUA	95.3	100.0	0.1	2.0	0.035	5.0	0.6	2.0	0.113	14.3	9.1	192.6	192.6
ZAIRE	96.5	100.0	0.1	0.0	0.001	0.3	4.0	1.9	0.049	15.5	2.6	183.5	183.5
SWEDEN	65.6	100.0	7.1	33.3	1.395	36.0	7.6	28.5	7.350	52.6	16.9	166.0	166.0
SENEGAL	93.0	100.0	0.0	0.0	0.000	0.9	0.0	-1.4	0.007	18.1	7.0	153.8	153.8
SRI LANKA	82.4	100.0	2.6	0.5	0.369	2.0	6.0	4.2	0.676	29.2	8.2	153.8	153.8
MARTINIQUE	99.1	100.0	0.0	0.1	0.002	0.1	..	..	..	..	.0	146.3	146.3
CZECH & SLOVAK CU	52.4	100.0	24.8	67.3	4.402	78.7	0.1	35.2	0.005	64.3	35.3	146.1	146.1
FIJI	6.9	100.0	18.6	128.0	0.941	128.0	100.0	82.0	5.348	82.0	16.9	139.6	139.6
SAUDI ARABIA	26.8	100.0	18.2	30.7	17.732	78.7	28.5	9.0	30.014	91.2	81.0	138.9	138.9
JAMAICA	41.0	100.0	0.0	85.9	..	86.1	0.0	-0.4	..	50.4	.5	137.9	137.9
MOROCCO	21.8	100.0	0.0	1.5	0.001	3.1	0.1	4.8	0.001	6.8	.9	137.6	137.6
GUADELOUPE	71.0	100.0	0.0	43.0	..	43.0	0.0	0.0	..	0.0	.0	134.1	134.1
VIETNAM	16.1	100.0	20.1	19.3	3.617	36.1	28.2	27.1	4.933	50.8	92.6	131.3	131.3
SWAZILAND	25.2	100.0	5.0	110.2	0.885	110.2	99.9	70.6	21.966	70.6	4.0	130.5	130.5
TUNISIA	5.0	100.0	0.0	0.2	0.000	0.6	0.0	-0.2	..	40.9	.9	130.0	130.0
SINGAPORE	41.3	100.0	26.6	19.1	1.407	27.2	58.0	38.6	3.058	56.0	58.6	129.0	129.0
RWANDA	98.6	100.0	0.0	0.0	0.001	0.0	..	..	..	..	.0	121.8	121.8
JAPAN	38.4	100.0	14.0	6.6	1.937	11.7	10.9	25.5	2.133	54.5	21.5	121.8	121.8
NORWAY	46.7	100.0	3.7	90.9	0.597	92.6	0.6	12.2	0.097	57.6	3.5	120.4	120.4
FINLAND	64.9	100.0	4.0	77.0	0.176	82.7	0.0	10.8	..	56.5	12.8	118.2	118.2
ROMANIA	36.8	100.0	3.0	36.1	0.454	47.2	0.5	3.7	0.014	60.8	13.6	115.8	115.8
MADAGASCAR	87.4	100.0	0.2	14.2	0.024	15.8	0.0	0.0	..	48.5	2.7	107.3	107.3
BURUNDI	99.7	100.0	0.0	0.0	0.000	0.2	0.0	1.7	..	15.1	.9	104.0	104.0
BULGARIA	73.3	100.0	5.4	22.1	0.578	32.2	0.0	-0.9	..	60.7	8.7	88.5	88.5
GUYANA	0.3	100.0	0.1	132.5	0.011	133.0	0.0	36.4	..	94.2	.9	83.1	83.1
TOGO	94.4	100.0	0.0	-0.1	0.000	2.1	0.0	-1.2	..	31.8	5.2	81.2	81.2
MALI	73.6	100.0	1.1	0.0	0.156	1.6	0.0	-0.3	..	5.1	19.5	67.5	67.5
BOLIVIA	47.9	100.0	1.6	-10.3	0.172	48.7	1.4	-24.6	0.094	83.8	34.1	63.5	63.5
DOMINICA	100.0	100.0	0.0	0.0	..	0.0	..	..	..	..	.0	63.2	63.2
VENEZUELA	93.0	100.0	0.6	-0.6	0.008	6.9	7.3	-6.7	0.090	77.7	5.5	63.1	63.1
SURINAME	30.5	100.0	0.0	54.7	..	54.8	0.0	2.0	..	30.0	.2	62.9	62.9
CYPRUS	10.3	100.0	2.4	6.2	0.434	14.7	31.7	29.6	5.819	134.9	4.6	62.5	62.5
HONG KONG	46.1	100.0	17.3	8.2	2.218	9.7	20.5	16.2	2.491	19.6	22.2	54.6	54.6
BELIZE	46.5	100.0	0.0	77.3	..	83.1	0.0	-1.6	..	48.6	6.4	54.6	54.6
CHAD	97.0	100.0	0.0	0.0	..	0.9	0.0	0.0	..	20.6	2.4	53.8	53.8
HAITI	99.7	100.0	0.0	0.0	..	0.1	0.0	0.0	..	40.0	.0	51.1	51.1
BURKINA FASO	78.5	100.0	0.2	0.0	0.029	0.5	0.0	0.0	..	5.6	4.4	49.2	49.2

Notes: 1. Value of exports from reporter countries that do not participate in Free Trade Agreements.

2. Weighted average tariff reduction measured by dT / (1 + T) in percent.

3. Estimate based on Merlinda Ingco's tarrif equivalents of non tariff barriers.

Agriculture, exc. Fish: Estimate 1[3] (continued)

Export market	% of exports GATT bount — Total pre-UR	Total post-UR	Average levels and changes weighted by value of exports to: the World exc. FTA[1] — % of exports affected	Post-UR applied rate	Tariff reduc-tion[2]	Post-UR bound rate	LMIEs exc. FTA[1] — % of exports affected	Post-UR applied rate	Tariff reduc-tion[2]	Post-UR bound rate	Value of exports in $ million — To IDB LMIEs exc. FTA[1]	To all IDB Ctrys exc. FTA[1]	To all IDB Ctrys inc. FTA
TRINIDAD AND TOBAGO	28.8	100.0	0.0	90.6	..	108.7	0.0	-26.6	..	81.9	7.3	43.5	43.5
SYRIA	68.1	100.0	0.0	1.8	0.001	33.9	0.0	2.9	..	62.9	21.6	40.4	40.4
CENTRAL AFRICAN REP.	97.1	100.0	0.0	0.0	..	0.1	0.0	0.0	..	8.7	.4	36.7	36.7
IRAQ	2.6	100.0	1.8	15.4	0.264	60.5	0.0	17.7	..	70.1	30.6	35.9	35.9
BANGLADESH	62.1	99.7	0.7	-0.4	0.093	8.2	0.1	-1.4	0.001	22.2	12.7	34.8	34.8
MOZAMBIQUE	60.5	100.0	12.6	27.3	1.812	31.8	0.0	24.4	..	67.2	3.4	31.9	31.9
BENIN	79.4	100.0	0.6	0.2	0.080	0.6	0.0	0.0	..	2.6	4.6	31.2	31.2
ANGOLA	100.0	100.0	0.0	0.0	..	0.3	..	..	..	..	.0	30.7	30.7
BARBADOS	6.8	100.0	0.0	139.4	0.008	139.5	0.0	0.0	..	100.0	.0	29.7	29.7
ALBANIA	63.1	100.0	0.0	6.5	..	24.0	0.0	8.8	..	20.5	21.7	29.7	29.7
BOTSWANA	74.1	100.0	95.4	60.8	8.087	61.0	0.0	0.0	..	150.0	.0	29.6	29.6
SOMALIA	99.9	100.0	0.0	0.0	..	0.1	0.0	0.0	..	43.7	.1	29.4	29.4
SIERRA LEONE	100.0	100.0	0.0	0.0	..	0.1	..	..	..	..	.0	26.5	26.5
GUINEA	93.5	100.0	0.2	1.9	0.019	2.8	0.0	-6.1	..	19.0	.7	24.3	24.3
ZAMBIA	81.6	100.0	0.0	-0.1	..	5.5	0.0	-6.5	..	128.9	.7	18.0	18.0
LIBERIA	97.8	100.0	1.4	1.3	1.050	1.4	100.0	95.0	74.598	95.0	.2	15.1	15.1
EQUATORIAL GUINEA	99.8	100.0	0.0	0.0	..	0.0	0.0	0.0	..	0.0	.0	15.1	15.1
GAMBIA, THE	59.5	100.0	0.0	39.4	..	39.4	0.0	0.0	..	30.0	.0	14.9	14.9
VANUATU	80.0	100.0	0.0	9.2	..	9.2	0.0	0.0	..	0.0	.0	13.5	13.5
ALGERIA	25.6	100.0	0.1	4.3	0.013	4.4	0.0	0.0	..	54.2	.0	13.0	13.0
GUINEA-BISSAU	23.2	100.0	0.0	0.0	..	76.6	0.0	0.0	..	99.8	9.7	12.7	12.7
GRENADA	100.0	100.0	0.0	0.0	..	0.0	..	..	..	..	.0	11.7	11.7
LEBANON	69.8	100.0	1.1	2.4	0.128	41.3	0.0	-1.6	..	130.2	3.4	11.5	11.5
NEPAL	23.3	100.0	0.3	12.0	0.043	79.4	0.2	14.7	0.002	98.9	9.2	11.5	11.5
MYANMAR	31.1	94.9	16.4	18.3	2.200	39.7	12.3	14.3	1.422	64.7	5.0	11.0	11.0
CONGO	32.1	100.0	0.0	101.9	..	101.9	..	..	..	..	.0	9.4	9.4
JORDAN	11.9	100.0	0.0	0.0	..	19.5	0.0	-0.1	..	26.8	5.6	7.9	'.9
GABON	97.7	100.0	0.0	2.9	..	4.0	0.0	0.0	..	59.0	.1	7.4	7.4
BERMUDA	12.2	100.0	0.8	0.5	0.345	94.4	0.0	..	..	106.0	6.3	7.2	7.2
AFGHANISTAN	75.2	100.0	0.0	2.8	..	56.9	0.0	1.8	..	86.6	3.9	6.1	6.1
ICELAND	23.1	100.0	0.5	110.6	0.032	110.7	0.0	0.0	..	0.8	.4	6.0	6.0
UNTD ARAB EMRTS	48.9	100.0	8.0	1.7	1.145	16.2	0.0	0.0	..	47.5	1.3	4.2	4.2
KIRIBATI	90.0	100.0	0.0	10.3	..	10.3	..	..	..	..	.0	4.0	4.0
YEMEN	97.8	100.0	0.0	0.0	..	0.0	..	..	..	..	.0	3.3	3.3
MALTA	47.5	100.0	6.4	5.5	0.473	10.3	..	..	..	..	.0	2.1	2.1
CAMBODIA	3.2	100.0	95.8	58.4	1.182	58.4	100.0	61.0	1.235	61.0	1.9	2.0	2.0
ARUBA	100.0	100.0	0.0	0.0	..	0.0	..	..	..	..	.0	1.8	1.8
TONGA	97.1	100.0	0.0	0.0	..	0.2	..	..	..	..	.0	1.6	1.6
LAO PDR	83.8	100.0	4.7	2.9	0.058	3.5	98.6	60.2	1.218	60.2	.1	1.6	1.6
NIGER	89.0	100.0	0.4	0.1	0.269	0.3	..	..	..	..	.0	1.5	1.5
PUERTO RICO	41.1	100.0	19.3	33.3	2.134	35.9	0.0	0.0	..	0.2	.5	1.5	1.5
OMAN	5.5	100.0	2.8	4.4	0.604	69.8	0.0	0.0	..	98.8	.9	1.3	1.3
MACAU	2.9	100.0	0.0	0.9	..	0.9	..	..	..	..	.0	1.2	1.2
NETHERLANDS ANTILLES	87.0	100.0	0.0	19.5	..	47.3	0.0	0.0	..	83.7	.3	.8	.8
EAST TIMOR	0.0	100.0	100.0	10.0	14.346	10.0	..	..	..	..	.0	.7	.7

Notes: 1. Value of exports from reporter countries that do not participate in Free Trade Agreements.

2. Weighted average tariff reduction measured by dT / (1 + T) in percent.

3. Estimate based on Merlinda Ingco's tarrif equivalents of non tariff barriers.

Agriculture, exc. Fish: Estimate 2³ Extent of other countries' MFN tariff reductions on exports from:

Export market	% of exports GATT bount		Average levels and changes weighted by value of exports to: the World exc. FTA¹				LMIEs exc. FTA¹				Value of exports in $ million		
	Total pre-UR	Total post-UR	% of exports affected	Post-UR applied rate	Tariff reduc-tion²	Post-UR bound rate	% of exports affected	Post-UR applied rate	Tariff reduc-tion²	Post-UR bound rate	To IDB LMIEs exc. FTA¹	To all IDB Ctrys exc. FTA¹	To all IDB Ctrys inc. FTA
UNITED STATES	66.0	100.0	19.5	6.9	1.068	27.7	14.6	18.8	1.687	91.5	4,179.6	23,176.5	28,402.6
EUROPEAN UNION	61.5	100.0	42.5	9.2	1.319	19.9	21.7	19.4	1.161	54.7	4,140.4	20,420.0	20,420.0
BRAZIL	86.8	100.0	36.8	5.7	1.607	7.8	10.5	15.8	0.630	32.7	781.7	8,732.9	8,869.3
CHINA	38.9	99.9	28.2	4.3	1.509	7.9	21.3	8.9	0.847	34.6	866.3	6,599.3	6,599.3
CANADA	76.7	100.0	8.9	2.6	0.587	6.8	6.7	9.7	0.344	42.8	455.1	2,780.1	6,119.2
AUSTRALIA	46.6	100.0	21.3	13.0	1.449	26.3	23.0	8.8	0.823	33.0	963.8	4,564.3	4,803.2
ARGENTINA	72.0	100.0	17.6	5.2	0.832	15.0	7.8	16.3	0.476	37.7	634.6	3,542.6	4,213.2
THAILAND	48.6	99.8	29.4	13.6	1.374	44.6	15.1	8.6	0.400	96.2	729.3	3,374.5	3,374.5
NEW ZEALAND	63.7	100.0	20.7	5.6	0.929	10.4	10.4	13.3	0.383	33.6	486.3	3,096.3	3,336.8
MEXICO	69.2	100.0	8.8	4.4	2.738	7.6	12.7	14.1	0.641	60.0	76.1	484.6	2,936.4
MALAYSIA	32.2	100.0	54.5	26.4	5.783	55.8	10.9	73.8	0.701	170.6	777.3	2,705.2	2,705.2
COLOMBIA	90.1	100.0	48.3	2.3	2.072	3.7	11.5	10.6	0.487	27.3	190.2	2,551.5	2,551.5
TAIWAN (CHINA)	29.5	100.0	70.7	7.3	2.294	9.1	28.6	16.5	1.345	36.5	173.0	1,891.1	1,891.1
INDONESIA	76.1	100.0	37.4	6.7	1.569	12.5	24.2	25.6	1.110	60.2	256.0	1,758.8	1,758.8
TURKEY	62.7	100.0	70.0	6.2	1.593	13.5	20.8	14.3	0.429	60.3	230.2	1,578.2	1,578.2
PHILIPPINES	57.5	100.0	56.7	9.2	4.866	10.4	44.4	14.9	1.770	39.5	72.9	1,550.9	1,550.9
COTE D'IVOIRE	94.9	100.0	73.9	2.0	2.894	2.8	21.7	9.1	0.782	23.6	74.8	1,484.0	1,484.0
CHILE	76.4	99.7	28.2	3.9	0.559	6.7	9.9	11.7	0.197	29.4	197.0	1,478.6	1,478.6
SWITZERLAND	78.4	100.0	25.6	13.2	1.380	20.5	22.8	27.6	1.882	47.5	194.9	1,410.3	1,410.3
INDIA	70.6	100.0	26.4	3.1	1.462	8.4	24.8	8.0	1.109	26.8	331.7	1,273.3	1,273.3
HUNGARY	59.7	100.0	38.6	7.8	1.405	14.9	18.9	12.9	0.533	45.2	180.7	1,207.5	1,207.5
SOUTH AFRICA	61.9	100.0	25.6	23.8	0.907	62.8	0.6	14.8	0.016	150.1	128.0	1,131.1	1,131.1
ISRAEL	81.7	100.0	48.0	8.7	2.157	10.0	14.5	12.4	0.510	39.6	14.7	961.7	1,033.2
COSTA RICA	91.3	100.0	34.0	2.5	1.595	4.2	9.8	12.7	0.896	35.0	57.7	1,029.7	1,029.7
JAPAN	45.2	99.6	31.1	4.4	1.733	8.2	45.2	17.1	2.702	34.6	160.8	1,010.7	1,010.7
KOREA, REPUBLIC OF	35.5	99.7	57.4	7.3	2.484	10.3	9.4	23.9	0.722	68.8	58.8	1,007.9	1,007.9
FORMER YUGOSLAVIA	76.3	100.0	40.0	10.9	1.322	34.9	24.8	21.2	0.731	102.7	179.4	975.1	975.1
POLAND	70.8	100.0	46.3	8.8	1.265	17.8	29.5	22.4	0.630	72.0	109.5	973.4	973.4
AUSTRIA	76.5	100.0	22.9	9.8	1.029	24.6	26.4	18.2	0.872	55.9	181.1	971.2	971.2
ECUADOR	85.4	100.0	13.6	3.3	1.100	7.5	6.1	12.7	0.196	44.1	98.2	937.7	937.7
SWEDEN	79.0	100.0	43.8	15.2	2.127	27.4	31.5	11.0	0.780	33.8	34.2	751.7	751.7
MOROCCO	57.3	100.0	37.3	8.2	1.322	9.8	1.4	30.7	0.033	82.8	10.2	652.7	652.7
KENYA	91.5	100.0	49.1	3.1	2.269	3.8	18.2	19.0	0.689	45.7	8.2	637.5	637.5
SINGAPORE	36.6	100.0	23.7	6.4	1.075	11.3	22.5	16.7	1.217	35.1	152.5	618.0	618.0
HONDURAS	93.5	100.0	25.1	2.5	1.091	3.1	54.2	11.4	1.848	19.5	30.1	612.9	612.9
PARAGUAY	74.2	100.0	10.1	1.1	0.611	13.0	0.7	12.0	0.495	45.9	32.2	441.8	565.3
CAMEROON	98.8	100.0	86.0	1.0	3.230	1.2	58.8	7.6	2.734	21.7	6.5	483.6	483.6
PERU	75.5	99.0	20.2	4.2	0.730	12.8	12.7	7.8	0.351	36.7	135.4	449.2	449.2
PANAMA	98.5	100.0	12.6	4.3	0.898	7.2	11.4	17.8	0.456	49.7	18.2	424.2	424.2
URUGUAY	40.2	100.0	8.2	4.5	1.225	34.2	0.8	6.9	0.134	44.6	32.7	213.3	423.7
NIGERIA	96.2	100.0	69.5	0.6	2.172	2.4	21.6	3.8	0.861	49.6	15.7	413.7	413.7
DOMINICAN REPUBLIC	68.6	100.0	29.8	5.8	1.158	6.3	0.8	18.7	0.130	86.2	2.6	393.4	393.4
EL SALVADOR	95.7	100.0	46.7	0.5	2.269	0.9	32.7	10.8	1.136	68.7	1.3	380.1	380.1
CUBA	45.7	100.0	35.3	44.2	3.141	79.7	22.5	23.9	1.013	72.1	114.7	372.9	372.9
HONG KONG	51.2	100.0	44.0	7.7	2.424	9.8	27.0	12.1	1.644	18.4	88.6	355.7	355.7

Notes: 1. Value of exports from reporter countries that do not participate in Free Trade Agreements.

2. Weighted average tariff reduction measured by dT / (1 + T) in percent.

3. Estimate based on available ad valorem tariff rates in the IDB. The available AVEs cover only 85% of all agricultural exports.

Agriculture, exc. Fish: Estimate 2[3] (continued)

Export market	% of exports GATT bount Total pre-UR	Total post-UR	World exc. FTA[1] % of exports affected	Post-UR applied rate	Tariff reduction[2]	Post-UR bound rate	LMIEs exc. FTA[1] % of exports affected	Post-UR applied rate	Tariff reduction[2]	Post-UR bound rate	To IDB LMIEs exc. FTA[1]	To all IDB Ctrys exc. FTA[1]	To all IDB Ctrys inc. FTA
ZIMBABWE	79.1	100.0	54.1	12.4	2.138	13.2	53.6	22.5	1.837	30.2	28.7	348.8	348.8
GHANA	95.9	100.0	64.4	1.4	2.235	1.4	67.1	10.5	4.104	11.6	11.3	345.2	345.2
CZECH & SLOVAK CU	57.4	100.0	33.4	9.9	1.614	21.6	9.6	18.5	0.383	42.6	82.5	338.4	338.4
FINLAND	66.3	100.0	22.2	6.7	0.589	19.0	15.4	17.3	0.394	54.8	30.7	332.8	332.8
MAURITIUS	8.2	100.0	4.0	48.8	0.774	49.1	2.3	3.9	0.089	18.2	.1	320.4	320.4
PAPUA NEW GUINEA	78.4	100.0	61.4	1.5	2.354	2.1	26.4	10.0	1.330	17.6	19.0	317.6	317.6
NORWAY	60.3	99.6	16.3	7.7	0.820	12.3	9.5	12.8	0.305	47.6	17.2	311.8	311.8
FORMER USSR	52.5	100.0	46.3	15.8	2.414	29.8	43.4	21.6	1.392	56.3	107.8	295.7	295.7
UGANDA	99.6	100.0	79.6	0.1	3.844	0.2	98.0	4.8	3.815	4.9	3.7	277.6	277.6
IRAN, ISLAMIC REP.	23.7	100.0	64.2	2.5	0.784	4.9	15.7	20.1	0.408	60.0	16.4	272.8	272.8
PAKISTAN	39.0	100.0	12.2	12.1	0.451	17.6	6.5	31.1	0.203	46.3	63.3	251.9	251.9
ETHIOPIA	97.4	100.0	52.2	0.5	2.498	0.8	0.4	10.4	0.031	52.4	1.2	244.6	244.6
BULGARIA	56.0	100.0	39.9	16.3	1.743	27.5	20.2	31.1	0.884	61.9	58.4	238.6	238.6
JAMAICA	60.3	100.0	35.8	5.2	1.112	6.9	0.0	4.7	..	83.7	2.3	221.8	221.8
MALAWI	67.8	100.0	41.6	6.8	1.395	7.9	13.8	10.1	0.542	88.1	2.7	214.0	214.0
TANZANIA	73.1	100.0	61.8	2.6	3.690	13.6	14.5	4.9	0.588	73.1	32.3	210.2	210.2
SRI LANKA	78.8	100.0	31.5	4.1	1.252	7.9	24.3	18.2	0.576	39.1	37.3	208.5	208.5
SAUDI ARABIA	47.7	100.0	36.5	5.4	0.617	47.0	15.1	7.8	0.682	83.5	86.8	206.9	206.9
CYPRUS	49.7	100.0	49.9	12.1	1.939	27.0	14.8	32.8	0.781	95.1	20.5	204.7	204.7
SUDAN	69.3	100.0	15.9	3.1	0.651	5.4	71.7	23.3	3.826	47.0	15.7	203.3	203.3
MADAGASCAR	80.9	100.0	68.0	2.3	4.240	3.3	44.5	17.0	1.790	63.0	3.7	196.4	196.4
ZAIRE	96.6	100.0	91.0	0.5	4.296	1.4	15.3	15.5	0.547	73.5	2.7	192.5	192.5
MARTINIQUE	98.6	100.0	21.3	13.2	1.378	13.2	..	..	..	..	.0	184.5	184.5
SWAZILAND	43.7	100.0	18.4	15.9	1.047	16.6	18.0	0.8	0.553	13.1	4.1	180.6	180.6
ROMANIA	48.7	100.0	34.9	8.4	1.444	21.6	14.0	13.8	0.358	74.8	21.0	177.3	177.3
VIETNAM	19.1	100.0	9.9	8.3	0.447	23.0	4.7	13.7	0.172	38.4	103.9	176.1	176.1
TUNISIA	15.4	100.0	32.1	7.6	1.367	7.8	52.6	7.2	1.185	13.8	1.7	163.4	163.4
SENEGAL	92.9	100.0	56.3	3.8	1.820	4.3	0.2	0.0	0.012	40.5	1.9	158.1	158.1
FIJI	11.4	100.0	3.8	27.6	0.218	52.1	2.9	0.3	0.226	14.9	17.4	156.2	156.2
NICARAGUA	95.2	100.0	57.9	2.1	2.910	3.1	6.7	16.9	0.084	27.2	7.5	148.7	148.7
GUADELOUPE	70.4	100.0	6.7	14.4	0.478	14.7	0.0	10.0	..	15.0	.0	144.8	144.8
EGYPT, ARAB REP.	48.7	100.0	51.8	9.0	1.830	15.1	40.7	17.8	0.937	42.5	28.8	136.9	136.9
RWANDA	98.6	100.0	86.1	0.2	4.153	0.2	..	..	..	..	.0	125.5	125.5
ICELAND	74.8	91.4	7.6	4.8	0.327	15.7	1.9	2.3	0.025	65.1	10.9	115.7	115.7
GUYANA	16.2	100.0	15.0	13.2	0.995	16.4	0.8	38.5	0.087	68.4	2.2	103.5	103.5
BURUNDI	99.4	100.0	83.8	0.2	3.972	0.3	69.1	5.0	2.682	15.3	.9	103.0	103.0
PUERTO RICO	45.3	100.0	81.5	5.6	1.862	7.0	22.5	16.5	6.410	50.0	4.0	100.9	100.9
VENEZUELA	78.2	100.0	41.4	4.0	1.567	14.7	1.5	13.7	0.089	76.2	15.9	96.6	96.6
TRINIDAD AND TOBAGO	51.6	100.0	41.5	19.4	3.445	33.7	0.0	35.3	..	84.6	19.0	92.7	92.7
BELIZE	60.1	100.0	17.4	15.4	0.613	20.8	0.0	24.3	..	47.1	9.5	78.9	78.9
BOLIVIA	48.2	100.0	12.7	7.6	0.692	45.9	0.0	13.8	..	84.3	36.4	68.2	68.2
DOMINICA	99.8	100.0	1.7	4.0	0.048	5.3	0.0	38.6	..	88.3	.1	64.4	64.4
SURINAME	31.1	100.0	3.2	8.4	0.099	9.3	0.0	15.0	..	30.0	.2	63.9	63.9
HAITI	98.8	100.0	87.7	1.2	3.684	1.3	0.0	12.1	..	35.4	.0	56.2	56.2
SYRIA	47.2	100.0	11.1	21.6	0.391	48.1	11.3	33.5	0.393	75.1	32.7	51.5	51.5

Notes: 1. Value of exports from reporter countries that do not participate in Free Trade Agreements.

2. Weighted average tariff reduction measured by dT / (1 + T) in percent.

3. Estimate based on available ad valorem tariff rates in the IDB. The available AVEs cover only 85% of all agricultural exports.

Agriculture, exc. Fish: Estimate 2[3] (continued)

	% of exports GATT bound		Average levels and changes weighted by value of exports to: the World exc. FTA[1]				LMIEs exc. FTA[1]				Value of exports in $ million		
Export market	Total pre-UR	Total post-UR	% of exports affected	Post-UR applied rate	Tariff reduc-tion[2]	Post-UR bound rate	% of exports affected	Post-UR applied rate	Tariff reduc-tion[2]	Post-UR bound rate	To IDB LMIEs exc. FTA[1]	To all IDB Ctrys exc. FTA[1]	To all IDB Ctrys inc. FTA
ALBANIA	66.9	99.9	30.9	12.1	0.921	30.9	42.1	17.2	1.261	44.9	29.4	48.9	48.9
TOGO	95.6	100.0	78.9	0.9	3.312	3.9	5.6	1.5	0.632	95.1	1.4	43.6	43.6
MOZAMBIQUE	56.3	100.0	17.2	3.7	1.807	6.9	12.3	14.1	0.412	45.8	3.8	42.4	42.4
BOTSWANA	75.9	100.0	23.0	4.8	3.294	22.2	2.3	1.3	0.171	24.7	9.6	40.7	40.7
IRAQ	4.7	100.0	24.0	45.2	1.141	73.9	11.4	53.3	0.638	87.8	33.1	39.9	39.9
LEBANON	75.7	100.0	26.8	19.8	0.953	34.1	1.3	40.8	0.023	72.4	16.7	39.9	39.9
BARBADOS	19.1	100.0	19.7	9.9	0.645	20.8	0.0	31.6	..	100.0	1.6	38.9	38.9
MYANMAR	30.8	98.4	14.8	8.3	1.326	52.3	10.6	10.9	0.451	81.9	20.5	35.7	35.7
SOMALIA	93.1	100.0	1.5	1.7	0.065	2.0	45.7	21.3	4.953	37.8	.1	34.7	34.7
CENTRAL AFRICAN REP.	96.0	100.0	91.1	1.1	4.500	1.2	..	..	..	..	.0	34.4	34.4
AFGHANISTAN	58.6	100.0	30.7	17.1	0.234	46.9	2.6	33.3	0.047	92.1	17.5	33.0	33.0
NEPAL	10.4	100.0	5.8	47.5	0.478	94.9	0.6	52.7	0.034	105.6	28.9	32.3	32.3
BANGLADESH	70.7	100.0	14.3	3.9	0.658	7.0	3.7	17.0	0.232	38.4	4.1	30.9	30.9
ANGOLA	100.0	100.0	95.6	0.7	4.494	0.9	..	..	..	..	.0	30.9	30.9
ALGERIA	49.1	99.8	40.0	5.7	1.936	6.0	0.0	32.5	..	113.0	.1	30.2	30.2
BAHAMAS, THE	98.4	100.0	89.5	13.1	6.751	13.1	0.0	21.8	..	33.9	.2	29.0	29.0
SIERRA LEONE	99.6	100.0	77.5	0.1	3.052	0.3	32.5	41.2	1.226	73.3	.0	27.3	27.3
GUINEA	92.1	100.0	56.9	0.8	2.542	1.3	14.7	9.8	1.236	18.1	.9	24.2	24.2
GRENADA	98.2	100.0	39.5	0.4	3.244	1.3	28.4	8.1	1.319	32.7	.5	23.6	23.6
ZAMBIA	80.9	100.0	65.0	7.8	2.176	14.6	0.2	3.1	0.011	129.0	.9	18.1	18.1
CONGO	51.5	100.0	20.5	0.4	0.898	0.4	100.0	30.0	3.774	30.0	.0	16.1	16.1
LIBERIA	97.7	100.0	92.7	0.9	3.454	5.4	1.0	19.4	0.206	191.9	.4	15.7	15.7
EQUATORIAL GUINEA	100.0	100.0	98.8	0.0	3.086	0.0	..	..	..	..	.0	15.1	15.1
GAMBIA, THE	59.3	100.0	43.7	4.7	1.565	4.7	0.0	12.6	..	23.3	.0	15.0	15.0
VANUATU	78.8	100.0	7.3	4.5	0.283	8.9	91.3	12.2	7.085	12.6	.2	13.7	13.7
BURKINA FASO	50.5	100.0	63.7	5.4	1.944	5.4	0.0	15.0	..	30.0	.0	13.2	13.2
GUINEA-BISSAU	15.1	100.0	0.8	0.0	0.040	84.9	0.0	0.0	..	99.8	9.7	11.5	11.5
BENIN	75.6	99.9	67.7	4.2	2.612	4.8	57.0	19.0	6.333	49.6	.2	11.4	11.4
GABON	91.0	100.0	63.6	0.6	2.327	0.6	0.0	16.4	..	35.2	.0	11.4	11.4
UNTD ARAB EMRTS	56.5	100.0	46.3	11.4	2.552	15.1	27.0	40.5	1.337	56.8	1.8	9.1	9.1
BERMUDA	27.8	100.0	13.9	12.9	0.434	106.2	0.0	15.7	..	144.0	6.4	8.9	8.9
JORDAN	18.6	100.0	80.6	27.0	2.678	27.9	96.5	34.9	3.247	36.1	5.8	8.9	8.9
MALI	82.9	100.0	59.7	3.8	3.036	7.1	0.8	18.8	0.005	48.5	.8	7.7	7.7
MACAU	15.6	100.0	12.8	0.8	0.790	0.8	11.5	41.8	1.631	41.8	.0	5.9	5.9
MALTA	75.6	100.0	60.4	9.6	2.887	10.9	21.5	39.5	0.827	61.1	.2	5.4	5.4
LESOTHO	27.7	100.0	26.6	13.6	0.971	30.7	0.1	12.5	0.004	36.2	3.6	5.0	5.0
CHAD	98.2	100.0	32.8	2.1	1.103	2.1	..	..	..	..	.0	4.8	4.8
KIRIBATI	90.2	100.0	4.0	0.3	0.093	0.3	0.0	20.4	..	27.0	.0	4.2	4.2
TONGA	98.5	100.0	24.4	1.5	0.662	1.6	100.0	11.0	7.792	11.0	.0	3.7	3.7
YEMEN	96.6	100.0	3.1	0.4	0.043	1.2	0.0	21.6	..	71.5	.1	3.7	3.7
ANTIGUA & B ARBUDA	26.4	100.0	87.8	8.9	2.364	8.9	0.0	50.0	..	50.0	.0	3.5	3.5
NETHERLANDS ANTILLES	92.5	100.0	58.8	7.9	2.378	16.1	0.0	18.6	..	67.4	.5	3.3	3.3
LAO PDR	47.8	99.1	53.2	13.2	2.043	13.8	89.9	28.3	3.261	29.3	1.4	3.0	3.0
CAMBODIA	11.6	100.0	0.1	0.4	0.004	8.1	0.0	0.5	..	10.5	1.9	2.5	2.5
ARUBA	99.5	100.0	96.5	1.3	4.386	1.3	..	..	..	..	.0	2.1	2.1

Notes: 1. Value of exports from reporter countries that do not participate in Free Trade Agreements.

2. Weighted average tariff reduction measured by dT / (1 + T) in percent.

3. Estimate based on available ad valorem tariff rates in the IDB. The available AVEs cover only 85% of all agricultural exports.

Fish and Fish Products Extent of other countries' MFN tariff reductions on exports from:

Export market	% of exports GATT bound Total pre-UR	% of exports GATT bound Total post-UR	Average levels and changes weighted by value of exports to: the World exc. FTA[1] % of exports affected	Post-UR applied rate	Tariff reduction[2]	Post-UR bound rate	LMIEs exc. FTA[1] % of exports affected	Post-UR applied rate	Tariff reduction[2]	Post-UR bound rate	Value of exports in $ million To IDB LMIEs exc. FTA[1]	To all IDB Ctrys exc. FTA[1]	To all IDB Ctrys inc. FTA
UNITED STATES	86.6	97.5	63.2	4.5	2.629	4.3	76.7	10.5	16.411	8.4	279.8	2,847.9	3,120.2
CANADA	94.2	98.9	28.3	2.7	1.478	2.8	30.3	11.5	4.588	16.2	16.2	1,147.8	2,361.2
THAILAND	75.1	94.8	38.7	6.6	1.044	7.0	7.3	9.7	1.170	34.5	79.6	1,869.2	1,869.2
KOREA, REPUBLIC OF	71.8	97.1	71.4	5.6	2.304	5.5	90.8	7.0	37.361	6.5	34.0	1,731.5	1,731.5
NORWAY	89.7	92.8	9.0	1.9	0.797	6.0	6.6	3.0	0.815	7.5	95.3	398.9	1,538.9
TAIWAN (CHINA)	84.4	98.8	50.0	4.5	2.504	4.7	78.3	8.3	32.493	5.9	82.4	1,533.0	1,533.0
CHINA	47.9	99.4	46.1	1.9	1.204	2.0	40.7	7.4	15.259	4.7	19.0	1,290.8	1,290.8
EUROPEAN UNION	68.5	88.2	31.9	2.7	3.309	2.8	59.8	6.6	16.220	6.7	115.9	755.7	1,177.1
ICELAND	99.0	99.4	24.1	1.2	1.076	8.3	14.7	4.5	0.945	6.0	10.6	291.2	929.5
JAPAN	43.8	95.5	34.6	4.2	8.306	4.5	77.0	7.9	29.687	8.0	199.2	773.9	773.9
INDONESIA	75.7	97.9	75.0	2.9	3.288	2.9	67.1	6.0	25.758	7.7	52.5	767.9	767.9
AUSTRALIA	76.2	99.4	50.4	2.3	1.302	2.5	45.2	12.7	18.368	5.9	6.9	566.5	568.8
MEXICO	37.4	100.0	11.0	0.8	0.938	2.0	74.5	8.1	29.475	10.3	1.0	137.2	533.1
INDIA	74.9	98.8	66.8	2.3	1.564	2.8	6.4	2.5	2.018	41.5	9.1	494.0	494.0
GREENLAND	96.0	96.0	34.6	9.6	0.913	10.0	0.0	20.0	..	..	.0	473.8	473.8
PHILIPPINES	81.0	99.9	59.7	3.8	1.414	3.9	71.9	10.3	29.473	12.0	3.7	461.3	461.3
FORMER USSR	81.5	91.7	49.7	6.3	2.133	6.5	24.0	12.7	8.315	10.9	48.6	458.5	458.5
ECUADOR	23.5	99.9	12.3	1.4	0.431	2.3	0.0	13.5	..	34.3	7.2	429.0	429.0
MOROCCO	64.3	100.0	67.0	9.3	2.460	10.1	0.1	10.4	0.024	34.5	10.7	403.7	403.7
NEW ZEALAND	79.3	99.6	30.5	1.3	1.630	1.6	88.6	7.8	25.428	7.0	14.7	334.0	382.6
ARGENTINA	79.5	97.8	45.0	6.5	2.172	9.7	3.1	16.3	0.973	33.9	6.6	328.1	371.0
CHILE	84.6	99.4	27.8	8.2	0.955	9.7	5.6	12.3	0.486	37.9	20.9	357.1	357.1
SINGAPORE	49.3	97.5	31.9	2.7	7.226	2.7	87.6	7.3	33.136	6.9	52.9	253.9	253.9
MALAYSIA	56.3	99.6	40.9	3.8	2.567	5.7	69.4	9.7	27.100	12.2	13.1	251.7	251.7
BRAZIL	67.6	100.0	28.8	1.9	0.972	3.3	0.1	15.4	0.202	35.0	.4	222.5	227.4
MAURITANIA	26.0	99.9	90.8	7.0	2.551	7.1	0.0	15.0	..	30.0	.4	222.0	222.0
PANAMA	63.0	99.8	32.4	2.4	0.614	5.3	10.6	18.9	4.380	20.4	.4	217.4	217.4
SENEGAL	95.8	100.0	52.1	12.9	2.074	15.1	..	..	..	..	.0	216.1	216.1
VIETNAM	54.7	96.4	46.8	1.8	1.090	1.3	16.8	13.8	6.114	8.4	.6	212.2	212.2
HONG KONG	70.8	98.2	60.5	2.7	1.941	2.9	44.1	7.1	15.796	4.9	12.0	189.2	189.2
BANGLADESH	67.4	98.3	63.1	4.3	2.296	4.5	4.8	0.2	1.983	5.0	3.4	188.0	188.0
POLAND	99.3	99.3	40.9	7.0	1.914	7.0	94.1	5.2	39.068	5.0	.0	157.0	157.0
CUBA	98.0	100.0	75.9	9.6	3.580	9.7	0.0	15.0	..	30.0	1.5	148.0	148.0
SEYCHELLES	80.9	100.0	17.8	4.9	7.153	18.4	100.0	5.0	41.509	5.0	24.8	144.4	144.4
COTE D'IVOIRE	99.7	100.0	5.5	17.4	0.276	22.3	0.0	15.0	..	..	.0	138.3	138.3
SOUTH AFRICA	84.7	99.9	28.8	7.9	1.437	8.5	0.0	0.1	..	3.1	.2	130.8	130.8
VENEZUELA	45.4	100.0	13.4	0.9	0.221	5.3	..	..	..	..	.0	129.2	129.2
SWEDEN	97.3	99.6	25.5	1.9	1.509	6.7	64.5	6.3	4.448	7.9	.5	34.6	127.0
TUNISIA	98.1	100.0	61.6	9.4	2.706	9.4	0.0	17.9	..	17.9	.3	108.4	108.4
PAKISTAN	53.5	99.4	50.6	2.9	1.875	13.1	3.1	0.2	1.274	48.6	21.1	100.3	100.3
HONDURAS	70.1	100.0	31.5	1.8	0.798	1.9	..	..	..	..	.0	89.3	89.3
URUGUAY	62.1	99.6	26.3	3.7	1.756	12.8	0.3	16.2	2.361	34.9	.4	52.0	72.9
TURKEY	95.5	99.9	34.8	9.1	1.165	9.1	0.0	24.7	..	25.0	.1	71.9	71.9
MOZAMBIQUE	87.7	99.9	96.0	7.9	7.421	8.0	81.7	4.2	33.917	4.1	7.6	68.0	68.0
PERU	49.1	99.1	20.6	6.6	0.889	9.9	1.5	17.9	0.009	32.7	14.2	65.0	65.0

Notes: 1. Value of exports from reporter countries that do not participate in Free Trade Agreements.

2. Weighted average tariff reduction measured by dT / (1 + T) in percent.

Fish and Fish Products (continued)

Export market	% of exports GATT bount		Average levels and changes weighted by value of exports to:								Value of exports in $ million		
			the World exc. FTA[1]				LMIEs exc. FTA[1]						
	Total pre-UR	Total post-UR	% of exports affected	Post-UR applied rate	Tariff reduc-tion[2]	Post-UR bound rate	% of exports affected	Post-UR applied rate	Tariff reduc-tion[2]	Post-UR bound rate	To IDB LMIEs exc. FTA[1]	To all IDB Ctrys exc. FTA[1]	To all IDB Ctrys inc. FTA
COLOMBIA	51.7	100.0	32.4	1.3	0.866	2.3	..	..	..	..	.0	59.6	59.6
GAMBIA, THE	30.9	99.8	87.3	5.8	2.260	5.8	0.0	15.0	..	30.0	.0	56.3	56.3
COSTA RICA	77.6	100.0	50.8	2.2	0.504	3.4	0.0	30.0	..	50.0	3.0	55.4	55.4
MADAGASCAR	94.0	100.0	90.1	5.4	3.280	5.9	..	..	..	..	.0	49.5	49.5
MACAU	44.0	100.0	39.9	0.7	0.862	0.7	..	..	..	..	.0	39.6	39.6
BAHAMAS, THE	99.2	100.0	31.2	3.7	3.043	3.7	..	..	..	..	.0	34.9	34.9
MYANMAR	15.7	97.5	16.2	0.7	1.280	3.5	47.1	2.8	19.212	5.9	1.6	33.1	33.1
FIJI	84.0	100.0	32.0	14.6	1.201	14.7	100.0	5.0	41.509	5.0	.0	33.0	33.0
PAPUA NEW GUINEA	33.8	44.0	30.2	11.5	0.633	2.1	0.0	19.7	..	..	18.4	32.9	32.9
FORMER YUGOSLAVIA	88.3	91.1	30.2	10.9	0.933	9.8	0.0	15.3	..	6.8	6.2	31.8	31.8
ANGOLA	100.0	100.0	80.1	11.3	4.449	11.3	..	..	..	..	.0	30.1	30.1
GHANA	51.7	100.0	46.0	2.9	0.825	2.9	0.0	15.0	..	..	.0	30.1	30.1
SRI LANKA	73.5	99.1	62.3	1.9	1.555	3.0	27.5	2.1	11.103	6.3	.4	29.4	29.4
SURINAME	90.8	100.0	87.6	2.5	2.088	2.5	..	..	..	..	.0	27.7	27.7
IRAN, ISLAMIC REP.	89.9	100.0	55.5	10.0	3.861	10.4	100.0	0.0	0.499	0.0	.0	26.1	26.1
MAURITIUS	96.2	99.9	8.5	13.3	0.200	13.9	0.0	1.7	..	7.5	.0	23.7	23.7
OMAN	70.1	99.8	17.4	1.9	1.735	5.7	96.1	4.8	39.880	5.0	.5	22.4	22.4
NAMIBIA	99.9	100.0	99.5	1.0	1.948	1.0	..	..	..	..	.0	22.3	22.3
FINLAND	40.0	42.5	25.9	1.3	1.709	4.6	0.0	6.1	..	47.3	.1	6.1	21.8
BULGARIA	98.1	99.9	25.6	6.0	1.278	6.0	60.2	7.2	24.249	7.4	.7	21.3	21.3
GABON	100.0	100.0	98.6	11.9	5.041	12.0	0.0	15.0	..	30.0	.0	19.8	19.8
EL SALVADOR	4.7	100.0	3.5	0.0	0.029	0.0	..	..	..	..	.0	19.1	19.1
GUYANA	23.6	100.0	19.6	0.7	0.527	0.7	..	..	..	..	.0	17.8	17.8
KENYA	63.1	99.5	36.4	4.5	1.805	5.9	0.0	0.0	..	0.0	.1	16.3	16.3
NIGERIA	58.6	100.0	45.5	3.2	1.499	3.2	0.0	0.0	..	..	.0	15.9	15.9
YEMEN	84.1	100.0	85.1	7.5	4.670	8.8	0.0	0.0	..	50.0	.0	14.6	14.6
NETHERLANDS ANTILLES	97.0	99.8	4.1	0.4	0.192	0.5	..	..	..	..	.0	13.9	13.9
VANUATU	2.4	100.0	2.4	0.3	0.124	0.3	..	..	..	..	.0	13.9	13.9
SWITZERLAND	80.1	99.2	12.5	4.4	13.542	10.0	86.3	6.8	35.517	6.4	1.9	5.0	13.8
SIERRA LEONE	99.6	100.0	91.1	10.9	4.450	10.9	0.0	15.0	..	30.0	.0	13.5	13.5
EGYPT, ARAB REP.	94.8	100.0	88.3	12.0	1.365	12.1	0.0	21.7	..	28.3	.0	12.3	12.3
TANZANIA	40.0	99.9	38.3	3.0	1.604	3.8	0.0	0.0	..	0.0	.0	9.9	9.9
KUWAIT	94.6	100.0	93.2	1.0	1.832	1.0	..	..	..	..	.0	9.7	9.7
SOMALIA	97.3	99.8	65.4	8.3	4.659	8.7	0.0	5.0	..	..	.0	9.6	9.6
CAMEROON	100.0	100.0	99.4	11.7	5.134	11.7	..	..	..	..	.0	9.3	9.3
UNTD ARAB EMRTS	56.4	100.0	33.8	3.3	1.814	9.5	14.8	4.4	6.157	43.3	1.2	9.2	9.2
NICARAGUA	99.7	100.0	58.8	5.2	2.286	5.4	0.0	20.5	..	40.9	.1	9.2	9.2
TRINIDAD AND TOBAGO	60.5	99.9	7.3	0.7	0.222	0.7	0.0	43.0	..	..	.0	8.9	8.9
BELIZE	84.7	100.0	15.6	1.9	1.555	1.9	..	..	..	..	.0	8.0	8.0
CZECH & SLOVAK CU	85.4	95.4	2.7	7.9	0.148	7.7	0.0	16.5	..	24.0	.5	7.3	7.3
TOGO	90.8	100.0	78.2	9.4	4.146	9.4	..	..	..	..	.0	6.9	6.9
BOTSWANA	91.7	91.7	55.2	9.1	3.703	9.9	0.0	3.3	..	7.5	1.0	6.6	6.6
HUNGARY	90.5	93.2	26.4	5.4	0.870	4.2	1.7	6.5	0.045	0.3	1.6	6.5	6.5
ISRAEL	98.7	100.0	6.6	4.1	0.150	4.5	0.0	9.5	..	14.4	.0	5.3	5.6
SAUDI ARABIA	94.7	100.0	70.9	12.4	3.778	14.3	0.0	5.0	..	50.0	.2	4.6	4.6

Notes: 1. Value of exports from reporter countries that do not participate in Free Trade Agreements.

2. Weighted average tariff reduction measured by dT / (1 + T) in percent.

Fish and Fish Products (continued)

Export market	% of exports GATT bount — Total pre-UR	Total post-UR	World exc. FTA[1] — % of exports affected	Post-UR applied rate	Tariff reduction[2]	Post-UR bound rate	LMIEs exc. FTA[1] — % of exports affected	Post-UR applied rate	Tariff reduction[2]	Post-UR bound rate	Value of exports in $ million — To IDB LMIEs exc. FTA[1]	To all IDB Ctrys exc. FTA[1]	To all IDB Ctrys inc. FTA
EQUATORIAL GUINEA	100.0	100.0	100.0	12.0	5.217	12.0	..	..	..	..	.0	4.2	4.2
AUSTRIA	92.1	93.0	2.4	13.3	0.099	9.0	3.2	17.1	0.053	15.1	1.8	1.9	4.0
GUINEA	37.1	100.0	35.3	2.0	0.613	2.0	..	..	..	..	.0	3.7	3.7
HAITI	92.0	100.0	7.8	0.9	0.636	1.0	..	..	..	..	.0	3.1	3.1
GUINEA-BISSAU	99.3	100.0	74.7	11.1	3.744	11.1	0.0	15.0	..	30.0	.0	3.1	3.1
CYPRUS	100.0	100.0	6.1	6.1	0.219	6.1	..	..	..	..	.0	2.7	2.7
CONGO	82.1	100.0	80.1	9.6	4.182	9.6	0.0	0.0	..	0.0	.0	2.7	2.7
ROMANIA	86.0	99.6	14.1	10.8	0.243	11.0	0.0	24.9	..	25.0	.6	2.7	2.7
UGANDA	1.9	99.9	0.7	0.1	0.015	0.1	..	..	..	..	.0	2.2	2.2
JAMAICA	100.0	100.0	1.4	0.4	0.027	0.4	..	..	..	..	.0	1.7	1.7
LIBYA	98.6	100.0	88.7	6.8	1.943	6.8	..	..	..	..	.0	1.7	1.7
ALBANIA	90.6	90.6	40.1	7.8	1.168	4.7	0.0	37.3	..	24.0	.2	1.6	1.6
ALGERIA	72.3	100.0	61.2	5.2	1.385	5.2	..	..	..	..	.0	1.3	1.3
ZAIRE	99.9	100.0	0.4	0.1	0.027	0.1	..	..	..	..	.0	1.3	1.3
BAHRAIN	89.3	100.0	82.0	8.5	3.789	8.6	0.0	5.0	..	50.0	.0	1.2	1.2
DOMINICAN REPUBLIC	94.6	100.0	27.2	0.2	0.212	0.2	..	..	..	..	.0	1.2	1.2
BENIN	100.0	100.0	99.2	12.0	5.173	12.0	..	..	..	..	.0	.9	.9
BARBADOS	82.0	100.0	9.5	0.6	0.391	0.6	..	..	..	..	.0	.8	.8
NIGER	100.0	100.0	15.7	10.2	0.783	10.2	..	..	..	..	.0	.5	.5
ANTIGUA & B ARBUDA	99.6	100.0	16.2	0.0	0.101	0.0	..	..	..	..	.0	.5	.5
MALAWI	91.8	91.8	16.7	0.6	0.321	0.7	0.0	0.0	..	0.0	.1	.4	.4
GRENADA	25.3	100.0	8.9	0.2	0.048	0.2	..	..	..	..	.0	.4	.4
SYRIA	100.0	100.0	0.3	5.7	0.019	5.7	..	..	..	..	.0	.4	.4
MALI	96.1	100.0	89.9	9.3	3.361	10.9	0.0	5.0	..	50.0	.0	.4	.4
TONGA	97.1	100.0	84.1	0.2	0.460	0.2	..	..	..	..	.0	.3	.3
BOLIVIA	59.9	100.0	56.6	6.7	2.905	6.7	..	..	..	..	.0	.3	.3
BURUNDI	100.0	100.0	0.0	0.0	..	0.0	..	..	..	..	.0	.3	.3
PARAGUAY	100.0	100.0	47.6	6.1	1.312	9.2	0.0	11.0	..	25.0	.1	.3	.3
ZAMBIA	100.0	100.0	17.1	2.2	1.152	2.2	0.0	0.0	..	0.0	.0	.2	.2
KIRIBATI	84.2	100.0	1.6	0.0	0.008	0.0	..	..	..	..	.0	.2	.2
GUADELOUPE	97.0	100.0	83.5	7.4	5.632	7.4	..	..	..	..	.0	.2	.2
LIBERIA	53.6	100.0	17.2	1.8	0.536	5.4	..	..	..	..	.0	.2	.2
LEBANON	19.7	92.4	0.0	15.1	..	37.3	0.0	15.2	..	37.6	.1	.1	.1
DJIBOUTI	0.0	100.0	1.2	0.1	0.483	9.6	100.0	5.0	41.509	5.0	.0	.1	.1
CHAD	100.0	100.0	95.4	3.3	1.372	3.3	..	..	..	..	.0	.1	.1
BHUTAN	100.0	100.0	100.0	10.0	4.444	10.0	..	..	..	..	.0	.1	.1
QATAR	100.0	100.0	100.0	12.0	5.217	12.0	..	..	..	..	.0	.1	.1
MALTA	100.0	100.0	21.1	13.8	0.276	13.8	..	..	..	..	.0	.1	.1
BRUNEI	3.9	100.0	0.0	10.2	..	14.7	0.0	18.6	..	19.3	.0	.1	.1
CAMBODIA	8.5	100.0	0.0	7.8	..	35.1	0.0	10.0	..	50.0	.0	.0	.0
GIBRALTAR	95.1	95.1	0.0	0.5	..	21.4	..	..	..	..	.0	.0	.0
MARTINIQUE	100.0	100.0	94.6	7.8	5.479	7.8	..	..	..	..	.0	.0	.0
MONGOLIA	97.1	100.0	97.1	0.4	0.624	0.7	..	..	..	..	.0	.0	.0
ETHIOPIA	100.0	100.0	6.3	0.8	0.658	0.8	..	..	..	..	.0	.0	.0
NEPAL	19.4	19.4	0.0	0.0	..	0.0	0.0	0.0	..	..	.0	.0	.0

Notes: 1. Value of exports from reporter countries that do not participate in Free Trade Agreements.

2. Weighted average tariff reduction measured by dT / (1 + T) in percent.

Petroleum Oils[3] Extent of other countries' MFN tariff reductions on exports from:

| Export market | % of exports GATT bound | | Average levels and changes weighted by value of exports to: | | | | | | | | Value of exports in $ million | | |
| | | | the World exc. FTA[1] | | | | LMIEs exc. FTA[1] | | | | | | |
	Total pre-UR	Total post-UR	% of exports affected	Post-UR applied rate	Tariff reduction[2]	Post-UR bound rate	% of exports affected	Post-UR applied rate	Tariff reduction[2]	Post-UR bound rate	To IDB LMIEs exc. FTA[1]	To all IDB Ctrys exc. FTA[1]	To all IDB Ctrys inc. FTA
SAUDI ARABIA	25.3	31.4	0.6	1.5	0.008	2.9	0.1	7.4	0.006	31.5	2,825.4	22,534.4	22,534.4
FORMER USSR	85.9	90.7	1.3	0.8	0.016	1.1	0.6	1.0	0.008	0.5	2,545.0	11,406.3	11,406.3
IRAQ	30.7	50.9	0.2	0.4	0.002	3.6	0.0	0.0	..	25.6	4,178.6	10,521.9	10,521.9
EUROPEAN UNION	42.8	45.9	0.5	1.7	0.010	2.5	3.9	14.0	0.071	28.8	608.9	5,814.9	8,420.4
NIGERIA	34.3	36.6	0.0	0.8	0.000	1.1	0.0	19.9	..	29.8	307.0	8,419.6	8,419.6
UNTD ARAB EMRTS	9.1	14.3	0.1	4.9	0.001	2.0	0.0	11.8	..	33.6	1,908.2	7,955.3	7,955.3
VENEZUELA	50.7	55.3	0.1	1.0	0.002	3.9	0.0	8.4	..	35.0	514.3	7,494.2	7,494.2
MEXICO	23.9	25.8	0.0	1.7	0.000	4.1	0.0	11.8	..	41.4	242.9	2,655.2	6,824.2
IRAN, ISLAMIC REP.	49.6	65.6	0.0	2.6	0.000	6.1	0.0	11.2	..	33.1	1,776.7	6,440.6	6,440.6
LIBYA	90.2	92.2	1.1	0.3	0.013	1.3	0.0	2.0	..	22.0	458.6	6,037.7	6,037.7
NORWAY	81.7	81.8	0.0	0.2	0.000	0.3	0.0	9.5	0.001	0.0	38.2	1,108.6	5,939.3
KUWAIT	39.0	45.5	2.2	1.7	0.028	2.4	0.0	8.6	..	40.0	741.3	5,900.4	5,900.4
ALGERIA	85.8	88.7	4.8	0.7	0.060	1.2	0.0	1.6	..	4.9	518.3	5,687.4	5,687.4
INDONESIA	9.6	12.8	0.0	1.2	0.000	0.4	0.0	5.7	..	..	238.7	5,179.9	5,179.9
CANADA	33.0	33.0	0.1	6.7	0.094	1.3	0.1	11.9	0.005	38.0	18.0	90.3	4,778.9
SINGAPORE	5.3	18.3	0.4	2.6	0.012	19.6	0.4	10.4	0.022	36.8	1,624.5	4,222.5	4,222.5
CHINA	1.3	3.9	0.1	7.6	0.001	7.4	0.0	12.3	..	28.3	255.2	3,369.7	3,369.7
OMAN	3.8	5.0	0.0	5.3	..	0.1	0.0	7.8	..	15.0	799.6	2,836.6	2,836.6
MALAYSIA	0.8	9.2	0.0	5.9	0.000	16.4	0.0	13.1	0.000	36.0	946.2	2,836.0	2,836.0
ANGOLA	27.9	29.6	0.0	0.6	..	0.3	0.0	5.9	..	3.5	117.1	2,496.7	2,496.7
UNITED STATES	36.8	49.8	8.2	4.8	0.215	22.4	1.8	11.6	0.174	37.1	422.2	1,357.9	2,066.4
EGYPT, ARAB REP.	59.9	71.8	2.7	2.5	0.034	7.0	0.0	8.1	..	32.4	503.8	1,740.2	1,740.2
QATAR	4.0	16.0	0.0	6.5	..	0.0	0.0	13.5	..	..	319.4	1,570.5	1,570.5
COLOMBIA	26.6	26.9	0.0	0.8	..	4.2	0.0	9.5	..	33.9	37.0	1,177.0	1,177.0
ECUADOR	12.2	12.2	0.0	2.3	0.000	13.0	0.0	5.9	..	27.8	308.8	972.4	972.4
ROMANIA	98.5	98.5	6.7	3.0	0.084	3.4	24.0	9.6	0.273	4.7	26.5	960.3	960.3
GABON	45.3	50.2	0.0	1.7	0.000	0.4	0.0	11.3	..	7.0	151.2	903.4	903.4
SWEDEN	94.1	94.2	0.0	0.5	0.002	2.7	0.0	12.0	0.000	31.3	12.1	139.7	896.3
BRUNEI	7.0	8.4	0.0	10.1	..	0.4	0.0	13.6	..	..	443.6	882.2	882.2
YEMEN	44.1	44.1	0.0	1.6	..	1.1	0.0	7.1	..	45.0	140.7	795.5	795.5
CAMEROON	65.0	65.0	0.0	0.3	..	0.1	0.0	1.8	..	0.0	25.5	777.0	777.0
BRAZIL	97.0	98.4	0.9	2.5	0.014	2.4	0.0	10.1	..	35.1	2.2	700.9	709.3
TRINIDAD AND TOBAGO	21.6	28.5	0.0	1.7	0.000	9.6	0.0	15.6	..	36.1	45.8	666.5	666.5
KOREA, REPUBLIC OF	2.6	2.8	0.5	4.5	0.006	4.6	0.0	19.5	..	39.7	81.5	645.8	645.8
TURKEY	46.9	48.6	1.5	1.0	0.018	3.5	0.0	7.1	..	35.2	10.0	623.5	623.5
AUSTRALIA	11.0	31.4	0.6	1.6	0.019	11.1	1.3	7.3	0.080	38.9	94.7	501.1	616.2
NETHERLANDS ANTILLES	69.8	93.8	2.4	5.5	0.052	13.5	0.0	14.1	..	37.1	192.7	592.7	592.7
SYRIA	82.6	86.0	3.5	0.8	0.043	2.2	0.0	1.3	..	35.0	23.9	504.4	504.4
BAHRAIN	3.5	10.4	0.0	4.2	..	1.5	0.0	2.0	..	5.0	14.9	448.8	448.8
INDIA	76.5	81.1	1.5	0.6	0.018	0.6	0.0	2.2	..	5.0	4.8	390.8	390.8
FINLAND	100.0	100.0	0.0	0.0	..	1.7	0.0	10.2	..	13.0	.0	.0	373.6
CONGO	83.3	83.3	0.0	0.4	0.000	0.1	0.0	5.0	..	..	21.7	328.4	328.4
TUNISIA	81.8	81.8	1.6	0.3	0.020	0.6	..	..	..	..	.0	323.0	323.0
JAPAN	5.0	17.8	12.0	10.3	0.654	11.6	27.8	14.9	1.582	15.0	122.9	304.7	304.7
ARGENTINA	54.3	79.1	5.7	3.7	0.082	10.5	0.5	14.5	0.036	34.6	42.3	224.0	246.4

Notes: 1. Value of exports from reporter countries that do not participate in Free Trade Agreements.

2. Weighted average tariff reduction measured by dT / (1 + T) in percent.

3. The available AVE tariff rates used in this product category cover only 72% of the petrol exports to the 40 IDB countries

Petroleum Oils[3] (continued)

Export market	% of exports GATT bound Total pre-UR	Total post-UR	the World exc. FTA[1] % of exports affected	Post-UR applied rate	Tariff reduc-tion[2]	Post-UR bound rate	LMIEs exc. FTA[1] % of exports affected	Post-UR applied rate	Tariff reduc-tion[2]	Post-UR bound rate	To IDB LMIEs exc. FTA[1]	To all IDB Ctrys exc. FTA[1]	To all IDB Ctrys inc. FTA
PERU	96.9	96.9	0.0	2.0	0.000	6.6	0.0	9.1	..	33.0	38.3	218.3	218.3
CZECH & SLOVAK CU	62.3	86.8	7.7	8.2	0.093	3.8	0.0	8.8	..	4.5	9.9	199.5	199.5
HUNGARY	30.0	79.7	6.9	25.1	0.086	4.8	0.2	10.2	0.002	34.8	6.6	187.3	187.3
FORMER YUGOSLAVIA	90.0	99.0	4.3	1.6	0.047	4.2	79.5	4.8	0.905	4.7	6.0	173.5	173.5
ZAIRE	1.0	1.0	0.0	0.6	..	0.7	..	..	..	..	.0	147.5	147.5
AUSTRIA	73.3	75.1	37.5	6.8	0.640	5.5	55.8	6.9	0.640	6.0	90.7	90.7	134.9
TAIWAN (CHINA)	4.1	8.8	7.2	5.6	0.298	10.4	26.0	13.5	1.562	14.6	22.7	134.1	134.1
BAHAMAS, THE	94.8	94.8	0.0	0.4	0.000	0.7	..	..	..	..	.0	118.1	118.1
THAILAND	97.1	98.6	0.0	0.8	0.000	1.0	0.3	10.8	0.019	39.2	1.9	96.0	96.0
NEW ZEALAND	4.8	68.1	0.0	0.0	0.001	0.0	0.0	..	..	..	.0	35.0	95.2
SWITZERLAND	74.5	92.1	0.4	0.8	0.008	7.9	0.4	1.0	0.006	10.5	54.1	62.3	84.9
PUERTO RICO	81.2	100.0	0.0	10.8	..	36.2	0.0	10.8	..	36.2	76.8	76.8	76.8
BULGARIA	80.1	85.4	0.5	1.5	0.006	4.0	0.0	11.3	..	29.3	7.1	64.4	64.4
POLAND	99.8	100.0	4.3	1.4	0.044	2.0	0.6	4.3	0.007	16.4	.8	60.3	60.3
PHILIPPINES	0.1	21.9	0.2	12.4	0.013	4.9	0.9	3.2	0.048	5.2	15.7	57.7	57.7
MOROCCO	89.2	91.5	39.7	4.9	0.593	4.5	0.0	36.0	..	..	5.8	54.1	54.1
COTE D'IVOIRE	72.5	77.7	0.1	0.7	0.002	0.9	0.0	4.0	..	4.0	.1	53.5	53.5
CUBA	100.0	100.0	33.9	1.6	0.418	3.9	..	..	..	..	.0	51.3	51.3
VIETNAM	0.0	0.0	0.0	..	..	..	..	..	..	..	.0	50.5	50.5
SOUTH AFRICA	71.7	71.7	1.4	6.6	0.031	6.8	0.0	32.4	..	42.1	18.4	46.5	46.5
BANGLADESH	13.2	25.5	0.0	1.2	..	4.2	0.0	2.0	..	5.0	4.0	32.9	32.9
ISRAEL	85.3	85.5	7.5	2.9	0.271	2.1	0.0	10.2	..	35.0	4.3	16.2	29.8
PAKISTAN	0.0	8.1	0.0	1.9	0.000	5.0	0.0	6.6	..	5.0	5.8	26.4	26.4
TANZANIA	0.0	0.0	0.0	0.6	..	..	..	..	..	..	.0	22.1	22.1
SRI LANKA	9.3	18.6	0.0	0.0	..	0.0	..	..	..	..	.0	15.2	15.2
ANTIGUA & B ARBUDA	0.0	47.4	0.0	7.4	..	35.0	0.0	15.0	..	35.0	6.8	14.3	14.3
CYPRUS	100.0	100.0	0.0	24.6	0.000	24.6	0.0	45.0	..	45.0	7.5	13.7	13.7
NICARAGUA	0.1	0.1	0.0	0.0	..	40.0	0.0	5.0	..	40.0	.0	12.5	12.5
GHANA	100.0	100.0	0.0	0.9	..	1.2	..	..	..	..	.0	11.5	11.5
PANAMA	58.4	97.9	0.0	12.1	..	28.7	0.0	16.1	..	38.7	7.6	10.3	10.3
ALBANIA	100.0	100.0	0.1	0.0	0.002	4.7	..	..	..	..	.0	9.8	9.8
JORDAN	1.9	1.9	1.9	3.7	0.042	3.7	..	..	..	..	.0	9.5	9.5
NAMIBIA	98.4	98.4	0.0	0.4	..	0.7	..	..	..	..	.0	9.1	9.1
MARTINIQUE	100.0	100.0	0.0	2.4	..	2.4	..	..	..	..	.0	9.0	9.0
MAURITANIA	100.0	100.0	48.6	2.3	0.599	4.7	..	..	..	..	.0	7.9	7.9
ZIMBABWE	100.0	100.0	0.0	0.0	..	0.0	..	..	..	..	.0	7.3	7.3
CHILE	67.0	99.8	0.0	3.7	..	12.0	0.0	10.3	..	34.7	2.4	7.3	7.3
TOGO	100.0	100.0	0.0	0.0	..	0.1	..	..	..	..	.0	6.5	6.5
BENIN	0.0	0.0	0.0	0.4	..	..	..	..	..	..	.0	6.5	6.5
NAURU	100.0	100.0	0.0	2.4	..	2.4	..	..	..	..	.0	4.9	4.9
HONG KONG	17.1	51.3	4.0	3.8	0.080	11.8	1.1	5.5	0.064	21.0	2.3	3.8	3.8
LIBERIA	100.0	100.0	3.6	3.5	0.080	3.5	..	..	..	..	.0	3.4	3.4
KIRIBATI	100.0	100.0	0.0	0.0	..	3.5	..	..	..	..	.0	3.2	3.2
KENYA	0.0	0.0	0.0	0.0	..	..	0.0	0.0	..	..	.4	3.2	3.2
ARUBA	16.1	16.1	0.0	0.4	..	2.4	..	..	..	..	.0	2.0	2.0

Notes: 1. Value of exports from reporter countries that do not participate in Free Trade Agreements.

2. Weighted average tariff reduction measured by dT / (1 + T) in percent.

3. The available AVE tariff rates used in this product category cover only 72% of the petrol exports to the 40 IDB countries

Petroleum Oils[3] (continued)

Export market	% of exports GATT bount		Average levels and changes weighted by value of exports to: the World exc. FTA[1]				LMIEs exc. FTA[1]				Value of exports in $ million		
	Total pre-UR	Total post-UR	% of exports affected	Post-UR applied rate	Tariff reduc-tion[2]	Post-UR bound rate	% of exports affected	Post-UR applied rate	Tariff reduc-tion[2]	Post-UR bound rate	To IDB LMIEs exc. FTA[1]	To all IDB Ctrys exc. FTA[1]	To all IDB Ctrys inc. FTA
BERMUDA	80.5	99.8	0.0	2.0	..	10.2	0.0	10.0	..	35.0	.3	1.5	1.5
DOMINICAN REPUBLIC	100.0	100.0	0.0	0.5	..	0.5	..	..	..	..	.0	1.0	1.0
BARBADOS	0.0	0.0	0.0	0.0	..	..	..	..	..	..	.0	.7	.7
HONDURAS	100.0	100.0	0.0	0.4	..	0.7	..	..	..	..	.0	.6	.6
MALTA	100.0	100.0	1.6	0.6	0.035	3.5	..	..	..	..	.0	.4	.4
MAURITIUS	0.0	10.0	0.2	0.6	0.015	0.3	33.3	7.7	2.003	13.0	.0	.4	.4
AFGHANISTAN	100.0	100.0	0.0	3.5	..	3.5	..	..	..	..	.0	.2	.2
DOMINICA	100.0	100.0	0.0	0.0	..	3.5	..	..	..	..	.0	.2	.2
ZAMBIA	0.0	0.0	0.0	..	..	..	0.0	..	..	..	.1	.1	.1
ICELAND	96.9	96.9	3.1	0.3	1.948	0.4	..	..	..	..	.0	.0	.1
MOZAMBIQUE	0.0	0.0	0.0	36.0	..	..	0.0	36.0	..	..	.1	.1	.1
COSTA RICA	16.3	16.3	0.0	0.8	..	9.6	0.0	5.0	..	40.0	.0	.1	.1
LEBANON	0.0	100.0	0.0	3.0	..	35.0	0.0	3.0	..	35.0	.1	.1	.1
MALI	100.0	100.0	100.0	3.7	2.194	3.7	..	..	..	..	.0	.0	.0
GREENLAND	100.0	100.0	0.0	0.0	..	3.5	..	..	..	..	.0	.0	.0
PARAGUAY	33.3	100.0	0.0	3.5	..	24.5	0.0	..	..	35.0	.0	.0	.0
URUGUAY	33.3	33.3	33.3	3.3	0.193	3.3	..	..	..	..	.0	.0	.0
SEYCHELLES	0.0	0.0	0.0	..	..	..	..	..	..	..	.0	.0	.0
JAMAICA	0.0	0.0	0.0	0.0	..	..	..	..	..	..	.0	.0	.0
HAITI	0.0	0.0	0.0	0.6	..	..	..	..	..	..	.0	.0	.0
BOTSWANA	0.0	0.0	0.0	0.0	..	..	0.0	0.0	..	..	.0	.0	.0
BELIZE	100.0	100.0	0.0	0.4	..	0.7	..	..	..	..	.0	.0	.0
GAMBIA, THE	100.0	100.0	0.0	7.0	..	7.0	0.0	7.0	..	7.0	.0	.0	.0
BOLIVIA	100.0	100.0	0.0	11.0	..	25.0	0.0	11.0	..	25.0	.0	.0	.0
GUINEA-BISSAU	100.0	100.0	100.0	3.7	2.194	3.7	..	..	..	..	.0	.0	.0
SURINAME	100.0	100.0	100.0	3.7	2.194	3.7	..	..	..	..	.0	.0	.0

Notes: 1. Value of exports from reporter countries that do not participate in Free Trade Agreements.
2. Weighted average tariff reduction measured by dT / (1 + T) in percent.
3. The available AVE tariff rates used in this product category cover only 72% of the petrol exports to the 40 IDB countries

Wood, Pulp, Paper and Furniture Extent of other countries' MFN tariff reductions on exports from:

Export market	% of exports GATT bount		Average levels and changes weighted by value of exports to: the World exc. FTA[1]				LMIEs exc. FTA[1]				Value of exports in $ million		
	Total pre-UR	Total post-UR	% of exports affected	Post-UR applied rate	Tariff reduc-tion[2]	Post-UR bound rate	% of exports affected	Post-UR applied rate	Tariff reduc-tion[2]	Post-UR bound rate	To IDB LMIEs exc. FTA[1]	To all IDB Ctrys exc. FTA[1]	To all IDB Ctrys inc. FTA
CANADA	90.9	94.4	5.9	0.2	1.136	0.7	26.8	4.6	1.825	18.4	616.8	6,045.3	20,427.4
UNITED STATES	67.0	80.0	16.7	1.3	1.331	4.0	29.2	6.8	2.850	18.6	2,162.2	11,580.4	15,815.9
EUROPEAN UNION	87.6	97.9	23.8	2.2	2.486	3.2	28.6	13.5	2.277	19.5	1,255.8	6,184.5	13,285.2
SWEDEN	96.7	99.6	3.2	0.4	2.118	0.8	27.3	10.4	2.413	18.0	315.4	934.8	10,229.1
FINLAND	94.8	99.5	7.1	0.5	2.281	1.2	23.8	10.3	2.182	18.3	321.0	1,282.8	8,551.8
MALAYSIA	30.3	98.7	12.7	1.6	0.706	2.9	17.3	5.9	1.358	8.7	754.4	3,863.8	3,863.8
AUSTRIA	96.9	99.4	4.3	0.8	1.643	1.4	42.6	9.9	1.295	8.2	247.6	357.1	3,721.3
TAIWAN (CHINA)	80.2	96.6	77.1	1.5	3.099	1.8	32.7	11.5	2.521	20.1	154.5	3,364.6	3,364.6
INDONESIA	65.7	90.8	49.5	5.6	1.699	5.1	16.8	13.8	1.481	11.0	268.3	2,540.6	2,540.6
FORMER USSR	71.0	76.4	10.3	0.9	0.378	2.0	16.3	6.2	0.473	10.6	287.1	2,414.2	2,414.2
JAPAN	51.7	96.8	45.9	2.5	3.338	2.6	51.6	12.8	7.513	15.4	357.8	2,269.9	2,269.9
SWITZERLAND	97.7	99.4	4.0	0.5	2.229	1.5	38.1	10.5	2.392	17.6	66.1	161.6	1,707.7
BRAZIL	92.0	99.8	35.5	1.5	2.022	3.3	10.9	11.0	1.449	26.7	81.0	1,492.3	1,554.2
NORWAY	95.5	98.7	3.8	0.6	2.120	1.1	14.5	14.1	2.327	22.3	67.8	187.8	1,554.0
CHINA	34.5	93.8	29.9	0.9	1.374	1.0	23.2	11.3	0.912	21.4	56.3	1,430.4	1,430.4
MEXICO	98.4	99.7	2.7	0.1	3.412	0.7	38.2	2.2	1.895	15.3	36.3	63.5	1,214.4
FORMER YUGOSLAVIA	95.2	99.7	72.2	1.9	4.060	1.9	68.0	13.4	5.285	13.7	74.9	1,036.1	1,036.1
KOREA, REPUBLIC OF	55.7	91.0	50.8	1.8	2.457	1.4	12.5	26.3	1.337	31.4	33.8	769.3	769.3
SINGAPORE	57.1	95.3	37.4	3.7	2.085	5.9	21.9	11.0	2.119	23.0	187.2	768.6	768.6
NEW ZEALAND	33.3	81.1	9.1	1.3	0.511	5.7	20.7	4.9	1.012	18.4	145.0	439.3	741.7
AUSTRALIA	21.8	43.0	7.2	0.8	0.454	4.4	26.5	8.8	1.662	22.9	62.0	567.4	697.5
CHILE	61.0	81.0	10.3	2.8	0.409	8.7	7.2	6.4	0.436	21.5	257.0	659.3	659.3
PHILIPPINES	79.7	97.4	66.4	2.0	3.288	2.1	61.9	13.0	5.004	12.1	4.0	639.1	639.1
HONG KONG	73.7	90.6	31.8	2.1	2.037	2.1	12.6	8.7	1.470	14.7	123.5	629.1	629.1
CZECH & SLOVAK CU	96.3	99.5	35.0	1.0	1.744	1.1	38.2	5.2	1.881	3.7	53.4	594.2	594.2
THAILAND	76.1	97.8	72.0	1.6	2.898	1.7	27.4	12.8	1.842	16.1	24.2	495.3	495.3
SOUTH AFRICA	74.5	85.3	33.5	1.9	1.868	3.3	6.2	9.2	0.498	22.5	76.3	470.9	470.9
POLAND	96.0	98.2	50.8	1.6	2.444	1.7	31.7	11.2	1.150	12.6	33.0	461.5	461.5
ROMANIA	98.4	99.6	88.0	1.8	4.749	1.9	47.6	13.6	2.784	13.7	32.5	442.4	442.4
COTE D'IVOIRE	92.0	95.9	18.7	1.9	0.538	1.5	3.6	17.7	0.300	24.2	26.8	335.7	335.7
HUNGARY	96.1	99.9	57.3	1.7	2.580	2.0	66.2	9.3	2.339	11.7	19.8	238.1	238.1
CAMEROON	96.6	99.3	13.5	0.9	0.457	0.8	46.9	9.6	3.840	8.9	10.7	219.2	219.2
GABON	95.8	99.3	15.9	1.4	0.571	1.6	40.8	10.4	3.407	18.9	8.4	181.1	181.1
ARGENTINA	87.5	100.0	16.2	1.0	0.762	7.0	0.4	2.1	0.321	16.1	19.0	119.7	174.0
MYANMAR	20.9	99.6	33.2	4.6	1.810	8.1	66.2	9.4	3.622	13.6	82.5	167.0	167.0
PAPUA NEW GUINEA	88.6	95.7	1.1	0.8	0.056	1.5	1.7	2.1	0.080	3.5	59.7	159.3	159.3
GHANA	100.0	100.0	13.1	0.4	0.355	0.4	20.0	0.2	1.206	0.2	1.2	143.1	143.1
CONGO	94.0	99.2	17.9	1.0	0.535	1.0	15.5	5.5	1.223	6.3	12.3	141.5	141.5
LIBERIA	92.5	98.5	6.2	0.9	0.425	0.8	72.5	12.0	5.367	12.3	10.3	137.0	137.0
ISRAEL	96.7	99.7	60.5	1.9	5.217	1.9	12.8	23.5	0.433	24.3	1.6	60.2	89.1
MOROCCO	78.8	99.1	21.6	5.2	0.970	5.4	22.8	17.4	1.217	18.6	19.7	71.8	71.8
INDIA	66.4	82.2	53.2	7.3	2.395	2.3	29.3	22.1	1.049	8.6	17.6	60.1	60.1
PARAGUAY	34.2	100.0	21.9	0.5	2.163	13.3	0.2	0.0	2.310	19.9	.1	19.5	54.7
ZAIRE	99.6	100.0	13.8	0.6	0.391	0.6	40.2	9.0	3.360	6.2	.4	51.4	51.4
SWAZILAND	42.5	47.9	33.1	4.4	1.557	1.8	27.1	6.1	1.310	3.5	37.6	51.4	51.4

Notes: 1. Value of exports from reporter countries that do not participate in Free Trade Agreements.

2. Weighted average tariff reduction measured by dT / (1 + T) in percent.

Wood, Pulp, Paper and Furniture (continued)

Export market	% of exports GATT bound Total pre-UR	Total post-UR	World exc. FTA¹ % of exports affected	Post-UR applied rate	Tariff reduction²	Post-UR bound rate	LMIEs exc. FTA¹ % of exports affected	Post-UR applied rate	Tariff reduction²	Post-UR bound rate	To IDB LMIEs exc. FTA¹	To all IDB Ctrys exc. FTA¹	To all IDB Ctrys inc. FTA
COLOMBIA	88.9	100.0	28.2	2.6	1.255	12.8	2.4	6.4	0.144	32.7	19.4	50.1	50.1
BULGARIA	89.9	99.2	53.2	2.4	2.950	2.1	31.9	16.7	1.568	14.3	3.9	37.2	37.2
COSTA RICA	97.0	100.0	70.9	4.6	2.335	8.0	0.0	20.6	..	38.8	6.8	36.3	36.3
VENEZUELA	89.8	100.0	65.6	1.7	3.925	4.9	1.6	11.8	0.534	34.4	4.3	30.4	30.4
BOLIVIA	59.5	100.0	8.0	4.7	0.452	12.0	8.6	9.5	0.688	25.0	13.5	28.9	28.9
EQUATORIAL GUINEA	100.0	100.0	8.9	0.3	0.219	0.3	0.0	0.0	..	0.0	.0	28.8	28.8
URUGUAY	50.7	100.0	14.6	2.3	0.979	19.4	0.0	5.4	0.009	29.7	1.7	11.4	27.0
HONDURAS	93.3	95.2	35.1	1.9	1.125	4.1	0.0	16.2	..	35.9	2.7	26.4	26.4
ECUADOR	88.6	99.3	42.6	2.8	1.451	4.8	2.7	9.3	0.210	31.8	2.4	24.8	24.8
DOMINICAN REPUBLIC	99.7	99.9	86.7	0.6	4.395	0.6	35.7	34.9	1.528	42.0	.1	24.5	24.5
VIETNAM	30.4	85.4	37.1	2.7	1.731	3.7	69.8	5.5	3.156	7.9	9.9	23.4	23.4
FIJI	23.4	65.4	25.8	3.0	2.800	5.4	4.6	4.0	0.171	12.2	1.9	20.0	20.0
TURKEY	79.1	99.8	67.5	4.2	2.989	4.8	22.3	17.3	0.369	20.8	3.2	17.7	17.7
LAO PDR	21.6	81.6	56.0	4.6	4.031	5.6	99.9	8.2	7.205	8.2	9.7	17.4	17.4
TUNISIA	97.4	99.3	44.5	1.1	2.391	1.6	8.4	7.8	0.312	36.5	.4	17.0	17.0
ALGERIA	99.0	99.0	18.7	0.9	0.644	0.7	0.0	26.3	..	43.0	.1	13.2	13.2
MALTA	81.6	100.0	44.8	0.3	2.312	7.4	2.8	0.7	0.236	39.8	2.1	11.6	11.6
CYPRUS	89.2	90.3	72.9	8.0	5.164	1.4	28.0	52.8	2.290	21.6	1.6	11.1	11.1
LEBANON	60.3	64.9	41.3	4.8	2.674	3.6	9.1	10.6	1.078	28.2	4.5	10.6	10.6
PUERTO RICO	92.9	99.9	4.7	5.4	0.318	33.8	0.1	5.7	0.003	35.7	9.0	9.6	9.6
SAUDI ARABIA	59.3	96.1	6.9	5.5	0.506	28.9	0.9	6.9	0.105	36.7	7.4	9.4	9.4
PANAMA	62.5	98.9	22.5	2.7	1.115	19.4	3.2	3.8	0.269	29.5	6.1	9.2	9.2
UNTD ARAB EMRTS	18.6	98.6	15.9	12.1	0.761	31.5	1.5	14.8	0.166	38.6	7.5	9.2	9.2
CENTRAL AFRICAN REP.	99.7	100.0	5.8	0.2	0.183	0.2	1.6	2.0	0.046	3.3	.2	8.7	8.7
SRI LANKA	82.5	90.9	36.0	1.1	1.713	1.4	12.1	14.6	0.668	21.5	.4	8.2	8.2
HAITI	99.9	100.0	99.6	0.4	4.930	0.4	..	..	..	..	.0	7.9	7.9
MOZAMBIQUE	37.4	97.0	10.9	9.1	0.781	10.9	4.4	12.4	0.593	15.0	5.7	7.7	7.7
MACAU	60.6	99.6	63.0	1.0	2.900	1.0	52.4	22.0	7.865	21.7	.1	7.5	7.5
BANGLADESH	6.0	99.7	4.1	1.1	0.246	23.4	0.4	5.1	0.048	24.9	6.9	7.4	7.4
PERU	96.1	100.0	26.4	4.6	1.033	9.6	9.5	12.2	0.229	25.9	2.6	7.0	7.0
TANZANIA	82.2	99.0	9.4	1.4	0.414	5.6	1.9	8.4	0.189	26.4	1.5	6.9	6.9
EGYPT, ARAB REP.	80.1	87.4	70.8	1.4	2.596	3.1	2.4	5.9	0.305	32.9	1.3	6.4	6.4
NIGERIA	89.1	98.6	16.7	1.0	0.877	2.3	0.2	9.4	0.010	23.4	.6	5.8	5.8
EL SALVADOR	99.7	100.0	97.4	0.3	4.526	0.5	5.1	2.6	0.147	11.4	.1	5.8	5.8
TRINIDAD AND TOBAGO	13.3	100.0	5.4	30.2	0.244	44.7	0.0	33.1	0.001	49.1	5.2	5.7	5.7
ZIMBABWE	99.7	100.0	75.1	1.7	3.001	7.7	0.0	0.0	..	30.0	.8	4.0	4.0
BELIZE	80.0	100.0	3.6	9.4	0.159	26.9	0.0	13.3	..	38.4	2.5	3.6	3.6
SURINAME	98.7	100.0	3.8	0.5	0.130	0.8	0.0	30.0	..	50.0	.0	3.5	3.5
GUYANA	88.2	100.0	1.6	3.0	0.057	6.2	0.0	23.9	..	49.4	.4	3.5	3.5
PAKISTAN	86.8	96.8	71.4	2.2	3.609	1.4	39.9	17.1	5.603	12.2	.3	3.5	3.5
CUBA	81.9	100.0	53.7	1.9	4.146	7.0	10.6	6.2	0.298	28.4	.8	3.4	3.4
KENYA	81.9	86.2	74.9	7.4	2.557	1.7	1.1	41.5	0.036	6.3	.4	3.0	3.0
KUWAIT	72.4	97.5	7.6	3.3	0.528	8.5	0.3	13.4	0.023	39.2	.7	2.9	2.9
ALBANIA	92.0	99.8	73.2	1.8	3.388	1.8	97.9	7.2	3.342	7.3	.4	2.8	2.8
NAURU	100.0	100.0	0.9	0.0	0.022	0.0	..	..	..	..	.0	2.3	2.3

Notes: 1. Value of exports from reporter countries that do not participate in Free Trade Agreements.

2. Weighted average tariff reduction measured by dT / (1 + T) in percent.

Wood, Pulp, Paper and Furniture (continued)

Export market	% of exports GATT bount		Average levels and changes weighted by value of exports to: the World exc. FTA[1]				LMIEs exc. FTA[1]				Value of exports in $ million		
	Total pre-UR	Total post-UR	% of exports affected	Post-UR applied rate	Tariff reduction[2]	Post-UR bound rate	% of exports affected	Post-UR applied rate	Tariff reduction[2]	Post-UR bound rate	To IDB LMIEs exc. FTA[1]	To all IDB Ctrys exc. FTA[1]	To all IDB Ctrys inc. FTA
ICELAND	91.7	98.6	9.8	0.4	1.592	1.7	5.5	2.3	0.798	3.1	.1	.7	2.3
JAMAICA	98.3	100.0	81.6	0.1	3.039	0.2	25.0	13.7	0.980	32.9	.0	2.3	2.3
GUINEA	35.4	100.0	9.2	6.7	0.259	16.4	0.0	9.7	..	24.3	1.4	2.1	2.1
MAURITIUS	97.9	100.0	89.4	0.3	5.008	0.3	25.0	25.0	0.980	25.0	.0	2.1	2.1
BARBADOS	9.5	100.0	6.0	16.4	0.289	43.7	0.0	18.1	..	48.3	1.8	2.0	2.0
NETHERLANDS ANTILLES	99.3	99.9	79.6	3.0	4.128	6.5	4.0	16.4	0.113	35.0	.4	1.9	1.9
JORDAN	94.8	97.1	34.1	7.9	3.299	7.5	83.6	29.5	10.772	30.6	.5	1.9	1.9
BRUNEI	56.0	99.3	12.5	3.2	1.095	3.9	28.0	18.2	5.080	22.4	.3	1.7	1.7
BOTSWANA	19.9	19.9	10.5	11.3	0.588	1.8	0.0	12.9	..	4.0	1.4	1.6	1.6
BAHAMAS, THE	100.0	100.0	7.5	0.1	0.361	0.1	0.0	0.3	..	1.2	.0	1.5	1.5
CAMBODIA	13.5	99.9	0.8	0.0	0.042	0.1	0.0	0.0	..	0.5	.1	1.3	1.3
NICARAGUA	99.9	100.0	8.7	10.6	0.583	26.8	0.0	12.1	..	30.5	1.0	1.1	1.1
BAHRAIN	68.8	97.6	6.5	3.6	0.398	8.2	0.4	16.2	0.030	39.9	.2	1.1	1.1
OMAN	82.4	99.4	13.4	2.8	0.657	6.8	0.0	15.8	..	40.0	.2	.9	.9
SENEGAL	100.0	100.0	40.2	0.1	2.239	0.1	..	..	..	..	.0	.9	.9
GUINEA-BISSAU	97.0	97.0	13.4	0.6	0.460	0.2	0.0	11.0	..	0.0	.0	.8	.8
NEPAL	51.7	94.0	61.4	10.4	4.596	11.9	24.5	23.5	3.694	29.3	.3	.7	.7
MADAGASCAR	77.2	99.9	28.7	0.2	1.483	1.3	0.0	15.0	..	..	.0	.7	.7
VANUATU	81.3	100.0	2.4	2.4	0.212	3.1	0.0	1.5	..	2.0	.4	.7	.7
BERMUDA	100.0	100.0	21.8	0.0	1.324	0.0	..	..	..	..	.0	.6	.6
GIBRALTAR	80.8	97.5	71.5	3.3	4.591	3.4	0.0	0.0	..	0.0	.0	.5	.5
TOGO	99.6	99.6	83.9	1.4	3.305	1.9	0.0	10.8	..	35.0	.0	.5	.5
SIERRA LEONE	100.0	100.0	12.8	0.0	0.500	0.0	0.0	0.0	..	0.0	.0	.4	.4
GUADELOUPE	100.0	100.0	50.7	1.2	2.988	7.9	0.0	5.0	..	35.0	.1	.4	.4
IRAN, ISLAMIC REP.	98.3	99.8	61.5	0.5	3.068	1.0	0.0	1.9	..	30.0	.0	.4	.4
MALAWI	88.1	89.3	75.7	0.4	4.005	0.5	0.0	0.0	..	0.0	.0	.4	.4
MARTINIQUE	100.0	100.0	34.4	0.3	1.872	0.3	..	..	..	..	.0	.4	.4
NIGER	60.6	69.1	28.6	3.1	1.898	0.0	0.0	10.0	..	..	.1	.4	.4
BHUTAN	99.7	100.0	37.4	0.1	2.118	0.1	..	..	..	..	.0	.4	.4
DOMINICA	100.0	100.0	79.4	1.8	4.687	2.1	0.0	10.0	..	35.0	.0	.4	.4
IRAQ	93.2	100.0	48.4	0.5	2.747	0.5	100.0	30.0	7.407	30.0	.0	.4	.4
RWANDA	99.4	100.0	15.6	0.1	1.101	0.1	100.0	13.0	6.009	13.0	.0	.3	.3
GAMBIA, THE	100.0	100.0	31.0	0.5	1.386	0.5	..	..	..	..	.0	.3	.3
LIBYA	74.2	79.0	55.1	3.6	2.830	1.0	40.4	8.4	0.276	3.6	.1	.3	.3
MALI	93.2	98.3	55.4	1.3	1.924	1.0	58.3	11.9	1.264	9.6	.0	.3	.3
BENIN	96.2	96.2	6.5	0.8	0.248	0.2	0.0	15.0	..	..	.0	.3	.3
ANGOLA	99.6	100.0	18.6	0.3	0.824	0.4	0.0	0.0	..	30.0	.0	.3	.3
CHAD	100.0	100.0	81.0	6.3	2.458	6.3	..	..	..	..	.0	.3	.3
SYRIA	82.8	88.1	72.8	2.0	2.804	3.1	0.0	2.5	..	26.2	.0	.3	.3
MONGOLIA	48.4	91.1	53.8	4.1	1.858	7.4	34.0	9.1	0.864	21.8	.0	.2	.2
SOMALIA	100.0	100.0	8.4	0.0	0.462	0.0	..	..	..	..	.0	.2	.2
BURKINA FASO	100.0	100.0	80.8	2.1	4.064	2.1	..	..	..	..	.0	.2	.2
QATAR	94.6	97.5	69.8	0.7	3.166	0.2	10.0	13.5	1.818	8.0	.0	.2	.2
ETHIOPIA	38.9	98.3	12.6	15.3	0.679	20.4	0.0	22.4	..	30.2	.1	.2	.2
SEYCHELLES	30.2	43.8	27.2	8.2	1.741	3.1	0.0	14.7	..	..	.1	.2	.2

Notes: 1. Value of exports from reporter countries that do not participate in Free Trade Agreements.

2. Weighted average tariff reduction measured by dT / (1 + T) in percent.

Textiles and Clothing[3] Extent of other countries' MFN tariff reductions on exports from:

Export market	% of exports GATT bount		Average levels and changes weighted by value of exports to: the World exc. FTA[1]				LMIEs exc. FTA[1]				Value of exports in $ million		
	Total pre-UR	Total post-UR	% of exports affected	Post-UR applied rate	Tariff reduc-tion[2]	Post-UR bound rate	% of exports affected	Post-UR applied rate	Tariff reduc-tion[2]	Post-UR bound rate	To IDB LMIEs exc. FTA[1]	To all IDB Ctrys exc. FTA[1]	To all IDB Ctrys inc. FTA
CHINA	35.7	42.2	31.7	4.6	0.930	11.2	48.8	16.2	4.407	20.8	864.7	26,173.2	26,173.2
EUROPEAN UNION	77.9	93.4	34.7	11.4	2.798	12.2	44.0	23.4	2.972	27.9	2,665.7	10,493.3	19,919.0
KOREA, REPUBLIC OF	73.7	82.2	71.7	11.3	2.201	13.3	47.1	31.9	5.664	29.4	599.5	12,250.8	12,250.8
TAIWAN (CHINA)	54.3	69.3	58.1	11.4	2.026	15.8	60.3	27.9	6.339	26.9	1,423.5	12,239.0	12,239.0
HONG KONG	81.6	93.4	84.6	14.7	2.322	14.7	42.0	22.9	4.388	24.7	1,319.6	10,302.1	10,302.1
JAPAN	41.9	75.0	52.2	8.6	3.071	12.2	63.8	19.6	5.752	22.1	1,388.8	5,620.7	5,620.7
UNITED STATES	75.7	93.6	40.7	9.7	2.805	14.1	26.8	21.5	4.300	32.7	907.4	3,485.9	5,034.8
INDIA	89.0	95.4	79.4	10.3	1.913	10.4	56.1	21.5	3.508	17.5	172.8	3,087.5	3,087.5
AUSTRIA	95.1	99.2	10.3	10.2	2.757	8.3	66.5	11.8	2.762	12.0	299.8	420.1	2,822.2
TURKEY	96.8	99.9	94.0	10.4	1.916	10.6	31.6	12.2	1.014	18.8	69.1	2,813.1	2,813.1
SWITZERLAND	94.8	98.9	8.9	8.1	2.456	7.7	52.4	15.2	2.611	17.6	141.7	386.2	2,798.9
AUSTRALIA	82.7	97.6	17.9	1.4	0.747	3.3	50.7	5.0	3.410	8.6	492.9	2,587.0	2,704.3
PAKISTAN	70.1	79.6	67.7	8.4	1.901	9.6	69.5	23.6	6.125	16.7	184.8	2,204.5	2,204.5
THAILAND	79.4	90.6	76.7	11.8	2.132	12.8	37.9	26.6	2.565	21.4	103.7	2,080.0	2,080.0
INDONESIA	77.5	86.7	80.1	14.4	2.064	16.2	65.0	22.9	5.083	19.6	119.4	1,517.5	1,517.5
MALAYSIA	56.6	90.0	55.0	11.4	1.367	14.0	40.1	33.2	5.782	29.1	57.5	1,416.5	1,416.5
PHILIPPINES	93.2	97.7	89.3	14.1	1.771	14.5	69.3	19.8	6.187	18.8	17.6	1,404.5	1,404.5
FORMER YUGOSLAVIA	94.4	99.8	92.9	10.5	2.319	10.6	72.8	12.3	3.788	12.9	120.9	1,204.8	1,204.8
BRAZIL	88.5	97.3	75.9	8.3	2.044	9.9	15.8	11.5	0.947	25.0	76.4	1,099.7	1,130.7
MACAU	87.8	92.4	85.4	14.3	1.943	15.5	97.6	20.8	6.526	20.9	.8	1,120.3	1,120.3
SINGAPORE	88.4	96.3	92.9	18.9	1.996	19.2	64.7	25.3	5.590	22.6	89.1	1,064.9	1,064.9
MEXICO	96.8	99.9	7.5	3.9	2.967	13.5	11.6	12.8	1.550	32.4	37.7	114.6	1,016.2
CANADA	87.9	98.3	16.5	7.1	3.165	9.4	38.8	14.7	3.351	21.7	76.0	254.2	913.5
MOROCCO	98.5	99.9	89.3	10.9	1.506	11.2	2.7	20.3	0.095	43.2	10.8	794.0	794.0
SWEDEN	94.2	98.7	7.2	9.4	2.589	9.1	41.1	22.7	2.546	22.3	34.5	88.8	776.7
DOMINICAN REPUBLIC	100.0	100.0	96.3	16.6	1.666	16.6	56.5	18.9	2.512	37.0	.1	754.8	754.8
FINLAND	90.6	99.8	5.4	9.3	5.649	9.8	70.2	18.8	9.609	21.1	21.3	50.1	731.6
BANGLADESH	93.8	98.5	87.9	12.1	1.762	12.5	48.3	10.3	3.033	18.6	33.6	707.8	707.8
ISRAEL	96.7	98.0	67.0	9.6	1.862	10.9	10.9	23.8	1.747	32.0	11.7	485.5	639.4
TUNISIA	99.7	100.0	92.7	10.9	1.625	10.9	33.5	21.2	1.001	18.0	.4	620.9	620.9
SRI LANKA	95.7	99.4	92.9	14.9	1.558	15.0	85.6	10.1	5.092	8.8	3.1	576.7	576.7
MAURITIUS	98.0	99.5	95.8	12.8	1.507	13.0	42.5	12.3	2.382	13.0	.3	502.2	502.2
SOUTH AFRICA	83.6	85.7	29.6	2.4	0.650	2.7	39.5	15.7	4.590	21.7	15.5	454.5	454.5
CZECH & SLOVAK CU	87.2	98.2	84.2	10.6	3.041	10.7	60.6	13.3	3.572	11.8	73.3	452.5	452.5
NEW ZEALAND	62.5	98.3	16.4	1.5	0.860	6.4	53.1	5.2	3.094	8.2	52.1	306.0	452.1
IRAN, ISLAMIC REP.	98.0	99.1	28.6	4.4	0.758	4.5	74.4	23.9	10.179	23.9	.6	435.1	435.1
ROMANIA	95.3	99.1	94.4	12.9	3.161	12.6	80.4	23.4	10.860	20.1	33.9	398.3	398.3
EGYPT, ARAB REP.	85.3	94.7	76.7	10.3	1.621	9.9	21.2	24.2	1.041	24.0	62.4	368.8	368.8
COSTA RICA	99.6	100.0	98.8	17.7	2.174	17.8	0.3	23.5	0.012	37.5	2.5	347.6	347.6
POLAND	92.4	97.5	90.9	12.2	2.774	11.6	61.9	22.5	4.377	13.2	28.0	334.8	334.8
URUGUAY	62.1	89.6	45.8	6.2	1.704	15.5	6.8	4.6	2.185	29.0	29.2	250.8	329.9
HUNGARY	92.7	99.3	85.1	10.9	2.691	12.2	55.4	9.7	1.926	20.2	39.6	317.5	317.5
ARGENTINA	78.2	96.1	49.5	6.7	1.511	12.2	5.2	12.9	1.167	30.5	21.9	247.9	296.4
PERU	92.1	99.5	68.7	9.0	1.544	11.9	6.8	13.9	0.404	30.5	45.7	265.9	265.9
COLOMBIA	95.2	100.0	77.2	14.7	1.427	15.5	35.1	24.1	1.281	32.3	24.7	249.5	249.5

Notes: 1. Value of exports from reporter countries that do not participate in Free Trade Agreements.

2. Weighted average tariff reduction measured by dT / (1 + T) in percent.

3. MFN tariff rates only. This table does not report any levels or changes in quota rents due to the abolishion of the MFA.

Textiles and Clothing[3] (continued)

Export market	% of exports GATT bount — Total pre-UR	Total post-UR	the World exc. FTA[1] — % of exports affected	Post-UR applied rate	Tariff reduction[2]	Post-UR bound rate	LMIEs exc. FTA[1] — % of exports affected	Post-UR applied rate	Tariff reduction[2]	Post-UR bound rate	Value of exports in $ million — To IDB LMIEs exc. FTA[1]	To all IDB Ctrys exc. FTA[1]	To all IDB Ctrys inc. FTA
JAMAICA	98.9	99.9	98.9	18.8	1.628	18.8	9.6	22.3	0.349	47.8	.6	241.1	241.1
HAITI	99.9	100.0	92.9	16.9	1.704	16.9	0.0	5.0	..	40.0	.0	202.3	202.3
NORWAY	94.2	98.9	5.2	6.3	2.469	8.3	22.7	19.3	0.962	23.4	3.1	14.7	185.8
FORMER USSR	65.0	83.9	54.9	10.6	2.416	9.7	53.6	21.6	3.825	15.1	48.4	162.6	162.6
NEPAL	89.9	96.6	42.0	12.1	0.778	10.1	9.6	68.8	2.549	40.0	7.0	144.0	144.0
MALTA	98.9	100.0	93.5	10.3	1.867	10.3	97.6	17.0	2.455	17.0	.2	139.6	139.6
CYPRUS	98.0	99.5	94.8	11.6	1.820	11.4	61.9	18.6	2.591	14.1	5.7	127.3	127.3
PANAMA	88.9	99.8	76.3	23.2	1.842	26.7	58.0	29.0	2.113	35.3	62.8	114.4	114.4
UNTD ARAB EMRTS	93.3	99.5	93.2	14.6	1.292	14.9	11.6	27.9	0.867	29.6	3.0	101.1	101.1
HONDURAS	99.9	100.0	95.5	18.6	1.610	18.7	0.0	25.4	..	43.0	.6	91.1	91.1
CHILE	86.5	93.6	62.2	10.1	1.127	12.4	12.2	11.6	0.702	31.9	6.5	83.6	83.6
EL SALVADOR	99.9	100.0	86.8	13.4	1.454	13.5	15.8	18.6	2.228	35.4	.4	66.3	66.3
BULGARIA	85.3	99.3	88.6	12.3	2.882	12.3	61.4	16.3	3.207	16.0	6.9	64.2	64.2
VIETNAM	59.9	88.6	74.3	11.3	2.108	13.3	83.2	13.7	2.515	14.4	33.9	50.2	50.2
COTE D'IVOIRE	95.9	98.1	92.8	8.6	1.679	9.0	3.6	11.5	0.204	20.9	2.8	47.4	47.4
AFGHANISTAN	98.3	99.1	35.2	3.7	0.755	3.7	21.3	5.1	1.107	2.6	.9	42.5	42.5
FIJI	43.9	99.6	56.4	36.2	2.213	45.0	100.0	7.0	3.128	7.0	.0	41.5	41.5
ZIMBABWE	99.7	100.0	97.5	9.8	1.746	9.8	..	..	..	..	.0	37.6	37.6
LEBANON	97.0	100.0	83.6	12.2	1.395	12.3	43.8	20.0	0.968	21.3	3.3	34.5	34.5
MADAGASCAR	97.9	100.0	79.0	7.1	1.581	7.2	4.1	37.6	0.227	52.3	.1	24.3	24.3
LESOTHO	99.9	100.0	98.6	15.5	1.652	15.6	0.0	10.4	..	25.0	.2	24.0	24.0
TANZANIA	81.3	98.9	73.4	6.4	2.939	6.7	35.0	6.4	2.572	17.5	.9	23.8	23.8
ECUADOR	77.8	99.9	30.8	8.8	0.668	14.2	1.4	18.2	0.138	36.6	6.8	23.7	23.7
PARAGUAY	80.8	100.0	80.1	13.8	1.142	17.8	0.8	6.2	5.545	34.7	.0	18.3	22.5
VENEZUELA	70.0	99.4	54.4	13.2	1.022	20.5	0.3	14.3	0.023	33.5	8.1	21.6	21.6
KENYA	81.2	94.4	40.7	4.8	1.441	4.3	59.6	11.3	4.003	10.9	4.2	20.8	20.8
ICELAND	99.3	100.0	31.2	8.8	3.813	9.3	75.4	8.7	0.915	9.7	.2	6.8	20.7
SYRIA	67.0	94.2	42.0	18.7	0.846	15.3	2.2	36.5	0.108	30.7	8.7	20.2	20.2
BOTSWANA	19.6	42.5	42.2	26.9	2.235	24.6	28.1	30.9	2.350	36.7	16.2	20.2	20.2
CAMEROON	98.1	99.0	97.6	8.6	1.646	8.9	9.6	40.2	1.076	55.5	.2	20.0	20.0
BELIZE	99.9	100.0	99.4	16.0	1.096	16.1	0.0	24.0	..	37.4	.1	15.7	15.7
BAHRAIN	95.2	95.4	94.8	16.5	1.079	16.6	0.8	16.0	0.108	48.2	.6	13.4	13.4
MONGOLIA	80.3	100.0	50.0	4.3	1.590	5.0	55.6	7.4	3.074	9.1	5.1	12.3	12.3
MALAWI	95.3	95.4	93.3	10.9	1.782	10.6	0.0	17.5	..	50.0	.6	11.9	11.9
BOLIVIA	38.0	100.0	34.4	11.2	0.813	26.6	0.2	10.2	0.006	35.0	7.2	11.7	11.7
NETHERLANDS ANTILLES	98.9	100.0	94.1	34.2	3.411	34.9	94.2	34.4	3.427	35.1	10.3	10.4	10.4
ALBANIA	96.8	100.0	56.4	8.3	1.408	8.3	75.7	14.3	3.744	14.3	1.4	9.7	9.7
SWAZILAND	87.3	99.8	85.8	14.4	3.375	16.5	6.4	21.4	0.416	29.6	.5	9.2	9.2
MYANMAR	87.1	98.4	88.0	16.6	1.513	17.9	28.7	19.4	5.962	36.0	.4	9.1	9.1
ZAMBIA	81.3	82.5	82.5	7.5	1.567	8.5	17.7	12.7	0.695	25.0	.6	8.7	8.7
CUBA	93.0	100.0	82.0	12.5	3.359	13.2	36.8	12.1	0.722	17.4	1.2	8.6	8.6
BARBADOS	99.9	100.0	85.0	12.0	4.872	12.0	0.0	45.0	..	50.0	.0	7.5	7.5
SAUDI ARABIA	75.5	90.6	42.3	7.4	1.996	6.4	70.2	22.5	7.274	17.1	1.4	7.0	7.0
OMAN	99.3	99.6	98.4	17.0	1.205	17.1	100.0	29.9	10.587	29.9	.0	6.7	6.7
BRUNEI	89.7	97.4	89.2	17.0	2.628	18.4	7.5	12.0	1.022	46.9	.1	6.0	6.0

Notes: 1. Value of exports from reporter countries that do not participate in Free Trade Agreements.

2. Weighted average tariff reduction measured by dT / (1 + T) in percent.

3. MFN tariff rates only. This table does not report any levels or changes in quota rents due to the abolishion of the MFA.

Textiles and Clothing[3] (continued)

Export market	% of exports GATT bount		Average levels and changes weighted by value of exports to: the World exc. FTA[1]				LMIEs exc. FTA[1]				Value of exports in $ million		
	Total pre-UR	Total post-UR	% of exports affected	Post-UR applied rate	Tariff reduction[2]	Post-UR bound rate	% of exports affected	Post-UR applied rate	Tariff reduction[2]	Post-UR bound rate	To IDB LMIEs exc. FTA[1]	To all IDB Ctrys exc. FTA[1]	To all IDB Ctrys inc. FTA
ETHIOPIA	99.8	100.0	97.6	9.8	1.424	9.8	100.0	2.5	3.023	2.5	.7	6.0	6.0
IRAQ	99.4	99.8	27.8	2.7	1.712	2.8	95.5	8.6	10.134	9.4	.6	5.3	5.3
QATAR	98.6	98.6	96.2	15.5	1.285	15.7	100.0	8.0	10.526	8.0	.0	5.0	5.0
NIGERIA	98.6	100.0	13.7	9.1	0.395	9.2	85.3	35.9	11.236	37.3	.1	4.2	4.2
JORDAN	96.7	99.0	93.6	12.0	2.679	12.2	89.4	10.4	9.458	10.1	.7	3.7	3.7
KUWAIT	93.1	97.2	58.2	10.2	1.508	8.9	48.6	30.7	3.981	17.5	.3	3.4	3.4
TRINIDAD AND TOBAGO	58.5	100.0	56.8	20.1	0.699	28.4	0.0	31.6	..	51.8	1.4	3.4	3.4
GRENADA	99.6	99.9	87.0	12.4	1.324	12.5	0.0	35.8	..	60.0	.0	3.0	3.0
DOMINICA	85.4	100.0	98.4	16.6	3.520	16.6	..	..	..	..	.0	3.0	3.0
SENEGAL	99.6	100.0	95.3	6.1	1.759	6.1	0.0	40.0	..	40.0	.0	2.8	2.8
SUDAN	96.9	100.0	96.9	4.3	1.868	4.4	0.0	0.3	..	5.0	.1	2.5	2.5
LIBYA	90.9	100.0	9.4	5.3	0.111	8.3	0.0	25.9	..	45.2	.4	2.3	2.3
MOZAMBIQUE	97.9	98.8	65.4	4.9	1.347	4.9	83.3	37.8	22.092	43.3	.0	2.2	2.2
LAO PDR	89.7	94.5	93.9	12.8	2.433	13.6	..	..	..	..	.0	1.8	1.8
PUERTO RICO	85.8	99.9	64.5	17.4	2.992	21.6	23.2	22.5	0.796	32.5	.7	1.6	1.6
GUYANA	99.9	100.0	99.7	16.1	1.338	16.1	75.0	12.5	4.506	16.0	.0	1.6	1.6
PAPUA NEW GUINEA	27.7	99.9	16.4	36.3	0.484	38.3	2.3	5.8	0.303	40.0	.1	1.6	1.6
NIGER	98.2	99.9	36.9	12.7	1.489	15.8	0.9	15.2	0.122	20.2	1.0	1.6	1.6
ANTIGUA & B ARBUDA	99.7	100.0	99.7	4.5	2.827	4.5	0.0	44.0	..	55.0	.0	1.5	1.5
ALGERIA	99.7	100.0	96.2	7.7	2.414	7.7	100.0	40.0	13.333	40.0	.0	1.5	1.5
MALI	97.6	99.9	50.2	13.7	1.278	16.1	0.0	15.0	..	20.0	.7	1.4	1.4
ZAIRE	100.0	100.0	93.9	13.0	3.155	13.0	100.0	8.5	3.709	8.5	.0	1.2	1.2
BURKINA FASO	100.0	100.0	97.7	5.4	0.217	5.4	100.0	5.0	0.095	5.0	.7	.7	.7
TONGA	47.7	100.0	99.4	38.0	10.522	38.0	..	..	..	..	.0	.7	.7
DJIBOUTI	100.0	100.0	99.7	12.5	2.028	12.5	..	..	..	..	.0	.7	.7
CAMBODIA	23.7	28.8	23.4	4.0	0.328	11.4	0.0	19.4	..	19.3	.1	.7	.7
CENTRAL AFRICAN REP.	100.0	100.0	88.5	2.5	0.658	2.5	..	..	..	..	.0	.7	.7
ARUBA	100.0	100.0	99.8	34.4	3.609	34.4	99.8	35.0	3.630	35.0	.6	.6	.6
BENIN	71.0	71.0	59.8	10.6	1.152	6.2	30.1	16.5	0.647	10.5	.3	.5	.5
MARTINIQUE	98.4	100.0	91.4	10.9	1.682	11.5	0.0	10.0	..	50.0	.0	.5	.5
GHANA	99.6	100.0	19.9	13.5	0.399	28.6	0.0	15.1	..	35.1	.3	.5	.5
BAHAMAS, THE	90.5	100.0	87.6	17.3	4.714	17.3	100.0	40.0	13.333	40.0	.0	.4	.4
SURINAME	98.4	99.7	97.6	15.3	1.630	15.3	50.0	25.0	6.667	28.3	.0	.4	.4
SIERRA LEONE	94.5	100.0	97.2	12.5	3.472	12.5	..	..	..	..	.0	.4	.4
MAURITANIA	100.0	100.0	86.6	10.1	1.634	10.2	93.5	6.5	2.008	7.1	.0	.3	.3
GUADELOUPE	100.0	100.0	87.1	10.7	1.880	10.7	..	..	..	..	.0	.3	.3
TOGO	81.6	86.5	66.5	9.9	1.352	12.4	0.0	43.0	..	60.0	.0	.3	.3
LIBERIA	78.1	97.7	59.6	13.0	1.732	14.9	0.0	23.7	..	28.1	.1	.3	.3
YEMEN	90.3	100.0	86.3	11.2	3.084	13.2	0.0	36.2	..	56.7	.0	.2	.2
BHUTAN	90.2	100.0	94.9	12.3	2.415	12.4	..	..	..	..	.0	.2	.2
BURUNDI	79.8	100.0	79.8	5.1	1.604	6.1	..	..	..	..	.0	.2	.2
NICARAGUA	100.0	100.0	76.1	7.6	1.115	7.6	..	..	..	..	.0	.2	.2
CONGO	99.4	100.0	40.9	8.1	1.193	8.3	21.3	10.0	0.747	10.2	.1	.2	.2
ANGOLA	80.2	80.2	80.2	8.6	1.464	10.8	100.0	6.0	2.699	6.0	.0	.2	.2
KIRIBATI	86.4	100.0	86.4	17.2	1.404	22.4	0.0	10.0	..	50.0	.0	.2	.2

Notes: 1. Value of exports from reporter countries that do not participate in Free Trade Agreements.

2. Weighted average tariff reduction measured by dT / (1 + T) in percent.

3. MFN tariff rates only. This table does not report any levels or changes in quota rents due to the abolition of the MFA.

Leather, Rubber, Footwear Extent of other countries' MFN tariff reductions on exports from:

Export market	% of exports GATT bound		Average levels and changes weighted by value of exports to: the World exc. FTA[1]				LMIEs exc. FTA[1]				Value of exports in $ million		
	Total pre-UR	Total post-UR	% of exports affected	Post-UR applied rate	Tariff reduction[2]	Post-UR bound rate	% of exports affected	Post-UR applied rate	Tariff reduction[2]	Post-UR bound rate	To IDB LMIEs exc. FTA[1]	To all IDB Ctrys exc. FTA[1]	To all IDB Ctrys inc. FTA
EUROPEAN UNION	81.6	94.0	25.1	8.0	1.522	8.0	49.0	18.0	3.113	18.0	1,143.8	6,451.4	10,078.7
KOREA, REPUBLIC OF	88.0	95.3	38.4	9.3	1.086	9.7	12.6	21.4	0.932	31.0	136.0	7,118.4	7,118.4
CHINA	27.3	56.3	16.5	3.4	0.410	6.2	64.2	9.1	1.725	11.4	164.7	6,490.7	6,490.7
TAIWAN (CHINA)	80.1	91.8	52.7	8.7	1.391	9.5	45.1	18.6	3.764	23.0	191.2	4,556.2	4,556.2
UNITED STATES	77.9	94.2	26.3	6.0	1.540	10.2	29.6	15.0	2.868	28.0	583.1	2,257.0	3,531.6
JAPAN	62.8	84.1	57.3	6.3	1.828	7.4	55.7	18.4	4.197	19.9	613.5	3,355.1	3,355.1
MALAYSIA	58.5	95.5	24.1	1.8	1.617	3.9	70.2	7.9	7.503	9.3	392.6	2,379.5	2,379.5
BRAZIL	92.2	96.6	28.5	7.9	0.763	8.6	40.1	11.1	4.012	22.9	61.6	1,947.3	1,961.4
THAILAND	77.8	94.8	25.5	3.3	0.797	4.2	56.6	7.6	5.190	7.0	68.8	1,600.9	1,600.9
CANADA	96.4	99.3	5.2	2.4	1.647	4.1	42.9	12.4	3.068	24.2	46.7	150.5	1,330.6
INDONESIA	89.4	98.4	14.7	2.1	0.529	2.3	47.8	7.4	3.678	10.4	98.3	1,234.2	1,234.2
AUSTRIA	95.4	99.8	6.7	3.3	1.442	5.4	69.6	8.8	2.571	9.9	63.5	176.1	988.1
INDIA	85.7	92.5	66.9	5.7	1.280	6.0	64.4	17.4	4.361	13.4	31.5	881.9	881.9
HONG KONG	90.5	96.7	45.4	11.8	1.168	12.1	22.3	20.6	1.949	26.2	32.3	848.3	848.3
ARGENTINA	72.6	88.9	41.2	4.2	1.283	8.4	37.5	9.3	4.414	23.8	71.9	594.0	649.0
TURKEY	99.0	99.9	92.4	4.5	2.391	4.5	27.9	17.3	1.262	18.7	9.9	542.0	542.0
FORMER YUGOSLAVIA	95.7	99.4	70.2	7.1	1.583	6.4	76.1	18.6	2.040	8.0	35.9	524.2	524.2
PAKISTAN	84.8	93.1	75.7	5.5	1.437	5.7	71.9	14.8	5.740	13.0	26.4	459.6	459.6
SWITZERLAND	90.4	97.8	10.9	6.1	1.889	6.4	41.3	15.8	2.009	19.6	22.7	120.5	453.7
SWEDEN	94.0	99.0	13.3	3.9	2.426	4.9	37.6	17.5	2.793	23.3	17.7	81.9	447.9
MEXICO	97.1	99.2	5.8	3.6	0.661	8.9	8.4	8.1	0.619	30.0	18.0	80.7	419.7
URUGUAY	46.0	98.4	30.8	4.5	1.387	20.5	2.1	14.4	3.725	34.4	6.3	178.0	367.2
SINGAPORE	40.1	92.8	18.6	7.6	0.732	19.9	6.0	11.3	0.611	32.7	168.0	293.3	293.3
FINLAND	81.5	99.5	11.2	4.6	2.467	5.4	79.7	13.9	6.498	15.6	11.6	46.4	225.0
CZECH & SLOVAK CU	88.8	99.5	57.1	7.9	1.828	8.1	55.4	9.9	3.237	11.2	23.7	191.3	191.3
POLAND	93.8	99.8	56.2	7.0	1.548	7.0	77.2	9.6	1.681	9.6	27.4	188.8	188.8
PHILIPPINES	80.6	97.6	56.8	10.9	1.889	11.3	58.8	6.8	5.839	9.4	5.5	181.1	181.1
AUSTRALIA	66.6	86.0	34.4	3.8	1.265	8.6	60.3	15.1	5.265	19.0	18.7	145.8	176.0
NEW ZEALAND	48.9	92.4	19.0	2.4	0.951	7.5	96.2	11.3	8.391	10.6	6.8	103.4	167.7
BANGLADESH	66.1	80.2	36.7	2.8	0.563	7.7	4.1	6.6	0.334	33.3	19.8	158.3	158.3
HUNGARY	90.1	99.5	68.8	6.6	1.652	6.8	61.0	14.4	1.772	15.6	21.9	151.4	151.4
NIGERIA	66.7	97.2	32.6	1.3	0.253	3.6	1.5	9.6	0.103	5.1	8.6	133.9	133.9
FORMER USSR	81.7	99.5	20.9	2.1	0.708	2.6	23.1	3.6	1.099	4.8	45.2	124.5	124.5
LIBERIA	92.8	100.0	0.2	0.7	0.005	3.6	0.3	7.9	0.017	33.5	10.6	119.2	119.2
ROMANIA	94.4	99.5	41.4	7.1	1.093	7.2	41.3	11.1	1.749	9.8	3.0	117.4	117.4
NORWAY	96.9	99.4	4.1	3.5	0.589	5.2	7.7	17.0	0.548	38.5	2.4	19.6	112.5
MOROCCO	97.3	99.7	66.9	6.3	1.575	6.3	17.9	20.8	0.133	30.1	1.0	103.5	103.5
ISRAEL	93.2	99.2	62.9	5.9	2.269	5.7	72.4	24.1	6.577	25.4	2.9	66.8	101.0
SRI LANKA	77.4	98.6	33.5	3.2	0.949	6.1	17.0	4.4	1.071	17.5	17.8	100.8	100.8
SOUTH AFRICA	90.8	93.4	47.9	3.2	0.815	3.2	21.6	15.2	2.184	17.7	4.7	85.2	85.2
COLOMBIA	95.5	99.6	27.0	7.4	0.597	8.5	36.1	20.5	0.986	31.7	7.5	77.3	77.3
COTE D'IVOIRE	99.4	100.0	0.7	0.1	0.012	0.3	0.0	9.9	..	33.7	.4	69.2	69.2
KENYA	95.5	97.0	56.5	2.5	0.470	2.5	8.5	16.0	0.606	27.4	1.4	50.6	50.6
CAMEROON	96.2	100.0	7.6	0.5	0.061	1.5	0.0	8.9	..	35.0	1.6	42.5	42.5
CHILE	75.7	81.5	17.4	6.8	0.280	9.6	4.7	14.7	0.182	32.8	1.9	35.9	35.9

Notes: 1. Value of exports from reporter countries that do not participate in Free Trade Agreements.

2. Weighted average tariff reduction measured by dT / (1 + T) in percent.

Leather, Rubber, Footwear (continued)

Export market	% of exports GATT bound		Average levels and changes weighted by value of exports to: the World exc. FTA[1]				LMIEs exc. FTA[1]				Value of exports in $ million		
	Total pre-UR	Total post-UR	% of exports affected	Post-UR applied rate	Tariff reduc-tion[2]	Post-UR bound rate	% of exports affected	Post-UR applied rate	Tariff reduc-tion[2]	Post-UR bound rate	To IDB LMIEs exc. FTA[1]	To all IDB Ctrys exc. FTA[1]	To all IDB Ctrys inc. FTA
PARAGUAY	88.6	96.0	61.4	5.1-	0.970	7.2	30.9	10.6	3.724	23.2	3.0	31.8	33.0
DOMINICAN REPUBLIC	100.0	100.0	51.8	5.4	0.952	5.4	0.0	20.4	..	35.0	.0	32.2	32.2
ETHIOPIA	99.1	99.8	83.8	2.5	0.933	2.6	100.0	9.8	8.430	9.8	.7	28.0	28.0
TUNISIA	91.9	93.1	85.8	11.7	1.418	5.9	13.4	75.7	0.040	6.2	2.3	27.8	27.8
MALTA	99.5	100.0	96.6	2.9	1.649	2.9	50.0	18.7	2.679	9.0	.0	27.4	27.4
PANAMA	61.8	99.9	41.8	18.0	1.139	24.9	42.6	24.8	1.455	34.7	18.4	26.3	26.3
MACAU	72.0	77.5	46.6	7.2	0.956	9.3	100.0	8.2	3.434	8.2	.1	25.5	25.5
VENEZUELA	82.1	98.8	27.0	4.9	0.498	9.1	0.0	12.8	..	34.8	4.1	22.2	22.2
EGYPT, ARAB REP.	95.2	98.9	32.3	7.6	0.583	8.2	13.0	14.6	0.191	15.8	8.2	19.4	19.4
BOLIVIA	56.4	100.0	23.4	4.9	0.384	15.9	0.0	9.3	0.000	34.4	8.2	18.7	18.7
COSTA RICA	92.4	99.4	34.4	8.6	0.452	16.2	4.3	12.7	0.160	32.3	6.8	17.7	17.7
HAITI	100.0	100.0	67.9	6.1	1.595	6.1	..	..	..	..	.0	17.1	17.1
BULGARIA	86.0	98.8	42.2	4.6	0.968	5.8	52.6	11.9	1.552	18.3	3.3	17.1	17.1
ZIMBABWE	96.8	100.0	26.2	1.5	0.354	1.5	100.0	10.0	8.696	10.0	.0	13.3	13.3
ZAIRE	99.6	100.0	0.3	0.0	0.003	0.2	0.0	8.9	..	35.0	.1	12.4	12.4
MYANMAR	0.2	89.7	0.3	3.3	0.012	6.8	0.2	4.6	0.015	5.3	8.6	12.1	12.1
ICELAND	99.7	99.8	3.3	1.1	1.283	2.8	98.1	9.9	3.207	9.6	.1	.7	11.8
SAUDI ARABIA	48.7	62.3	56.6	36.6	1.944	4.5	39.7	57.4	2.701	8.1	6.7	10.6	10.6
PUERTO RICO	96.6	100.0	95.9	7.7	2.129	8.3	3.0	18.0	0.102	39.4	.3	10.6	10.6
CYPRUS	83.1	98.0	57.0	7.3	1.599	6.9	14.0	18.5	0.100	12.7	.8	10.4	10.4
BOTSWANA	97.0	97.0	61.7	2.7	0.987	2.2	0.0	19.2	..	..	.3	9.9	9.9
UNTD ARAB EMRTS	93.7	99.8	91.9	4.5	1.333	4.8	67.4	13.7	3.218	14.3	.4	9.8	9.8
PERU	86.7	100.0	50.5	6.0	0.937	11.1	5.8	9.6	0.066	21.6	3.5	8.1	8.1
VIETNAM	28.0	88.7	21.1	7.9	0.705	11.5	21.8	8.9	0.777	11.7	6.3	7.6	7.6
LEBANON	93.7	99.6	75.0	6.4	1.661	6.8	13.8	22.5	0.517	27.4	.5	7.3	7.3
MONGOLIA	86.6	100.0	89.5	4.9	1.456	6.2	90.0	5.0	1.598	6.6	5.1	6.0	6.0
NEPAL	86.8	99.6	96.3	3.7	1.417	4.3	92.9	4.9	3.085	6.6	1.6	5.2	5.2
SYRIA	78.9	99.6	1.8	22.7	0.042	25.2	0.1	24.4	0.004	27.1	4.7	5.1	5.1
NETHERLANDS ANTILLES	79.7	100.0	75.0	28.7	2.249	32.9	73.4	30.2	2.297	34.7	4.6	5.0	5.0
EL SALVADOR	100.0	100.0	10.4	8.2	0.203	9.1	0.0	10.8	..	25.7	.2	4.0	4.0
MAURITIUS	99.0	99.1	88.5	6.1	1.577	6.2	0.0	30.0	..	30.0	.0	3.6	3.6
PAPUA NEW GUINEA	91.5	100.0	7.8	0.5	0.066	0.6	100.0	10.0	8.696	10.0	.0	3.5	3.5
JAMAICA	100.0	100.0	2.1	6.0	0.029	6.6	16.5	15.1	0.231	31.3	.1	2.8	2.8
MADAGASCAR	98.6	98.8	90.2	5.8	0.587	5.9	0.0	15.0	..	30.0	.0	2.5	2.5
FIJI	70.4	95.6	20.9	36.6	1.653	38.4	..	..	..	..	.0	2.3	2.3
TANZANIA	51.7	51.9	6.5	0.2	0.068	0.3	..	..	..	..	.0	2.1	2.1
IRAN, ISLAMIC REP.	89.7	97.7	65.1	6.7	1.650	5.5	17.1	36.7	0.440	28.4	.2	2.1	2.1
IRAQ	9.8	10.0	5.2	86.8	0.131	6.9	0.0	94.8	..	31.7	1.9	2.0	2.0
SUDAN	66.7	66.7	27.7	27.6	1.318	2.2	28.3	67.4	2.460	10.0	.7	1.7	1.7
JORDAN	79.1	91.6	73.9	10.3	1.259	7.2	23.7	31.6	1.657	22.5	.3	1.6	1.6
BURKINA FASO	100.0	100.0	97.0	2.3	0.853	2.3	..	..	..	..	.0	1.6	1.6
AFGHANISTAN	91.9	100.0	99.0	3.3	1.491	3.4	92.2	10.5	8.015	12.0	.1	1.6	1.6
ZAMBIA	98.3	99.9	20.3	0.4	0.189	0.8	0.0	0.0	..	25.0	.0	1.6	1.6
CAMBODIA	21.0	100.0	17.5	3.8	0.138	3.9	17.3	4.0	0.134	4.0	1.4	1.5	1.5
SOMALIA	100.0	100.0	20.6	0.4	0.139	0.4	..	..	..	..	.0	1.5	1.5

Notes: 1. Value of exports from reporter countries that do not participate in Free Trade Agreements.

2. Weighted average tariff reduction measured by dT / (1 + T) in percent.

Leather, Rubber, Footwear (continued)

Export market	% of exports GATT bound		the World exc. FTA[1]				LMIEs exc. FTA[1]				Value of exports in $ million		
	Total pre-UR	Total post-UR	% of exports affected	Post-UR applied rate	Tariff reduction[2]	Post-UR bound rate	% of exports affected	Post-UR applied rate	Tariff reduction[2]	Post-UR bound rate	To IDB LMIEs exc. FTA[1]	To all IDB Ctrys exc. FTA[1]	To all IDB Ctrys inc. FTA
ECUADOR	83.6	96.8	11.8	7.8	0.255	5.4	0.0	40.9	..	32.1	.2	1.4	1.4
ALBANIA	86.4	100.0	45.7	3.1	0.903	3.2	85.5	5.7	1.860	6.1	.3	1.0	1.0
NIGER	91.8	91.8	80.3	3.6	0.614	2.5	21.1	12.5	0.163	3.0	.1	.9	.9
TRINIDAD AND TOBAGO	14.2	100.0	1.3	25.9	0.024	42.9	0.0	30.1	..	50.0	.7	.9	.9
SENEGAL	95.7	99.3	51.8	5.9	0.761	6.0	..	..	..	..	.0	.8	.8
TONGA	10.7	100.0	88.2	34.4	7.345	34.4	..	..	..	..	.0	.8	.8
MALAWI	88.7	94.8	6.6	1.3	0.165	5.8	0.0	0.3	..	5.0	.7	.8	.8
ALGERIA	91.7	91.7	82.6	5.2	1.396	3.3	0.0	26.1	..	..	.1	.7	.7
TOGO	100.0	100.0	96.0	4.4	1.416	4.4	..	..	..	..	.0	.7	.7
HONDURAS	79.8	100.0	13.5	14.1	0.337	28.6	6.8	18.6	0.257	38.3	.5	.6	.6
CONGO	100.0	100.0	100.0	6.0	0.747	6.0	..	..	..	..	.0	.6	.6
NICARAGUA	100.0	100.0	5.1	7.6	0.155	37.7	0.2	7.8	0.005	39.9	.5	.6	.6
CUBA	70.5	100.0	94.7	5.5	2.353	5.9	90.1	10.3	3.626	11.6	.2	.5	.5
LESOTHO	88.5	88.5	78.7	8.4	0.550	7.5	0.0	15.9	..	..	.1	.5	.5
GHANA	67.9	71.6	1.3	3.7	0.018	0.7	0.0	15.0	..	..	.1	.5	.5
GAMBIA, THE	93.3	100.0	14.1	0.9	0.142	2.9	0.0	5.5	..	35.0	.0	.5	.5
LIBYA	12.6	55.6	8.5	25.0	0.055	33.7	0.0	28.3	..	43.0	.4	.5	.5
MALI	87.0	87.0	31.3	1.4	0.848	0.5	0.0	90.0	..	..	.0	.4	.4
KUWAIT	70.3	80.7	39.0	29.4	0.639	3.2	16.5	126.4	0.790	7.2	.1	.4	.4
GREENLAND	93.5	100.0	98.1	4.0	1.804	4.0	..	..	..	..	.0	.4	.4
BRUNEI	81.9	97.8	29.0	7.1	0.575	20.2	0.9	11.0	0.074	34.8	.2	.4	.4
YEMEN	100.0	100.0	95.0	2.2	1.056	2.2	100.0	0.4	0.100	0.4	.0	.4	.4
GUINEA	99.7	99.7	12.2	0.3	0.112	0.3	..	..	..	..	.0	.3	.3
BELIZE	99.7	99.7	20.7	7.1	1.098	11.2	0.0	19.0	..	35.0	.1	.3	.3
BAHRAIN	81.5	90.8	78.2	3.9	1.241	5.2	..	..	..	..	.0	.3	.3
SWAZILAND	51.2	99.7	49.2	6.6	2.923	6.5	99.3	13.3	5.977	13.1	.1	.3	.3
GUYANA	95.7	100.0	60.5	2.3	0.985	2.3	..	..	..	..	.0	.3	.3
OMAN	84.7	100.0	84.7	4.3	1.588	4.3	100.0	5.0	4.651	5.0	.0	.2	.2
QATAR	100.0	100.0	63.5	4.9	0.789	4.9	..	..	..	..	.0	.2	.2
MOZAMBIQUE	100.0	100.0	68.4	4.0	1.433	4.0	..	..	..	..	.0	.2	.2
DOMINICA	85.3	100.0	48.1	8.7	0.797	21.8	0.0	14.2	..	39.3	.1	.1	.1
UGANDA	56.8	92.4	16.9	16.0	0.455	20.8	0.0	43.0	..	52.0	.0	.1	.1
ANTIGUA & B ARBUDA	100.0	100.0	81.2	10.6	5.092	10.6	..	..	..	..	.0	.1	.1
MARTINIQUE	97.2	100.0	94.4	7.3	0.817	7.3	..	..	..	..	.0	.1	.1
RWANDA	80.4	100.0	100.0	18.1	1.803	18.1	..	..	..	..	.0	.1	.1
NAURU	100.0	100.0	1.1	8.5	0.014	8.5	..	..	..	..	.0	.1	.1
KIRIBATI	68.2	100.0	96.5	10.2	2.458	10.3	100.0	6.0	2.699	6.0	.0	.1	.1
SURINAME	89.3	100.0	14.3	8.8	0.130	13.8	0.0	5.6	..	47.5	.0	.1	.1
BHUTAN	100.0	100.0	100.0	15.5	3.630	15.5	..	..	..	..	.0	.1	.1
CENTRAL AFRICAN REP.	55.3	100.0	100.0	6.9	4.832	6.9	100.0	10.0	8.696	10.0	.0	.1	.1
GIBRALTAR	81.4	100.0	58.6	7.1	0.982	7.5	0.0	14.8	..	16.0	.0	.1	.1
GUADELOUPE	100.0	100.0	61.4	10.9	1.995	10.9	..	..	..	..	.0	.1	.1
MAURITANIA	40.6	75.0	75.0	10.6	1.168	9.1	20.0	13.9	0.433	9.6	.0	.1	.1
BURUNDI	63.5	100.0	100.0	8.7	2.316	8.7	..	..	..	..	.0	.1	.1
SEYCHELLES	100.0	100.0	38.0	4.4	0.258	4.4	..	..	..	..	.0	.1	.1

Notes: 1. Value of exports from reporter countries that do not participate in Free Trade Agreements.

2. Weighted average tariff reduction measured by dT / (1 + T) in percent.

Metals Extent of other countries' MFN tariff reductions on exports from:

Export market	% of exports GATT bound		Average levels and changes weighted by value of exports to:								Value of exports in $ million		
			the World exc. FTA[1]				LMIEs exc. FTA[1]						
	Total pre-UR	Total post-UR	% of exports affected	Post-UR applied rate	Tariff reduction[2]	Post-UR bound rate	% of exports affected	Post-UR applied rate	Tariff reduction[2]	Post-UR bound rate	To IDB LMIEs exc. FTA[1]	To all IDB Ctrys exc. FTA[1]	To all IDB Ctrys inc. FTA
EUROPEAN UNION	79.0	92.9	30.7	5.2	2.805	5.4	26.0	16.2	2.594	23.1	5,527.8	15,072.8	25,945.7
UNITED STATES	79.1	92.4	25.7	3.1	1.351	6.4	18.0	9.0	1.866	22.3	2,777.1	9,137.0	14,538.2
JAPAN	46.8	88.7	56.1	4.8	3.832	6.2	44.4	10.9	5.655	15.8	5,263.7	14,047.5	14,047.5
CANADA	95.5	98.6	6.6	0.6	0.512	1.2	21.9	6.9	1.799	14.1	682.6	4,762.3	13,365.9
AUSTRALIA	82.1	95.6	25.9	1.3	0.679	2.4	25.1	6.1	1.592	9.7	1,407.1	7,037.5	7,244.3
BRAZIL	77.5	93.6	33.3	2.0	1.281	4.1	11.4	7.9	1.202	21.3	1,478.9	6,960.9	7,133.6
SWEDEN	94.3	99.0	11.2	1.0	3.636	2.4	26.7	12.1	2.670	24.7	263.9	1,112.6	5,917.4
KOREA, REPUBLIC OF	74.7	92.0	71.3	3.0	2.758	3.2	6.4	17.5	0.723	32.4	591.0	4,667.2	4,667.2
TAIWAN (CHINA)	72.1	90.1	58.2	3.9	1.850	4.5	37.8	13.5	3.509	17.9	475.2	4,468.9	4,468.9
NORWAY	96.7	99.0	5.8	1.5	0.947	3.6	16.4	16.1	1.604	10.6	132.3	874.9	4,465.0
AUSTRIA	95.2	98.8	10.3	1.8	2.371	2.9	55.7	9.4	1.866	11.6	346.9	618.1	3,904.6
CHINA	49.8	70.7	34.8	2.1	0.941	3.4	9.6	11.1	0.622	19.4	405.0	3,744.2	3,744.2
CHILE	80.0	97.8	13.4	1.0	0.385	4.7	13.4	3.4	1.129	22.1	703.7	3,410.5	3,410.5
SWITZERLAND	95.6	98.6	6.1	2.2	1.579	3.9	32.5	16.8	1.577	20.3	118.0	437.0	3,123.0
SOUTH AFRICA	82.0	90.8	30.9	2.4	0.825	2.4	0.8	9.5	0.038	31.3	380.9	3,111.5	3,111.5
FORMER USSR	76.0	94.8	23.2	1.4	0.510	3.3	13.9	3.5	0.259	8.9	1,024.6	3,058.1	3,058.1
FORMER YUGOSLAVIA	82.3	90.6	51.4	6.2	1.936	4.8	27.3	15.9	1.182	13.8	570.1	1,995.9	1,995.9
FINLAND	94.5	99.3	11.4	0.9	4.007	1.8	45.9	11.0	7.455	12.9	102.2	405.1	1,984.0
MEXICO	89.1	99.4	7.2	1.9	1.424	4.3	17.3	9.3	1.905	26.8	204.8	533.4	1,795.0
INDONESIA	88.0	94.0	32.8	1.3	0.695	0.8	15.4	11.1	1.203	12.7	154.6	1,420.4	1,420.4
PERU	80.9	97.7	13.8	1.3	0.360	5.6	3.0	3.7	0.240	22.8	311.2	1,398.1	1,398.1
VENEZUELA	82.7	97.6	42.7	3.3	1.033	6.4	8.9	13.3	0.934	32.5	263.6	1,359.7	1,359.7
INDIA	80.8	95.5	27.0	1.6	0.821	2.5	2.0	4.8	0.108	11.0	182.2	1,123.1	1,123.1
POLAND	90.0	98.3	43.3	1.7	1.346	2.0	38.7	5.3	0.461	6.4	264.6	1,078.8	1,078.8
ZAMBIA	72.2	88.6	39.4	2.0	0.672	4.9	4.2	4.3	0.342	22.1	240.2	1,000.8	1,000.8
PHILIPPINES	81.2	99.6	27.4	1.7	1.041	2.8	61.0	7.3	5.301	12.5	122.0	917.5	917.5
MALAYSIA	46.9	88.5	11.1	2.3	0.789	4.1	34.2	13.7	3.584	16.7	146.5	917.4	917.4
HONG KONG	75.4	91.5	56.3	4.1	1.891	4.8	31.6	10.6	2.483	14.7	172.4	858.0	858.0
ZAIRE	83.9	88.3	8.1	0.8	0.259	0.7	11.7	7.6	1.226	6.8	115.3	803.5	803.5
CZECH & SLOVAK CU	77.6	96.2	70.6	3.7	3.063	4.1	39.0	10.8	1.265	12.7	259.1	783.4	783.4
SINGAPORE	42.4	78.7	32.7	8.3	1.593	10.8	16.0	15.1	1.500	23.0	387.4	762.8	762.8
PAPUA NEW GUINEA	81.2	93.1	0.0	0.8	0.000	0.1	0.0	4.3	..	1.0	139.8	750.0	750.0
ARGENTINA	72.8	97.8	48.7	4.3	2.282	10.9	5.5	14.4	1.174	29.6	146.0	620.0	743.3
ROMANIA	69.0	82.2	48.1	6.1	2.027	3.1	8.6	19.1	0.602	18.0	208.2	712.1	712.1
NEW ZEALAND	82.1	98.9	72.3	0.6	1.397	1.5	23.6	10.9	1.588	13.0	25.5	596.5	696.6
TURKEY	89.9	98.9	64.8	2.5	2.786	2.9	34.1	17.9	4.558	25.5	55.6	644.8	644.8
HUNGARY	84.4	95.6	62.8	3.1	2.320	2.8	20.0	8.8	0.651	8.3	136.5	585.3	585.3
ZIMBABWE	97.4	99.9	47.1	2.2	1.212	2.5	7.5	6.4	1.012	13.3	14.4	455.2	455.2
THAILAND	60.6	86.0	28.5	2.1	0.984	3.7	14.4	10.1	1.341	21.5	45.6	437.4	437.4
LIBERIA	97.8	99.2	0.0	0.0	0.002	0.5	1.0	1.8	0.097	34.5	7.8	355.6	355.6
UNTD ARAB EMRTS	93.9	96.7	74.4	1.2	1.017	0.9	48.2	10.3	2.818	8.0	37.4	343.5	343.5
GUINEA	98.4	100.0	0.3	0.0	0.012	0.6	0.0	2.8	..	32.9	5.3	300.0	300.0
DOMINICAN REPUBLIC	97.4	98.2	23.5	0.9	0.626	1.3	0.0	0.5	..	35.4	7.3	275.7	275.7
BAHRAIN	79.1	90.5	51.9	6.9	1.180	3.8	49.2	21.0	3.024	7.5	63.8	263.5	263.5
EGYPT, ARAB REP.	95.9	98.9	24.7	5.8	0.818	5.8	23.4	20.5	2.103	24.0	12.2	260.0	260.0

Notes: 1. Value of exports from reporter countries that do not participate in Free Trade Agreements.

2. Weighted average tariff reduction measured by dT / (1 + T) in percent.

Metals (continued)

Export market	% of exports GATT bound		Average levels and changes weighted by value of exports to:								Value of exports in $ million		
			the World exc. FTA[1]				LMIEs exc. FTA[1]						
	Total pre-UR	Total post-UR	% of exports affected	Post-UR applied rate	Tariff reduc-tion[2]	Post-UR bound rate	% of exports affected	Post-UR applied rate	Tariff reduc-tion[2]	Post-UR bound rate	To IDB LMIEs exc. FTA[1]	To all IDB Ctrys exc. FTA[1]	To all IDB Ctrys inc. FTA
ISRAEL	94.2	96.3	46.0	3.1	1.916	2.9	33.0	22.0	1.656	16.8	8.2	156.3	252.8
GHANA	96.8	99.7	0.4	4.8	0.022	5.0	15.4	6.3	1.267	29.7	2.9	250.6	250.6
BOTSWANA	87.6	87.6	0.1	0.1	0.001	0.0	0.0	0.7	..	0.0	34.1	209.1	209.1
ICELAND	99.8	100.0	10.5	0.5	2.021	4.1	4.6	1.5	0.342	1.4	2.7	31.3	202.0
MAURITANIA	99.8	99.8	0.0	0.0	0.000	0.0	0.0	15.0	..	25.0	.3	176.8	176.8
BOLIVIA	85.5	99.6	2.9	0.8	0.086	3.1	0.0	4.2	..	17.4	30.1	169.7	169.7
COLOMBIA	89.3	95.1	13.4	1.8	0.329	3.6	0.4	8.9	0.013	27.9	25.4	163.9	163.9
ALGERIA	72.0	93.2	55.5	4.1	2.247	6.3	9.0	12.5	0.858	24.1	49.7	163.0	163.0
GABON	93.5	96.0	0.4	0.1	0.025	0.0	4.4	2.1	0.651	1.8	3.8	162.4	162.4
SAUDI ARABIA	69.9	91.8	30.9	3.9	1.685	1.6	59.4	13.3	4.876	5.4	44.1	160.9	160.9
BULGARIA	66.0	93.5	47.1	4.9	1.696	8.1	9.8	11.1	0.177	21.2	64.6	145.8	145.8
TRINIDAD AND TOBAGO	83.4	100.0	39.2	2.8	1.795	19.1	0.0	5.5	0.001	37.8	63.7	126.1	126.1
MOROCCO	94.7	97.7	26.5	1.7	0.383	1.8	3.6	15.9	0.314	26.6	7.8	123.6	123.6
CAMEROON	99.3	99.4	0.8	5.9	0.042	5.8	14.3	14.6	1.946	20.0	1.0	122.0	122.0
JAMAICA	99.9	100.0	0.6	0.0	0.034	0.0	0.0	18.4	..	38.2	.0	112.2	112.2
SIERRA LEONE	95.5	100.0	0.0	0.7	0.001	2.5	0.0	0.9	..	35.1	5.1	97.5	97.5
MOZAMBIQUE	20.2	92.4	2.1	1.2	0.100	11.6	0.7	4.0	0.108	37.2	26.4	90.0	90.0
GUYANA	97.2	100.0	0.0	1.0	0.000	6.2	0.0	4.9	..	31.9	15.1	78.1	78.1
ALBANIA	98.0	100.0	37.7	1.7	1.145	2.0	10.9	1.0	0.234	1.9	17.6	71.3	71.3
IRAN, ISLAMIC REP.	42.2	94.2	3.4	0.3	0.139	14.5	0.1	0.6	0.000	32.7	27.2	69.8	69.8
CUBA	93.7	94.7	16.3	1.0	0.573	3.4	0.0	2.2	0.000	10.6	21.6	64.8	64.8
GREENLAND	99.9	99.9	0.2	0.0	0.004	0.0	0.0	29.8	..	30.0	.1	60.5	60.5
KUWAIT	59.5	95.1	26.0	1.5	1.974	1.4	50.8	3.8	4.444	3.5	17.5	43.8	43.8
VIETNAM	47.0	96.1	7.0	0.9	0.263	18.3	12.1	1.6	0.460	33.0	20.9	37.2	37.2
TUNISIA	97.2	98.9	37.8	1.0	1.438	1.0	51.8	6.1	4.775	7.5	1.0	33.8	33.8
LEBANON	88.9	98.6	46.2	2.3	1.781	2.2	84.8	1.9	7.808	1.4	3.5	33.0	33.0
SRI LANKA	82.9	95.8	34.6	2.9	1.166	3.6	29.8	16.5	4.022	23.9	2.6	30.2	30.2
TANZANIA	92.4	96.2	14.3	0.8	0.186	0.3	6.9	20.3	0.861	28.0	1.1	26.6	26.6
PAKISTAN	77.7	95.6	40.1	3.4	2.234	5.6	35.0	6.6	3.380	21.6	4.1	24.2	24.2
MALTA	98.2	100.0	83.5	3.1	2.121	3.1	68.7	9.5	6.540	11.3	.1	24.0	24.0
URUGUAY	16.4	99.9	10.3	2.7	0.949	29.8	0.0	3.9	..	34.5	3.4	6.4	21.0
HONDURAS	99.6	100.0	3.2	0.8	0.033	1.3	0.0	22.8	..	41.4	.6	21.0	21.0
NIGERIA	79.3	99.1	4.3	1.1	0.194	1.0	7.4	4.8	0.600	4.4	3.9	19.1	19.1
COSTA RICA	93.2	100.0	23.4	9.1	1.098	15.4	12.3	17.1	1.150	32.0	8.0	19.0	19.0
CYPRUS	78.4	92.0	54.3	3.6	2.033	1.6	56.9	13.3	4.601	2.5	3.4	18.3	18.3
OMAN	60.9	87.6	51.4	3.1	2.105	3.4	51.1	8.4	4.437	9.3	6.5	18.3	18.3
PANAMA	72.6	100.0	11.0	5.0	0.753	12.6	17.1	11.3	1.551	28.9	7.4	17.1	17.1
MYANMAR	45.8	91.7	4.1	3.2	0.335	8.4	4.8	7.5	0.633	17.5	6.9	15.6	15.6
SURINAME	99.8	100.0	5.1	3.8	0.143	3.8	0.0	27.4	..	46.4	.0	15.4	15.4
JORDAN	79.1	89.9	26.8	3.2	1.327	1.1	37.7	29.3	3.982	11.5	2.5	14.9	14.9
CONGO	60.1	100.0	2.8	0.0	0.162	0.0	..	..	..	..	.0	13.2	13.2
BAHAMAS, THE	100.0	100.0	3.9	0.3	0.269	8.6	1.5	0.2	0.068	9.4	12.0	13.2	13.2
PUERTO RICO	59.4	99.6	17.3	4.2	1.167	17.9	8.7	7.3	0.686	34.3	6.3	12.5	12.5
LAO PDR	49.1	99.6	0.0	6.0	..	7.9	0.0	6.1	..	8.0	11.0	11.1	11.1
MADAGASCAR	87.9	87.9	3.3	0.1	0.034	0.1	0.0	32.0	..	..	.0	9.7	9.7

Notes: 1. Value of exports from reporter countries that do not participate in Free Trade Agreements.

2. Weighted average tariff reduction measured by dT / (1 + T) in percent.

Metals (continued)

Export market	% of exports GATT bound Total pre-UR	Total post-UR	the World exc. FTA[1] % of exports affected	Post-UR applied rate	Tariff reduction[2]	Post-UR bound rate	LMIEs exc. FTA[1] % of exports affected	Post-UR applied rate	Tariff reduction[2]	Post-UR bound rate	Value of exports in $ million To IDB LMIEs exc. FTA[1]	To all IDB Ctrys exc. FTA[1]	To all IDB Ctrys inc. FTA
COTE D'IVOIRE	44.4	52.0	6.7	7.6	0.286	3.0	2.4	14.0	0.210	26.0	5.0	9.4	9.4
IRAQ	89.1	96.7	9.3	0.6	0.449	3.9	0.0	4.2	..	38.9	.9	7.3	7.3
NETHERLANDS ANTILLES	39.0	100.0	11.9	0.8	0.231	22.6	0.1	0.6	0.005	35.0	4.0	6.3	6.3
NICARAGUA	100.0	100.0	3.0	12.5	0.142	39.6	0.0	14.2	..	45.1	5.4	6.2	6.2
MONGOLIA	99.4	99.4	0.0	0.0	0.000	0.0	0.0	0.0	..	0.0	1.6	6.1	6.1
BARBADOS	54.6	99.7	36.3	9.7	1.017	24.1	0.0	18.0	..	50.0	2.6	5.8	5.8
DOMINICA	57.6	97.7	44.5	3.4	1.211	3.5	0.0	4.8	..	5.1	2.3	5.5	5.5
EL SALVADOR	98.4	99.9	17.4	3.6	0.259	8.2	1.5	11.5	0.009	30.1	1.1	4.6	4.6
BRUNEI	6.0	80.9	4.7	0.3	0.140	21.3	0.1	0.5	0.002	34.5	1.8	4.5	4.5
ECUADOR	65.4	100.0	33.1	4.8	1.140	13.5	0.0	11.8	..	33.8	1.8	4.5	4.5
SENEGAL	99.4	100.0	4.3	0.1	0.135	0.1	100.0	3.0	6.573	3.0	.0	4.2	4.2
KENYA	49.4	80.8	20.9	4.2	1.535	3.6	30.0	16.6	4.001	24.8	1.0	3.7	3.7
MAURITIUS	93.2	97.0	79.6	2.5	2.059	2.6	97.4	23.8	10.090	24.4	.2	3.7	3.7
NIGER	100.0	100.0	5.7	0.8	0.206	0.8	..	..	..	..	.0	3.6	3.6
HAITI	99.7	100.0	31.8	3.4	0.925	3.6	0.0	10.0	..	35.0	.0	3.5	3.5
LIBYA	50.6	52.4	21.8	4.4	0.575	2.0	0.0	7.8	..	30.7	1.6	3.2	3.2
SWAZILAND	90.6	96.7	91.9	4.1	2.531	4.0	54.0	15.6	3.242	19.7	.2	2.6	2.6
SUDAN	49.1	49.1	2.8	2.6	0.068	0.9	0.1	5.0	0.005	23.0	1.2	2.3	2.3
MACAU	34.2	73.9	22.8	0.4	0.339	0.6	100.0	10.0	8.696	10.0	.0	2.3	2.3
QATAR	87.4	100.0	80.4	3.5	2.817	7.2	0.0	5.0	..	40.0	.2	2.0	2.0
NAMIBIA	100.0	100.0	9.0	0.2	0.113	0.2	..	..	..	..	.0	1.8	1.8
GUADELOUPE	100.0	100.0	37.1	1.0	1.180	1.0	..	..	..	..	.0	1.6	1.6
BELIZE	61.8	100.0	23.0	2.3	1.401	4.1	3.2	16.9	0.237	34.2	.3	1.6	1.6
ARUBA	65.6	85.5	11.2	3.9	0.343	13.4	0.0	14.2	..	35.0	.4	1.3	1.3
GAMBIA, THE	99.4	100.0	0.3	4.8	0.007	5.0	0.0	10.0	..	35.0	.0	1.3	1.3
GIBRALTAR	95.8	100.0	53.3	2.5	1.761	2.5	0.0	30.0	..	30.0	.0	1.2	1.2
YEMEN	38.5	42.7	25.8	5.0	0.947	0.9	2.1	73.8	0.136	9.8	.3	1.2	1.2
NEPAL	71.3	74.1	45.7	1.0	1.310	1.5	0.0	2.0	..	..	.0	1.0	1.0
BANGLADESH	19.3	28.6	11.0	0.8	0.313	1.5	0.0	8.9	..	..	.0	1.0	1.0
SYRIA	82.2	98.6	47.0	1.5	2.197	0.9	88.7	4.3	8.394	1.1	.2	.8	.8
FIJI	43.6	100.0	14.0	3.2	0.818	3.9	100.0	3.0	6.573	3.0	.0	.8	.8
MARTINIQUE	100.0	100.0	38.7	1.3	0.754	1.3	..	..	..	..	.0	.7	.7
TOGO	99.8	100.0	16.9	0.8	0.659	0.9	0.0	10.0	..	50.0	.0	.6	.6
CENTRAL AFRICAN REP.	100.0	100.0	10.5	0.5	0.420	2.0	0.0	5.0	..	30.0	.0	.6	.6
DJIBOUTI	100.0	100.0	18.5	0.3	0.767	0.3	..	..	..	..	.0	.5	.5
ETHIOPIA	97.9	98.3	7.1	1.5	0.192	3.4	0.0	9.5	..	28.3	.1	.5	.5
ANTIGUA & B ARBUDA	100.0	100.0	31.4	2.1	1.014	2.1	..	..	..	..	.0	.4	.4
AFGHANISTAN	88.8	88.8	34.2	8.8	0.723	16.4	2.5	15.4	0.055	34.1	.2	.3	.3
PARAGUAY	68.8	100.0	47.4	2.3	3.476	12.4	0.0	12.5	..	35.0	.0	.2	.3
GUINEA-BISSAU	100.0	100.0	2.7	0.0	0.116	0.0	..	..	..	..	.0	.3	.3
BENIN	100.0	100.0	35.1	1.1	1.033	1.1	..	..	..	..	.0	.3	.3
RWANDA	100.0	100.0	5.2	0.2	0.124	0.2	..	..	..	..	.0	.2	.2
ANGOLA	100.0	100.0	100.0	2.3	2.498	2.3	..	..	..	..	.0	.2	.2
BURKINA FASO	100.0	100.0	38.3	2.2	0.831	2.2	..	..	..	..	.0	.2	.2
GRENADA	58.6	100.0	14.3	2.3	0.611	14.7	0.0	5.0	..	35.0	.1	.2	.2

Notes: 1. Value of exports from reporter countries that do not participate in Free Trade Agreements.

2. Weighted average tariff reduction measured by dT / (1 + T) in percent.

Chemical & Photographic Suppl. Extent of other countries' MFN tariff reductions on exports from:

| Export market | % of exports GATT bount | | Average levels and changes weighted by value of exports to: | | | | | | | | Value of exports in $ million | | |
| | Total pre-UR | Total post-UR | the World exc. FTA1 | | | | LMIEs exc. FTA1 | | | | To IDB LMIEs exc. FTA1 | To all IDB Ctrys exc. FTA1 | To all IDB Ctrys inc. FTA |
			% of exports affected	Post-UR applied rate	Tariff reduction2	Post-UR bound rate	% of exports affected	Post-UR applied rate	Tariff reduction2	Post-UR bound rate			
EUROPEAN UNION	73.8	93.5	31.3	5.2	2.574	6.6	35.5	13.5	3.131	19.7	10,882.0	31,276.8	46,415.5
UNITED STATES	70.3	94.5	39.9	4.9	2.253	9.0	27.1	11.4	3.552	23.5	6,257.0	23,196.1	29,742.2
JAPAN	52.0	84.0	44.2	5.9	2.898	8.1	54.4	11.8	5.827	15.6	4,650.0	14,490.4	14,490.4
SWITZERLAND	87.0	96.3	18.4	3.2	2.648	5.8	24.7	11.4	1.709	20.9	1,413.0	3,808.3	10,847.8
CANADA	87.5	97.7	14.6	1.8	2.964	3.9	53.0	7.5	4.916	17.4	434.6	1,370.6	5,253.1
TAIWAN (CHINA)	49.9	62.9	36.4	4.0	1.281	7.2	28.7	16.9	3.634	25.5	479.1	4,614.0	4,614.0
CHINA	43.3	50.4	27.3	2.5	0.879	5.8	20.4	14.6	1.898	24.2	323.2	4,400.2	4,400.2
SWEDEN	93.0	98.9	10.1	2.0	2.527	4.4	34.8	13.5	2.778	19.6	182.2	713.6	3,438.3
AUSTRALIA	66.9	94.5	9.2	1.9	0.660	7.2	16.1	8.0	1.934	29.4	577.5	2,453.4	2,841.8
AUSTRIA	92.7	99.0	11.9	4.1	2.066	5.7	47.6	7.9	2.145	11.2	481.9	690.8	2,686.2
KOREA, REPUBLIC OF	51.4	65.5	38.9	4.7	1.466	8.3	15.1	18.5	2.250	30.9	335.5	2,145.2	2,145.2
SINGAPORE	36.1	72.4	31.9	8.4	2.173	15.5	21.7	13.9	2.724	26.6	905.0	1,759.9	1,759.9
SAUDI ARABIA	52.8	84.9	66.2	6.5	3.683	8.1	43.8	11.4	4.291	16.3	614.5	1,757.8	1,757.8
NORWAY	93.0	97.2	10.2	3.9	2.118	5.3	27.8	14.4	2.479	19.2	102.7	334.3	1,546.0
BRAZIL	68.0	96.4	38.1	4.7	2.073	10.7	7.6	11.4	1.525	25.4	265.0	1,269.9	1,507.5
MEXICO	76.1	96.3	17.3	6.0	1.443	9.0	13.6	10.8	1.032	22.6	453.5	711.2	1,427.9
FORMER USSR	75.4	98.7	30.3	4.3	1.745	4.6	51.7	12.6	3.707	13.6	337.9	1,224.7	1,224.7
FINLAND	93.8	98.4	8.4	3.6	2.477	5.7	34.5	13.9	3.452	22.3	74.0	192.8	1,064.9
ISRAEL	88.4	96.3	52.6	5.6	2.452	6.1	21.6	14.6	1.417	20.6	92.8	673.1	881.7
HONG KONG	57.8	89.4	45.1	7.5	2.320	8.5	20.0	16.3	2.667	22.8	235.0	836.8	836.8
FORMER YUGOSLAVIA	67.9	93.8	61.4	7.0	2.522	7.8	45.6	11.4	2.323	14.4	272.3	721.4	721.4
MALAYSIA	44.0	83.3	27.5	2.8	1.266	6.3	32.0	13.7	2.824	23.9	89.1	647.8	647.8
SOUTH AFRICA	51.4	69.8	15.0	4.2	0.486	6.7	0.5	9.4	0.028	33.6	204.9	617.8	617.8
ARGENTINA	58.5	99.3	27.6	5.1	2.500	14.0	4.5	10.9	1.266	23.2	96.7	345.4	547.2
HUNGARY	74.6	93.1	56.1	6.7	2.436	7.4	44.3	14.7	2.777	18.1	161.7	505.4	505.4
INDIA	62.4	84.9	49.7	5.0	2.250	8.2	18.5	9.0	1.008	18.7	138.3	478.5	478.5
CZECH & SLOVAK CU	75.8	95.9	56.2	4.9	2.229	6.0	45.4	8.3	1.945	11.7	136.3	471.5	471.5
PUERTO RICO	80.2	99.9	70.7	3.8	2.895	7.7	2.6	9.9	0.249	26.5	95.0	418.3	418.3
POLAND	83.6	96.4	43.9	5.2	1.724	6.6	32.6	8.7	1.594	11.2	140.1	382.6	382.6
BAHAMAS, THE	98.8	100.0	97.0	5.6	1.038	5.9	8.4	9.4	0.660	27.2	5.8	381.7	381.7
THAILAND	39.9	71.5	35.0	5.7	1.494	9.3	19.5	17.6	2.192	23.5	53.6	367.1	367.1
JAMAICA	95.5	100.0	30.4	1.3	0.444	2.2	0.2	1.4	0.005	21.7	15.9	353.1	353.1
MOROCCO	41.1	93.7	73.5	18.1	9.009	22.1	64.5	27.8	12.481	35.6	180.1	312.6	312.6
NIGER	61.2	100.0	0.2	0.0	0.005	0.2	2.3	34.0	0.063	28.2	.0	285.2	285.2
LIBYA	74.8	96.6	50.5	3.4	3.849	2.8	72.3	7.2	6.898	5.2	69.4	270.0	270.0
SURINAME	86.8	100.0	37.9	1.7	0.531	3.6	18.3	1.8	0.167	16.0	34.7	262.4	262.4
ROMANIA	62.0	91.7	53.5	7.9	2.368	8.6	30.0	17.3	2.092	18.9	78.6	225.8	225.8
TURKEY	80.4	96.2	56.7	5.7	2.936	6.7	45.9	11.5	4.171	16.7	51.4	221.2	221.2
NEW ZEALAND	55.6	95.8	33.5	2.0	3.440	6.7	48.5	7.4	2.838	16.1	14.9	97.3	193.8
TRINIDAD AND TOBAGO	92.3	99.7	48.9	4.4	3.522	5.4	0.1	19.2	0.002	32.0	16.8	191.5	191.5
INDONESIA	25.4	49.2	29.0	7.0	2.447	8.9	33.9	15.7	4.217	16.3	66.9	175.5	175.5
VENEZUELA	47.3	100.0	11.8	7.6	0.460	19.7	0.0	10.9	0.002	30.3	108.7	174.6	174.6
PHILIPPINES	51.2	85.2	31.9	3.1	1.127	12.6	19.6	4.0	1.952	31.0	47.5	168.4	168.4
CHILE	74.3	99.2	26.2	4.1	1.830	8.3	8.2	9.3	1.379	23.8	45.5	157.3	157.3
QATAR	13.2	49.9	32.1	14.6	3.716	12.0	25.4	18.7	3.825	16.6	94.5	121.3	121.3

Notes: 1. Value of exports from reporter countries that do not participate in Free Trade Agreements.

2. Weighted average tariff reduction measured by dT / (1 + T) in percent.

Chemical & Photographic Suppl. (continued)

Export market	% of exports GATT bount Total pre-UR	Total post-UR	the World exc. FTA¹ % of exports affected	Post-UR applied rate	Tariff reduc-tion²	Post-UR bound rate	LMIEs exc. FTA¹ % of exports affected	Post-UR applied rate	Tariff reduc-tion²	Post-UR bound rate	To IDB LMIEs exc. FTA¹	To all IDB Ctrys exc. FTA¹	To all IDB Ctrys inc. FTA
BULGARIA	71.2	98.4	64.0	6.5	3.658	7.7	52.2	10.9	4.576	13.8	46.5	117.8	117.8
COLOMBIA	65.4	99.5	16.3	10.2	0.894	22.2	0.8	13.0	0.054	29.1	83.5	113.3	113.3
URUGUAY	11.8	100.0	5.4	3.7	3.936	21.3	0.1	4.8	0.031	22.6	3.9	10.3	107.4
TUNISIA	65.7	97.9	60.3	7.6	4.237	19.2	23.4	10.4	4.021	36.8	41.6	92.6	92.6
GABON	59.7	99.4	0.1	0.1	0.003	0.0	0.0	13.8	..	41.0	.5	80.5	80.5
PANAMA	48.4	99.9	20.5	7.7	0.969	24.1	4.5	9.3	0.285	30.3	60.3	77.2	77.2
GUINEA	96.1	100.0	78.5	3.1	1.140	3.8	0.0	0.0	..	17.5	2.0	52.9	52.9
PERU	68.0	99.7	18.2	4.4	0.724	13.3	2.6	7.9	0.323	26.7	23.6	49.9	49.9
EGYPT, ARAB REP.	73.2	99.8	10.5	9.5	0.596	15.4	2.1	11.0	0.409	19.2	35.2	48.8	48.8
BAHRAIN	72.7	99.9	87.1	7.3	7.896	8.1	82.1	12.6	9.757	15.3	13.9	44.9	44.9
COSTA RICA	91.2	99.2	25.2	8.3	0.966	16.2	0.0	16.0	0.000	34.9	14.9	35.4	35.4
ALGERIA	92.7	97.2	58.3	4.8	3.732	· 4.5	3.2	20.0	0.422	22.1	2.4	31.8	31.8
CUBA	7.3	100.0	0.9	7.8	0.037	32.3	0.4	8.0	0.018	33.5	30.3	31.5	31.5
UNTD ARAB EMRTS	25.1	88.2	74.1	16.4	16.542	18.0	79.7	23.3	22.883	26.0	20.1	29.3	29.3
IRAQ	80.8	88.7	75.0	13.8	3.496	16.0	79.0	14.5	3.689	17.0	23.6	25.0	25.0
MACAU	61.9	64.7	35.1	2.6	1.040	4.1	0.0	4.7	..	6.6	.4	24.1	24.1
KENYA	21.0	73.3	5.6	9.1	0.283	17.9	1.3	10.5	0.135	21.8	15.7	18.3	18.3
KUWAIT	62.3	99.9	47.7	9.4	11.690	9.4	99.6	25.0	30.332	24.9	6.6	18.0	18.0
DOMINICAN REPUBLIC	99.0	100.0	27.2	2.6	0.758	4.3	0.0	7.5	..	36.7	.9	16.6	16.6
PARAGUAY	28.0	99.7	1.8	2.8	0.403	15.9	0.8	9.8	0.961	20.8	1.3	5.3	16.5
CYPRUS	71.3	79.5	37.7	6.4	1.692	5.8	19.3	20.0	1.316	16.0	4.0	15.0	15.0
MALTA	95.4	97.9	88.3	3.8	3.069	4.0	74.5	8.6	2.658	6.9	.3	14.0	14.0
JORDAN	19.3	91.6	7.3	2.1	0.200	30.8	0.2	1.7	0.027	38.2	9.8	12.3	12.3
ZAIRE	98.8	100.0	63.4	1.9	5.442	1.9	0.0	20.0	..	20.0	.1	11.7	11.7
SRI LANKA	76.7	96.2	27.2	4.1	1.100	6.1	31.0	17.4	4.488	27.5	.9	11.6	11.6
ICELAND	95.6	98.3	8.6	3.8	3.546	4.8	33.6	9.4	3.448	9.0	.3	1.4	10.7
PAKISTAN	77.1	89.8	25.0	7.4	1.176	6.5	8.2	10.5	0.933	9.2	5.0	10.4	10.4
MOZAMBIQUE	2.7	94.9	7.3	2.3	0.566	5.7	25.5	8.8	2.220	19.7	2.3	9.5	9.5
SENEGAL	2.9	100.0	99.0	38.8	18.761	39.0	99.4	39.8	19.247	40.0	9.0	9.3	9.3
LEBANON	98.3	99.6	78.8	6.6	2.883	6.5	9.9	19.2	0.390	18.8	1.4	8.8	8.8
HONDURAS	91.8	94.8	3.2	9.1	0.142	19.0	0.0	14.7	..	32.4	4.2	8.5	8.5
BERMUDA	62.8	99.9	41.0	7.4	0.928	16.1	0.0	9.7	..	28.1	3.9	8.3	8.3
DOMINICA	20.7	100.0	14.2	36.3	0.663	40.9	0.0	43.9	..	49.5	6.6	8.1	8.1
NAMIBIA	100.0	100.0	0.0	0.2	0.002	5.8	0.0	11.1	..	25.0	.1	7.8	7.8
ECUADOR	30.9	98.7	14.7	10.5	0.485	31.9	0.5	13.2	0.020	42.2	5.6	7.6	7.6
IRAN, ISLAMIC REP.	72.4	98.2	63.3	4.4	1.433	5.7	17.6	13.7	1.177	11.0	.4	6.8	6.8
NIGERIA	93.5	94.3	88.1	6.1	4.485	5.5	12.1	17.8	1.869	37.8	.4	6.2	6.2
NETHERLANDS ANTILLES	89.0	99.4	22.5	5.7	0.977	14.5	0.7	9.5	0.011	31.8	2.3	5.7	5.7
NEPAL	1.7	97.8	97.1	38.3	15.791	38.9	97.7	38.8	16.040	39.5	5.3	5.4	5.4
ZIMBABWE	39.1	39.8	33.4	8.4	0.532	6.7	1.2	10.1	0.173	32.0	2.7	4.4	4.4
GUYANA	91.5	100.0	86.2	7.2	1.147	10.0	0.0	19.3	..	48.7	.4	3.9	3.9
BOTSWANA	3.0	4.1	0.3	17.4	0.013	45.9	0.0	17.7	..	86.9	3.7	3.8	3.8
SWAZILAND	23.9	86.6	37.8	12.8	3.585	11.3	45.2	15.4	4.413	14.1	2.6	3.3	3.3
HAITI	99.0	100.0	74.7	3.9	1.729	4.1	0.0	13.7	..	39.6	.0	3.1	3.1
SYRIA	95.8	99.1	17.8	10.5	1.363	11.0	21.3	17.9	1.828	19.1	1.6	3.0	3.0

Notes: 1. Value of exports from reporter countries that do not participate in Free Trade Agreements.

2. Weighted average tariff reduction measured by dT / (1 + T) in percent.

Chemical & Photographic Suppl. (continued)

Export market	% of exports GATT bount		Average levels and changes weighted by value of exports to: the World exc. FTA[1]				LMIEs exc. FTA[1]				Value of exports in $ million		
	Total pre-UR	Total post-UR	% of exports affected	Post-UR applied rate	Tariff reduc-tion[2]	Post-UR bound rate	% of exports affected	Post-UR applied rate	Tariff reduc-tion[2]	Post-UR bound rate	To IDB LMIEs exc. FTA[1]	To all IDB Ctrys exc. FTA[1]	To all IDB Ctrys inc. FTA
VIETNAM	14.2	76.6	60.0	7.8	3.478	12.6	78.5	10.5	4.550	13.1	2.1	2.9	2.9
BARBADOS	22.4	100.0	11.6	28.8	0.784	39.8	0.0	35.6	..	49.8	2.1	2.7	2.7
BOLIVIA	78.8	92.9	18.7	3.2	0.270	3.4	0.0	11.1	..	14.7	.7	2.5	2.5
TANZANIA	31.0	53.4	3.6	9.1	0.224	11.9	1.8	13.3	0.196	29.2	1.7	2.5	2.5
ETHIOPIA	92.5	100.0	91.4	0.2	3.752	4.1	0.0	1.3	..	48.8	.2	2.2	2.2
BANGLADESH	26.7	81.8	12.9	3.9	0.357	21.1	1.4	6.2	0.058	31.1	1.2	2.2	2.2
NICARAGUA	99.5	100.0	17.0	9.6	0.863	28.3	0.5	11.6	0.063	36.7	1.5	2.0	2.0
LIBERIA	97.5	100.0	8.4	1.4	0.575	2.3	88.2	11.9	7.838	14.8	.1	2.0	2.0
ALBANIA	95.9	96.4	54.8	9.7	3.087	9.8	53.5	17.0	4.582	17.8	.9	1.9	1.9
COTE D'IVOIRE	66.8	68.2	34.3	7.5	1.433	4.8	0.0	14.8	..	24.5	.6	1.6	1.6
GIBRALTAR	95.4	99.0	55.5	3.3	2.147	3.5	0.0	8.9	..	15.2	.1	1.5	1.5
EL SALVADOR	77.8	100.0	42.0	5.3	1.599	12.5	10.4	10.4	0.103	26.8	.6	1.5	1.5
MYANMAR	93.5	95.8	76.7	2.5	3.080	2.3	16.1	20.3	0.774	29.8	.1	1.5	1.5
MAURITIUS	78.7	81.5	52.0	5.9	0.826	4.3	8.3	18.9	0.178	6.5	.2	1.4	1.4
MAURITANIA	100.0	100.0	87.8	5.6	4.417	5.6	0.0	11.0	..	25.0	.0	1.3	1.3
ZAMBIA	10.4	10.6	0.0	3.4	..	2.6	0.0	3.8	..	150.0	1.0	1.1	1.1
CAMEROON	99.7	100.0	97.1	5.4	2.192	5.4	0.0	5.0	..	5.0	.0	.9	.9
OMAN	17.1	17.7	11.4	0.8	0.531	2.4	0.0	48.9	..	30.0	.0	.9	.9
GRENADA	100.0	100.0	73.8	1.2	3.562	1.2	..	..	..	..	.0	.7	.7
MALI	99.3	100.0	42.9	4.3	1.179	4.3	66.7	9.5	3.024	9.5	.0	.7	.7
GUADELOUPE	100.0	100.0	81.3	5.4	1.421	5.4	..	..	..	..	.0	.7	.7
PAPUA NEW GUINEA	9.2	92.7	11.8	4.1	0.510	12.8	41.6	15.0	1.771	23.6	.2	.6	.6
MARTINIQUE	100.0	100.0	63.2	2.8	2.208	2.8	..	..	..	..	.0	.4	.4
FIJI	53.2	100.0	23.4	12.5	1.471	16.0	20.0	27.6	1.935	35.6	.1	.4	.4
MONGOLIA	96.4	100.0	83.1	3.6	2.190	3.6	87.5	3.7	2.339	3.7	.3	.4	.4
GAMBIA, THE	97.4	100.0	97.9	5.4	5.001	5.4	100.0	30.0	3.774	30.0	.0	.3	.3
RWANDA	97.0	100.0	19.4	2.7	0.803	4.7	..	..	..	..	.0	.3	.3
GREENLAND	98.3	100.0	49.1	3.6	2.188	7.7	14.3	8.8	0.283	42.9	.0	.3	.3
BELIZE	94.7	100.0	39.6	11.0	1.346	23.6	0.0	15.4	..	36.3	.2	.3	.3
GHANA	99.6	100.0	25.6	6.1	1.354	12.1	1.7	7.7	0.046	34.4	.1	.3	.3
YEMEN	26.1	100.0	25.3	1.4	3.137	7.3	77.9	3.2	9.935	12.0	.1	.2	.2
BENIN	98.1	98.1	86.9	2.5	4.258	2.3	0.0	15.0	..	..	.0	.2	.2
SEYCHELLES	57.1	100.0	42.4	2.7	1.326	5.5	..	..	..	..	.0	.2	.2
NAURU	21.6	99.0	21.6	1.4	0.539	9.4	0.0	2.5	..	35.0	.0	.2	.2
BURKINA FASO	100.0	100.0	73.0	3.0	3.427	3.0	..	..	..	..	.0	.2	.2
UGANDA	76.1	91.0	74.5	9.1	4.928	11.3	65.7	11.0	5.712	14.3	.1	.2	.2
ANTIGUA & B ARBUDA	92.4	100.0	26.5	3.4	0.320	3.9	..	..	..	..	.0	.2	.2
ARUBA	100.0	100.0	65.0	4.8	5.410	12.9	0.0	9.5	..	35.0	.1	.2	.2
BRUNEI	38.7	53.3	23.4	4.3	0.637	11.0	0.0	10.1	..	28.6	.0	.1	.1
SUDAN	87.4	100.0	40.0	3.2	1.812	3.2	100.0	9.0	2.397	9.0	.0	.1	.1
CENTRAL AFRICAN REP.	95.3	100.0	89.1	3.1	5.593	3.1	100.0	6.6	9.632	6.6	.0	.1	.1
SIERRA LEONE	89.0	98.2	13.8	1.4	1.222	1.3	0.0	4.1	..	3.9	.0	.1	.1
TOGO	94.4	99.1	87.9	6.9	3.159	7.1	0.0	30.8	..	36.4	.0	.1	.1
KIRIBATI	81.9	100.0	81.9	6.2	4.474	6.2	..	..	..	..	.0	.1	.1
CONGO	72.0	81.7	45.2	11.6	1.064	7.7	2.0	18.4	0.197	12.2	.0	.1	.1

Notes: 1. Value of exports from reporter countries that do not participate in Free Trade Agreements.

2. Weighted average tariff reduction measured by dT / (1 + T) in percent.

Transport Equipment Extent of other countries' MFN tariff reductions on exports from:

Export market	% of exports GATT bound Total pre-UR	Total post-UR	World exc. FTA[1] % of exports affected	Post-UR applied rate	Tariff reduc-tion[2]	Post-UR bound rate	LMIEs exc. FTA[1] % of exports affected	Post-UR applied rate	Tariff reduc-tion[2]	Post-UR bound rate	To IDB LMIEs exc. FTA[1]	To all IDB Ctrys exc. FTA[1]	To all IDB Ctrys inc. FTA
JAPAN	84.6	91.2	21.9	8.3	0.741	8.5	22.3	34.2	3.442	43.4	4,315.3	58,524.4	58,524.4
UNITED STATES	90.8	93.8	10.7	2.3	1.022	5.9	6.3	7.2	0.318	19.1	3,310.1	14,283.9	36,932.2
EUROPEAN UNION	89.1	93.1	12.5	5.0	0.622	6.1	18.4	18.7	1.625	21.5	3,953.6	23,531.5	36,357.1
CANADA	99.7	99.9	0.7	1.0	1.734	6.7	3.5	13.1	0.354	28.8	71.1	440.2	27,980.4
SWEDEN	95.2	97.4	4.1	4.8	0.698	7.6	20.9	29.7	5.566	35.6	154.8	2,480.3	6,721.2
MEXICO	99.2	100.0	0.9	3.4	0.648	3.8	5.1	12.0	0.221	30.2	43.3	99.2	3,201.3
KOREA, REPUBLIC OF	91.9	96.2	13.0	4.3	0.310	4.0	1.5	23.3	0.105	48.9	79.7	2,416.2	2,416.2
BRAZIL	93.8	99.3	33.3	5.7	0.510	8.4	9.3	16.7	0.291	29.3	195.8	1,802.1	1,920.6
TAIWAN (CHINA)	76.4	82.4	45.3	5.5	1.152	6.7	28.9	19.1	1.826	26.1	98.0	1,828.7	1,828.7
AUSTRIA	94.4	95.8	6.4	7.9	1.006	6.0	38.3	14.5	0.837	16.5	121.1	170.3	1,260.5
SWITZERLAND	96.4	97.9	5.5	2.3	0.846	6.3	25.0	22.9	0.467	20.3	43.7	122.3	1,044.4
FORMER USSR	73.3	83.3	35.6	9.0	0.754	9.1	26.2	12.5	0.548	15.7	356.9	971.1	971.1
FINLAND	98.7	99.1	1.6	1.6	1.725	5.8	25.6	9.1	0.443	15.7	13.3	30.0	768.5
NORWAY	80.3	97.2	3.2	0.9	0.595	2.9	4.3	8.4	0.237	29.0	24.7	188.1	705.7
FORMER YUGOSLAVIA	90.7	92.7	49.0	7.6	1.085	7.8	23.1	7.4	0.418	10.6	83.6	671.8	671.8
CHINA	19.0	23.2	11.3	2.6	0.263	12.3	1.3	16.9	0.115	29.2	29.8	514.5	514.5
AUSTRALIA	85.1	93.5	17.4	3.4	0.910	11.9	16.9	25.3	5.006	39.7	31.8	273.5	399.3
SINGAPORE	56.7	81.0	14.9	2.7	0.501	4.9	8.4	10.1	0.838	25.6	70.9	356.5	356.5
CZECH & SLOVAK CU	49.9	62.7	35.4	8.6	2.005	7.2	17.7	11.9	0.961	13.9	199.6	343.9	343.9
POLAND	91.9	95.3	33.2	6.7	0.833	7.3	71.2	9.1	0.793	10.9	55.8	326.9	326.9
GABON	100.0	100.0	0.1	0.1	0.001	0.1	..	..	..	..	.0	270.1	270.1
SAUDI ARABIA	98.7	98.8	4.8	0.4	0.036	0.2	0.1	0.3	0.004	0.1	157.6	204.5	204.5
HUNGARY	68.3	80.4	58.1	8.6	0.795	8.5	46.7	12.5	0.568	14.3	110.4	186.7	186.7
INDIA	26.9	33.7	22.0	10.9	0.586	11.1	2.1	14.7	0.131	25.5	92.2	137.0	137.0
ARGENTINA	56.3	100.0	24.9	7.5	0.844	20.9	2.4	14.0	0.596	27.6	21.8	58.7	130.6
ROMANIA	77.3	91.5	59.3	8.8	1.956	8.9	66.2	12.9	1.691	14.2	55.1	129.2	129.2
ISRAEL	98.9	99.0	10.2	0.9	1.517	1.1	1.5	9.5	0.006	11.6	4.0	20.0	120.8
THAILAND	81.9	85.5	67.7	6.5	1.770	7.2	2.9	17.3	0.330	26.9	8.6	117.3	117.3
IRAN, ISLAMIC REP.	97.6	99.8	0.8	0.8	0.037	0.9	18.3	27.1	1.088	31.6	2.2	77.1	77.1
SOUTH AFRICA	88.8	89.9	28.3	2.3	0.703	2.2	0.6	8.8	0.117	20.0	7.8	69.5	69.5
HONG KONG	57.9	61.9	18.4	6.2	0.378	4.8	2.3	13.1	0.134	17.8	19.9	62.8	62.8
NIGERIA	100.0	100.0	1.8	0.1	0.053	0.1	0.0	64.1	..	22.1	.0	58.1	58.1
TURKEY	71.5	82.6	51.1	9.1	1.276	8.7	2.4	20.7	0.191	33.1	16.3	52.8	52.8
VENEZUELA	81.6	100.0	70.8	6.1	0.747	11.4	0.4	14.8	0.013	36.3	12.3	50.6	50.6
MOROCCO	95.7	99.7	35.0	3.0	0.751	3.1	0.0	25.8	..	28.6	2.5	50.2	50.2
SYRIA	100.0	100.0	0.3	0.1	0.008	0.1	20.0	24.6	0.193	28.6	.0	45.8	45.8
MALAYSIA	31.5	37.8	6.8	7.3	0.532	13.2	17.6	41.5	4.927	45.7	3.5	45.7	45.7
NEW ZEALAND	77.8	94.1	52.4	2.1	0.660	5.1	0.2	8.7	0.009	23.9	.7	29.5	40.7
INDONESIA	32.6	36.6	15.9	1.9	0.466	4.6	8.1	14.1	1.358	12.6	1.7	36.4	36.4
BERMUDA	100.0	100.0	34.2	0.1	0.070	0.1	..	..	..	..	.0	29.6	29.6
PANAMA	37.9	91.2	4.6	6.8	0.139	16.7	4.9	11.4	0.190	29.3	18.2	27.9	27.9
BULGARIA	96.4	98.1	92.5	5.1	1.063	4.9	93.1	5.1	1.028	4.8	26.6	27.8	27.8
EGYPT, ARAB REP.	31.9	99.8	3.9	21.0	0.107	24.4	0.0	30.0	..	35.0	14.1	20.7	20.7
CHILE	92.6	99.9	2.9	13.9	0.040	32.0	0.0	15.0	..	34.6	16.4	17.9	17.9
PHILIPPINES	80.5	93.8	22.7	11.2	2.101	11.0	25.7	68.9	12.216	78.9	2.6	17.4	17.4

Notes: 1. Value of exports from reporter countries that do not participate in Free Trade Agreements.

2. Weighted average tariff reduction measured by dT / (1 + T) in percent.

Transport Equipment (continued)

Export market	% of exports GATT bound		Average levels and changes weighted by value of exports to: the World exc. FTA[1]				LMIEs exc. FTA[1]				Value of exports in $ million		
	Total pre-UR	Total post-UR	% of exports affected	Post-UR applied rate	Tariff reduction[2]	Post-UR bound rate	% of exports affected	Post-UR applied rate	Tariff reduction[2]	Post-UR bound rate	To IDB LMIEs exc. FTA[1]	To all IDB Ctrys exc. FTA[1]	To all IDB Ctrys inc. FTA
COTE D'IVOIRE	100.0	100.0	6.7	1.1	0.290	1.1	0.0	5.5	..	5.5	.0	17.0	17.0
PERU	93.9	99.9	15.7	9.8	0.111	22.0	0.5	11.2	0.003	25.7	12.2	14.6	14.6
TUNISIA	100.0	100.0	95.7	4.5	2.574	4.5	97.3	9.8	16.222	10.4	.1	13.4	13.4
LIBYA	97.0	97.0	2.8	0.4	0.016	0.1	0.0	10.0	..	25.0	.3	10.0	10.0
URUGUAY	18.0	99.8	10.3	3.9	0.844	29.8	0.7	10.1	0.085	34.6	.2	1.7	9.8
ALGERIA	72.7	100.0	40.5	15.1	1.841	15.1	0.0	28.5	..	28.5	2.8	9.4	9.4
MALTA	97.5	97.5	17.9	1.1	0.273	1.0	0.0	6.9	..	..	.2	9.3	9.3
DJIBOUTI	100.0	100.0	0.2	0.1	0.007	0.1	..	..	..	..	.0	8.8	8.8
CYPRUS	99.4	99.4	19.4	7.8	0.372	7.8	0.0	17.7	..	22.4	.1	7.7	7.7
BENIN	100.0	100.0	1.0	0.2	0.019	0.2	0.0	16.5	..	50.0	.0	6.9	6.9
SWAZILAND	97.6	97.6	0.0	0.2	0.000	0.0	0.0	9.9	..	..	.2	6.4	6.4
HONDURAS	4.0	4.5	0.5	2.8	0.009	12.3	0.2	2.8	0.006	33.2	6.2	6.4	6.4
OMAN	75.9	76.0	14.3	1.6	0.350	1.8	0.0	69.0	..	10.0	.0	6.4	6.4
PAKISTAN	98.6	98.9	11.1	1.8	0.302	1.7	0.0	19.3	..	21.5	.1	5.7	5.7
ICELAND	98.8	98.8	2.8	0.4	1.056	5.4	..	..	..	..	.0	.4	5.5
NETHERLANDS ANTILLES	17.0	100.0	7.8	3.3	0.193	31.3	3.9	3.3	0.142	34.9	4.6	5.1	5.1
COSTA RICA	93.1	94.9	7.9	4.7	0.099	6.6	0.0	32.2	..	46.0	.6	4.8	4.8
UNTD ARAB EMRTS	80.8	87.4	48.5	9.0	1.859	6.0	49.1	51.0	6.250	23.7	.5	4.5	4.5
JORDAN	79.8	83.4	18.9	8.9	0.899	8.5	0.5	11.3	0.008	11.0	1.7	3.9	3.9
KUWAIT	86.0	93.9	48.6	8.5	1.233	6.7	7.4	54.8	0.512	31.3	.2	3.7	3.7
SUDAN	100.0	100.0	0.4	0.1	0.001	0.1	..	..	..	..	.0	3.6	3.6
MARTINIQUE	100.0	100.0	85.4	1.8	1.096	1.8	..	..	..	..	.0	3.2	3.2
GIBRALTAR	100.0	100.0	19.2	3.8	0.426	3.8	0.0	30.0	..	..	.0	3.1	3.1
GUADELOUPE	100.0	100.0	18.8	1.4	0.389	1.4	..	..	..	..	.0	2.9	2.9
CAMEROON	98.3	99.9	20.2	9.0	0.705	9.0	19.0	24.3	0.887	29.3	.0	2.5	2.5
BAHRAIN	80.5	85.4	3.0	2.0	0.083	5.1	0.0	115.3	..	3.0	.0	2.5	2.5
COLOMBIA	95.2	100.0	15.0	11.3	0.323	23.6	5.3	13.3	0.095	28.5	1.8	2.2	2.2
SENEGAL	100.0	100.0	15.2	7.6	0.397	7.6	100.0	9.5	0.456	9.5	.0	1.9	1.9
KENYA	88.1	89.5	29.1	8.9	0.885	4.3	0.0	73.5	..	..	.2	1.8	1.8
BOLIVIA	47.7	99.2	0.0	3.1	..	18.2	0.0	6.0	..	35.0	.9	1.7	1.7
LEBANON	98.7	100.0	39.3	7.3	0.737	7.6	0.0	16.4	..	25.7	.0	1.7	1.7
ECUADOR	37.7	100.0	7.4	15.0	0.175	30.5	0.0	16.6	..	35.1	1.4	1.6	1.6
TRINIDAD AND TOBAGO	14.5	85.4	3.8	6.6	0.034	34.5	0.2	6.6	0.011	40.3	1.3	1.5	1.5
ANTIGUA & B ARBUDA	100.0	100.0	1.4	1.3	0.034	1.3	..	..	..	..	.0	1.3	1.3
ZAMBIA	99.8	99.8	18.6	0.7	0.187	0.6	0.0	21.8	..	33.5	.0	1.2	1.2
SRI LANKA	55.3	87.4	47.3	4.0	0.275	17.5	26.4	4.7	0.083	31.5	.5	1.2	1.2
IRAQ	92.7	99.9	50.1	5.3	2.772	6.4	0.0	15.3	..	30.4	.1	1.0	1.0
CENTRAL AFRICAN REP.	100.0	100.0	1.3	4.0	0.014	4.0	..	..	..	..	.0	.8	.8
MAURITIUS	81.6	98.6	70.5	2.4	1.427	11.1	0.0	0.0	..	50.0	.1	.8	.8
CONGO	100.0	100.0	18.7	7.7	0.295	7.7	0.0	15.0	..	15.0	.0	.8	.8
FIJI	75.9	100.0	2.5	4.9	0.187	5.8	..	..	..	..	.0	.7	.7
LIBERIA	89.1	100.0	3.2	5.2	0.094	5.7	0.0	35.3	..	39.2	.1	.7	.7
MACAU	95.4	97.5	93.9	3.4	2.203	3.7	0.0	25.0	..	30.0	.0	.6	.6
PAPUA NEW GUINEA	73.7	87.8	4.7	6.9	0.326	8.1	0.3	10.1	0.021	10.1	.3	.6	.6
BRUNEI	10.1	10.5	5.8	17.7	0.179	8.7	4.8	21.4	1.013	31.1	.0	.6	.6

Notes: 1. Value of exports from reporter countries that do not participate in Free Trade Agreements.

2. Weighted average tariff reduction measured by dT / (1 + T) in percent.

Transport Equipment (continued)

Export market	% of exports GATT bound		Average levels and changes weighted by value of exports to:								Value of exports in $ million		
			the World exc. FTA[1]				LMIEs exc. FTA[1]						
	Total pre-UR	Total post-UR	% of exports affected	Post-UR applied rate	Tariff reduc-tion[2]	Post-UR bound rate	% of exports affected	Post-UR applied rate	Tariff reduc-tion[2]	Post-UR bound rate	To IDB LMIEs exc. FTA[1]	To all IDB Ctrys exc. FTA[1]	To all IDB Ctrys inc. FTA
ETHIOPIA	87.7	87.9	31.8	3.9	0.143	2.5	1.5	13.6	0.092	13.0	.1	.5	.5
ZAIRE	99.6	100.0	52.0	6.6	0.539	6.6	93.8	10.6	0.427	10.6	.0	.5	.5
GREENLAND	100.0	100.0	2.9	6.1	0.039	6.3	..	..	..	..	.0	.5	.5
BARBADOS	96.1	100.0	93.8	11.7	2.104	13.2	84.5	33.8	1.522	39.4	.1	.4	.4
SOMALIA	100.0	100.0	0.7	18.6	0.016	18.6	..	..	..	..	.0	.4	.4
HAITI	92.4	100.0	79.6	5.8	1.237	5.8	0.0	40.0	..	40.0	.0	.4	.4
ANGOLA	97.9	100.0	28.0	0.8	0.285	0.8	..	..	..	..	.0	.4	.4
GUINEA	48.3	97.9	67.3	19.9	2.296	20.3	100.0	35.0	3.636	35.0	.2	.4	.4
MAURITANIA	100.0	100.0	54.5	5.5	0.592	9.5	4.5	10.6	0.044	24.0	.1	.4	.4
QATAR	100.0	100.0	56.6	5.7	1.210	5.7	..	..	..	..	.0	.4	.4
GAMBIA, THE	99.4	99.4	95.0	3.9	2.268	4.0	..	..	..	..	.0	.3	.3
EL SALVADOR	60.9	91.4	15.1	11.0	0.209	15.6	0.7	18.3	0.003	30.5	.1	.3	.3
BELIZE	98.3	98.3	52.2	12.2	1.478	21.0	0.0	19.3	..	38.0	.1	.3	.3
GHANA	99.3	100.0	84.5	3.7	1.577	3.7	0.0	27.5	..	27.5	.0	.3	.3
YEMEN	95.5	95.5	6.6	6.9	0.176	2.2	0.0	90.2	..	25.0	.0	.3	.3
DOMINICAN REPUBLIC	92.0	98.2	4.7	8.1	0.027	24.3	0.0	11.6	..	35.2	.2	.3	.3
MOZAMBIQUE	83.0	84.1	7.0	14.1	0.085	16.8	0.0	11.0	..	27.5	.0	.3	.3
MALI	100.0	100.0	9.8	10.1	0.304	10.1	..	..	..	..	.0	.2	.2
MYANMAR	13.7	14.6	4.9	25.5	0.450	6.1	1.0	29.4	0.513	80.0	.2	.2	.2
DOMINICA	100.0	100.0	90.7	3.7	0.754	6.9	0.0	12.8	..	50.0	.0	.2	.2
CUBA	99.5	100.0	19.8	6.1	0.472	6.1	50.0	17.0	0.621	27.0	.0	.2	.2
LAO PDR	100.0	100.0	1.1	0.5	0.020	1.4	..	..	..	..	.0	.2	.2
ZIMBABWE	97.3	97.3	65.1	9.4	1.920	5.6	0.0	150.0	..	..	.0	.2	.2
GUYANA	100.0	100.0	9.5	18.9	0.068	18.9	..	..	..	..	.0	.2	.2
TANZANIA	97.5	97.5	72.0	5.8	7.116	2.1	0.0	150.0	..	..	.0	.2	.2
NIGER	100.0	100.0	34.6	8.1	1.114	8.1	..	..	..	..	.0	.2	.2
PARAGUAY	93.9	100.0	14.2	8.9	0.519	12.9	0.0	13.2	..	31.6	.0	.1	.1
SURINAME	60.9	62.5	14.8	13.7	0.087	8.8	0.0	30.0	..	50.0	.0	.1	.1
BURUNDI	100.0	100.0	5.7	9.8	0.138	10.2	0.0	11.0	..	25.0	.0	.1	.1
BURKINA FASO	100.0	100.0	18.8	9.5	0.615	9.5	0.0	5.0	..	5.0	.0	.1	.1
UGANDA	100.0	100.0	8.7	3.6	0.188	3.6	..	..	..	..	.0	.1	.1
BAHAMAS, THE	90.1	91.0	59.5	1.9	0.547	2.3	0.0	2.7	..	50.0	.0	.1	.1
NICARAGUA	100.0	100.0	66.4	10.8	1.819	12.3	0.0	35.0	..	43.9	.0	.1	.1
TOGO	100.0	100.0	27.0	9.8	0.693	9.8	..	..	..	..	.0	.1	.1
PUERTO RICO	76.5	100.0	54.1	14.3	1.602	19.0	2.4	25.5	0.043	36.5	.0	.1	.1
VIETNAM	24.5	29.6	9.2	14.0	0.225	11.2	0.0	42.0	..	33.3	.0	.1	.1
SIERRA LEONE	100.0	100.0	92.2	2.5	1.784	2.5	..	..	..	..	.0	.1	.1
MADAGASCAR	100.0	100.0	6.0	9.5	0.149	9.5	..	..	..	..	.0	.1	.1
JAMAICA	51.2	56.1	9.8	15.0	0.503	18.7	1.8	22.0	0.008	36.5	.1	.1	.1
SEYCHELLES	67.9	98.8	18.5	2.3	0.191	1.3	0.0	78.0	..	..	.0	.1	.1
BOTSWANA	74.7	74.7	8.9	10.4	0.164	24.7	0.0	14.0	..	34.9	.1	.1	.1
BANGLADESH	85.5	85.5	40.8	2.7	0.951	0.8	0.0	50.0	..	..	.0	.1	.1
CHAD	100.0	100.0	1.4	9.8	0.046	9.8	..	..	..	..	.0	.1	.1
EQUATORIAL GUINEA	100.0	100.0	48.4	6.4	2.780	6.4	..	..	..	..	.0	.1	.1
NEPAL	54.2	54.2	2.1	0.1	0.060	0.2	..	..	..	..	.0	.0	.0

Notes: 1. Value of exports from reporter countries that do not participate in Free Trade Agreements.

2. Weighted average tariff reduction measured by $dT / (1 + T)$ in percent.

Non-Electric Machinery Extent of other countries' MFN tariff reductions on exports from:

Export market	% of exports GATT bound		Average levels and changes weighted by value of exports to:								Value of exports in $ million		
			the World exc. FTA[1]				LMIEs exc. FTA[1]						
	Total pre-UR	Total post-UR	% of exports affected	Post-UR applied rate	Tariff reduction[2]	Post-UR bound rate	% of exports affected	Post-UR applied rate	Tariff reduction[2]	Post-UR bound rate	To IDB LMIEs exc. FTA[1]	To all IDB Ctrys exc. FTA[1]	To all IDB Ctrys inc. FTA
UNITED STATES	82.6	97.0	38.5	3.0	2.020	6.0	23.2	13.6	2.362	25.5	7,492.1	37,975.2	54,219.6
EUROPEAN UNION	80.5	95.1	38.5	5.4	2.021	6.1	41.5	13.9	1.958	19.9	12,616.5	36,304.0	53,832.3
JAPAN	72.7	90.5	65.1	3.9	2.432	5.2	48.7	14.5	4.000	19.3	9,806.6	51,002.3	51,002.3
TAIWAN (CHINA)	76.1	89.2	59.6	2.4	2.057	3.9	32.8	12.1	2.774	22.3	1,091.0	10,348.0	10,348.0
SWITZERLAND	91.1	98.0	17.5	5.3	1.972	4.0	45.8	13.0	1.984	18.9	1,143.3	2,810.6	9,055.4
CANADA	96.6	99.7	7.9	0.8	2.023	2.0	29.0	12.4	2.365	26.3	266.4	1,237.9	8,531.6
SWEDEN	92.6	98.7	17.4	2.8	2.173	3.4	40.4	12.8	1.888	19.7	621.5	2,277.7	7,848.6
SINGAPORE	81.2	94.5	53.1	2.7	2.687	3.4	58.2	15.6	7.890	20.5	999.8	6,898.7	6,898.7
AUSTRIA	93.4	99.0	21.8	4.2	1.568	3.7	73.7	7.1	1.334	9.0	1,030.7	1,491.7	5,090.5
KOREA, REPUBLIC OF	84.6	94.6	67.1	2.0	2.143	3.0	21.3	15.2	1.892	28.2	308.5	4,269.0	4,269.0
MEXICO	98.1	99.7	10.0	1.0	1.613	2.3	8.7	13.5	0.665	29.3	62.6	424.5	2,948.1
CHINA	22.4	52.0	16.5	1.8	0.516	5.2	27.4	13.7	1.296	26.6	216.9	2,601.2	2,601.2
HONG KONG	78.9	97.4	67.0	2.2	2.389	3.2	28.5	12.7	2.582	21.4	258.0	2,420.2	2,420.2
FINLAND	94.4	99.2	21.0	2.3	2.005	2.6	49.8	11.0	1.893	16.4	153.3	823.9	2,143.9
BRAZIL	87.7	97.8	64.6	3.1	1.707	7.0	5.4	12.0	0.465	29.8	231.4	1,628.3	1,723.0
THAILAND	54.8	85.0	22.8	0.9	0.978	1.3	29.6	11.3	3.952	15.5	67.5	1,413.0	1,413.0
NORWAY	94.4	98.9	12.9	2.0	2.581	2.3	56.2	12.8	4.516	17.1	71.9	259.3	1,113.2
MALAYSIA	38.6	73.8	26.7	1.3	0.891	4.5	19.6	18.1	1.966	31.0	63.8	1,043.8	1,043.8
AUSTRALIA	68.3	94.1	55.0	3.6	2.193	6.9	39.8	14.7	3.358	21.9	134.6	711.1	843.1
FORMER USSR	59.4	96.6	70.3	8.3	2.257	10.2	65.6	10.3	2.505	12.9	535.4	732.2	732.2
FORMER YUGOSLAVIA	90.0	99.4	92.0	3.4	2.079	3.8	81.5	6.1	1.831	7.4	136.4	576.5	576.5
CZECH & SLOVAK CU	49.9	93.4	54.3	8.4	1.455	10.6	31.3	12.1	1.163	15.9	321.7	516.3	516.3
ISRAEL	94.6	99.6	42.1	1.7	2.130	2.3	53.9	11.7	1.828	18.2	25.5	285.1	512.8
POLAND	86.6	94.3	82.9	6.7	1.472	6.1	80.1	8.8	1.186	8.0	302.9	461.5	461.5
PHILIPPINES	36.7	90.5	64.6	7.9	6.885	9.1	95.1	18.7	14.681	19.7	159.4	383.3	383.3
HUNGARY	82.3	95.0	83.0	5.5	1.465	4.9	73.4	7.9	0.871	7.1	208.2	377.0	377.0
ARGENTINA	57.3	98.7	23.9	4.4	1.523	19.1	4.7	11.2	1.739	30.6	59.2	180.2	297.5
INDIA	53.8	88.1	50.1	3.9	1.986	6.2	29.9	11.1	3.567	19.7	61.0	228.3	228.3
NEW ZEALAND	65.6	92.3	21.0	1.8	1.483	9.6	19.8	10.7	1.404	22.6	11.0	80.2	198.3
BULGARIA	57.3	90.0	68.1	7.1	1.402	8.2	61.4	8.4	1.354	10.1	143.1	189.8	189.8
ROMANIA	68.0	93.7	72.1	6.1	1.690	8.0	57.0	8.7	1.545	11.7	85.1	161.3	161.3
SOUTH AFRICA	78.2	82.1	66.3	2.2	2.181	2.9	0.4	3.5	0.016	16.1	25.6	134.2	134.2
TURKEY	90.2	99.1	86.2	3.8	2.169	4.8	7.7	19.1	0.203	29.6	10.3	96.3	96.3
PUERTO RICO	90.5	99.6	71.2	2.7	2.397	4.1	1.7	8.4	0.078	30.0	3.3	59.6	59.6
SAUDI ARABIA	84.4	98.7	54.5	1.8	2.057	1.7	18.5	8.5	1.603	8.2	6.3	43.7	43.7
PANAMA	41.2	99.7	8.0	10.9	0.167	31.2	1.0	11.7	0.007	33.6	27.8	30.1	30.1
VENEZUELA	44.8	99.9	39.5	7.3	0.801	18.4	0.3	11.9	0.003	31.4	15.4	27.0	27.0
EGYPT, ARAB REP.	70.4	99.5	35.4	6.9	0.890	12.6	2.2	17.5	0.041	32.5	9.0	24.6	24.6
INDONESIA	67.1	82.3	67.1	4.4	2.163	4.8	38.3	19.0	3.311	18.7	4.0	24.0	24.0
COLOMBIA	90.7	100.0	51.7	10.7	1.243	18.8	17.2	18.1	0.300	33.3	11.7	22.1	22.1
MOROCCO	85.6	96.8	53.0	4.0	1.553	3.8	0.2	21.9	0.011	24.8	3.1	21.1	21.1
ALGERIA	98.7	100.0	95.0	1.3	3.460	1.4	0.0	11.0	..	15.4	.4	18.6	18.6
UNTD ARAB EMRTS	73.5	98.4	72.6	2.4	2.859	4.1	82.3	17.2	6.672	18.9	1.7	17.8	17.8
JORDAN	80.9	94.5	83.9	3.7	2.477	2.8	57.9	12.4	8.547	5.8	2.4	16.2	16.2
BAHRAIN	98.1	99.9	33.9	0.9	0.712	1.0	5.9	39.2	0.670	16.0	.0	14.8	14.8

Notes: 1. Value of exports from reporter countries that do not participate in Free Trade Agreements.

2. Weighted average tariff reduction measured by dT / (1 + T) in percent.

Non-Electric Machinery (continued)

Export market	% of exports GATT bound		Average levels and changes weighted by value of exports to: the World exc. FTA[1]				LMIEs exc. FTA[1]				Value of exports in $ million		
	Total pre-UR	Total post-UR	% of exports affected	Post-UR applied rate	Tariff reduc-tion[2]	Post-UR bound rate	% of exports affected	Post-UR applied rate	Tariff reduc-tion[2]	Post-UR bound rate	To IDB LMIEs exc. FTA[1]	To all IDB Ctrys exc. FTA[1]	To all IDB Ctrys inc. FTA
ICELAND	97.7	100.0	16.7	2.1	2.113	2.1	95.4	4.0	0.532	3.6	.4	2.5	11.7
TUNISIA	99.8	100.0	92.7	2.7	2.296	2.7	15.3	6.0	0.623	7.0	.1	11.6	11.6
MALI	100.0	100.0	51.0	0.1	1.115	0.1	0.0	5.0	..	5.0	.0	10.8	10.8
CYPRUS	81.3	82.8	67.6	8.7	2.025	3.2	28.7	26.3	1.056	14.1	3.1	10.4	10.4
URUGUAY	39.9	100.0	5.5	8.7	0.747	31.4	0.6	10.8	0.041	33.0	1.3	1.7	8.6
CHILE	54.3	97.9	31.5	7.5	0.883	18.0	0.1	12.4	0.005	30.6	4.8	8.4	8.4
COSTA RICA	93.1	98.9	56.6	8.2	1.300	14.1	0.0	19.9	..	36.5	2.7	7.8	7.8
KUWAIT	89.5	99.7	75.9	1.3	2.883	1.6	95.9	16.6	4.847	16.5	.3	7.8	7.8
IRAN, ISLAMIC REP.	97.0	99.6	31.7	0.7	0.575	0.6	89.7	9.4	3.452	5.8	.2	7.5	7.5
DOMINICAN REPUBLIC	99.1	99.6	86.1	0.4	2.975	0.7	0.0	7.8	..	31.8	.1	7.1	7.1
MALTA	97.4	98.0	95.3	2.1	1.860	2.1	97.4	4.5	1.386	4.3	1.3	6.6	6.6
OMAN	81.2	99.9	51.4	0.6	1.621	2.4	16.7	9.0	2.114	13.5	.0	6.0	6.0
BAHAMAS, THE	99.0	100.0	60.8	5.9	1.602	14.1	0.3	12.7	0.001	34.8	2.2	5.9	5.9
MACAU	68.6	69.0	61.7	0.7	1.956	1.0	90.9	3.6	3.651	3.6	.0	5.4	5.4
PERU	72.5	98.9	56.0	5.6	1.025	13.8	2.6	11.4	0.051	31.4	2.2	5.3	5.3
IRAQ	97.4	99.7	55.8	1.0	2.281	1.6	26.9	14.9	1.526	30.6	.2	5.2	5.2
COTE D'IVOIRE	99.8	100.0	98.9	1.6	2.712	1.8	27.3	12.1	1.125	26.0	.1	5.1	5.1
TRINIDAD AND TOBAGO	34.7	100.0	18.5	25.8	0.598	35.9	0.9	31.4	0.005	43.8	3.4	4.2	4.2
KENYA	86.8	98.2	42.5	0.9	1.495	1.4	55.7	6.6	3.696	17.1	.3	4.2	4.2
SRI LANKA	71.3	94.8	25.4	1.1	0.727	2.7	17.9	12.4	1.540	19.0	.2	4.0	4.0
CUBA	79.5	99.8	73.9	2.6	0.340	4.1	73.6	2.8	0.155	4.4	3.6	3.9	3.9
NIGERIA	99.1	99.2	87.5	1.1	3.670	1.1	33.1	12.2	2.646	15.2	.1	3.7	3.7
LEBANON	90.6	99.9	87.9	2.8	2.504	4.5	5.8	13.1	0.292	31.0	.3	3.5	3.5
SWAZILAND	68.0	98.7	85.0	5.1	10.325	5.0	91.2	5.9	12.293	5.9	2.9	3.5	3.5
MAURITIUS	85.3	87.6	63.8	1.7	1.834	0.8	28.7	0.8	0.952	2.6	.1	3.5	3.5
ECUADOR	59.1	99.9	40.8	7.1	1.017	19.3	0.1	11.1	0.003	32.1	1.8	3.2	3.2
PAPUA NEW GUINEA	21.9	95.6	9.4	1.9	0.535	5.1	23.0	12.0	2.028	31.2	.3	3.1	3.1
PAKISTAN	70.1	79.0	62.0	2.9	1.733	2.3	13.4	7.6	0.877	13.4	.8	3.0	3.0
BRUNEI	31.7	85.0	21.9	0.3	0.928	2.2	15.3	7.5	0.744	8.1	.1	3.0	3.0
CAMEROON	99.2	100.0	97.3	1.3	2.954	1.4	97.2	4.1	1.118	4.4	.4	2.9	2.9
MARTINIQUE	99.6	100.0	87.6	1.2	2.631	1.3	..	..	..	..	.0	2.8	2.8
SUDAN	97.4	100.0	5.3	0.1	0.152	0.3	..	..	..	..	.0	2.7	2.7
GUADELOUPE	99.8	100.0	74.5	1.2	2.252	1.3	..	..	..	..	.0	2.6	2.6
GABON	99.8	100.0	93.4	1.2	3.802	2.1	0.0	13.8	..	35.1	.1	2.5	2.5
GUYANA	74.2	100.0	73.4	11.6	4.549	13.1	0.8	44.0	0.028	49.3	.7	2.5	2.5
GIBRALTAR	97.8	100.0	97.8	2.1	2.641	2.2	0.0	2.5	..	5.0	.0	2.2	2.2
GRENADA	100.0	100.0	100.0	0.2	2.945	0.2	100.0	6.0	3.085	6.0	.0	2.2	2.2
VIETNAM	51.2	56.2	45.6	1.2	0.178	7.4	79.8	2.1	0.176	8.0	1.1	2.2	2.2
SENEGAL	98.8	100.0	53.0	1.4	1.194	1.7	22.2	15.1	0.810	31.7	.0	2.1	2.1
DOMINICA	96.8	97.7	76.0	3.5	2.847	5.2	4.6	12.4	0.041	25.6	.3	2.0	2.0
ANGOLA	100.0	100.0	52.1	0.9	1.295	0.9	..	..	..	..	.0	1.9	1.9
GHANA	99.8	100.0	96.5	2.2	4.216	2.9	6.7	12.6	0.467	33.8	.1	1.9	1.9
JAMAICA	91.5	99.6	61.2	2.7	1.503	8.2	19.6	7.7	0.188	24.8	.6	1.9	1.9
NETHERLANDS ANTILLES	95.8	99.9	23.6	9.4	0.655	24.5	1.3	12.2	0.020	32.5	1.4	1.8	1.8
LIBYA	82.6	96.5	81.5	5.1	2.752	3.6	50.3	21.6	2.974	16.0	.3	1.8	.8

Notes: 1. Value of exports from reporter countries that do not participate in Free Trade Agreements.

2. Weighted average tariff reduction measured by $dT / (1 + T)$ in percent.

Non-Electric Machinery (continued)

Export market	% of exports GATT bount		Average levels and changes weighted by value of exports to:								Value of exports in $ million		
			the World exc. FTA[1]				LMIEs exc. FTA[1]						
	Total pre-UR	Total post-UR	% of exports affected	Post-UR applied rate	Tariff reduc-tion[2]	Post-UR bound rate	% of exports affected	Post-UR applied rate	Tariff reduc-tion[2]	Post-UR bound rate	To IDB LMIEs exc. FTA[1]	To all IDB Ctrys exc. FTA[1]	To all IDB Ctrys inc. FTA
TOGO	99.5	100.0	68.8	0.7	2.197	0.8	0.0	20.0	..	40.0	.0	1.7	1.7
MOZAMBIQUE	19.4	99.9	16.1	0.5	0.582	0.6	0.0	15.5		29.7	.0	1.7	1.7
SEYCHELLES	98.4	100.0	83.7	1.1	2.397	1.2	..	..	..	..	.0	1.6	1.6
BANGLADESH	18.6	92.4	18.7	1.9	0.602	2.1	23.5	26.5	3.915	15.5	.1	1.5	1.5
LIBERIA	83.1	100.0	62.1	7.5	3.287	13.4	0.0	19.3	..	35.0	.5	1.5	1.5
SYRIA	90.9	98.7	73.2	2.5	2.064	3.6	9.9	5.9	0.422	9.9	.4	1.5	1.5
NIGER	100.0	100.0	98.9	3.7	2.960	3.7	..	..	..	..	.0	1.3	1.3
HONDURAS	84.7	100.0	9.4	17.1	0.254	25.6	2.3	25.0	0.137	37.4	.8	1.2	1.2
ZIMBABWE	88.7	93.8	70.2	3.5	2.675	4.2	6.1	10.7	0.130	23.9	.1	1.2	1.2
CONGO	99.4	99.8	96.5	1.8	2.703	1.8	89.8	4.5	0.653	3.6	.0	1.2	1.2
GREENLAND	100.0	100.0	96.4	1.9	3.091	1.9	..	..	..	..	.0	1.1	1.1
YEMEN	55.5	93.1	54.5	0.6	2.238	6.8	1.3	0.9	0.028	38.9	.2	1.1	1.1
ANTIGUA & B ARBUDA	99.5	100.0	20.2	0.4	0.504	0.5	0.0	15.4	..	31.4	.0	1.0	1.0
TANZANIA	99.9	100.0	65.5	0.8	2.284	0.8	..	..	..	..	.0	1.0	1.0
MAURITANIA	100.0	100.0	99.4	2.4	1.633	2.5	83.3	6.1	1.069	8.5	.0	.9	.9
GAMBIA, THE	95.1	100.0	95.1	0.2	4.824	0.7	0.0	15.0	..	30.0	.0	.9	.9
ETHIOPIA	99.2	100.0	32.7	2.4	0.796	5.2	0.0	14.7	..	36.1	.1	.9	.9
BARBADOS	99.6	100.0	67.6	2.2	1.709	2.5	0.0	13.2	..	37.3	.0	.9	.9
NEPAL	28.8	74.4	25.1	0.9	0.409	1.4	75.0	3.8	2.735	5.0	.0	.8	.8
ALBANIA	99.4	100.0	96.6	4.4	2.104	4.7	94.6	6.0	1.512	6.4	.5	.8	.8
BELIZE	99.3	100.0	16.7	13.2	0.580	28.4	0.2	15.6	0.013	34.2	.6	.7	.7
GUINEA	96.4	98.2	60.5	1.1	2.030	1.2	0.0	15.0	..	..	.0	.7	.7
NICARAGUA	97.2	100.0	73.1	3.8	1.564	6.4	0.0	7.3	..	17.7	.2	.7	.7
BOTSWANA	34.9	34.9	31.1	1.9	0.822	4.9	0.0	1.2	..	30.4	.4	.7	.7
PARAGUAY	72.0	95.1	28.6	8.6	1.410	23.2	0.0	14.4	..	33.3	.3	.5	.7
SOMALIA	99.5	100.0	87.5	0.8	2.414	0.9	83.3	8.2	4.438	9.5	.0	.6	.6
MALAWI	82.2	94.3	21.8	1.7	0.561	6.9	9.7	6.6	0.353	43.9	.1	.6	.6
HAITI	65.5	96.6	59.4	1.6	1.571	2.7	0.0	14.1	..	35.0	.0	.6	.6
BOLIVIA	79.1	100.0	10.6	4.8	0.241	11.3	0.0	13.1	..	31.7	.2	.6	.6
ZAMBIA	92.4	99.7	73.8	2.1	3.006	2.1	0.0	19.1	..	20.0	.0	.6	.6
ZAIRE	100.0	100.0	76.3	1.6	1.990	1.6	0.0	5.0	..	5.0	.0	5	.5
MYANMAR	88.4	99.8	53.9	1.5	1.931	2.9	0.0	5.0	..	17.7	.0	.5	.5
SURINAME	97.9	100.0	95.3	0.5	3.445	1.4	0.0	10.1	..	47.7	.0	.5	.5
QATAR	97.0	99.8	97.3	1.8	2.621	2.5	10.0	4.5	1.818	36.0	.0	.4	.4
BENIN	89.9	100.0	48.3	1.7	1.524	4.7	0.0	10.0	..	40.0	.0	.4	.4
BURKINA FASO	100.0	100.0	98.9	1.5	2.534	1.5	..	..	..	..	.0	.4	.4
LESOTHO	97.9	97.9	95.8	3.6	1.743	4.1	0.0	5.4	..	30.0	.0	.3	.3
BERMUDA	60.5	98.2	88.3	5.5	4.133	5.3	95.5	13.4	5.898	13.1	.1	.3	.3
NAURU	91.4	99.7	91.4	1.7	1.758	2.5	0.0	27.0	..	..	.0	.3	.3
FIJI	74.3	100.0	11.2	3.1	0.240	5.2	0.0	22.0	..	22.0	.0	.3	.3
MADAGASCAR	100.0	100.0	99.3	2.2	2.329	2.2	..	..	..	..	.0	.3	.3
AFGHANISTAN	85.1	100.0	74.3	1.4	1.955	2.0	0.0	12.7	..	35.0	.0	.2	.2
EL SALVADOR	56.3	79.6	37.9	4.2	1.355	16.5	10.2	10.3	0.166	32.0	.1	.2	.2
BURUNDI	99.1	99.1	97.7	0.7	3.626	0.8	28.6	11.0	1.042	17.0	.0	.2	.2
SIERRA LEONE	100.0	100.0	15.0	0.1	0.661	0.1	..	..	..	..	.0	.2	.2

Notes: 1. Value of exports from reporter countries that do not participate in Free Trade Agreements.

2. Weighted average tariff reduction measured by dT / (1 + T) in percent.

Electric Machinery Extent of other countries' MFN tariff reductions on exports from:

Export market	% of exports GATT bount		Average levels and changes weighted by value of exports to:								Value of exports in $ million		
			the World exc. FTA[1]				LMIEs exc. FTA[1]						
	Total pre-UR	Total post-UR	% of exports affected	Post-UR applied rate	Tariff reduc-tion[2]	Post-UR bound rate	% of exports affected	Post-UR applied rate	Tariff reduc-tion[2]	Post-UR bound rate	To IDB LMIEs exc. FTA[1]	To all IDB Ctrys exc. FTA[1]	To all IDB Ctrys inc. FTA
JAPAN	66.8	86.6	55.2	4.7	2.098	5.6	53.6	14.0	4.547	14.8	7,778.8	45,087.0	45,087.0
UNITED STATES	69.0	91.7	35.8	4.9	2.378	6.6	41.2	12.8	3.455	16.9	6,100.1	19,845.8	26,699.1
EUROPEAN UNION	73.6	90.5	27.1	7.9	1.682	7.6	29.6	17.7	1.953	22.5	5,135.5	13,448.7	21,556.8
TAIWAN (CHINA)	66.3	82.3	44.0	3.4	1.574	4.6	41.7	16.3	3.884	19.4	833.6	10,555.1	10,555.1
KOREA, REPUBLIC OF	77.7	92.7	41.2	4.1	1.413	4.7	28.6	20.0	2.598	23.1	738.5	9,896.2	9,896.2
CHINA	24.0	29.2	15.7	1.1	0.576	4.0	27.4	18.1	3.418	28.2	96.5	8,800.7	8,800.7
MEXICO	99.2	99.8	0.7	0.8	1.595	3.5	14.6	14.3	1.181	30.3	43.8	125.4	6,802.3
SINGAPORE	66.0	86.9	45.0	5.2	2.157	5.3	42.2	14.7	4.476	14.9	1,336.0	6,483.1	6,483.1
MALAYSIA	54.7	94.0	24.0	1.5	1.001	4.5	60.0	11.8	6.077	10.5	197.1	6,341.7	6,341.7
CANADA	93.9	97.7	8.4	2.4	2.213	2.9	27.9	17.8	2.675	22.3	164.2	645.8	4,188.8
HONG KONG	80.9	96.2	62.6	4.6	2.612	5.2	55.7	11.6	4.886	11.9	567.7	3,890.7	3,890.7
SWITZERLAND	91.6	97.2	15.3	7.5	1.871	4.6	35.5	17.9	2.431	22.5	298.1	930.0	3,637.1
SWEDEN	87.0	97.0	16.3	8.4	2.671	6.4	28.4	15.3	2.198	23.7	375.2	1,029.5	3,351.6
AUSTRIA	94.4	98.7	9.7	8.0	1.628	6.6	64.5	10.8	1.687	11.5	361.4	483.0	2,915.4
PHILIPPINES	71.6	92.0	25.6	1.3	0.942	2.2	55.8	1.5	1.931	0.8	109.8	1,326.7	1,326.7
THAILAND	63.1	88.6	31.4	2.0	0.997	2.9	71.8	6.1	2.459	4.6	146.6	1,321.7	1,321.7
FINLAND	92.8	97.5	9.5	8.5	3.324	6.2	63.7	19.6	5.911	21.0	60.1	158.9	961.8
BRAZIL	81.0	97.8	68.6	5.7	1.780	11.4	5.0	14.2	1.261	32.7	79.0	641.4	736.5
ISRAEL	89.5	98.0	28.5	4.3	2.234	4.3	3.3	18.0	0.320	21.7	60.8	268.0	659.5
FORMER YUGOSLAVIA	83.8	97.8	81.5	5.2	2.222	5.5	41.0	10.2	1.773	11.5	145.2	586.2	586.2
NORWAY	87.1	97.5	7.7	10.7	1.419	5.6	16.9	19.4	1.143	26.1	41.8	117.0	533.8
AUSTRALIA	35.7	81.3	27.1	5.5	1.247	14.6	17.1	18.4	1.490	28.5	52.1	203.2	296.3
POLAND	92.2	95.9	90.1	5.6	2.275	5.7	85.5	8.7	2.205	8.8	99.5	244.6	244.6
FORMER USSR	70.7	98.9	52.4	9.5	2.105	11.1	48.1	11.8	1.383	14.1	159.1	238.2	238.2
HUNGARY	82.4	95.3	75.5	9.4	2.211	8.6	61.8	18.4	2.370	17.0	83.6	227.9	227.9
MALTA	85.5	100.0	45.8	3.7	2.009	5.0	19.4	16.3	0.722	29.7	.3	227.5	227.5
CZECH & SLOVAK CU	64.0	97.2	62.4	6.7	1.698	8.2	35.4	10.8	1.332	13.5	75.2	163.8	163.8
PANAMA	52.9	99.9	4.8	17.9	0.094	33.9	3.8	18.2	0.072	34.4	95.4	96.9	96.9
NEW ZEALAND	50.3	94.1	13.4	4.2	1.874	15.2	23.3	17.8	1.927	23.9	3.5	22.5	94.4
MOROCCO	84.9	99.8	72.2	4.5	3.466	5.9	0.9	17.2	0.056	13.7	.7	92.6	92.6
INDONESIA	45.5	64.0	46.3	2.8	1.939	3.5	76.1	6.3	3.290	4.0	18.5	84.4	84.4
TURKEY	96.6	99.6	56.9	10.1	1.457	10.6	17.4	26.6	0.829	33.4	7.2	84.1	84.1
DOMINICAN REPUBLIC	100.0	100.0	97.3	3.3	1.893	3.3	33.3	13.1	2.003	22.7	.0	83.7	83.7
TUNISIA	99.8	100.0	94.6	3.6	2.380	3.6	15.3	9.4	1.772	9.6	.3	75.4	75.4
INDIA	59.4	81.8	52.3	6.9	1.640	8.6	34.9	15.6	1.614	20.2	21.3	68.9	68.9
ROMANIA	81.6	93.2	80.8	6.5	2.902	4.8	36.1	16.1	0.667	11.4	18.2	64.9	64.9
COSTA RICA	98.0	99.2	78.0	4.1	2.126	5.5	10.8	20.6	0.862	36.8	5.0	61.8	61.8
HAITI	100.0	100.0	67.5	3.3	1.754	3.3	100.0	4.6	1.612	4.6	.1	58.4	58.4
BULGARIA	72.9	97.7	67.2	6.7	1.468	8.8	55.0	8.4	1.195	11.3	39.0	57.1	57.1
SOUTH AFRICA	63.1	67.4	54.8	4.2	1.667	5.5	2.0	7.5	0.060	15.1	12.3	41.8	41.8
EL SALVADOR	99.8	100.0	98.6	8.6	1.293	8.7	19.4	10.6	0.366	20.5	.2	26.9	26.9
ARGENTINA	47.9	99.8	23.1	7.9	1.008	24.4	0.2	12.0	0.032	31.6	6.7	13.6	26.3
MACAU	66.9	68.1	56.4	3.6	2.061	5.3	34.0	19.9	7.027	27.4	.1	24.9	24.9
BARBADOS	100.0	100.0	73.8	3.6	1.935	3.6	..	..	..	..	.0	24.4	24.4
VENEZUELA	79.4	95.1	53.5	5.7	0.865	9.6	0.4	13.3	0.034	36.6	4.2	24.1	24.1

Notes: 1. Value of exports from reporter countries that do not participate in Free Trade Agreements.

2. Weighted average tariff reduction measured by dT / (1 + T) in percent.

Electric Machinery (continued)

Export market	% of exports GATT bount		Average levels and changes weighted by value of exports to:								Value of exports in $ million		
			the World exc. FTA[1]				LMIEs exc. FTA[1]						
	Total pre-UR	Total post-UR	% of exports affected	Post-UR applied rate	Tariff reduction[2]	Post-UR bound rate	% of exports affected	Post-UR applied rate	Tariff reduc[2]	Post-UR bound rate	To IDB LMIEs exc. FTA[1]	To all IDB Ctrys exc. FTA[1]	To all IDB Ctrys inc. FTA
PERU	93.7	100.0	8.9	6.6	0.163	10.2	0.9	11.5	0.010	24.9	5.2	20.1	20.1
PUERTO RICO	83.5	96.0	66.8	6.3	2.914	9.3	2.4	14.7	0.110	31.3	2.4	16.9	16.9
EGYPT, ARAB REP.	31.9	96.2	16.8	11.8	0.506	26.1	0.0	14.5	..	31.6	12.8	16.5	16.5
URUGUAY	26.3	100.0	15.8	3.0	2.337	26.8	0.0	12.1	..	31.8	.1	2.0	11.1
COLOMBIA	84.6	98.8	30.2	18.0	0.569	27.0	13.7	22.3	0.071	33.4	7.7	9.9	9.9
CHILE	52.7	85.7	25.8	9.5	0.541	24.3	1.9	14.9	0.015	34.1	5.4	9.2	9.2
UNTD ARAB EMRTS	84.6	95.5	67.4	3.8	1.432	5.8	20.8	13.1	0.730	26.4	.9	8.3	8.3
SAUDI ARABIA	95.4	97.7	77.6	3.4	2.050	3.3	31.6	12.0	2.270	10.5	.5	7.7	7.7
SRI LANKA	32.9	57.4	24.4	10.8	0.364	5.7	0.2	22.4	0.024	10.6	3.1	6.9	6.9
LEBANON	84.5	99.9	73.7	7.5	1.724	11.2	0.0	20.7	..	35.9	1.3	5.5	5.5
VIETNAM	25.2	77.8	25.5	11.2	0.234	15.1	32.5	14.4	0.293	15.1	3.9	5.1	5.1
ECUADOR	64.1	98.8	10.2	14.7	0.254	28.7	0.0	16.4	..	31.9	4.1	4.7	4.7
KENYA	76.7	85.2	62.2	4.9	3.155	2.6	9.7	23.8	1.423	28.8	.8	4.7	4.7
BELIZE	99.9	100.0	0.1	11.7	0.001	25.6	0.0	16.0	..	35.0	2.8	3.8	3.8
KUWAIT	99.6	99.8	96.9	3.2	2.680	3.2	0.0	20.0	..	10.0	.0	3.6	3.6
CYPRUS	78.8	98.2	60.2	7.3	1.603	9.8	4.7	23.3	0.490	32.8	.5	3.4	3.4
NETHERLANDS ANTILLES	75.2	100.0	52.1	9.4	0.919	15.4	17.2	18.6	0.280	34.9	1.2	3.3	3.3
JORDAN	71.7	87.8	50.5	3.8	1.539	3.8	0.3	19.9	0.002	2.2	.3	3.2	3.2
JAMAICA	97.1	99.8	80.4	3.7	1.889	4.7	0.6	15.1	0.001	21.1	.3	2.7	2.7
GUADELOUPE	100.0	100.0	91.9	4.1	2.492	4.1	..	..	..	..	.0	2.7	2.7
TRINIDAD AND TOBAGO	32.4	98.4	7.4	24.2	0.351	34.7	0.0	33.2	..	48.5	1.8	2.6	2.6
PAKISTAN	82.1	87.8	50.6	9.9	1.686	18.1	5.8	14.0	0.351	33.8	1.3	2.6	2.6
IRAQ	98.5	100.0	98.1	3.8	2.682	4.0	57.6	23.7	3.503	31.8	.1	2.5	2.5
ALGERIA	72.2	96.8	68.3	11.6	2.094	13.1	0.1	34.8	0.004	43.7	.7	2.4	2.4
CONGO	99.8	100.0	98.7	2.7	2.235	2.7	0.0	15.6	..	35.0	.0	2.4	2.4
MAURITIUS	47.9	84.7	40.0	2.8	0.993	6.0	1.0	19.3	0.058	13.0	.1	2.2	2.2
NIGERIA	91.5	100.0	85.7	4.6	1.715	4.9	0.0	9.9	..	9.9	.1	1.8	1.8
ICELAND	87.0	93.2	17.7	2.9	3.521	3.6	87.3	16.3	10.593	16.6	.1	.5	1.7
BANGLADESH	69.4	97.6	63.6	2.3	1.494	5.3	6.9	19.3	0.414	32.6	.1	1.6	1.6
BAHRAIN	99.8	99.8	88.2	3.6	1.874	3.6	2.8	7.8	0.346	7.7	.2	1.6	1.6
SENEGAL	100.0	100.0	49.5	2.6	1.562	2.7	0.0	13.1	..	35.0	.0	1.5	1.5
COTE D'IVOIRE	97.6	99.1	81.9	2.4	3.137	2.3	13.9	8.4	3.950	7.9	.2	1.5	1.5
IRAN, ISLAMIC REP.	90.2	96.0	52.8	6.2	1.509	7.1	13.2	14.0	0.338	14.2	.4	1.4	1.4
OMAN	100.0	100.0	96.2	3.1	2.227	3.1	..	..	..	..	.0	1.3	1.3
MALI	99.8	99.8	71.6	3.8	2.403	3.8	0.0	7.0	..	7.0	.0	1.2	1.2
NICARAGUA	97.6	100.0	21.7	1.5	0.500	2.6	0.0	12.2	..	35.0	.1	1.2	1.2
SYRIA	85.9	99.6	83.0	6.8	2.335	7.9	23.3	21.5	0.135	27.0	.2	1.1	1.1
MARTINIQUE	99.6	100.0	90.6	3.7	2.604	3.9	0.0	10.0	..	50.0	.0	1.1	1.1
BAHAMAS, THE	90.9	100.0	26.9	9.5	0.837	27.2	0.0	12.0	..	36.6	.8	1.1	1.1
GIBRALTAR	96.9	97.7	95.6	2.9	2.074	3.0	0.0	10.0	..	10.0	.0	.9	.9
PAPUA NEW GUINEA	78.4	89.0	43.4	10.0	1.537	19.1	0.0	17.1	..	35.0	.4	.9	.9
BENIN	99.6	100.0	5.4	7.4	0.158	14.2	0.0	15.5	..	35.1	.3	.8	.8
ZAIRE	100.0	100.0	83.1	3.8	0.687	3.8	0.0	10.5	..	35.0	.0	.8	.8
SURINAME	99.6	99.7	84.8	3.1	1.481	3.0	0.0	40.0	..	50.0	.0	.7	.7
DOMINICA	99.3	99.3	71.8	6.0	1.947	7.0	0.0	15.4	..	34.5	.0	.7	.7

Notes: 1. Value of exports from reporter countries that do not participate in Free Trade Agreements.

2. Weighted average tariff reduction measured by dT / (1 + T) in percent.

Electric Machinery (continued)

Export market	% of exports GATT bount — Total pre-UR	Total post-UR	Average levels and changes weighted by value of exports to: the World exc. FTA[1] — % of exports affected	Post-UR applied rate	Tariff reduc-tion[2]	Post-UR bound rate	LMIEs exc. FTA[1] — % of exports affected	Post-UR applied rate	Tariff reduc-tion[2]	Post-UR bound rate	Value of exports in $ million — To IDB LMIEs exc. FTA[1]	To all IDB Ctrys exc. FTA[1]	To all IDB Ctrys inc. FTA
SEYCHELLES	97.0	97.0	75.7	2.8	2.225	2.9	..	..	..	..	.0	.7	.7
GABON	98.8	99.9	79.6	2.9	1.969	3.1	0.0	17.1	..	31.4	.0	.7	.7
CAMEROON	99.4	100.0	91.2	2.9	2.423	2.9	30.0	8.8	1.803	8.8	.0	.7	.7
KIRIBATI	100.0	100.0	100.0	5.3	7.805	5.3	..	..	..	..	.0	.6	.6
TOGO	100.0	100.0	50.7	7.0	1.589	12.8	0.0	13.6	..	29.8	.2	.6	.6
GHANA	98.2	98.3	94.8	4.1	2.797	4.4	0.0	18.4	..	35.0	.0	.6	.6
SWAZILAND	51.1	62.2	47.2	10.8	1.233	5.7	43.2	15.4	1.170	10.7	.4	.6	.6
ZIMBABWE	99.3	99.3	93.4	3.1	2.766	3.2	..	..	..	..	.0	.6	.6
ALBANIA	11.2	99.8	10.7	11.7	0.119	24.8	5.7	12.1	0.011	26.0	.6	.6	.6
QATAR	99.5	99.5	93.4	2.3	4.358	2.1	0.0	41.7	..	..	.0	.6	.6
BRUNEI	57.7	74.5	47.7	4.2	1.482	8.8	2.3	19.9	0.332	34.2	.0	.6	.6
ZAMBIA	100.0	100.0	54.1	3.2	1.981	3.2	..	..	..	..	.0	.4	.4
GUINEA	65.5	100.0	60.5	2.5	1.814	5.9	..	..	..	..	.0	.4	.4
LIBERIA	94.3	99.8	94.3	3.6	2.335	4.1	0.0	20.0	..	..	.0	.4	.4
MOZAMBIQUE	80.2	88.9	29.8	6.3	0.805	4.8	0.0	27.0	..	..	.0	.4	.4
HONDURAS	96.5	100.0	8.7	6.0	0.230	11.3	0.0	16.1	..	36.3	.1	.4	.4
GREENLAND	100.0	100.0	95.3	3.7	5.236	3.7	..	..	..	..	.0	.4	.4
NEPAL	81.7	98.8	5.5	2.8	0.241	4.4	66.7	10.3	4.006	13.0	.0	.3	.3
MADAGASCAR	100.0	100.0	95.2	3.1	1.667	3.1	..	..	..	..	.0	.3	.3
SIERRA LEONE	100.0	100.0	99.4	9.3	1.643	9.3	..	..	..	..	.0	.3	.3
NIGER	100.0	100.0	85.0	3.7	2.727	3.7	100.0	13.9	5.227	13.9	.0	.3	.3
YEMEN	73.3	74.0	41.6	1.2	1.265	1.8	0.0	5.0	..	25.0	.0	.3	.3
VANUATU	1.1	100.0	98.2	10.0	4.361	10.3	0.0	10.0	..	35.0	.0	.3	.3
BOTSWANA	89.5	89.5	71.9	5.1	2.108	3.2	0.0	21.9	..	..	.0	.3	.3
CUBA	57.9	88.8	28.3	7.2	0.833	16.3	0.7	10.0	0.013	21.9	.1	.2	.2
TANZANIA	100.0	100.0	71.5	7.5	1.512	7.5	0.0	20.0	..	20.0	.1	.2	.2
LAO PDR	0.0	0.0	0.0	0.0	..	..	..	..	..	..	.0	.2	.2
TONGA	98.0	100.0	97.0	3.8	4.055	3.8	..	..	..	..	.0	.2	.2
ANGOLA	100.0	100.0	96.4	2.8	1.958	2.8	..	..	..	..	.0	.2	.2
GUINEA-BISSAU	100.0	100.0	22.5	14.5	0.651	28.0	0.0	17.7	..	35.0	.1	.2	.2
AFGHANISTAN	67.2	67.2	39.3	1.3	1.171	1.9	0.0	8.0	..	8.0	.0	.2	.2
BERMUDA	90.1	100.0	89.0	4.7	2.063	5.9	48.1	17.6	4.684	25.4	.0	.2	.2
MALAWI	100.0	100.0	85.1	2.6	1.957	2.6	..	..	..	..	.0	.2	.2
LIBYA	93.5	99.4	81.1	3.4	1.218	3.9	0.0	13.3	..	18.0	.0	.2	.2
MAURITANIA	99.4	99.4	95.1	3.8	2.222	3.8	94.8	5.7	1.697	5.9	.1	.2	.2
GRENADA	100.0	100.0	37.0	5.1	0.743	5.6	0.0	12.6	..	35.0	.0	.2	.2
BOLIVIA	13.2	71.1	7.5	9.1	0.160	27.9	0.0	14.7	..	32.2	.1	.2	.2
CENTRAL AFRICAN REP.	100.0	100.0	88.3	3.0	2.516	3.0	..	..	..	..	.0	.2	.2
DJIBOUTI	100.0	100.0	100.0	4.1	1.643	4.1	..	..	..	..	.0	.2	.2
PARAGUAY	48.0	100.0	25.3	12.0	1.091	20.8	0.0	18.9	..	31.6	.1	.1	.2
FIJI	81.2	100.0	12.8	5.1	0.331	6.4	0.0	17.5	..	25.0	.0	.1	.1
CAMBODIA	42.4	63.9	17.4	0.6	0.405	1.0	..	..	..	..	.0	.1	.1
BURUNDI	100.0	100.0	35.8	8.2	1.098	17.2	0.0	11.0	..	25.0	.1	.1	.1
ARUBA	100.0	100.0	83.5	3.9	2.111	4.9	0.0	10.2	..	35.0	.0	.1	.1
RWANDA	86.0	100.0	70.2	2.4	2.379	3.8	..	..	..	..	.0	.1	.1

Notes: 1. Value of exports from reporter countries that do not participate in Free Trade Agreements.

2. Weighted average tariff reduction measured by dT / (1 + T) in percent.

Mineral Prod.,Prec. Stones & Metal Extent of other countries' MFN tariff reductions on exports from:

	% of exports GATT bount		Average levels and changes weighted by value of exports to: the World exc. FTA[1]				LMIEs exc. FTA[1]				Value of exports in $ million		
Export market	Total pre-UR	Total post-UR	% of exports affected	Post-UR applied rate	Tariff reduc-tion[2]	Post-UR bound rate	% of exports affected	Post-UR applied rate	Tariff reduc-tion[2]	Post-UR bound rate	To IDB LMIEs exc. FTA[1]	To all IDB Ctrys exc. FTA[1]	To all IDB Ctrys inc. FTA
EUROPEAN UNION	74.1	82.3	22.5	3.1	1.063	4.0	16.4	7.2	1.293	18.2	3,566.4	14,682.7	20,756.2
SOUTH AFRICA	88.5	89.8	5.1	0.3	0.051	0.2	1.2	28.1	0.117	28.5	138.5	14,566.6	14,566.6
UNITED STATES	79.1	89.9	21.4	1.8	0.480	4.1	10.4	9.7	1.110	20.6	2,114.7	10,963.4	14,516.4
CANADA	78.6	95.4	2.3	0.4	0.096	1.1	7.0	3.5	0.315	8.9	880.4	4,102.2	9,628.7
AUSTRALIA	49.6	87.8	16.1	0.8	0.355	2.1	8.1	5.2	0.995	12.7	990.5	6,259.6	6,305.1
FORMER USSR	74.2	95.7	9.2	1.5	0.174	3.8	3.0	4.4	0.202	12.8	1,862.4	6,007.0	6,007.0
SWITZERLAND	90.5	92.8	2.2	0.4	0.206	1.0	23.9	9.8	2.686	21.2	148.2	2,842.9	5,038.0
ISRAEL	79.8	82.2	2.9	0.3	0.253	0.8	18.0	3.9	2.523	11.6	161.7	2,136.3	3,664.7
INDONESIA	83.3	95.0	5.5	1.1	0.217	0.8	3.2	7.4	0.240	5.8	485.0	3,654.5	3,654.5
INDIA	76.4	79.4	7.6	0.4	0.475	0.4	71.1	4.4	8.780	3.2	148.5	3,438.7	3,438.7
JAPAN	53.9	83.5	47.4	5.2	2.061	7.4	42.2	13.0	3.775	20.3	883.2	3,407.8	3,407.8
CHINA	41.9	64.2	19.5	1.9	0.556	3.9	11.5	8.4	0.667	23.7	225.7	2,563.6	2,563.6
NORWAY	97.9	98.4	0.3	0.5	0.184	1.3	4.4	17.0	0.143	26.9	67.5	117.1	2,456.3
ALGERIA	92.0	95.1	16.2	0.3	0.261	0.8	0.0	2.8	0.001	15.2	145.4	1,820.4	1,820.4
MEXICO	94.3	99.7	7.6	0.3	0.873	1.9	21.4	6.1	2.716	26.2	43.2	419.6	1,812.6
HONG KONG	92.9	97.2	56.5	3.3	1.386	3.5	42.9	10.3	4.922	14.5	91.1	1,655.6	1,655.6
TAIWAN (CHINA)	80.6	92.5	70.5	4.7	2.256	5.4	18.0	14.9	1.922	23.3	95.3	1,512.0	1,512.0
KOREA, REPUBLIC OF	78.8	85.4	47.2	4.3	1.632	3.5	9.1	21.0	1.925	24.6	163.2	1,471.3	1,471.3
SAUDI ARABIA	83.9	96.8	68.3	1.2	2.930	1.4	0.6	6.6	0.032	9.7	280.8	1,435.5	1,435.5
POLAND	94.0	99.6	36.8	1.5	0.430	3.8	5.7	3.0	0.127	11.1	403.3	1,419.7	1,419.7
AUSTRIA	88.4	97.6	13.4	2.8	1.605	3.7	49.0	10.5	1.973	13.1	167.2	398.9	1,384.7
MALAYSIA	87.0	91.1	7.3	0.9	0.264	0.8	6.8	17.0	0.506	20.6	54.6	1,343.1	1,343.1
THAILAND	82.8	87.9	43.8	2.8	0.963	3.6	13.9	11.8	1.537	25.0	52.4	1,311.2	1,311.2
BRUNEI	100.0	100.0	20.0	0.5	0.196	0.5	0.0	16.5	..	28.6	.1	1,102.7	1,102.7
UNTD ARAB EMRTS	90.2	93.9	51.0	1.4	2.264	0.5	11.5	13.9	1.511	9.4	102.1	1,056.0	1,056.0
BRAZIL	81.4	89.7	22.7	2.6	0.854	5.3	10.5	12.2	1.104	28.8	77.1	841.6	870.3
SWEDEN	97.5	99.2	3.8	0.8	1.443	2.4	27.7	13.7	1.583	18.4	13.6	81.9	868.2
URUGUAY	97.2	99.9	1.5	0.1	0.058	0.8	0.2	2.3	0.285	25.5	1.0	702.7	722.4
MOROCCO	90.0	98.3	15.3	1.6	0.052	4.5	2.2	3.0	0.044	21.6	114.7	698.6	698.6
SINGAPORE	42.3	81.6	34.2	3.2	1.319	7.8	5.2	6.1	1.005	15.7	335.3	668.1	668.1
PHILIPPINES	43.5	47.4	16.4	1.5	0.617	1.6	32.0	22.1	1.453	12.3	30.1	634.0	634.0
BERMUDA	99.9	100.0	0.0	0.1	0.000	0.1	0.6	10.1	0.035	34.9	.3	607.6	607.6
CZECH & SLOVAK CU	87.6	97.1	49.4	3.7	1.331	4.3	29.9	6.7	1.506	8.6	127.9	584.9	584.9
COLOMBIA	93.6	96.0	22.4	0.6	0.301	1.5	7.5	9.6	0.398	29.1	24.7	512.8	512.8
FORMER YUGOSLAVIA	89.0	95.4	68.8	4.8	1.132	5.5	41.2	10.5	0.926	17.3	92.8	497.0	497.0
TURKEY	94.4	98.2	39.9	3.0	0.809	3.5	19.0	8.8	1.308	20.6	30.9	496.6	496.6
ZAIRE	97.9	98.0	0.4	0.1	0.017	0.0	1.9	6.5	0.072	24.9	7.8	425.8	425.8
BOLIVIA	18.7	100.0	2.5	8.3	0.031	28.7	0.0	10.0	..	35.0	345.0	422.4	422.4
KUWAIT	67.6	81.5	61.1	3.7	2.445	1.8	0.0	10.3	0.000	8.1	142.4	405.4	405.4
FINLAND	97.0	98.8	4.3	0.9	1.159	2.5	21.8	11.9	0.921	16.5	12.4	39.0	371.9
VENEZUELA	82.5	100.0	13.9	1.4	0.429	4.2	0.0	8.0	..	33.2	67.6	354.8	354.8
JORDAN	40.1	72.8	12.9	7.1	0.139	9.5	1.7	8.8	0.143	13.7	252.6	352.2	352.2
CHILE	79.9	98.9	7.4	0.4	0.213	5.7	2.9	1.2	0.328	27.1	66.8	331.9	331.9
LIBERIA	99.8	99.9	1.7	0.0	0.008	0.0	61.1	8.9	2.856	5.0	.6	316.5	316.5
ROMANIA	57.4	67.5	47.7	11.8	0.981	9.9	12.3	17.5	0.225	20.3	154.4	302.7	302.7

Notes: 1. Value of exports from reporter countries that do not participate in Free Trade Agreements.

2. Weighted average tariff reduction measured by dT / (1 + T) in percent.

Mineral Prod.,Prec. Stones & Metal (continued)

Export market	% of exports GATT bound		Average levels and changes weighted by value of exports to:								Value of exports in $ million		
	Total pre-UR	Total post-UR	the World exc. FTA[1]				LMIEs exc. FTA[1]				To IDB LMIEs exc. FTA[1]	To all IDB Ctrys exc. FTA[1]	To all IDB Ctrys inc. FTA
			% of exports affected	Post-UR applied rate	Tariff reduc-tion[2]	Post-UR bound rate	% of exports affected	Post-UR applied rate	Tariff reduc-tion[2]	Post-UR bound rate			
TUNISIA	82.3	96.3	49.7	3.8	0.366	8.5	0.0	2.1	..	33.0	48.6	265.3	265.3
PERU	79.0	100.0	48.6	3.2	0.787	10.5	0.6	2.1	0.022	34.9	58.0	261.2	261.2
HUNGARY	91.0	94.9	67.7	4.8	1.275	4.6	42.1	11.5	0.960	14.2	30.9	239.8	239.8
ANGOLA	91.7	100.0	0.0	0.0	0.000	0.0	0.0	..	..	..	17.0	203.6	203.6
DOMINICAN REPUBLIC	99.8	100.0	41.5	3.2	0.458	3.3	0.0	15.2	..	41.0	.5	184.7	184.7
SRI LANKA	80.6	93.3	19.6	1.0	0.963	1.5	31.6	1.8	3.107	5.1	23.1	162.8	162.8
LIBYA	99.8	99.8	14.5	1.5	0.180	1.9	97.9	13.6	1.372	13.4	16.8	154.1	154.1
QATAR	78.8	91.1	55.5	3.2	2.410	1.4	0.0	14.0	..	8.7	35.8	153.9	153.9
PANAMA	98.0	99.7	1.9	0.6	0.060	1.4	6.2	6.5	0.229	15.5	12.7	148.4	148.4
ZIMBABWE	93.4	98.1	5.3	1.6	0.178	2.6	13.1	12.4	1.243	23.6	17.4	142.5	142.5
TOGO	76.6	98.5	0.1	0.9	0.002	1.5	0.0	3.6	..	6.3	33.5	134.8	134.8
ARGENTINA	46.6	99.7	20.1	3.6	1.373	21.9	0.0	3.6	0.007	33.5	16.9	57.7	119.0
NEW ZEALAND	51.1	87.5	7.8	0.7	0.489	5.3	42.8	8.7	2.181	11.5	3.3	49.4	108.9
PAPUA NEW GUINEA	62.7	94.9	6.4	0.3	0.849	0.4	99.6	5.0	13.278	5.1	6.9	108.5	108.5
IRAQ	24.3	45.9	11.1	18.6	0.144	19.9	5.6	22.1	0.080	30.5	86.9	105.9	105.9
SENEGAL	86.0	99.3	10.5	1.9	0.014	2.6	0.0	5.6	..	8.8	22.6	104.3	104.3
LEBANON	99.7	99.9	25.8	1.4	0.299	1.3	1.0	49.5	0.065	34.5	.3	101.7	101.7
COTE D'IVOIRE	98.5	98.6	0.7	0.0	0.011	0.1	0.0	0.4	..	40.0	1.3	85.5	85.5
GHANA	66.0	67.0	0.3	0.1	0.043	0.5	1.0	0.2	0.134	29.2	26.5	84.5	84.5
NAURU	91.2	100.0	0.1	0.6	0.001	0.6	0.0	6.4	..	6.4	7.0	79.3	79.3
CONGO	96.0	96.1	0.2	0.0	0.016	0.0	3.3	0.0	0.423	1.1	2.7	74.9	74.9
NIGERIA	91.2	99.5	35.0	2.5	1.598	2.9	24.4	4.5	2.729	7.9	7.4	74.0	74.0
GUINEA	97.6	97.7	0.1	0.0	0.002	0.0	0.0	0.0	..	40.0	1.6	67.5	5 '.5
ECUADOR	98.7	100.0	5.7	0.5	0.123	1.6	2.7	8.0	0.098	36.4	2.6	67.5	67.5
SIERRA LEONE	97.7	97.7	0.1	0.0	0.004	0.0	0.0	0.0	..	..	.6	67.2	67.2
CUBA	99.4	100.0	0.6	0.1	0.015	0.2	25.5	5.1	0.626	14.4	.9	62.1	62.1
VIETNAM	4.8	18.3	4.1	15.2	0.143	1.9	3.3	19.5	0.137	7.8	46.4	59.9	59.9
BULGARIA	83.5	95.0	44.8	4.0	1.096	3.9	30.6	7.8	0.768	7.9	14.5	54.3	54.3
CENTRAL AFRICAN REP.	100.0	100.0	3.1	0.0	0.016	0.0	..	..	..	..	.0	51.2	51.2
TRINIDAD AND TOBAGO	92.8	99.8	23.3	3.0	0.821	5.9	0.0	12.6	..	36.4	6.3	50.5	50.5
BURUNDI	99.8	100.0	2.2	0.3	0.011	0.6	0.0	9.3	..	19.0	1.6	48.1	48.1
BURKINA FASO	100.0	100.0	0.1	0.0	0.003	0.0	..	..	..	..	.0	43.0	43.0
BAHRAIN	94.1	94.8	28.8	0.2	1.261	1.1	0.0	0.4	0.003	13.2	5.1	41.7	41.7
EGYPT, ARAB REP.	61.0	87.5	28.4	3.7	0.736	10.2	0.3	7.1	0.018	29.3	16.5	41.3	41.3
TANZANIA	59.4	61.8	1.0	6.1	0.035	1.5	0.0	16.3	..	37.1	12.6	33.8	33.8
CYPRUS	85.5	95.5	69.1	4.7	0.478	7.3	2.2	8.3	0.288	29.9	5.4	32.9	32.9
KENYA	88.3	94.2	9.3	1.4	0.279	0.5	4.4	14.0	0.545	6.7	2.7	32.1	32.1
MYANMAR	41.4	43.3	7.7	0.3	0.410	0.6	78.9	5.1	7.532	5.4	1.3	31.7	31.7
SYRIA	65.6	78.4	5.7	4.0	0.092	5.8	0.0	11.3	..	35.0	10.6	31.0	31.0
COSTA RICA	92.2	97.6	72.2	6.4	1.447	7.7	0.0	18.1	0.002	34.8	3.3	29.8	29.8
FIJI	0.2	99.9	0.1	0.0	0.006	0.1	..	..	..	..	.0	28.7	28.7
ZAMBIA	79.5	83.9	1.7	1.0	0.113	2.3	5.3	7.1	0.486	30.4	3.8	28.0	28.0
OMAN	86.8	86.8	82.7	7.3	0.812	2.4	0.0	40.0	..	..	3.6	27.0	27.0
GAMBIA, THE	100.0	100.0	0.2	0.0	0.001	0.0	..	..	..	..	.0	26.9	26.9
PAKISTAN	79.2	87.8	33.6	4.2	1.514	3.8	64.3	36.2	11.518	36.3	2.1	25.2	25.2

Notes: 1. Value of exports from reporter countries that do not participate in Free Trade Agreements.

2. Weighted average tariff reduction measured by $dT / (1 + T)$ in percent.

Mineral Prod.,Prec. Stones & Metal (continued)

| | % of exports GATT bount | | Average levels and changes weighted by value of exports to: | | | | | | | | Value of exports in $ million | | |
| | Total pre-UR | Total post-UR | the World exc. FTA[1] | | | | LMIEs exc. FTA[1] | | | | | | |
Export market			% of exports affected	Post-UR applied rate	Tariff reduc-tion[2]	Post-UR bound rate	% of exports affected	Post-UR applied rate	Tariff reduc-tion[2]	Post-UR bound rate	To IDB LMIEs exc. FTA[1]	To all IDB Ctrys exc. FTA[1]	To all IDB Ctrys inc. FTA
MAURITIUS	98.3	98.3	17.9	0.7	0.199	0.7	..	..	..	..	.0	20.9	20.9
BAHAMAS, THE	99.9	99.9	1.4	0.2	0.023	0.3	2.0	12.2	0.270	36.1	.1	20.3	20.3
IRAN, ISLAMIC REP.	14.5	97.0	4.9	12.5	0.108	19.3	0.0	14.3	0.001	22.1	16.9	19.6	19.6
NETHERLANDS ANTILLES	99.7	99.9	4.2	0.6	0.076	1.6	1.0	11.5	0.037	35.5	.8	19.2	19.2
LESOTHO	100.0	100.0	0.2	0.0	0.003	0.0	..	..	..	..	.0	17.5	17.5
SWAZILAND	83.7	95.3	35.1	1.0	0.177	0.5	0.1	11.0	0.008	10.0	1.5	17.1	17.1
MOZAMBIQUE	17.6	77.8	0.5	5.8	0.005	19.6	0.0	6.9	..	20.4	14.1	16.7	16.7
HAITI	100.0	100.0	87.5	4.7	1.354	4.7	..	..	..	..	.0	16.5	16.5
ICELAND	99.2	99.7	1.2	0.1	0.164	0.4	25.0	11.6	1.546	10.1	.1	3.8	15.8
MADAGASCAR	99.4	100.0	4.7	0.1	0.123	0.1	58.5	2.5	3.959	8.5	.1	15.3	15.3
MALI	95.5	95.5	3.6	0.0	0.034	0.0	..	..	..	..	.0	15.2	15.2
NICARAGUA	100.0	100.0	0.1	0.5	0.001	0.8	0.0	21.9	..	34.0	.3	14.2	14.2
BOTSWANA	86.4	86.5	0.1	1.1	0.002	0.3	0.0	4.6	..	1.9	3.5	13.9	13.9
MACAU	62.4	92.0	61.1	3.1	2.513	3.4	0.0	20.0	..	30.0	.0	13.1	13.1
BANGLADESH	10.5	70.1	8.9	10.0	0.120	5.8	0.0	10.1	..	5.0	10.2	11.9	11.9
GUYANA	97.6	98.2	0.0	0.0	0.001	0.2	0.0	0.0	..	40.0	.3	11.3	11.3
MALTA	97.4	99.1	72.3	3.9	1.046	3.9	42.9	21.7	1.482	8.0	.0	10.3	10.3
ALBANIA	39.0	94.0	12.7	6.4	0.414	10.0	9.7	8.3	0.264	13.7	4.2	5.8	5.8
SUDAN	99.9	99.9	16.7	1.1	0.038	1.1	..	..	..	..	.0	5.4	5.4
GABON	96.0	98.0	57.6	2.5	0.952	2.3	60.0	22.5	7.979	27.7	.2	4.3	4.3
PUERTO RICO	64.4	99.7	21.8	5.0	0.646	21.4	11.7	9.5	0.430	46.5	1.5	3.5	3.5
HONDURAS	90.5	100.0	19.0	2.1	0.573	4.9	0.0	10.7	..	36.8	.3	2.8	2.8
BARBADOS	89.2	100.0	0.0	1.6	0.003	3.3	0.0	15.0	..	30.0	.3	2.5	2.5
YEMEN	1.3	1.3	0.8	9.1	0.006	2.6	0.0	9.2	..	..	2.4	2.5	2.5
NEPAL	78.1	91.7	87.9	8.8	4.132	9.8	96.4	38.6	18.664	39.5	.2	1.5	1.5
NIGER	99.2	100.0	30.9	1.7	0.391	1.7	..	..	..	..	.0	1.5	1.5
CAMEROON	87.3	87.3	8.4	2.3	0.252	0.4	0.0	15.0	..	..	.2	1.5	1.5
MONGOLIA	79.2	100.0	2.0	4.2	0.027	4.4	0.0	4.2	..	4.4	1.2	1.3	1.3
AFGHANISTAN	89.3	91.6	32.7	0.5	0.964	1.0	4.0	1.6	0.774	21.8	.0	1.1	1.1
GREENLAND	98.2	100.0	2.2	0.3	0.052	0.7	0.0	15.0	..	35.0	.0	1.1	1.1
UGANDA	99.9	100.0	6.7	0.6	0.488	0.6	100.0	16.0	11.382	16.0	.0	.8	.8
GUADELOUPE	100.0	100.0	90.4	2.4	1.463	2.4	..	..	..	..	.0	.8	.8
JAMAICA	58.5	100.0	28.8	10.0	0.931	25.4	34.4	15.3	1.250	39.7	.5	.8	.8
ETHIOPIA	49.0	49.0	3.9	2.9	0.075	1.0	0.0	5.1	..	25.0	.4	.7	.7
NAMIBIA	90.1	100.0	27.1	0.9	0.553	0.9	100.0	5.0	4.651	5.0	.1	.5	.5
DOMINICA	65.5	96.6	11.4	1.8	0.335	16.9	0.0	0.0	..	50.0	.1	.5	.5
ARUBA	100.0	100.0	1.8	7.2	0.046	26.2	0.0	9.5	..	35.0	.3	.4	.4
MARTINIQUE	100.0	100.0	80.6	2.7	1.264	2.7	0.0	0.0	..	0.0	.0	.4	.4
EL SALVADOR	95.1	97.4	21.3	6.6	0.648	7.1	0.0	7.3	..	10.6	.1	.4	.4
BELIZE	77.2	78.0	36.7	6.6	0.659	4.2	0.0	12.3	..	9.8	.2	.4	.4
RWANDA	100.0	100.0	28.3	1.5	0.535	1.5	..	..	..	..	.0	.4	.4
KIRIBATI	100.0	100.0	77.4	5.0	3.091	5.0	100.0	7.0	2.583	7.0	.0	.3	.3
PARAGUAY	32.7	100.0	34.5	3.3	3.164	21.5	12.3	2.1	4.651	30.0	.0	.1	.3
GRENADA	100.0	100.0	0.9	0.1	0.028	0.1	..	..	..	..	.0	.3	.3
GUINEA-BISSAU	68.2	68.2	0.0	0.0	..	0.0	0.0	0.0	..	..	.1	.3	.3

Notes: 1. Value of exports from reporter countries that do not participate in Free Trade Agreements.

2. Weighted average tariff reduction measured by dT / (1 + T) in percent.

Manufactured Articles nes. Extent of other countries' MFN tariff reductions on exports from:

Export market	% of exports GATT bound		Average levels and changes weighted by value of exports to:								Value of exports in $ million		
			the World exc. FTA[1]				LMIEs exc. FTA[1]						
	Total pre-UR	Total post-UR	% of exports affected	Post-UR applied rate	Tariff reduction[2]	Post-UR bound rate	% of exports affected	Post-UR applied rate	Tariff reduction[2]	Post-UR bound rate	To IDB LMIEs exc. FTA[1]	To all IDB Ctrys exc. FTA[1]	To all IDB Ctrys inc. FTA
JAPAN	70.5	87.7	61.8	3.5	2.381	4.2	54.0	15.9	5.269	17.8	3,525.2	34,468.7	34,468.7
UNITED STATES	78.1	97.1	37.8	2.5	2.065	4.6	37.8	9.5	2.856	17.6	3,942.2	19,847.3	24,271.3
EUROPEAN UNION	83.0	95.9	32.0	3.1	1.899	4.1	41.1	13.6	2.538	21.7	3,269.4	16,296.2	23,774.5
CHINA	42.2	52.8	31.1	1.2	1.531	3.1	39.7	11.0	1.449	26.9	409.5	13,461.1	13,461.1
TAIWAN (CHINA)	80.8	87.6	58.1	3.4	2.374	4.0	40.0	21.1	4.538	24.7	333.5	7,966.6	7,966.6
SWITZERLAND	79.1	94.3	8.2	1.6	0.936	2.8	49.9	16.4	3.233	20.9	394.5	3,256.3	7,893.3
KOREA, REPUBLIC OF	86.7	92.0	66.7	3.0	2.497	3.3	29.7	24.1	2.848	30.9	189.6	5,700.1	5,700.1
HONG KONG	84.2	93.4	67.3	4.7	2.456	4.3	26.7	23.5	2.847	23.3	406.2	4,187.8	4,187.8
AUSTRIA	93.2	98.3	22.9	2.8	2.303	3.9	67.7	7.9	2.163	10.8	385.2	849.4	2,631.5
CANADA	72.7	98.9	12.8	0.9	1.656	1.6	57.6	9.0	3.235	15.3	103.4	741.2	2,570.2
SWEDEN	94.4	98.8	14.8	1.2	2.400	2.2	43.7	8.9	2.336	14.2	108.7	530.5	2,130.0
AUSTRALIA	76.6	97.7	18.6	1.3	0.930	3.1	41.0	4.8	2.828	10.8	406.2	1,817.6	1,906.1
SINGAPORE	66.9	82.6	50.7	4.2	2.952	4.2	45.5	18.4	6.989	17.7	271.2	1,604.5	1,604.5
FORMER USSR	76.7	99.4	8.3	1.4	0.298	5.1	8.9	2.7	0.356	10.4	730.1	1,568.6	1,568.6
MEXICO	97.0	99.8	3.5	0.9	1.024	2.6	9.3	9.0	0.118	21.9	68.4	183.6	1,467.9
NEW ZEALAND	70.6	99.8	22.0	1.5	1.107	2.3	82.3	9.0	5.126	12.6	132.7	934.7	1,035.8
THAILAND	75.3	93.4	51.4	3.0	1.998	3.5	24.9	16.6	1.773	22.2	17.0	995.5	995.5
MALAYSIA	47.5	72.2	42.6	1.0	2.077	3.8	36.8	17.6	3.034	20.4	12.8	990.2	990.2
FINLAND	95.1	99.6	14.2	1.9	1.309	4.2	15.6	9.8	0.639	29.6	88.3	308.8	892.2
PANAMA	73.2	88.5	2.0	3.8	0.073	6.1	4.5	15.4	0.162	33.0	199.8	806.5	806.5
PAKISTAN	63.0	99.9	23.6	1.2	0.747	4.9	34.4	3.1	0.223	16.3	212.5	760.7	760.7
NORWAY	88.5	91.9	10.5	5.8	1.683	2.6	17.7	35.4	1.726	23.5	72.0	185.2	704.5
LIBERIA	86.9	91.3	0.0	0.1	0.000	0.7	0.0	2.9	..	35.0	25.7	679.1	679.1
ISRAEL	87.5	97.6	29.5	2.4	1.907	4.0	19.0	11.4	0.561	25.5	77.5	358.7	590.3
BRAZIL	85.7	99.1	52.6	3.2	1.889	9.4	14.5	6.7	0.269	29.9	110.9	483.8	502.1
PHILIPPINES	84.8	93.8	64.6	3.3	2.737	4.0	53.7	15.2	5.770	18.5	9.7	407.4	407.4
POLAND	93.1	99.9	43.8	2.7	1.118	4.6	77.9	6.3	1.282	11.1	68.6	365.6	365.6
FORMER YUGOSLAVIA	81.7	99.0	52.0	3.4	1.818	6.9	25.4	8.6	1.533	25.2	79.1	361.8	361.8
PARAGUAY	23.2	100.0	0.7	0.8	0.330	36.9	0.0	0.9	0.001	45.8	32.2	100.6	347.5
MACAU	94.0	96.5	73.6	3.1	4.014	3.3	11.6	15.1	2.051	28.4	1.2	315.8	315.8
SOUTH AFRICA	88.9	95.6	8.2	1.1	0.429	1.7	16.6	13.7	2.040	28.1	29.2	314.4	314.4
EGYPT, ARAB REP.	89.8	99.8	5.0	0.5	0.183	0.8	13.0	2.1	0.560	3.9	55.2	285.5	285.5
BAHAMAS, THE	89.8	96.7	0.9	0.1	0.016	0.9	0.3	7.5	0.009	13.5	2.2	263.8	263.8
ARGENTINA	79.0	99.9	16.2	1.8	0.569	7.4	18.8	6.3	0.441	23.8	51.1	233.4	258.0
SUDAN	58.7	100.0	30.1	1.8	0.238	2.2	71.6	4.2	0.521	5.2	89.7	214.9	214.9
INDIA	69.3	91.2	34.3	2.9	1.482	5.6	16.7	5.9	0.770	20.6	36.3	196.3	196.3
INDONESIA	79.4	87.4	56.4	3.4	1.167	4.0	42.9	23.4	3.138	30.7	12.5	183.2	183.2
TURKEY	78.0	98.9	20.8	2.0	0.515	7.1	1.9	3.1	0.034	15.0	77.5	181.3	181.3
CZECH & SLOVAK CU	75.1	97.5	74.0	4.4	2.488	5.2	48.3	8.6	1.945	11.4	49.8	178.2	178.2
HUNGARY	77.0	98.7	66.3	5.8	1.763	7.3	59.5	9.3	1.085	12.4	76.1	155.8	155.8
CYPRUS	81.4	99.7	5.4	0.5	0.232	2.3	33.0	24.5	4.664	27.6	1.8	129.9	129.9
MALTA	98.4	98.6	34.3	1.6	1.277	1.1	57.7	20.7	0.663	6.1	3.1	115.6	115.6
COTE D'IVOIRE	69.9	99.2	18.9	1.9	0.430	6.6	37.3	4.2	0.178	17.0	41.5	112.2	112.2
IRAN, ISLAMIC REP.	95.7	97.5	3.6	0.4	0.172	0.4	89.4	20.9	7.640	21.7	1.5	96.5	96.5
COLOMBIA	89.6	100.0	17.2	6.7	1.088	17.8	3.6	11.8	0.477	33.8	47.6	94.2	94.2

Notes: 1. Value of exports from reporter countries that do not participate in Free Trade Agreements.

2. Weighted average tariff reduction measured by dT / (1 + T) in percent.

Manufactured Articles nes. (continued)

Export market	% of exports GATT bount		Average levels and changes weighted by value of exports to: the World exc. FTA[1]				LMIEs exc. FTA[1]				Value of exports in $ million		
	Total pre-UR	Total post-UR	% of exports affected	Post-UR applied rate	Tariff reduction[2]	Post-UR bound rate	% of exports affected	Post-UR applied rate	Tariff reduction[2]	Post-UR bound rate	To IDB LMIEs exc. FTA[1]	To all IDB Ctrys exc. FTA[1]	To all IDB Ctrys inc. FTA
SENEGAL	12.6	18.4	1.7	4.9	0.042	17.7	0.4	13.7	0.002	51.1	72.4	82.3	82.3
DOMINICAN REPUBLIC	99.9	100.0	94.9	0.2	6.421	0.2	48.0	14.5	0.438	20.2	.2	75.3	75.3
URUGUAY	61.8	100.0	13.4	1.6	0.244	16.5	4.9	3.7	0.221	36.1	11.7	52.8	75.0
ZIMBABWE	96.9	97.1	1.3	0.0	0.045	0.2	0.0	0.7	..	27.0	2.3	72.8	72.8
MALI	74.9	99.8	11.2	2.4	0.216	7.3	34.7	8.1	0.166	25.7	19.2	68.4	68.4
PERU	62.9	99.9	8.3	2.9	0.285	14.6	0.2	5.1	0.005	27.2	34.1	64.5	64.5
TANZANIA	74.2	99.9	12.5	1.2	1.667	2.4	0.0	0.2	..	12.9	5.4	56.7	56.7
HAITI	99.5	99.9	80.0	1.5	2.610	1.5	86.4	9.3	0.992	9.7	.4	55.7	55.7
CHAD	97.1	100.0	2.1	0.3	0.027	1.2	35.8	6.1	0.171	27.3	2.4	54.3	54.3
SAUDI ARABIA	64.5	98.0	41.8	11.3	5.302	11.7	92.8	32.6	14.464	33.6	18.2	52.7	52.7
AFGHANISTAN	99.7	100.0	4.2	0.1	0.037	0.1	2.7	1.0	0.364	1.2	2.2	48.3	48.3
CHILE	79.3	97.9	10.6	2.4	0.517	6.5	6.0	10.0	0.596	30.8	10.1	48.2	48.2
ROMANIA	86.4	99.7	92.5	3.9	3.248	3.9	94.7	8.1	4.537	8.0	8.7	48.0	48.0
NICARAGUA	95.4	100.0	2.8	0.2	0.092	0.8	0.0	1.8	..	12.3	2.9	47.6	47.6
MOROCCO	98.4	98.7	35.2	1.8	1.080	1.5	5.3	25.7	0.021	21.2	.7	45.7	45.7
BURKINA FASO	90.6	99.9	3.0	1.4	0.069	4.9	16.7	13.0	0.079	47.8	4.5	43.9	43.9
MONGOLIA	98.7	100.0	1.7	0.2	0.015	0.8	3.2	1.9	0.035	9.4	3.8	43.5	43.5
PUERTO RICO	93.5	100.0	14.7	0.8	0.649	2.2	16.4	10.6	0.514	30.4	2.9	43.4	43.4
TOGO	92.5	99.8	4.6	0.8	0.096	2.4	46.8	8.7	0.938	25.7	3.9	41.1	41.1
BULGARIA	64.1	99.0	43.3	3.9	1.495	11.7	27.1	7.5	0.846	26.9	16.6	41.0	41.0
SYRIA	85.8	100.0	9.0	1.4	0.352	3.6	30.4	5.3	1.160	14.3	10.0	40.6	40.6
CAMEROON	69.6	99.7	17.2	2.5	1.037	7.5	46.2	8.8	1.744	29.0	9.8	39.6	39.6
ALGERIA	99.5	99.5	3.5	0.2	0.136	0.1	2.2	26.4	0.007	0.9	.2	37.9	37.9
ETHIOPIA	97.0	99.9	8.5	0.4	0.180	4.9	0.0	1.2	..	41.9	4.0	36.9	36.9
LEBANON	89.6	99.9	7.3	2.8	0.641	4.4	27.9	19.6	4.026	30.8	5.0	36.3	36.3
NIGERIA	98.2	99.8	2.8	0.2	0.125	2.0	12.8	9.1	1.887	153.9	.5	35.9	35.9
MAURITIUS	94.8	99.0	82.7	3.6	2.525	3.6	0.0	11.9	..	30.0	.1	29.9	29.9
EL SALVADOR	12.5	13.1	8.1	4.5	0.375	8.2	0.7	15.3	0.100	38.8	24.4	27.4	27.4
ICELAND	94.7	99.9	5.8	1.2	6.401	1.6	79.8	29.2	12.501	34.3	.9	2.7	26.4
SRI LANKA	94.2	99.0	77.1	3.6	2.702	3.9	47.5	24.4	1.714	36.0	.5	25.5	25.5
BRUNEI	83.4	87.8	64.5	3.0	0.876	3.4	87.7	9.7	13.835	9.9	.5	25.4	25.4
VIETNAM	44.4	99.6	54.5	6.5	2.105	15.9	74.5	9.8	3.061	24.7	13.8	22.0	22.0
BENIN	79.4	99.6	6.8	2.8	0.155	8.8	26.1	12.7	0.125	41.3	4.6	21.6	21.6
IRAQ	74.9	99.9	37.8	10.4	4.620	10.4	94.4	31.2	13.247	31.3	7.0	21.4	21.4
UNTD ARAB EMRTS	75.5	94.8	41.5	6.2	2.260	7.5	44.6	23.2	5.868	26.0	4.8	21.4	21.4
VENEZUELA	77.4	99.5	30.3	5.1	0.896	8.3	29.2	15.2	0.683	25.9	6.1	20.8	20.8
UGANDA	99.0	100.0	0.6	0.0	0.021	0.0	100.0	16.0	11.382	16.0	.0	20.5	20.5
TUNISIA	98.9	99.1	84.8	1.5	4.430	1.4	43.5	12.7	2.168	10.7	.3	20.4	20.4
KENYA	91.2	97.4	35.4	2.4	1.101	6.9	14.1	12.7	2.170	116.7	1.2	17.9	17.9
GIBRALTAR	100.0	100.0	11.0	0.6	0.329	0.6	0.0	0.0	..	0.0	.0	16.0	16.0
ZAMBIA	28.0	36.2	1.3	0.0	0.038	0.1	0.0	0.0	..	32.3	10.1	15.8	15.8
COSTA RICA	99.9	100.0	79.3	2.3	3.395	2.9	0.0	26.4	..	39.1	.9	15.7	15.7
YEMEN	93.9	100.0	9.3	0.9	1.015	0.9	17.7	6.8	2.818	7.9	.5	11.0	11.0
BERMUDA	99.0	100.0	6.0	0.3	0.217	0.3	65.3	12.1	3.924	20.6	.0	10.8	10.8
LIBYA	95.8	99.9	94.8	2.4	0.942	5.7	3.5	17.6	0.575	96.0	.5	10.6	10.6

Notes: 1. Value of exports from reporter countries that do not participate in Free Trade Agreements.

2. Weighted average tariff reduction measured by $dT / (1 + T)$ in percent.

Manufactured Articles nes. (continued)

| Export market | % of exports GATT bound | | Average levels and changes weighted by value of exports to: | | | | | | | | Value of exports in $ million | | |
| | Total pre-UR | Total post-UR | the World exc. FTA[1] | | | | LMIEs exc. FTA[1] | | | | To IDB LMIEs exc. FTA[1] | To all IDB Ctrys exc. FTA[1] | To all IDB Ctrys inc. FTA |
			% of exports affected	Post-UR applied rate	Tariff reduction[2]	Post-UR bound rate	% of exports affected	Post-UR applied rate	Tariff reduction[2]	Post-UR bound rate			
KUWAIT	90.2	99.6	32.6	3.2	1.930	3.2	96.2	29.1	12.602	28.9	1.0	10.4	10.4
ECUADOR	57.8	100.0	40.4	4.3	1.306	16.2	0.7	6.7	0.008	31.8	4.3	9.1	9.1
OMAN	99.5	99.7	79.3	2.4	1.525	2.4	0.0	80.0	..	..	.0	9.0	9.0
HONDURAS	94.4	100.0	59.7	2.3	1.746	6.7	0.0	6.6	..	37.8	1.2	8.6	8.6
MADAGASCAR	98.8	99.8	64.0	1.3	1.665	1.7	0.0	69.3	..	111.3	.1	8.0	8.0
PAPUA NEW GUINEA	90.9	97.3	9.5	0.6	0.430	0.9	0.4	3.8	0.037	33.7	.2	7.4	7.4
BANGLADESH	60.8	93.4	40.1	3.2	1.618	48.1	5.8	5.1	0.333	135.5	2.1	6.3	6.3
RWANDA	99.9	99.9	1.2	0.1	0.037	0.1	22.2	16.0	2.529	16.0	.0	6.2	6.2
SOMALIA	99.0	99.8	6.6	0.5	0.302	0.5	98.1	35.5	15.904	36.0	.1	6.0	6.0
CENTRAL AFRICAN REP.	84.6	91.5	3.6	0.7	0.040	2.5	28.4	7.5	0.135	27.6	.5	5.7	5.7
JAMAICA	98.0	99.4	49.1	2.5	1.756	2.7	19.8	11.5	0.374	27.8	.1	5.7	5.7
NETHERLANDS ANTILLES	97.8	100.0	19.3	2.7	0.535	4.8	10.7	17.4	0.376	33.0	.8	5.5	5.5
GUINEA	98.7	99.1	45.2	0.9	1.217	0.9	0.0	..	..	..	.0	5.5	5.5
ZAIRE	98.9	99.7	24.9	1.7	0.684	1.9	0.0	1.0	..	25.0	.1	5.3	5.3
BOLIVIA	69.6	99.7	3.0	2.6	0.160	14.8	0.0	4.8	..	28.9	2.7	5.2	5.2
BAHRAIN	58.1	65.3	46.9	3.5	2.437	4.9	88.5	32.6	12.624	30.6	.4	5.1	5.1
BURUNDI	98.9	98.9	2.9	0.1	0.100	0.1	0.0	..	..	..	.0	4.9	4.9
TRINIDAD AND TOBAGO	88.1	100.0	82.0	2.3	3.713	4.1	13.6	18.1	0.049	33.0	.5	4.6	4.6
NIGER	99.5	99.5	15.3	0.4	0.482	0.4	0.0	..	..	..	.0	4.5	4.5
MOZAMBIQUE	95.8	97.6	8.4	1.0	0.506	5.6	6.8	4.0	1.012	27.5	1.0	4.5	4.5
CUBA	86.4	95.4	14.1	1.7	0.429	4.3	29.5	7.9	0.837	23.5	.7	4.4	4.4
BOTSWANA	43.6	53.4	7.6	12.2	0.197	22.8	1.9	22.0	0.013	110.3	2.4	4.2	4.2
GUYANA	96.6	100.0	84.5	4.7	5.080	4.9	0.0	42.5	..	48.9	.1	4.1	4.1
JORDAN	59.6	94.2	55.1	11.7	4.901	11.9	69.5	24.0	9.133	23.7	1.8	4.0	4.0
ALBANIA	77.1	100.0	56.7	3.7	1.304	10.4	25.2	5.8	0.426	27.3	1.1	3.7	3.7
QATAR	61.6	100.0	43.9	11.6	5.414	12.3	99.9	35.9	16.173	35.9	1.2	3.7	3.7
BARBADOS	99.4	99.7	65.8	1.6	2.003	1.7	0.0	45.0	..	50.0	.0	3.5	3.5
GABON	94.9	94.9	62.8	1.1	2.844	2.5	0.0	1.4	..	27.6	.3	3.0	3.0
SWAZILAND	73.6	97.0	67.2	3.6	3.359	3.8	76.6	7.0	7.954	8.4	.4	2.9	2.9
DJIBOUTI	99.2	99.2	7.4	0.4	0.223	0.4	0.0	..	..	..	.0	2.9	2.9
ANTIGUA & B ARBUDA	100.0	100.0	10.3	0.4	0.276	0.4	..	..	..	..	.0	2.3	2.3
BELIZE	99.3	100.0	14.2	11.8	0.440	25.0	0.7	13.7	0.006	30.2	1.8	2.2	2.2
CONGO	97.4	99.3	47.1	1.5	1.460	1.6	21.4	11.0	0.244	5.0	.6	2.0	2.0
NEPAL	61.7	88.3	11.3	1.3	1.018	8.1	2.3	2.7	0.778	19.5	.6	2.0	2.0
DOMINICA	98.5	99.6	71.5	1.9	3.178	1.9	64.7	21.0	2.869	29.4	.0	1.9	1.9
MALAWI	87.2	97.0	12.1	1.1	0.410	18.5	0.0	2.0	..	74.0	.5	1.9	1.9
GRENADA	100.0	100.0	27.8	0.3	1.572	0.3	..	..	..	..	.0	1.8	1.8
MARTINIQUE	100.0	100.0	56.1	1.8	2.408	1.8	..	..	..	..	.0	1.8	1.8
GUINEA-BISSAU	99.7	99.7	1.1	0.1	0.059	0.1	0.0	12.0	..	..	.0	1.4	1.4
ARUBA	26.5	100.0	85.8	8.9	10.713	11.3	0.0	8.9	..	32.0	.2	1.4	1.4
LESOTHO	30.6	100.0	20.8	42.3	0.335	70.2	0.0	59.9	..	100.1	.9	1.4	1.4
MAURITANIA	95.4	95.4	29.8	3.1	0.585	1.5	83.5	10.1	1.344	4.9	.4	1.4	1.4
SURINAME	99.4	100.0	11.9	1.3	0.238	1.4	0.0	10.0	..	50.0	.0	1.4	1.4
GUADELOUPE	99.1	99.9	54.6	1.5	2.061	1.5	..	..	..	..	.0	1.2	1.2
FIJI	72.0	100.0	22.2	4.2	0.871	4.6	100.0	13.0	6.009	13.0	.0	1.2	1.2

Notes: 1. Value of exports from reporter countries that do not participate in Free Trade Agreements.

2. Weighted average tariff reduction measured by dT / (1 + T) in percent.

Industrial Goods Extent of other countries' MFN tariff reductions on exports from:

Export market	% of exports GATT bound		Average levels and changes weighted by value of exports to: the World exc. FTA[1]				LMIEs exc. FTA[1]				Value of exports in $ million		
	Total pre-UR	Total post-UR	% of exports affected	Post-UR applied rate	Tariff reduction[2]	Post-UR bound rate	% of exports affected	Post-UR applied rate	Tariff reduction[2]	Post-UR bound rate	To IDB LMIEs exc. FTA[1]	To all IDB Ctrys exc. FTA[1]	To all IDB Ctrys inc. FTA
EUROPEAN UNION	79.7	93.1	28.9	5.3	1.925	6.3	33.6	14.9	2.336	21.0	50,016.5	173,742.0	271,921.0
JAPAN	70.0	88.5	49.0	5.4	2.057	6.4	47.9	16.2	4.703	19.5	38,582.7	232,274.0	232,274.0
UNITED STATES	78.5	93.4	30.1	3.3	1.822	6.3	26.2	11.2	2.597	21.7	35,646.0	152,572.0	225,301.0
CANADA	92.9	97.8	5.1	0.6	1.050	3.2	25.0	7.1	1.973	16.0	3,342.1	19,750.3	94,190.2
CHINA	35.5	48.0	26.9	2.9	0.925	6.4	33.0	13.3	2.281	22.5	2,792.4	70,179.7	70,179.7
TAIWAN (CHINA)	69.1	82.4	54.9	5.3	1.921	6.7	42.4	18.7	4.190	23.2	5,175.0	61,453.2	61,453.2
KOREA, REPUBLIC OF	78.8	89.3	54.9	6.2	1.836	6.9	23.3	21.7	2.555	28.3	3,175.5	50,703.7	50,703.7
SWITZERLAND	88.9	96.5	12.1	2.7	1.568	4.2	36.1	13.3	2.075	20.2	3,789.3	14,875.7	45,599.4
SWEDEN	94.1	98.6	9.6	1.9	2.045	3.7	32.7	14.1	2.512	21.4	2,087.5	9,331.5	41,729.0
AUSTRIA	94.2	98.8	12.8	3.1	1.907	4.4	61.4	8.9	1.781	10.6	3,505.1	5,655.6	27,405.0
HONG KONG	81.5	94.2	70.0	8.6	2.269	8.8	37.7	18.0	3.762	20.0	3,225.9	25,691.3	25,691.3
AUSTRALIA	68.2	91.9	20.2	1.4	0.669	3.6	24.9	6.5	1.932	14.1	4,173.3	22,056.0	23,413.8
MEXICO	96.0	99.5	4.9	1.6	1.415	4.0	14.5	10.3	1.211	25.0	1,011.7	2,755.6	22,105.4
SINGAPORE	67.3	88.2	47.5	5.2	2.289	6.5	34.9	14.3	4.254	20.4	4,749.9	20,660.4	20,660.4
SOUTH AFRICA	85.8	89.2	11.5	0.9	0.272	0.9	2.6	12.4	0.243	28.6	895.7	19,866.4	19,866.4
BRAZIL	83.2	95.9	40.1	3.8	1.363	6.6	10.6	9.8	1.128	25.4	2,657.1	18,167.3	19,039.8
MALAYSIA	50.6	91.6	23.4	2.3	1.041	4.5	36.6	9.8	3.661	11.9	1,771.9	18,989.5	18,989.5
FINLAND	94.4	99.3	9.5	1.1	2.428	2.8	35.9	11.7	3.168	19.2	857.4	3,337.7	17,695.5
FORMER USSR	73.6	92.6	18.9	2.6	0.575	4.4	19.4	6.1	0.795	11.8	5,387.2	16,501.0	16,501.0
NORWAY	94.4	98.1	5.8	1.7	1.420	3.1	21.4	17.7	1.946	19.1	586.2	2,298.1	13,376.8
INDONESIA	78.2	91.8	32.5	4.3	0.990	4.2	20.5	11.4	1.681	9.9	1,229.2	10,870.7	10,870.7
THAILAND	71.3	89.6	44.5	4.4	1.409	5.3	40.6	13.0	2.699	14.3	587.8	10,139.2	10,139.2
INDIA	79.5	87.6	42.5	4.8	1.211	5.4	32.2	11.1	2.791	13.7	901.6	9,700.3	9,700.3
FORMER YUGOSLAVIA	87.0	95.9	68.1	6.1	2.197	6.0	43.1	12.4	1.851	13.5	1,611.1	8,175.5	8,175.5
ISRAEL	85.9	90.2	24.3	2.3	1.282	3.3	19.2	10.9	1.574	19.4	446.7	4,510.0	7,512.1
PHILIPPINES	74.4	90.4	50.1	5.3	1.893	6.5	64.9	11.2	7.054	16.1	508.2	6,079.2	6,079.2
POLAND	91.6	98.0	50.8	3.8	1.327	4.6	45.0	6.7	0.923	9.5	1,423.4	5,264.7	5,264.7
TURKEY	94.1	99.2	79.5	7.4	1.957	7.9	23.4	11.7	1.828	19.8	331.4	5,150.0	5,150.0
CHILE	77.2	95.4	13.9	1.6	0.437	5.7	10.8	4.6	0.896	22.9	1,118.2	4,762.2	4,762.2
CZECH & SLOVAK CU	76.7	94.2	57.0	5.5	2.139	6.0	35.3	10.4	1.506	12.6	1,319.9	4,280.1	4,280.1
NEW ZEALAND	61.3	94.2	28.2	1.4	1.126	4.5	48.3	7.3	2.927	14.2	395.5	2,658.7	3,729.7
SAUDI ARABIA	68.9	90.9	61.4	4.1	3.085	4.6	28.0	9.4	2.782	11.8	1,137.4	3,689.8	3,689.8
PAKISTAN	70.7	86.0	58.5	6.3	1.585	7.7	51.2	12.8	3.146	16.3	437.3	3,499.3	3,499.3
ARGENTINA	68.9	96.7	34.9	4.3	1.642	12.3	8.2	10.1	1.529	26.6	511.3	2,470.4	3,241.3
HUNGARY	83.6	95.2	67.7	6.0	2.041	6.2	51.9	11.4	1.411	12.6	888.7	2,984.9	2,984.9
ROMANIA	78.2	89.4	65.8	7.4	2.549	6.4	30.1	16.5	1.571	16.1	677.7	2,602.1	2,602.1
MOROCCO	86.6	98.4	55.1	7.5	2.061	9.0	36.3	18.3	6.687	29.7	341.1	2,313.5	2,313.5
ALGERIA	90.6	95.1	20.6	0.8	0.508	1.3	2.3	6.7	0.217	22.2	201.7	2,099.1	2,099.1
PERU	81.5	98.4	25.3	2.8	0.573	7.7	2.8	5.1	0.207	25.6	498.1	2,094.7	2,094.7
VENEZUELA	79.1	98.4	36.1	3.6	0.905	7.7	5.2	12.3	0.512	32.1	494.4	2,085.7	2,085.7
URUGUAY	69.1	97.6	17.9	2.2	0.651	11.1	2.6	5.0	1.535	30.5	58.8	1,218.0	1,679.5
LIBERIA	92.8	96.0	1.0	0.2	0.043	0.7	14.4	5.7	1.054	27.5	55.7	1,612.2	1,612.2
UNTD ARAB EMRTS	89.2	94.9	59.4	2.6	2.183	2.2	28.3	14.9	4.305	15.2	178.3	1,601.0	1,601.0
MACAU	87.6	92.1	80.6	11.3	2.347	12.3	39.8	15.3	3.468	21.5	2.7	1,539.4	1,539.4
DOMINICAN REPUBLIC	99.4	99.7	73.5	9.6	1.600	9.7	2.0	3.0	0.045	35.5	9.4	1,454.8	1,454.8

Notes: 1. Value of exports from reporter countries that do not participate in Free Trade Agreements.

2. Weighted average tariff reduction measured by $dT / (1 + T)$ in percent.

Industrial Goods (continued)

Export market	% of exports GATT bount		Average levels and changes weighted by value of exports to:								Value of exports in $ million		
			the World exc. FTA[1]				LMIEs exc. FTA[1]						
	Total pre-UR	Total post-UR	% of exports affected	Post-UR applied rate	Tariff reduc-tion[2]	Post-UR bound rate	% of exports affected	Post-UR applied rate	Tariff reduc-tion[2]	Post-UR bound rate	To IDB LMIEs exc. FTA[1]	To all IDB Ctrys exc. FTA[1]	To all IDB Ctrys inc. FTA
PANAMA	72.7	92.9	10.8	6.9	0.313	12.0	12.4	16.5	0.463	32.6	508.9	1,354.0	1,354.0
ZAIRE	89.5	92.2	6.5	0.6	0.235	0.5	11.2	7.5	1.158	7.1	123.7	1,313.2	1,313.2
COLOMBIA	90.4	97.7	32.0	5.6	0.703	9.0	7.6	13.4	0.329	30.9	254.1	1,295.1	1,295.1
TUNISIA	92.8	98.8	78.1	7.9	1.661	9.7	11.6	7.7	1.842	34.3	95.1	1,178.2	1,178.2
BRUNEI	98.9	99.5	21.3	0.7	0.228	0.7	17.8	5.9	2.822	28.9	3.2	1,145.0	1,145.0
EGYPT, ARAB REP.	85.5	97.3	36.7	6.4	0.900	7.2	11.2	14.4	0.611	19.4	226.8	1,091.9	1,091.9
ZAMBIA	71.9	87.6	38.1	1.9	0.655	4.8	4.1	4.2	0.330	22.2	255.7	1,058.5	1,058.5
PAPUA NEW GUINEA	80.2	93.8	1.0	0.8	0.105	0.5	3.9	3.7	0.471	2.4	208.0	1,035.4	1,035.4
SRI LANKA	89.6	97.7	69.1	10.1	1.387	10.8	27.8	5.8	2.350	11.7	52.1	928.0	928.0
BANGLADESH	86.5	94.7	76.4	10.3	1.508	12.1	23.3	9.0	1.485	26.7	73.9	898.0	898.0
BULGARIA	70.7	95.2	61.6	6.2	1.981	7.9	49.6	9.1	1.508	13.0	364.8	752.1	752.1
ZIMBABWE	96.3	98.9	36.8	2.3	0.916	2.7	9.0	9.5	0.972	19.0	37.9	731.8	731.8
JAMAICA	97.3	99.9	49.1	7.0	0.801	7.5	2.2	3.2	0.059	23.3	18.3	722.5	722.5
IRAN, ISLAMIC REP.	89.6	98.4	19.6	3.2	0.533	4.9	5.2	7.8	0.429	28.1	49.6	716.2	716.2
GABON	92.8	98.8	5.2	0.4	0.187	0.5	27.8	8.2	2.453	13.7	13.3	704.6	704.6
BAHAMAS, THE	95.4	98.7	54.9	3.2	0.607	4.0	3.1	4.9	0.224	17.7	23.3	688.0	688.0
COTE D'IVOIRE	89.8	96.8	20.1	2.0	0.495	2.6	21.3	9.8	0.226	19.0	78.7	684.5	684.5
BOLIVIA	39.8	99.9	4.1	6.1	0.090	20.8	0.3	9.5	0.023	33.3	408.6	661.6	661.6
BERMUDA	99.4	100.0	2.3	0.2	0.024	0.3	3.9	10.0	0.248	28.1	4.5	657.6	657.6
MALTA	93.1	99.6	60.4	4.7	1.804	5.2	48.2	11.2	0.850	18.7	7.6	585.9	585.9
PUERTO RICO	82.4	99.7	64.3	3.7	2.566	7.7	3.3	9.6	0.257	28.2	121.4	576.0	576.0
COSTA RICA	97.8	99.7	82.6	13.1	1.983	14.6	3.6	17.8	0.286	35.2	51.5	575.9	575.9
MAURITIUS	97.5	99.2	91.5	11.6	1.528	11.8	29.1	13.3	2.195	26.4	1.1	570.2	570.2
KUWAIT	68.0	84.4	57.0	3.8	2.707	2.3	10.0	10.5	1.739	9.0	169.1	499.4	499.4
GHANA	92.3	94.0	4.8	2.6	0.149	3.0	3.1	1.0	0.277	23.0	31.2	483.0	483.0
PARAGUAY	32.0	99.7	11.3	1.7	0.744	30.5	0.5	1.0	0.354	41.7	37.0	176.6	475.7
LIBYA	84.2	97.4	37.9	2.7	2.397	2.5	74.5	8.7	5.603	7.8	89.7	452.9	452.9
CAMEROON	95.0	99.4	14.4	2.8	0.434	3.2	42.4	9.6	2.540	20.4	24.0	451.8	451.8
GUINEA	97.6	99.6	10.7	0.5	0.174	1.0	1.8	3.4	0.064	28.1	10.5	430.0	430.0
JORDAN	44.2	75.6	17.8	6.8	0.380	9.5	3.3	8.9	0.350	15.0	272.6	413.9	413.9
TRINIDAD AND TOBAGO	86.5	99.7	41.4	4.6	2.472	11.4	0.1	11.6	0.002	38.1	101.1	391.0	391.0
BAHRAIN	81.1	92.2	53.9	6.2	1.954	4.4	51.2	18.3	3.956	10.0	84.3	388.8	388.8
CYPRUS	87.6	97.2	52.0	6.0	1.210	6.4	31.8	19.5	2.002	18.3	26.3	366.3	366.3
HAITI	99.8	100.0	84.8	10.7	1.891	10.7	65.7	10.6	0.801	16.7	.6	365.4	365.4
NIGERIA	83.4	98.6	24.6	1.4	0.627	2.6	11.2	7.3	1.204	10.6	21.7	342.8	342.8
ICELAND	98.9	99.8	10.8	1.6	2.396	3.9	33.5	8.1	2.996	8.9	4.8	50.9	308.6
NIGER	62.9	99.9	1.6	0.1	0.044	0.3	5.1	15.1	0.253	19.7	1.3	299.4	299.4
QATAR	51.4	74.1	46.5	7.9	2.985	5.0	19.1	17.4	2.889	14.2	131.7	287.6	287.6
SURINAME	87.8	100.0	35.8	1.8	0.511	3.6	18.3	1.8	0.167	16.1	34.8	284.7	284.7
BOTSWANA	80.2	82.1	6.0	2.8	0.220	1.4	7.4	11.0	0.614	15.4	62.1	263.7	263.7
LEBANON	93.9	98.2	40.1	3.9	1.012	4.2	32.0	15.1	2.800	22.3	20.3	242.9	242.9
MYANMAR	27.5	90.9	28.5	4.4	1.426	7.9	56.1	8.9	3.151	13.2	100.2	238.5	238.5
CONGO	92.9	98.3	13.1	0.7	0.387	0.7	13.5	4.6	1.070	6.3	15.2	236.8	236.8
SUDAN	61.1	99.2	29.5	1.9	0.254	2.1	70.3	4.7	0.529	5.2	91.7	233.5	233.5
VIETNAM	34.3	69.9	32.6	8.8	1.083	12.7	39.5	12.5	1.379	19.0	138.4	210.5	210.5

Notes: 1. Value of exports from reporter countries that do not participate in Free Trade Agreements.

2. Weighted average tariff reduction measured by $dT / (1 + T)$ in percent.

Industrial Goods (continued)

Export market	% of exports GATT bount		Average levels and changes weighted by value of exports to: the World exc. FTA[1]				LMIEs exc. FTA[1]				Value of exports in $ million		
	Total pre-UR	Total post-UR	% of exports affected	Post-UR applied rate	Tariff reduc-tion[2]	Post-UR bound rate	% of exports affected	Post-UR applied rate	Tariff reduc-tion[2]	Post-UR bound rate	To IDB LMIEs exc. FTA[1]	To all IDB Ctrys exc. FTA[1]	To all IDB Ctrys inc. FTA
SENEGAL	54.5	67.6	13.0	4.7	0.918	6.6	9.0	15.1	1.669	22.7	104.1	210.1	210.1
ANGOLA	91.8	100.0	1.0	0.0	0.024	0.0	0.2	6.2	0.010	14.9	17.1	207.1	207.1
MAURITANIA	99.7	99.7	1.8	0.2	0.052	0.1	40.2	11.8	0.666	9.3	1.1	181.5	181.5
TOGO	80.8	98.8	2.8	0.9	0.071	1.8	4.9	4.2	0.097	8.5	37.7	180.5	180.5
CUBA	79.7	97.9	13.5	2.5	0.484	8.1	6.4	5.6	0.065	23.3	59.3	179.7	179.7
IRAQ	47.0	64.6	26.6	15.7	1.342	14.2	25.5	22.0	1.599	25.8	121.2	175.9	175.9
HONDURAS	94.1	95.3	61.8	11.5	1.172	13.3	0.4	11.3	0.016	35.6	17.2	167.0	167.0
SIERRA LEONE	96.4	99.1	0.7	0.4	0.018	1.5	0.4	0.8	0.013	34.8	5.7	166.7	166.7
NEPAL	85.8	96.3	45.6	12.4	1.358	10.8	51.1	47.4	7.580	32.9	15.0	161.1	161.1
KENYA	80.7	92.4	35.4	3.6	0.787	4.3	13.1	12.7	1.075	23.2	27.9	157.1	157.1
TANZANIA	74.8	89.3	19.8	3.2	1.156	2.8	1.9	11.7	0.167	18.8	23.3	153.9	153.9
SYRIA	83.4	94.7	11.6	4.8	0.316	5.4	10.4	17.6	0.465	23.9	36.5	149.4	149.4
ECUADOR	83.9	99.7	20.3	3.9	0.580	8.5	0.9	13.2	0.059	35.4	30.9	148.0	148.0
EL SALVADOR	82.0	82.6	68.4	10.6	1.257	11.2	1.3	12.5	0.129	29.9	27.4	137.5	137.5
MOZAMBIQUE	23.9	91.4	4.4	2.4	0.206	11.5	2.2	6.0	0.252	29.2	49.5	133.1	133.1
GUYANA	96.2	99.8	10.0	1.8	0.373	6.0	0.1	7.4	0.004	33.5	17.0	105.4	105.4
MALI	81.7	99.1	16.1	2.0	0.346	5.4	33.5	8.4	0.161	25.5	19.9	99.0	99.0
ALBANIA	92.8	99.6	40.6	3.0	1.235	3.7	19.8	4.1	0.660	6.6	27.1	97.7	97.7
SWAZILAND	60.2	70.6	41.0	4.8	1.851	4.1	31.8	7.3	2.184	6.5	46.4	97.4	97.4
FIJI	28.0	92.5	30.8	17.3	1.606	23.0	10.9	5.3	0.549	13.2	2.1	96.0	96.0
AFGHANISTAN	98.6	99.3	20.5	1.8	0.406	1.9	10.6	3.1	0.801	3.6	3.4	94.3	94.3
BURKINA FASO	95.4	99.9	5.0	0.8	0.083	2.5	27.4	11.9	0.081	42.2	5.1	90.4	90.4
NAURU	91.3	100.0	0.8	0.6	0.014	0.6	0.1	6.4	0.008	6.5	7.0	82.7	82.7
OMAN	81.3	89.4	66.7	5.5	1.284	4.1	32.6	22.8	2.824	10.4	10.3	76.6	76.6
ETHIOPIA	97.3	99.3	46.1	2.1	0.668	4.4	21.7	3.4	1.254	33.2	6.3	76.0	76.0
NICARAGUA	97.0	100.0	4.0	1.8	0.133	5.6	0.1	10.6	0.008	34.0	11.9	73.9	73.9
MONGOLIA	93.9	99.9	18.3	1.4	0.434	2.1	45.4	4.5	1.432	7.2	17.3	69.9	69.9
CENTRAL AFRICAN REP.	98.6	99.3	5.0	0.2	0.075	0.3	23.5	6.3	0.590	20.5	.8	68.2	68.2
GREENLAND	99.8	99.9	3.7	0.2	0.119	0.2	4.1	18.7	0.080	38.9	.1	65.3	65.3
NETHERLANDS ANTILLES	83.0	99.9	33.4	9.8	1.107	16.8	45.1	19.8	1.566	34.6	30.3	64.2	64.2
MADAGASCAR	96.6	98.0	46.4	3.3	0.943	3.5	27.2	29.7	1.832	47.8	.3	61.3	61.3
CHAD	97.1	100.0	2.9	0.4	0.049	1.3	35.0	6.3	0.167	27.5	2.5	54.9	54.9
BURUNDI	99.5	99.9	3.2	0.4	0.052	0.7	0.1	9.4	0.004	19.3	1.8	53.9	53.9
BARBADOS	86.3	99.9	60.9	7.2	2.051	10.7	1.4	23.6	0.026	48.5	6.9	49.6	49.6
LESOTHO	97.5	99.8	56.3	9.9	0.940	10.9	0.0	46.2	..	81.8	1.3	43.9	43.9
LAO PDR	35.7	88.5	38.1	5.8	2.416	7.3	47.9	7.5	3.351	8.5	21.2	31.5	31.5
GAMBIA, THE	99.5	100.0	6.0	0.3	0.256	0.4	4.5	7.9	0.172	34.5	.0	31.2	31.2
BENIN	85.1	99.2	8.2	2.4	0.213	6.7	24.6	13.0	0.144	40.1	5.2	31.2	31.2
EQUATORIAL GUINEA	99.9	100.0	10.0	0.4	0.257	0.5	0.0	12.1	..	32.2	.1	29.5	29.5
BELIZE	94.9	99.7	58.7	13.2	0.788	19.0	0.2	14.8	0.009	34.8	8.6	29.0	29.0
GIBRALTAR	98.7	99.8	29.0	1.6	0.875	1.6	0.0	16.3	..	21.1	.2	25.9	25.9
DOMINICA	57.9	99.1	47.2	16.9	1.696	19.4	0.4	32.1	0.012	38.1	9.6	22.4	22.4
UGANDA	98.0	99.6	2.3	0.3	0.107	0.3	32.1	16.6	2.806	20.4	.3	22.1	22.1
YEMEN	73.0	81.1	16.1	2.6	1.004	2.0	4.6	10.2	0.595	18.8	3.6	17.3	17.3
MALAWI	91.8	94.1	74.5	8.6	1.526	10.8	0.8	7.4	0.031	33.6	2.2	16.2	16.2

Notes: 1. Value of exports from reporter countries that do not participate in Free Trade Agreements.

2. Weighted average tariff reduction measured by dT / (1 + T) in percent.

All Merchandise Trade Extent of other countries' MFN tariff reductions on exports from:

	% of exports GATT bound		*the World exc. FTA[1]*				*LMIEs exc. FTA[1]*				*Value of exports in $ million*		
Export market	Total pre-UR	Total post-UR	% of exports affected	Post-UR applied rate	Tariff reduction[2]	Post-UR bound rate	% of exports affected	Post-UR applied rate	Tariff reduction[2]	Post-UR bound rate	To IDB LMIEs exc. FTA[1]	To all IDB Ctrys exc. FTA[1]	To all IDB Ctrys inc. FTA
EUROPEAN UNION	77.4	92.2	29.0	5.5	1.813	7.0	32.4	15.2	2.251	24.0	54,881.7	200,732.0	301,939.0
UNITED STATES	76.9	93.9	29.2	3.8	1.726	8.7	24.7	12.0	2.573	31.5	40,527.5	179,954.0	258,890.0
JAPAN	69.7	88.4	48.9	5.4	2.075	6.4	47.9	16.1	4.813	19.5	39,065.7	234,363.0	234,363.0
CANADA	89.4	95.0	5.6	0.8	1.013	3.3	22.4	7.5	1.781	20.1	3,831.4	23,768.5	107,450.0
CHINA	34.6	51.2	26.2	3.0	0.939	6.5	28.3	12.2	1.880	25.8	3,933.0	81,439.4	81,439.4
TAIWAN (CHINA)	68.1	83.1	55.1	5.3	1.943	6.7	42.5	18.4	4.516	23.4	5,453.0	65,011.4	65,011.4
KOREA, REPUBLIC OF	76.8	88.7	54.8	6.1	1.841	6.9	23.2	21.6	2.815	29.1	3,349.8	54,088.9	54,088.9
SWITZERLAND	88.6	96.6	12.5	3.0	1.550	4.4	35.0	13.9	2.053	21.5	4,040.2	16,353.2	47,108.4
SWEDEN	93.8	98.6	10.0	2.2	2.021	4.0	32.5	14.1	2.471	21.6	2,134.3	10,257.5	43,504.0
MEXICO	77.4	84.1	4.3	1.9	0.888	4.3	11.8	10.8	0.980	29.5	1,331.7	6,032.6	32,399.1
AUSTRALIA	63.6	92.1	20.5	3.1	0.798	7.2	24.1	7.0	1.716	18.0	5,238.6	27,687.9	29,402.0
BRAZIL	84.5	97.3	38.0	4.3	1.403	6.8	10.6	11.2	1.014	27.1	3,441.5	27,823.6	28,845.8
FORMER USSR	78.4	91.9	12.6	2.1	0.397	3.4	13.8	5.1	0.600	9.5	8,088.6	28,661.5	28,661.5
AUSTRIA	93.5	98.7	13.2	3.4	1.762	4.8	59.6	9.3	1.709	12.8	3,778.7	6,719.4	28,515.0
SAUDI ARABIA	31.6	40.3	9.4	2.0	0.443	4.2	8.3	8.2	0.800	23.0	4,049.7	26,435.8	26,435.8
HONG KONG	81.0	94.3	69.6	8.6	2.269	8.8	37.4	17.8	3.747	19.9	3,328.7	26,240.1	26,240.1
SINGAPORE	56.2	77.1	39.1	5.0	1.935	7.1	26.5	13.9	3.371	22.3	6,579.9	25,754.8	25,754.8
MALAYSIA	42.9	83.2	24.3	5.2	1.455	11.2	21.2	24.7	2.105	62.8	3,508.5	24,782.4	24,782.4
SOUTH AFRICA	84.5	89.8	12.4	1.7	0.313	3.3	2.3	12.8	0.210	64.0	1,042.3	21,174.8	21,174.8
NORWAY	90.0	93.2	4.6	1.1	0.932	2.7	18.1	15.2	1.661	17.7	736.9	4,117.4	21.166.7
INDONESIA	58.7	70.8	25.7	4.1	0.864	4.9	19.7	12.5	2.084	21.0	1,776.3	18,577.3	18,577.3
FINLAND	94.0	99.2	9.6	1.2	2.261	2.9	35.2	11.9	3.072	20.5	888.2	3,676.6	18,423.5
THAILAND	66.9	92.5	40.3	6.2	1.348	12.5	25.4	10.6	1.410	63.4	1,398.6	15,478.9	15,478.9
INDIA	78.3	89.2	40.4	4.4	1.213	5.5	30.0	10.2	2.328	18.1	1,247.1	11,858.3	11,858.3
IRAQ	30.9	51.3	0.7	1.1	0.028	4.7	0.8	7.0	0.050	29.6	4,332.9	10,737.7	10,737.7
VENEZUELA	56.9	65.5	8.4	1.6	0.213	5.3	2.5	10.7	0.249	34.2	1,024.7	9,805.7	9,805.7
UNTD ARAB EMRTS	22.6	27.9	10.1	4.1	0.370	2.2	2.4	12.2	0.372	21.6	2,089.5	9,574.6	9,574.6
FORMER YUGOSLAVIA	86.0	96.4	63.9	6.4	2.062	8.1	41.3	13.3	1.730	24.6	1,802.7	9,356.0	9,356.0
NIGERIA	39.0	41.9	4.1	0.8	0.124	1.4	1.7	17.4	0.115	29.6	344.4	9,192.0	9,192.0
ISRAEL	85.4	91.3	27.0	2.9	1.431	4.0	18.9	11.0	1.526	20.2	465.8	5,493.1	8,580.8
PHILIPPINES	71.0	92.3	51.5	6.0	2.418	7.1	60.8	11.4	6.367	19.0	600.4	8,149.1	8,149.1
ARGENTINA	70.5	97.9	25.4	4.8	1.178	13.5	7.7	13.4	0.914	32.4	1,194.8	6,565.2	8,071.9
ALGERIA	86.9	90.5	9.2	0.8	0.187	1.2	0.6	3.7	0.061	9.5	720.2	7,818.0	7,818.0
NEW ZEALAND	62.6	96.7	24.7	3.0	1.047	6.4	28.4	10.3	1.916	24.4	896.5	6,124.0	7,544.3
IRAN, ISLAMIC REP.	52.6	70.1	4.4	2.7	0.093	5.9	0.3	11.2	0.015	33.3	1,842.7	7,455.8	7,455.8
TURKEY	83.5	95.1	70.5	6.6	1.709	8.9	22.0	12.7	1.232	37.4	571.6	7,423.6	7,423.6
CHILE	77.4	96.6	17.8	2.4	0.492	6.1	10.5	5.8	0.785	24.2	1,338.5	6,605.2	6,605.2
LIBYA	89.8	92.6	3.7	0.5	0.180	1.5	12.2	4.2	0.916	18.0	549.2	6,493.3	6,493.3
POLAND	88.7	98.3	49.4	4.4	1.320	6.1	43.9	7.8	0.902	14.2	1,533.7	6,455.3	6,455.3
KUWAIT	41.3	48.6	6.7	1.9	0.240	2.3	1.9	9.3	0.324	18.3	911.0	6,410.5	6,410.5
COLOMBIA	75.0	82.5	32.8	2.8	1.230	5.4	8.5	12.0	0.366	29.7	481.3	5,083.2	5,083.2
CZECH & SLOVAK CU	74.7	94.3	53.3	5.8	2.014	6.7	33.5	10.9	1.429	14.7	1,412.8	4,825.2	4,825.2
HUNGARY	74.7	95.8	57.0	6.8	1.781	8.1	46.0	11.6	1.253	18.9	1,077.5	4,386.1	4,386.1
PAKISTAN	67.7	86.7	54.9	6.5	1.508	8.4	43.4	14.4	2.683	21.6	527.6	3,878.0	3,878.0
ROMANIA	82.0	92.3	49.1	6.3	1.862	6.0	29.4	16.1	1.488	18.6	725.7	3,742.3	3,742.3

Notes: 1. Value of exports from reporter countries that do not participate in Free Trade Agreements.

2. Weighted average tariff reduction measured by dT / (1 + T) in percent.

All Merchandise Trade (continued)

Export market	% of exports GATT bound — Total pre-UR	% of exports GATT bound — Total post-UR	World exc. FTA[1] — % of exports affected	World exc. FTA[1] — Post-UR applied rate	World exc. FTA[1] — Tariff reduction[2]	World exc. FTA[1] — Post-UR bound rate	LMIEs exc. FTA[1] — % of exports affected	LMIEs exc. FTA[1] — Post-UR applied rate	LMIEs exc. FTA[1] — Tariff reduction[2]	LMIEs exc. FTA[1] — Post-UR bound rate	Value of exports $ million — To IDB LMIEs exc. FTA[1]	Value of exports $ million — To all IDB Ctrys exc. FTA[1]	Value of exports $ million — To all IDB Ctrys inc. FTA
MOROCCO	78.4	98.8	52.8	7.8	1.944	9.2	33.7	18.6	6.203	31.5	367.8	3,424.0	3,424.0
EGYPT, ARAB REP.	68.9	82.6	17.8	4.3	0.439	7.5	4.9	10.6	0.218	27.5	759.4	2,981.3	2,981.3
OMAN	6.4	8.0	1.9	5.3	0.048	2.5	0.5	8.0	0.062	22.9	811.3	2,937.2	2,937.2
PERU	81.0	98.4	22.4	3.0	0.561	8.5	4.6	6.2	0.220	28.3	686.0	2,827.1	2,827.1
ANGOLA	34.3	36.4	2.0	0.7	0.100	0.6	0.0	5.9	0.001	3.5	134.2	2,764.9	2,764.9
ECUADOR	46.0	65.6	8.5	2.6	0.524	6.5	1.4	8.0	0.047	37.7	445.1	2,487.1	2,487.1
COTE D'IVOIRE	93.2	98.6	52.7	2.9	1.979	3.9	21.5	9.4	0.497	21.6	153.6	2,360.4	2,360.4
URUGUAY	63.2	98.1	16.3	2.5	0.772	14.8	2.0	5.8	1.040	35.0	91.9	1,483.3	2,176.1
BRUNEI	58.8	59.9	12.1	3.9	0.136	0.7	0.2	13.6	0.022	28.8	447.0	2,028.7	2,028.7
PANAMA	77.0	95.2	13.5	6.1	0.468	10.7	12.2	16.5	0.459	33.4	535.1	2,005.9	2,005.9
QATAR	11.3	25.0	7.2	7.1	0.463	3.5	5.6	15.1	0.843	14.2	451.1	1,858.5	1,858.5
DOMINICAN REPUBLIC	92.9	99.7	64.2	8.8	1.505	9.0	1.8	6.4	0.063	54.1	12.0	1,850.4	1,850.4
TUNISIA	84.0	95.9	58.9	6.5	1.399	8.1	12.3	7.8	1.825	33.8	97.1	1,773.1	1,773.1
CAMEROON	82.5	84.0	28.5	1.2	1.049	1.5	25.0	5.8	1.405	13.1	56.0	1,721.6	1,721.6
COSTA RICA	93.1	99.9	51.4	6.7	1.693	8.2	6.7	15.5	0.592	35.5	112.2	1,661.1	1,661.1
ZAIRE	82.4	85.0	15.7	0.6	0.686	0.6	11.3	7.8	1.145	11.3	126.4	1,654.5	1,654.5
GABON	66.7	72.0	3.9	1.2	0.157	0.7	2.3	11.0	0.199	9.3	164.6	1,639.1	1,639.1
LIBERIA	92.8	96.1	1.9	0.2	0.076	0.8	14.3	5.8	1.047	29.7	56.1	1,631.5	1,631.5
MACAU	86.2	92.3	79.3	11.0	2.304	11.9	39.5	15.6	3.450	21.7	2.7	1,585.0	1,585.0
PAPUA NEW GUINEA	78.7	94.0	15.6	1.2	0.633	0.9	5.3	5.4	0.502	4.0	245.4	1,385.9	1,385.9
ICELAND	96.9	98.8	19.6	2.0	1.033	7.8	12.8	4.2	0.927	11.7	26.2	457.8	1,353.9
SRI LANKA	86.3	97.1	61.4	8.8	1.350	10.1	26.3	10.8	1.648	23.4	89.7	1,181.1	1,181.1
TRINIDAD AND TOBAGO	46.2	58.8	17.3	3.7	1.111	12.9	0.1	15.4	0.001	42.9	166.0	1,159.1	1,159.1
BANGLADESH	80.8	93.5	70.4	9.0	1.571	10.6	20.5	8.7	1.375	26.0	85.5	1,149.9	1,149.9
ZIMBABWE	90.8	99.2	42.1	5.0	1.301	5.5	28.3	15.3	1.345	24.5	66.5	1,087.8	1,087.8
ZAMBIA	72.0	87.8	38.5	2.0	0.680	4.9	4.1	4.1	0.328	22.8	256.7	1,076.9	1,076.9
BULGARIA	68.5	95.7	52.4	7.6	1.796	11.0	44.8	12.2	1.435	20.5	431.0	1,076.4	1,076.4
PARAGUAY	55.0	99.9	10.6	1.4	0.649	21.0	0.5	2.3	0.419	43.0	69.3	618.7	1,041.3
JAMAICA	88.6	100.0	45.9	6.7	0.873	7.4	2.0	3.4	0.053	30.0	20.6	946.0	946.0
MAURITIUS	66.1	99.5	58.7	14.2	1.229	14.4	26.5	12.6	1.990	25.4	1.2	914.8	914.8
BAHAMAS, THE	95.6	98.3	47.7	3.2	0.826	3.9	3.1	5.1	0.222	17.9	23.5	870.0	870.0
GHANA	92.4	96.7	29.8	2.1	0.998	2.3	20.1	3.6	1.294	15.0	42.5	869.9	869.9
HONDURAS	91.2	99.1	32.8	4.4	1.075	5.1	34.6	11.3	1.181	23.9	47.4	869.8	869.8
BAHRAIN	39.6	48.5	25.1	5.5	0.911	4.1	43.6	16.1	3.358	9.1	99.4	839.8	839.8
YEMEN	45.7	46.1	1.8	1.7	0.103	1.4	0.1	7.2	0.015	42.6	144.3	831.1	831.1
KENYA	88.5	98.1	46.0	3.2	1.965	3.9	14.1	14.1	0.974	30.3	36.7	814.0	814.0
PUERTO RICO	77.3	99.8	60.1	4.7	2.210	10.5	2.4	10.2	0.281	31.7	202.3	753.7	753.7
CUBA	67.8	99.5	37.9	23.8	2.407	42.5	16.9	17.6	0.684	55.9	175.5	751.8	751.8
BOLIVIA	40.6	99.9	4.9	6.2	0.147	23.1	0.3	9.9	0.021	37.5	445.0	730.1	730.1
SYRIA	80.2	88.9	5.8	3.2	0.126	6.7	8.1	19.0	0.321	48.9	93.1	705.7	705.7
NETHERLANDS ANTILLES	71.7	94.5	5.7	5.9	0.167	13.6	6.1	14.9	0.212	36.8	223.4	674.1	674.1
BERMUDA	98.4	100.0	2.4	0.4	0.029	1.8	1.5	13.2	0.099	94.8	11.2	668.1	668.1
VIETNAM	34.2	81.3	28.6	6.1	0.829	11.5	24.6	13.0	0.874	29.1	242.9	649.4	649.4
MALTA	93.0	99.6	60.3	4.7	1.812	5.3	47.4	12.0	0.849	20.1	7.8	591.9	591.9
CYPRUS	74.8	98.3	49.9	8.0	1.431	12.2	21.0	28.0	1.265	55.9	54.3	587.3	587.3

Notes: 1. Value of exports from reporter countries that do not participate in Free Trade Agreements.

2. Weighted average tariff reduction measured by $dT / (1 + T)$ in percent.

All Merchandise Trade (continued)

Export market	% of exports GATT bount		Average levels and changes weighted by value of exports to:								Value of exports in $ million		
			the World exc. FTA[1]				LMIEs exc. FTA[1]						
	Total pre-UR	Total post-UR	% of exports affected	Post-UR applied rate	Tariff reduc-tion[2]	Post-UR bound rate	% of exports affected	Post-UR applied rate	Tariff reduc-tion[2]	Post-UR bound rate	To IDB LMIEs exc. FTA[1]	To all IDB Ctrys exc. FTA[1]	To all IDB Ctrys inc. FTA
SENEGAL	80.2	88.4	39.2	7.9	1.590	9.5	8.8	14.4	1.640	23.6	106.0	584.3	584.3
CONGO	86.3	89.9	6.3	0.6	0.201	0.4	5.6	4.8	0.440	6.3	36.9	584.0	584.0
GREENLAND	96.4	96.5	30.9	8.4	0.818	8.7	3.8	18.8	0.074	38.9	.1	540.0	540.0
EL SALVADOR	88.9	95.5	50.7	2.8	1.930	3.2	2.8	12.0	0.175	40.4	28.7	536.6	536.6
GUINEA	96.8	99.6	13.4	0.5	0.302	1.0	2.8	3.9	0.159	27.2	11.4	457.8	457.8
SUDAN	64.9	99.6	23.2	2.4	0.439	3.5	70.5	7.4	1.012	11.4	107.4	436.8	436.8
JORDAN	42.7	74.5	18.7	7.2	0.420	10.0	5.2	9.4	0.410	15.7	278.4	432.3	432.3
HAITI	99.6	100.0	84.6	9.4	2.119	9.4	65.0	10.6	0.792	17.0	.6	424.7	424.7
MAURITANIA	59.9	99.8	50.5	3.9	1.406	4.0	22.0	10.5	0.364	13.1	2.0	412.9	412.9
TANZANIA	68.8	90.3	41.5	2.7	2.447	9.1	9.2	7.7	0.411	61.2	55.7	396.1	396.1
SURINAME	78.4	100.0	34.1	2.0	0.558	3.5	18.2	1.9	0.167	16.2	34.9	376.3	376.3
ETHIOPIA	97.4	99.8	50.8	0.9	2.065	1.6	18.3	4.6	1.059	36.5	7.5	320.6	320.6
BOTSWANA	79.9	84.7	9.2	3.1	0.696	3.3	6.6	9.6	0.548	18.8	72.6	311.0	311.0
MYANMAR	26.6	92.5	25.6	4.4	1.399	12.5	48.3	9.2	2.904	24.7	122.3	307.3	307.3
MADAGASCAR	86.1	99.6	67.3	3.0	3.427	3.8	43.2	18.0	1.793	61.8	4.0	307.3	307.3
UGANDA	98.8	100.0	73.3	0.2	3.543	0.2	93.3	5.6	3.742	5.8	4.0	301.9	301.9
NIGER	63.1	99.9	2.0	0.2	0.055	0.4	4.5	15.1	0.223	21.2	1.5	301.8	301.8
FIJI	25.4	97.5	16.2	20.0	0.799	30.8	3.8	0.9	0.263	14.7	19.5	285.2	285.2
LEBANON	91.3	98.4	38.2	6.0	1.003	8.3	18.1	26.6	1.538	47.8	37.2	283.0	283.0
SWAZILAND	49.5	89.7	26.3	10.4	1.329	11.3	30.7	6.7	2.053	7.7	50.5	278.0	278.0
NICARAGUA	91.0	94.9	38.7	2.0	1.898	4.2	2.6	13.0	0.037	31.4	19.4	244.2	244.2
MOZAMBIQUE	47.3	95.2	32.2	4.2	2.498	9.7	12.7	6.3	4.444	27.0	61.0	243.7	243.7
TOGO	84.3	99.1	18.9	1.2	0.783	2.3	4.9	4.1	0.116	11.8	39.1	237.6	237.6
MALAWI	69.6	99.6	43.9	7.0	1.402	8.1	7.8	8.7	0.306	69.3	5.0	230.6	230.6
GUYANA	54.0	99.9	13.1	3.3	0.669	6.8	0.2	11.0	0.014	37.6	19.2	226.7	226.7
SIERRA LEONE	97.0	99.3	16.7	1.1	0.706	2.0	0.6	1.1	0.022	35.1	5.8	207.5	207.5
MARTINIQUE	98.8	100.0	23.4	9.5	1.347	9.5	0.0	2.5	..	12.7	.1	205.0	205.0
NEPAL	73.2	96.9	39.0	18.2	1.211	25.1	17.8	50.9	2.609	86.8	44.0	193.4	193.4
GUADELOUPE	72.9	100.0	11.3	7.6	0.583	7.8	0.0	5.2	..	34.0	.1	158.2	158.2
ALBANIA	85.2	99.6	35.1	5.5	1.061	11.6	31.3	11.0	0.970	26.7	56.7	158.0	158.0
BURUNDI	99.5	100.0	56.0	0.3	2.620	0.5	24.1	7.9	0.934	17.9	2.7	157.2	157.2
SEYCHELLES	81.2	99.7	19.5	4.8	6.999	17.9	98.1	5.1	40.704	5.2	25.3	149.3	149.3
RWANDA	98.6	100.0	81.5	0.3	3.922	0.3	30.0	15.0	2.877	15.0	.0	133.4	133.4
AFGHANISTAN	88.3	99.5	23.1	5.4	0.361	12.8	3.9	27.6	0.170	76.3	20.9	127.5	127.5
BELIZE	70.5	99.9	27.6	13.2	0.722	18.2	0.1	19.8	0.004	41.3	18.2	115.9	115.9
MALI	81.9	99.2	19.5	2.1	0.549	5.6	32.2	8.8	0.155	26.4	20.8	107.0	107.0
BURKINA FASO	89.7	99.9	12.4	1.4	0.320	2.8	27.4	11.9	0.081	42.2	5.1	103.5	103.5
CENTRAL AFRICAN REP.	97.7	99.5	33.9	0.5	1.557	0.6	23.5	6.3	0.590	20.5	.8	102.6	102.6
GAMBIA, THE	56.0	99.9	56.1	3.9	1.548	4.0	2.3	10.7	0.087	30.1	.1	102.5	102.5
BARBADOS	56.5	99.1	42.2	7.5	1.413	12.2	1.2	25.1	0.021	58.2	8.5	90.0	90.0
NAURU	91.7	100.0	1.1	0.7	0.022	0.7	0.1	6.4	0.008	6.5	7.0	87.8	87.8
DOMINICA	89.0	99.8	13.4	15.7	0.472	18.0	0.4	32.1	0.012	38.4	9.6	87.0	87.0
MONGOLIA	93.5	99.9	18.2	1.4	0.427	2.1	45.4	4.6	1.404	7.3	17.8	71.9	71.9
CHAD	97.1	100.0	5.4	0.5	0.135	1.4	35.0	6.3	0.167	27.5	2.5	59.8	59.8
SOMALIA	94.9	99.9	15.5	4.5	0.961	4.7	64.4	20.5	6.825	29.6	.2	53.3	53.3

Notes: 1. Value of exports from reporter countries that do not participate in Free Trade Agreements.

2. Weighted average tariff reduction measured by dT / (1 + T) in percent.

Distributors of World Bank Publications

Prices and credit terms vary from country to country. Consult your local distributor before placing an order.

ALBANIA
Adrion Ltd.
Perlat Rexhepi Str.
Pall. 9, Shk. 1, Ap. 4
Tirana
Tel: (1) 815-8156
Fax: (1) 815-8354

ARGENTINA
Oficina del Libro Internacional
Av. Cordoba 1877
1120 Buenos Aires
Tel: (1) 815-8156
Fax: (1) 815-8354

AUSTRALIA, FIJI, PAPUA NEW GUINEA, SOLOMON ISLANDS, VANUATU, AND WESTERN SAMOA
D.A. Information Services
648 Whitehorse Road
Mitcham 3132
Victoria
Tel: (61) 3 9210 7777
Fax: (61) 3 9210 7788
URL: http:www.dadirect.com.au

AUSTRIA
Gerold and Co.
Graben 31
A-1011 Wien
Tel: (1) 533-50-14-0
Fax: (1) 512-47-31-29

BANGLADESH
Micro Industries Development
Assistance Society (MIDAS)
House 5, Road 16
Dhanmondi R/Area
Dhaka 1209
Tel: (2) 326427
Fax: (2) 811188

BELGIUM
Jean De Lannoy
Av. du Roi 202
1060 Brussels
Tel: (2) 538-5169
Fax: (2) 538-0841

BRAZIL
Publicacoes Tecnicas Internacionais Ltda.
Rua Peixoto Gomide, 209
01409 Sao Paulo, SP.
Tel: (11) 259-6644
Fax: (11) 258-6990

CANADA
Renouf Publishing Co. Ltd.
1294 Algoma Road
Ottawa, Ontario K1B 3W8
Tel: 613-741-4333
Fax: 613-741-5439

CHINA
China Financial & Economic
Publishing House
8, Da Fo Si Dong Jie
Beijing
Tel: (1) 333-8257
Fax: (1) 401-7365

COLOMBIA
Infoenlace Ltda.
Apartado Aereo 34270
Bogotá D.E.
Tel: (1) 285-2798
Fax: (1) 285-2798

COTE D'IVOIRE
Centre d'Edition et de Diffusion
Africaines (CEDA)
04 B.P. 541
Abidjan 04 Plateau
Tel: 225-24-6510
Fax: 225-25-0567

CYPRUS
Center of Applied Research
Cyprus College
6, Diogenes Street, Engomi
P.O. Box 2006
Nicosia
Tel: 244-1730
Fax: 246-2051

CZECH REPUBLIC
National Information Center
prodejna, Konviktska 5
CS – 113 57 Prague 1
Tel: (2) 2422-9433
Fax: (2) 2422-1484
URL: http://www.nis.cz/

DENMARK
SamfundsLitteratur
Rosenoerns Allé 11
DK-1970 Frederiksberg C
Tel: (31)-351942
Fax: (31)-357822

ECUADOR
Facultad Latinoamericana de
Ciencias Sociales
FLASCO-SEDE Ecuador
Calle Ulpiano Paez 118
y Av. Patria
Quito, Ecuador
Tel: (2) 542 714; 542 716; 528 200
Fax: (2) 566 139

EGYPT, ARAB REPUBLIC OF
Al Ahram
Al Galaa Street
Cairo
Tel: (2) 578-6083
Fax: (2) 578-6833

The Middle East Observer
41, Sherif Street
Cairo
Tel: (2) 393-9732
Fax: (2) 393-9732

FINLAND
Akateeminen Kirjakauppa
P.O. Box 23
FIN-00371 Helsinki
Tel: (0) 12141
Fax: (0) 121-4441
URL: http://booknet.cultnet.fi/aka/

FRANCE
World Bank Publications
66, avenue d'Iéna
75116 Paris
Tel: (1) 40-69-30-55
Fax: (1) 40-69-30-68

GERMANY
UNO-Verlag
Poppelsdorfer Allee 55
53115 Bonn
Tel: (228) 212940
Fax: (228) 217492

GREECE
Papasotiriou S.A.
35, Stournara Str.
106 82 Athens
Tel: (1) 364-1826
Fax: (1) 364-8254

HONG KONG, MACAO
Asia 2000 Ltd.
Sales & Circulation Department
Seabird House, unit 1101-02
22-28 Wyndham Street, Central
Hong Kong
Tel: 852 2530-1409
Fax: 852 2526-1107
URL: http://www.sales@asia2000.com.hk

HUNGARY
Foundation for Market
Economy
Dombovari Ut 17-19
H-1117 Budapest
Tel: 36 1 204 2951 or
36 1 204 2948
Fax: 36 1 204 2953

INDIA
Allied Publishers Ltd.
751 Mount Road
Madras – 600 002
Tel: (44) 852-3938
Fax: (44) 852-0649

INDONESIA
Pt. Indira Limited
Jalan Borobudur 20
P.O. Box 181
Jakarta 10320
Tel: (21) 390-4290
Fax: (21) 421-4289

IRAN
Kowkab Publishers
P.O. Box 19575-511
Tehran
Tel: (21) 258-3723
Fax: 98 (21) 258-3723

Ketab Sara Co. Publishers
Khaled Eslamboli Ave.,
6th Street
Kusheh Delafrooz No. 8
Tehran
Tel: 8717819 or 8716104
Fax: 8862479

IRELAND
Government Supplies Agency
Oifig an tSolathair
4-5 Harcourt Road
Dublin 2
Tel: (1) 461-3111
Fax: (1) 475-2670

ISRAEL
Yozmot Literature Ltd.
P.O. Box 56055
Tel Aviv 61560
Tel: (3) 5285-397
Fax: (3) 5285-397

R.O.Y. International
PO Box 13056
Tel Aviv 61130
Tel: (3) 5461423
Fax: (3) 5461442

Palestinian Authority/Middle East
Index Information Services
P.O.B. 19502 Jerusalem
Tel: (2) 271219

ITALY
Licosa Commissionaria Sansoni SPA
Via Duca Di Calabria, 1/1
Casella Postale 552
50125 Firenze
Tel: (55) 645-415
Fax: (55) 641-257

JAMAICA
Ian Randle Publishers Ltd.
206 Old Hope Road
Kingston 6
Tel: 809-927-2085
Fax: 809-977-0243

JAPAN
Eastern Book Service
Hongo 3-Chome,
Bunkyo-ku 113
Tokyo
Tel: (03) 3818-0861
Fax: (03) 3818-0864
URL: http://www.bekkoame.or.jp/-svt-ebs

KENYA
Africa Book Service (E.A.) Ltd.
Quaran House, Mfangano Street
P.O. Box 45245
Nairobi
Tel: (2) 23641
Fax: (2) 330272

KOREA, REPUBLIC OF
Daejon Trading Co. Ltd.
P.O. Box 34
Yeoeida
Seoul
Tel: (2) 785-1631/4
Fax: (2) 784-0315

MALAYSIA
University of Malaya Cooperative
Bookshop, Limited
P.O. Box 1127
Jalan Pantai Baru
59700 Kuala Lumpur
Tel: (3) 756-5000
Fax: (3) 755-4424

MEXICO
INFOTEC
Apartado Postal 22-860
14060 Tlalpan,
Mexico D.F.
Tel: (5) 606-0011
Fax: (5) 606-0386

NETHERLANDS
De Lindeboom/InOr-Publikaties
P.O. Box 202
7480 AE Haaksbergen

NEW ZEALAND
EBSCO NZ Ltd.
Private Mail Bag 99914
New Market
Auckland
Tel: (9) 524-8119
Fax: (9) 524-8067

NIGERIA
University Press Limited
Three Crowns Building Jericho
Private Mail Bag 5095
Ibadan
Tel: (22) 41-1356
Fax: (22) 41-2056

NORWAY
Narvesen Information Center
Book Department
P.O. Box 6125 Etterstad
N-0602 Oslo 6
Tel: (22) 57-3300
Fax: (22) 68-1901

PAKISTAN
Mirza Book Agency
65, Shahrah-e-Quaid-e-Azam
P.O. Box No. 729
Lahore 54000
Tel: (42) 7353601
Fax: (42) 7585283

Oxford University Press
5 Bangalore Town
Sharae Faisal
PO Box 13033
Karachi-75350
Tel: (21) 446307
Fax: (21) 454-7640

PERU
Editorial Desarrollo SA
Apartado 3824
Lima 1
Tel: (14) 285380
Fax: (14) 286628

PHILIPPINES
International Booksource Center Inc.
Suite 720, Cityland 10
Condominium Tower 2
H.V dela Costa, corner
Valero St.
Makati, Metro Manila
Tel: (2) 817-9676
Fax: (2) 817-1741

POLAND
International Publishing Service
Ul. Piekna 31/37
00-577 Warzawa
Tel: (2) 628-6089
Fax: (2) 621-7255

PORTUGAL
Livraria Portugal
Rua Do Carmo 70-74
1200 Lisbon
Tel: (1) 347-4982
Fax: (1) 347-0264

ROMANIA
Compani De Librarii Bucuresti S.A.
Str. Lipscani no. 26, sector 3
Bucharest
Tel: (1) 613 9645
Fax: (1) 312 4000

RUSSIAN FEDERATION
Isdatelstvo <Ves Mir>
9a, Lolpachrui pereulok
Moscow 101831
Tel: (95) 917 87 49
Fax: (95) 917 92 59

SAUDI ARABIA, QATAR
Jarir Book Store
P.O. Box 3196
Riyadh 11471
Tel: (1) 477-3140
Fax: (1) 477-2940

SINGAPORE, TAIWAN, MYANMAR, BRUNEI
Asahgate Publishing Asia
Pacific Pte. Ltd.
41 Kallang Pudding Road #04-03
Golden Wheel Building
Singapore 349316
Tel: (65) 741-5166
Fax: (65) 742-9356

SLOVAK REPUBLIC
Slovart G.T.G. Ltd.
Krupinska 4
852 99 Bratislava 5
Tel: (7) 839472
Fax: (7) 839485

SOUTH AFRICA, BOTSWANA
For single titles:
Oxford University Press
Southern Africa
P.O. Box 1141
Cape Town 8000
Tel: (21) 45-7266
Fax: (21) 45-7265

For subscription orders:
International Subscription Service
P.O. Box 41095
Craighall
Johannesburg 2024
Tel: (11) 880-1448
Fax: (11) 880-6248

SPAIN
Mundi-Prensa Libros, S.A.
Castello 37
28001 Madrid
Tel: (1) 431-3399
Fax: (1) 575-3998
http://www.tsai.es/mprensa

Libreria Internacional AEDOS
Consell de Cent, 391
08009 Barcelona
Tel: (3) 488-3009
Fax: (3) 487-7659

SRI LANKA, THE MALDIVES
Lake House Bookshop
P.O. Box 244
100, Sir Chittampalam A.
Gardiner Mawatha
Colombo 2
Tel: (1) 32105
Fax: (1) 432104

SWEDEN
Fritzes Customer Service
Regeringsgaton 12
S-106 47 Stockholm
Tel: (8) 690 90 90
Fax: (8) 21 47 77

Wennergren-Williams AB
P.O. Box 1305
S-171 25 Solna
Tel: (8) 705-97-50
Fax: (8) 27-00-71

SWITZERLAND
Librairie Payot
Service Institutionnel
Côtes-de-Montbenon 30
1002 Lausanne
Tel: (021)-320-2511
Fax: (021)-320-2514

Van Diermen Editions Technique
Ch. de Lacuez 41
CH1807 Blonay
Tel: (021) 943 2673
Fax: (021) 943 3605

TANZANIA
Oxford University Press
Maktaba Street
PO Box 5299
Dar es Salaam
Tel: (51) 29209
Fax (51) 46822

THAILAND
Central Books Distribution
306 Silom Road
Bangkok
Tel: (2) 235-5400
Fax: (2) 237-8321

TRINIDAD & TOBAGO, JAMAICA
Systematics Studies Unit
#9 Watts Street
Curepe
Trinidad, West Indies
Tel: 809-662-5654
Fax: 809-662-5654

UGANDA
Gustro Ltd.
Madhvani Building
PO Box 9997
Plot 16/4 Jinja Rd.
Kampala
Tel/Fax: (41) 254763

UNITED KINGDOM
Microlnfo Ltd.
P.O. Box 3
Alton, Hampshire GU34 2PG
England
Tel: (1420) 86848
Fax: (1420) 89889

ZAMBIA
University Bookshop
Great East Road Campus
P.O. Box 32379
Lusaka
Tel: (1) 213221 Ext. 482

ZIMBABWE
Longman Zimbabwe (Pte.)Ltd.
Tourle Road, Ardbennie
P.O. Box ST125
Southerton
Harare
Tel: (4) 662711
Fax: (4) 662716